Lecture Notes in Computer Science 2391

Edited by G. Goos, J. Hartmanis and J. van Leeuwen

Springer
Berlin
Heidelberg
New York
Barcelona
Hong Kong
London
Milan
Paris
Tokyo

Lars-Henrik Eriksson
Peter Alexander Lindsay (Eds.)

FME 2002:
Formal Methods –
Getting IT Right

International Symposium of Formal Methods Europe
Copenhagen, Denmark, July 22-24, 2002
Proceedings

 Springer

Series Editors

Gerhard Goos, Karlsruhe University, Germany
Juris Hartmanis, Cornell University, NY, USA
Jan van Leeuwen, Utrecht University, The Netherlands

Volume Editors

Lars-Henrik Eriksson
Uppsala University, Department of Information Technology
P.O. Box 337, 751 05 Uppsala, Sweden
E-mail: lhe@csd.uu.se

Peter Alexander Lindsay
The University of Queensland, Software Verification Research Centre
Queensland 4072, Australia
E-mail: Peter.Lindsay@svrc.uq.edu.au

Cataloging-in-Publication Data applied for

Die Deutsche Bibliothek - CIP-Einheitsaufnahme

Formal methods - getting IT right : proceedings / FME 2002, International
Symposium of Formal Methods Europe, Copenhagen, Denmark, July 22 - 24,
2002. Lars-Henrik Eriksson ; Peter Alexander Lindsay (ed.). - Berlin ;
Heidelberg ; New York ; Barcelona ; Hong Kong ; London ; Milan ; Paris ;
Tokyo : Springer, 2002
    (Lecture notes in computer science ; Vol. 2391)
    ISBN 3-540-43928-5

CR Subject Classification (1998): F.3, D.2, D.3, D.1, J.1, K.6, F.4.1

ISSN 0302-9743
ISBN 3-540-43928-5 Springer-Verlag Berlin Heidelberg New York

Springer-Verlag Berlin Heidelberg New York
a member of BertelsmannSpringer Science+Business Media GmbH
© Springer-Verlag Berlin Heidelberg 2002
Printed in Germany

Typesetting: Camera-ready by author, data-conversion by PTP-Berlin, Stefan Sossna e.K.
Printed on acid-free paper   SPIN: 10873502   06/3142   5 4 3 2 1 0

Lars-Henrik Eriksson
Peter Alexander Lindsay (Eds.)

FME 2002:
Formal Methods –
Getting IT Right

International Symposium of Formal Methods Europe
Copenhagen, Denmark, July 22-24, 2002
Proceedings

 Springer

Series Editors

Gerhard Goos, Karlsruhe University, Germany
Juris Hartmanis, Cornell University, NY, USA
Jan van Leeuwen, Utrecht University, The Netherlands

Volume Editors

Lars-Henrik Eriksson
Uppsala University, Department of Information Technology
P.O. Box 337, 751 05 Uppsala, Sweden
E-mail: lhe@csd.uu.se

Peter Alexander Lindsay
The University of Queensland, Software Verification Research Centre
Queensland 4072, Australia
E-mail: Peter.Lindsay@svrc.uq.edu.au

Cataloging-in-Publication Data applied for

Die Deutsche Bibliothek - CIP-Einheitsaufnahme

Formal methods - getting IT right : proceedings / FME 2002, International
Symposium of Formal Methods Europe, Copenhagen, Denmark, July 22 - 24,
2002. Lars-Henrik Eriksson ; Peter Alexander Lindsay (ed.). - Berlin ;
Heidelberg ; New York ; Barcelona ; Hong Kong ; London ; Milan ; Paris ;
Tokyo : Springer, 2002
    (Lecture notes in computer science ; Vol. 2391)
    ISBN 3-540-43928-5

CR Subject Classification (1998): F.3, D.2, D.3, D.1, J.1, K.6, F.4.1

ISSN 0302-9743
ISBN 3-540-43928-5 Springer-Verlag Berlin Heidelberg New York

Springer-Verlag Berlin Heidelberg New York
a member of BertelsmannSpringer Science+Business Media GmbH
© Springer-Verlag Berlin Heidelberg 2002
Printed in Germany

Typesetting: Camera-ready by author, data-conversion by PTP-Berlin, Stefan Sossna e.K.
Printed on acid-free paper   SPIN: 10873502   06/3142   5 4 3 2 1 0

Preface

This volume contains the proceedings of the 2002 symposium Formal Methods Europe (FME 2002). The symposium was the 11th in a series that began with a VDM Europe symposium in 1987. The symposia are traditionally held every 18 months. In 2002 the symposium was held at the University of Copenhagen, as part of the 2002 Federated Logic Conference (FLoC 2002), which brought together in one event seven major conferences related to logic in computer science, as well as their affiliated workshops, tutorials, and tools exhibitions.

Formal Methods Europe (www.fmeurope.org) is an independent association which aims to stimulate the use of, and research on, formal methods for software development. FME symposia have been notably successful in bringing together a community of users, researchers, and developers of precise mathematical methods for software development.

The theme of FME 2002 was "Formal Methods: Getting IT Right". The double meaning was intentional. On the one hand, the theme acknowledged the significant contribution formal methods can make to Information Technology, by enabling computer systems to be described precisely and reasoned about with rigour. On the other hand, it recognized that current formal methods are not perfect, and further research and practice are required to improve their foundations, applicability, and effectiveness.

FME 2002 covered many aspects of the use of formal methods for development of software in many different application areas. As with previous FME symposia, FME 2002 covered a wide range of activities, from development of fundamental theory of description and reasoning, to particulars of practice and experience.

A total of 31 papers were accepted out of 95 submissions from 30 countries, half of which are outside Europe, making this a truly international event. In addition to authors of submitted papers, Natarajan Shankar, Anthony Hall, and David Basin were invited to give keynote presentations at the symposium.

A symposium session on Semantics and Logic was dedicated to the memory of John Dawes, who was a founding member of VDM Europe and a long-time active contributor to FME.

May 2002   Lars-Henrik Eriksson, Peter Lindsay

Organization

FME 2002 was organized by Formal Methods Europe and the third Federated Logic Conference (FLoC 2002). It was hosted jointly by the IT University of Copenhagen, the Technical University of Denmark, and the University of Copenhagen. We would like to thank the FME Board (John Fitzgerald, Nico Plat, and Kees Pronk) for their support, and the FLoC Organizing Committee for making local arrangements. Moshe Vardi was FLoC General Chair and Neil Jones was FLoC Conference Chair. We particularly thank Henning Makholm, Andrzej Filinski, and Sebastian Skalberg of the FLoC Local Committee for their help in organizing the web pages, the printed program, and the tool demonstration facilities.

Organizing Committee

Organizing Chair:	Dines Bjørner (Technical University of Denmark)
Program Co-chairs:	Lars-Henrik Eriksson (Industrilogik, Sweden)
	Peter Lindsay (University of Queensland, Australia)
Tool Demonstrations:	Paul Mukherjee
	(Systematic Software Engineering A/S, Denmark)

Program Committee

Bernhard Aichernig	Graz University of Technology, Austria
Juan Bicarregui	Rutherford Appleton Laboratory, UK
Ernie Cohen	Microsoft Research, Cambridge, UK
Ben Di Vito	NASA Langley Research Center, USA
Cindy Eisner	IBM Haifa Research Laboratory, Israel
Lars-Henrik Eriksson (co-chair)	Industrilogik, Sweden
John Fitzgerald	Transitive Technologies Ltd, UK
Jim Grundy	Intel Corporation, USA
Yves Ledru	IMAG Grenoble, France
Peter Lindsay (co-chair)	University of Queensland, Australia
Markus Montigel	University of New Orleans, USA
Richard Moore	IFAD, Denmark
Tobias Nipkow	Technische Universität München, Germany
Colin O'Halloran	QinetiQ, UK
Jose Oliveira	Universidade do Minho, Portugal
Nico Plat	West Consulting, The Netherlands
Jeannette Wing	Carnegie Mellon University, USA
Jim Woodcock	University of Kent, UK
Joakim von Wright	Åbo Akademi University, Finland
Pamela Zave	AT&T Laboratories, USA

External Referees

All submitted papers were peer reviewed by at least three referees. In addition to the Program Committee, the following people contributed reviews:

Referees

Parosh Aziz Abdulla
James M Armstrong
Clemens Ballarin
Luís S. Barbosa
Sharon Barner
Leonor Barroca
Shoham Ben-David
Pierre Berlioux
Didier Bert
Eerke Boiten
Roland Bol
Gregory Bond
Michael Butler
Martin Büchi
Orieta Celiku
Michel Chaudron
David Clark
Pieter Cuipers
Anat Dahan
John Derrick
Jeremy Dick
Theo Dimitrakos
Lydie du Bousquet
Steve Dunne
Sophie Dupuy-Chessa
Andy Evans
João M. Fernandes
Jean-Claude Fernandez
Arnaud Fevrier
Colin Fidge
Daniel Geist
Anna Gerber
Rob Gerth
Stephen Gilmore
Stefan Gruner

Alan Hartman
David Hemer
Dang Van Hung
Tomasz Janowski
He Jifeng
Robert B. Jones
Jan Jürjens
Steve King
Andre S. E. Koster
Linas Laibinis
K. Lano
Johan Lilius
Zhiming Liu
Anthony MacDonald
Ricardo J. Machado
Brian Matthews
C. A. Middelburg
Anna Mikhailova
Tim Miller
N. Moffat
Paul Mukherjee
Markus Müller-Olm
Marco Nijdam
John O'Leary
Jeff Z. Pan
P. K. Pandya
Joachim Parrow
Stephen Paynter
Paul Pettersson
Sibylle Peuker
Andrej Pietschker
Ivan Porres
Marie-Laure Potet
Viorel Preoteasa
Alex Pretschner

Kees Pronk
Xu Qiwen
S Riddle
Brian Ritchie
Ken Robinson
Alexander Romanovsky
Kaisa Sere
W. Simmonds
David Sinclair
Graeme Smith
M. A. Smith
Baruch Sterin
Martin Strecker
Kim Sunesen
Francis Tang
Jan Tretmans
John Turner
Rachel Tzoref
Shmuel Ur
Gertjan van Oosten
Marcel Verhoef
Arjan Vermeij
M. Voorhoeve
Jos Vrancken
Hagen Völzer
Marina Waldén
Heike Wehrheim
Markus Wenzel
Alan Cameron Wills
Guido Wimmel
Kirsten Winter
Jin Yang
Emmanuel Zarpas

Table of Contents

Little Engines of Proof*

Natarajan Shankar

Computer Science Laboratory
SRI International
Menlo Park CA 94025 USA
shankar@csl.sri.com
http://www.csl.sri.com/~shankar/
Phone: +1 (650) 859-5272 Fax: +1 (650) 859-2844

Abstract. The automated construction of mathematical proof is a basic activity in computing. Since the dawn of the field of automated reasoning, there have been two divergent schools of thought. One school, best represented by Alan Robinson's resolution method, is based on simple uniform proof search procedures guided by heuristics. The other school, pioneered by Hao Wang, argues for problem-specific combinations of decision and semi-decision procedures. While the former school has been dominant in the past, the latter approach has greater promise. In recent years, several high quality inference engines have been developed, including propositional satisfiability solvers, ground decision procedures for equality and arithmetic, quantifier elimination procedures for integers and reals, and abstraction methods for finitely approximating problems over infinite domains. We describe some of these "little engines of proof" and a few of the ways in which they can be combined. We focus in particular on combining different decision procedures for use in automated verification.

Its great triumph was to prove that the sum of two even numbers is even.

Martin Davis [Dav83] (on his Presburger arithmetic procedure)

The most interesting lesson from these results is perhaps that even in a fairly rich domain, the theorems actually proved are mostly ones which call on a very small portion of the available resources of the domain.

Hao Wang (quoted by Davis [Dav83])

* Funded by NSF Grants CCR-0082560 and CCR-9712383, DARPA/AFRL Contract F33615-00-C-3043, and NASA Contract NAS1-20334. John Rushby, Sam Owre, Ashish Tiwari, and Tomás Uribe commented on earlier drafts of this paper.

L.-H. Eriksson and P. Lindsay (Eds.): FME 2002, LNCS 2391, pp. 1–20, 2002.
© Springer-Verlag Berlin Heidelberg 2002

1   Introduction

At a very early point in its development, the field of automated reasoning took an arguably wrong turn. For nearly forty years now, the focus in automated reasoning research has been on *big iron*: general-purpose theorem provers based on uniform proof procedures augmented with heuristics. These efforts have not been entirely fruitless. As success stories, one might list an impressive assortment of open problems that have succumbed to semi-brute-force methods, and spin-off applications such as logic programming. However, there has been very little discernible progress on the problem of automated proof construction in any significant mathematical domain. Proofs in these domains tend to be delicate artifacts whose construction requires a collection of well-crafted instruments, little engines of proof, working in tandem. In other disciplines such as numerical analysis, computer algebra, and combinatorial algorithms, it is quite common to have libraries of useful routines. Such software libraries have not taken root in automated deduction because the scientific and engineering challenges involved are quite significant. We examine some of the successes in building and combining little deduction engines for building proofs and refutations (e.g., counterexamples), and survey some of the challenges that still lie ahead.

The tension between general-purpose proof search and special-purpose decision procedures has been with us from very early on. Automated reasoning had its beginnings in the pioneering Logic Theorist system of Newell, Shaw, and Simon [NSS57]. The theorems they proved were shown by Hao Wang [Wan60b] to fall within simply decidable fragments like propositional logic and the $\forall^*\exists^*$ Bernays-Schönfinkel fragment of first-order logic [BGG97]. Many technical ideas from the Logic Theorist such as subgoaling, substitution, replacement, and forward and backward chaining, have been central to automated reasoning, but the dogma that human-oriented heuristics are the key to effective theorem proving has not been vindicated. Hao Wang [Wan60a] proposed an entirely different approach that he called *inferential analysis* as a parallel to numerical analysis. Central to his approach was the use of domain-specific decision and semi-decision procedures, so that proofs could be constructed by means of reductions to some combination of problems that could each be easily solved. Due to the prevailing bias in artificial intelligence, Wang lost the debate at that point in time, but, as we argue here, his ideas still make plenty of sense. As remarked by Martin Davis [Dav83]:

> *The controversy referred to may be succinctly characterized as being between the two slogans: "Simulate people" and "Use mathematical logic".*
> *... Thus as early as 1961 Minsky [Min63] remarked*
>> ... it seems clear that a program to solve real mathematical problems will have to combine the mathematical sophistication of Wang with the heuristic sophistication of Newell, Shaw, and Simon.

The debate between human-oriented and logic-oriented approaches is beside the point. The more significant debate in automated reasoning is between two approaches that in analogy with economics can be labelled as *macrological* and *micrological*. The macrological approach takes a language and logic such as first-order logic as given, and attempts to find a uniform (i.e., problem-independent) method for constructing proofs of conjectures stated in the logic. The micrological approach attacks a class of problems and attempts to find the most effective way of validating or refuting conjectures in this problem class. In his writings, Hao Wang was actually espousing a micrological viewpoint. He wrote [Wan60a]

> *In contrast with pure logic, the chief emphasis of inferential analysis is on the efficiency of algorithms, which is usually obtained by paying a great deal of attention to the detailed structure of problems and their solutions, to take advantage of possible systematic short cuts.*

Automated reasoning got off to a running start in the 1950s. Already in 1954, Davis [Dav57] had implemented a decision procedure for Presburger arithmetic [Pre29]. Davis and Putnam [DP60], during 1958–60, devised a decision procedure for CNF satisfiability (SAT) based on inference rules for propagation of unit clauses, ground resolution, deletion of clauses with pure literals, and splitting. The ground resolution rule turned out to be space-inefficient and was discarded in the work of Davis, Logemann, and Loveland [DLL62]. Variants of the latter procedure are still employed in modern SAT solvers. Gilmore [Gil60] and Prawitz [Pra60] examined techniques for first-order validity based on Herbrand's theorem. Many of the techniques from the 1950s still look positively modern.

Robinson's introduction [Rob65] of the resolution principle (during 1963–65) based on unification brought about a qualitative shift in automated theorem proving. From that point on, the field of automated reasoning never looked forward. Resolution provides a simple inference rule for refutational proofs for first-order statements in skolemized, prenex form. It spawned a multitude of strategies, heuristics, and extensions. Nearly forty years later, resolution [BG01] remains extremely popular as a general-purpose proof search method primarily because the basic method can be implemented and extended with surprising ease. Resolution-based methods have had some success in proving open problems in certain domains where general-purpose search can be productive. The impact of resolution on theorem proving in mathematically rich domains has not been all that encouraging.

The popularity of uniform proof methods like resolution stems from the simple dogma that since first-order logic is a generic language for expressing statements, generic first-order proof search methods must also be adequate for finding proofs. This central dogma seems absurd on the face of it. Stating a problem and solving it are two quite separate matters. But the appeal of the dogma is obvious. A simple, generic method for proving theorems basically hits the jackpot by fulfilling Leibniz's dream of a reasoning machine. A more sophisticated version of the dogma is that a uniform proof method can serve as the basic structure for introducing domain-specific automation. There is little empirical evidence that even this dogma has any validity.

On the other hand, certain domain-specific automated theorem provers have been quite effective. The Boyer-Moore line of theorem provers [BM79,KMM00] has had significant success in the area of inductive proofs of recursively defined functions. Various geometry theorem provers [CG01] based on both algebraic and non-algebraic, machine-oriented and human-oriented methods, have been able to automatically prove theorems that would tax human ingenuity. Both of these classes of theorem provers owe their success to domain-specific automation rather than general-purpose theorem proving.

Main Thesis. Automated reasoning has for too long been identified with uniform proof search procedures in first-order logic. This approach shows very little promise. The basic seduction of uniform theorem proving techniques is that phenomenal gains could be achieved with very modest implementation effort. Hao Wang [Wan60b,Wan60a,Wan63] in his early papers on automated reasoning sketched the vision of a field of inferential analysis that would take a deeper look at the problem of automating mathematical reasoning while exploiting domain-specific decision procedures. He wrote [Wan63]

> *That proof procedures for elementary logic can be mechanized is familiar. In practice, however, were we slavishly to follow these procedures without further refinements, we should encounter a prohibitively expansive element. ... In this way we are led to a closer study of reduction procedures and of decision procedures for special domains, as well as of proof procedures of more complex sorts.*

Woody Bledsoe [Ble77] made a similar point in arguing for semantic theorem proving techniques as opposed to resolution.

Decision procedures [Rab78], and more generally inference procedures, are crucial to the approach advocated here. Few problems are stated in a form that is readily decidable, but proof search strategies, heuristics, and human guidance can be used to decompose these problems into decidable subproblems. Thus, even though not many interesting problems are directly expressible in Presburger arithmetic, a great many of the naturally arising proof obligations and subproblems do fall into this decidable class.

Building a library of automated reasoning routines along the lines of numerical analysis and computer algebra, is not as easy as it looks. A theorem prover has a simple interface in that it is given a conjecture and it returns a proof or a disproof. The lower-level procedures often lack clear interface specifications of this sort. Even if they did, building a theorem prover out of modular components may not be as efficient as a more monolithic system. Boyer and Moore [BM86] indicate how even a simple decision procedure can have a complex interaction with the other components, so that it is not merely a black box that returns *proved* or *disproved.* The construction of modular inference procedures is a challenging research issues in automated reasoning.

Work on little engines of proof has been gathering steam lately Many groups are actively engaged in the construction of little proof engines, while others are putting in place the train tracks on which these engines can run. PVS [ORSvH95] itself can be seen as an attempt to unify many different inference procedures: typechecking, ground decision procedures, simplification, rewriting, MONA [EKM98], model checking [CGP99], abstraction, and static analysis, within a single system with an expressive language for writing mathematics.

2   Propositional Logic

The very first significant metamathematical results were those on the soundness, completeness, and decidability of propositional logic [Pos21]. Since boolean logic has applications in digital circuit design, a lot of attention has been paid to the problem of propositional satisfiability. A propositional formula ϕ is built from propositional atoms p_i by means of negation $\neg\phi$, disjunction $\phi_1 \vee \phi_2$, and conjunction $\phi_1 \wedge \phi_2$. Further propositional connectives can be defined in terms of basic ones like $\neg$ and $\vee$. A propositional formula can be placed in *negation normal form*, where all the negations are applied only to propositional atoms. A literal l is an atom p or its negation $\neg p$. A clause C is a disjunction of literals. By labelling subformulas with atoms and using distributivity, any propositional formula can be efficiently transformed into one that is in conjunctive normal form (CNF) as a conjunction of clauses. A CNF formula can be viewed as a bag Γ of clauses. The Davis–Putnam method (DP) [DP60] consisted of the following rules:

1. Unit propagation: l, Γ is satisfiable if $\Gamma[l \mapsto \top, \neg l \mapsto \bot]$ is satisfiable.
2. Pure literal: Γ is satisfiable if $\Gamma - \Delta$ is satisfiable, for $\neg l \notin \llbracket \Gamma \rrbracket$, where $\llbracket \Gamma \rrbracket$ are the subformulas of Γ, and $l \in C$ for each $C \in \Delta$.
3. Splitting: Γ is satisfiable if l, Γ and $\neg l, \Gamma$ are satisfiable.
4. Ground resolution: $l \vee C_1, \neg l \vee C_2, \Gamma$ is satisfiable if $C_1 \vee C_2, \Gamma$ is satisfiable.

The Davis–Logemann–Loveland (DLL) variant [DLL62] drops the ground resolution rule since it turned out to be space-inefficient. Several modern SAT solvers such as SATO [Zha97], GRASP [MSS99], and Chaff [MMZ+01], are based on the DLL method. They are capable of solving satisfiability problems with hundreds of thousands of propositional variables and clauses. With this kind of performance, many significant applications become feasible including invariant-checking for systems of bounded size, bounded model checking, i.e., the search for counterexamples of length k for a temporal property, and boolean equivalence checking where two circuits are checked to have the same input/output behavior.

Stålmarck's method [SS00] does not employ a CNF representation. Truth values are propagated from formulas to subformulas through a method known as saturation. There is a splitting rule similar to that of DP, but it can be applied to subformulas and not just propositions. The key component of Stålmarck's method is the dilemma rule which considers the intersection of the two subformula truth assignments derived from splitting. Further splitting is carried out with respect to this intersection.

Binary Decision Diagrams. Reduced Ordered Binary Decision Diagrams (ROB-DDs) [Bry86] are a canonical representation for boolean functions, i.e., functions from $[B^n \rightarrow B]$. BDDs are binary branching directed acyclic graphs where the nodes are variables and the outgoing branches correspond to the assignment of $\top$ and $\bot$ to the variable. There is a total ordering of variables that is maintained along any path in the graph. The graph is kept in reduced form so that if there is a node such that both of its branches lead to the same subgraph, then the node is eliminated.

Standard operations like negation, conjunction, disjunction, composition, and boolean quantification, have efficient implementations using BDDs. The BDD data structure has primarily been used for boolean equivalence checking and symbolic model checking. The main advantage of BDDs over other representations is that checking equivalence is easy. Boolean quantification is also handled more readily using BDDs. BDDs can also be used for SAT solving since it is in fact a compact representation for all solutions of a boolean formula. But the strength of BDDs is in representing boolean functions of a low communication complexity, i.e., where it is possible to partition the variables so that there are few dependencies between variables across the partition. BDDs have been popular for symbolic model checking [CGP99] and boolean equivalence checking.

Quantified Boolean Formulas and Transition Systems. In a propositional logic formula, all variables are implicitly universally quantified. One obvious extension is the introduction of Boolean existential and universal quantification. The resulting fragment is called quantified boolean formulas (QBF). This kind of quantification can be expressed purely in propositional logic. For example, the formula $(\exists p : Q)$ is equivalent to $(Q[p \mapsto \top] \vee Q[p \mapsto \bot])$. The language of QBF is of course exponentially more succinct than propositional logic. The decision procedure for QBF validity is a PSPACE-complete problem. Many interesting problems that can be cast as interactive games can be mapped to QBF.

Finite-state transition systems can be defined in QBF. A finite state type consists of a finite number of distinct variables over types such as booleans, scalars, subranges, and finite arrays over a finite element type. A finite state type can be encoded in binary form. A transition system over a finite state type that is represented by n boolean variables then consists of an initialization predicate I that is an n-ary boolean function, and a transition relation N that is a $2n$-ary boolean function. The nondeterministic choice between two transition relations N_1 and N_2 is easily expressed as $N_1 \vee N_2$. Internal state can be hidden through boolean quantification. The composition $(N_1; N_2)$ of two transition relations N_1 and N_2 can be captured as $\exists \overline{y} : N_1(\overline{x}, \overline{y}) \wedge N_2(\overline{y}, \overline{x}')$.

Fixpoints and Model Checking. QBF can be further extended through the addition of fixpoint operators that can capture the transitive closure of a transition relation. Given a transition relation N, the reflexive-transitive closure of N can be written as $\mu Q : \overline{x}' = \overline{x} \vee (\exists \overline{y} : N(\overline{x}, \overline{y}) \wedge Q(\overline{y}, \overline{x}'))$. Similarly, the set of states reachable from the initial set of state can be represented as $\mu Q : I(\overline{x}) \vee (\exists \overline{y} : Q(\overline{y}) \wedge N(\overline{y}, \overline{x}))$. The boolean function represented by a fixpoint formula can be computed by unwinding the fixpoint until convergence is reached. For this, the ROBDD representation of the boolean function is especially convenient since it makes it easy to detect convergence through an equivalence test, and to represent boolean quantification [BCM+92,McM93]. The boolean fixpoint calculus can easily represent the temporal operators of the branching-time temporal logic CTL where one can for example assert that a property always (or eventually) holds on all (or some) computation paths leading out of a state. The boolean fixpoint calculus can also represent different fairness constraints on paths. The emptiness problem for Büchi automaton over infinite words can be expressed using fairness constraints. This in turn captures the model checking problem for linear-time temporal logics [VW86,Kur93].

Weak monadic second-order logic of a single successor (WS1S). WS1S has a successor operation for constructing natural numbers, first-order quantification over natural numbers, and second-order quantification over finite sets of natural numbers. WS1S is a natural formalism for many applications, particularly for parametric systems. The logic can be used to capture interesting datatypes such as regular expressions, lists, queues, and arrays. There is a direct mapping between the logic and finite automata. A finite set X of natural numbers can be represented as a bit-string where a 1 in the i'th position indicates that i is a member of X. A formula with free set variables $X_1, \ldots, X_n$ is then a set of strings over B^n. The logical operations have automata theoretic counterparts so that negation is complementation, conjunction is the product of automata, and existential quantification is projection. The MONA library [EKM98] uses an ROBDD representation for the automaton corresponding to the formula.

3   Equality and Inequality

Equality introduces some of the most significant challenges in automated reasoning [HO80]. Many subareas of theorem proving are devoted to equality including rewriting, constraint solving, and unification. In this section we focus on ground decision procedures for equality. Many theorem proving systems are based around decision procedures for equality. The language now includes terms which are built from variables x, and applications $f(a_1, \ldots, a_n)$ of an n-ary function symbol f to n terms $a_1, \ldots, a_n$. The *ground* fragment can be seen as an extension of propositional logic where the propositional atoms are of the form

$a = b$, for terms a and b. The literals are now either equations $a = b$ or disequations $a \neq b$. The variables in a formula are taken to be universally quantified. The validity of a formula ϕ that is a propositional combination of equalities can be decided by first transforming $\neg \phi$ into disjunctive normal form $D_1 \vee \ldots \vee D_n$, and checking that each disjunct D_i, which is a conjunction of literals, is refutable. The refutation of a conjunction D_i of literals can be carried out by partitioning the terms in D_i into equivalence classes of terms with respect to the equalities in D_i. If for some disequation $a \neq b$ in D_i, a and b appear in the same equivalence class, then we have a contradiction and D_i has been refuted. The original claim ϕ is verified if each such disjunct D_i has been refuted.

If the function symbols are all uninterpreted, then congruence closure can be used to construct the equivalence classes corresponding to the conjunction of literals D_i. Let the set of subterms of D_i be $\lceil D_i \rceil$. The initial partition P_0 is the set $\{\{c\} \mid c \in \lceil D_i \rceil\}$. When an equality of the form $a = b$ from D_i is processed, it results in the merging of the equivalence classes corresponding to a and b. As a result of this merge, other equivalence classes might become mergeable. For example, one equivalence might contain $f(a_1, \ldots, a_n)$ while the other contains $f(b_1, \ldots, b_n)$, and each a_j is in the same equivalence class as the corresponding b_j. The merging of equivalence classes is performed until no further mergeable pairs of equivalence classes remain, and the partition P_1 is constructed. The equalities in D_i are successively processed and the resulting partition is returned as P_m. If for some disequality $a \neq b$, a and b are in the same equivalence class in P_m, then a contradiction is returned. Otherwise, the conjunction D_i is satisfiable.

Linear arithmetic. A large fraction of the subgoals that arise in verification condition generation, typechecking, array-bounds checking, and constraint solving involve linear arithmetic constraints [BW01]. Linear arithmetic equalities in n variables have the form $c_0 + c_1 * x_1 + \ldots + c_n * x_n = 0$, where the coefficients c_i range over the rationals, and the variables x_i range over the rationals or reals. It is easy to isolate a single variable, say x_1, as $x_1 = -c_0/c_1 - (c_2/c_1) * x_2 - \ldots - (c_n/c_1) * x_n$. This solved form for x_1 can then be substituted into the remaining linear equations thus eliminating the variable x_1. Gaussian elimination is based on the same idea where the set of linear equations is represented by $A * X = B$, and the matrix representation of the linear equations is transformed into row echelon form in order to solve for the variables.

Linear inequalities are of the form $c_0 + c_1 * x_1 + \ldots + c_n * x_n \# 0$, where $\#$ is either $<$, $\leq$, $>$, or $\geq$. Note that linear inequalities, unlike equalities, are closed under negation. Any linear equality can also be easily transformed into a pair of inequalities. As with linear equalities, linear inequalities can also be transformed into a form where a single variable is isolated. A pair of inequalities, $x \leq a$ and $x \geq b$ can be resolved to obtain $b \leq a$ thus eliminating x. This kind of Fourier-Motzkin elimination [DE73] can be used as a quantifier elimination procedure to decide the first-order theory of linear arithmetic by repeatedly reducing any quantified formula of the form $\exists x : P(x)$ where $P(x)$ is a conjunction of inequalities, into the form P', where x has been eliminated. By eliminating quantifiers in an inside-out order while transforming universal quantification $\forall x : A$ into $\neg \exists x : \neg A$, we arrive at an equivalent variable-free formula that directly evaluates to true or false. Linear programming techniques like Simplex [Nel81] can also be used for solving linear arithmetic inequality constraints. Separation predicates are linear inequalities of the form $x - y \leq c$ or $x - y < c$ for some constant c, and these can be decided with graph-theoretic techniques [Sho81]. This simple class of linear inequalities is useful in model checking timed automata [ACD93].

Presburger arithmetic [Pre29] is the first-order theory of linear arithmetic over the integers. Solving constraints over the integers is harder than over the rationals and reals. Cooper [Coo72,Opp78] gives an efficient quantifier elimination algorithm for Presburger arithmetic. Once again, we need only consider quantifiers of the form $\exists x : P(x)$ where $P(x)$ is a conjunction of inequalities. We add divisibility assertions of the form $k|a$, where k is a positive integer. An inequality of the form $c_0 + c_1 * x_1 + \ldots + c_n * x_n \geq 0$ can be transformed to $c_1 * x_1 \geq -c_0 - c_2 * x_n - \ldots - c_n * x_n$, and similarly for other inequality relations. Since we are dealing with integers, a nonstrict inequality like $a \leq b$ can be transformed to $a < b + 1$. Having isolated all occurrences of x_1, we can compute the least common multiple α_1 of the coefficients corresponding to each occurrence of x_i. Now $P(x_1)$ is of the form $P'(\alpha_1 * x_1)$, and $\exists x_1 : P(x_1)$ can be replaced by $\exists x_1 : P'(x_1) \wedge \alpha_1 | x_1$. Here, $P'(x)$ is a conjunction of formulas of the forms: $x < a$, $x > b$, $k|x+d$, and $j \nmid x+e$. Let $A = \{a \mid x < a \in P'(x)\}$, $B = \{b \mid x > b \in P'(x)\}$, $K = \{k \mid (k|x+d) \in P'(x)$, and $J = \{j \mid (j \nmid x+e) \in P'(x)\}$. Let G be the least common multiple of $K \cup J$. If A is nonempty, then $\exists x : P'(x)$ can be transformed to $\bigvee_{a \in A} \exists x : a - G \leq x < a \wedge P'(x)$. The bounded existential quantification in the latter formula can easily be eliminated. Essentially, if m satisfies the constraints in $K \cup J$, then so does $m + r * j$ for any integer r. Hence, if $P'(m)$ holds for some m and A is nonempty, then there is an m in the interval $[a - G, a)$ for some $a \in A$ such that $P'(m)$ holds. Similarly, if B is nonempty, $\exists x : P'(x)$ can also be transformed to $\bigvee_{b \in B} \exists x : b < x \leq b + G \wedge P'(x)$. If both A and B are empty, then $\exists x : P'(x)$ is transformed to $\exists x : 0 < x \leq G \wedge P'(x)$. For example, the claim that x is an even integer can be expressed as $\exists u : 2 * u = x$ if we avoid the divisibility predicate. The quantifier elimination transformation above would convert this to $u' > x - 1 \wedge u' < x + 1 \wedge (2|u')$ which eventually yields $(x > x - 1 \wedge x < x + 1 \wedge 2|x) \vee (x + 1 > x - 1 \wedge x + 1 < x + 1 \wedge (2|x+1))$. The latter formula easily simplifies to $(2|x)$. The claim that the sum of two even numbers is even then has the form $(\forall x : \forall y : 2|x \wedge 2|y \supset 2|(x + y))$. Converting universal quantification to existential quantification yields $\neg \exists x : \exists y : 2|x \wedge 2|y \wedge 2 \nmid (x + y)$. Quantifier elimination yields $\neg \exists x : 0 < x \leq 2 \wedge \exists y : 0 < y \leq 2 \wedge (2|x) \wedge (2|y) \wedge (2 \nmid x + y)$, which is clearly valid. The decidability of Presburger arithmetic can also be reduced to that of WS1S, and even though the latter theory has nonelementary complexity, this reduction using MONA works quite efficiently in practice [SKR98].

By the unsolvability of Hilbert's tenth problem, even the quantifier-free fragment of nonlinear arithmetic over the integers or rationals is undecidable. However, the first-order theory of nonlinear arithmetic over the reals and the complex numbers is decidable. Tarski [Tar48] gave a decision procedure for this theory. Collins [Col75] gave an improved quantifier elimination procedure that is the basis for a popular package called QEPCAD [CH91]. These procedures have been successfully used in proving theorems in algebraic geometry. Buchberger's Gröbner basis method for testing membership in polynomial ideals has also been successful in computer algebra and geometry theorem proving [CG01,BW01].

Constraint solving and quantifier elimination methods in linear and nonlinear arithmetic over integers, reals, and rationals, are central to a large number of applications of theorem proving that involve numeric constraints.

4   The Combination Problem

The application of decision procedures for individual theories is constrained by the fact that few natural problems fall exactly within a single theory. Many of the proof obligations that arise out of extended typechecking or verification condition generation involve arithmetic equalities and inequalities, tuples, arrays, datatypes, and uninterpreted function symbols. There are two basic techniques for constructing decision procedures for checking the satisfiability of conjunctions of literals in combinations of disjoint theories: the Nelson–Oppen method [NO79, TH96] and the Shostak method [Sho84].

Nelson and Oppen's Method. The Nelson–Oppen method combines decision procedures for disjoint theories by using variable abstraction to purify a formula containing operations from a union of theories, so that the formula can then be partitioned into subgoals that can be handled by the individual decision procedures. Let B represent the formula whose satisfiability is being checked in the union of disjoint theories θ_1 and θ_2. First variable abstraction is used to convert B into $B' \wedge V$, where V contains equalities of the form $x = t$, where x is a fresh variable and t contains function symbols exclusively from θ_1 or from θ_2, and B' contains x renaming t. In particular, if $V[B']$ is the result of replacing each occurrence of x in B' by the corresponding t for each $x = t$ in V, then B must the result of repeatedly applying V to B' and eliminating all the newly introduced variables. Next, $V \wedge B'$ can be partitioned as $B_1 \wedge B_2$, where each B_i only contains function symbols from the theory θ_i. Let X be the free variables that are shared between B_1 and B_2. Guess a partition $X_1, \ldots, X_m$ on the variables in X. Let E be an arrangement corresponding to this partition so that E contains $x = y$ for each pair of distinct variables x, y in some X_j, and $u \neq v$ for each pair of variables u, v, such that $u \in X_j, v \in X_k$ for $j \neq k$. Check if $E \wedge B_1$ is satisfiable in θ_1 and $E \wedge B_2$ is satisfiable in θ_2. If that is the case, then B is satisfiable in $\theta_1 \cup \theta_2$, provided θ_1 and θ_2 are *stably infinite*. A theory θ is stably infinite if whenever a formula is satisfiable in θ, then it is satisfiable in an infinite model.

Shostak's Method. The Nelson–Oppen combination is a way of combining black box decision procedures. Shostak's method is an optimization of the Nelson–Oppen combination for a restricted class of equational theories. A theory θ is said to be canonizable if there is a canonizer σ such that the equality $a = b$ is valid in θ iff $\sigma(a) \equiv \sigma(b)$. A theory θ is said to be solvable if there is an operation *solve* such that $solve(a = b)$ returns a set S of equalities $\{x_1 = t_1, \ldots, x_n = t_n\}$ equivalent in some sense to $a = b$, where each x_i occurs in $a = b$ but not in t_j for $1 \leq i, j \leq n$. A Shostak theory is one that is canonizable and solvable. Shostak's combination method can be used to combine one or more Shostak theories with the theory of equality over uninterpreted terms. The method essentially maintains a set S of solutions $S_0, \ldots, S_N$, where each set S_i contains equalities of the form $x = t$ for some term t in θ_i. The theory θ_0 is used for the uninterpreted function symbols. Two variables x and y are said to be merged in S_i if $x = t$ and $y = t$ are both in S_i. It is possible to define a global canonical form $S[\![a]\!]$ for a term a with respect to the solution state S using the individual canonizers σ_i.

Shostak's original algorithm [Sho84] and its proof were both incorrect. The algorithm, as corrected by the author and Harald Ruess [RS01,SR02], checks the validity of a sequent $T \vdash c = d$. It does this by processing each equality $a = b$ into its solved form. If S is the current solution state, then an unprocessed equality $a = b$ in T is processed by first transforming it to $a' = b'$, where $a' = S[\![a]\!]$ and $b' = S[\![b]\!]$. The equality $a' = b'$ is variable abstracted and the variable abstraction equalities $x = t$ are added to the solution S_i, where t is a term in the theory θ_i. The algorithm then repeatedly reconciles the solutions S_i so that whenever two variables x and y are merged in S_i but not in S_j, for $i \neq j$, then they are merged in S_j by solving $t_x = t_y$ in θ_j, for $x = t_x$ and $y = t_y$ in S_j, and composing the solution with S_j to obtain a new solution set S_j. When all the input equalities from T have been processed and we have the resulting solution state S, we check if $S[\![c]\!] = S[\![d]\!]$. A conjunction of literals $\bigwedge_i a_i = b_i \wedge \bigwedge_j c_j = d_j$ is satisfiable iff $S \neq \bot$ and $S[\![c_j]\!] \not\equiv S[\![d_j]\!]$, for each j, where $S = process(T)$.

Ground Satisfiability. The Nelson–Oppen and Shostak decision procedures check the satisfiability of conjunctions of literals drawn from a combination of theories. These procedures can be extended to handle propositional combinations of atomic formulas by transforming these formulas to disjunctive normal form. This method can be inefficient when the propositional case analysis involved is heavy. It is usually more efficient to combine a SAT solver with a ground decision procedure [BDS02,dMRS02]. There are various ways in which such a combination can be executed. Let ϕ be the formula whose satisfiability is being checked. Let L be an injective map from fresh propositional variables to the atomic subformulas of ϕ such that $L^{-1}[\phi]$ is a propositional formula. We can use a SAT solver to check that $L^{-1}[\phi]$ is satisfiable, but the resulting truth assignment, say $l_1 \wedge \ldots \wedge l_n$, might be spurious, that is $L[l_1 \wedge \ldots \wedge l_n]$ might not be ground-satisfiable. If that is the case, we can repeat the search with the added lemma $(\neg l_1 \vee \ldots \vee \neg l_n)$ and invoke the SAT solver on $(\neg l_1 \vee \ldots \vee \neg l_n) \wedge L^{-1}[\phi]$. This ensures that the next satisfying assignment returned is different from the previous assignment that was found to be ground-unsatisfiable. The lemma that is added can be minimized to find the minimal unsatisfiable set of literals l_i. This means that the lemma that is added is smaller, and the pruning of spurious assignments is more effective. The ground decision procedure can be also be used to precompute a set Λ of lemmas (clauses) of the form $l_1 \vee \ldots \vee l_n$, where

$\neg L[l_1] \wedge \ldots \neg L[l_n]$ is unsatisfiable according to the ground decision procedures. The SAT solver can then be reinvoked with $\Lambda \wedge L^{-1}[\phi]$.

A tighter integration of SAT solvers and ground decision procedures would allow the decision procedures to check the consistency of the case analysis during an application of splitting in the SAT solver and avoid cases that are ground-unsatisfiable. Through a tighter integration, it would also be possible to resume the SAT solver with the added conflict information without starting the SAT solving process from scratch. We address the challenge of integrating inference procedures below.

Applications. Ground decision procedures, ground satisfiability, and quantifier elimination have many applications.

Symbolic Execution: Given a transition system, symbolic execution is the process of computing preconditions or postconditions of the transition system with respect to an assertion. For example, the strongest postcondition of an assertion p with respect to a transition N is the assertion $\lambda s : \exists s_0 : p(s_0) \wedge N(s_0, s)$. For certain choices of p and N, this assertion can be computed by means of a quantifier elimination. This is useful in analyzing timed and hybrid systems [ACH+95].

Infinite-State Bounded Model Checking: Bounded model checking checks for the existence of counterexamples of length upto a bound k for a given temporal property. With respect to certain temporal properties, it is possible to reduce the bounded model checking problem for such systems to a ground satisfiability problem [dMRS02].

Abstraction and Model Checking: The early work on abstraction in the context of model checking was on reducing finite-state systems to smaller finite-state systems, i.e., systems with fewer possible states [Kur93,CGL92, LGS+95]. Graf and Saïdi [GS97] were the first to consider the use of a theorem prover for reducing (possibly) infinite-state systems to finite-state (hence, model-checkable) form. Their technique of *predicate abstraction* constructs an abstract counterpart of a concrete transition system where the truth values of certain predicates over the concrete state space are simulated by boolean variables. Data abstraction replaces a variable over an infinite state space by one over a finite domain. Predicate and data abstraction based on theorem proving are widely used [BLO98b,CU98,DDP99,SS99, BBLS00,CDH+00,TK02,HJMS02,FQ02]. The finite-state abstraction can exhibit spurious counterexamples that are not reproducible on the concrete system. Ground decision procedures are also useful here for detecting spurious counterexamples and suggesting refinements to the abstraction predicates [BLO98a,SS99,DD01].

Software Engineering: Ground decision procedures are central to a number of analysis tools for better engineered software including array-bounds checking, extended static checking [DLNS98], typechecking [SO99], and static analysis [BMMR01,Pug92].

5   Challenges

We have enumerated some of the progress in developing, integrating, and deploying various inference procedures. A great many challenges remain. We discuss a few of these below.

The Complexity Challenge. Many decision procedures are of exponential, superexponential, or non-elementary complexity. However, this complexity often does not manifest itself on practical examples. Modern SAT solvers can solve very large practical problems, but they can also run aground on small instances of simple challenges like the propositional pigeonhole principle. MONA deals with a logic that is known to have a non-elementary lower bound, yet it performs quite well in practice. The challenge here is to understand the ways in which one can overcome complexity bounds on the problems that arise in practice through heuristic or algorithmic means.

The Theory Challenge. Inference procedures are hard to build, extend, and maintain. The past experience has been that good theory leads to simpler decision procedures with greater efficiency. A well-developed theory can also help devise uniform design patterns for entire classes of decision procedures. Such design patterns can contribute to both the efficiency and modularity of these procedures. Methods derived by specializing general-purpose methods like resolution and rewriting can also simplify the construction of decision procedures.

The Modularity Challenge. As we have already noted, inference procedures need rich programmer interfaces (APIs) [BM86,FORS01]. Boyer and Moore [BM86] write:

> ... the black box nature of the decision procedure is frequently destroyed by the need to integrate it. The integration forces into the theorem prover much knowledge of the inner workings of the procedure and forces into the procedure many features that are unnecessary when the problem is considered in isolation.

For example, a ground decision procedure can be used in an online manner so that atomic formulas are added to a context incrementally, and claims are tested against the context. The API should include operations for asserting and retracting information, testing claims, and for creating, deleting, and browsing contexts. The decision procedures might need to exchange information with other inference procedures such as a rewriter, typechecker, or an external constraint solver. We already saw how the desired interaction between ground decision procedures and SAT solvers was such that neither of these could be treated as a black box procedure.

The modularity challenge is a significant one. Butler Lampson has argued that software components have always failed at low levels of granularity (see http://research.microsoft.com/users/blampson/Slides/ReusableComponentsAbstract.htm). He says that successful software components are those at the level of a database, a compiler, or a theorem prover, but not decision procedures, constraint solvers, or unification procedures. For interoperation between inference components, we also need compatible logics, languages, and term and proof representations.

The Integration Challenge. The availability of good inference components is a prerequisite for integration, but we also need to find effective ways of combining these components in complementary ways. The combination of decision procedures with model checking in predicate and data abstraction is a case where such a complementary integration is remarkably effective. Other such examples include the combination of unification/matching procedures and constraint solving, and typechecking and ground decision procedures.

The Verification Challenge. How do we know that our inference procedures are sound? This question is often asked by those who wish to apply inference procedures in contexts where a high level of manifest assurance is required. This question has been addressed in a number of ways. The LCF approach [GMW79] requires inference procedures to be constructed as tactics that generate a fully expanded proof in terms of low level inferences when applied. Proof objects have also been widely used as a way of validating inference procedures and securing mobile code [Nec97]. Reflection [Wey80,BM81] is a way of reasoning about the metatheory of a theory within the theory itself. The difficult tradeoff with reflection is that the theory has to be simple in order to be reasoned about, but rich enough to reason with. The verification of decision procedures is actually well within the realm of feasible, and recently, there have been several successful attempts in this direction [Thé98,FS02].

6   Conclusions

We have argued for a reappraisal of Hao Wang's programme [Wan60b,Wan60a] of inferential analysis as a paradigm for automated reasoning. The key element of this paradigm is the use of problem-driven combinations of sophisticated and efficient low-level decision procedures. Such an approach runs counter to the traditional thinking in automated reasoning which is centered around uniform proof search procedures. Similar ideas are also central to the automated reasoning schools of Bledsoe [Ble77] and Boyer and Moore [BM79,BM86].

The active use of decision procedures in automated reasoning began with the *west-coast* theorem proving approach pioneered by Boyer and Moore [BM79], Shostak [SSMS82], and Nelson and Oppen [LGvH+79,NO79]. The PVS system is in this tradition [ORS92,Sha01], as are STeP [MT96], SIMPLIFY [DLNS98], and SVC [BDS00].

In recent years there has been a flurry of interest in the development of verification tools that rely quite heavily on sophisticated decision procedures. The quality and efficiency of many of these decision procedures is impressive. The underlying theory is also advancing rapidly [Bjø99,Tiw00]. Such theoretical advances will make it easier to construct correct decision procedures and integrate them more easily with other inference mechanisms. Contrary to the impression that decision procedures are black boxes, they need rich interfaces [BM86, FORS01,GNTV02] in order to be deployed most efficiently. The theory, construction, integration, verification, and deployment of inference procedures is likely to be a rich source of challenges for automated reasoning in mathematically rich domains.

References

[ACD93]   Rajeev Alur, Costas Courcoubetis, and David Dill. Model-checking in dense real-time. *Information and Computation*, 104(1):2–34, May 1993.

[ACH+95] R. Alur, C. Courcoubetis, N. Halbwachs, T. A. Henzinger, P.-H. Ho, X. Nicollin, A. Olivero, J. Sifakis, and S. Yovine. The algorithmic analysis of hybrid systems. *Theoretical Computer Science*, 138(1):3–34, 6 February 1995.

[BBLS00] Kai Baukus, Saddek Bensalem, Yassine Lakhnech, and Karsten Stahl. Abstracting WS1S systems to verify parameterized networks. In Susanne Graf and Michael Schwartzbach, editors, *Tools and Algorithms for the Construction and Analysis of Systems (TACAS 2000)*, number 1785 in Lecture Notes in Computer Science, pages 188–203, Berlin, Germany, March 2000. Springer-Verlag.

[BCM+92] J. R. Burch, E. M. Clarke, K. L. McMillan, D. L. Dill, and L. J. Hwang. Symbolic model checking: 10^{20} states and beyond. *Information and Computation*, 98(2):142–170, June 1992.

[BDS00]   Clark W. Barrett, David L. Dill, and Aaron Stump. A framework for cooperating decision procedures. In David McAllester, editor, *Automated Deduction—CADE-17*, volume 1831 of *Lecture Notes in Artificial Intelligence*, pages 79–98, Pittsburgh, PA, June 2000. Springer-Verlag.

[BDS02]   Clark W. Barrett, David L. Dill, and Aaron Stump. Checking satisfiability of first-order formulas by incremental translation to SAT. In *Computer-Aided Verification, CAV '02*, Lecture Notes in Computer Science. Springer-Verlag, July 2002.

[BG01]   Leo Bachmair and Harald Ganzinger. Resolution theorem proving. In Robinson and Voronkov [RV01], pages 19–99.

[BGG97]   Egon Börger, Erich Grädel, and Yuri Gurevich. *The Classical Decision Problem*. Perspectives in Mathematical Logic. Springer, 1997.

[Bjø99]   Nikolaj Bjørner. *Integrating Decision Procedures for Temporal Verification*. PhD thesis, Stanford University, 1999.

[Ble77]   W. W. Bledsoe. Non-resolution theorem proving. *Artificial Intelligence*, 9:1–36, 1977.

[BLO98a] Saddek Bensalem, Yassine Lakhnech, and Sam Owre. Computing abstractions of infinite state systems compositionally and automatically. In Hu and Vardi [HV98], pages 319–331.

[BLO98b] Saddek Bensalem, Yassine Lakhnech, and Sam Owre. InVeSt: A tool for the verification of invariants. In Hu and Vardi [HV98], pages 505–510.

[BM79]   R. S. Boyer and J S. Moore. *A Computational Logic*. Academic Press, New York, NY, 1979.

[BM81]   R. S. Boyer and J S. Moore. Metafunctions: Proving them correct and using them efficiently as new proof procedures. In R. S. Boyer and J S. Moore, editors, *The Correctness Problem in Computer Science*. Academic Press, London, 1981.

[BM86]   R. S. Boyer and J S. Moore. Integrating decision procedures into heuristic theorem provers: A case study with linear arithmetic. In *Machine Intelligence*, volume 11. Oxford University Press, 1986.

[BMMR01] T. Ball, R. Majumdar, T. Millstein, and S. Rajamani. Automatic predicate abstraction of C programs. In *Proceedings of the SIGPLAN '01 Conference on Programming Language Design and Implementation, 2001*, pages 203–313. ACM Press, 2001.

[Bry86]   R. E. Bryant. Graph-based algorithms for Boolean function manipulation. *IEEE Transactions on Computers*, C-35(8):677–691, August 1986.

[BW01]   Alexander Bockmayr and Volker Weispfenning. Solving numerical constraints. In Robinson and Voronkov [RV01], pages 751–742.

[CDH+00] James Corbett, Matthew Dwyer, John Hatcliff, Corina Pasareanu, Robby, Shawn Laubach, and Hongjun Zheng. Bandera: Extracting finite-state models from Java source code. In *22nd International Conference on Software Engineering*, pages 439–448, Limerick, Ireland, June 2000. IEEE Computer Society.

[CG01]   Shang-Ching Chou and Xiao-Shan Gao. Automated reasoning in geometry. In Robinson and Voronkov [RV01], pages 707–749.

[CGL92]   E. M. Clarke, O. Grumberg, and D. E. Long. Model checking and abstraction. In *Nineteenth Annual ACM Symposium on Principles of Programming Languages*, pages 343–354, 1992.

[CGP99]   E. M. Clarke, Orna Grumberg, and Doron Peled. *Model Checking*. MIT Press, 1999.

[CH91]   G. E. Collins and H. Hong. Partial cylindrical algebraic decomposition. *Journal of Symbolic Computation*, 12(3):299–328, 1991.

[Col75]   G. E. Collins. Quantifier elimination for real closed fields by cylindrical algebraic decomposition. In *Second GI Conference on Automata Theory and Formal Languages*, number 33 in Lecture Notes in Computer Science, pages 134–183, Berlin, 1975. Springer-Verlag.

[Coo72]   D. C. Cooper. Theorem proving in arithmetic without multiplication. In *Machine Intelligence 7*, pages 91–99. Edinburgh University Press, 1972.

[CU98]   M. A. Colón and T. E. Uribe. Generating finite-state abstractions of reactive systems using decidion procedures. In Hu and Vardi [HV98], pages 293–304.

[Dav57]   M. Davis. A computer program for Presburger's algorithm. In *Summaries of Talks Presented at the Summer Institute for Symbolic Logic*, 1957. Reprinted in Siekmann and Wrightson [SW83], pages 41–48.

[Dav83]   M. Davis. The prehistory and early history of automated deduction. In Siekmann and Wrightson [SW83], pages 1–28.

[DD01]   Satyaki Das and David L. Dill. Successive approximation of abstract transition relations. In *Annual IEEE Symposium on Logic in Computer Science01*, pages 51–60. The Institute of Electrical and Electronics Engineers, 2001.

[DDP99]   Satyaki Das, David L. Dill, and Seungjoon Park.   Experience with
            predicate abstraction. In Nicolas Halbwachs and Doron Peled, editors,
            Computer-Aided Verification, CAV '99, volume 1633 of *Lecture Notes
            in Computer Science*, pages 160–171, Trento, Italy, July 1999. Springer-
            Verlag.

[DE73]   George B. Dantzig and B. Curtis Eaves. Fourier-Motzkin elimination and
            its dual. *Journal of Combinatorial Theory (A)*, 14:288–297, 1973.

[DLL62]   M. Davis, G. Logemann, and D. Loveland. A machine program for the-
            orem proving. *Communications of the ACM*, 5(7):394–397, July 1962.
            Reprinted in Siekmann and Wrightson [SW83], pages 267–270, 1983.

[DLNS98]   David L. Detlefs, K. Rustan M. Leino, Greg Nelson, and James B. Saxe.
            Extended static checking. Technical Report 159, COMPAQ Systems Re-
            search Center, 1998.

[dMRS02]   Leonardo de Moura, Harald Rueß, and Maria Sorea. Lazy theorem prov-
            ing for bounded model checking over infinite domains. In A. Voronkov,
            editor, *International Conference on Automated Deduction (CADE'02)*,
            Lecture Notes in Computer Science, Copenhagen, Denmark, July 2002.
            Springer-Verlag.

[DP60]   M. Davis and H. Putnam. A computing procedure for quantification
            theory. *JACM*, 7(3):201–215, 1960.

[EKM98]   Jacob Elgaard, Nils Klarlund, and Anders Möller. Mona 1.x: New tech-
            niques for WS1S and WS2S. In Hu and Vardi [HV98], pages 516–520.

[FORS01]   J.-C. Filliâtre, S. Owre, H. Rueß, and N. Shankar. ICS: Integrated Can-
            onization and Solving. In G. Berry, H. Comon, and A. Finkel, editors,
            Computer-Aided Verification, CAV '2001, volume 2102 of *Lecture Notes
            in Computer Science*, pages 246–249, Paris, France, July 2001. Springer-
            Verlag.

[FQ02]   Cormac Flanagan and Shaz Qadeer. Predicate abstraction for software
            verification. In *ACM Symposium on Principles of Programming Lan-
            guages02*, pages 191–202. Association for Computing Machinery, January
            2002.

[FS02]   Jonathan Ford and Natarajan Shankar. Formal verification of a combina-
            tion decision procedure. In A. Voronkov, editor, *Proceedings of CADE-19*,
            Berlin, Germany, 2002. Springer-Verlag.

[Gil60]   P. C. Gilmore. A proof method for quantification theory: Its justification
            and realization. *IBM Journal of Research and Development*, 4:28–35,
            1960.   Reprinted in Siekmann and Wrightson [SW83], pages 151–161,
            1983.

[GMW79]   M. Gordon, R. Milner, and C. Wadsworth. *Edinburgh LCF: A Mechanized
            Logic of Computation*, volume 78 of *Lecture Notes in Computer Science*.
            Springer-Verlag, 1979.

[GNTV02]   Enrico Giunchiglia, Massimo Narizzano, Armando Tacchella, and
            Moshe Y. Vardi. Towards an efficient library for SAT: a manifesto. To
            appear, 2002.

[GS97]   S. Graf and H. Saïdi. Construction of abstract state graphs with PVS.
            In *Conference on Computer Aided Verification CAV'97*, LNCS 1254,
            Springer Verlag, 1997.

[HJMS02]   Thomas A. Henzinger, Ranjit Jhala, Rupak Majumdar, and Gregoire
            Sutre. Lazy abstraction. In *ACM Symposium on Principles of Program-
            ming Languages02*, pages 58–70. Association for Computing Machinery,
            January 2002.

[HO80]   G. Huet and D. C. Oppen. Equations and rewrite rules: a survey. In
           R. Book, editor, *Formal Language Theory: Perspectives and Open Prob-
           lems*, pages 349–405. Academic Press, ny, 1980.

[HV98]   Alan J. Hu and Moshe Y. Vardi, editors. *Computer-Aided Verification,
           CAV '98*, volume 1427 of *Lecture Notes in Computer Science*, Vancouver,
           Canada, June 1998. Springer-Verlag.

[KMM00]   Matt Kaufmann, Panagiotis Manolios, and J Strother Moore. *Computer-
           Aided Reasoning: An Approach*, volume 3 of *Advances in Formal Methods*.
           Kluwer, 2000.

[Kur93]   R.P. Kurshan. *Automata-Theoretic Verification of Coordinating Pro-
           cesses*. Princeton University Press, Princeton, NJ, 1993.

[LGS+95]   C. Loiseaux, S. Graf, J. Sifakis, A. Bouajjani, and S. Bensalem. Property
           preserving abstractions for the verification of concurrent systems. *Formal
           Methods in System Design*, 6:11–44, 1995.

[LGvH+79] D. C. Luckham, S. M. German, F. W. von Henke, R. A. Karp, P. W.
           Milne, D. C. Oppen, W. Polak, and W. L. Scherlis. Stanford Pascal
           Verifier user manual. CSD Report STAN-CS-79-731, Stanford University,
           Stanford, CA, March 1979.

[McM93]   K.L. McMillan. *Symbolic Model Checking*. Kluwer Academic Publishers,
           Boston, 1993.

[Min63]   Marvin Minsky. Steps toward artificial intelligence. In E. A. Feigenbaum
           and J. Feldman, editors, *Computers and Thought*. McGraw-Hill Book
           Company, New York, 1963.

[MMZ+01]   Matthew W. Moskewicz, Conor F. Madigan, Ying Zhao, Lintao Zhang,
           and Sharad Malik. Chaff: Engineering an efficient SAT solver. In *Design
           Automation Conference*, pages 530–535, 2001.

[MSS99]   J. Marques-Silva and K. Sakallah. GRASP: A search algorithm for propo-
           sitional satisfiability. *IEEE Transactions on Computers*, 48(5):506–521,
           May 1999.

[MT96]   Zohar Manna and The STeP Group. STeP: Deductive-algorithmic verifi-
           cation of reactive and real-time systems. In Rajeev Alur and Thomas A.
           Henzinger, editors, *Computer-Aided Verification, CAV '96*, volume 1102
           of *Lecture Notes in Computer Science*, pages 415–418, New Brunswick,
           NJ, July/August 1996. Springer-Verlag.

[Nec97]   George C. Necula. Proof-carrying code. In *24th ACM Symposium on
           Principles of Programming Languages*, pages 106–119, Paris, France, Jan-
           uary 1997. Association for Computing Machinery.

[Nel81]   G. Nelson. Techniques for program verification. Technical Report CSL-
           81-10, Xerox Palo Alto Research Center, Palo Alto, Ca., 1981.

[NO79]   G. Nelson and D. C. Oppen. Simplification by cooperating decision pro-
           cedures. *ACM Transactions on Programming Languages and Systems*,
           1(2):245–257, 1979.

[NSS57]   A. Newell, J. C. Shaw, and H. A. Simon. Empirical explorations with
           the logic theory machine: A case study in heuristics. In *Proc. West.
           Joint Comp. Conf.*, pages 218–239, 1957. Reprinted in Siekmann and
           Wrightson [SW83], pages 49–73, 1983.

[Opp78]   Derek C. Oppen. A $2^{2^{2^{pn}}}$ upper bound on the complexity of Presburger
           arithmetic. *Journal of Computer and System Sciences*, 16:323–332, 1978.

[ORS92]   S. Owre, J. M. Rushby, and N. Shankar. PVS: A prototype verification
            system. In Deepak Kapur, editor, *11th International Conference on Au-
            tomated Deduction (CADE)*, volume 607 of *Lecture Notes in Artificial
            Intelligence*, pages 748–752, Saratoga, NY, June 1992. Springer-Verlag.

[ORSvH95]   Sam Owre, John Rushby, Natarajan Shankar, and Friedrich von Henke.
            Formal verification for fault-tolerant architectures: Prolegomena to the
            design of PVS. *IEEE Transactions on Software Engineering*, 21(2):107–
            125, February 1995.

[Pos21]   E. L. Post. Introduction to a general theory of elementary propositions.
            American Journal of Mathematics, 43:163–185, 1921. Reprinted in [vH67,
            pages 264–283].

[Pra60]   D. Prawitz. An improved proof procedure. *Theoria*, 26:102–139, 1960.
            Reprinted in Siekmann and Wrightson [SW83], pages 162–201, 1983.

[Pre29]   M. Presburger. Uber die vollständigkeit eines gewissen systems der arith-
            metik ganzer zahlen, in welchem die addition als einzige operation hervor-
            tritt. *Compte Rendus du congrés Mathématiciens des Pays Slaves*, pages
            92–101, 1929.

[Pug92]   W. Pugh. A practical algorithm for exact array dependence analysis.
            Communications of the ACM, 35(8):102–114, 1992.

[Rab78]   Michael O. Rabin. Decidable theories. In Jon Barwise, editor, *Handbook
            of Mathematical Logic*, volume 90 of *Studies in Logic and the Foundations
            of Mathematics*, chapter C8, pages 595–629. North-Holland, Amsterdam,
            Holland, 1978.

[Rob65]   J. A. Robinson. A machine-oriented logic based on the resolution prin-
            ciple. *JACM*, 12(1):23–41, 1965. Reprinted in Siekmann and Wright-
            son [SW83], pages 397–415.

[RS01]   Harald Rueß and Natarajan Shankar. Deconstructing Shostak. In *16th
            Annual IEEE Symposium on Logic in Computer Science*, pages 19–28,
            Boston, MA, July 2001. IEEE Computer Society.

[RV01]   A. Robinson and A. Voronkov, editors. *Handbook of Automated Reason-
            ing*. Elsevier Science, 2001.

[Sha01]   Natarajan Shankar. Using decision procedures with a higher-order logic.
            In *Theorem Proving in Higher Order Logics: 14th International Confer-
            ence, TPHOLs 2001*, volume 2152 of *Lecture Notes in Computer Sci-
            ence*, pages 5–26, Edinburgh, Scotland, September 2001. Springer-Verlag.
            Available at
            `ftp://ftp.csl.sri.com/pub/users/shankar/tphols2001.ps.gz`.

[Sho81]   Robert E. Shostak. Deciding linear inequalities by computing loop
            residues. *Journal of the ACM*, 28(4):769–779, October 1981.

[Sho84]   Robert E. Shostak. Deciding combinations of theories. *Journal of the
            ACM*, 31(1):1–12, January 1984.

[SKR98]   T. R. Shiple, J. H. Kukula, and R. K. Ranjan. A comparison of Presburger
            engines for EFSM reachability. In Hu and Vardi [HV98], pages 280–292.

[SO99]   Natarajan Shankar and Sam Owre. Principles and pragmatics of subtyp-
            ing in PVS. In D. Bert, C. Choppy, and P. D. Mosses, editors, *Recent
            Trends in Algebraic Development Techniques, WADT '99*, volume 1827
            of *Lecture Notes in Computer Science*, pages 37–52, Toulouse, France,
            September 1999. Springer-Verlag.

[SR02]   N. Shankar and H. Rueß. Combining Shostak theories. In *International
            Conference on Rewriting Techniques and Applications (RTA '02)*, Lecture
            Notes in Computer Science. Springer-Verlag, July 2002. Invited Paper.

[SS99]   Hassen Saïdi and Natarajan Shankar. Abstract and model check while
             you prove. In *Computer-Aided Verification, CAV '99*, Trento, Italy, July
             1999.
[SS00]   Mary Sheeran and Gunnar Stålmarck. A tutorial on Stålmarck's proof
             procedure for propositional logic. *Formal Methods in Systems Design*,
             16(1):23–58, January 2000.
[SSMS82]   R. E. Shostak, R. Schwartz, and P. M. Melliar-Smith. STP: A mecha-
             nized logic for specification and verification. In D. Loveland, editor, *6th
             International Conference on Automated Deduction (CADE)*, volume 138
             of *Lecture Notes in Computer Science*, New York, NY, 1982. Springer-
             Verlag.
[SW83]   J. Siekmann and G. Wrightson, editors. *Automation of Reasoning: Clas-
             sical Papers on Computational Logic, Volumes 1 & 2*. Springer-Verlag,
             1983.
[Tar48]   A. Tarski. *A Decision Method for Elementary Algebra and Geometry*.
             University of California Press, 1948.
[TH96]   Cesare Tinelli and Mehdi Harandi. A new correctness proof of the Nelson-
             Oppen combination procedure. In Frans Baader and Klaus U. Schulz, edi-
             tors, *Frontiers of Combining Systems: First International Workshop*, vol-
             ume 3 of *Applied Logic Series*, pages 103–119, Munich, Germany, March
             1996. Kluwer.
[Thé98]   Laurent Théry. A certified version of Buchberger's algorithm. In H. Kirch-
             ner and C. Kirchner, editors, *Proceedings of CADE-15*, number 1421 in
             Lecture Notes in Artificial Intelligence, pages 349–364, Berlin, Germany,
             July 1998. Springer-Verlag.
[Tiw00]   Ashish Tiwari. *Decision Procedures in Automated Deduction*. PhD thesis,
             State University of New York at Stony Brook, 2000.
[TK02]   Ashish Tiwari and Gaurav Khanna. Series of abstractions for hybrid au-
             tomata. In C.J. Tomlin and M.R. Greenstreet, editors, *Hybrid Systems:
             Computation and Control, 5th International Workshop, HSCC 2002*, vol-
             ume 2289 of *Lecture Notes in Computer Science*, pages 465–478, Stanford,
             CA, March 2002. Springer-Verlag.
[vH67]   J. van Heijenoort, editor. *From Frege to Gödel: A Sourcebook of Math-
             ematical Logic, 1879–1931*. Harvard University Press, Cambridge, MA,
             1967.
[VW86]   Moshe Y. Vardi and Pierre Wolper. An automata-theoretic approach to
             automatic program verification (preliminary report). In *Proceedings 1st
             Annual IEEE Symp. on Logic in Computer Science*, pages 332–344. IEEE
             Computer Society Press, 1986.
[Wan60a]   H. Wang. Proving theorems by pattern recognition — I. *Communi-
             cations of the ACM*, 3(4):220–234, 1960. Reprinted in Siekmann and
             Wrightson [SW83], pages 229–243, 1983.
[Wan60b]   Hao Wang. Toward mechanical mathematics. *IBM Journal*, 4:2–22, 1960.
[Wan63]   H. Wang. Mechanical mathematics and inferential analysis. In P. Braffort
             and D. Hershberg, editors, *Computer Programming and Formal Systems*.
             North-Holland, 1963.
[Wey80]   Richard W. Weyhrauch. Prolegomena to a theory of mechanized formal
             reasoning. *Artificial Intelligence*, 13(1 and 2):133–170, April 1980.
[Zha97]   Hantao Zhang. SATO: An efficient propositional prover. In *Conference
             on Automated Deduction*, pages 272–275, 1997.

Automated Boundary Testing from Z and B

Bruno Legeard, Fabien Peureux, and Mark Utting*

Laboratoire d'Informatique
Université de Franche-Comté
16, route de Gray - 25030 Besançon, France
Tel.: (33) 381 666 664
{legeard,peureux,utting}@lifc.univ-fcomte.fr

Abstract. We present a method for black-box boundary testing from B and Z formal specifications. The basis of the method is to test every operation of the system at every boundary state using all input boundary values of that operation. The test generation process is highly automated. It starts by calculating boundary goals from Pre/Post predicates derived from the formal model. Then each boundary goal is instantiated to a reachable boundary state, by searching for a sequence of operations that reaches the boundary goal from the initial state. This process makes intensive use of a set-oriented constraint technology, both for boundary computation and to traverse the state space. The method was designed on the basis of industrial applications in the domain of critical software (Smart card and transportation). Application results show the effectiveness and the scalability of the method. In this paper, we give an overview of the method and focus on the calculation of the boundary goals and states.

Keywords: specification-based testing, boundary values, set constraint solving, B method, Z notation.

1 Introduction

Automated formal-specification-based test generation is a very promising way to improve functional software testing. On the one hand, it offers the opportunity to give a rational for better covering the requirements, and on the other hand, the automation is able to reduce the cost of test design. This is particularly true in application domains of critical software, such as smart cards, aeronautics and transportation, where more than 50% of the development is devoted to the validation of the software product. Thus the effort for specification formalization can easily be recouped. We have trialled this on a large scale industrial application, the Smart Card GSM 11-11 case-study, with test case generation from a B formal model [1]. This showed that the generated test suites had good coverage, and that the test design effort was reduced by 30%.

During the last decade, test generation from formal specification has been a very active research area [2,3]. For model-based specification, as in Z [4],

---

* On sabbatical leave from the University of Waikato, New Zealand.

L.-H. Eriksson and P. Lindsay (Eds.): FME 2002, LNCS 2391, pp. 21–40, 2002.
© Springer-Verlag Berlin Heidelberg 2002

VDM [5] or B [6], a now classical method was presented by Jeremy Dick and Alain Faivre [7]. It consists of two steps:

1. generating an abstract Finite State Automaton – FSA – from the formal model by partition analysis of the state space and operations;
2. selecting test cases as paths in the FSA using various test selection criteria like all-transitions or all-transition-pairs.

This approach is followed by numerous authors, for Z specifications [8] [9], for B specifications [10] and also for Abstract State Machine specifications [11]. In the Dick and Faivre paper, this test generation process was defined, but only the partition analysis was automated. Currently, there is still no proposal which automates the full process. This is due to the difficulties inherent to this method. At the first step of FSA generation, there is the possible state explosion and the non-discovery problem which make it difficult to determine all the FSA states and transitions [11]. At the second step, the problem of finding the shortest sequences of operations which cover all the transitions of the FSA is equivalent to the well known NP-complete Chinese Postman Problem [12].

We present a new method, for *boundary value* test generation from a B or Z formal specification. This method was designed during the last three years on the basis of industry collaboration on real applications. Three projects, concerning Smart Card software (GSM 11-11 Standard [13], Java Card Virtual Machine and Transaction mechanism [14]) and transport system software (Ticket Validation Algorithm [15]) have been realized. We started these projects with a set constraint solver, called CLPS-B [16,17], which could animate B specifications. This solver constitutes the basis of our test generation method, both for bounds computation (using propagation of interval constraints over integer and set domains) and for traversing the constrained reachability graph of the abstract model to generate test cases as sequences of operations. Now, the solver is being extended to handle Z constructs and incorporated into a tool-set, called BZ-Testing-Tools (BZ-TT), which is able to compute boundary values, generate test cases and produce executable test scripts.

The unique features of the BZ-TT method are that it:

- takes both B and Z specifications as an input;
- avoids the construction of the complete FSA;
- produces boundary-value test cases (both boundary states and boundary input values);
- produces both negative and positive test cases;
- is fully supported by tools.

The main objectives of this paper are to introduce the BZ-Testing-Tools test generation method and to focus on boundary calculation. The next section presents an overview of the method. Section 3 introduces the specification model used as an input for the method, and an example. Section 4 details boundary goal calculation and the following section describes test generation steps. The final sections discuss related work and conclusions.

2   Overview of the BZ-TT Test Generation Method

Our goal is to test some implementation, which is not derived via refinement from the formal model. The implementation is usually a state machine with hidden state. We specify this state machine by a B or Z formal specification, which has a state space (consisting of several state variables) and a number of operations that modify this state.

A behavior of such a system can be described in terms of a sequence of operations (a trace) where the first is activated from the initial state of the machine. However, if the precondition of an operation is false, the effect of the operation is unknown, and any subsequent operations are of no interest, since it is impossible to determine the state of the machine. Thus, we define a positive test case to be any legal trace, i.e. any trace where all preconditions are true. A positive test case corresponds to a sequence of system states presenting the value of each state variable after each operation invocation. The submission of a legal trace is a success if all the output values returned by the concrete implementation during the trace are equivalent (through a function of abstraction) to the output values returned by its specifications during the simulation of the same trace (or included in the set of possible values if the specification is non-deterministic). A negative test case is defined as a legal trace plus a final operation whose precondition is false. The generation of negative test cases is useful for robustness testing.

2.1   Principles of the Method

The BZ-TT method consists of testing the system when it is in a *boundary state*, which is a state where at least one state variable has a value at an extremum – minimum or maximum – of its sub domains.

At this boundary state, we are interested to test all the possible behaviors of the specification. That is, the goal is to invoke each *update operation* with extremum values of the subdomains of the input parameters. The test engineer partitions the operations into *update operations*, which may modify the system state, and *observation operations*, which may not.

We divide the trace constituting the test case into four subsequences[1] (see Fig.1):

Preamble: this takes the system from its initial state to a boundary state.
Body: this invokes one update operation with input boundary values.
Identification: this is a sequence of observation operations to enable a pass/fail verdict to be assigned.
Postamble: this takes the system back to the boundary state, or to an initial state. This enables test cases to be concatenated.

---

[1] The vocabulary follows the ISO9646 standard [18].

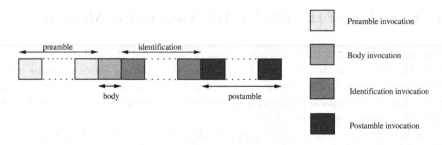

Fig. 1. Test case constitution

The body part is the critical test invocation of the test case. Update operations are used in the preamble, body and postamble and observation operations in the identification part.

The BZ-TT generation method is defined by the following algorithm, where $\{bound_1, bound_2, ..., bound_n\}$ and $\{op_1, op_2, ..., op_m\}$ respectively define the set of all boundary states and the set of all the update operations of the specification:

```
for i=1 to n              % for each boundary state
    preamble(bound_i);    % reach the boundary state
    for j=1 to m          % for each update operation
        body(op_j);       % test op_j
        identification;   % observe the state
        postamble(bound_i); % return to the boundary state
    endfor
    postamble(init);      % return to the initial state
endfor
```

This algorithm computes positive test cases with valid boundary input values at body invocations. Figure 2 shows how the state space is traversed during the generation method. A set of one or more test cases, concatenated together, defines a test sequence. For negative test cases, the body part is generated with invalid input boundary values, and no identification or postamble parts are generated, because the system arrives at an indeterminate state from the formal model point of view.

After positive and negative test cases are generated by this procedure, they are automatically translated into executable test scripts, using a test script pattern and a reification relation between the abstract and concrete operation names, inputs and outputs.

3   Specification Model

This section describes the specification model that we use, for Z and B.

Z is a model-oriented formal specification notation that was developed at Oxford University in the 1980s, with extensive industry collaboration. It has

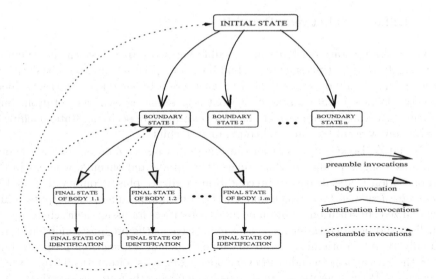

Fig. 2. Traversal of the state space during the test sequence generation.[2]

become quite widely known and used, and is in the process of becoming an ISO standard. Z is essentially typed set theory, plus a *schema* notation that allows specifications to be built up incrementally.

One of the early designers of Z was Jean-Raymond Abrial, who later developed the B method [6], which places more emphasis on refinement to code and on tool support. B has been used for the formal development of several significant safety-critical systems, such as the driverless Metro line in Paris [19].

There are many similarities between B and Z. They have basically the same notation for expressions and predicates (over 90% of their toolkit operators are identical), the same type system and the same approach to undefinedness.

The main difference between B and Z is that Z is primarily a specification notation, whereas B is a complete method that covers the whole lifecycle, including specification, refinement and code generation. For specification, Z is more flexible, since schemas can be used in many different ways, whereas the B specification constructs are more tailored to specifying state machines and to supporting refinement.

Because of the similarity between the B and Z toolkits, and our use of a set-oriented constraint technology which is convenient for B and Z notations, we decided to provide test-generation tools for both notations. Our approach is to translate both notations into a common subset, which is suitable for test-generation and convenient for our tools. The remainder of this section describes the major differences between the B and Z notations, the limitations that we impose, the common subset and our translation process.

---

[2] The final state of the body and the final state of identification are generally the same, because observation operations may not affect the value of the state variables.

3.1   Differences between B and Z

B and Z specify state machines in very different ways. In Z, the schema calculus is typically used to (incrementally) build a state space schema, an initialisation schema and several operation schemas, but there is no language construct which directly defines a state machine. In contrast, B has no schema notation, but provides a sophisticated *abstract machine notation* for specifying state machines, with many ways of layering and combining machines.

B and Z also specify operations in different ways: in Z an operation schema contains a single predicate which relates the inputs and outputs, whereas in B, an operation is specified by a precondition predicate plus a command (called a *generalized substitution*) which updates the state and produces the outputs. This generalized substitution notation includes constructs for assignment, choice, parallelism and non-determinism, so is as expressive as the pre/postcondition style. Finally, B and Z both allow a state machine to include an *invariant predicate*, but in Z the invariant is included in every operation, so is automatically preserved, whereas in B the operations are specified independently from the invariant, and it is a proof obligation to show that each operation preserves the invariant.

3.2   How We Use B and Z

Our test generation method takes as an input an abstract model of the requirements. For B, that means that only the machine level is used (no refinement or implementation level). For simplicity, and to improve the scalability of the test generation process, we impose three restrictions on the input specification:

1. It must specify a single state machine. For B, this means that we allow only one abstract machine, without layering etc. For our industrial case-studies, this was not a problem.

   For Z, it is necessary to identify which schemas represent the state and the operations. We do this by using a *schema* to represent a state machine. This *machine* schema must have fields called *state* and *init* (which are themselves schemas), plus other schema-valued fields which are the operations. A machine schema is an ordinary Z schema, so can be typechecked and manipulated using standard Z tools, but our tools give it the additional (machine) interpretation, and apply extra typechecking rules to make sure that the machine is well-formed. So it is necessary to write this schema before using our method.

2. Operations must have explicit preconditions. Both Z and B allow the precondition to be implicit within the operation. They both have laws for calculating preconditions, but these typically give complex predicates with existential quantifiers. To ensure more tractable preconditions, we restrict the syntactic form of B operations so that all preconditions appear at the beginning of each operation, and for each Z operation we require the engineer to provide an explicit precondition. These explicit preconditions are written

using the conjecture syntax of standard Z, as follows, and should be verified using a Z prover.

$$\vdash? \, pre \; Op = [State; \; Inputs \mid Simplified\_Precondition]$$

This emphasis on explicit preconditions is a requirement of our method, but is generally considered good engineering practice.

3. Given sets must be replaced by finite enumerated sets (free types in Z) for the purposes of test generation. This makes it possible for our CLP-based tools to perform much stronger reasoning about the specification, and this is usually necessary for the test-generation process to be tractable.

3.3 Translation Architecture

Figure 3 shows how we translate B and Z specifications into our common subset, which we call the *BZ-Prolog* format (BZP). The BZP format is a Prolog-readable syntax, which is similar to the Atelier-B ASCII notation for B (*.mch syntax). Semantically, the BZP format is equivalent to a single B machine (no imports), where all operations are specified in a standard pre/postcondition format:[3]

$$outputs \leftarrow opname(inputs)$$
$$\mathrel{\widehat{=}} Pre \mid @s', outputs' \bullet Post \implies outputs, s := outputs', s'$$

where s is the state variable of the machine, Pre is the precondition (a predicate over $inputs$ and s) and $Post$ is the postcondition (a predicate over $inputs, s, s'$ and $outs'$). The rules for translating an arbitrary generalized substitution command into this pre/post format are taken from the B book [6, Chap. 6]. So, in the BZP file, each operation is specified by: its name, the names and types of its inputs and outputs, and its precondition and postcondition predicates.

As noted above, invariants have different roles in B and Z. This difference is visible in the resulting BZP file, because when we translate a Z operation, we include the (primed) invariant in its postcondition (because it often contributes to the effect of the operation), but when we translate a B operation we do not include the invariant. However, the well-formedness proofs for a B machine check that every operation preserves the invariant, so discharging these proofs ensures that the B and Z approaches are equivalent.

3.4 Process Scheduler Example

As a running example, we use a simple scheduler that manages a set of processes (taken from [7]). Figure 4 shows the B model of the scheduler. For test generation, the set of processes *PID* is restricted to the finite set $\{p_1, p_2, p_3, p_4\}$. The active process is represented by a singleton set or an empty set. The usual well-formedness conditions of this B model were proved using Atelier B [20], 50 proof obligations were generated and proved automatically.

---

[3] The @ non-deterministically chooses any $s', outputs'$ values that satisfy *Post*.

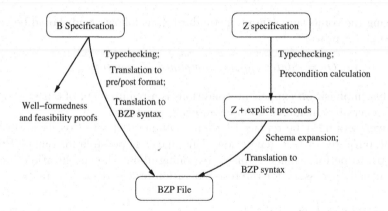

Fig. 3. Translation of B and Z specifications into common BZP format.

MACHINE
   SCHEDULER
SETS
   $PID = \{p1, p2, p3, p4\}$
VARIABLES
   active, ready, waiting
INVARIANT
   active $\subseteq PID \wedge$
   ready $\subseteq PID \wedge$
   waiting $\subseteq PID \wedge$
   $card(active) \leq 1 \wedge$
   ready $\cap$ *waiting* $= \varnothing \wedge$
   active $\cap$ *waiting* $= \varnothing \wedge$
   active $\cap$ *ready* $= \varnothing \wedge$
   $(active = \varnothing) \Rightarrow (ready = \varnothing)$
INITIALIZATION
   active, ready, waiting $:= \varnothing, \varnothing, \varnothing$

OPERATIONS
   NEW(pp)
     PRE
       $pp \in PID \wedge$
       $pp \notin (ready \cup waiting \cup active)$
     THEN
       waiting $:= (waiting \cup \{pp\})$
     END;

READY(rr)
   PRE
     $rr \in waiting$
   THEN
     waiting $:= (waiting - \{rr\}) \|$
     IF $(active = \varnothing)$ **THEN**
       active $:= \{rr\}$
     ELSE
       ready $:= ready \cup \{rr\}$
     END
   END;
SWAP
   PRE
     active $\neq \varnothing$
   THEN
     waiting $:= waiting \cup active \|$
     IF $(ready = \varnothing)$ **THEN**
       active $:= \varnothing$
     ELSE
       ANY pp
       WHERE $pp \in ready$ **THEN**
         active $:= \{pp\}$
         ready $:= ready - \{pp\}$
       END
     END
   END;

Fig. 4. Scheduler B abstract machine

4 Boundary Goal Calculation

Our method works by computing a set of *boundary goals* from the Disjunctive
Normal Form (DNF) of the specification, then instantiating each boundary goal

into a *boundary state*. A *boundary goal* is a predicate that describes a subset of the state space. A *boundary state* is a fully instantiated state (or set of states) obtained by traversal of the state space.

4.1 Partition Analysis

For test generation purposes, we transform the pre/post predicates into DNF, obtaining $\bigvee_i Pre_i$ and $\bigvee_j Post_j$. This means an operation is equivalent to:

$$(\textstyle\bigvee_i Pre_i) \mid @s', outputs' \bullet (\textstyle\bigvee_j Post_j) \Longrightarrow outputs, s := outputs', s'$$
$$= \{\textit{By the laws of generalized substitutions [6, Sect. 6.1].}\}$$
$$(\textstyle\bigvee_i Pre_i) \mid ([]_j (@s', outputs' \bullet Post_j \Longrightarrow outputs, s := outputs', s')) \,.$$

This shows that the operation is a demonic choice between the alternative postconditions, which are the different *effects* of the operation. We want to test each effect separately. This is essentially an implementation of the *cause-effect* test-generation strategy [21].

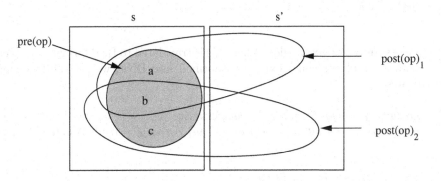

Fig. 5. Analysis of input state space using precondition subdomains

To illustrate this further, Fig. 5 shows a simple operation *op* whose postcondition has two disjuncts, $post(op)_1$ and $post(op)_2$, and whose precondition, $pre(op)$ is represented by the shaded circle, which is a subset of the state space s. If we considered only the precondition, we would choose boundary values within the circle $(a \cup b \cup c)$. This does not usually give sufficiently detailed tests, especially for industry applications where many operations are robust, so have trivial preconditions (*true*). However, using the cause-effect strategy, we project each of the postcondition disjuncts onto the initial state space, by hiding all input, output and final-state variables. Then we generate tests for each of the resulting state subsets, which we call *precondition subdomains*. The jth subdomain is:

$$(\exists\, inputs, s', outputs' \bullet (\textstyle\bigvee_i Pre_i) \wedge Post_j) \,.$$

For the example in Fig. 5, this means we generate tests for two precondition subdomains: one is the region $a \cup b$ and the other is $b \cup c$. We test boundary values within each of these subsets.

Note that the union of all the precondition subdomains (over all operations) covers all the *interesting* states for generating positive tests, because if a state is outside all precondition subdomains, then there are no operations enabled at that state, so no positive testing is possible.

Fig. 5 illustrates that other interpretations of the cause-effect strategy are possible. It appears attractive to insist on testing each of the a, b, c subsets separately. However, we currently do not do this, because

- it can give a number of tests that is exponential in the number of postcondition disjuncts;
- in industrial practice, region b is often empty (e.g., when op is deterministic), so testing regions a and c is sufficient to ensure that both postconditions are exercised. This is the case for the scheduler example, and our three industrial case-studies.
- our focus on *boundary* values (described in the next section) is a strong heuristic that typically forces some values within a or c to be chosen, rather than just b.

Process scheduler example: When this is translated to BZP format, and each precondition and postcondition is transformed into DNF, we get the following predicates:

$pre(new)_1 == pp \notin waiting \cup ready \cup active$
$post(new)_1 == waiting' = waiting \cup \{pp\} \wedge ready' = ready \wedge active' = active$

$pre(ready)_1 == pp \in waiting$
$post(ready)_1 == active = \{\} \wedge waiting' = waiting - \{pp\}$
$\qquad \wedge ready' = ready \wedge active' = \{pp\}$
$post(ready)_2 == active \neq \{\} \wedge waiting' = waiting - \{pp\}$
$\qquad \wedge ready' = ready \cup \{pp\} \wedge active' = active$

$pre(swap)_1 == active \neq \{\}$
$post(swap)_1 == ready = \{\} \wedge waiting' = waiting$
$\qquad \wedge ready' = ready \wedge active' = \{\}$
$post(swap)_2 == ready \neq \{\} \wedge (\exists pp \in ready \mid waiting' = waiting$
$\qquad \wedge ready' = ready - \{pp\} \wedge active' = \{pp\})$

This gives five precondition subdomains, which are equivalent to the following predicates. In practice, the BZ-TT solver reduces each subdomain to a set of constraints, which is equivalent to the predicate shown in Table 1.

Table 1. Results of pre/post predicate partition on the process scheduler example.

Name	Op,Pre,Post	Predicate
PS_1	$new, 1, 1$	$Inv \wedge \#(waiting \cup ready \cup active) < \#PID$
PS_2	$ready, 1, 1$	$Inv \wedge waiting \neq \{\} \wedge active = \{\}$
PS_3	$ready, 1, 2$	$Inv \wedge waiting \neq \{\} \wedge \#active = 1$
PS_4	$swap, 1, 1$	$Inv \wedge active \neq \{\} \wedge ready = \{\}$
PS_5	$swap, 1, 2$	$Inv \wedge active \neq \{\} \wedge ready \neq \{\}$

4.2 Boundary Goals

We compute boundary goals on the basis of the partition analysis by minimization and maximization using a suitable metric function (e.g., minimize or
maximize the sum of the cardinalities of the sets). This results in one or several
minimal and maximal boundary goals for each predicate.

Given the invariant properties Inv, a precondition subdomain predicate PS_i,
a vector of variables V_i which comprises all the free state variables within PS_i,
and f an optimization function, the boundary goals are computed as follows:

$$BG_i^{min} = minimize(f(V_i), Inv \wedge PS_i) \tag{1}$$
$$BG_i^{max} = maximize(f(V_i), Inv \wedge PS_i) \tag{2}$$

According to the optimization function used to compute the boundary goals,
we may obtain one or several boundary goals per minimization or maximization
calculus. We include the whole invariant, Inv, within this computation because
it contains important background information such as the types and ranges of
all the state variables.

The optimization function $f(V_i)$, where V_i is a vector of variables $v_1 \ldots v_m$,
is defined as $g_1(v_1) + g_2(v_2) + \ldots + g_m(v_m)$, where each function g_i is chosen
according to the type of the variable v_i. Table 2 shows examples of the various
functions that we use. The choice of functions can be customized by the test
engineer.

Process scheduler example: From each pre/post predicate PS_i of the process
scheduler example (Table 1), boundary goals BG_i^{min} and BG_i^{max} are computed
with the optimization function $f(V_i) = \sum_{v \in V_i} \#v$. The results of this boundary
goal computation on the scheduler example is shown in Table 3. The result of
constraint solving is a set of constraints on the cardinalities of the set variables
$waiting$, $ready$ and $active$. In Table 3, each X_i variable stands for an arbitrary
member of PID, so we always have the following constraints:

$$(\forall i \bullet X_i \in \{p_1, p_2, p_3, p_4\}) \wedge$$
$$(\forall i, j \bullet i \neq j \Rightarrow X_i \neq X_j) .$$

When a state variable does not appear in a line of Table 3, its value is unconstrained, so it can take any value of its domain that satisfies the invariant.

Table 2. Simple examples of optimization functions

Type	Possible optimization functions
set V_i of integers	$\sum_{v \in V_i} v$ $\sum_{v \in V_i} v^2$ $\sum_{v \in V_i} \sqrt{v}$
set V_i of couples	$g_j(dom(V_i))$ $g_k(ran(V_i))$ $g_j(dom(V_i)) \circ g_k(ran(V_i))$
set V_i of sets	$\sum_{v \in V_i} \#v$ $\sum_{v \in V_i} \#v^2$ $\sum_{v \in V_i} \sqrt{\#v}$

Boundary goals 8 and 12 are subsumed by boundary goal 5, and boundary goals 10 and 11 are subsumed by boundary goal 9. So we keep the nine boundary goals 1...7, 9 and 13 to generate test sequences.

Table 3. Results of boundary goal computation on the process scheduler example.

BG N°	BG Name	Boundary Goal Predicate
1	BG_1^{min}	$waiting = \{\} \wedge ready = \{\} \wedge active = \{\}$
2	BG_1^{max}	$waiting = \{X_1, X_2, X_3\} \wedge ready = \{\} \wedge active = \{\}$
3		$waiting = \{\} \wedge ready = \{X_1, X_2\} \wedge active = \{X_3\}$
4		$waiting = \{X_1, X_2\} \wedge ready = \{\} \wedge active = \{X_3\}$
5		$waiting = \{X_1\} \wedge ready = \{X_2\} \wedge active = \{X_3\}$
6	BG_2^{min}	$waiting = \{X_1\} \wedge ready = \{\} \wedge active = \{\}$
7	BG_2^{max}	$waiting = \{X_1, X_2, X_3, X_4\} \wedge ready = \{\} \wedge active = \{\}$
8	BG_3^{min}	$waiting = \{X_1\} \wedge active = \{X_2\}$
9	BG_3^{max}	$waiting = \{X_1, X_2, X_3\} \wedge ready = \{\} \wedge active = \{X_4\}$
10	BG_4^{min}	$ready = \{\} \wedge active = \{X_1\}$
11	BG_4^{max}	$ready = \{\} \wedge active = \{X_1\}$
12	BG_5^{min}	$ready = \{X_1\} \wedge active = \{X_2\}$
13	BG_5^{max}	$waiting = \{\} \wedge ready = \{X_1, X_2, X_3\} \wedge active = \{X_4\}$

It should be noted that other optimization functions could be used. For example, from BG_1^{max}, with the optimization function $f(V_i) = \sum_{v \in V_i} \#v^2$, only boundary goal N°2 is generated, and with the optimization function $f(V_i) = \sum_{v \in V_i} \sqrt{v}$, only boundary goal N°5 is generated.

5   Test Generation

This section describes how test cases are generated from boundary goals. The generation process follows the structure of each test case: preamble, body, identification and postamble.

5.1   Preamble Computation

Each boundary goal is instantiated to one or more reachable boundary states by exploring the reachable states of the system, starting from the initial state. The BZ-TT solver simulates the execution of the system, recording the set of possible solutions after each operation. A best-first search [22] is used to try and reach a boundary state that satisfies a given boundary goal. Preamble computation can thus be viewed as a traversal of the reachability graph, whose nodes represent the constrained states built during the simulation, and whose transitions represent an operation invocation. A consequence of this preamble computation is that state variables which are not already assigned a value by the boundary goal, are assigned a reachable value of their domain.

Some boundary goals may not be reachable via the available operations (this happens when the invariant is weaker than it could be). By construction, every boundary goal satisfies the invariant, which is a partial reachability check. In addition to this, we bound the search for the boundary state during the preamble computation, so that unreachable boundary goals (and perhaps some reachable goals) are reported to the test engineer as being unreachable. This feedback may suggest ways of improving the specification by strengthening the invariant, thus eliminating those goals. If all boundary goals in a precondition subdomain P are unreachable, we relax our boundary testing criterion and search for any preamble that reaches a state satisfying P. Finally, the test engineer can add and delete boundary goals, to customise the test generation, or to satisfy other test objectives.

Process scheduler example: For each boundary goal of the scheduler example (Table 3), preambles are generated with the BZ-TT solver. It should be noted that we take only one path to reach a state verifying the boundary goal. Therefore, we obtain only one preamble per boundary goal. The result of this computation is shown in Table 4.

5.2   Input Variable Boundary Analysis and Body Computation

The purpose of the body computation is to test, for a given boundary state, all the update operations, with all boundary values of their input variables. For the boundary values which satisfy the precondition, we get a positive test case, otherwise we get a negative test case. Note that, from the same preamble and boundary state, several bodies are usually obtained for each operation, with differing input values.

Table 4. Results of preamble computation on the system process scheduler example.

Boundary goal	Preamble
1	True at initial state: empty preamble
2	new(p_1), new(p_2), new(p_3)
3	new(p_1), new(p_2), new(p_3), ready(p_1), ready(p_2), ready(p_3)
4	new(p_1), new(p_2), new(p_3), ready(p_1)
5	new(p_1), new(p_2), new(p_3), ready(p_1), ready(p_2)
6	new(p_1)
7	new(p_1), new(p_2), new(p_3), new(p_4)
9	new(p_1), new(p_2), new(p_3), new(p_4), ready(p_1)
13	new(p_1), new(p_2), new(p_3), new(p_4), ready(p_1), ready(p_2), ready(p_3), ready(p_4)

The process of boundary analysis for input variables is similar to that for state variables, except that invalid input values are kept, which is not the case for unreachable boundary states. Given an operation Op with a set of input variables I_i and a precondition Pre, let BG_i be one of the boundary goals of Op. Note that BG_i is a set of constraints over the state variables, typically giving a value to each state variable. Then, given f an optimization function, the input variable boundaries are computed as follows:

- for positive test cases:

$$minimize(f(I_i), Inv \wedge Pre \wedge BG_i) \qquad (3)$$
$$maximize(f(I_i), Inv \wedge Pre \wedge BG_i) \qquad (4)$$

- for negative test cases:

$$minimize(f(I_i), Inv \wedge \neg Pre \wedge BG_i) \qquad (5)$$
$$maximize(f(I_i), Inv \wedge \neg Pre \wedge BG_i) \qquad (6)$$

Process scheduler example: Results of body computation on the scheduler example are shown in Table 5 for the positive test cases, and in the appendix for the negative test cases.

Some positive test case bodies already appear in the preamble of another test case (for example, PC_1 in preamble 2, PC_2 in preamble 7, etc.). These redundant test cases are removed. That is why only the test cases with bold-faced names in Table 5 are retained. For each positive test case, the oracle is composed of the possible output values (none in this example) and state variable values after each operation invocation.

The BZ-TT method generates 9 different positive test cases containing a total of 53 operation invocations. For the same example, Dick and Faivre [7] define a FSA with six states and 16 transitions, and manually create a single (optimal) test sequence containing 19 operation invocations that exercises all these transitions.

The CASTING test generation method [10] also uses an FSA-based approach, but proposes an algorithm for efficiently covering all the transitions. When applied to the scheduler using the same FSA as Dick and Faivre, this results in six test sequences with a total of 27 operation invocations. BZ-TT has around double this number of invocations, which is not surprising, because its aim is to test each transition with both minimum and maximum boundary values.

The BZ-TT method generates 31 negative test cases for the system process scheduler example. The generation of negative test cases is a user choice and the test engineer must provide the oracle for each final invocation operation of each negative test case.

Table 5. Positive test cases

BG N°	Preamble	Body	test N°
1		new(p_1)	PC_1
2	new(p_1), new(p_2), new(p_3)	new(p_4)	PC_2
		ready(p_1)	PC_3
3	new(p_1), new(p_2), new(p_3), ready(p_1), ready(p_2), ready(p_3)	new(p_4)	**PC_4**
		swap	**PC_5**
4	new(p_1), new(p_2), new(p_3), ready(p_1)	new(p_4)	**PC_6**
		ready(p_2)	PC_7
		swap	**PC_8**
5	new(p_1), new(p_2), new(p_3), ready(p_1), ready(p_2)	new(p_4)	**PC_9**
		ready(p_3)	PC_{10}
		swap	**PC_{11}**
6	new(p_1)	new(p_2)	PC_{12}
		ready(p_1)	**PC_{13}**
7	new(p_1), new(p_2), new(p_3), new(p_4)	ready(p_1)	PC_{14}
9	new(p_1), new(p_2), new(p_3), new(p_4), ready(p_1)	ready(p_2)	PC_{15}
		swap	**PC_{16}**
13	new(p_1), new(p_2), new(p_3), new(p_4), ready(p_1), ready(p_2), ready(p_3), ready(p_4)	swap	**PC_{17}**

5.3   Identification and Postamble

The identification part of a test case is simply a sequence of all observation operations whose preconditions are true after the body. The postamble part is computed similarly to the preamble, using best-first search.

As this process scheduler specification is a toy example from the literature, there is no observation operations, so we cannot generate an identification part and the system is not testable. Real-life applications are generally testable, so provide observation operations. For example, a realistic scheduler would provide a function to determine whether a given process is active or waiting.

There is also no operation to put the system in the initial state (no delete operation), so no postamble part is possible in this example.

5.4   Observability and Executable Test Scripts Reification

Automatic generation of executable test scripts from generated test cases is of major importance to fully support the testing process. Generated test cases define sequences of operation invocations at an abstract level. More precisely, the operation appears with the signature of the formal model and the input values are those from the abstract data model. In the Java Card case-study [14], we defined and implemented a solution to bridge the gap between generated test cases and executable scripts. This solution is as follows. The tester defines two inputs: a test script pattern and a table of equivalence and observability. This table is similar to the representation mappings defined in [23].

The script pattern is a source file in the target language in which the test will be built. This source file includes all the declaration and code prerequisites for testing, and contains some tags indicating where to insert sequences of operation invocations and sequences of observation. For example, in the Java Card case study, the script pattern is a Java Card source file and the operation sequences to be inserted are API or Byte-code [24]. The table of equivalence and observability gives, for each operation of the abstract model, the callable expression of the system under test. Also, it gives expressions to compute the value of state variables when this is possible. For negative test cases, this table defines the oracle. If necessary, this table is completed by a table giving the equivalences between abstract input and output values and concrete values (for example, correspondence between symbolic values and hexadecimal). A module computes executable test scripts by inserting concrete expressions in the script pattern following the generated test cases and the equivalence and observability expression. This process is deterministic.

The verdict assignment is achieved by comparing both operation output values and observable state variables using observability expressions, from test cases with test script passing results. Our experience on the Java Card case-study show that automatic verdict assignment is one of the main difficult points. This is, on one hand, due to well-known theoretical problems [2] such as the possibility of non-determinism of the specification. On the other hand, there are also practical problems in comparing generated oracle values (values of abstract state variables) and concrete execution results. Automatic verdict assignment is still an important research area for specification-based test generation.

For negative test cases, the final state, after the body invocation with invalid input values, means nothing from a specification point of view. In the implementation, the response to negative test case stimuli depends highly on how defensive programming has been achieved. The oracle for these kind of test cases must be defined manually by the tester. For example, if the swap operation of a scheduler implementation is meant to be robust, then the oracle for the invalid test case $new(p1);\ new(p2);\ new(p3);\ swap$ might check that the correct exception is raised. Alternatively, a more detailed specification could specify exception behaviours, then this negative test would become a positive test whose oracle would be generated from the specification.

6 Conclusion

We have presented techniques for automatic boundary testing from model-oriented formal specifications. The main novelty lies in the systematic use of bounds to compute tests using constraint technology. This approach gives rise to the BZ-TT test generation process which allows one to test an implementation in four main stages:

1. produce the formal model of the system, verify it using proof and validate it using animation;
2. compute boundary goals from the formal model;
3. generate a preamble for each boundary goal, then body parts, identification parts and postamble parts;
4. generate executable test scripts given a target pattern file.

In the last three years, we have conducted three industrial case-studies using the BZ-TT test generation method. These case-studies demonstrated the effectiveness of the BZ-TT method and helped to define usable functionalities for the test engineers. Each of these studies focused on particular goals and results. The first one was the Smart Card GSM 11-11 Standard, which gave the opportunity to compare generated test cases from the BZ-TT process with a very mature and high quality manually-designed test suite. The results showed coverage of more 85% compared to the manually-designed test suites, while 50% of generated tests supplemented the manual test suites, with the possibility of detecting different faults. The second case-study, a ticket validation algorithm for transportation, used test generation on a single operation model using bounds on input variables. The third case-study tested part of the Java Card Virtual Machine - JCVM - and Run-Time Environment - JCRE - focusing on the transaction mechanism. This case study allowed us to produce executable test scripts and to evaluate them on the test bed.

These case studies showed that the effort for specification formalization is directly recouped by the benefit of test generation: the automation reduces the time for test design and coding, and test generation from the formal model gives a good rational for deciding the scope of testing and when testing should end. Moreover, automated boundary testing based on constraint technology makes it possible to define a scalable method and tools. It avoids the complete construction of an abstract Finite State Automaton from the B or Z formal model.

The boundary goal and preamble computation uses set-based constraint solving. This allows automation of the test generation process, including the generation of executable test scripts, under the control of the test engineer. Indeed, the test engineer drives the generation process at several points: producing the formal model, validating boundary goals (boundary goals can be seen as test objectives), defining the oracle for negative test cases, overriding the default preamble computation (for example by defining some state in the state space to be reached during the graph traversal) and defining the reification mapping and the pattern source file for executable test script generation. Driving the test generation process, the test engineer exploits his/her test expertise to optimize the generated test suite.

Currently, the main limitations of the BZ-TT test generation method and tool are the following; these points are our ongoing research:

- at the formal model level: the restriction of one single machine is too strong – we want to take as an input multi-layered B machines, including refinement levels.
- for boundary goals, we need a stronger reachability test before beginning the preamble computation. For the moment, each boundary goal verifies the invariant predicate and the search is bounded during preamble computation. But this is not ideal. We are investigate the use of more precise techniques for ensuring the reachability of each boundary goal.
- we want to better address the question of coverage measure for boundary test generation.

The BZ-TT environment is currently being consolidated for delivery to the scientific community. All the interfaces are developed in Java and the kernel (boundary goal computation, test generation and constraint solving) are developed in SICStus Prolog.

Acknowledgment. This research was supported in part by a grant of the French ANVAR - Agence Nationale de Valorisation des Actions de Recherche. The visit of Mark Utting was supported under the French/New Zealand scientific cooperation program. We wish to thank Bruno Marre for useful discussions concerning this work.

References

1. E. Bernard, B. Legeard, X. Luck, and F. Peureux. Generation of test sequences from formal specifications: GSM 11.11 standard case-study. *Submitted to the Journal of Software Practice and Experience*, 2002.
2. M-C. Gaudel. Testing can be formal too. *TAPSOFT'95: Theory and Practice of Software Development*, LNCS 915:82–96, May 1995.
3. J. Tretmans. Test generation with inputs, outputs and repetitive quiescence. *Software-Concepts and Tools*, 17(3):103–120, 1996.
4. J.M. Spivey. *The Z notation: A Reference Manual.* Prentice-Hall, 2nd edition, 1992. ISBN 0 13 978529 9.

5. C.B. Jones. *Systematic Software Development Using VDM.* Prentice-Hall, 2nd edition, 1990.
6. J-R. Abrial. *The B-BOOK: Assigning Programs to Meanings.* Cambridge University Press, 1996. ISBN 0 521 49619 5.
7. J. Dick and A. Faivre. Automating the generation and sequencing of test cases from model-based specifications. *FME'93: Industrial-Strength Formal Methods,* LNCS 670 Springer-Verlag:268–284, April 1993.
8. R. Hierons. Testing from a Z specification. *The Journal of Software Testing, Verification and Reliability,* 7:19–33, 1997.
9. L. Murray, D. Carrington, I. MacColl, J. McDonald, and P. Strooper. Formal derivation of finite state Machines for class testing. In *Proceedings of the Z User Meeting (ZUM'98): The Z Formal Specification Notation,* pages 42–59, Berlin, Germany, September 1998. Springer-Verlag.
10. L. van Aertryck, M. Benveniste, and D. le Metayer. CASTING: a formally based software test generation method. *In 1st IEEE International Conference on Formal Engineering Methods (ICFEM'97),* pages 99–112, 1997.
11. W. Grieskamp, Y. Gurevich, W. Schulte, and M. Veanes. Testing with abstract state machines. In *Formal Methods and Tools for Computer Science (EURO-CAST'01) - Extended Abstracts,* february 2001.
12. Jonathan Gross and Jay Yellen. *Graph Theory and its Applications.* The CRC Press Series on Discrete Mathematics and its Applications. CRC Press, Boca Raton, Florida, 1999.
13. B. Legeard and F. Peureux. Generation of functional test sequences from B formal specifications – Presentation and industrial case-study. In 16th *IEEE International Conference on Automated Software Engineering (ASE'01),* San Diego, USA, November 2001.
14. F. Bouquet, J. Julliand, B. Legeard, and F. Peureux. Automatic reconstruction and generation of functional test patterns - application to the Java card transaction mechanism (confidential). Technical Report TR-01/02, LIFC - University of Franche-Comt and Schlumberger Montrouge Product Center, 2002.
15. N. Caritey, L. Gaspari, B. Legeard, and F. Peureux. Specification-based testing – Application on algorithms of Metro and RER tickets (confidential). Technical Report TR-03/01, LIFC - University of Franche-Comt and Schlumberger Besan on, 2001.
16. F. Ambert, B. Legeard, and E. Legros. Constraint Logic Programming on Sets and Multisets. In *Proceedings of ICLP'94 - Workshop on Constraint Languages and their use in Problem Modeling,* pages 151–165, Ithaca, New York, November 1994.
17. F. Bouquet, B. Legeard, and F. Peureux. CLPS-B – A constraint solver for B. In *Proceedings of the conference on Tools and Algorithms for the Construction and Analysis of Systems (TACAS'02),* Grenoble, France, April 2002.
18. ISO. Information Processing Systems, Open Systems Interconnection. *OSI Conformance Testing Methodology and Framework – ISO 9646.*
19. P. Behm, P. Desforges, and J.M. Meynadier. METEOR : An Industrial Success in Formal Development. In *Second conference on the B method,* Montpellier, France, 1998.
20. Clearsy, Europarc de Pichaury 13856 Aix-en-Provence Cedex 3 - France. *Atelier B Technical Support version 3,* May 2001 – http://www.atelierb.societe.com.
21. G.J. Myers. *The Art of Software Testing.* Wiley-InterScience, 1979.

22. A. Pretschner. Classical search strategies for test case generation with Constraint Logic Programming. In BRICS, editor, *Proceedings of the Workshop on Formal Approaches to Testing of Software (FATES'01)*, pages 47–60, Aalborg, Denmark, August 2001.

23. D.J. Richardson and S.L. Aha T.O. O'Malley. Specification-based test oracles for reactive systems. In *Proceedings of the 14th International Conference on Software Engineering (ICSE'92)*, pages 105–118, Melbourne, Australia, May 1992. ACM Press.

24. Sun microsystems. *Java Card 2.1.1 Virtual Machine Specification.* http://java.sun.com/products/javacard/javacard21.html#specification, May 2000.

A   Negative Test Cases for the Scheduler Example

BG N°	Preamble	Body	test N°
1		new($invalid$)	NC_1
		ready($invalid$)	NC_2
		swap	NC_3
2	new(p_1), new(p_2), new(p_3)	new($invalid$)	NC_4
		new(p_1)	NC_5
		ready($invalid$)	NC_6
		swap	NC_7
3	new(p_1), new(p_2), new(p_3), ready(p_1),ready(p_2), ready(p_3)	new($invalid$)	NC_8
		new(p_1)	NC_9
		ready($invalid$)	NC_{10}
4	new(p_1), new(p_2), new(p_3), ready(p_1)	new($invalid$)	NC_{11}
		new(p_1)	NC_{12}
		ready($invalid$)	NC_{13}
5	new(p_1), new(p_2), new(p_3), ready(p_1), ready(p_2)	new($invalid$)	NC_{14}
		new(p_1)	NC_{15}
		ready($invalid$)	NC_{16}
6	new(p_1)	new($invalid$)	NC_{17}
		new(p_1)	NC_{18}
		ready($invalid$)	NC_{19}
		swap	NC_{20}
7	new(p_1), new(p_2), new(p_3), new(p_4)	new($invalid$)	NC_{21}
		new(p_1)	NC_{22}
		ready($invalid$)	NC_{23}
		swap	NC_{24}
9	new(p_1), new(p_2), new(p_3), new(p_4), ready(p_1)	new($invalid$)	NC_{25}
		new(p_1)	NC_{26}
		ready($invalid$)	NC_{27}
13	new(p_1), new(p_2), new(p_3), new(p_4), ready(p_1), ready(p_2), ready(p_3), ready(p_4)	new($invalid$)	NC_{28}
		new(p_1)	NC_{29}
		ready($invalid$)	NC_{30}

Improvements in Coverability Analysis

Gil Ratsaby, Baruch Sterin, and Shmuel Ur

IBM Haifa Research Labs, Israel
{rgil,baruch,ur}@il.ibm.com

Abstract. In simulation-based verification users are faced with the challenge of maximizing test coverage while minimizing testing costs. Sophisticated techniques are used to generate clever test cases and to determine the quality attained by the tests. The latter activity, which is essential for locating areas of the design that need to have more tests, is called *test coverage analysis*.

We have previously introduced the notion of coverability, which refers to the degree to which a model can be covered when subjected to testing. We showed how a coverability analyzer enables naive users to take advantage of the power of symbolic model checking with a 'one-button' interface for coverability analysis.

In this work, we present several heuristics, based on static program analysis and on simulation of counter examples, for improving the efficiency of coverability analysis by symbolic model checking. We explain each heuristic independently and suggest a way to combine them. We present an experiment that shows improvements based on using random simulation in the analysis of coverability.

1   Introduction

We introduced the notion of coverability in [6]. Informally, coverability is a property of a State-machine model that refers to the degree to which the model can be tested using simulation. Formally, a *coverability model* is defined by creating a *coverability goal* for every coverage goal in the coverage model of interest. The coverability goal is met if, and only if, a test that covers the corresponding coverage goal exists. Thus, a tool for determining coverability can help assess whether a given fragment of HDL code contains dead-code or whether all branches of a particular control-flow statement can be taken. A coverability analyzer is a tool that enables naive users to take advantage of the power of model checkers with a 'one-button' interface for coverability analysis.

To compare coverability analysis and coverage analysis, consider the implementation of statement coverage. In statement coverage, the coverage model is composed of a goal for each statement which can be satisfied by a test whose control passes through that statement. Here, a coverage tool typically implements statement coverage by adding a counter after every statement and initializing the counter to zero. Every time a test is simulated, some of the counters are modified. The coverage tool outputs all the counters that remain zero, as they are indicative of either dead-code or holes in the test plan. In coverability analysis, a rule for every statement would be automatically generated to check that it can be reached. These rules are executed by the model checker on the program (or instrumented program) and a warning on the existence of dead-code is created for every statement that cannot be reached. While it is often reasonable to leave

L.-H. Eriksson and P. Lindsay (Eds.): FME 2002, LNCS 2391, pp. 41–56, 2002.

dead-code in the model to ease the testing of future modifications, this dead-code should not be considered 'uncovered' in the coverage analysis. The concept of coverability captures this point.

We implemented coverability analysis by building on symbolic model checking techniques which provide a framework for reasoning about Finite-state systems [20]. The implementation is based on two key observations. The first is that a coverage model is composed of coverage goals, each of which is mappable to a corresponding coverability goal. The second observation is that a State-machine model can be instrumented with control variables and related transitions. On one hand, they retain the original model behavior as reflected on the original state variables and, on the other hand, they can be used for coverability analysis of the model. The analysis is carried out by formulating special rules on the instrumented model and presenting these rules (with the instrumented model) to a symbolic model checker. Then, the symbolic model checker either verifies that the task is coverable and presents a proof in the form of a counter example, or states that the task is uncoverable and a bug is found.

Coverability analyzers are computationally intensive tools that automatically execute a large number of rules. In this paper, we show a number of techniques that reduce the number of rules that need to be run, as well as improve the efficiency of each rule as it is executed. One idea is based on the observation that a test that was generated to cover one coverability goal may cover other goals as well. There are a number of techniques for determining which other tasks are covered; some techniques are based on static analysis and some on the simulation of counter examples. If one takes into account that covering one task may cause others to be covered, the order chosen to cover the tasks is of importance. The second idea, which has applications for other domains in model checking, is that given a rule R and a program P, it is sometimes possible to create a simpler program P' on which R yields the same reply.

Unlike recent coverage work for the Finite State-machine (FSM) citeFSMCover, where coverage is calculated for formal rules on the FSM and is measured on the FSM (e.g., percentage of the FSM states covered), our measurement is on the program itself. Our tool's feedback is expressed in a language that is natural to the developer, with clear action items based on the tool's outputs.

The rest of this paper is organized as follows: in Section 2, we define the common terms used throughout the paper. In Section 3, we describe the context in which our work was created. In Section 4, we show how coverability can be implemented for several coverability models. In Section 5, the main section, we show a number of algorithms and a general methodology used to improve the efficiency of coverability analysis. In Section 6, we explain how CAT — our Coverability Analysis Tool — was implemented. In Section 7, we discuss our experience using CAT and present our conclusions in Section 8.

2   Definitions

An FSM is an abstract model of a system where, at any given time, the outputs are a function of the inputs and values of the state variables at that time. The relationship between the inputs of the FSM, present state (represented as a vector of state values), and next state is described by a transition relation. Hereafter, we use the terms *FSM*, *State-machine model*, and *program* interchangeably.

A *symbolic model checker* [20] is an algorithm that takes a State-machine model and a set of temporal logic properties (rules) as input. It computes the truth or falsity of the property by traversal of the State-machine. Whenever the property is not satisfied by the model, the model checker produces a counter-example, namely, a sample execution sequence of the model where the property is violated.

A *coverage goal* is a binary function on test patterns. This function specifies whether some event occurred when the test pattern is simulated against the State-machine model.

A *coverage model* is a set of goals. The statement coverage model, for example, is a model that contains a goal for every statement and indicates whether this statement has been executed in simulation.

Every coverage model has a corresponding *coverability model*. A coverability model is defined by creating, for every coverage goal in the coverage model, a coverability goal, which is a binary function on the state-machine model. The coverability goal is true if there exists a test on the State-machine model for which the corresponding coverage goal is true.

A *basic block* is a sequence of non-branching statements. Basic block A *dominates* basic block B ($Dom(A, B)$) if, whenever the control goes through basic block B, it *must* go through A. Basic block A *predominates* basic block B ($Pre(A, B)$) if, before the control gets to B, it *must* go through A. Basic block A is reachable from basic block B ($Reach(B, A)$), if there is a path from B to A. Calculating dominance, predominance, and reachability is fast. For more information on basic blocks, dominating blocks, and their uses in compilation, see[1].

In the next section, we describe how to efficiently implement coverability analysis in a model checker, such that the implementation is invisible to the user.

3   Background

State-machines are simple yet powerful modeling techniques used in a variety of areas, including hardware [29] and software design [5] [19], protocol development, and other applications citeHol91. As a normal part of the modeling process, State-machine models need to be analyzed with regard to their function, performance, complexity, and other properties.

Formal verification techniques, especially symbolic model checking, are a natural means for reasoning about State-machines. However, most tools available today require specialized training, not available to all designers. Further, due to the state explosion problem, the tools are limited to relatively small designs or design components. As a result, functional simulation is the most commonly used technique for verification. In simulation-based verification, the model is simulated against its expected real world stimuli and the simulated results are compared with the expected results. Simulation, by its very nature, cannot and does not guarantee complete exhaustive coverage of all execution sequences. Furthermore, some parts of the model code, such as error handling, may be inherently hard to cover. Simulation and simulation coverage analysis also suffers from several significant limitations:

- Analysis can only start after 'system integration', when the simulation environment can receive stimuli. This occurs fairly late in the development process.
- Simulation requires a process of test pattern generation (i.e., test cases or vectors), which is often costly, as it involves the creation of a suitable test-bench.
- Simulation Coverage Analysis is, by definition, an analysis of the test suite, rather than of the model under investigation. Therefore, it is essentially limited in its ability to provide deep insight into the model.

In recent years, symbolic model checking and formal verification have been successfully used in the verification of communication protocols, as well as software and hardware systems [3]. Our work may be viewed as an extension of the recent research trend to bring together simulation-based verification and formal verification. Some recent works, for example, have focused on improving the quality of simulation by using formal verification methods to generate test sequences that ensure transition coverage [9,18]. Some researchers [22] have used formal methods to specify simulation targets at the micro-architecture level, while others have used formal verification as part of the simulation process [10]. Indeed, with the ever-increasing complexity and diversity of systems under development, we view the paradigm of integrating formal methods with simulation as a powerful and practical approach.

4   Coverability Analysis via Model Checking

This section uses two simple examples to describe how coverability can be implemented. We focus on two types of coverability models: one that relates to the values of variables, which only requires auxiliary rules, and one that relates to dead-code analysis, which requires code instrumentation (the insertion of some additionl code) in addition to auxiliary rules.

4.1   Attainability of All the Values of a Variable

This coverability model checks whether all variable values, in binary or enumerated types, in a code fragment are attainable. For each variable declaration, we automatically create a collection of auxiliary rules of the form !EF $(var = V_i)$ — one for each value V_i of var — which specifies that V_i cannot be attained by var.

The conjunction of these rules is a property that requires all possible values of var to be attainable by var. This rule is presented to the underlying model checker, which, in turn, decides on the attainability of these values. If the formula passes, an example is also produced, which demonstrates how the value is attained. Checking for this kind of coverability does not require code instrumentation; the tool only needs the information about the variable declaration that enables the auxiliary rule to be created.

4.2   Statement Coverability Analysis

This coverability model checks whether all statements can be reached. To this end, the program is instrumented separately for each statement S_i in the following manner:

- Create an auxiliary variable V_i and initialize it to 0.
- Replace statement S_i with $\{V_i = 1; S_i\}$.

The model checker is then presented with the following rule: $!EF(V_i = 1)$, which indicates whether S_i can be reached.

5   Improvements in Coverability

5.1   Optimizing Coverability Analysis by Reducing the Rules to Be Checked

When performing coverability analysis, there are a large number of temporal rules that have to be checked. In our previous implementation [6], we created a list of these rules and presented each of them, in turn, to the model checker. Since running a rule in a symbolic model checker is a time consuming task, we looked for ways to reduce the number of rules that have to be checked, based on static analysis and on simulation of counter examples.

Using Inflation: The following simple optimization is natural; start by creating a list of coverability tasks. Randomly choose one of the coverability tasks from the list, create a corresponding rule, and present it to the model checker. The model checker yields a counter example if the task, as expected, is reachable. If the task is reachable, it can be removed from the list. Then, the counter example can be examined to see if it contains evidence that can be used to remove additional tasks. If it contains such evidence, the examination is rewarded since running a rule is more time-consuming than examining the counter example, and the total execution time is reduced.

Currently, symbolic model checking performs many optimizations to improve efficiency. One of these optimizations, called *cone of influence*, retains those variables referred to in the rule, as well as any variable that affect them. After a rule is run, the counter example only contains values for the variables of the reduced model. This causes the examination of the counter example to yield very few additional tasks.

To overcome this problem, we use *inflation*. Inflation is a method for adding variables to a trace created from the counter example, so that it contains legal values for all the variables in the design. This is accomplished by using simulation and randomly selecting values for any variables not contained in the trace and not deterministically set by the program. For example, the value of the model inputs not contained in the trace, and of random or non-deterministic operations, is selected at random. The inflator can be used to create such a trace by itself or to expand a counter example. A random choice is consistent with the counter example since all variables in the counter examples were chosen using the cone of influence reduction. Therefore, variables outside that cone cannot influence them. Such an inflator is part of the RuleBase package [3][26].

We can improve the simple idea of observing the counter example by using the inflator. The counter example is inflated, using a set of variables mentioned in the coverability tasks. All the coverability tasks that are covered by the inflated trace are removed from the list. This reduces the number of rules and the execution time, since running the inflator is faster than checking a rule.

In our implementation, we have two types of rules: rules that check if some auxiliary Boolean variables reached the value of 1 (related to statement coverability and multi-condition coverability) and rules that check that each model variable received all of its possible values (a rule for each variable-value combination). We instrument the program only at basic blocks where we have not yet ascertained if the blocks are reachable (a decreasing number). After receiving a counter example, we use the inflator to expand the trace with all the auxiliary variables and all the variables for which some value has not yet been achieved. For each auxiliary variable, we check whether it attained the value 1. For each variable, we check whether it reached new values. After we remove all the coverability tasks that have been attained through inflation, we run the next rule. Before running a rule, we instrument the program at all the locations that have not yet been reached. As this list shrinks, the execution speed increases and the inflator is used on a decreasing number of variables. Although many auxiliary variables are added in the instrumentation, they hardly affect the speed of execution, since all but one are removed by the cone of influence heuristics. The algorithm, expanded with some steps from the next subsection, is described in the left side of Figure 2.

The inflator chooses random values for the model inputs and for non-deterministic operations. Therefore, it is possible that repeated runs of the inflator would yield different inflated traces for the same counter example that contains additional coverability tasks. A possible strategy for deciding how to run the inflator is to re-run the inflator and, after each run, to randomly (e.g., at 0.5 probability) decide whether to continue re-running the inflator or move to the next rule. A more intelligent strategy would be to re-run the inflator as long as the total time of the re-runs is less than the average time it took to run the model checker. This way we have the chance of covering many coverability tasks in the time it would take to model-check one coverability task. In addition, we can modify the inflator to receive a list of variables and the values we would like to cover, and to bias its random choice toward achieving the supplied values.

There are a number of additional ways in which the inflator can be used to improve performance. The first, which is simple to implement, but very useful, is to create a long random trace for the program and examine it to remove the tasks seen in it. In this case, we use only the random simulation capabilities of the inflator. The advantage is that after a few seconds of execution, many of the tasks are eliminated. The number of the tasks eliminated is larger than initially expected due to the highly parallel nature of the HDL code. The second way is to extend every trace created for a counter example by a number of cycles. The idea is that there may be other tasks 'hiding' next to the one we found and we want to increase the chances of finding them. This is based on the coupling effect [23].

Static Reduction of the Number of Rules: Static analysis can show the relationship between coverage tasks. For example, dominating block analysis shows which additional blocks are always executed if a block is executed. This information may be presented in a list in which each entry contains a block and the block that are always executed whenever the former block is executed. This list may be used to find a small set of blocks that dominate the entire program. Therefore, instead of directly covering the entire program, we only have to cover this small set of blocks.

Techniques for solving the Set Cover problem [12] can then be used to find a subset of tasks, which if covered, imply that all the tasks are covered.

For example, a list for the program on the left side of Figure 1 will appear as follows:

```
{ A, {A, B, F}}
{ B, (A, B, F}}
{ C, {A, B, C, E, F}}
{ D, {A, B, D, F}}
{ E, {A, B, C, E, F}}
{ F, (A, B, F}}
{ G, {A, B, C, E, F, G}}
```

From the list we can see that if we created a task that covers C we can remove A, B, E, and F from the list of blocks to cover. It can be seen that D and G are necessary and sufficient to cover everything. If this analysis was not used, it is possible we would have tried to cover a random block in the beginning and would have ended up using three tests. For example, the tests used could have tested for D passing through A, B, D, F and then for E passing through A, B, C, E, B, D, F and finally for G passing through A, B, C, E, G, B, D, F.

A number of papers have been published on the similar problem of modeling test compression as the Set Cover Problem [14]. In general, the problem of finding a minimal set cover is NP-Complete [12] Finding a good solution turns out to be easy.

If this technique is used, even without inflation, it is possible to use coverability only on a subset of the tasks and thus reduce the performance requirements.

5.2   Faster Execution of Rules

Given a program A and a question (rule) Q on program A, we create an auxiliary program A' such that the question Q on A' yields the same reply as the question Q on A. If A' is simpler than A, Q may execute faster on A'.

Other than the guarantee that Q will have the same reply on A and A', we make no other claims on A'. For example, it is possible that A' will not terminate and that a trace on A' is not expandable to a trace on A. A similar idea was used in [18], where A' was constructed for specific rules that have to do with tuning tests on pipelines.

We created an auxiliary program based on this idea to improve statement coverability analysis. When checking if basic block B is reachable in program A, program A' is created by removing all basic blocks X from A such that either X is in the set $Pre(B, X)$ or X is in $!Reach(X, B)$. Then, we can check if B is reachable in A'. In many cases, A' is much simpler than A and we expect the rule to run faster. Furthermore, this heuristic is orthogonal to the more common cone of influence heuristics and provides different and disjoint improvements.

We can remove all X, such that X is in the set $Pre(B, X)$ (including B itself) because we know before the control reaches X it will go through B. Since we only care if the control can reach B, we know that the control can reach B in A' if and only if it can reach B in A. If there is no way to get to B (X in $!Reach(X, B)$) from X, then we do not care what is done in X. Since the control will never reach B after it reaches

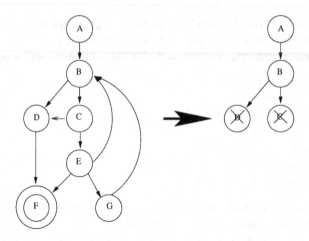

Fig. 1. Creating an Auxilary Program

X, X can be removed. When a block is removed, its entire content can be removed. If a block that was not removed points to a removed block in the control flow diagram, a stub (empty block) needs to be maintained for consistency.

An example of creating an auxiliary program can be seen in Figure ref-fig:ShortProgram. The original program on the left is composed of seven basic blocks, each containing any number of statements. The execution of the program can be complex and terminates once the control reaches block F. If the question is ' Is basic block C' reachable?,' we can reduce the program to a much simpler program. Basic blocks E and G can be eliminated because, in order to reach them, the control has to pass through C first; stated differently, they belong to $Pre(C, X)$. Blocks D and F may be removed since if the control reaches them it will not reach block C. The content of block C can be removed, because we only care whether it was reached, and, it can become an empty block. We have to keep an empty block for block D to maintain a legal program, since it is pointed to by some part of the program. The auxiliary program does nothing and probably terminates abnormally; however, the reply to the rule 'block C can be reached' is the same for the original and the auxiliary program. The rule will almost certainly run faster on the auxilary program because it is much simpler.

Similar optimizations may be used when we want to check if variable y can attain the value y_0. Assume there are n locations in which the assignment happens (i.e., it can happen in these specific locations and cannot happen in any other location). In essence, we want to check if we can reach one of a set of basic blocks. When checking if a group B of basic blocks is reachable in program A, program A' is created by removing all basic blocks X from A such that either X is in $Pre(b, X)$ (b in B) or X is in $!Reach(X, b)$ for all b in B. Then we can check if B is reachable in A'.

Similar reasoning to that of the first application shows the correctness of this reduction.

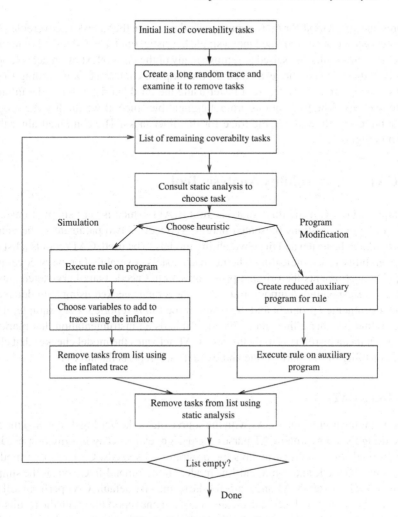

Fig. 2. Combining Heuristics

The power of this idea is not limited to rules that originate in coverability. We found a number of other general cases in which such reduction can be applied; however, these cases are beyond the scope of this paper.

5.3 Combining Heuristics

We presented heuristics based on three distinct ideas. First, we explained how simulation may be used. Initially, random simulation can be used to remove many tasks. Then, given a counter example, we can try to expand it to find similar tasks that are coverable. Next, we show that for each coverability task, we can statically evaluate other tasks, such that if that task is covered, these tasks will also be covered. We showed that we can choose a subset of the tasks such that if they are coverable, all the tasks are coverable. In addition, we presented a method for more rapidly calculating whether a task is coverable. All of these heuristics can be combined into a single heuristic. First, a list of tasks is calculated. Then, random simulation is used to remove many of the tasks. Next, we reach a loop that we follow until all tasks are evaluated. In the loop we choose a task according to static analysis. Next, we either execute it faster using the third heuristic or use the inflator to inflate the trace. The two options are not compatible since, if we modify the program, we cannot correctly evaluate the trace for the other tasks. The combined algorithm is shown in Figure 2.

6   CAT — Coverability Analysis Tool

We improved our Coverability Analysis Tool (CAT), which is very simple to use, with some of the optimizations presented here. CAT receives two parameters: the name of the program to be tested and the coverability models to be used. CAT outputs a list of all the coverability tasks, indicating whether each task is coverable. For every coverability goal, CAT instruments the original program with the needed auxiliary statements and creates a corresponding temporal rule. The rule is then checked using a model checker on the instrumented program and the result of the run is reported. For example, if CAT wants to find whether a line can be reached, it adds an instrumentation that marks this line so that it can be referred to by the rule. CAT activates the model checker that checks the attainability of the marked line and extracts and reports the answer.

6.1   Using CAT

To use CAT, the user invokes CAT with the source file of the Verilog design and the name of the design's top module. CAT parses the design, extracts any information needed to create formal rules, and instruments the program to its needs. CAT has two modes of operation: GUI mode and command-line mode. The command-line mode is the simplest, where the user activates CAT and waits for the results. By default, CAT performs all three types of coverability analyses, and creates unique-name report files with the results. CAT also has a graphic interface, which allows the user to choose the kind of coverability analysis to be performed and the parts of the design on which to perform them.

The user may also choose to create an environment for the design, view the details of the design details based on the CAT parser, and activate a heuristic run of the coverability analysis. The left side of Figure 3 shows the CAT reachability screen, which presents the statements that are potentially reachable. The user can change the list of statements to be checked using the Custom option, and may choose between running a regular full check, or a heuristic check — which can run faster.

Figure 4 presents the results of running the heuristic reachability analysis and shows which of the statements are reachable and which are not. It also reports the running time, the number of full runs needed, and the number of rules found using simulation. It reports that two lines, line 21 and line 30, are not coverable. Line 21 is not coverable since $int1$ and $int2$ are updated at every cycle and are never equal to each other. Line 30 demonstrates a typical error; writing *or* in line 27 instead of *and* causes line 30 to be unreachable.

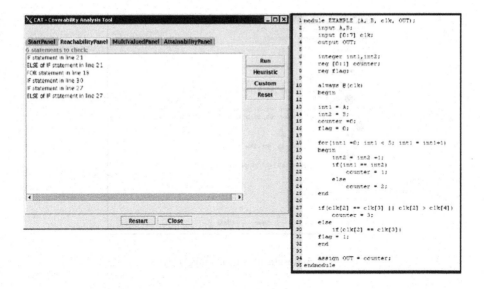

Fig. 3. Source Code and Reachability Analysis Screen

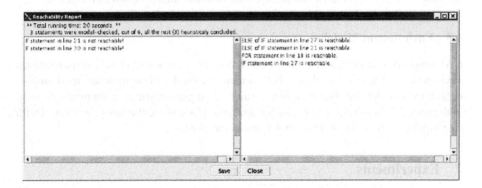

Fig. 4. Results of Reachability with Simulation on Counter Examples

Figure 5 shows the attainability analysis report. For each variable the user may check which values are attainable and which are not.

6.2 Supporting Software

CAT uses RuleBase, a symbolic model checker developed by the IBM Haifa Research Labs ([3]), as its underlying engine. RuleBase can analyze models formulated in several hardware description languages, including VHDL and Verilog. The basis for CAT is Koala, the RuleBase Verilog parser. CAT parses the input Verilog design, extracts the information needed in the current coverability goal, and constructs the auxiliary SUGAR

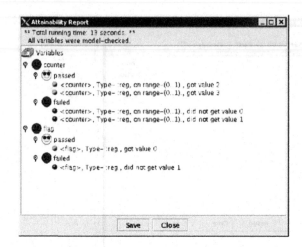

Fig. 5. Results of Attainability Analysis

citeSUGAR rules on demand. CAT then transforms the design so that it includes the relevant auxiliary statements and presents the instrumented program to RuleBase.

6.3 Environment Modeling

CAT supports default non-deterministic behavior environments, as well as user-defined environments. The user can choose between the two modes of environment modeling — default or user-defined. For example, default non-deterministic environments are used in the application of CAT for dead-code analysis. If a statement cannot be covered with free inputs, it cannot be reached under any circumstances.

7   Experiments

We ran coverability analysis on several designs, ranging from trivial examples to large complex designs consisting of thousands of lines of Verilog code. All the tests were run with a non-deterministic environment, covering all possible behaviors of the inputs.

Designs were collected from several sources: [2], internal IBM, and a customer supplied design. All the tests were executed on a 375 MHz PowerPC 604e machine with 1GB of RAM. Table 1 provides a summary of our results. Each row contains parameters that describe a design and the experimental results for that design. The design is described using its name, number of lines, number of reachability tasks, and number of flip flops. For each design, we measured the run time without any heuristics. We measured the total run time when the simulator is used to inflate the counter examples which are then inspected to remove tasks. In the next column, we show the number of statements that were removed using that inspection. Next, we present the total time if random simulation is used to remove statements before the FSM is model checked. The last column details the number of tasks removed when simulation is used first.

As seen in Table 1 , coverability analysis on the smaller designs is usually very fast; CAT was able to perform a full analysis in a matter of minutes. Medium-size designs were processed in less than an hour, which suggests that CAT can be used early in the development process of such modules to efficiently find some initial design problems. The largest designs we tried (such as ac97_ctl), were too much of a challenge for the model checker, and made it impossible to process even the simplest queries.

All designs benefited from running the simulation first and then inflating the tests. As designs become larger, the use of heuristics to improve the performance of coverability analysis becomes a must; without them, the analysis is either too slow or does not terminate. For example, for DLX, running the simulation made it possible to complete the coverability analysis. After simulation, only four tasks remained which were model checked. The model checker alone could not handle the entire design.

Simulation works so well is because of the parallel nature of HDL code, where many statements execute in parallel, leading even the shortest simulation to find many reachable statements. Inflation of counter traces works well, even after simulation was used to remove the tasks, because of the coupling effect.

Table 1. Performance with and without heuristics

Design	Lines	Statements	FF	Regular	Heuristic	Statements Removed	Simulation First	Tasks Removed
Example	35	6	5	34sec	21 sec	3	15 sec	4
MEM	50	5	54	26sec	13 sec	2	0.5 sec	5
VEND	100	14	16	69 sec	41 sec	6	0.5 sec	14
PG_FIFO	1200	74	816	42 Min	18 Min	57	20 Min	43
PCI(norm)	1700	264	646	62 Min	52 Min	103		102
DLX	1700	57	2274	N/A	N/A	N/A	181 sec	54
Prime Arbiter	1365	62	173	517 Min	15 Min	57	11 Min	55

8   Conclusions

In [6], we introduced the concept of coverability analysis and described how a number of coverability metrics, which correspond to some commonly-used coverage metrics, can be implemented via symbolic model checking. The same ideas can be used to implement many additional coverability metrics (e.g., define-use, mutation, and loop [19][15]).

Tools that measure coverability have a strong appeal; they are very simple to use, the reports generated are easy to uderstand without any training, and the tool can be used as soon as the code is written — when verification by simulation is not yet an option. Further, the reports have the additional benefit that every bug reported is a real bug with no false alarms. However, the naive implementation proved slow.

We have therefore started to work on heuristics that improve the implementation of coverability analysis. We recognize a number of avenues that may be pursued in order to improve performance:

1. Observing the counter examples. We can put all the coverability tasks into a pool of tasks. Whenever a counter example is created to demonstrate that a task is coverable, we can check if there are additional tasks, not yet covered, that are covered by that counter example. If we find such tasks we remove them from the pool.
2. Using random simulation. Simulation is fast and can be used to generate traces of possible execution of the program. However, unlike functional coverage, simulation cannot be efficiently directed to cover specific tasks. Before we begin to look for specific tasks, we can run simulation on the program a few times and remove all the observed tasks. In addition, simulation may be used to expand any counter example to contain all the values, referred to in the remaining coverability tasks, to improve the likelihood of detecting and removing these tasks.
3. Using static analysis. For each task we can identify a list (which may be empty) of additional tasks, such that, if this task is covered, all the additional tasks are covered. Using algorithms for set cover [7], we can select a subset of the tasks and try to cover only these tasks, thereby reducing the number of the tasks that need to be covered.
4. Using program transformations. The rules used for coverability analysis, especially statement coverability analysis lend themselves to optimizations based on modifying the program. We can create an auxiliary program that is simpler, in which running the rule on the auxiliary program yields the same results.

We have already implemented item one and two of the above heuristics. The results are very promising and it seems that coverability can be measured on modules that are at the size limit used for model checking, or that have slightly surpassed it. One reason is that many of the tasks are eliminated using fast simulation. Another is that many of the reductions used in model checking engines apply to the simple rules used in coverability analysis.

In the future, we plan to implement and test the remaining heuristics, see how to efficiently combine all the heuristics, and most importantly see how many bugs we can find in real, designer written code.

References

1. A.V. Aho, R. Sethi, J.D. Ullman. Compilers: Principles, Techniques and Tools. Addison-Wesley, 1986.
2. Adnan Aziz. Example of Hardware Verification Using VIS, The benchmark PCI Local BUS, URL http://www-cad.eecs.berkeley.edu/Respep/Research/vis/texas-97/.
3. I. Beer, S. Ben-David, C. Eisner, A. Landver. RuleBase: an Industry-Oriented Formal Verification Tool. Proc. DAC'96, pp. 655–660.
4. I. Beer, M. Yoeli, S. Ben-David, D. Geist and R. Gewirtzman. Methodology and System for Practical Formal Verification of Reactive Systems. CAV94, LNCS818, pp 182-193.
5. Boris Beizer. Software Testing Technique. New York: Van Nostrand Reinhold, second edition, 1990.

6. G Ratzaby, S. Ur and Y. Wolfsthal. Coverability Analysis Using Symbolic Model Checking. CHARME2001, September, 2001.

7. E. Buchink and S. Ur. Compacting Regression Suites On-The-Fly. Joint Asia Pacific Software Engineering Conference and International Computer Science Conference, Hong Kong, December, 1997.

8. E.M. Clarke, O. Grumberg. D.A. Peled. Model Checking, MIT Press, 1999.

9. D. Geist, M. Farkas, A. Landver, Y. Lictenstein, S. Ur and Y Wolfsthal. Coverage-directed test generation using symbolic techniques. In Proc. Int. Conf. Formal methods in Computer-Aided Design, pages 143–158, 1996.

10. Y. Abarbanel, I. Beer, L. Gluhovsky, S. Keidar, and Y. Wolfsthal. FoCs - Automatic Generation of Simulation Checkers from Formal Specifications. In Proc. 12th International Conference on Computer Aided Verification (CAV), 2000.

11. Y. Hoskote, T. Kam , P. Ho and X. Zhao. Coverage Estimation for Symbolic Model Checking. DAC'99, pp300-305, June 1999.

12. M.R. Garey and D. S. Johnson. Computers and Intractability: A Guide to the Theory of NP-Completeness. W.H. Freeman, 1979.

13. G. J. Holtzman. Design and Validation of Computer Protocols. Prentice Hall, 1991.

14. D.S. Hochbaum. An Optimal Test Compression Procedure for Combinational Circuits. IEEE Transactions on Computer-Aided Design of Integrated Circuits and Systems, 15:10, 1294-1299, 1996.

15. C. Kaner. Software Negligence & Testing Coverage. Software QA Quarterly, Vol 2, #2, pp 18, 1995.

16. M. Kantrowitz, L. M. Noack. I'm Done Simulating; Now What? Verification Coverage Analysis and Correctness Checking of the DECchip 21164 Alpha Microprocessor. Proc. DAC'96.

17. S. Kajihara, I. Pomerantz, K. Kinoshita and S. M. Reddy. .Cost Effective Generation of Minimal Test Sets for Stack-At Faults in Combinatorial Logic Circuits. 30th ACM/IEEE DAC, pp. 102-106, 1993.

18. D. Levin, D. Lorentz and S. Ur. A Methodology for Processor Implementation Verification. FMCAD 96: Int. Conf. on Formal Methods in Computer-Aided Design, November 1996.

19. B. Marick. The Craft of Software Testing: Subsystem Testing Including Object-Based and Object-Oriented Testing. Prentice-Hall, 1995.

20. K. L. McMillan. Symbolic Model Checking. Kluwer Academic Publishers, 1993.

21. Raymond E. Miller. Protocol Verification: The first ten years, the next ten years; some personal observations. In Protocol specification, Testing, and Verification X, 1990.

22. Y.V. Hoskote, D. Moundanos and J.A. Abraham. Automatic Extraction of the Control Flow Machine and Application to Evaluating Coverage of Verification Vectors. IEEE International Conference on Computer Design (ICCD '95), October 1995.

23. A. J. Offutt. Investigation of the software testing coupling effect. ACM Transactions on Software Engineering Methodology, 1(1):3–18, January 1992.

24. F. Orava. Formal Semantics of SDL Specifications. In Protocol Specification, Testing, and Verification VIII, 1988.

25. RuleBase User Manual V1.0, IBM Haifa Research Laboratory, 1996.

26. I. Beer, S. Ben-David, C. Eisner, D. Geist, L. Gluhovsky, T. Heyman, A. Landver, P. Paanah, Y. Rodeh, G. Ronin, and Y. Wolfsthal. RuleBase: Model Checking at IBM. Proc. 9th International Conference on Computer Aided Verification (CAV), 1997.

27. I. Beer, S. Ben-David, C. Eisner, D. Fisman, A. Gringauze, and Y. Rodeh. The Temporal Logic Sugar. Proc. 13th International Conference on Computer Aided Verification (CAV), 2001.

28. I. Beer, M. Dvir, B. Kozitsa. Y. Lichtenstein, S. Mach, W.J. Nee, E. Rappaport. Q. Schmierer, Y. Zandman. VHDL Test Coverage in BDLS/AUSSIM Environment. IBM HRL Technical Report 88.342, December 1993.
29. D. L. Perry. VHDL Second Edition. McGraw-Hill Series on Computer Engineering, 1993.
30. Telecordia Software Visualization and Analysis Tool. URL http://xsuds.argreenhouse.com/.
31. E. Weyuker, T. Goradia and A. Singh. Automatically Generating Test Data from a Boolean Specification. IEEE Transaction on Software Engineering, Vol 20, No 5 May 1994.

Heuristic-Driven Test Case Selection from Formal Specifications. A Case Study

Juan C. Burguillo-Rial, Manuel J. Fernández-Iglesias,
Francisco J. González-Castaño, and Martín Llamas-Nistal

Grupo de Ingeniería de Sistemas Telemáticos
Departamento de Ingeniería Telemática
Universidade de Vigo, Spain
jrial@det.uvigo.es,
http://www-gist.det.uvigo.es/

Abstract. We propose an approach to testing that combines formal methods with practical criteria, close to the testing engineer's experience. It can be seen as a framework to evaluate and select test suites using formal methods, assisted by informal heuristics. This proposal is illustrated with a practical case study: the testing of a protocol for mobile auctions in a distributed, wireless environment.

Keyword: formal testing, heuristics for testing, test case selection, risk and cost of testing.

1 Introduction

Test generation algorithms [31] are used to obtain a set of test cases from a given specification, trying to provide an adequate coverage. Test cases are intended to detect errors in non-conforming implementations, insofar the initial specification is concerned. However, the number of test cases needed to guarantee an exhaustive coverage may be too large, even infinite. This means that execution of all potential test cases may be infeasible due to time limitations or resource availability. As a consequence, in practical cases it is necessary to select a subset of all possible test cases prior to conformance testing. The reduction of the initially generated test case set is known in the literature as *test case selection* [5].

Test case selection should not be performed at random. An appropriate strategy should be applied to obtain a valuable test case collection, in the sense that it should detect as many non-conforming implementations as possible. For software testing, some criteria are available, like the division in equivalence partitions [25] or the test proposal selection in communication protocol testing [14].

On the other side, test case selection should not be based only on the system's formal specification. To select the most valuable test cases, additional information, external to the corresponding specification formalism, should also be used. Such information may consider most frequent errors committed by implementors, most harmful errors, most difficult to implement features, critical basic functionalities, etc. Although there is no general method available, there

L.-H. Eriksson and P. Lindsay (Eds.): FME 2002, LNCS 2391, pp. 57–76, 2002.
© Springer-Verlag Berlin Heidelberg 2002

are some results for the classification and problem decomposition based on statistical and mathematical analysis [24].

In the field of Formal Description Techniques some proposals have been made to address the test case selection problem [5,30,10,33,1,32,35,36]. T. Robles [27] introduced the concepts of risk, cost and efficiency for a test case collection or suite, which are revisited in this paper. This approach is based on the estimation, from the testing engineer's experience, of the risk involved when testing a system implementation. It formalises and simplifies the selection of test cases, and can be applied to most practical problems. This approach is similar to that presented in [33].

Thus, this paper proposes a method to evaluate and select test cases from practical criteria, close to the testing engineer's experience. This proposal is illustrated with a practical case study: the testing of a protocol for mobile auctions in a distributed, wireless environment. Our aim is to provide implementable, and computationally feasible criteria. Additionally, we want the proposed methodology to be easily configurable for testing engineers, who can provide their experience through the introduction of heuristics to facilitate the testing of key aspects in a system, or specific parts of a system that are more prone to errors.

The next two sections discuss the theoretical background that serves as the foundation of our experience. Section 2 presents some general definitions and notation about the supporting representation framework and formal testing, and Sect. 3 presents our approach to test case selection. Section 4 discusses the proposed case study. Finally, Sect. 5 offers a summary of the work described and some conclusions.

2 General Definitions and Notation

Along the next paragraphs we discuss basic theoretical concepts and notation related to testing and test case selection. First, we briefly introduce Labelled Transition Systems. Then, we present some basic concepts from formal testing, like conformance, test case, verdicts or complete test suites. After this, we introduce risk, coverage, cost and efficiency as the supporting heuristics to assist the testing engineer along test case selection (Sect. 2.3) and *a priori* and *a posteriori* values for these parameters (Sect. 2.4).

2.1   Labelled Transition Systems

Labelled Transition Systems (LTS) will be the basic model to describe the behaviour of processes, such as specifications, implementations and tests.

Definition 1. *A labelled transition system is a 4-tuple $< Stat, L, T, s_0 >$ where Stat is a countable, non-empty set of states; L is a countable set of labels; $T \subseteq Stat \times (L \cup \{i\}) \times Stat$ is the countable set of transitions and i denotes a special internal action, referred as τ in some models [23]; and $s_0 \in Stat$ is the initial state.*

An element $(s, \mu, s') \in T$ is represented as $s - \mu \to s'$. We use the following relations (sets) derived (constructed) from the transition relation:

$s = \epsilon \Rightarrow s'$: $s = s'$ or $s - i - \ldots \to s'$

$s = a \Rightarrow s'$: $\exists s_1, s_2 \in Stat$ such that $s = \epsilon \Rightarrow s_1 - a \to s_2 = \epsilon \Rightarrow s'$

$s = \sigma \Rightarrow s'$: $\exists \{s_1, \ldots, s_{n-1}\} \subseteq Stat$, and a trace $\sigma = a_1 \ldots a_n$
            such that $s = a_1 \Rightarrow s_1 = \cdots \Rightarrow s_{n-1} = a_n \Rightarrow s'$.

$s = \sigma \Rightarrow$: $\exists s' \in Stat$ such that $s = \sigma \Rightarrow s'$

$s \neq \sigma \Rightarrow$: $\nexists s' \in Stat$ such that $s = \sigma \Rightarrow s'$

$\mathbf{Tr}(P)$: $\{\sigma \in L^* \mid P = \sigma \Rightarrow\}$

$\mathbf{Init}(P)$: $\{a \in L \mid P = a \Rightarrow\}$

P **after** σ : $\{s' \mid P = \sigma \Rightarrow s'\}$

$\mathbf{Ref}(P, \sigma)$: $\{A \subseteq L \mid \exists s' \in (P \text{ after } \sigma) \text{ and } \forall a \in A, s' \neq a \Rightarrow\}$

L^* is the set of strings (sequences, traces) constructed using elements from L. A trace $\sigma \in L^*$ is a finite sequence of observable actions over L, where ϵ denotes the empty sequence. The special label $i \notin L$ represents an unobservable, internal action, thus $= \epsilon \Rightarrow$ represents a null transition or a sequence of transitions including only internal actions (i.e. traces do not have internal actions). Internal actions are used to model non-determinism. The difference between $s - a \to s'$ and $s = a \Rightarrow s'$ is that, for the first case, the system evolves from s to s' through transition a, whereas for the second case evolution from s to s' may include any number of internal actions before and after observable action a.

We represent an LTS by a tree or a graph, where nodes represent states and edges represent transitions. Given an LTS $P = < Stat, L, T, s_0 >$, we write $P = \sigma \Rightarrow$ instead of $s_0 = \sigma \Rightarrow$ to represent transitions from the initial state of P (i.e. traces initially accepted by P) when we find it convenient for the sake of clarity. Note that this is only syntax sugar to stress the fact that we are representing transitions accepted by process P. When a given state does not accept further actions (i.e. deadlock state), we label it as **stop**.

$\mathbf{Tr}(P)$ is the set of traces accepted by process P, $\mathbf{Init}(P)$ the set of labels from L accepted by P, and $\mathbf{Ref}(P, \sigma)$ is the set of refusals of P after trace σ. We denote the class of all labelled transition systems over L by $LTS(L)$. LTS model the semantics of languages used to describe distributed and concurrent systems like LOTOS [13], CSP [3] or CCS [23], among others.

2.2 Formal Testing Concepts

Concerning testing, it is important to define a relation to model the conformance of a implementation with its specification. There are several relations in the literature that may be selected [31]. As we want to compare our framework with other approaches and reuse the existing theory, we selected the conformance relation **conf** described in [4,31] to model such implementation relation. It has the advantage that only the behaviour contained in the specification must be tested, reducing the test space. Besides, the relation **conf** allows us to extend the functionality specified, but does not force the implementation of specification options. Its only requisite is to implement correctly the compulsory parts of the specification. The relation **conf** is defined as follows:

Definition 2 (Conformance: conf). *Let* $I, S \in LTS(L)$, *we say that* I **conf** S *if and only if for every trace* $\sigma \in \mathbf{Tr}(S)$ *and for every subset* $A \subseteq L$ *the following proposition holds:*

If $A \in \mathbf{Ref}(I, \sigma)$ *then* $A \in \mathbf{Ref}(S, \sigma)$

In case $\sigma \notin \mathbf{Tr}(I)$ *we assume* $\mathbf{Ref}(I, \sigma)$ *is empty.*

Obviously, we desire to perform test or experiments over the implementation that should terminate in finite time, so the corresponding test cases should have finite behaviour. Moreover, a tester executing a test case should have as much control as possible over the testing process, so nondeterminism in a test case is also undesirable. To decide about the success of a test case we use *verdicts*. Reference [16] proposes three possible verdicts:

- **Pass** (**pass**): The observed behaviour satisfies the test and the result is a valid specification behaviour.
- **Fail** (**fail**): The observed behaviour is an invalid specification behaviour.
- **Inconclusive** (**inc**): The observed behaviour is valid so far, but it has not been possible to complete the test.

These concepts are formalised below [31]:

Definition 3 (Test case). *A test case tc is a 5-tuple* $< Stat, L, T, v, s_0 >$, *such that* $< Stat, L, T, s_0 >$ *is a deterministic transition system with finite behaviour, and* $v : Stat \rightarrow \{\mathbf{fail}, \mathbf{pass}, \mathbf{inc}\}$ *is a function to assign verdicts.*
The class of test cases over L *is denoted by* $LTS_t(L)$.

Definition 4 (Test suite). *A test suite or test collection ts is a set of test cases:*
$$ts \in PowerSet(LTS_t(L))$$

The execution of a test case is modelled by the parallel synchronous execution of the test case with the implementation under test (IUT), that is, every action in a test case tries to synchronize with the corresponding observable action in the IUT. Such execution continues until there are no more interactions, i.e. until a deadlock is reached. Such deadlock may appear because the test case tc reaches a final state, or when the combination of tc and the IUT reaches a state where the actions offered by tc are not accepted.

An implementation passes the execution of a test case if and only if the verdict of the test case is **pass** when reaching a deadlock. As the implementation may have nondeterministic behaviour, different executions of the same test case with the same IUT may reach different final states, and as a consequence different verdicts. An implementation passes a test case tc if and only if all possible executions of tc carry to a **pass** verdict. This means that we should execute every test case several times to obtain a final verdict, ideally an infinite number of times.

Test generation algorithms provide test suites from specifications. Ideally, an implementation must pass a test suite if and only if it conforms. In such case, the test suite obtained is called *complete*. Unfortunately, in practice, such test suites would have infinitely many test cases. As a consequence, in the real world we have to restrict ourselves to (finite-size) test suites that can only detect non-conformance, but cannot detect conformance. Such test suites are called *sound*. In other words, if a sound test suite detects the presence of one or more errors, then the implementation is wrong. On the other side, if a sound test suite does *not* detect the presence of errors, then we increase our confidence in the implementation, but we cannot say that it is correct, as there could be errors not discovered yet. This is the typical situation when testing software products.

2.3   Risk, Coverage, Cost, and Efficiency

Through the next few paragraphs we introduce the concepts of *error weight* or *risk*, *coverage*, *cost* and *efficiency*, which will support the comparison and selection of test cases to be passed to an implementation.

To analyse the coverage obtained after testing an implementation we have to take into account several factors. On one side, test cases are derived from a formal object, i. e. the formal specification. As a consequence, after testing an implementation we get a specific coverage level for the behaviours in the specification. On the other side, coverage depends on the implementation itself because, given a formal specification, the selected implementation technology (i.e. programming language or programming tools) will be more or less prone to errors.

Table 1. Error weighting

Target	Parameter	Range
Event	$R_I(e) = E_I(e) \times I_I(e)$	$(0, \infty)$
Implementation	$R_I(S)$	$(0, \infty)$
Measurement, Event	$MR_I(e, ts)$	$[0, \infty)$
Measurement, Implementation	$MR_I(S, ts)$	$[0, \infty)$

Legend. I: implementation under test; e: event in I; ts: test suite; S: specification corresponding to I.

Table 1 proposes some heuristics to *a priori* evaluate the influence of errors in a given implementation, which will be used to select an adequate test suite. $R_I(e)$ assigns a weight to a (possible) error, i.e. estimates the risk involved in committing errors when implementing event e. It is calculated from two values: an estimation of the chances of event e being erroneously implemented ($E_I(e)$), and an estimation of the impact of the corresponding error in the rest of the system ($I_I(e)$). $R_I(S)$ estimates the chances for the implementation not to conform to the corresponding specification, and measures the risk of erroneously implementing S.

$MR_I(e, ts)$ represents the amount of risk for event e that can be detected through a testing process using test suite ts, and $MR_I(S, ts)$ represents the amount of risk for implementation I that can be detected using test suite ts. Risk measurement for a single test case is a particular case where suite ts is composed by a single test case. Note that, from the definitions above, $MR_I(e, ts) \leq R_I(e)$ and $MR_I(S, ts) \leq R_I(S)$.

Table 2. Coverage parameters

Target	Parameter	Range
Event	$K_I(e, ts) = \frac{MR_I(e,ts)}{R_I(e)}$	$[0, 1]$
Implementation	$K_I(S, ts) = \frac{MR_I(S,ts)}{R_I(S)}$	$[0, 1]$

The underlying mathematical model we need is considerably simplified through the assumption of independence among errors. However, in practice, errors are not independent from each other, as erroneous sentences in a program may affect the evolution of other parts of the program. As a solution, correlation among errors is reflected in our model as error weight values, that is, we model such interdependence through parameter $I_I(e)$. Then, testing engineers will estimate the correlation among errors, using available error statistics and their own expertise, to define $I_I(e)$ accordingly.

This can be seen as a compromise between a convenient mathematical foundation and the need to consider error correlation in real cases. Note that, independently of being supported by the underlying mathematical model or through explicit parameters, getting the correlations between failures right is crucial to get the most of the approach discussed in this paper.

From the parameters above, we define *coverage* as the quotient between a measurement of the detection power of a test suite and a measurement of the risk (c.f. Table 2). $K_I(e, ts)$ represents the coverage for event e using test suite ts, whereas $K_I(S, ts)$ represents the coverage for implementation I, corresponding to specification S, using test suite ts.

Table 3. Cost parameters

Target	Parameter	Range
Event	$C_I(e) = P_I(e) + X_I(e)$	$(0, \infty)$
Implementation	$C_I(S, ts)$	$(0, \infty)$

When executing a test suite ts on an IUT we are checking whether some of the error possibilities estimated have been materialised into actual errors. If errors appear, they should be corrected. Conversely, if errors are not found, our confidence increases. Given two test suites ts_1 and ts_2, using the parameters above we can compare their coverage, and therefore their ability to detect errors in an IUT. However, there is another factor when comparing test suites that should be taken into account: the resources needed. To estimate this aspect, we introduce a new parameter: the *cost* (c.f. Table 3). $C_I(e)$ estimates the cost of testing event e as the sum of the cost due to its implementation in a test case $(P_I(e))$ and the cost of executing that event on the implementation $(X_I(e))$. $C_I(S, ts)$ represents the cost of testing an implementation I using test suite ts generated from specification S.

Using cost values we can better discriminate among several test suites. Therefore, the next step will be to relate the parameters defined above to obtain another reference to facilitate the selection of test cases. For this, we define the *efficiency* of a test suite ts obtained from S $(F_I(S, ts))$ as the quotient between the coverage of that suite and the cost associated to its use to test I.

$$F_I(S, ts) = \frac{K_I(S, ts)}{C_I(S, ts)} \tag{1}$$

The values of this new parameter are in the range $[0, \infty)$. Its values increase when coverage increases and with cost reduction.

We need a procedure to calculate values for the heuristics above taking into account our representation formalism, namely Labelled Transition Systems. We try to assess conformance for a system implementation from its formal specification. Thus, we will take as a reference the risk involved when implementing all events in the specification. In this way, we can formulate the risk for a IUT as the sum of the risk values for its events.

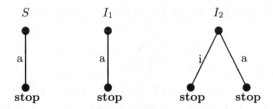

Fig. 1. S, I_1 and I_2

On the other side, due to nondeterminism, practical test cases should be executed several times to gain confidence on the testing process. For example, consider the specification S in Fig. 1 and its implementations I_1 and I_2. While the implementation I_1 is equal to S and will always accept event a as stated by S, implementation I_2 sometimes executes an internal action and then refuses event a. Obviously, this latter implementation does not conform with S.

If we are testing a physical implementation, which may behave as I_1 or I_2, we will need to execute several times a from the initial state in order to discover if it conforms with S. Each time event a is accepted we increase our confidence on the implementation. Conversely, if we obtain a single refusal we can guarantee

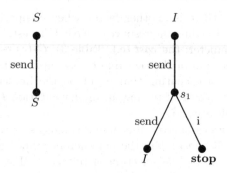

Fig. 2. S and I are recursive processes

that the IUT does not conform. In other words, estimated risk values vary along the testing process.

Additionally, the presence of recursive behaviours makes testing dependent on the level of recursion where the test is passed. We name recursive behaviours those ones that are self-instantiated. Consequently, the recursion level will be the number of times a behaviour has been instantiated. For instance, specification S in Fig. 2 contains a recursive behaviour and never stops. Again, to check a physical implementation of S that behaves as I in Fig. 2, we might need to execute many times event *send* to detect that sometimes such event is refused. As a consequence, the risk involved when testing an event is spread along the successive levels of recursion (i.e. successive event instantiations).

Taking into account both aspects, we can decompose the risk of every event in an LTS (i.e. the weight assigned to errors in events) as:

$$R_I(e) = \sum_{r=1}^{\infty} \sum_{n=1}^{\infty} R_I^{r,n}(e) \le \infty \qquad (2)$$

where $R_I^{r,n}(e)$ represents the risk of event e when being tested for the n-th time at recursion level r using a given test case. Then, the risk detection power of a test suite ts becomes:

$$MR_I(S,ts) = \sum_{tc \in ts} \sum_{e \in E(tc)} \sum_{r=1}^{Rc_e} \sum_{n=0}^{N_e(r)} R_I^{r,n}(e) \qquad (3)$$

where Rc_e and $N_e(r)$ are respectively the deepest recursion level where event e has been tested and the number of times we tested such event for every recursion level. If test cases $tc \in ts$ have a tree structure we can obtain several possible values for every successful run of the test case. So, we may measure the risk, *a priori*, using available statistics. This will be illustrated when discussing the proposed case study below.

2.4   A Priori and a Posteriori Values

As the IUT is an entity whose behaviour is unknown, there may be differences between what we desire to test and what we really test in practice. These differences may be due to:

- **Nondeterminism**: due to nondeterministic behaviour in the implementation or as a result of its interaction with other entities, it is possible that, in a first try, we cannot test those behaviours we are interested in. Even divergent behaviours may appear [19]. Because of this, it may be needed to execute test cases several times until we reach an appropriate result. New executions modify coverage values.
- **Failures**: if we detect a non-conforming implementation, it may not be possible to achieve the expected coverage because some test cases may not be executable due to errors in the implementation.

As a consequence we can identify [12] two classes of cost and coverage values:

- **A priori values**, which are obtained when we estimate the risk measurement and the cost to execute a test case *tc* assuming all possible implementation responses, as defined by the corresponding specification.
- **A posteriori values**, which are obtained after executing the test case *tc* over the IUT.

3   Test Case Selection

Now, we will discuss our approach to test case selection, which is based on a classical approach, as discussed below. But first we introduce Enriched Transition Systems as a way to keep track of the structural information needed to know those parts of the specification already tested.

3.1   Enriched Transition Systems

When we try to execute several test cases over an implementation, it would be desirable to have access to the values of risk, cost and coverage obtained along the process. For this, as discussed above, we need information about recursion levels and testing iterations. Besides, if these values were available, we could select new test cases depending on the results obtained from the ones that have been already executed.

To maintain the information gathered after the execution of test cases we define a new type of transition systems [6]:

Definition 5 (Enriched Transition System). *An enriched transition system (ETS) is a 5-tuple denoted by $S = < Stat, L, T, N(t,r), s_0 >$, such that $< Stat, L, T, s_0 >$ is a labelled transition system and $N(t,r)$ is the number of times transition $t \in T$ is executed at recursion level $r \in [1, \infty)$.*

The set of enriched transitions systems over the label set L is denoted by $ETS(L)$. Available notation and definitions for $LTS(L)$ are extended to $ETS(L)$ defining them over the underlying transition system. Unlike classical LTS, ETS are dynamic, i.e. for every transition $t \in T$, function $N(t, r)$ changes its values along the test process.

As we execute a test case on an implementation I generated from a specification S, events in the enriched specification $S_E \in ETS(L)$ are updated with the number of executions in every recursion level. In this way, we maintain information concerning which behaviours or specification parts have not been sufficiently tested.

Note that from the specifications described as ETS we can easily obtain risk and coverage values. For this, we assume that every transition has its own risk value. We also assume the existence of an heuristic function for measuring risks $f_{MR}(e, r, n) \rightarrow [0, R_I(e)]$ provided by the test engineer. This function will provide the risk measured for individual executions in a given level of recursion. This function must be convergent, and the sum over r and n of all risk measurements for a single event e must be less than or equal to the risk of that event.

Example 1. A suitable risk measurement function can be defined as

$$MR_I^{r,n}(e) = \frac{R_I(e)}{2^{r+n}} \ \ for \ r, n \geq 1 \tag{4}$$

Up to now, we have been considering transition systems without any additional information about which parts may be recursively called, which parts correspond to the main process, etc. In other words, when we traverse a plain LTS we do not know which states are recursively accessed from other states. With ETS, we consider every transition as a potential process (i.e. as a potential destination for a recursive call). Every time we reach a previously visited state, we assume that we have increased by one the recursive level for the next transition. In this way, we just need to check how many times we have visited a state to obtain the level of recursion.

Example 2. Suppose that we have the recursive specification $S_E \in ETS(L)$ appearing in Fig. 3. Function $N(t, r)$ appears next to the corresponding label for every transition. We have represented the function $N(t, r)$ as a sequence where the first element is the number of times we executed the transition in the first recursion level, the second element corresponds to the second level of recursion and so on. Initially, all values in the sequence are zero because we did not execute any test case over the IUT.

Suppose also that we have a physical object I that implements correctly the behaviour described in the specification, i.e. $I = S_E$, and that we want to execute test cases tc_1 and tc_2 described in Fig. 3.

S_{bis} represents a snapshot of $S_E \in ETS(L)$ after the execution of both test cases. Event a has been tested twice in the first level of recursion, one for each test case. Besides, this event has also been tested in the second level of recursion, which corresponds to the last transition of tc_1. The rest of the events have been executed only once in the first level of recursion.

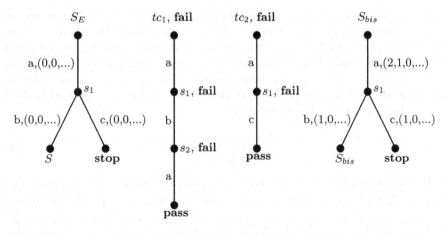

Fig. 3. S, tc_1, tc_2 and S_{bis}

3.2   An Algorithm for Risk-Driven Test Case Selection

For test generation and selection, we adopted a classical testing algorithm and modified it to take into account risk and coverage values. The classical approach selected was Tretmans' [31], which constructs tree-like deterministic test cases recursively selecting at random a subset of all possible specification transitions from a given state. This algorithm assigns a verdict to every generated state in the test case that corresponds to the expected result if the synchronous execution of test case and IUT gets blocked in that specific state.

Given $S \in ETS(L)$, we construct a test case $tc := \sum\{a; tc_a \mid a \in A_{MR}\}$ recursively as follows:

1. Construct the set $C_S := \{\mathbf{Init}(S') \mid S = \epsilon \Rightarrow S'\}$
2. Among all possible sets $A \subseteq \mathbf{Init}(S)$, select the set A_{MR} having a maximum value of $\dfrac{\sum_{e \in A} MR_I^{r,n}(e)}{Card(A)}$ and satisfying one of the following:
   a) $\forall C \in C_S : A_{MR} \bigcap C \neq \emptyset$ and $v(tc) = \mathbf{fail}$, or
   b) $\emptyset \in C_S$ and $A_{MR} = \mathbf{Init}(S)$ and $v(tc) = \mathbf{pass}$, or
   c) $A_{MR} = \emptyset$ and $v(tc) = \mathbf{pass}$
3. Construct recursively tc_a as a test case for $\sum\{i; S' \mid S = a \Rightarrow S'\}$

(*) When representing a test case, $\sum$ represents branching and $a; s$ is short notation for transitions (i.e. $-a \rightarrow s$).

Fig. 4. Generating test cases for S

The original Tretmans algorithm did not presume a strategy to select those transitions to be added to the (being constructed) test case when several subsets are available. In our case (c.f. Fig. 4), we introduced risk measures calculated from the information available in an ETS (i.e. the specification ETS) to include specific transitions into a new test case, instead of selecting branches at random. For example, we can select those branches able to detect more risk, as computed from $MR_I^{r,n}(e)$. Specifically, when we have several candidate successor states to be added to a test case (i.e. when event e corresponds to an unstable or branching state s) we will select (considering the conditions expressed in [31]) the set $A_{MR} \subseteq \mathbf{Init}(s)$ that maximises:

$$\frac{\sum_{e \in A_{MR}} MR_I^{r,n}(e)}{Card(A_{MR})} \tag{5}$$

Before we generate any test case, we make a copy of $S_E \in ETS(L)$ and name it S_E^{bcp}. During the generation process we will work with S_E^{bcp} instead of S_E. Then, each time a new set A_{MR} is selected, the values of $N(t,r)$ in copy S_E^{bcp} are updated accordingly as they are executed. For example, if due to recursion the same transition is selected for a second time in the being generated test case, the corresponding value for $N(t,r)$ will reflect that now we are in the second level of recursion. These values are updated in S_E^{bcp} and are considered a priori values (c.f Sect. 2.4). In other words, a priori values are updated along the generation of a test case over the copy, and they guide the construction of the test case in a dynamic fashion.

Once a test case has been completely generated, we recover the original ETS specification, formerly S_E, and execute the test case. After the execution of the test case, values of $N(t,r)$ in S_E are updated according to the execution sequence obtained a posteriori.

This cycle (i.e. test generation using a priori values, test execution to obtain a posteriori values, which are used as the initial values for the next iteration) is repeated until test cases with the desired coverage or cost are obtained. This way, we construct dynamically test cases to cover those parts less adequately tested so far. This approach is illustrated along the case study below and described extensively in [6].

4   A Case Study: Auction Protocol for Mobile Auction Facilities

Our case study is based on a wireless automated auction setting developed by the authors. Each user owns a mobile terminal with a unique serial number. When the user enters a new auction room, the terminal initiates an automatic dialog with the base station placed there, and obtains a local working code. Once users are registered they can participate in all forthcoming auctions, provided they have enough credit. For a comprehensive technical discussion of this system see [29].

This automated auction facility is being deployed in several fishing fraternities in Galicia, Spain. The system had around 1,500 users by end 2001, and generated revenues around 120,000 Euro/year. The main objective of our formal approach to testing was to develop a testing methodology to simplify validation at two levels: acceptance testing for devices (terminals, base stations) to be installed in fraternities, and global (field) testing involving real users and system managers. The outcome of this work is a standard set of testing procedures and test suites, which have been selected according to their cost and coverage, as discussed in this paper.

Once tests were selected, they were translated into executable sentences for the real system and instructions for the system operators and users. The testing process was iterated until our confidence on the implementation was adequate, that is, until no errors were detected.

4.1   System Description

Entities participating in the auction are:

- *Cell.* A cell is an auction room. All active terminals entering a cell are assigned to it.
- *Base station.* The core of the bid system. It is responsible of assigning transmission slots to user terminals, resolving conflicts, recognising present terminals, transmitting messages to them, and deciding who wins an auction.
- *Terminal.* A terminal is a mobile hand held computer that sends bids to the base station and receives messages from it.
- *Clock computer.* During auctions, it displays a price count-down. A terminal bid stops the clock computer when a user is interested in the current price. Also, the clock computer sets terminal recognition mode or auction mode in the base station, transmits a list of valid users and their balance to the base station, receives the list of present users, and generates messages to be transmitted to terminals.

We implemented system control on a Motorola MC68HC11 microcontroller [22]. An underlying source coding (with one start bit and one stop bit per byte) is injected in the radiofrequency (RF) module. The mobile terminal has a display for user messages, and four buttons for bidding, user message interfacing and set-up. Wireless communications are supported by 433 MHz modems, and follow the Time Domain Multiplex (TDM) model, i.e. different time slots are assigned to the base station and terminals to support communications among them. The system can handle two simultaneous auction processes.

4.2   Protocol Discussion

The auction protocol TDM has a $B \to T$ channel, which is transmitted from the base station to the terminals, and one smaller channel per auction in the opposite sense, $T \to B_1$ and $T \to B_2$. We chose this structure due to the simplicity of our RF module. Other mobile systems with a complex RF interface, such as GSM, have a different TDM per transmission sense, in separate carriers [7].

All auction protocol frames have the same structure: a synchronisation burst, an idle byte, a frame start byte, and a data load (2 bytes for $T \to B$ and 17 bytes for $B \to T$). Here, a *byte* is a source-level byte (10 bits), including start and stop bits. A $T \to B$ frame is any frame placed in channel $T \to B$ (a $B \to T$ frame is defined accordingly). All terminals in the same auction compete for the same $T \to B$ channel, in a slotted ALOHA fashion [2]. Collisions are detected as serial transmission error exceptions. To locate the correct $T \to B$ channel for an auction, terminals use $B \to T$ frame starting time as a reference (the base station injects a new $B \to T$ frame immediately after the last $T \to B$ channel).

Depending on frame type, there are two different data loads:

1. A $T \to B$ user frame has a two-byte data load. The first byte is the user local code. The second one is a checksum, for robustness.
2. A $B \to T$ base station frame has a 17-byte data load. Additional *MODE* bits control auction working mode: *Terminal recognition*, *Auction activation*, *Winner identification*, *Winner acknowledgement*, or *Purchase mode*.

The auction protocol includes the possibility of sending ASCII messages to the terminals, to be shown on their displays. Typical messages are current account balance and the total amount of items purchased. Any $B \to T$ frame can be used to send a 12-byte message to any terminal, by setting the adequate control bits.

Bidirectional handshake ensures that all bids arrive to their destination, which guarantees a finite bid time for a given number of present users, which is a basic characteristic of real-time systems.

4.3   System Modelling in LOTOS

The mobile auction facility was modelled using LOTOS. To avoid state explosion and to keep the problem tractable, the system was modelled at a higher level of abstraction. Specifically, the obtained formal specification described the system from the end-user point of view. All top-level procedures were included, both user or operator-initiated, and automatically triggered (e.g. user registration, auction initiation and termination, bidding, purchase, roaming, automatic disconnection or reconnection, etc.), but lower level details were abstracted away (e.g. low-level error recovery procedures, wireless specific communication details, etc.).

The LOTOS model was validated using simulation and model checking using the tools provided by the LOTOS TOPO tool set[20,21]. The final LOTOS specification was obtained through several iterations in a classical cyclic design process.

The interested reader can download the corresponding formal specification from:

`http://www-gist.det.uvigo.es/auction/auction.tar.gz`

As discussed above, test case selection was based on a version of the Tretmans algorithm [31], modified to include risk and cost values to construct test cases. This activity was further organised into two stages: tuning up and actual generation and selection.

4.4   Tuning Up the Testing Process

From the LOTOS specification we generated a simplified version in basic LOTOS (i.e. no data structures) that abstracted away some details of the system. For example, protocol frames were simplified to one single frame per message. This simplified version of the system was used to select *a priori* risk values for all relevant events in the system. Table 4 offers some details of both specifications.

Table 4. Original spec. vs. Tuning up spec.

Specification	States	Transitions
Terminal, Original	29	41
Terminal, Tuning Up	11	17
Base Station, Original	132	181
Base Station, Tuning Up	36	56
System (base and 2 terminals), Original	4649	6648
System (base and 2 terminals), Tuning Up	76	120

From this *tuning up* specification we generated the corresponding LTS using the tool LOLA[26]. Then, the obtained LTS were converted into ETS, which were used to keep track of measured risk values for all configurations analysed. We analysed the behaviour of the selected testing algorithm for different risk and cost calculation strategies, and for several test settings: testing of isolated terminals, isolated base station, testing of the interactions of a base station with a variable number of terminals, etc.

The selected risk measurement function during the tuning up stage was $MR_I^{r,n}(e) = \frac{R_I(e)}{2^n}$, where $R_I(e)$ represents the weight assigned to a given event and n the number of times this event is executed. The influence of recursion into the risk values was not taken into account. Initial cost and risk values for single events were supposed equal to one (i.e. $C_I(e) = R_I(e) = 1$ for all events e, see Tables 1 and 3).

To check the efficiency of test case generation over the different system components, either isolated or integrated into a complete system, we developed a test case execution simulator. This simulator composes in parallel the generated test cases with any tentative implementation of the system, modelled also as an LTS.

When running the system composed by the synchronous execution of the tunning up specification and the being analyzed test case, the simulator generates execution paths, selecting a transition randomly in any state with several choices available. As a consequence, different values of coverage and cost may be obtained in different executions of the same test case. As the test case is being executed, the simulator updates the values of $N(t, r)$ for the related transitions. This allows the generation of new test cases taking into account the previous execution.

```
java tools.AlgSelMR term1 impterm1 /K 0.8 /C 1000
Detecting maximum depth...
Max. Depth: 6

Generating TC 1 ...    Executing TC 1 ...    K=0.11111111    C=2
Generating TC 2 ...    Executing TC 2 ...    K=0.19444445    C=4
Generating TC 3 ...    Executing TC 3 ...    K=0.3611111     C=7
Generating TC 4 ...    Executing TC 4 ...    K=0.4027778     C=9
Generating TC 5 ...    Executing TC 5 ...    K=0.4236111     C=11
Generating TC 6 ...    Executing TC 6 ...    K=0.48958334    C=14
Generating TC 7 ...    Executing TC 7 ...    K=0.5173611     C=15
Generating TC 8 ...    Executing TC 8 ...    K=0.5763889     C=18
Generating TC 9 ...    Executing TC 9 ...    K=0.6041667     C=20
Generating TC 10 ...   Executing TC 10 ...   K=0.6197917     C=22
Generating TC 11 ...   Executing TC 11 ...   K=0.6267361     C=23
Generating TC 12 ...   Executing TC 12 ...   K=0.7378472     C=25
Generating TC 13 ...   Executing TC 13 ...   K=0.7934028     C=27
Generating TC 14 ...   Executing TC 14 ...   K=0.828125      C=29

END:    Num.TCs=14    Global Risk=9.0    Coverage=0.828125    Cost=29

GLOBAL Verdict: PASS
```

Fig. 5. Sample execution of the test case selection tool

The process was automated through a program that generates test cases using the algorithm described in Sect. 3, executes the simulator over a correct implementation, and updates the values of $N(t, r)$ over the specification considered as an ETS. This cyclic procedure was iterated until the desired coverage or the maximum bearable cost was reached. The whole process was integrated into a single Java application, AlgSelMR, which is also included in the accompanying package. Figure 5 illustrates the use of this tool. Parameter K represents the desired coverage in percentage, and C represents the maximum cost supported.

4.5 Testing the Automated Auction System

For test generation and selection several testing architectures were tried for an 80% coverage level. Table 5 reflects the results obtained when testing a simplified setting composed by two terminals and a base station, and when testing its components separately. 10 different test suites were generated. We can see that testing the complete system is in average 55% more expensive than testing the system components separately.

Table 5. Cost analysis. Base station and 2 terminals

System	States	Transitions	Avg. Cost
Term 1	11	17	100.2
Term 2	11	17	100.2
Base	36	56	680.0
Aggregate Avg. Cost			880.4
Composed System	76	120	1380

In general, one of the key factors which increases cost is the size of the transition space when testing a given system. Table 4 shows that the original system has a larger transition space when compared with the tuning up one, and therefore the real cost will be comparatively higher with respect to the one presented in Table 5.

The cost associated to a given coverage level increases when global system specifications are tested, reducing considerably the test suite efficiency. Besides, the problem becomes intractable for a setting with more than six terminals due to state explosion. We can conclude that it is cheaper to test system components separately, prior to their inclusion into the overall system. Obviously, when integrating the system components new errors may appear due to interoperability failures, or due to the integration process itself. A compromise solution could be based on the generation of global test cases targeted to specific events related to synchronisation among components, to complement isolated component testing. Concerning this, we were influenced by the work described in [18], which proposes the combination of *ad-hoc* partition techniques and instrumentation-related techniques used for integrated circuits testing [34]. Basically, it discusses a scalable approach to testing for systems composed by modules. First, the basic modules are tested isolated, and then they are combined into more complex modules to be tested.

To sum up, we proceeded as follows:

1. Test each system component separately. Concentrate on key resources or features assigning risk and cost values accordingly.
2. Integrate all components into the system.
3. Proceed to interoperability testing. Generate test sequences targeted to interoperation-related events and transitions.

For the first part we chose the variation of Tretmans algorithm described above, using ETS risk information for test case generation. As we had no previous information concerning specification errors, we assumed equal error probability for all component transitions except those considered basic in the component execution. For those values we assigned double risk (double weight) and then we tried to reach at least the coverage level specified. Cost values for every transition were assigned considering the time needed to execute such component transition.

For the second part, the generation of test cases from the original system specification was very slow due to the great amount of states and transitions involved (c.f. Table 4). Instead of that, we used the technique described in [28] that

provides a language to formalize test purposes, and an algorithm that permits
to merge the reference specification, plus the test purposes, to yield a test suite.
The obtained test suite is consistent with the purposes defined, and is guaranteed to be correct and complete with respect to the reference specification.
This technique provided very good results when testing the integrated system,
as it was fast enough considering the specification size. For this second part,
we assumed that the external actions for every system component were tested
exhaustively during the isolated testing stage.

Global system testing was focused on those interaction-related events more
prone to errors, assuming that external actions were already tested during (isolated) component testing. Obviously, this was the case. This decision also helped
to reduce the costs, as the external actions appear in multiple transitions of the
global systems, due to concurrence.

Thus, we decided to check those interoperability sequences more common
in normal operation: terminal recognition, base auction, winner identification
with and without collision, winner acknowledgement, purchasing, etc. Besides,
the robustness of the system has also been tested introducing errors in specific
components or modules to check the behaviour of the rest of the system.

In all cases, once a suitable test suite was obtained, the corresponding test was
translated back into executable code to be fed to the auction system components,
or into specific instructions given to users and operators to play *test auctions*
or *biddings*. The former was typically the case for isolated component testing,
whereas the latter was more common for interoperability testing based on the
strategy described above.

5   Conclusions

We have presented in this paper an approach to testing supported by formal
methods, which also includes non-formal heuristics to introduce the experience
of the testing engineer to evaluate the costs of the testing process.

LOTOS was selected as the supporting formal language. Nevertheless, the
ideas discussed here are not specific to LOTOS, but applicable to a wide range
of formal techniques. For example, any formal description technique with comparable expressive power, like ESTELLE [15], SDL [17], or PROMELA [11], could
be equally suitable to implement the ideas discussed here. In our case, LOTOS
was used because a broad selection of tools was available to support the testing
process. Additionally, our group had previous experience using LOTOS [8,9].

Our experience showed us that this approach based on error weighting and
cost values was appropriate from two different points of view. On one side,
it provided a way to assign values to different test cases, which permitted us
to classify them according to different criteria, taking into account the desired
coverage and supported cost. Test generation was directed by these heuristics to
obtain context-adapted test suites.

On the other side, it supported the analysis of several testing strategies to
compare global system testing with isolated component testing. For the case

study discussed, our final approach to testing was organised into two stages. First, we tested individual components. Then, we tested the global system targeting our efforts into the interoperation-related functionality.

Acknowledgements. We would like to thank Prof. Tomás Robles from the Politechnical University of Madrid for his comments and fruitful discussion.

References

1. Alilovic-Curgus, J., Vuong, S.T.: A Metric Based Theory of Test Selection and Coverage. Protocol Specification, Testing and Verification XIII. Elsevier Science Publishers B.V. IFIP, 1993.
2. Bertsekas, D., Gallagher, R.: Data Networks, Prentice-Hall International Ed., 1992.
3. Brookes, S.D., Hoare, C.A.R., Roscoe, A.W.: A Theory of Communicating Sequential Processes. Journal of the ACM 31, 1984
4. Brinksma, E.: A Theory for the Derivation of Tests. Protocol Specification, Testing and Verification VIII, 63-74. 1988.
5. Brinksma, E., Tretmans J., Verhaard, L.: A Framework for Test Selection. Protocol Specification, Testing and Verification, XI. Elsevier Science Publishers B.V. 233-248, 1991.
6. Burguillo-Rial, J.C.: Contribución a la Fase de Prueba de Sistemas Concurrentes y Distribuidos mediante Técnicas de Descripción Formal. Ph. D. Dissertation (in Spanish), Universidad de Vigo, Spain, 2001.
7. ETSI: "Digital cellular telecommunications system (phase 2+); Multiplexing and multiple access on the radio path (GSM 05.02 version 5.4.1)". ETSI technical report ETR 300 908, 1997.
8. Fernández-Iglesias, M. J., Llamas-Nistal, M.: Algebraic Specification through Expression Transformation, in: Mizuno, T., Shiratori, N., Higashino, T., Togashi, A., (Eds.), Procs. of the Joint Conference FORTE/PSTV'97, Chapman & Hall, 1997, 355-366.
9. Fernández-Iglesias, M. J., González-Castaño, F. J., Pousada-Carballo, J. M., Llamas-Nistal, M., and Romero-Feijoo, A.: From Complex Specifications to a Working Prototype. A Protocol Engineering Case Study. Procs. of FME 2001. Lecture Notes on Computer Science 2021, 436-448.
10. Heerink, L., Tretmans, J.: Formal Methods in Conformance Testing: a Probabilistic Refinement. In B. Baumgarten, H.J. Burkhardt, and A. Giessler, editors, Int. Workshop on Testing of Communicating Systems IX, Chapman & Hall, 1996, 261-276.
11. Holzmann, G.: Design and Validation of Computer Protocols, Prentice Hall, 1991.
12. Huecas, G.: Contribución a la Formalización de la Fase de Ejecución de Pruebas. Ph. D. Dissertation (in Spanish), Universidad Politécnica de Madrid, Spain, 1995.
13. Information Processing Systems - Open Systems Interconnections: LOTOS: A Formal Description Technique Based on the Temporal Ordering of Observational Behaviour. IS 8807, ISO, 1989.
14. Information Processing Systems - Open Systems Interconnections: Conformance Testing Methodology and Framework. IS 9646, ISO, 1991.
15. Information Processing Systems - Open Systems Interconnections: ESTELLE: A formal description technique based on the extended state transition model. IS 9074, ISO, 1989.

16. ITU-T: Recommendation Recommendation Z.500. Framework on Formal Methods in Conformance Testing. ISO ITU-T, Mayo 1997.
17. ITU-T: SDL: Specification and Description Language, CCITT Recommendation Z.100, International Telecommunication Union, 1993.
18. Koenig, H., Ulrich, A., Heiner, M.: Design for Testability: a Step-Wise Approach to Protocol Testing. Testing of Communicating Systems. Volume 10. 1997
19. Leduc, G.: Failure-based Congruences, Unfair Divergences and New Testing Theory. Proceedings of PSTV XIV, Vancouver, Canadá, Junio 1994. Chapman & Hall, 252-267, 1995.
20. Mañas, J. A., de Miguel, T.: From LOTOS to C, in: K. J. Turner, (Ed), Procs. of FORTE'88, North Holland, 1988, 79-84.
21. Mañas, J. A., de Miguel, T., Salvachúa, J., Azcorra, A.: Tool support to implement LOTOS specifications, Computer Networks and ISDN Systems, 25 (1993) 79-84.
22. Miller, G. H: Microcomputer Engineering, Prentice Hall, 1993.
23. Milner, R.: Communication and Concurrency. Prentice-Hall International, London, 1989
24. Musa, J.D., Ackerman, A.F.: Quantifying Software Validation: When to Stop Testing?. IEEE Trans. Soft. Eng., 19-26, 1989.
25. Myers, G.L.: The Art of Software Testing. John Wiley & Sons Inc., 1979.
26. Quemada, J., Pavón, S., Fernández, A.: Transforming LOTOS specification with LOLA, in: Turner, K. J., (Ed), Procs. of FORTE'88, North Holland, 1988.
27. Robles, T.: Contribución al Tratamiento Formal de la Fase de Pruebas del Ciclo Software en Ingeniería de Protocolos. Ph. D. Dissertation (in Spanish), Universidad Politécnica de Madrid, Spain, 1991.
28. Robles, T., Mañas, J. A., Huecas, G.: Specification and Derivation of OSI Conformance Test Suites. Protocol Test Systems, V. Elsevier Science Publishers. 177 - 188. IFIP, 1993.
29. Rodríguez-Hernández, P. S., González-Castaño, F. J., Pousada-Carballo, J. M., Fernández-Iglesias, M. J., García-Reinoso, J.: Cellular Network for Real-Time Mobile Auction. Wireless Personal Communications (Submitted).
30. Tretmans, J.: A Formal Approach to Conformance Testing. Ph. D. Dissertation, University of Twente, Enschede, The Netherlands, 1992.
31. Tretmans, J.: Conformance Testing with Labelled Transition Systems: Implementation Relations and Test Generation. Computer Networks and ISDN Systems, 29: 49-79, 1996.
32. Ulrich, A., Koenig, H.: Test Derivation from LOTOS using Structure Information. Protocol Test Systems VI. 1994.
33. Velthuys, R.J., Schneider, J.M., Zoerntlein, G.: A Test Derivation Method Based on Exploiting Structure Information. Protocol Specification, Testing and Verification XII, 1992.
34. Williams, T.W., Parker, K.P.: Design for Testability - A Survey. IEEE Trans. on Computers C-31, 1, 2-15. 1982.
35. Zju, J., Vuong, S.T.: Generalized Metric Based Test Selection and Coverage Measure for Communication protocols. Formal Description Techniques and Protocol Specification, Testing and Verification. FORTE X/PSTV XVII. IFIP 1997.
36. Zju, J., Vuong, S.T., Chanson, S.T.: Evaluation of Test Coverage for Embedded System Testing. 11th International Workshop on Testing of Communicating Systems. 1998.

The Next 700 Synthesis Calculi

David Basin

Universität Freiburg
Freiburg Germany

Abstract. Over the last decade I have worked with colleagues on different projects to develop, implement, and automate the use of calculi for program synthesis and transformation. These projects had different motivations and goals and differed too in the kinds of programs synthesized (e.g., functional programs, logic programs, and even circuit descriptions). However, despite their differences they were all based on three simple ideas. First, calculi can be formally derived in a rich enough logic (e.g., higher-order logic). Second, higher-order resolution is the central mechanism used to synthesize programs during proofs of their correctness. And third, synthesis proofs have a predictable form and can be partially or completely automated. In the talk I explain these ideas and illustrate the general methodology employed.

L.-H. Eriksson and P. Lindsay (Eds.): FME 2002, LNCS 2391, p. 430, 2002.

UniTesK Test Suite Architecture

Igor B. Bourdonov, Alexander S. Kossatchev, Victor V. Kuliamin, and
Alexander K. Petrenko

Institute for System Programming of Russian Academy of Sciences (ISPRAS),
B. Communisticheskaya, 25, Moscow, Russia
{igor,kos,kuliamin,petrenko}@ispras.ru
http://www.ispras.ru/~RedVerst/

Abstract. The article presents the main components of the test
suite architecture underlying UniTesK test development technology,
an automated specification based test development technology for
use in industrial testing of general-purpose software. The architecture
presented contains such elements as automatically generated oracles,
components to monitor formally defined test coverage criteria, and test
scenario specifications for test sequence generation with the help of
an automata based testing mechanism. This work stems from the ISP
RAS results of academic research and 7-years experience in industrial
application of formal testing techniques [1].

Keywords: specification based testing, partition testing, automata
based testing, test suite architecture.

1   Introduction

An automated technology of industrial test development applicable for general
purpose software is a dream of several generations of test designers and testers.
During past decades many views concerning both the possibility of such a technology and various approaches to its implementation were expressed in research
community. At the same time, the industry has attained such a level of software
complexity that some rigorous testing technology is recognized as an urgent need.

But the industry is not in a hurry to accept the first technology to appear. Industrial software development processes require some "critical mass" of features
from test development techniques to benefit actually from them. RedVerst [1]
group of ISP RAS proposes UniTesK test development technology as a candidate.
UniTesK is a successor of KVEST test development technology [2,3] developed
by RedVerst group of ISP RAS for Nortel Networks. UniTesK is based on a
ground experience in specification based testing obtained from 7-years work in
several software verification projects performed with the help of KVEST technology. The total size of software tested in these projects is about 0.5 million
lines of code. UniTesK tries to keep all the positive experience of KVEST usage.
It also introduces some improvements in flexibility of technology, heightens the
reusability of various artifacts of test development process, and lessens the skills
required to start using the technology in an effective way.

L.-H. Eriksson and P. Lindsay (Eds.): FME 2002, LNCS 2391, pp. 77–88, 2002.

To be successful, a test development technology should be based on considered test suite architecture. Test suite architecture should consist of clearly described components with neatly defined responsibilities, interfaces, relations, and interactions with each other, but all this is not sufficient. UniTesK technology is based on a new approach to automated test development: it proposes some architecture framework that can be used to construct effective tests for almost any kind of software system and makes testing process completely automated. The technology determines the immutable part of this framework and components depending on target system or test goals. Then, it defines the procedures that help to minimize the amount of manual work necessary to develop these components.

Although completely automated test generation is impossible, except for some very simple or very special cases, our experience shows that the work required to produce the manual components is usually much more simple than the one required to develop the similar test suite in traditional approaches. The use of the UniTesK technology is similar to the use of rich libraries of templates and classes — the developer specifies only actually important details and control specifics, uses library elements for routine tasks, and obtains the result without doing much tedious and mechanical work.

UniTesK technology can be used to produce tests for any kind of software. For each reasonable criterion of correctness of the system behavior we can construct a test, which convinces us of this correctness if it is successful, or can find some incorrectness. In simple case we can produce such a test at once, in more complex ones several iterative steps of test development is required.

This article presents the main elements of the test suite architecture underlying UniTesK test development technology. We also tried to provide the definitions of the main concepts used in UniTesK method and to supply each concept and architecture component with comments containing arguments in favor of the architecture decisions proposed. See [8] for some additional arguments.

2   Goals of Testing Determine Test Suite Structure

Since there is no sense in discussion of test suite architecture used in a technology irrespective from testing goals and main techniques used to test something in this technology, we start with some general considerations that clarify the goals of UniTesK and methods used to reach them.

The main question, the answer to which lies in the heart of each testing technology, is "What is the main goal of testing?" The short form of this answer accepted by UniTesK test development technology is that *testing should demonstrate that the system under test works correctly.* This answer raises more questions: "What is a correct work of the system under test? And how it can be demonstrated?" Let us try to give detailed answers.

The system under test works correctly if it behaves according to its requirements. This statement holds for all kinds of requirements, but UniTesK technology pays more attention on so-called *functional requirements.* They describe what the system should do regardless of methods used and such issues as scalability, performance, dependability, etc. To make requirements more clear and to enable automatic checking of system's behavior accordance to requirements, they should be formulated in a rigorous, clear, and unambiguous form. Such form is often called *formal specifications*. So, UniTesK approach is a kind of *conformance testing* — it presumes that we have formal specifications of the system behavior and they are given in such a form that enables us to generate *an oracle*, a program that can check the results of the target system's work against the constraints given in specifications.

Unfortunately for testing, most software systems are so complex and can interoperate with their environment in so many different ways, that there is a huge, often infinite, set of possible testing situations. To demonstrate the correct work of the system by trying all possible situations in such a case is obviously impossible. The only way to actually rigorous and convincing arguments in favor of correct or incorrect work of the system is to consider the structure of the system implementation and specifications and to look for some natural equivalence on the set of all possible situations induced by this structure. The main thesis of *partition testing*, also used by UniTesK technology, is that there are often a finite number of equivalence classes of all situations, which possess the following property: if the system behaves in correspondence with its specifications in one situation of such a class, then it behaves so in every situation of the same class, and, conversely, if it behaves improperly in one situation of a class, then it does the same way in every situation of the same class. Obviously, if this statement holds, we can test the behavior of the target system only in a finite number of situations representing all the equivalence classes.

The percent of situations (from some set of testing situations) that are tested during some test is called *test coverage*. The corresponding set of testing situations is called *coverage model* or *test coverage criterion*. The partition described in the previous paragraph can be used to define coverage model. For practical reasons we cannot restrict our consideration by only one coverage model. In an industrial project other coverage models are often considered as a base measure of the effectiveness of a test. So, to be useful in the industry a test development method should be able to provide tests based on different test coverage criteria for target component's domain. UniTesK technology does so. The criterion chosen as a test coverage criterion for a test we call *the target criterion* of this test.

Since we want to be able to test the component with different target criteria, we need to generate a kind of *universal oracle* from its specifications. Such an oracle should be able to check the correctness of the component's behavior for an arbitrary input (see [3,4,5] for more details on automatic generation of such kind of oracles). It is different from commonly implied by the term "oracle" *input/outcome oracle*, which can be used only for the prescribed input.

Let us have a more detailed look at possible mechanism of testing that is intended to achieve some coverage criterion. In most cases the only interesting part of the system's behavior is its interactions with its environment, when an environment acts on it in some way and the system reacts in some way. Other aspects, as the internal state of the system, are considered only in so far as they have an influence on possible system's reactions. So, from this point of view the system can be adequately modeled by some *automaton* having some states and transitions. Each transition is caused by some external action, or input, and, along with moving the automaton into other state, produces some reaction, or output.

The target coverage criterion defines some equivalence relation on the transitions of the modeling automaton of the system under test. We often can transform this automaton into an other one in the following way: a state of the resulting automaton corresponds to some set of states of the initial one, a transition of the resulting automaton corresponds to a set of equivalent transitions of the initial one, one for each state corresponding to the starting state of the transition in the resulting automaton, and each equivalence class of initial transitions has at least one corresponding resulting transition in some resulting state (the particular case of such transformation, factorization technique, is discussed in [6]). If we can construct a traversal of the resulting automaton (a path that contains each transition at least once) and we can find the corresponding path on the initial automaton and execute the corresponding sequence of calls, we shall achieve the target criterion. Obviously, we cover all the transitions of the resulting automaton; hence, on the initial one we cover at least one transition of every equivalence class as we need.

So, we see that the general purpose testing mechanism can be based on traversal of finite automata. This is one of the main points of UniTesK technology.

Let us now look at the details of UniTesK test suite architecture.

3   Details of UniTesK Test Suite Architecture

The core of UniTesK test suite is the traversal mechanism for finite automata. To provide additional flexibility, it is divided into two parts: *a test engine component* encapsulating a traversal algorithm of finite automata of some wide class, and *a test sequence iterator component,* which contains all the details of the particular automaton. Test engine and test sequence iterator interact via well-defined interface consisting of three following operations defined in test sequence iterator.

- **State getState()**. This operation returns the identifier of the current state of the automaton. State identifiers can be stored by test engine to facilitate a traversal, but the only thing it can do with them is comparison, which shows whether two identifiers designate one state of the automaton under traversal or two different states.
- **Input next()**. This operation seeks for the next input symbol in the current state, which has not been applied yet during this traversal. If there exists some, it returns anyone of such symbols, else it returns **null**. The objects of **Input** type are identifiers of input symbols. As state identifiers, they also may be stored by test engine and can be compared with each other.

- `void call(Input param)`. This operation applies the input symbol identified by the `param` object in the current state. It actually performs the
corresponding transition in the automaton under traversal.

Notice, that the interface specified requires that the traversal algorithm implemented by test engine component is able to work on base of only data provided by these operations. This means, in particular, that test engine has no
full description of the automaton under traversal. It can use only the structure
of already traversed part of it. We call algorithms of automata traversal that
require only this information *undemanding*.

Why the use of undemanding automata traversal algorithms is justified? It
may seem that more traditional automata testing based on full description of
the state-transition graph is more appropriate. But, notice, that undemanding
traversal algorithm requires only the information on applicable input symbols in
each state, and traditional approach needs also to know the end of each transition
(for nondeterministic automata — all possible ends). Our experience shows that
the first way to describe an automaton is much simpler and more scalable on the
size of the automaton under test. To obtain the information on all the possible
ends of each transition we need to examine deeply the specifications. So, along
with additional data, full description of an automaton requires much more human
work, because such an analysis can hardly be automated in usual case. But, if we
already have the specifications, why don't describe only applicable input and let
oracles generated from these specifications check the correctness automatically,
instead of hard manual work?

UniTesK technology is intended to use implicit specifications that describe
only properties of admissible input. So, the specifications contain enough information to generate inputs only for very simple software components. In general
case, it takes much less effort to specify necessary input by hand than to derive it from such specifications (see below the discussion of the structure of test
sequence iterator component).

The main idea of UniTesK testing technique is separating test sequence generation from the behavior verification. Test engine and test sequence iterator are
responsible for test sequence generation and require only a part of description
of an automaton under test — the set of states and applicable input symbols
for each state. Oracles of target components are called during the work of test
sequence iterator's `call()` method and, in turn, call the corresponding target
methods and perform the verification of their behavior against the specifications.

Fig. 1 shows the basic architecture of UniTesK test suite. We do not consider here auxiliary components responsible for trace gathering and run-time
test support, because they have no UniTesK specifics.

Let us say some words on the origin of the components presented. Test engine
component is a predefined part of a test suite. There are several test engine
components intended to traverse different classes of finite automata. The test
developer does not need to write such a component himself, instead it should
use one of the existing ones. Oracles are supposed to be generated automatically
from specifications, which in turn are always developed by hand.

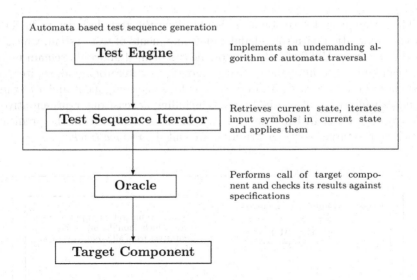

Fig. 1. Basic architecture of UniTesK test suite

Now we consider test sequence iterator component structure in more details paying more attention to the mechanism of iteration of applicable input symbols.

Test sequence iterator should provide all possible input symbols for each state of the automaton under traversal. Remember, that we construct this automaton from the behavior of the system under test and target coverage criterion. Input symbol of the automaton under traversal corresponds to some class of possible inputs for the system under test.

An arbitrary coverage criterion can be described by a number of predicates depending on the target operation identifier, a list of its input parameters, and system's state. Each of these predicates determines one coverage task. The set of predicates, describing the criterion based on the structure of implementation or specification could be extracted from them, but it is not an easy task in general case. To facilitate this work, UniTesK technology requires specification designer to emphasize the basic functionality partition of the specified operation domain by means of special constructs, **branch** operators. The elements of this basic partition correspond to subdomains where the specified operation has substantially different functionality.

But how can we use the predicates describing coverage criterion? In most simple cases we can consider and solve the corresponding boolean equations to produce automatically the set of test cases that ensures the test coverage needed. We have seen that it is impossible in general and even for common software components used in the industry, because, for example, the equations obtained can be unsolvable by an algorithm. In spite of the fact that all the data in real computers are from some finite sets, such equations are practically unsolvable due to enormous amount of time required for that.

Thus, the general case solution should allow the test designer to facilitate test case generation with some handmade components of test system, which are called *iterators* in UniTesK. But the predicates defined above do remain useful. They can be used to filter the test cases provided by iterators, and, so, iterators need not to be very precise. An iterator used for some component under test may provide a wide range of possible inputs, including at least one representative of each coverage class. In UniTesK test case filters generated from the predicates describing the target coverage criterion are called *coverage trackers.*

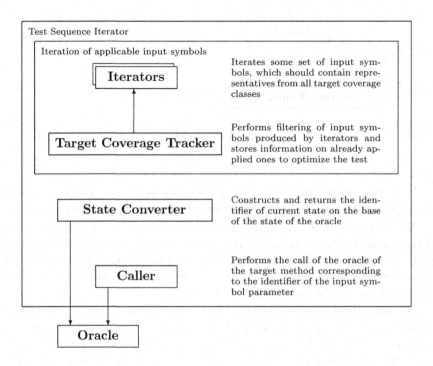

Fig. 2. Typical structure of a test sequence iterator component

Such coverage tracker is used as a part of test sequence iterator component. It determines the coverage task corresponding to a call of the target operation generated by an iterator and checks whether this task has been achieved before during the test. If not, this call is considered as the next unapplied input symbol, and the tracker marks the corresponding coverage task as covered (because the test engine actually performs this call later), else the coverage tracker pushes the iterator for the next call. When all the coverage tasks are achieved, the coverage tracker reports that there are no unapplied input symbols and the test can be finished.

Other functionality of test system iterator is represented by methods `getState()` and `call()`. As our experience shows, in some cases both of them can be generated automatically from the specification of the target component. When we consider the coverage criteria based only on coverages of component's operations domains, the method `call()` can be generated in general case. For most testing tasks it is enough, but sometimes, when we need to cover some specific sequences of target operation invocations, we should write part of this method by hand. For these reasons the possibility to do so exists in the UniTesK technology.

Fig. 2 shows the structure of mechanism iterating applicable input symbols used in UniTesK.

So, as we see, test sequence iterator has a complex structure, a bulk of which is usually generated automatically — target coverage trackers and caller implementing `call()` method. Sometimes a caller needs some manual code and sometimes state converter component and iterators can also be generated. To provide a comprehensible description of all the parts of test sequence iterator UniTesK method proposes a form of *test scenario,* which can be written by hand entirely or generated and then tuned up as needed. Test scenario serves as a source for test sequence iterator generation. For more detailed description of the structure and possible syntax of test scenarios see [7,10]. Our experience shows that the ratio of generated code size to manual code size in test sequence iterator component is usually more than 4:1.

One more important point of UniTesK test suite architecture is the use of adapter pattern (see [9] on detailed description of this pattern) to bind specification and implementation of the target component. For historical reasons we call adapters, which have specification interface and implement it on the base of the implementation under test, *mediators.*

To be able to produce reusable and repeatable tests is crucial for industrial test development technology. UniTesK supports reusability of tests and specifications by using more abstract specifications, which can be applicable to several versions of the target component. To perform a test in such a situation, we should have something to bind the immutable specification with changing implementation. One of the most simple and at the same time flexible solutions is to use mediator component having the interface of specification and implementing it with the help of implementation. Such an approach allows us to change the level of abstraction of specifications and tests developed with the help of UniTesK technology in almost arbitrary way.

Along with implementation of the specification interface, mediator is responsible for synchronization of model state defined in specifications with the state of the implementation, which can have entirely different form. This is important to support *open state testing,* which assumes that on each step (between two calls of target methods) we can determine exactly what the current state of the component's implementation is.

Fig. 3 demonstrates the complete set of the main components of UniTesK test suite architecture. Test sequence iterator component details are not presented, look at Figure 2 for them. Auxiliary components of test suite responsible for tracing and run-time test support are not showed too.

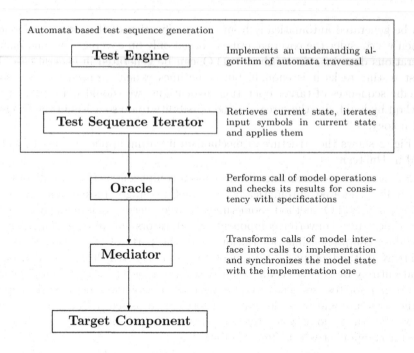

Fig. 3. Complete architecture of UniTesK test suite

Mediator components are usually written by hand. This fact increases the total size of manual work, but in return we have the possibility to develop really reusable specifications and tests, sometimes comprising the complete and ready-to-use suite for regression testing.

4   Comparison with Existing Approaches

The need of well-scalable systematic approach to industrial test development is generally recognized. The discussion of JUnit [11] testing framework in Java world shows that once more. It also demonstrates that the mere set of base classes and interfaces of the test suite components and a reasonable guide on creating tests on the base of this framework can significantly improve unit testing procedures commonly used in the industry.

UniTesK approach makes several more steps. Like JUnit, it gives test developers a flexible architecture of test suite. But in addition it determines a minimum data set required to generate all of the test suite components automatically. After that it proposes a simple representation of these data and gives tools for its automatic transformation into a ready-to-use test suite.

UniTesK test suite architecture also have many similarities with other model based testing approaches emerged during last decade, like the one used in CADP [12,13,14] tool or the one proposed in AGEDIS [15] project and based on GOTCHA-TCBeans [16,17] tool. These approaches also propose a flexible architecture of test suite supporting reuse of behavior models. Both of them use FSM based mechanism of test generation. GOTCHA tool, similar to UniTesK approach, supports coverage driven test generation. AGEDIS test architecture also proposes the components similar to UniTesK mediators.

The main differences between UniTesK and CADP/GOTCHA approaches are the following.

First, these approaches use some universal modeling language. CADP is on LOTOS and some specific notation for FSM description, and GOTCHA proposes specific GOTCHA Definition Language for description of automata models along with test cases and coverage tasks. UniTesK supposes to use uniformly defined extensions of well-known programming languages, like Java, C/C++, and so on. The uniformity of these extensions is guaranteed by the coincidence of extension constructs sets. We should add special constructs to express pre- and postconditions of operations, data type invariants, and several constructs making possible implicit FSM description (specifying only the state data structure and possible input symbols for each state) in the form of test scenarios.

Second, both CADP and AGEDIS methods suppose that the single automata model expresses both the constraints on the target system behavior and is used for test case generation. This is not convenient in general case, so we often need to use different models of the target system depending on the level of test coverage we want to achieve.

UniTesK proposes strict distinction between the model of behavior used to check its correctness and the testing model used for test generation. We need only one behavior model, which is represented in our case in the form of pre- and postconditions of operations and data type invariants. One can also notice that UniTesK behavior model can be implicit, while CADP or GOTCHA always requires an executable one.

A testing model encoded in test sequence iterator component is always FSM. We can use different testing models depending on the goals of testing. But in UniTesK approach it is much more convenient, because a testing model should not include information on correct or incorrect behavior, like in other FSM based testing techniques. So, the description of such a model is more compact and easier to use and maintain.

The only approach we know that uses two different models for behavior correctness checking and for test design is used in Rational Test RealTime [18] tool for functional testing. But this tool lacks any support for automated test generation based on FSM models.

Although most elements of UniTesK test suite architecture can be found in other approaches, none of them combines all the UniTesK features and provides the similar level of flexibility and automation support.

5   Conclusion

As we see from the previous sections the test suite architecture proposed possesses such features as full support for conformance testing, test coverage monitoring and dynamic test optimization according to the target coverage criterion, support for user-developed test scenarios, flexibility, reusability of the most part of the components, high level of automation combined with the possibility to tune up the test suite in many ways, and, last but not least, rigorous theoretical base.

This set of features along with our experience in industrial testing makes sound our hope that UniTesK test development technology based on the architecture presented can bring many benefits in industrial software testing.

We can also notice that this architecture is developed in conjunction with tools for an automatic generation of all the components that are marked above as able to be generated. So, from its origin, the architecture is intended for industrial use and has been already demonstrated its capabilities in several industrial testing projects.

Just now we have tools supporting UniTesK test development for Java and C (lite version); we also developed the similar tool for testing models developed in VDM++ [19]. This tool is implemented as an add-in for VDM Toolbox. The list of research and industrial project performed with the help of these tools and more information on UniTesK technology can be found on [1].

References

1. http://www.ispras.ru/~RedVerst/
2. http://www.fmeurope.org/databases/fmadb088.html
3. I. Bourdonov, A. Kossatchev, A. Petrenko, and D. Galter. KVEST: Automated Generation of Test Suites from Formal Specifications. *FM'99: Formal Methods. LNCS,* volume 1708, Springer-Verlag, 1999, pp. 608–621.
4. D. Peters, D. Parnas. Using Test Oracles Generated from Program Documentation. *IEEE Transactions on Software Engineering,* 24(3):161–173, 1998.
5. M. Obayashi, H. Kubota, S. P. McCarron, L. Mallet. The Assertion Based Testing Tool for OOP: ADL2, available via http://adl.xopen.org/exgr/icse/icse98.htm
6. I. B. Burdonov, A. S. Kossatchev, and V. V. Kulyamin. Application of finite automatons for program testing. *Programming and Computer Software,* 26(2):61–73, 2000.
7. A. Petrenko, I. Bourdonov, A. Kossatchev, and V. Kuliamin. Experiences in using testing tools and technology in real-life applications. *Proceedings of SETT'01,* India, Pune, 2001.
8. A. K. Petrenko. Specification Based Testing: Towards Practice. *Proceedings of PSI'01. LNCS,* Springer-Verlag. To be printed.
9. E. Gamma, R. Helm, R. Johnson, and J. Vlissides. Design Patterns: Elements of Reusable Object-Oriented Software. Reading, MA: Addison-Wesley, 1995.
10. Igor B. Bourdonov, Alexey V. Demakov, Andrew A. Jarov, Alexander S. Kossatchev, Victor V. Kuliamin, Alexander K. Petrenko, Sergey V. Zelenov. Java Specification Extension for Automated Test Development. *Proceedings of PSI'01. LNCS,* Springer-Verlag. To be printed.

11. http://junit.sourceforge.net/
12. http://www.inrialpes.fr/vasy/cadp/
13. J.-C. Fernandez, H. Garavel, A. Kerbrat, R. Mateescu, L. Mounier, and M. Sighire-anu. CADP: A Protocol Validation and Verification Toolbox. Proceedings of the 8-th Conference on Computer-Aided Verification (New Brunswick, New Jersey, USA), 1996, pp. 437–440.
14. H. Garavel, F. Lang, and R. Mateescu. An overview of CADP 2001. INRIA Technical Report TR-254, December 2001.
15. http://www.agedis.de/
16. http://www.haifa.il.ibm.com/projects/verification/gtcb/documentation.html
17. E. Farchi, A. Hartman, and S. S. Pinter. Using a model-based test generator to test for standard conformance. IBM Systems Journal, volume 41, Number 1, 2002, pp. 89–110.
18. http://www.rational.com/products/testrt/index.jsp
19. http://www.ifad.dk/

Hoare Logic for NanoJava: Auxiliary Variables, Side Effects, and Virtual Methods Revisited

David von Oheimb and Tobias Nipkow

Fakultät für Informatik, Technische Universität München
http://isabelle.in.tum.de/Bali/

Abstract. We define NanoJava, a kernel of Java tailored to the investigation of Hoare logics. We then introduce a Hoare logic for this language featuring an elegant approach for expressing auxiliary variables: by universal quantification on the outer logical level. Furthermore, we give simple means of handling side-effecting expressions and dynamic binding within method calls. The logic is proved sound and (relatively) complete using Isabelle/HOL.

Keywords: Hoare logic, Java, Isabelle/HOL, auxiliary variables, side effects, dynamic binding.

1   Introduction

Java appears to be the first widely used programming language that emerged at a time at which formal verification was mature enough to be actually feasible. For that reason the past few years have seen a steady stream of research on Hoare logics for sequential parts of Java [24,7,6,9,21,22], mostly modeled and analyzed with the help of a theorem prover. Since even sequential Java is a formidable language in terms of size and intricacies, there is no Hoare logic for all of it as yet. In terms of language constructs, von Oheimb [22] covers the largest subset of Java. However, as a consequence, this Hoare logic is quite complex and it is difficult to see the wood for the trees. Therefore Nipkow [17] selected some of the more problematic or technically difficult language features (expressions with side effects, exceptions, recursive procedures) and dealt with their Hoare logics in isolation. Although each of these features admits a fairly compact proof system, it remains to demonstrate that their combination in one language is still manageable.

In a sense, NanoJava has been designed with the same aim as Featherweight Java [8]: to have a kernel language for studying a certain aspect of Java. In the case of Featherweight Java, Java's module system is under scrutiny, in NanoJava it is Hoare logic. This explains why, despite of some similarities, we could not just start with Featherweight Java: it was designed for a different purpose; being purely functional, it would not have done us any good.

Starting from μJava [18] we have isolated NanoJava, a Java-like kernel of an object-oriented language. The purpose of this paper is to present the language

L.-H. Eriksson and P. Lindsay (Eds.): FME 2002, LNCS 2391, pp. 89–105, 2002.

NanoJava as a vehicle to convey new techniques for representing Hoare logics (for partial correctness). Next to the Hoare logic we give also an operational semantics such that we can conduct soundness and completeness proofs. Because such proofs have a checkered history in the literature (e.g. the proof system for recursive procedures by Apt [3] was later found to be unsound [2]), the whole development was carried out in the theorem prover Isabelle/HOL [19]. In fact, this very paper is generated from the Isabelle theories, which are documents that can both be machine-checked and rendered in LaTeX. Thus every formula quoted in this paper as a theorem actually is one. The full formalization including all proofs is available online from http://isabelle.in.tum.de/library/HOL/NavoJava/.

Our general viewpoint on Hoare logic is that when conducting rigorous analysis (using a theorem prover or not), in particular metatheory, making the dependency of assertions on the program state is indispensable. Furthermore, syntactic treatments of assertions lead to awkward technical complications, namely term substitutions and syntactic side conditions like variable freshness hard to deal with in a fully formal way. Thirdly, for our purposes, constructing and using an assertion language of its own rather than re-using the metalogic for expressing assertions would only add unnecessary clutter. For these reasons, we use a semantic representation of assertions. Doing so, we can in particular replace fresh variables by (universally) bound variables and term substitutions by suitable state transformations.

Compared with previous Hoare logics, in particular fully rigorous ones like [10,21], we introduce the following technical innovations: auxiliary variables are hidden via universal quantification at the meta-level; side-effecting expressions are treated more succinctly; the treatment of dynamic binding by von Oheimb is combined with the idea of virtual methods (a conceptually important abstraction enabling modular proofs) by Poetzsch-Heffter [24]. The latter technique may be applied to other object-oriented languages as well, whereas the enhanced treatment of side effects and in particular of auxiliary variables applies to Hoare logics for imperative languages in general.

1.1 Related Work

Both Huisman and Jacobs [7] and Jacobs and Poll [9] base their work on a kind of denotational semantics of Java and derive (in PVS and Isabelle/HOL) a set of proof rules from it. They deal with many of the complexities of Java's state space, exception handling etc., but without (recursive) method calls. Therefore their rules and ours are quite incomparable. Neither do they investigate completeness. Their rationale is that they can always fall back on the denotational semantics if necessary.

Poetzsch-Heffter and Müller [24] present a Hoare logic for a kernel of Java and prove its soundness. In contrast to our semantic approach to assertions, which is most appropriate for meta theory as our primary concern, they emphasize tool support for actual program verification and use a syntactic approach. This has drawbacks for meta theory, but in the other hand side allows a more or less implicit use of auxiliary variables. More recently, Poetzsch-Heffter [23] has extended this work to a richer language and has also proved completeness. His rules are quite different from ours. In particular he does not use our extended rule of consequence but combines the usual consequence rule with substitution and invariance rules.

Other axiomatic semantics for object-oriented languages include the one by Leino [13], who does not discuss soundness or completeness because he considers only a weakest precondition semantics, and the object-calculus based language by Abadi and Leino [1], who state soundness but suspect incompleteness.

Kleymann [10,11] gives a machine-checked Hoare logic for an imperative language with a single procedure without parameters, in particular motivating the use of auxiliary variables.

2   NanoJava

We start with an informal exposition of NanoJava. Essentially, NanoJava is Java with just classes. Statements are `skip`, sequential composition, conditional, `while`, assignments to local variables and fields. Expressions are `new`, cast, access to local variables and fields, and method call. The most minimal aspect is the type system: there are no basic types at all, only classes. Consequently there are no literals either; the `null` reference can be obtained because variables and fields are initialized to `null` (and need not be initialized by the programmer). As there are no booleans either, conditionals and loops test references for being `null` (in which case the loop terminates or the `else`-case is taken).

Because of the restriction to references as the only type, it may not be immediately apparent that NanoJava is computationally complete. Figure 1 shows how natural numbers can be simulated by a linked list of references. The natural number n is implemented by a linked list of $n + 1$ `Nat`-objects: 0 is implemented by `new Nat()` (initializing `pred` to `null`), and +1 by `suc` (which appends one object to the list). Given two `Nat`-objects m and n, `m.eq(n)` determines if m and n represent the same number, and `m.add(n)` adds m to n non-destructively, i.e. by creating new objects.

3   Abstract Syntax

Here we begin with the formal description of NanoJava. We do not show the full formalization in Isabelle/HOL but only the most interesting parts of it.

3.1   Terms

Programs contain certain kinds of names, which we model as members of some not further specified types. For the names of classes, methods, fields and local variables we use the Isabelle types *cname*, *mname*, *fname* and *vname*. It is convenient to extend the range of "normal" local variables with special ones

```
class Nat {

  Nat pred;

  Nat suc()
    { Nat n = new Nat(); n.pred = this; return n; }

  Nat eq(Nat n)
    { if (this.pred) if (n.pred) return this.pred.eq(n.pred);
                     else return n.pred;
      else if (n.pred) return this.pred; else return this.suc(); }

  Nat add(Nat n)
    { if (this.pred) return this.pred.add(n.suc()); else return n; }
}
```

Fig. 1. Emulating natural numbers

holding the *This* pointer, the (single) parameter and the result of the current method invocation, whereby for simplicity we assume that each method has exactly one parameter, called *Par*.

Using the concepts just introduced, we can define statements and expressions as

datatype *stmt*
  = *Skip*
  | *Comp stmt stmt*   (_; _)
  | *Cond expr stmt stmt*   (*If* '(_') _ *Else* _)
  | *Loop vname stmt*   (*While* '(_') _)
  | *LAss vname expr*   (_ = _)   — local assignment
  | *FAss expr fname expr*   (_.._ = _)   — field assigment
  | *Meth cname* × *mname*   — virtual method
  | *Impl cname* × *mname*   — method implementation
and *expr*
  = *NewC cname*   (*new* _)
  | *Cast cname expr*
  | *LAcc vname*   — local access
  | *FAcc expr fname*   (_.._)   — field access
  | *Call cname expr mname expr* ({_}_._'(_'))

The symbols in parentheses on the right hand side specify alternative mixfix syntax for some of the syntactic entities. Virtual methods *Meth* and method implementations *Impl* are intermediate statements that we use for modeling method calls, as will be explained in §4.2. The first subterm C of a method call expression $\{C\}e.m(p)$ is a class name holding the static type of the second subterm e. It will be used as an upper bound for the type dynamically computed during a method call.

3.2   Declarations

The only types we care about are classes and the type of the null pointer:

datatype $ty = NT \mid Class\ cname$

Programs are modeled as lists of class declarations, which contain field and method declarations. The details of their definition and the functions for accessing them are suppressed here as they are of little relevance for the Hoare logic. Also for reasons of space, we gloss over the definitions of type relations as well as the few concepts of well-structuredness required for technical reasons [21, §2.6.4].

Due to our defensive operational semantics given next, the typical notions of well-formedness and well-typedness are not required at all.

4   Operational Semantics

We employ an operational semantics as the primary semantical description of NanoJava. It is more or less standard and thus we can afford to give just the most essential and interesting aspects here.

4.1   Program State

The only values we deal with are references, which are either the null pointer or an address, i.e. a certain location (of some not further specified type loc) on the heap:

datatype $val = Null \mid Addr\ loc$

The program state can be thought of as an abstract datatype $state$ for storing the values of the local variables (of the current method invocation) as well as the heap, which is essentially a mapping from locations to objects. There are a number of access and modification functions on the state. We typically introduce them on demand, except for two simple ones: $s\langle x \rangle$ stands for the value of the program variable x within state s, and $lupd(x \mapsto v)\ s$ for the state s where the value v has been assigned to the local variable x. The actual definitions of these auxiliary functions are not needed for the meta-theoretic proofs in this paper.

4.2   Evaluation Rules

We write $s\ -c-n\rightarrow\ s'$ to denote that execution of the statement c from state s terminates with final state s'. The natural number n gives additional information about program execution, namely an upper bound for the recursive depth. This annotation will be required for the soundness proof of the Hoare logic. The evaluation of an expression e to a value v is written analogously as $s\ -e\succ v-n\rightarrow\ s'$.

Here we give only a selection of the most interesting non-standard execution rules.

For simplicity, and since we do not consider exceptions, we define our semantics in a defensive way: when things go wrong, program execution simply gets stuck. For example, evaluation of a field access $e.f$ from an initial state s terminates in state s' if (and only if) the reference expression e evaluates to an address a, transforming the state s into s', and yields the value $get\_field\ s'\ a\ f$ (which is the contents of field f within the object at heap location a of the state s'):

$FAcc$: $s\ -e\!\succ\!Addr\ a-n\!\to\ s'\implies s\ -e.f\!\succ\!get\_field\ s'\ a\ f-n\!\to\ s'$

The most complex rules of our Hoare logic are those concerning method calls. Therefore we give their operational counterparts here first, which should be easier to understand, in order to introduce the basic semantic concepts behind them. As opposed to the rules for method calls we gave in earlier work, the *Call* rule given here is restricted to argument and result value passing (i.e., the context switch between caller and callee) whereas dynamic binding is handled by the *Meth* rule given thereafter. This not only makes the (still rather formidable) rule a bit simpler, but — more importantly — supports the concept of *virtual methods* [24].

The virtual method $Meth(C,m)$ stands for the methods with name m available in class C (and possibly inherited in any subclass) as well as all methods overriding it in any subclass. In other words, the properties of $Meth(C,m)$ are the intersection of all properties of method implementations possibly invoked (through dynamic binding) for invocations of m from a reference with static type C. Virtual methods enable not only the usual method specifications from the callee's point of view (involving in particular the local names of the method parameters[1]) but uniform verification of method calls from the caller's view.

Call: $[\![\ s0\ -e1\!\succ\!a-n\!\to\ s1;\ s1\ -e2\!\succ\!p-n\!\to\ s2;$
$\quad\quad lupd(\mathit{This}\!\mapsto\!a)(lupd(Par\!\mapsto\!p)(del\_locs\ s2))\ -Meth(C,m)-n\!\to\ s3\ ]\!]\implies$
$\quad\quad s0\ -\{C\}e1.m(e2)\!\succ\!s3\langle Res\rangle-n\!\to\ set\_locs\ s2\ s3$

First a notational remark: in a rule of the form $[\![\ A_1;\ A_2;\ \dots\ A_n\ ]\!]\implies C$, the formulas A_i are the premises and C is the conclusion. After evaluating the reference expression $e1$ and the (single) argument expression $e2$, the local variables of the intermediate state $s2$ are deleted and the values of the parameter value and the *This* pointer are inserted as new local variables. After the corresponding virtual method has been called, its result is extracted as the value of the method call and the original local variables of $s2$ are restored in the final state $s3$. Note that the first parameter of the auxiliary function set_locs is the whole state value rather than just the local variable part of it. We decided to do so in order to be able to keep the structure of type *state* opaque.

Meth: $[\![\ s\langle\mathit{This}\rangle = Addr\ a;\ D = obj\_class\ s\ a;\ D \preceq_C C;$
$\quad\quad init\_locs\ (D,m)\ s\ -Impl(D,m)-n\!\to\ s'\ ]\!]\implies$
$\quad\quad s\ -Meth(C,m)-n\!\to\ s'$

---

[1] Note that here, as well as in [24], matters are somewhat simplified because the method parameter names are the same for all methods.

Evaluating the virtual method $Meth(C,m)$ means extracting the address a of the receiver object (from the *This* pointer), looking up its dynamic type D, which must be a subclass of C, and calling the implementation of m available in class D (after initializing its local variables).

$$Impl:\ s\ -body\ Cm-n\rightarrow s' \implies$$
$$s\ -Impl\ Cm-n+1\rightarrow s'$$

The only thing that remains to be done for a method call is to unfold the method body, using a suitable auxiliary function *body* which yields the corresponding (typically compound) statement. Note the increase of the recursive depth from n to $n + (1::'a)$. The pair of method class and name is represented by the single free variable Cm. One might think of merging the *Impl* and *Meth* rules, but it makes sense to keep virtual methods and method implementations apart in order to separate concerns, which pays off in particular for the axiomatic semantics.

5 Hoare Logic Concepts

This section and the following one form the core of this article. First, we describe important basic concepts of our axiomatic semantics of NanoJava.

5.1 Assertions

One of the most crucial concepts of a Hoare logic is the notion of *assertions* used as propositions on the program state before and after term execution. The assertion language and its underlying logic strongly determine the expressiveness and completeness of the resulting verification logic.

We take a semantic view of assertions, thus an assertion is nothing but a predicate on the state:

types $assn = state \Rightarrow bool$

This technique, already used in [15], short-circuits the logic used for the assertions with the logic of the underlying proof system, in our case Isabelle/HOL. Thus we do not have to invent a new assertion logic and worry about its expressiveness, and our notion of completeness will be *relative* in the sense of Cook [4].

5.2 Side Effects

Since expressions can have side effects, we need a Hoare logic for expression evaluation as well. For a review of different approaches to this issue, see [22, §4.3]. In essence, assertions used in connection with expressions must be able to refer to the expression results. Kowaltowski [12] shows how to achieve this for a syntactic view on assertions. Since we prefer a semantic view, we can avoid technical complications with substitutions and variable freshness conditions (cf. §6.3), and assertions simply receive the current result as an extra parameter:

types $vassn = val \Rightarrow assn$

Having decided on the assertion types, we can define the Hoare triples for statements and expressions as follows:

types

$$triple = assn \times stmt \times assn$$
$$etriple = assn \times expr \times vassn$$

In the approach that we promoted in [22, §4.3], the type *vassn* is used not only in the postconditions, but also in the preconditions of *etriples*. This was just for uniformity reasons, and in our definition of validity of such triples given in [22, §6.1], the value parameter was effectively ignored for the precondition. The variant given here is simpler.

5.3 Auxiliary Variables

The most notable novelty and simplification (as compared to the approach promoted by Kleymann [11]) achieved by the work presented here concerns the representation of *auxiliary variables*.

Auxiliary variables are required to relate values between pre- and postconditions. For example, in the triple $\{x=Z\}$ $y:=42$ $\{x=Z\}$ the (logical) variable Z is used to remember the value of the program variable x, such that one can express that x does not change while y is assigned to. From the logical point of view, Z is implicitly universally quantified, which has to take place somewhere outside the triple such that both occurrences are bound. In case the whole triple occurs negatively (e.g., as an assumption as will be required for handling recursive methods), care is needed to put the quantifier not too far outside.

In [22, §4.2 and §6.1], we followed Kleymann implementing auxiliary variables by extra parameters of assertions that are universally quantified within the definition of validity. Here, in contrast, we leave auxiliary variables and the universal quantifications on them as implicit as possible. That is, auxiliary variables are mentioned in assertions only when they are actually needed, and explicit universal quantification is used only if the concerning triple appears negatively. In other words, we leave the mechanism for dealing with auxiliary variables to the outer logical level.

6 Hoare Logic Rules

This section gives the full list of Hoare logic rules the constitute the axiomatic semantics of NanoJava.

We write $A \Vdash C$ to denote that from the *antecedent* A (acting as a set of assumptions) the consequent C can be derived. Both sets consist of statement triples, i.e. the relation $\_ \Vdash \_$ has type $(triple\ set \times triple\ set)\ set$. If the set C contains just a single triple, we write $A \vdash \{P\}\ c\ \{Q\}$. For expression triples, we use the relation $\_ \vdash_e \_$ of type $(triple\ set \times etriple)\ set$.

6.1 Structural Rules

We require only a few structural, i.e. non-syntax-directed rules. The first one is the assumption rule:

Asm: $[\![\ a \in A\ ]\!] \Longrightarrow A \Vdash \{a\}$

The next two are used to construct and destruct sets in the consequent, i.e. to introduce and eliminate conjunctions on the right-hand side:

ConjI: $[\![\ \forall c \in C.\ A \Vdash \{c\}\ ]\!] \Longrightarrow A \Vdash C$

ConjE: $[\![\ A \Vdash C;\ c \in C\ ]\!] \Longrightarrow A \Vdash \{c\}$

The final two rules are a further development of the consequence rule due to Morris [14], championed by Kleymann [11], and re-formulated by Nipkow [17].

Conseq: $[\![\ \forall Z.\ A \vdash \{P'\ Z\}\ c\ \{Q'\ Z\};$
$\qquad\qquad \forall s\ t.\ (\forall Z.\ P'\ Z\ s \longrightarrow Q'\ Z\ t) \longrightarrow (P\ s \longrightarrow Q\ t)\ ]\!] \Longrightarrow$
$\qquad\qquad A \vdash \{P\}\ c\ \{Q\ \}$

eConseq: $[\![\ \forall Z.\ A \vdash_e \{P'\ Z\}\ e\ \{Q'\ Z\};$
$\qquad\qquad \forall s\ v\ t.\ (\forall Z.\ P'\ Z\ s \longrightarrow Q'\ Z\ v\ t) \longrightarrow (P\ s \longrightarrow Q\ v\ t)\ ]\!] \Longrightarrow$
$\qquad\qquad A \vdash_e \{P\}\ e\ \{Q\ \}$

Within these two rules, as usual the use of auxiliary variables Z partially has to be made explicit in order to allow the adaptation (i.e., specialization with different values) of auxiliary variables for the assertions P' and Q'. The explicit universal quantification on Z in the first premise of each rule is required just because the appearances of Z are on the implication-negative side and thus implicit quantification would be existential rather than universal. Still, due to our new approach to auxiliary variables and side-effecting expressions, these rules are simpler than those given e.g. in [21,22]: they are closer to the well-known standard form of the consequence rule and require fewer explicit quantifications.

6.2 Standard Rules

The rules for standard statements and expressions appear (almost) as usual, except that side effects are taken into account for the condition of *If _ Then _ Else* and for variable assignments. Thus we comment only on those parts of the rules deviating from the standard ones.

Skip: $A \vdash \{P\}\ Skip\ \{P\}$

Comp: $[\![\ A \vdash \{P\}\ c1\ \{Q\};\ A \vdash \{Q\}\ c2\ \{R\}\ ]\!] \Longrightarrow$
$\qquad\quad A \vdash \{P\}\ c1;\ c2\ \{R\}$

LAcc: $A \vdash_e \{\lambda s.\ P\ (s\langle x\rangle)\ s\}\ LAcc\ x\ \{P\}$

The rule for access to a local variable x is reminiscent of the well-known assignment rule: in order to derive the postcondition P, one has to ensure the precondition P where the current value of x is inserted for its result parameter. The lambda abstraction (and later application again) on s is used to peek at the program state.

LAss: $[\![\; A \vdash_e \{P\} \; e \; \{\lambda v \; s. \; Q \; (lupd(x \mapsto v) \; s)\} \;]\!] \Longrightarrow$
$\qquad A \vdash \{P\} \; x{=}e \; \{Q\}$

In the postcondition of the premise of the *LAss* rule, we can refer to the result of e via the lambda abstraction on v. This value is used to modify the state at the location x before it is fed to the assertion Q.

Cond: $[\![\; A \vdash_e \{P\} \; e \; \{Q\};$
$\qquad \forall v. \; A \vdash \{Q \; v\} \; (if \; v \neq Null \; then \; c1 \; else \; c2) \; \{R\} \;]\!] \Longrightarrow$
$\qquad A \vdash \{P\} \; If(e) \; c1 \; Else \; c2 \; \{R\}$

The second premise of the *Cond* rule can handle both branches of the conditional statement uniformly by employing the *if _ then _ else _* of the metalogic HOL. This is possible because the statement between the pre- and postcondition is actually a meta-level expression that can depend on the value v of the condition e, as obtained through the precondition $Q \; v$. Note that the universal quantification over v around the triple makes v available throughout the triple, in particular the statement expression in the middle.

This technique for describing the dependency of program terms on previously calculated values, which will be crucial for handling dynamic binding in the *Meth* rule below, has been introduced in [21, §5.5]. If we had standard Booleans, we could expand all possible cases for v (viz. *true* and *false*) and write the *Cond* rule in the more familiar way:

$[A \vdash_e \{P\} \; e \; \{Q\}; \; A \vdash \{Q \; true\} \; c1 \; \{R\}; \; A \vdash \{Q \; false\} \; c2 \; \{R\}]$
$\Longrightarrow A \vdash \{P\} \; If \; (e) \; c1 \; Else \; c2 \; \{R\}$

Loop: $[\![\; A \vdash \{\lambda s. \; P \; s \wedge s\langle x \rangle \neq Null\} \; c \; \{P\} \;]\!] \Longrightarrow$
$\qquad A \vdash \{P\} \; While(x) \; c \; \{\lambda s. \; P \; s \wedge s\langle x \rangle = Null\}$

The *Loop* rule appears almost as usual except that we consider the loop condition to be fulfilled as long as the given program variable holds a nonzero reference. Allowing for arbitrary side-effecting expressions as loop conditions is possible [22, §9.1] but not worth the technical effort.

6.3   Object-Oriented Rules

The rules dealing with object-oriented features are less common and therefore deserve more comments. Where needed, we introduce auxiliary functions on the program state on the fly.

FAcc: $[\![\; A \vdash_e \{P\} \; e \; \{\lambda v \; s. \; \forall a. \; v{=}Addr \; a \longrightarrow Q \; (get\_field \; s \; a \; f) \; s\} \;]\!] \Longrightarrow$
$\qquad A \vdash_e \{P\} \; e.f \; \{Q\}$

The operational semantics for field access given in §4.2 implies that in order to ensure the postcondition Q it is sufficient that as the postcondition of the reference expression e, Q holds for the contents of the field referred to, under the assumption that the value of e is some address a.

FAss: ⟦ $A \vdash_e \{P\}$ *e1* $\{\lambda v\ s.\ \forall a.\ v{=}Addr\ a \longrightarrow Q\ a\ s\}$;
    $\forall a.\ A \vdash_e \{Q\ a\}$ *e2* $\{\lambda v\ s.\ R\ (upd\_obj\ a\ f\ v\ s)\}$ ⟧ $\Longrightarrow$
    $A \vdash\ \{P\}$ *e1.f=e2* $\{R\}$

Field assignment handles the value of the reference expression *e1* in the same way except that the address a has to be passed to the triple in the second premise of the rule. We achieve this by passing a as an extra parameter to the intermediate assertion Q and universally quantifying over a around the second triple. This technique, which will be applied also for the *Call* rule below, uses only standard features of the metalogic and is therefore technically less involved than the substitutions to fresh intermediate variables, as employed by Kowaltowski [12]. The auxiliary function *upd_obj* $a\ f\ v\ s$ updates the state s by changing the contents of field f (within the object located) at address a to the value v.

NewC: $A \vdash_e \{\lambda s.\ \forall a.\ new\_Addr\ s = Addr\ a \longrightarrow P\ (Addr\ a)\ (new\_obj\ a\ C\ s)\}$
    new C $\{P\}$

The rule for object creation uses the functions *new_Addr* selecting a vacant location a on the heap (if possible) as well as *new_obj* $a\ C\ s$ which updates the state s by initializing an instance of class C and allocating it at address a. Note that the result of the *new C* expression is the value *Addr a*, given to P as its first argument.

Cast: ⟦ $A \vdash_e \{P\}$ e $\{\lambda v\ s.\ (case\ v\ of\ Null \Rightarrow True$
                    $|\ Addr\ a \Rightarrow obj\_class\ s\ a \preceq_C C) \longrightarrow Q\ v\ s\}$ ⟧ $\Longrightarrow$
    $A \vdash_e \{P\}$ *Cast C e* $\{Q\}$

In our operational semantics, evaluating a type cast gets stuck if the dynamic type of the object referred to is not a subtype of the given class C. Thus the postcondition Q in the rule's premise needs to be shown only if the value of the reference is a null pointer or the type given by *obj_class* $s\ a$ is a subclass of C.

Call: ⟦ $A \vdash_e \{P\}$ *e1* $\{Q\}$;
    $\forall a.\ A \vdash_e \{Q\ a\}$ *e2* $\{R\ a\}$;
    $\forall a\ p\ ls.\ A \vdash\ \{\lambda s'.\ \exists s.\ R\ a\ p\ s \land ls = s \land$
                    $s' = lupd(This{\mapsto}a)(lupd(Par{\mapsto}p)(del\_locs\ s))\}$
            Meth(C,m) $\{\lambda s.\ S\ (s\langle Res\rangle)\ (set\_locs\ ls\ s)\}$ ⟧ $\Longrightarrow$
    $A \vdash_e \{P\}$ $\{C\}$*e1.m(e2)* $\{S\}$

The rule for method calls closely resembles the operational semantics, too. The values of both subexpressions are passed on like in the *FAss* rule above. A third universal quantification is needed in order to transfer the value *ls* of the existentially quantified pre-state s (before the local variables are modified, resulting in state s') to the postcondition of the third triple where the original local variables have to be restored.

Meth: ⟦ $\forall D.\ A \vdash\ \{\lambda s'.\ \exists s\ a.\ s\langle This\rangle = Addr\ a \land D = obj\_class\ s\ a \land D \preceq_C C \land$
                    $P\ s \land s' = init\_locs\ (D,m)\ s\}$ *Impl*(D,m) $\{Q\}$ ⟧ $\Longrightarrow$
    $A \vdash\ \{P\}$ *Meth*(C,m) $\{Q\}$

The rule for virtual methods requires proving the desired property for all method implementations possibly called when taking dynamic binding into account. This is equivalent to the combination of the *class-rule* and *subtype-rule* (plus some structural rules) given in [24], except that the set of implementations is constrained not only by the dynamic type D of the *This* pointer, but also by the set of subclasses of C.

This new combination of techniques dealing with dynamic binding has the following advantages. In contrast to the rules given in [24], the variety of possible implementations is captured by a single rule, and the user may immediately exploit the fact that this variety is bound by the statically determined class C. In contrast to the version given in [21,22], the abstraction of a virtual method allows one to prove the properties of such methods once and for all (independently of actual method calls) and exploiting them for any number of method calls without having to apply the *Meth* rule again.

Method implementations are handled essentially by unfolding the method bodies. Additionally, as usual, the set of assumptions A has to be augmented in order to support recursive calls. For supporting mutual recursion, it is furthermore very convenient to handle a whole set of methods Ms simultaneously [20].

$$\llbracket \, A \, \cup \, (\bigcup Z. \, (\lambda Cm. \, (P \, Z \, Cm, \, Impl \, Cm, \, Q \, Z \, Cm)) \, `Ms) \, \Vdash$$
$$(\bigcup Z. \, (\lambda Cm. \, (P \, Z \, Cm, \, body \, Cm, \, Q \, Z \, Cm)) \, `Ms) \, \rrbracket \implies$$
$$A \, \Vdash \, (\bigcup Z. \, (\lambda Cm. \, (P \, Z \, Cm, \, Impl \, Cm, \, Q \, Z \, Cm)) \, `Ms)$$

Recall that each $Cm \in Ms$ is a method identifier consisting of a class and method name. For any f, the HOL expression $f \, ` \, Ms$ denotes the set of all $f \, Cm$ where $Cm \in Ms$. Thus each term $(\lambda Cm. \, (P \, Z \, Cm, \, ... \, Cm, \, Q \, Z \, Cm)) \, `Ms$ denotes a set of triples indexed by Cm ranging over Ms. The use of auxiliary variables Z has to be made explicit here because the additional assumptions, namely that the implementations involved in any recursive invocations already fulfill the properties to be proved, have to be available for all Z. Within antecedents, this universal quantification can be expressed using the set union operator $\bigcup Z$, and for uniformity we have written the other two quantifications the same way. Note that the semantics of forming a union of sets of Hoare triples is logical conjunction and thus is essentially the same as when using an universal quantifier, which is not possible within the antecedents part of the derivation relation $\Vdash$.

There is a variant of the above rule more convenient to apply. Wherever possible, it uses the standard universal quantifier or even makes quantification implicit:

$$Impl: \llbracket \, \forall Z2. \, A \cup (\bigcup Z1. \, (\lambda Cm. \, (P \, Z1 \, Cm, \, Impl \, Cm, \, Q \, Z1 \, Cm)) \, `Ms) \, \Vdash$$
$$(\lambda Cm. \, (P \, Z2 \, Cm, \, body \, Cm, \, Q \, Z2 \, Cm)) \, `Ms \, \rrbracket \implies$$
$$A \quad \Vdash \quad (\lambda Cm. \, (P \, Z3 \, Cm, \, Impl \, Cm, \, Q \, Z3 \, Cm)) \, `Ms$$

7   Example

As an example of a proof in our Hoare logic we formalize (part of) the definition of class Nat given in §2 and prove that the virtual method add is homomorphic wrt. lower bounds:

$$\{\} \vdash \{\lambda s. \, s{:}s\langle This\rangle \geq X \wedge s{:}s\langle Par\rangle \geq Y\} \, Meth(Nat,add) \, \{\lambda s. \, s{:}s\langle Res\rangle \geq X{+}Y\}$$

where the relation $s{:}v \geq n$ means that the value v represents at least the number n, i.e. within state s, the chain of Nat-objects starting with v has more than n elements. We consider the lower bound rather than the exact element count in order to avoid problems with non-well-founded chains, e.g. circular ones.

The above proposition is typical for a method specification, in two senses. First, it refers to local variables (including the pointer to the receiver of the method call, the parameter and the result variables) from the perspective of the called method. Second, it makes essential use of auxiliary variables (X and Y, bound at the meta-level): if *This* initially represents at least the number X and *Par* the number Y, then the result of the method represents at least $X + Y$.

The proof consists of 56 user interactions including 32 Hoare logic rule applications (with 6 explicit instantiations of assertion schemes, while all remaining ones are computed by unification). We further make use of many simple properties of the functions acting on the program state and a few properties of the relation $\_{:}\_ \geq \_$. We comment only on the most interesting of the 32 major steps here. For details see

http://isabelle.in.tum.de/library/HOL/NanoJava/Example.html.

Steps 1-3 are the application of the *Meth* and *Conseq* rule and the admissible rule $A \vdash \{\lambda s.\ False\}\ c\ \{Q\}$. Dynamic binding is trivial here because Nat does not have subclasses. Thus after some cleanup, our goal reduces to

$$\{\}\vdash \{\lambda s.\ s{:}s\langle This\rangle \geq X \wedge s{:}s\langle Par\rangle \geq Y\}\ Impl(Nat,add)\ \{\lambda s.\ s{:}s\langle Res\rangle \geq X{+}Y\}$$

Step 4 is to apply a derived variant of the *Impl* rule and to unfold the method body, which yields

$$(\bigcup(X,Y).\ \{A\ X\ Y\}) \vdash \{\lambda s.\ s{:}s\langle This\rangle \geq n \wedge s{:}s\langle Par\rangle \geq m\}$$
$$If\ (LAcc\ This.pred)\ Res = \{Nat\}LAcc\ This.pred.add(\{Nat\}LAcc\ Par.suc(<>))$$
$$Else\ Res = LAcc\ Par\ \{\lambda s.\ s{:}s\langle Res\rangle \geq n{+}m\}$$

where $A\ X\ Y$ is the single triple appearing as the conclusion of Step 3 which now acts as assumption for any recursive calls of *Impl(Nat,add)*.

Steps 5-12 simply follow the syntactic structure of the NanoJava terms and arrive at the recursive call of *add*:

$$v \neq Null \implies (\bigcup(X,Y).\ \{A\ X\ Y\}) \vdash_e \{\lambda s.\ s{:}s\langle This\rangle \geq n \wedge s{:}s\langle Par\rangle \geq m \wedge$$
$$(\exists a.\ s\langle This\rangle = Addr\ a \wedge v = get\_field\ s\ a\ pred)\}\ \{Nat\}LAcc\ This.pred.$$
$$add(\{Nat\}LAcc\ Par.suc(<>))\ \{\lambda v\ s.\ lupd(Res{\mapsto}v)\ s{:}v \geq n{+}m\}$$

Steps 13 applies the *Call* rule, giving suitable instantiations for the new intermediate assertions Q and R.

Steps 14-16 deal with evaluating the receiver expression of the call to add.

Steps 17-19 apply the *Meth* rule to the second subgoal, which concerns the term *Meth(Nat,add)*, and after some post-processing this subgoal becomes

$$v \neq Null \implies (\bigcup(X,Y).\ \{A\ X\ Y\}) \vdash \{?P\}\ Impl(Nat,add)\ \{?Q\}$$

where $?P$ and $?Q$ are assertion schemes that may depend on n and m.

Step 20 is the most interesting one of this example: It applies the *Asm* rule after explicitly specializing the universally quantified pair of values $(X,\ Y)$ to (*if n=0 then 0 else n−1*, *m+1*). Recall that n and m are the lower bounds for *This* and *Par* within the current invocation of add.

Steps 21-32 deal with evaluating the parameter expression of the call to add. This is analogous to the steps before except that no recursion is involved.

8   Equivalence of Operational and Axiomatic Semantics

8.1   Validity

We define validity of Hoare triples with respect to the operational semantics given in §4. The validity of statements is the usual one for partial correctness:

$$\models \{P\}\ c\ \{Q\} \;\equiv\; \forall s\ t.\ P\ s \longrightarrow (\exists n.\ s -c-n\rightarrow t) \longrightarrow Q\ t$$

The improvement here in comparison to [22, §6] is that the references to auxiliary variables Z are not required any more.

   The validity of expressions additionally passes the result of the expression to the postcondition:

$$\models_e \{P\}\ e\ \{Q\} \;\equiv\; \forall s\ v\ t.\ P\ s \longrightarrow (\exists n.\ s -e \succ v-n\rightarrow t) \longrightarrow Q\ v\ t$$

For the soundness proof we need variants of these definitions where the recursive depth is not existentially quantified over but exported as an extra numerical parameter of the judgments, e.g. $\models n\colon (P,\ c,\ Q) \equiv \forall s\ t.\ P\ s \longrightarrow s -c-n\rightarrow t \longrightarrow Q\ t$. This gives rise to the equivalences $\models \{P\}\ c\ \{Q\} = (\forall n.\ \models n\colon (P,\ c,\ Q))$ and $\models_e \{P\}\ e\ \{Q\} = (\forall n.\ \models n{:}_e\ (P,\ e,\ Q))$.

   The validity of a single (statement) triple canonically carries over to sets of triples:

$$\Vert\models n\colon T \;\equiv\; \forall t{\in}T.\ \models n\colon t$$

Finally, we extend the notion of validity to judgments with sets of statement triples in both the antecedent and consequent:

$$A \Vert\models C \;\equiv\; \forall n.\ \Vert\models n\colon A \longrightarrow \Vert\models n\colon C$$

and analogously to judgments with sets of statement triples in the antecedent and a single expression triple in the consequent:

$$A \Vert\models_e t \;\equiv\; \forall n.\ \Vert\models n\colon A \longrightarrow \models n{:}_e\ t$$

   Note that this handling of antecedents is stronger than the one that might be expected, viz. $(\forall n.\ \Vert\models n\colon A) \longrightarrow (\forall n.\ \Vert\models n\colon C)$. For an empty set of assumptions A, both variants are equivalent and coincide with the standard notion of validity.

8.2   Soundness

Soundness of the Hoare logic means that all triples derivable are valid, i.e. $\{\} \vdash \{P\}\ c\ \{Q\} \Longrightarrow \models \{P\}\ c\ \{Q\}$, and analogously for expressions.

   We prove soundness by simultaneous induction on the derivation of $\Vert\vdash$ and $\Vert\vdash_e$. All cases emerging during the proof are straightforward, except for the *Loop* rule where an auxiliary induction on the derivation of the evaluation judgment is required (in order to handle the loop invariant) and the *Impl* rule where an induction on the recursive depth is required (in order to justify the additional assumptions). The proof takes about 50 steps (user interactions).

For more details of the proof see [22, §10] though matters are simplified here because of our defensive operational semantics. In particular, the evaluation of *Meth* gets stuck if the dynamic type computed from the receiver expression of the method call does not conform to the expected static type. This relieves us from expressing, proving and exploiting type safety for NanoJava, a major endeavor that we had to make for the language(s) given in [21,22]. [2]

8.3   (Relative) Completeness

Relative completeness of the Hoare logic means that all valid triples are derivable from the empty set of assumptions (if we assume that all valid side conditions can be proved within the meta logic), i.e. $\models \{P\}\ c\ \{Q\} \implies \{\} \vdash \{P\}\ c\ \{Q\}$, and analogously for expressions.

We prove this property with the Most General Formula (MGF) approach due to Gorelick [5]. The Most General Triple for a statement c,
$MGT\ c\ Z\ \equiv\ \{\lambda s.\ Z = s\}\ c\ \{\lambda t.\ \exists n.\ Z\ -c-n\rightarrow\ t)$
expresses essentially the operational semantics of c: if we bind the initial state using the auxiliary variable Z then the final state t referred to in the postcondition is exactly the one obtained by executing c from Z. The MGF states that the MGT is derivable without assumptions for any Z: $\forall Z.\ \{\} \vdash \{MGT\ c\ Z\}$. The MGT and MGF for expressions are defined analogously.

In contrast to earlier applications of the MGF approach, in particular [22, §11], here the auxiliary variables Z are bound at the meta level and not within the assertions. This makes the MGFs easier to understand and manipulate.

If we manage to prove the MGF for all terms, relative completeness follows easily by virtue of the consequence rule and the definitions of validity. This has to be done basically by structural induction on the terms. The problem of structural expansion (rather than reduction) during method calls is solved by assuming first that the MGFs for all method implementations are fulfilled. Thus the main effort lies in proving the lemma $\forall M\ Z.\ A \vdash \{MGT\ (Impl\ M)\ Z\} \implies (\forall Z.\ A \vdash \{MGT\ c\ Z\}) \wedge (\forall Z.\ A \vdash_e MGT_e\ e\ Z)$. Note that the free variables c and e denote any statement or expression, irrespectively if they appear in M or not.

Using the lemma and applying the structural rules *Impl*, *ConjI*, *ConjE* and *Asm*, we can then prove $\{\} \vdash \{MGT\ (Impl\ M)\ Z\}$ and from this — and using the lemma again — the MGF and thus relative completeness is straightforward. The proof takes about 100 steps. More detail on the proof as well as some some proof-theoretical remarks may be found in [22, §11].

---

[2] Of course, the theorem prover would assist us in re-using the earlier developments, but still manual adaptations would be required, and it is of course better to avoid technically difficult matters entirely if possible.

9 Concluding Remarks

We have presented new solutions for technically difficult issues of Hoare logic and applied them to a Java-like object-oriented kernel language. Although this is unlikely to be the definitive word on the subject, it is a definite improvement over previous such Hoare logics, in particular regarding simplicity and succinctness. This is because we have tuned the logic towards ease of mathematical analysis. Thus we could show that soundness and completeness proofs need not be hard — they can even be machine-checked.

This brings us to a hidden theme of this research: analyzing logics with a theorem prover pays. Although the main benefit usually advertised is correctness (which is indeed an issue in the literature on Hoare logics), we feel the following two points are at least as valuable.

Occam's razor: the difficulty of machine-checked proofs enforces a no-frills approach and often leads to unexpected simplifications.

Incrementality: once you have formalized a certain body of knowledge, incremental changes are simplified: the prover will tell you which proofs no longer work, thus freeing you from the tedium of having to go through all the details once again, as you would have to on paper.

Finally we should comment on how to extend our work from partial to total correctness. Since NanoJava is deterministic, we conjecture that the rules for loops, recursion and consequence by Kleymann [11] should carry over easily. In the presence of unbounded nondeterminism, things become more difficult, but we have already treated this situation in isolation [16] and are confident that it should also carry over easily into an object-oriented context.

References

1. M. Abadi and K. R. M. Leino. A logic of object-oriented programs. In *Theory and Practice of Software Development*, volume 1214 of *Lect. Notes in Comp. Sci.*, pages 682–696. Springer-Verlag, 1997.
2. P. America and F. de Boer. Proving total correctness of recursive procedures. *Information and Computation*, 84:129–162, 1990.
3. K. R. Apt. Ten years of Hoare logic: A survey — part I. *ACM Trans. on Prog. Languages and Systems*, 3:431–483, 1981.
4. S. A. Cook. Soundness and completeness of an axiom system for program verification. *SIAM Journal on Computing*, 7(1):70–90, 1978.
5. G. A. Gorelick. A complete axiomatic system for proving assertions about recursive and non-recursive programs. Technical Report 75, Department of Computer Science, University of Toronto, 1975.
6. M. Huisman. *Java program verification in Higher-order logic with PVS and Isabelle*. PhD thesis, University of Nijmegen, 2001.
7. M. Huisman and B. Jacobs. Java program verification via a Hoare logic with abrupt termination. In *Fundamental Approaches to Software Engineering*, volume 1783 of *Lect. Notes in Comp. Sci.*, pages 284–303. Springer-Verlag, 2000.

8. A. Igarashi, B. Pierce, and P. Wadler. Featherweight Java: A minimal core calculus for Java and GJ. In *ACM Symposium on Object Oriented Programming: Systems, Languages, and Applications (OOPSLA)*, Oct. 1999. Full version in ACM Transactions on Programming Languages and Systems (TOPLAS), 2001.

9. B. Jacobs and E. Poll. A logic for the Java Modeling Language JML. In H. Hussmann, editor, *Fundamental Approaches to Software Engineering*, volume 2029 of *Lect. Notes in Comp. Sci.*, pages 284–299. Springer-Verlag, 2001.

10. T. Kleymann. Hoare logic and VDM: Machine-checked soundness and completeness proofs. Ph.D. Thesis, ECS-LFCS-98-392, LFCS, 1998.

11. T. Kleymann. Hoare logic and auxiliary variables. *Formal Aspects of Computing*, 11:541–566, 1999.

12. T. Kowaltowski. Axiomatic approach to side effects and general jumps. *Acta Informatica*, 7:357–360, 1977.

13. K. R. M. Leino. Ecstatic: An object-oriented programming language with an axiomatic semantics. In *Fourth International Workshop on Foundations of Object-Oriented Programming (FOOL 4)*, 1997.

14. J. Morris. Comments on "procedures and parameters". Undated and unpublished.

15. T. Nipkow. Winskel is (almost) right: Towards a mechanized semantics textbook. In V. Chandru and V. Vinay, editors, *Foundations of Software Technology and Theoretical Computer Science*, volume 1180 of *Lect. Notes in Comp. Sci.*, pages 180–192. Springer-Verlag, 1996.

16. T. Nipkow. Hoare logics for recursive procedures and unbounded nondeterminism. Draft, 2001.

17. T. Nipkow. Hoare logics in Isabelle/HOL. In *Proof and System-Reliability*, 2002.

18. T. Nipkow, D. v. Oheimb, and C. Pusch. μJava: Embedding a programming language in a theorem prover. In F. Bauer and R. Steinbrüggen, editors, *Foundations of Secure Computation*, pages 117–144. IOS Press, 2000.
    http://isabelle.in.tum.de/Bali/papers/MOD99.html.

19. T. Nipkow, L. C. Paulson, and M. Wenzel. *Isabelle/HOL — A Proof Assistant for Higher-Order Logic*, volume 2283 of *LNCS*. Springer, 2002.
    http://www4.in.tum.de/~nipkow/LNCS2283/.

20. D. v. Oheimb. Hoare logic for mutual recursion and local variables. In C. P. Rangan, V. Raman, and R. Ramanujam, editors, *Foundations of Software Technology and Theoretical Computer Science*, volume 1738 of *Lect. Notes in Comp. Sci.*, pages 168–180. Springer-Verlag, 1999.
    http://isabelle.in.tum.de/Bali/papers/FSTTCS99.html.

21. D. v. Oheimb. *Analyzing Java in Isabelle/HOL: Formalization, Type Safety and Hoare Logic*. PhD thesis, Technische Universität München, 2001.
    http://www4.in.tum.de/~oheimb/diss/.

22. D. v. Oheimb. Hoare logic for Java in Isabelle/HOL. *Concurrency and Computation: Practice and Experience*, 13(13), 2001.
    http://isabelle.in.tum.de/Bali/papers/CPE01.html.

23. A. Poetzsch-Heffter. Personal communication, Aug. 2001.

24. A. Poetzsch-Heffter and P. Müller. A programming logic for sequential Java. In S. Swierstra, editor, *Programming Languages and Systems (ESOP '99)*, volume 1576 of *Lect. Notes in Comp. Sci.*, pages 162–176. Springer-Verlag, 1999.

Do Not Read This

Juan C. Bicarregui

CLRC Rutherford Appleton Laboratory, Oxfordshire, UK
http://www.bitd.clrc.ac.uk/Person/J.C.Bicarregui

Abstract. We discuss the interpretation of read and write frames in model-oriented specification taking the B's generalised substitutions as the vehicle for the presentation. In particular, we focus on the interpretation of read frames, the semantics of which have not been considered by previous authors. We gives several examples of the relevance of read frames and show that a substitution admits a read respecting implementation if and only if a certain bisimulation condition is satisfied. We use this to motivate a richer semantic model for substitutions which interprets read and write constraints directly in the denotation of a substitution. This semantics yields some non-interference results between substitutions which cannot be given at this level without the use of read and write frames.

1 Introduction

In [Dun02], Dunne raises the question of whether $x := x$ and $skip$ are equivalent and argues that they should not be considered equivalent because they do not exhibit substitutivity of equals, in particular, when composed in parallel with another substitution writing x. For example, $skip \parallel x := x + 1$ is well formed, whereas $x := x \parallel x := x + 1$ is not. This and other considerations lead Dunne to develop a semantic model for generalised substitutions which strengthens the standard weakest precondition semantics with an explicit *write frame*[1]. This enables the distinction of the above substitutions at the semantic level and leads to the clarification of various properties of generalised substitutions.

The present author has previously advocated the explicit treatment of frames in the semantics of model oriented specifications and has proposed a number of models which extend the relational semantics of VDM[Jon86,Jon87] with explicit treatment of read and write frames [Bic93,Bic94,Bic95]. In this paper, we consider read frames in B and discuss the interpretation of the variables which can be read in a substitution. To continue the above example, a similar question to that raised by Dunne above is whether the substitution $x := 0$ is equivalent to $x := y - y$? In this case well formedness of the latter expression depends on which variables are in (read) scope and so substitutivity depends on the visibility rules employed in a structured specification.

---

[1] Dunne calls it the *active frame*

L.-H. Eriksson and P. Lindsay (Eds.): FME 2002, LNCS 2391, pp. 106–125, 2002.

In this paper we define the concept of read and write frames for B's generalised substitutions[Abr95] and show how they can be used to enrich the semantic model of substitutions to yield non-interference properties between substitutions and a richer definition of refinement.

1.1   Examples of the Relevance of Read Frames

Read frames and non-interference. Under what conditions is $S||T$ is refined by $S; T$ Clearly, a sufficient condition is *if T does not read and variables written by S*, but in view of the above example, $x := y - y$, this is clearly not a necessary condition and a more precise definition would be if T *does not depend* on any variable written by S.

One would like to be able formalise the semantic justification of syntactic sufficient conditions for non-interference such as:

$$\frac{reads(S2) \cap writes(S1) = \{\}}{S1||S2 \sqsubseteq S1; S2}$$

Read frames and initialisation. Consider the substitution which arbitrarily sets a boolean variable $(x := true[]x := false)$. Two obvious refinements of this substitution are $x := true$ and $x := false$. But there are also others such as $x := x$, $x := \neg x$ or $x := y$, for some other boolean variable y. If this substitution appeared in an initialisation, syntactic constraints would be applied which prohibited this latter set of implementations. However, all of these implementations are admitted by the standard semantics of refinement.

In this case, what we wish to say, is that the substitution should be refined by a substitution that *does not read any variable* thus permitting only the first two of the implementations given above.

Read frames and encapsulation. Consider the same substitution but in a context where x and y relate to separate aspects of the specification. In order to allow for separate development of the components related to x and y, the specifier may wish to indicate that the substitution should be refined without reference to y. That is, so as to allow the first 4 implementations which manipulate x according to its previous value, but not the fifth where the outcome is dependent on y.

Clearly, machine structuring could be used to give full hiding of the y variable in the machine manipulating x but this brings with it other constraints which may restrict the specifiers freedom. Furthermore, how is one to demonstrate formally that the syntactic conditions imposed by the structuring mechanisms actually ensure the desired semantic properties.

In this case, by specifying that the substitution must be refined by a substitution that *does not read y*, we can allow the first four refinements but disallow the last.

Read frames and underspecification. In B it is commmonplace to use machine CONSTANTS to specify that looseness present in a specification should be treated as underspecification, that is, that it must be implemented by a deterministic function. For example, the machine with a constant $c : 0, 1$, a variable, $x : 0, 1$, and an operation, $op == x := c$ admits implementations $x := 0$ and $x := 1$. That is, like the initialisation example above, it *does not read any variable* in its implementation.

Note that if we try to specify this range of implementations without the use of constants, for example by $(x := 0 [] x := 1)$, we also admit implementations such as *skip*, $x := x - 1$ etc,. as well as implementations which make use of state which is added as a result of refinement later in the development.

Again, specifying a read frame for the substitution could be a way to capture the required semantics. (Naturally, constants can be used more generally that this, for example to relate aspects of different substitutions in a machine, but this use exemplifies a reasonably common case.)

1.2   Read Frames and Refinement

For all of the above examples we would wish to formalise how such properties interact with refinement. Note that it is not the case that non-dependence on a variable is preserved by refinement since the refinement may resolve some non-determinism present in the specification by refence to a variable not referenced in the abstract description. For example when the above example is refined by $x := y$.

Ultimately, one would wish to give a definition of read respecting refinement which ensure no new read dependencies are introduced as a result of reduction of non-determinism. For example one would wish to give rules which restrict the usual definition of refinement, such as

$$\frac{vars(P) \subset reads(S)}{S \sqsubseteq (P \Longrightarrow S)}$$

Classical interpretations of specifications and refinements make it impossible to justify such rules.

1.3   Objective

In this paper we consider the semantic conditions required for such properties to hold. This leads us to propose a strengthening of the semantics to also include a second frame, a "read frame" which determines which variables can influence the outcome of a substitution or any refinement of it. This extended semantic model supports the formalisation, at specification time, of implementation constrains hitherto only captured by syntactic constraints implicit in the structuring of specifications and so clarifies some issues related to non-interference, initialisation, encapsulation, and underspecification in B developments.

2 Language

We consider a language similar to that in [Dun02] but with a slight change to the construct for (write) frame extension and with the addition of similar construct read frames. Thus language of substitutions is given by:

name	subst	default read frame	default write frame
skip	$skip$	empty	$\{\}$
simple assignment	$x := E$	vars E	$\{x\}$
preconditioned substitution	$P \mid S$	vars P $\cup$ reads S	writes S
guarded substitution	$G \Longrightarrow S$	vars G $\cup$ reads S	writes S
sequential substitution	$S; T$	reads S $\cup$ reads T	writes S $\cup$ writes T
bounded choice	$S[]T$	reads S $\cup$ reads T	writes S $\cup$ writes T
unbounded choice	$@z.S$	reads S $-\{z\}$	writes S $-\{z\}$
opening	$S^{\smallfrown}$	reads S	writes S
parallel composition	$S \parallel T$	reads S $\cup$ reads T	writes S $\cup$ writes T
set_reads	S_R	R	writes S
set_writes	$_W S$	reads S	W

The default frames are those which are calculated from the text of the substitution. The set_reads and set_writes constructs can be used to override the default frames. Note that set_reads and set_writes set the respective frames to those given whatever they were perviously. Thus the frames can be expanded or contracted by these constructs.

2.1 Abstract Syntax

In the abstract syntax, we make explicit the read and write frames for all substitutions and also incorporate the alphabet of variables in scope. Thus, formally, a substitution is a quadruple (F, R, W, S) where F is the set of all variables in scope, R is the subset of F which are readable, W is the subset of F which are writeable and S is the body of the generalised substitution. The first component declares and binds the variables appearing in the substitution. The second and third give information about access to the variables that must be respected by any implementation, and the last gives the body of the substitution[2]. We do not insist on any relationship between the *reads* and *writes* and the variables

---

[2] The exposition here does not deal with substitutions with parameters and results.

appearing in S. Nor do we require that *writes* $\subseteq$ *reads*. Note that variables that can be read and written appear in both *reads* and *writes* clauses.

3   Interpreting the Read Frame

We find it convenient to present the majority of this discussion in terms of a relational semantics composed of a termination predicate giving those states for which termination is guaranteed and a meaning relation which gives the possible state transitions. We consider first the meaning relation.

For a given substitution (F, R, W, S), we define four relations on the state space giving interpretations for the substitution respecting none, one or other or both frames. Let Σ be the state space spanned by F, then $M_\emptyset$ is the meaning relation not respecting either frame; M_W is the meaning relation which respects the write frame (only); M_R is the meaning relation which respects the read frame (only); and M_{RW} is the meaning relation which respects both read and write frames. For any $(\sigma, \sigma') \in \Sigma \times \Sigma$, we write $\sigma M_\emptyset \sigma'$ for $(\sigma, \sigma') \in M_\emptyset$ and $\sigma M_\emptyset$ for the relational image of σ under $M_\emptyset$ (and respectively for M_R, M_W M_{RW}).

The first two relations, $M_\emptyset$ and M_W, are simple to define. The third, M_R, is the subject of this section. We intend that M_R and M_W can each be defined independently of the other frame and that M_{RW} can be recovered as the intersection of the two: $M_{RW} = M_W \cap M_R$.

We define $M_\emptyset$ in the usual way as the "predicate" of a substitution:

$$M_\emptyset \;\triangleq\; \{(\sigma, \sigma') \in \Sigma \times \Sigma \,|\, prd(S, \sigma, \sigma')\}$$

where $prd(S, \sigma, \sigma') \;\triangleq\; \neg[S]\neg(\sigma = \sigma')$.

It is a simple matter to extend this definition to incorporate the semantics of the write frame. We simply remove from the meaning relation any transition which changes a value of a non-written variable[3].

$$M_W \;\triangleq\; M_\emptyset \cap \Xi_{F-W}$$

The task now remaining is to define the constraint on the meaning relation which interprets the constraint imposed by the read frame.

For a given substitution, the interpretation M_R, which respects the read frame but ignores the write frame, must be equivalent to a read-write respecting interpretation of a similar substitution with the same F, R and S but with a universal write frame. Clearly, this substitution may have a write frame which is bigger than its read frame and so, to make this definition, we will need to give an interpretation to variables which are in the write frame but not the read frame.

---

[3] We borrow a notation from Z and, generalising slightly, define for any set of identifiers $S \subseteq F$, a relation on states $\Xi_S \;\triangleq\; \{(\sigma, \sigma') : \Sigma \times \Sigma \,|\, \sigma|_S = \sigma'|_S\}$ where $\sigma|_S$ is the projection of σ onto S.

But how are we to make sense of such "write-only" variables? Although such variables are not normally used in substitutions, and arguably do not correspond to any useful programming concept, perhaps such unrealistic constructs, much like miracles in [Mor88], can play a *part* in defining useful substitutions and so help us to understand the underlying concepts.

The following subsections propose three alternative interpretations for write-only variables and discuss the merits of each. We begin by considering the strictest of the three interpretations.

Must-write semantics. The first interpretation we consider is that write-only variables *must* be written by the substitution with a value which depends only on the reads.

Consider a simple assignment, $x := E$, under read frame R where $x \notin R$. Clearly, this substitution can be implemented by $x := e$ where e is an equivalent expression only mentioning variables in R, and in particular x:=c where c is a constant expression not referring to any variables. However, in this case **skip**, which is akin to $x := x$ should be thought of as reading x and thus is not a valid implementation.

To formalise this definition, we consider a state with universal write frame and read frame R. In this case there are two sets of variables, one set is read-write and the other is write-only. In this interpretation, we require that two starting states which differ only in the WO component must have exactly the same possible final states - not just the same RW components. That is, any result state possible from a given start state should also be possible from any other start state that differs only in a write-only component[4] (Figure 1).

$$\forall \sigma_1, \sigma_2 \cdot \sigma_1 \Xi_R \sigma_2 \Rightarrow \sigma_1[S] = \sigma_2[S]$$

Note that this condition forces equality on the whole after states and so, in particular, on those components which are neither read nor written. Therefore, when we reintroduce the write frame, which requires identity on the unwritten components, this leads to infeasibility for initial states which differ on components which are neither read nor written because these must be made equal without changing them. Thus this interpretation of write-only variables is too strong for the orthogonal treatment of reads and writes which we seek.

May-write semantics. A second, slightly more liberal, alternative arises if we reintroduce the possibility of skip on the write-only variables. This corresponds more closely to what might be expected to arise from a static analysis of code ascertaining which variables are read and written. By allowing **skip** on unread variables, this interpretation would allow their final values to be the same as

---

[4] Here we consider S as a relation on states and take the relational image.

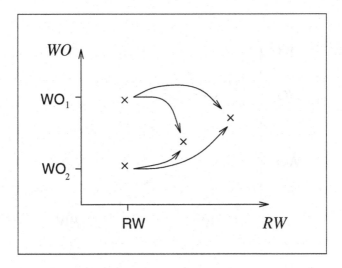

Fig. 1. "Must-write" semantics

their initial values, but it would not allow their original values to affect the final values in any other case. Thus we call this a *may*-write semantics.

This semantics can be formalised by explicitly adding to the must-write semantics the possibility of no change of value for the unread variables. However, in this case, the formulation is rather unwieldy[5] and so for brevity we simply observe that it doesn't exhibit the property we want when recombined with the write frame constraint.

Non-interference semantics. The third and most liberal alternative, not only allows **skip** on unread variables but also allows other statements that, whilst allowing the value of the unread variables to be changed, do not allow of any read variables to depend on any of the unread variables. Thus, the original values of the write-only variables can influence their own final values, and those of other write-only variables, but not the final values of any read variable. Examples of such statements include statements to increment a number, append to, or reverse a list, or even to swap the values in two variables which are both write-only.

This is clearly an information flow condition, and so is appropriate as a basis for defining non-interference between substitutions. For this reason we call it a 'non-interference' semantics.

---

[5] Roughly speaking, for each transition $\sigma \overset{\circ}{\longrightarrow} \sigma'$ and for each subset of the write-only variables, WO, we must add a transition of the form $\sigma \overset{\circ}{\longrightarrow} (\sigma|_{WO}, \sigma'|_{F-WO})$.

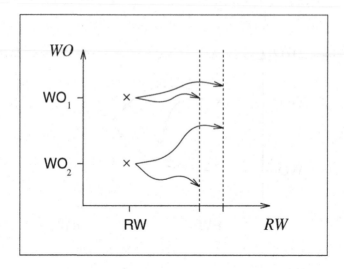

Fig. 2. "Non-interference" semantics

The condition required to yield this interpretation states that the initial values of write-only variables should be able to influence their own final values and those of any other write-only variables, but should not influence the final values of any read variables. For a substitution with universal write frame, this can be pictured as in Figure 2.

Here we see that it would be impossible to deduce the initial values of the write-only variables from the final values of only the read variables. This is formalised by weakening the predicate given above to require merely the existence of some state with the required read component[6].

$$\forall \sigma_1, \sigma_2 \cdot \sigma_1 M_R \sigma_2 \;\Rightarrow\; \sigma_1[S]\big|_R = \sigma_2[S]\big|_R$$

It is clear that when we reintroduce the write frame constraint, the freedom on the unwritten variables is constrained to the one value for which the final values are equal to the initial ones[7]. So this interpretation does indeed yield the orthogonality between the interpretations of the two frames that we seek.

$$M_{RW} = M_R \cap M_W$$

It is interesting to note that this constraint as akin to the definition of a (strong) bisimulation from process algebra (eg. [Mil89]). Recall that a relation S over agents is a (strong) bisimulation if

---

[6] Note that projection is lifted pointwise to sets of states in the relational image, and that this represents an implicit existential quantification in the set equality:
$S_1\big|_R = S_2\big|_R \;\overset{\triangle}{=}\; \forall e_1 \in S_1 \cdot \exists e_2 \in S_2 \cdot e_1\big|_R = e_2\big|_R \wedge vice\ versa.$

[7] To see this note that for $x \in W \subseteq R$ we have $\sigma'_1\big|_{\{x\}} = \sigma_1\big|_{\{x\}} = \sigma_2\big|_{\{x\}} = \sigma'_2\big|_{\{x\}}$.

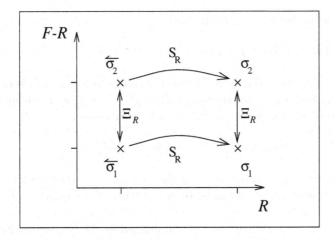

Fig. 3. Non-interfernce as a bisimulation

"For any agents P and Q such that $(P,Q) \in \mathcal{S}$, and for all actions $\alpha \in Act$ we have:

i) $P \xrightarrow{\alpha} P' \Rightarrow \exists Q' \cdot Q \xrightarrow{\alpha} Q'$ and $(P',Q') \in \mathcal{S}$, and

ii) $Q \xrightarrow{\alpha} Q' \Rightarrow \exists P' \cdot P \xrightarrow{\alpha} P'$ and $(P',Q') \in \mathcal{S}$"

Here P, Q, P', Q' correspond to $\sigma_1, \sigma_2, \sigma'_1, \sigma'_2$ and $(A, B) \in \mathcal{S}$ corresponds to $A|_R = B|_R$.

This yields the following theorem

Theorem

The relation M_R is the largest subrelation of $M_\emptyset$ such that Ξ_R is a strong bisimulation on M_R.

The fact that M_R is the *largest* subset of $M_\emptyset$ clearly corresponds to the definition of the weakest strong bisimulation, the existence of which is discussed for example in [Mil89].

This surprising result warrants some further investigation to understand its significance more fully. Consider that Ξ_R is the meaning of a substitution, call it $write_{F-R}$, which is the least refined substitution which has $F - R$ as write frame. Clearly, the above theorem indicates a relationship between any substitution that respects a read frame R and $write_{F-R}$.

For any substitution S_R with read frame R, since S_R does not read the values of variables in $F - R$, and $write_{F-R}$ only affects those variables, whatever behaviour was possible for S_R from a given state, will also be possible if preceded by the execution of $write_{F-R}$. The resulting states in the two cases again being equal on $F - R$.

This is formalised by the condition[8]

$$S_R; write_{F-R} \sqsubseteq write_{F-R}; S_R$$

In this light, the bisimulation condition can be recast in terms of relational algebra. Writing M_α for the relation $\{(P, P')|P \xrightarrow{\alpha} P'\}$, and writing S and M_α infixed, the definition of bisimulation can be written as (Figure 3)

$$\forall \alpha \in Act \cdot S^{-1}; M_\alpha \subseteq M_\alpha; S^{-1} \quad \wedge \quad S; M_\alpha \subseteq M_\alpha; S$$

Note that if S is symmetric (as is the case for Ξ_R), then we have $S = S^{-1}$, so either conjunct can be dropped from the body of the quantification without effect.

In our case, we have only one action defined by M. So, we finally achieve a concise characterisation of the condition for not reading outside R:

$$readsM(R, M) \quad \triangleq \quad \Xi_R; M \subseteq M; \Xi_R$$

Note that this definition is independent of W and so, unlike the write frame constraint, can be made without a closed world assumption.

3.1   Termination and Read Frames

Thus far, we have ignored the termination set in the semantic model. However, if the frames are to be interpreted as advanced information about the state accesses of implementing code, and if this code is to respect the read frame, then this will be reflected in the termination set of the substitution.

As might be expected, the criterion for read-respecting for a set is similar, but simpler, than that for a relation. It amounts to saying that a set T respects the frame R if it is a cylinder in the state space (Figure 4).

which can be formalised as a constraint on the relational image of T under Ξ_R:

$$readsT(R, T) \quad \triangleq \quad \Xi_R(\!|T|\!) \subseteq T$$

4   Interpreting Substitutions with Read and Write Frames

We have given an interpretation of read frames and have related this to the established concept of bisimulation. We now recombine this interpretation with the interpretation of the other components of the substitution to define a semantic model for substitutions.

---

[8] One should not be misled into believing that this containment is in fact an equality, for in the presence of an invariant the necessary intermediate state may not be valid.

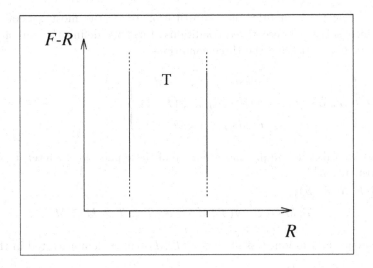

Fig. 4. The termination set must be a cylinder in the state space

In order to prepare the ground for the richer semantic model that will be used in the treatment of refinement later, we take a slightly indirect route to defining the substitution semantics. Rather than defining T and M directly from the components of the substitution definition, we consider the (T, M) for all the valid refinements of the substitution and take the most general of these.

Again consider a fixed substitution $S = (F, R, W, S)$. Below, we identify three separate compliance conditions for a pair $(T, M) : \mathcal{D}_o$.

subst which ensures that the termination set and meaning relation interpret the substitution:

$$subst_{(F,R,W,S)}(T, M) \quad \triangleq \quad T \supseteq [S]\textbf{true} \ \land \ M \subseteq \neg[S]\neg(\sigma = \sigma')$$

writes which ensures that the write frame is adhered to

$$writes_{(F,R,W,S)}(T, M) \quad \triangleq \quad M \subseteq \Xi_{F-W}$$

and

reads which ensures the same for the read frame

$$reads_{(F,R,W,S)}(T, M) \quad \triangleq \quad \Xi_R; M \subseteq M; \Xi_R \ \land \ \Xi_R (\!| T |\!) \subseteq T$$

We define the semantics of a substitution to be the most general (T, M) pair which satisfies these three conditions. First we define the set of all the interpretations satisfying the three conditions

$$
\mathcal{S} = \left\{ (T, M) : \mathcal{D}_o \left| \begin{array}{c} subst_{(F,R,W,S)}(T, M) \\ \wedge\ writes_{(F,R,W,S)}(T, M) \\ \wedge\ reads_{(F,R,W,S)}(T, M) \end{array} \right. \right\}
$$

Then we take the unique, most general of these pairs as the interpretation of the substitution[9]

$$
[\![(F, R, W, S)]\!]_o \ \triangleq
$$
$$
\iota(T, M) \in \mathcal{S} \cdot \forall (T_i, M_i) \in \mathcal{S} \cdot T \subseteq T_i \wedge M \supseteq M_i
$$

Existence and uniqueness of such a (T, M) pair is demonstrated in the next section.

4.1   Non-interference

We can now give our first non-interference result which we state without proof as it is superseded by a stronger result later.

Theorem For two substitutions over the same alphabet: $\mathsf{S}_i = (F, R_i, W_i, S_i)$,

$$
\frac{\begin{array}{c} R_1 \supseteq W_1 \wedge R_2 \supseteq W_2 \\ R_1 \cap W_2 = \{\} = R_2 \cap W_1 \end{array}}{[\![\mathsf{S}_1 \parallel \mathsf{S}_2]\!]_o = [\![\mathsf{S}_1 ; \mathsf{S}_2]\!]_o = [\![\mathsf{S}_2 ; \mathsf{S}_1]\!]_o}
$$

However, as stated earlier, it is not necessarily the case that non-interference is preserved by usual definition of refinement.

5   Refinement with Read Frames

As discussed above, the usual semantic model for substitutions is not rich enough to ensure the preservation of read-respecting behaviour by refinement. One approach to resolving this difficulty is to restrict the definition of refinement so that it is by the read frame. An alternative approach is to define a richer semantic model for specifications where substitutions are interpreted as the set of their valid refinements and this set is filtered by the read constraint. In effect, we encode the read frame into the semantics of the substitution as "advanced

---

[9] The suffix in $[\![\ ]\!]_o$ is used to distinguish this interpretation from that defined in the next section.

information" about the valid refinements. With this interpretation, a simple definition of refinement, as containment of implementations, does respect the read frame. This section gives such a semantics for substitutions and refinement.

5.1   Semantics for Substitutions with Refinement

Consider again a fixed substitution $S = (F, R, W, S)$ and, taking the three conditions defined above, instead of defining the semantics of a substitution to be the most general (T, M) pair which satisfies these conditions, we simply take the set itself as the semantics[10].

$$[\![(F, R, W, S)]\!]_1 \quad \triangleq \quad \left\{ (T, M) : \mathcal{D}_0 \,\middle|\, \begin{array}{l} subst_{(F,R,W,S)}(T, M) \\ \wedge \, writes_{(F,R,W,S)}(T, M) \\ \wedge \, reads_{(F,R,W,S)}(T, M) \end{array} \right\}$$

5.2   Semantics of Refinement

With this model, refinement is simply set containment

$$S \sqsubseteq_1 T \quad \triangleq \quad [\![S]\!]_1 \supseteq [\![T]\!]_1$$

5.3   Consistency

The semantics of Section 4 is thus a "retrieval" of this model defined by

$$retr : \mathcal{D}_1 \rightarrow \mathcal{D}_0$$
$$retr(\mathcal{S}) \quad \triangleq \quad (\bigcap_{(T_i, M_i) \in \mathcal{S}} T_i \quad , \bigcup_{(T_i, M_i) \in \mathcal{S}} M_i \quad)$$

then, for any substitutions S, we have $[\![S]\!]_0 = retr([\![S]\!]_1)$ and refinement in $\mathcal{D}_1$ is a sufficient condition for refinement in $\mathcal{D}_0$

$$\frac{S_a \sqsubseteq_1 S_c}{S_a \sqsubseteq_0 S_c}$$

where $\sqsubseteq_0$ is satisfaction in the $\mathcal{D}_0$ semantics defined in the usual way.

Note that the reverse is not the case since the new definition of refinement prohibits putative refinements which do not respect the read frame.

To see that these definitions are well-defined we need to show existence and uniqueness of such a (T, M) pair and preservation of refinement between the models. It is also necessary to show monotonicity of each substitution constructor with respect to refinement[BvW98,BB98].

---

[10] The suffix in $[\![\ ]\!]_1$ is used to distinguish this interpretation from that defined in the previous section.

Lemma For $\mathcal{S}$ defined as above we have

$$\exists!(T, M) \in \mathcal{S} \cdot \forall(T_i, M_i) \in \mathcal{S} \cdot T \subseteq T_i \wedge M \supseteq M_i$$

Proof Existence within $\mathcal{D}_0$ and uniqueness within $\mathcal{S}$ are both trivial on constructing $[\![S]\!]_o = retr([\![S]\!]_1)$.

To show "closure", that the pair constructed above is in the set $\mathcal{S}$, we must show that (T, M) satisfies the three properties defining $\mathcal{S}$. Each property follows easily from the assumption that all $(T_i, M_i) \in \mathcal{S}$ by various distributive properties of **dom** and $\lhd$ over $\subseteq$ and $\cup$. It is interesting to note that the proof of each property relies only on the assumption of the respective property for the (T_i, M_i).

The proof that *retr* preserves refinement is straightforward. In this setting, with refinement defined as set inclusion, monotonicity is also trivial since constructing a set comprehension over smaller sets clearly leads to smaller constructed set.

Miracles. Note that when no implementation is possible then $[\![S]\!]_1$ is empty. This corresponds to miracle [Mor88] since

$$retr(\{\,\}) = (\underset{\{\}}{\bigcap}, \underset{\{\}}{\bigcup}) = (\overline{\mathbf{true}}, \overline{\mathbf{false}}) = [\![\mathbf{miracle}]\!]_o$$

Incompleteness. Note that this semantics does not address issues arising from non-essential read and write accesses. For example, if y is not read, then the semantics will not allow $x \in \{0, 1\}$ to be refined by $x :=$ **if** $y = 0$ **then** 0 **else** 1, whilst the refinement $x :=$ **if** $y = 0$ **then** 0 **else** 0 is permitted since this is equivalent to $x := 0$. Thus the semantics does admit refinements which syntactically break the read and write frame provided that they are equivalent to substitutions that do respect them. On the other hand, proof rules which give syntactic sufficient conditions will prohibit refinements which break the frames even if such accesses have no effect on the resulting behaviour. This semantics will therefore not be complete with respect to such rules.

6   Examples

In order to illustrate properties of the above semantics, we consider some examples including those given in Section 1.1.

6.1   Filtering of Refinements

We first consider an extremely simple example which demonstrates the result of filtering the refinements in the semantics of a substitution. Consider two variables

x and y such that $x, y \in \{0, 1\}$ and the substitution $(\{x, y\}, \{x\}, \{y\}, y := 0 [] y := 1)$.

We calculate the most general (T, M) to be $(\{(0,0), (0,1), (1,0), (1,1)\},$ $\{(0,0) \mapsto (0,0), (0,0) \mapsto (0,1), (0,1) \mapsto (0,1), (0,1) \mapsto (0,0), (1,0) \mapsto (1,0), (1,0) \mapsto (1,1), (1,1) \mapsto (1,1), (1,1) \mapsto (1,0)\})$ as illustrated in the top circle of the following diagram. It has eight transitions and four points of non-determinacy. Note this relation satisfies the read frame constraint for $\{x\}$.

If the read frame were ignored, there would be eighty-nine different refinements of this substitution arising by reducing the non-determinacy by removing one, two, three, or four transitions whilst maintaining the totality of the substitution. (There are eight interpretations with seven transitions, forty-eight with six, twenty-four with five, and eight with four.) However, if we 'filter' these interpretations by the read frame constraint, we have to remove transitions in read respecting pairs, and so we remove all but eight of the subrelations. The ones remaining correspond to combinations of the interpretations of $y := 0$, $y := 1$, $y := x$ and $y := 1 - x$. So, for example, we have that $S \sqsubseteq y := 1 - x$ but not by $y := 1 - y$ or by *skip*. This illustrates how an explicitly stated read frame can restrict the valid implementations even when the substitution itself respects the read frame.

We now revisit the examples given in Section 1.1.

6.2   Read Frames and Non-interference

We are now in a position to prove the stronger form of the non-interference result from Section 4.1 which states that non-interference is preserved by refinement.

For two substitutions in the same context $S_i \triangleq (F, R_i, W_i, S_i)$, $i = 1, 2$, we have:

$$\frac{R_1 \cap W_2 = \{\} = R_2 \cap W_1 \qquad S_i \sqsubseteq_1 T_i}{T_1 ; T_2 = T_2 ; T_1 = T_1 \parallel T_2}$$

The proof, which is reasonably straightforward, relies on the four 'frame' properties of the semantics

$$readsM(R_1, M_1), \; writes(W_1, M_1), \; readsM(R_2, M_2), \; writes(W_2, M_2)$$

the non-interference conditions in a slightly different form

$$F - W_2 \supseteq R_1 \text{ and } F - W_1 \supseteq R_2$$

and on the 'global' conditions

$$R_1 \supseteq W_1 \text{ and } R_2 \supseteq W_2$$

The first example in Section 1.1 is simply one half of this result with the identity refinement.

It could reasonably be argued that non-interference should hold provided the write frame of each substitution does not intersect either frame of the other substitution, irrespective of whether it is contained in its own read frame. We later discuss (Section 7.1) a slight strengthening of the reads constraint which yields this stronger form of the non-interference result.

6.3   Read Frames and Initialisation

An initialisation is simply a substitution with empty read frame. For example, if we want to initialise to any state satisfying the invariant, we can simply give the substitution $(F, \{ \}, F, skip)$. The usual proofs for maintaining the invariant together with the requirement not to depend on the old value of any variable will ensure the invariant is established by the initialisation. Of course, skip itself does not now respect the read frame and must be implemented by code which does.

Even if the abstract initialisation mentions a variable on the right hand side of an assignment, we would require that by the time the initialisation is implemented the dependence on that variable is removed. For example, for invariant $x = y$, we can give the initialisation as $(F, \{ \}, F, x := y)$ which would then need to be implemented by something like $x := c; y := c$.

6.4   Read Frames and Encapsulation

It is a simple matter to specify that y is not used in the implementation of a substitution manipulating x by excluding y from the read frame. This can be used to suggest a decomposition of a specification without bringing in structuring mechanisms which ensure full hiding. Furthermore, such techniques may be a useful basis to define a form of structuring for *abstract* machines which employs full hiding and so permits separate development. (See Section 7.4.)

6.5   Read Frames and Underspecification

Using the read frame it is a simple matter to specify which variables can be used to resolve any looseness in an abstract substitution and so we can remove some uses of constants in specifications.

6.6   Read Frames and Refinement

In all of these examples, read-respecting refinement ensures that non-reading behaviour of an abstract substitution is preserved during refinement.

We now give some proof rules which give sufficient conditions for read-respecting refinement.

Strengthening the read and write frames. We can contract the read and write frames in refinement[11]

$$\frac{R_1 \supseteq R_2 \supseteq W}{(F, R_1, W, S) \sqsubseteq (F, R_2, W, S)} \qquad \frac{W_1 \supseteq W_2}{(F, R, W_1, S) \sqsubseteq (F, R, W_2, S)}$$

The proof of the latter is straightforward on noting that $W_1 \supseteq W_2 \Rightarrow \Xi_{F-W_1} \subseteq \Xi_{F-W_2}$.

To prove the former, we must show

$$\frac{R_1 \supseteq R_2}{\Xi_{R_2}; M \subseteq M; \Xi_{R_2}}{\Xi_{R_1}; M \subseteq M; \Xi_{R_1}}$$

which can be shown provided $M \subseteq \Xi_{F-W}$ since $R_1 \supseteq R_2 \Rightarrow \Xi_{R_1} \subseteq \Xi_{R_2}$ and $M \subseteq \Xi_{F-W} \subseteq \Xi_{R_1-R_2}$. This final proviso explaining the presence of the last containment in the hypothesis of the rule.

As for non-interference result given above, one might expect the contract reads rule to be valid irrespective of the write frame. Again, with the current definition *reads*, this is not the case. In order to weaken the hypothesis to allow the introduction of write-only variables we must take a stronger definition of *reads* as discussed in the next section.

Strengthening the substitution. We can strengthen the body of a substitution provided the new body does not introduce a new read dependency. Take for example guarded substitutions. Recall that in the standard semantics, we have $S \sqsubseteq G \Longrightarrow S$ for all substitutions S and guards G. The proof of this is straightforward from the definition of the weakest precondition of guarded substitution as $[G \Longrightarrow S]Q \triangleq G \Rightarrow [S]Q$.

To give a similar rule for read-respecting refinement, we must additionally show that $\Xi_R; M_{G \Longrightarrow S} \subseteq M_{G \Longrightarrow S}; \Xi_R$. On expanding $M_{G \Longrightarrow S}$ we are required to prove $\Xi_R;(G \wedge prd(S)) \subseteq (G \wedge prd(S)); \Xi_R$ which, on expanding the definition of sequence, follows provided $\Xi_R(|G|) \subseteq G$. This is the definition given of G read respects R. Thus we have

$$\frac{\Xi_R(|G|) \subseteq G}{(F, R, W, S) \sqsubseteq (F, R, W, G \Longrightarrow S)}$$

Similar rules can be defined for other constructs.

---

[11] The reader familiar with [Dun02] may at first be surprised by this as Dunne's approach allows expansion rather than contraction of write frames in refinement. The difference is not fundemental, it is simply due to the fact that different syntax is being used for the same concept. Dunne's conservative frame expansion conserves the values of the variables introduced to the frame by the frame expansion, whereas, here we conserve the variables outside the specified frame.

7   Further Work and Conclusions

7.1   Introducing Write-Only Variables

It is interesting to note that the proof of non-interference and of soundness for contracting the read frame requires that the reads should contain the writes for each substitution. This is perhaps surprising as it is reasonable to expect that a substitution reading fewer variables than permitted should be a valid refinement whatever the write frame might be. Furthermore, these is the only places where the orthogonality of the treatment of the *reads*, *writes* and *subst* is broken.

It turns out that with a slight adjustment to the definition of the read constraint, we can remove the requirement that the reads contain the writes. We record here without detailed justification a stronger version of the read predicate which exhibits this cleaner property.

$$reads_{wo}(R, M) \triangleq \forall S \supseteq R \cdot \Xi_S; M \subseteq M; \Xi_S$$

An informal understanding of this condition is that it does not allow information flow between the unread variables so read frame can be contracted within the writes without concern.

This interpretation yields a non-interference result for relations without recourse to the assumptions such as $R_i \supseteq W_i$. We give the result for arbitrary M_1 and M_2, for its use in practice, one of the M_i will be Ξ_{R_i}.

$$\frac{reads_{wo}(R_1, M_1) \wedge writes(W_1, M_1)}{reads_{wo}(R_2, M_2) \wedge writes(W_2, M_2)}{W_1 \cap (R_2 \cup W_2) = \{\} = W_2 \cap (R_1 \cup W_1)}{M_1; M_2 = M_2; M_1}$$

7.2   Weakest Precondition Semantics

It is not straightforward to present the concepts developed here in a standard weakest precondition framework[Dij76]. Rather, a more convenient form for a weakest precondition semantic model of these concepts is to give the sets of identifiers comprising the read and write frames directly as components of the semantics. Thus $[\![S]\!]$ is a triple $(R, W, [S])$ where $[S]$ is the usual weakest precondition semantics of S. This would be a relatively simple extension to the approach taken by Dunne in defining a semantics for substitutions with write frames as a pair $(W, [S])$.

7.3   Proof Rules for Read-Respecting Refinement

We have presented the key concepts required to interpret the fact that a substitution does not read outside a given frame of variables, and given a definition of refinement which respects this property. We have given a few examples of proof rules which give sufficient conditions for read respecting refinement. There is obviously more work to be done to give a comprehensive suite of proof rules which are sound with respect to this semantics.

7.4   Specification Structuring and Read-Respecting Refinement

There is also considerable work to be done to build these concepts into a useful development methodology which exploits read and write frames fully in the structuring of specifications. This work could be progressed in two directions. Firstly, the new semantics could be used to justify semantically the visibility rules in B's existing machine structuring mechanisms, and secondly, perhaps new structuring mechanisms could be found which give a more orthogonal treatment of horizontal and vertical structuring of developments. One might hope that with this would come more intuitively obvious visibility rules between components.

We have presented semantic conditions interpreting the concept that the outcome of a substitution does not depend on the value of variables outside a "read frame". We have taken care to ensure that this interpretation of the read frame is orthogonal to the interpretation of the write frame. This semantics supports the formalisation, at specification time, of implementation constraints previously only captured by visibility rules implicit in certain forms the structuring of specifications.

We have given some example proof rules for refinement which ensure that the read-respecting behaviour of an abstract substitution is preserved by its implementation. A more comprehensive treatment of such proof rules for the language of substitutions is still to be undertaken. We believe that such a treatment could lead to a more expressive and compositional development method with more orthogonal specification structuring constructs.

References

[Abr95]   J-R. Abrial. *The B-Book.* Cambridge University Press, 1995.
[BB98]   R.J.R. Back and M.J. Butler. Fusion and simultaneous substitution in the refinement calculus. *Acta Informatica*, 35(11):921–940, 1998.
[Bic93]   J.C. Bicarregui. Algorithm refinement with read and write frames. In J.C.P. Woodcock and P.G. Larsen, editors, *Proceedings of Formal Methods Europe '93*, volume 670 of *Lecture Notes in Computer Science*. Springer-Verlag, 1993.
[Bic94]   J.C. Bicarregui. Operation semantics with read and write frames. In *Sixth Refinement Workshop*, Workshops in Computer Science. Springer-Verlag, 1994.
[Bic95]   J.C. Bicarregui. *Intra-Modular Structuring in Model-oriented Specification: Expressing non-interference with read and write frames.* PhD thesis, Manchester University, Computer Science, June 1995. UMCS-95-10-1.
[BvW98] R.J.R. Back and J. von Wright. *Refinement Calculus: a Systematic Introduction.* Springer-Verlag, 1998.
[Dij76]   E.W. Dijkstra. *A Discipline of Programming.* Prentice Hall, 1976.

[Dun02] S. Dunne. A theory of generalised substitutions. In D. Bert et al, editor, *Proceedings of ZB2002.* Springer Verlag, LNCS 2272, 2002.

[Jon86] C.B. Jones. *Systematic Software Development using VDM.* Prentice Hall, 1986.

[Jon87] C.B. Jones. VDM proof obligations and their justification. In M. Mac an Airchinnigh D. Bjørner, C.B. Jones and E.J. Neuhold, editors, *Proceedings of VDM '87*, volume 252 of *Lecture Notes in Computer Science.* Springer-Verlag, 1987.

[Mil89] R. Milner. *Communication and Concurrency.* Prentice Hall, 1989.

[Mor88] C. Morgan. Data refinement by miracles. *Inf. Proc. Letters*, 26(5), Jan. 1988.

Safeness of Make-Based Incremental Recompilation

Niels Jørgensen

Department of Computer Science, Roskilde University
P.O. Box 260, DK-4000 Roskilde, Denmark
nielsj@ruc.dk

Abstract. The make program is widely used in large software projects to reduce compilation time. make skips source files that would have compiled to the same result as in the previous build. (Or so it is hoped.) The crucial issue of safeness of omitting a brute-force build is addressed by defining a semantic model for make. Safeness is shown to hold if a set of criteria are satisfied, including soundness, fairness, and completeness of makefile rules. Conditions are established under which a makefile can safely be modified by deleting, adding, or rewriting rules.

Keywords. Make, incremental recompilation, semantic model.

1 Introduction

The make program reads a makefile consisting of rules with the following meaning: "If file G is older than one or more of the files D_1, D_2, etc., then execute command C", where D_1, D_2, etc., are source files that G depends on, and the execution of C creates G by compiling the sources. This is characterized in [1] as *cascading* incremental recompilation, because recompilation spreads to other files along chains of dependency.

Safeness of make-based incremental compilation, the key result of this paper, can be stated as follows: Suppose we build a program brute-force, and then edit the source files, and possibly the makefile as well. Then under certain assumptions about the makefile rules and the kind of editing performed, the result of *make-based incremental recompilation* is equivalent to the result of a (second) *brute force build*. The result also applies to repeated cycles of editing and incremental recompilation.

The required properties of makefile rules are intuitively reasonable, for example, a fair rule may only create or update its own derived target. In confirming intuition about make, the safeness result provides formal justification for the existing practice of using make. Moreover, the result establishes that one may rely on make for incremental recompilation in situations where this is not obvious, for example upon certain modifications of the makefile.

L.-H. Eriksson and P. Lindsay (Eds.): FME 2002, LNCS 2391, pp. 126–145, 2002.
© Springer-Verlag Berlin Heidelberg 2002

Comparison with related work:

Historically, make originated [4] within the Unix/C community. It is the most useful with languages such as C that allow for splitting source files into implementation and interface (header) files, because then make's cascading recompilation can be instrumented as follows: Recompile a file either if the file itself changes, or an interface file on which it depends changes – but not if there is merely a change in the *implementation* of what is declared in the interface. Of course, the scheme is still extremely simple, and many files will be recompiled redundantly, for example, if a comment in a header file is modified.

A number of techniques exist for incremental recompilation which require knowledge about the syntax and semantics of the programming language being compiled. Tichy [17] coined the notion of *smart recompilation* to describe a scheme for recompilation based on analysis of the modifications made to a file, to determine whether recompilation of a file that depended on the file would be redundant, and applied the scheme to a variant of Pascal. A variant of smart recompilation was proposed by Elsman [3] to supplement various other techniques for compiling Standard ML programs, and incorporated into the ML Kit with Regions compiler. Syntax directed editors [2,5] have been developed which perform compilation-as-you-type, and where the unit of granularity may be language constructs such as an individual assignment.

The level of granularity in make-based incremental recompilation is the file, and make controls the recompilation of files merely on the basis of their time stamps. Indeed, make is useful for tasks involving file dependencies in general (see [13] for some interesting examples) not just those that arise in the compilation of programming languages. An analysis of make must take a similar "blackbox" approach to files. The analysis framework comprises a small formal machinery for reasoning about execution of commands that appear in makefile rules. The machinery allows for proving the equivalence of certain command sequences, comprising the same commands but in a different order and possibly duplicated. representing brute-force vs. incremental recompilation.

The analysis framework also comprises a semantic definition for make which is in some ways similar to the semantic definition for (constraint) logic programs given in [8]. Makefile execution resembles logic program execution because it is query-driven and does not assign values to global variables.

Despite the widespread use of make, there are only few scientific or other publications on make. They include presentation or analysis of tools and methods [4,18,9], standardization [6], and tutorials [11,12,16] on make and makefile generators such as mkmf and makedepend. In retrospect it can be seen that Stuart Feldman's original paper on make [4] tacitly assumed that makefile rules satisfy properties that guarantee safeness. Walden's [18] analysis revealed errors in makefile generators for C. In the terminology of this paper, he showed that they did not generate complete rules for targets whose dependencies were derived targets. The framework supplements work such as Walden's because the notion of rule completeness is defined formally and independently of C.

Contribution:

The main contribution is the definition of criteria that makefile rules should meet as prerequisites for safeness of make-based recompilation, and the proof that they are sufficient when editing of sources and makefile is constrained.

There are two ways that the rigorous formulation of criteria for makefile rules may be useful:

First, the criteria may be of interest in a modified, tutorial form directed at the makefile programmer. The criteria can be restated as three rules of thumb. Writing correct makefiles by hand is difficult, and existing tools only automate standard tasks such as the generation of rules for C files.

Second, the criteria are also of interest in the construction and verification of make-related tools. For example, the starting point for this paper was an attempt to verify that the Java compilation rules generated by the tool JavaDeps [14] were appropriate, which was a practically important problem in a large software development effort I was part of. It seemed that there were no criteria against which the rules generated could be measured.

Using make with new languages where rule-generating tools are not mature (or available at all) may be of interest for several reasons, even for languages having compilers with built-in features for incremental recompilation. First, make is useful if there are chains of dependencies due to compilation in multiple steps, analogous to the conventional use of make for C source files created by the parser-generator yacc. Second, in a sophisticated build system that monitors the compilation process, and writes configuration information to system-specific log files, make is useful because compilation of a file is invoked explicitly in makefile rules, as opposed to automatically inside a compiler.

Because a number of crucial questions about make whose answer require a rigorous, formal approach have apparently not been addressed previously, in many software projects there is little confidence in make. For example, the Mozilla browser project states that it builds incrementally *and* brute force, "*.. to make sure our dependencies are right, and out of sheer paranoia .. *" [10]. In Mozilla, incremental builds are used mainly as a regression test, to see whether the browser compiles successfully; if compilation succeeds, the browser is built brute force using the exact same sources.

Organization of the paper:

Sections 2-5 define notation, the subset of makefile syntax accounted for, the notion of a brute-force build, and the command execution model.

The semantic definitions in Sections 6-7 comprise rule satisfiability and semantics of make's execution of a makefile and an initial target.

Section 8 defines the notions of derivability and build rules in terms of rule completeness, fairness, and soundness. Section 9 contains the main result, safeness of make-based incremental recompilation. Section 10 discusses the validity of the make model, and Section 11 concludes. An appendix indicates how the main result is proven by listing and explaining intermediate results. For proof details see [7].

2   Notation

$X \rightarrow Y$ is the set of functions from X to Y, $X \times Y$ is the Cartesian product of X and Y, X^* is the set of finite sequences of elements of X, and $\wp\, X$ is the power set of X. nil is the empty sequence. The concatenation of sequences L and L' is written $L; L'$. We write $X \in L$ if X occurs in the sequence L, and $L \subseteq L'$ if $X \in L$ implies $X \in L'$, and $L' \setminus L$ for $\{X \mid X \in L' \wedge X \notin L\}$.

Functions are defined in curried from, i.e., having only a single argument. The function space $X \rightarrow (Y \rightarrow Z)$ is written as $X \rightarrow Y \rightarrow Z$. For a given function $F : X \rightarrow Y \rightarrow Y$, the symbol $\Sigma\, F$ is used for brevity to denote the function which has range $X^* \rightarrow Y \rightarrow Y$ and is defined as the following recursive application of F:

$$\Sigma\, F\, nil\, E = E$$
$$\Sigma\, F\, (D; L)\, E = \Sigma\, F\, L\, (F\, D\, E)$$

3   Syntax of Makefiles

For simplicity, the definitions given in this paper of syntax and semantics of makefiles are concerned only with a subset of the makefile language defined in the POSIX standard [6].

The basic syntax categories are *Name* and *Command*. *Command* contains a (neutral) command nil. A rule $R \in Rule$ is of the form

$$Ts : Ds; C$$

and contains a nonempty list of derived targets $Ts \in Name^*$, a (possibly empty) list of dependency targets $Ds \in Name^*$, and a command $C \in Command$. The rule is said to derive Ts, depend on Ds, and define C. A makefile $M \in Makefile$ is a finite set of rules no two of which derive the same target. An invocation of `make` comprises a makefile and an initial target. $targ\, M$ is the set of all targets occurring in M.

Macro rules are omitted; this is without loss of generality because macro rules are expanded in a preprocessing phase, leaving only target rules. Multiple rules deriving the same target are omitted; they can be rewritten into a single, and semantically equivalent rule. Finally, an invocation of `make` with multiple or zero initial targets can be modeled by adding an extra rule to the given makefile.

Among the syntactical constructs not captured is the special separator "::" of derived targets vs. dependency targets.

The rules shown in Figure 1 are as in Feldman's [4] C compilation example. In all makefile examples, command lines are indicated by tabulation, which is by far the most common in practice. In the formal model, the semicolon is used instead for brevity. (Both are POSIX compliant.) In all examples, rule commands comply with the syntax of the `Unix` Bourne shell, and rules derive only a single target. Additionally, in examples it is assumed that M consists of the rules listed in Figures 1 and 2, and the domain of targets *Name* is assumed to contain only names that occur as targets in M (and not names such as `cc`).

```
pgm: codegen.o parser.o library        # R_pgm
    cc codegen.o parser.o library -o pgm
codegen.o: codegen.c definitions       # R_codegen.o
    cc -c codegen.c
parser.o: parser.c definitions         # R_parser.o
    cc -c parser.c
parser.c: parser.y                     # R_parser.c
    yacc parser.y
    mv y.tab.c parser.c
```

Fig. 1. A makefile for building a C program **pgm**. We refer to the rules as R_{pgm}, etc.

4   Commands and Files

Execution of a rule's command changes the contents and time stamps of files. The formal framework must capture the distinction between file contents (the basis for defining safeness of incremental compilation) and the time-last-modified field in a file's directory entry (which determines whether a rule fires).

A *file* $F \in File = Time \times Content$ is a pair consisting of a time stamp and contents. A mapping $S \in State = Name \rightarrow File$ associates names with files; by abuse of notation, it is identified with its natural extension to $(\wp\, Name) \rightarrow (\wp\, File)$. For a given rule $R = (Gs : Ds; C)$, the set $\{S\, T \mid T \in Gs \vee T \in Ds)\}$ is written as $S\, R$.

No ordering relation on $Time$ is required. This is because the definition of rule satisfiability to be given below (Section 6) is abstract in the sense that it does not specify *how* time stamps determine satisfiability.

Command execution is modeled in terms of a function $exec : Command \rightarrow State \rightarrow State$. The value of $exec\, nil\, S$ is S. The function $exec$ is identified with $\Sigma\, exec$, so the following expressions denote the same file state:

$$exec\, (C; C')\, S = \Sigma\, exec\, (C; C')\, S = exec\, C'\, (exec\, C\, S)$$

Files $F, F' \in File$ are *equivalent*, written $F \equiv F'$, if they have the same contents, that is, if $F = \langle T, X \rangle$ and $F' = \langle T', X \rangle$. Equivalence is lifted to states as follows: $S \equiv S'$ holds if $S\, G \equiv S'\, G$ holds for all $G \in Name$.

When a makefile and a state is given in the context, a derived (or dependency) file is one that a derived (or dependency) target of a rule in the makefile maps to under the given state.

5   Brute Force Building

Safeness of **make**-based incremental recompilation is *defined* in terms of the reference notion of a brute-force build defined in this section. A brute-force build is the full, unconditional build in which everything is compiled. It is defined in terms of a given makefile, consistently with the common use of **make** to execute a brute-force build, for example when the developer uses targets such as `clobber` of Figure 2 to delete the files that were created in a previous build, and when the advanced user compiles source code before installation.

```
clean:              # R_clean
    rm *.o parser.c
clobber: clean      # R_clobber
    rm pgm
```

Fig. 2. Rules $R_{\texttt{clean}}$ and and $R_{\texttt{clobber}}$ may be added to the rules of Figure 1, for cleaning up prior to invoking a brute-force build by deleting intermediate and executable files. Example 3 discusses under what circumstances the commands of the rules are executed.

The command order in a brute-force build is derived from what is defined here as the induced make graph:

The *make graph* induced by a makefile M is a directed graph where a leaf node is a dependency target which is not derived by a rule in M, and a nonleaf node is the target(s) derived by a rule in M. There is an edge from node Ts to node Ds if there is a rule in M that derives a target in Ts and depends on a target in Ds. A make file is *well-formed* if the induced make graph is acyclic. Figure 3 shows the make graph induced by the makefile of Figure 1.

In the sequel all makefiles are assumed to be well-formed. This is consistent with, e.g., **gnumake** which in the presence of circularity will print a warning message and disregard one of the dependencies.

Rule R is a parent of rule R' if R' derives a target that R depends on. Predecessor/ancestor rules are defined accordingly. Predecessor/ancestor commands are defined in terms of the relationship between the rules that define the commands. We write $M|_T$ for the set of predecessor rules of the rule R deriving target T (including R); if T is not derived by a rule in M, $M|_T$ is the empty set.

Definition 1. *Let M be a makefile. Then command sequence Cs is a brute-force build with respect to M of the targets Ds if*

- *command C is in Cs if and only if for some rule R deriving a target $T \in Ds$, C is defined by a rule in $M|_T$.*
- *no command in Cs occurs before any of its predecessor commands.*
- *no command occurs more than once in Cs.*

Example 1. The command sequence
```
cc -c codegen.c;
yacc parser.y ; mv y.tab.c parser.c;
cc -c parser.c;
    cc codegen.o parser.o library -o pgm
```
is a brute-force build of target **pgm** wrt. to the makefile of Figure 1. So are two permutations of the sequence.

A brute-force build wrt. M is a command sequence which is a brute-force build wrt. M of *some* target list.

Definition 2 (Safeness). *File state S is* safe *wrt. makefile M if*

$$exec\,Cs\,S \equiv S$$

holds for any brute-force build Cs wrt. M.

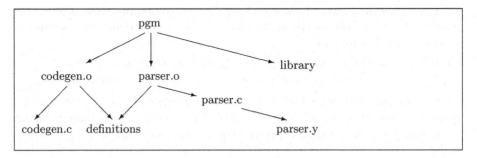

Fig. 3. The make graph induced by the makefile of Figure 1.

Thus a file state is safe if the contents of files will remain the same if a brute-force build is invoked. Such a state is what one wants as the outcome of make-based incremental recompilation. In practice, the set of rules relative to which one is interested in safeness is a subset of a given makefile, e.g., the subset $M|_T$ consisting of the rules relevant for building target T.

6   Satisfiability

Satisfiability of rules is important in the model because a rule fires if and only if it is unsatisfied.

The motivation for using the logical notion of satisfiability is the declarative reading of a makefile as a statement that certain rules must be satisfied. In addition to "rules" and "satisfiability", the informal language commonly used to describe make also contains the notion of "derived" targets. Both notions are used in the model because they may help explain make execution, not because results from logic are used to infer properties about make.

In the literature about make – including [4,16,12,6,18] – there is no definition of make's operational behavior which covers all the special cases. There may be some doubt as to whether a rule fires if, say, its list of dependency targets is empty and its derived file exists.

In order for the make-model not to be tied to a specific make-variant, the model is parameterized in the satisfiability relation $\models$.

Definition 3 (Satisfiability). *A satisfiability relation* $\models$ *is a subset of State* $\times$ *Rule such that for arbitrary states* S *and* S' *we have:*

- *If* $S\,R = S'\,R$, *then*

$$S \models R \Leftrightarrow S' \models R$$

- *If* R *is the rule* $(Gs : Ds; C)$, *where* $Ds \neq nil$, *and* R' *is the rule* $(Gs : Ds'; C')$, *where* $Ds \subseteq Ds'$, *then*

$$S \not\models R \Rightarrow S \not\models R'$$

Satisfiability is lifted to sets of rules: if $M = \{R, R', \dots\}$, then $S \models M$ means $S \models R$, $S \models R'$, etc.

Thus while real **make** decides satisfiability by comparing time stamps, the **make** model relies only on the above abstract notion of satisfiability, which can be summarized as follows:

- Satisfiability of a rule depends only on the rule's targets.
- Adding targets to a non-empty dependency list preserves unsatisfiability.

For example, the definition of soundness of a rule (see Section 8 below) requires that executing the rule's command renders the rule *satisfied* and its parent rules *unsatisfied* (rather than explicitly requiring a reset of the derived file's time stamp).

While not used inside the model, the following interpretation of satisfiability is assumed in the informal discussion and all examples given in the remainder of the paper. The definition has been reversely engineered from **gnumake**.

Definition 4 (Interpretation of satisfiability). *A rule is satisfied in a state if*

- *no dependency file is strictly newer than any derived file, and*
- *all derived files exist, and*
- *all dependency files exist, and*
- *the dependency list is non-empty.*

It may be noted that the above interpretation of satisfiability assumes that *Time* is linearly ordered (so that time-stamp comparison is well-defined) and that non-existence of files can be expressed. The abstract notion of interpretation is independent of these notions, so we omit their formalization.

Example 2. Assume that `codegen.c`, `definitions`, `parser.y`, and `library` exist in S, and that none of `codegen.o`, `parser.c`, `parser.o`, and `pgm` exist in S – in other words, only source files and the library exist. Then none of the rules in Figure 1 are satisfied in S, because their derived files don't exist.

So-called *phony* targets are targets that never (or practically never) exist as files. The intention is that since the rules that derive them are always unsatisfied, their commands will always be executed.

Example 3. See Figure 2. For all S we have $S \not\models R_{\texttt{clean}}$ because the rule has no dependencies. If we assume that `clobber` does not exist in S, then we also have that $S \not\models R_{\texttt{clobber}}$. Thus running **make** with target `clobber` will always delete all files except the source files and the external library.

7   Semantics of Make

The semantic definitions model the behavior of make in terms of what sequence of rule commands is executed when make is invoked.

Definition 5. *The semantics of invoking* make *with makefile M and initial target T is as follows:*

Perform a post order traversal of the nonleaf nodes of the induced make graph, starting with the node containing T. A visit of node Gs entails the following action: if Gs is derived by rule $R = (Gs : Ds; C) \in M$ and $S \not\models R$ holds, then command C is executed.

Visiting targets in post order reflects that make always processes a rule's dependency targets before testing whether the rule is satisfied.

In addition to the above graph-based definition, a denotational-style definition is given below. By Definition 6 below the value of an expression $\mathbf{M} \llbracket M \rrbracket S T$ is the list of commands executed when make is invoked with makefile M in the context of state S, and with initial target T. The denotational definition is more explicit than the graph-based, and it brings out the similarity with logic programs, eg. the semantic definition for constraint logic programs given in [8]. It can be seen from Definition 6 that the main mechanism is the reduction of a list of targets, and there are no references to global variables in the makefile.

More specifically, the format of the definition is partly in the style of denotational semantics [15], including the convention of using $\llbracket \cdot \rrbracket$ to distinguish arguments that are syntactical objects. On the other hand, because of the finite nature of make's graph traversal the full machinery of a fixpoint-based definition is not required.

In the definition of $\mathbf{M}$, a triplet $\langle V, Cs, S \rangle \in Dom$ represents the list of nodes visited so far (V), the commands executed (Cs), and the resulting state (S). The function $\mathbf{T}$ represents the evaluation of a dependency target; note that a makefile contains at most a single rule deriving a given target, so $\mathbf{T}$ is well-defined. The function $\mathbf{R}$ represents rule evaluation.

Definition 6. *The semantic function* $\mathbf{M}$ *is defined as follows.*

$$Dom = Name^* \times Command^* \times State$$
$$\mathbf{M} \ : \ Makefile \to State \to Name \to Command^*$$
$$\mathbf{T} \ : \ Makefile \to Name \to Dom \to Dom$$
$$\mathbf{R} \ : \ Rule \to Dom \to Dom$$

$$\mathbf{M} \llbracket M \rrbracket S T = \text{let } \langle V, Cs, S' \rangle = \Sigma \ (\mathbf{T} \llbracket M \rrbracket) \ T \ \langle nil, nil, S \rangle \text{ in } Cs$$
$$\mathbf{T} \llbracket M \rrbracket T \langle V, Cs, S \rangle = \text{if } T \notin V \text{ and } T \in Ts \text{ and } (Ts : Ds; C) \in M$$
$$\text{then } \mathbf{R} \llbracket Ts : Ds; C \rrbracket \ \langle (V; Ts), Cs, S \rangle$$
$$\text{else } \langle V, Cs, S \rangle$$
$$\mathbf{R} \llbracket Ts : Ds; C \rrbracket \langle V, Cs, S \rangle = \text{let } \langle V', Cs', S' \rangle = \Sigma \ (\mathbf{T} \llbracket M \rrbracket) \ Ds \ \langle V, Cs, S \rangle \text{ in }$$
$$\text{if } S' \models (Ts : Ds; C) \text{ then } \langle V', Cs', S' \rangle$$
$$\text{else } \langle V', (Cs'; C), exec \ C \ S' \rangle$$

8 Derivability

This section defines three desirable properties of makefile rules, and compounds them in the notion of a build rule. The properties may be summarized as follows:

Property of a build rule	Expressed as rule of thumb
Completeness	The rule's dependency list must contain all the files that the rule's target(s) depend on
Fairness	Executing the rule's command may not create or update any targets other than the rule's own
Soundness	Executing the rule's command must update the rule's target(s)

The first and core property of a rule is *completeness* wrt. to a given state. The definition says that the effect on the derived files of executing the rule's command remains the same as long as the content of the dependency files remain the same.

$$complete\ (Gs:Ds;C)\ S \Leftrightarrow \begin{cases} \forall S' : S'\ Ds \equiv S\ Ds \Rightarrow \\ exec\ C\ S'\ Gs \equiv exec\ C\ S\ Gs \end{cases}$$

Example 4. Rule R_{pgm} is complete wrt. any state S, because its command is
    cc codegen.o parser.o library -o pgm
and by the semantics of linking of C object files, definitions of external references are sought only in `parser.o` or `library`, which are both listed as dependency targets. In contrast, rule $R_{\text{codegen.o}}$ is complete only in certain states, because its command is
    cc -c codegen.c
and by the semantics of compilation of C source files, a preprocessor searches the file `codegen.c` recursively for include directives. Thus the rule, which lists `codegen.c`, and `definitions` as dependencies, is complete only if S is such that no other file than `definitions` is mentioned in an include directive in `codegen.c`, and `definitions` (if it is mentioned) contains no directives to include other files.

Second, *fairness* of a rule wrt. to a state means that executing the rule's command never changes the content or time stamp of any file other than those derived by the rule:

$$fair\ (Gs:Ds;C)\ S \Leftrightarrow \begin{cases} \forall S' : S'\ Ds \equiv S\ Ds \Rightarrow \\ exec\ C\ S'\ (Name \setminus Gs) = S'\ (Name \setminus Gs) \end{cases}$$

Example 5. Rules R_{pgm}, $R_{\text{codegen.o}}$, $R_{\text{parser.o}}$, and $R_{\text{parser.c}}$ are fair in any state. Rules R_{clean} and R_{clobber} are designed to remove the targets of other rules, and are unfair in any state. For example, firing R_{clobber} removes pgm, and even if pgm does not exist in the given state S there is a state S' satisfying S'clean $\equiv S$clean in which that file does exist, so that executing `rm pgm` makes a difference.

Third, *soundness* of a rule wrt. a state means that executing the rule's command renders the rule satisfiable and any parent rule unsatisfiable:

$$sound\,(Gs:Ds;C)\;S \Leftrightarrow \begin{cases} \forall S' : S'\,Ds \equiv S\,Ds \Rightarrow \\ exec\,C\,S' \models (Gs:Ds;C) \\ exec\,C\,S' \not\models R \text{ if } R \text{ is a parent of } (Gs:Ds;C) \end{cases}$$

Example 6. $R_{\text{codegen.o}}$ is sound wrt. S if the state meets the following two requirements: First, the process of compiling $R_{\text{codegen.c}}$ must succeed; then the object file $R_{\text{codegen.o}}$ is created or updated, having a time stamp showing that it is newer than the dependency targets $R_{\text{codegen.c}}$ and $R_{\text{definitions}}$, as well as newer than the target pgm derived by the parent rule R_{pgm}. Second, the file definitions must exist; otherwise $R_{\text{codegen.o}}$ is unsatisfied (before and) after executing cc -c codegen.c.

Definition 7 (Build rule). *Rule $R = (Gs:Ds;C)$ in makefile M is a build rule wrt. M and state S, if there is a brute-force build Cs of Ds wrt. M satisfying:*

- *R is complete wrt. $exec\,Cs\,S$*
- *R is fair wrt. $exec\,Cs\,S$*
- *R is sound wrt. $exec\,Cs\,S$*

Example 7. If S is as required in Examples 4 and 6, then $R_{\text{codegen.o}}$ is sound, fair, and complete wrt. S and M. Since none of the rule's dependencies are derived targets, the trivial command *nil* is a brute-force build of the dependency list, so $R_{\text{codegen.o}}$ is a build rule wrt. S and M.

Example 8. To determine whether R_{pgm} is a build rule wrt. S and M it is necessary to examine a state S' obtained from S by executing commands for brute-force building the three dependency targets of R_{pgm}. R_{pgm} is fair and complete wrt. any state (see Examples 4 and 5). Thus R_{pgm} is a build rule wrt. S if it is sound wrt. S'. The latter holds if S' is such that executing the link command of R_{pgm} does not fail, that is, any external reference of codegen.o must be defined in parser.o or library, with the object files being as created in S'.

Derivability ($\vdash$) expresses that all the rules in a makefile are build rules:

Definition 8 (Derivability ($\vdash$)). *The targets derived by rules in M are derivable in S, written $S \vdash M$, if M contains only build rules wrt. S and M.*

For the build rule concept to be useful in practice, determination of whether a rule is a build rule should be possible by considering only a single brute-force build of the rule's dependencies, and not the numerous permutations that may exist (see Example 1). For this it suffices that permutations of brute-force builds are equivalent in the sense established by the following lemma:

Lemma 1. *Assume $S \vdash M$ and let the permutations Cs and Cs' be brute-force builds wrt. M. Then $exec\, Cs'\, S \equiv exec\, Cs\, S$.*

This completes the formal framework. The key symbols are listed in the following table.

Symbol	Definition
$Gs : Ds; C$	Rule deriving Gs, depending on Ds, and defining C.
$S\,G$	The value of file name G in state S.
$S\,G \equiv S'\,G$	The contents of G is the same in S and S'.
$S\,G = S'\,G$	The contents and time stamp of G are the same in S and S'.
$M\|_G$	The set of rules in M that are predecessors of the rule deriving G.
$S \models M$	All rules in M are satisfied in context S.
$S \vdash M$	All rules in M are build rules in context S.
$\mathbf{M}\,[\![M]\!]\,S\,T$	The command sequence executed by make given makefile M, state S, and target T.

9   Safeness

This section contains the main result, Proposition 1 which states sufficient criteria for safeness of make-based incremental recompilation. The criteria include that the state against which make is invoked is partially safe wrt. the given makefile:

Definition 9 (Partial safeness). *File state S is partially safe wrt. M if*

$$\forall\, G \in targ\, M : S \models M\|_G \Rightarrow S \text{ is safe wrt. } M\|_G.$$

Clearly, make cannot attain safeness when invoked against an arbitrary state, even if the makefile's rules are build rules. For example, if by a mistake a rule's target is "touched" (cf. the Unix touch command) upon editing of the dependency files, the state would not qualify as partially safe. Indeed, the rule will not fire, and make will not attain safeness. In general, partial safeness shall guarantee that for any derived target G, if the rule deriving G does not fire, the state prior to make execution must be already safe wrt. the portion of the makefile containing the rule and its predecessors. Note also that a state is trivially safe if it is safe or if all rules are unsatisfied.

Example 9. Suppose $S_{safe} \models M$ where M contains the rules of Figures 1 and 2 as in the previous examples. Now assume parser.y is edited, yielding state S that satisfies all rules in M except for $R_{\text{parser.c}}$. Then $S \not\models M\|_{\text{parser.c}}$, $S \not\models M\|_{\text{parser.o}}$, and $S \not\models M\|_{\text{pgm}}$, while $S \models M\|_{\text{codegen.o}}$. Thus for S to be partially safe wrt. M, we require that S is safe wrt. $M\|_{\text{codegen.o}}$.

Proposition 1 (Safeness of make-based incremental recompilation).
Assume $S \vdash M$ and S is partially safe wrt. M. Let $C_{make} = \mathbf{M} [\![M]\!] S T$. Then exec $C_{make} S$ is safe wrt. $M|_T$.

The remainder of this section shows how partial safeness can be attained (so that Proposition 1 applies) prior to an initial, brute-force make invocation as well as prior to subsequent incremental make invocations. The difference is only in how partial safeness is attained, while make is invoked the same way in all cases.

The initial brute-force build:

A sufficient criteria for partial safeness is that no derived files exist. Then all rules are unsatisfied, and so by Proposition 1, if the relevant rules are build rules, the ensuing make invocation produces a safe state. To enforce partial safeness prior to an initial brute-force build, makefile rules such as R_{clobber} are sometimes used to delete all derived files.

Additionally, the following lemma shows that the command sequence produced by make is indeed a brute-force build if make is invoked when all rules are unsatisfied:

Lemma 2. *Assume $S \vdash M$ and $S \not\models R$ holds for all $R \in M$. Then the command sequence $\mathbf{M} [\![M]\!] S T$ is a brute-force build of T wrt. M.*

Subsequent incremental builds:

By Proposition 1 the result of the preceding make invocation is a state S_{safe} which is safe wrt. the corresponding makefile M_{safe}. Since a safe state is (trivially) partially safe, we essentially need to constrain editing so as to preserve partial safeness.

The following proposition gives a sufficient criteria for the new state to be partially safe S wrt. the new makefile M. (Recall that $S R \equiv S_{safe} R$ means that the rule's derived and dependency files have the same contents in S and S_{safe}):

Proposition 2 (Editing constraints). *Assume S_{safe} is safe wrt. M_{safe}, $S_{safe} \vdash M_{safe}$, and $S \vdash M$. Then S is partially safe wrt. M if*

$$\forall R \in M : S \models R \Rightarrow \begin{cases} S R \equiv S_{safe} R \\ M_{safe} \text{ contains a rule defining the same command as } R \end{cases}$$

Thus partial safeness is preserved when editing of source files and makefile is constrained as summarized in Table 1. It follows from Proposition 2 that we may safely apply make-based incremental recompilation upon such kind of editing.

For source files, Table 1 simply says that editing of a rule's dependency file is permissible if the rule becomes unsatisfied.

With regard to the more subtle question of editing a makefile rule, the table says that one may change the dependency list of a rule without enforcing unsatisfiability of the rule, if the rule's command is not alterned. This applies to removing redundant elements from the dependency list. In addition, it is permissible to add a new rule if the rule is unsatisfied, and to delete a rule.

Note that any number of modifications to source files and makefile may be combined, as long as each modification is permissible on its own.

Table 1. A field in the left column indicates a modification which is permissible if the corresponding criterion in the right column is met. Assumptions: $R = (T : Ds; C) \in M$, S_{safe} is safe wrt. M_{safe}, $S_{safe} \vdash M_{safe}$, and $S \vdash M$.

Type of editing	Sufficient criteria for partial safeness
$S\,D \not\equiv S_{safe}\,D$ (editing of dependency file $D \in Ds$)	$S \not\vdash R$
$R \notin M_{safe}$ (adding or modifying rule R)	$S\,R \equiv S_{safe}\,R$ and M_{safe} contains a rule defining the same command as R

Example 10. Suppose target `pgm` has been built, so that the state is safe wrt. M, and that in subsequent editing a portion of file `codegen.c` is moved to a new file `functions.c`. Accordingly M is modified by adding the rule $R_{\texttt{functions.o}}$ and changing $R_{\texttt{pgm}}$ to $R'_{\texttt{pgm}}$, yielding M' which is equal to M except for the fragments underlined below:

```
functions.o: functions.c definitions          # R_functions.o
    cc -c functions.c
pgm: codegen.o parser.o library function.o     # R'_pgm
    cc codegen.o parser.o function.o library -o pgm
```

Assume also that all rules are build rules (wrt. the respective states). Then by Proposition 2 the new state is partially safe wrt. M', since $R_{\texttt{codegen.o}}$, $R_{\texttt{functions.o}}$, and $R'_{\texttt{pgm}}$ are unsatisfied upon the editing. It follows from Proposition 1 that invoking `make` to rebuild `pgm` incrementally will produce a safe state. This avoids recompilation of two out of five derived files, even though editing has changed or created two source files, and changed or added two makefile rules.

If the criteria for preserving partial safeness are met, Proposition 1 guarantees that the state produced by incremental recompilation state is again safe, and so repeated cycles are feasible of editing + incremental recompilation.

10   Discussion

One may ask whether Definition 8 of build rules is too narrow. For the safeness result to apply to real `make`, the notions of completeness, fairness, and soundness should not (for safety) require build rules to fire too often, and so disqualify makefile rules that are appropriate in practice.

The analysis in Examples 4-8 of Stuart Feldman's example makefile provided indication that the definition is appropriate, because the verification that the rules are build rules made only reasonable assumptions about the contents of the relevant files.

Also, an argument for the validity of the build rule definition is the capture of "cascading" of rule firing from an unsatisfied rule to all its ancestors:

Lemma 3. *Let $S \vdash M$, let T be a derived target in M, and let $R = (Gs : Ds; C)$ $\in M|_T$. Then*

$$C \in \mathbf{M} \, [\![M]\!] \, S \, T$$
$$\Leftrightarrow \text{ for some predecessor } R' \text{ of } R, \; S \not\models R' \text{ holds.}$$

The above lemma captures "cascading" because $S \not\models M|_G$ holds if and only if $S \not\models R'$ for some predecessor R' of R. In particular, the lemma shows that no rules fire except those reached by cascading.

In addition, the following lemma shows that the model captures the fact that make creates a state wherein all rules visited are satisfiable (so that none of them will fire if make is invoked immediately after).

Lemma 4. *Let $S \vdash M$ and let T be a derived target in M. Then*

$$exec \, (\mathbf{M} \, [\![M]\!] \, S \, T) \, S \models M|_T$$

11   Conclusion

The main result is Proposition 1 which states sufficient criteria for make-based incremental recompilation to produce a safe state, that is, the same result as a brute-force build. Safeness is shown to hold subject to makefile rules being build rules, and partial safeness of the state against which make is invoked. For the use of make for incremental recompilation, Proposition 2 provides a constraint on the editing of sources and makefiles as performed upon a previous make invocation which ensures that partial safeness, as required by Proposition 1, is attained.

From a practical point of view, the analysis pursued here may be of interest as the basis for guidelines for writing makefiles. The definition of build rules may be translated into rules of thumb for makefile programming, as indicated in Section 8. Examples 4-8 indicate how the definition of build rules can be checked in the case of a makefile for a C program.

Also of practical interest are the editing constraints. The permissible modifications include deletion of rules and, under the stronger assumption that rules are rendered unsatisfiable, further changes to rules such as changing their commands. Any combination of these modifications may be performed, as long as each is permissible on its own.

Verification of makefiles is given a strong basis because of the formal approach.

Verification or construction of makefile rules must additionally use knowledge of the semantics of, for example, the commands for C compilation. As indicated in Example 4, completeness of a C compilation rule cannot be verified simply by checking that all files passed as parameters to the cc command are listed as dependencies. Because of the semantics of the cc command, verification or construction of the dependency list also involves parsing of source files, since include directives may establish dependency upon files not passed as parameters.

The definition of the build rule property in terms of a state attained upon execution of the commands of a given rule's predecessor rules (if any) pinpoints a major reason that automated tools for generation of makefile rules may be indispensable in practice. The reason is that a file which is passed as input to, for example, a cc command may be created by the command of a predecessor rule, and so is not available for inspection to check for include directives prior to make invocation.

The make model may support the verification or construction of such rule-generating tools, because the properties that makefile rules should comply with are stated generically in the sense of independently of any particular programming language.

Acknowledgment. Thanks to the anonymous referees for many valuable suggestions. The research was supported by the Development Center for Electronic Business and the IT-University, Copenhagen.

References

1. R. Adams, W. Tichy, and A. Weinert. The cost of selective recompilation and environment processing. *ACM Transactions on Software Engineering and Methodology*, Vol. 3 (1), January 1994, 3-28.
2. Demers, A., Reps, T., and Teitelbaum, T. Incremental evaluation for attribute grammars with application to syntax-directed editors. *Proc. Eighth ACM Symposium on Principles of Programming Languages,* Williamsburg, VA, January, 1981, 105-116.
3. M. Elsman. Static Interpretation of Modules. *Proc. International Conference on Functional Programming,* September 99, Paris, France.
4. S. I. Feldman. Make - a program for maintaining computer programs. *Software - Practice and Experience,* Vol. 9, 1979, 255-265.
5. R. Ford and D. Sawamiphakdi. A Greedy Concurrent Approach to Incremental Code Generation. *Proc. 12th Annual ACM Symposium on Principles of Programming Languages,* New Orleans, Louisiana, 1985, 165-178.
6. Institute of Electrical and Electronics Engineers. *Information technology - Portable Operating System Interface (POSIX) .* ANSI/IEEE Std. 1003.2, 1993, Part 2: Shell and Utilities, Volume 1, 1013-1020.
7. N. Jørgensen. *Safeness of Make-Based Incremental Recompilation.* URL: http://www.ruc.dk/~nielsj/research/papers/make.pdf.
8. K. Marriott and H. Søndergaard. Analysis of constraint logic programs, *Proc. North American Conference on Logic Programming,* Austin, 1988, 521-540.
9. P. Miller. *Recursive make considered harmful.* URL: http://www.pcug.org.au/~millerp/rmch/recu-make-cons-harm.html.
10. The Mozilla build process is described at the URL: http://www.mozilla.org/tinderbox.html in the context of a presentation of the build tool "Tinderbox".
11. P.J. Nicklin. Mkmf - makefile editor. *UNIX Programmer's Manual 4.2 BSD,* June 1983.
12. A. Oram and S. Talbott. *Managing projects with make.* O'Reilly, 1993.

13. R. Quinton. *Make and Makefiles*. URL:
    `http://www.ibiblio.org/pub/docs/unix-tutorials/courses/make.ps`.
14. S. Robbins. *JavaDeps - automatic dependency tracking for Java*.
    `http://www.cs.mcgill.ca/~stever/software/JavaDeps/`. The JavaDeps tool is
    a SourceForge project available at `http://sourceforge.net/projects/jmk`.
15. D.A. Schmidt. *Denotational semantics - a methodoogy for language development*.
    Allyn and Bacon, 1986.
16. R. Stallman and R. McGrath. *GNU Make, Version 3.77*. Free Software Foundation,
    1998.
17. W. F. Ticky. Smart recompilation. *ACM Transactions on Programming Languages
    and Systems*, Vol. 8 (3), July 1986, 273-291.
18. K. Walden. Automatic Generation of Make Dependencies. *Software - Practice and
    Experience*, Vol. 14 (6), June 1984, 575-585.

URLs available May 10, 2002.

Appendix

The appendix lists and comments the intermediate results used in [7] where full
proof details are given. A proof of Proposition 2 is included for illustration.

A   Algebra of Commands

Lemma 5-7 establish a command algebra in the sense of criteria that allow for
commuting or duplicating commands that are executed on a state.

Recall that by definition of *exec*, the value of $exec\,(C_1; C_2)\,S$ is the same as
$exec\,C_2\,(exec\,C_1\,S)$. The first form is preferred because it is more intuitive.

Lemma 5 (Commutativity of unrelated commands). *Suppose $S \vdash M$
where M contains $R = (Gs : Ds; C)$ and $R_1 = (Gs_1 : Ds_1; C_1)$, and R is complete,
fair, and sound wrt. S, and R' is complete, fair and sound wrt. $exec\,C\,S$. Also
assume that R_1 is neither predecessor nor ancestor of R. Then*

$$(i)\ \ R\ is\ complete,\ fair,\ and\ sound\ wrt.\ exec\,C_1\,S$$
$$(ii)\ exec\,(C; C_1)\,S \equiv exec\,(C_1; C)\,S$$

Lemma 6 (Generalized commutativity of unrelated commands). *Suppose $S \vdash M$ and $R, R_i \in M$ for $i = 1, \ldots, n$, where $R = (Gs : Ds; C)$ and
$R_i = (Gs_i : Ds_i; C_i)$, R is complete, fair, and sound wrt. S, and R_i is complete,
fair, and sound wrt. $exec\,(C_1 \ldots C_{i-1})\,S$. Then:*

$$\forall j : 1 \leq j \leq n \Rightarrow$$
$$(i)\ \ R\ is\ complete,\ fair,\ and\ sound\ wrt.\ exec\,(C_1 \ldots C_j)\,S$$
$$(ii)\ exec\,(C; C_1 \ldots C_n)\,S \equiv exec\,(C_1 \ldots C_j; C; C_{j+1} \ldots C_n)\,S$$

Lemma 7 (Idempotence). *Consider a rule $R = (Gs : Ds; C)$ which is complete and fair wrt. S. Then the equivalence $exec\,(C; C)\,S \equiv exec\,C\,S$ holds.*

B   Permutations of Commands in Brute-Force Builds

Lemma 1 of Section 8 stated that the execution of brute-force builds which are permutations produce equivalent file states. The lemma is part (ii) of the following lemma:

Lemma 8. *Let* $S \vdash M$. *Let* $Cs = (C_1 \ldots C_n)$ *and* Cs' *be permutations and brute-force builds wrt.* M. *Then*

> (i) *for each* $R_i = (Gs_i : Ds_i; C_i) \in M$:
> R_i *is complete, fair, and sound wrt.* $exec\,(C_1 \ldots C_{i-1})$
> (ii) $exec\,Cs'\,S \equiv exec\,Cs\,S$

Lemma 9 is a consequence of Lemma 8, and implies that if $S \vdash M$ and S is safe wrt. M, then all rules in M are complete, fair, and sound wrt. S.

Lemma 9 (Rule completeness + fairness + soundness in safe states). *Suppose* $S \vdash M$, *and consider a rule* R *where for each* R' *deriving a dependency* D *of* R, S *is safe wrt.* $M|_D$. *Then* R *is complete, fair, and sound wrt.* S.

C   Safeness: Proposition 1

Proposition 1 as well as Lemma 2-4 rely on Lemma 10-11.

Recall that safeness was defined in Definition 2 in terms of the execution of full brute-force builds. The proof of Proposition 1 is simplified by the following safeness-criterion which allows for considering only the execution of the individual commands in rules:

Lemma 10 (Safeness criterion). *Assume* $S \vdash M$. *Then* S *is safe wrt.* M *if and only if*
$$exec\,C\,S \equiv S$$
holds for any command C *occurring in a rule in* M.

Lemma 11. *Assume* $S \vdash M$ *and* S *is partially safe wrt.* M. *Let* N *be the number of nonleaf nodes in the make graph of* $M|_T$, *and consider a post order traversal of those* N *nodes starting with the node containing* T. *For* $0 \le n \le N$, *let* S_n *be the state attained upon visiting the first* n *nodes (with* $S_0 = S$), *and let* $R_n = (Gs_n : Ds_n; C_n)$ *be the rule deriving the targets of the* n'*th node. Let* $C_{make} = \mathbf{M}\,[\![M]\!]\,S\,T$, *and let* $p(n)$ *denote the conjunction of the following propositions:*

$$
\begin{aligned}
p_a(n) &: S \not\models M|_{R_n} & &\Leftrightarrow C_n \in C_{make} \\
p_b(n) &: \forall i : i \le n & &\Rightarrow S_n \models R_i \\
p_c(n) &: \forall i : i \le n \wedge S \models R_i & &\Rightarrow S_n\,Gs_i = S\,Gs_i \\
p_d(n) &: \forall i,j : i < n \wedge (j \le i \vee j > n) & &\Rightarrow S_n\,Gs_j = S_i\,Gs_j \\
p_e(n) &: \forall i : i \le n & &\Rightarrow exec\,C_i\,S_n \equiv S_n
\end{aligned}
$$

Then $p(n)$ *holds for all* n *where* $1 \le n \le N$.

Specifically, Proposition 1 is $p_e(N)$, Lemma 2 follows from $p_a(N)$, Lemma 3 is $p_a(N)$, and Lemma 4 is $p_b(N)$.

Lemma 11 says that during traversal of the induced make graph, upon visiting the n'th target G_n the following holds invariantly for $1 \le n \le N$:

$p_a(n)$ R_n fired if and only if R_n has a predecessor rule not satisfied in S.

$p_b(n)$ For any node visited so far, the corresponding rule is satisfied in the current state.

$p_c(n)$ For any node visited so far, if the corresponding rule was satisfied in S, its derived files remains unaltered.

$p_d(n)$ In the current state and the state attained upon the visit to the i'th node, all derived files are the same, except for derived files of rules corresponding to a node visited after the i'th visit.

$p_e(n)$ For any rule R corresponding to a node visited so far, the current state is safe wrt. $M|_R$.

The proof of Lemma 11 is by induction over n. The idea is to consider two distinct cases: First, in the case of $S \models M|_{R_n}$ use that $exec\, C_n\, S \equiv S$ holds by partial safeness, and second, in the case of $S \not\models M|_{R_n}$ use that R_n fires.

D   Editing Constraints: Proposition 2

This section proves Proposition 2 which says that S is partially safe wrt. M if

$$(*) \begin{cases} S_{safe} \text{ is safe wrt. } M_{safe} \\ S_{safe} \vdash M_{safe} \\ S \vdash M \\ \forall R \in M : S \models R \Rightarrow \begin{cases} S\,R \equiv S_{safe}\,R \\ \exists R' \in M_{safe} : R \text{ and } R' \text{ define the same command} \end{cases} \end{cases}$$

Proof. Assume $(*)$. By Definition 9, it suffices to show that for an arbitrary derived target T in M, where $S \models M|_T$ holds, we have that S is safe wrt. $M|_T$. By Lemma 10 this holds if

$$exec\, C\, S \equiv S \tag{1}$$

where C is the command occurring in an arbitrary rule $R = (Gs : Ds; C) \in M|_T$.
    The proof idea is to establish and use that

$$exec\, C\, S_{safe} \equiv S_{safe} \tag{2}$$

From assumption $S \models M|_T$ and $R \in M|_T$ we infer $S \models R$. Thus by $(*)$ there is a rule $R' \in M_{safe}$ defining the same command C, and by safeness of S_{safe} wrt. M_{safe} the equivalence (2) follows from Lemma 10.
    Moreover, by $S\,R \equiv S_{safe}\,R$ we have

$$S\,Ds \equiv S_{safe}\,Ds \tag{3}$$

$$S\,Gs \equiv S_{safe}\,Gs \tag{4}$$

Since R is fair and complete wrt. S_{safe} (by Lemma 9) we have

$$
\begin{aligned}
exec\,C\,S\,(Name \setminus Gs) &\equiv S\,(Name \setminus Gs) \quad \text{(by (3) and fairness of R wrt. S_{safe})} \\
exec\,C\,S\,Gs &\equiv exec\,C\,S_{safe}\,Gs \;\text{(by (3) and completeness of R wrt. S_{safe})} \\
&\equiv S_{safe}\,Gs \qquad \text{(by (2))} \\
&\equiv S\,Gs \qquad\quad \text{(by (4))}
\end{aligned}
$$

which establishes (1). $\qquad\qquad\qquad\qquad\qquad\qquad\qquad\qquad\qquad\qquad\qquad$ $\square$

An Algorithmic Approach to Design Exploration

Sharon Barner, Shoham Ben-David, Anna Gringauze, Baruch Sterin, and
Yaron Wolfsthal

IBM Research Laboratory in Haifa

Abstract. In recent years, the technique of symbolic model checking
has proven itself to be extremely useful in the verification of hardware.
However, after almost a decade, the use of model checking techniques
is still considered complicated, and is mostly practiced by experts. In
this paper we address the question of how model checking techniques
can be made more accessible to the hardware designer community.
We introduce the concept of *exploration* through model checking,
and demonstrate how, when differently tuned, the known techniques
can be used to easily obtain interesting traces out of the model,
rather than used for the discovery of hard-to-find bugs. We present a
set of algorithms, which support the exploration flavor of model checking.

Keywords: Model checking, hardware debugging, hardware exploration

1 Introduction

The application of model checking in industrial settings requires a high level of
user expertise to be able to withstand the state-space explosion problem. [2,14,
11,12]. The main reason is that many of the methods used for overcoming the
size problem are not completely automated. Rather, these methods frequently
draw on the insight and experience of the user for their success. User expertise
is also required to model input behavior. In this activity, the user must work
carefully to avoid false negative and false positive results when restricting input
behavior to avoid state-space explosion. These application challenges, together
with the need to master formal languages (in particular temporal languages),
have established industrial model checking as a domain where a high level of
expertise is required. Most of the research in this area has concentrated on attacking the state explosion problem. Some of these new methods [2,3,20,21],
however, require an even higher degree of expertise from users, as well as significant insights into the algorithmic nature of these methods. This has made model
checking accessible only to trained verification engineers, thus limiting prospects
for wide-scale deployment of model checking.

In this paper we take a different direction. Our investigation focuses on making model checking (and the associated benefits and impact) accessible to the
non-expert user. Specifically, we aimed our efforts at reaching the community of
design engineers, and providing them with a methodology and tools to develop
and debug newly written hardware design code; currently, no adequate cost-
effective means exist for this purpose. Indeed, contemporary hardware design

L.-H. Eriksson and P. Lindsay (Eds.): FME 2002, LNCS 2391, pp. 146–162, 2002.

methodologies involve the creation of relatively small design blocks, which are only subjected to verification at the unit level (unit is an ensemble of blocks). Block level verification is typically tedious and costly, and is thus generally skipped or reduced to a minimum; this has a detrimental impact on time-to-market and overall design quality.

To address the above problems, we propose the paradigm of *Design Exploration* through model checking. This paradigm provides a means for the designer to explore, debug and gain insight into the behaviors of the design at a very early stage of the implementation—before verification has even started. In this paradigm, the design engineer specifies a behavior of interest. The exploration tool then uses model checking techniques to find one or more execution sequences compliant with the specified behavior. When presented with such an execution sequence ("trace"), the designer is essentially furnished with an insight into the design behavior, and specifically with a concrete scenario in which the behavior of interest occurs. This scenario can then be closely inspected, refined, or abandoned in favor of another scenario. Using model checking for exploration provides two important advantages over traditional simulation. These are (1) the ability to specify scenarios of interest without specifying the inputs sequences required to reach them, and (2) the ability to reason about multiple executions in parallel, rather than one at a time.

The exploration paradigm presents some new challenges which were not raised in traditional model checking. First, as design exploration is geared for use by non-experts, it is important to hide the difficult parts of the technique, namely, the need to learn new languages and the need to accurately describe input behavior. Second, the model checker should be tuned to algorithmically support design exploration—in order for the new paradigm to be applicable and accepted, the underlying tool should quickly and easily provide as much information as possible to the design engineer exploring the hardware design. We present several algorithms which support the exploration paradigm. These include the generation of disjoint multiple traces, the production of maximal partial trace when no full trace exists, the interactive mode, where new requests can be made after all calculations ended, and the integration with a simulator.

Note that the size problem is not addressed in this paper. The struggle with size is minimized by restricting the application of exploration to small hardware models (which is consistent with the purpose of design exploration to serve as a block-level [1] design tool).

The rest of this paper is organized as follows: In the next section we compare our approach with related work. Section 3 describes the concept of design exploration. Section 4 presents the features developed to support the design exploration paradigm. In section 5 we present a short case study of the usage of our exploration system, and in section 6 we conclude and point to directions for future research.

---

[1] Blocks are small models of about 100 state variables

2   Comparison to Related Work

The problem of making model checking easier to access has been addressed before. Winters and Hu [23] propose the approach of automatic source-level optimizations, to make models written by novices more efficiently processed by the model checker Murφ. Fisler in [13] and Amla et al in [1] discuss the usage of *timing diagrams* for specification, as those are a commonly used and visually appealing specification method for hardware designers. De Palma et al [10] have approached the usability problem by restricting the specification repertoire to a finite set of graphical, intuitive templates. Like the above, we also propose a restricted visual language. However, it is designed for exploration rather than verification, which makes it different. Hardin et al in [16] mention a feature called "check-pointing", which provides for path exploration. Copty et al in [9] talk about *debugging* in a model checking environment. Unlike our use of this term, they refer to the problem of analyzing a counter example produced by a model checker. They also mention having an algorithm to produce multiple traces, as far as possible from one another. However, the algorithm is not presented in their paper.

In [15] a debugging method is presented by Gunter and Peled, which is close to our approach. They concentrate on the interactive process of finding the cause of a bug, in an explicit model checking environment. Although we also talk about debugging, our effort concentrates in making symbolic model checking methods easy to access.

3   Design Exploration – Basic Principles

The first challenge of the exploration approach is to make the model checking techniques easy to access to the non-experts. As discussed in the introduction, we view three aspects of the model checking process as problematic. These are: (1) the need to cope with size problems, (2) property specification and (3) modeling the environment.

Size problem handling will continue to demand great deal of expertise in the foreseeing future; our exploration approach is therefore aimed to be used on small blocks only, where size problem does not exist.

To avoid the need to master specification languages, we have developed a simple graphical specification formalism, which provides a natural way for designers to state their intent. The specification formalism, and its translation to a known language are shown in section 3.1

The need to accurately model environment behavior is avoided by the different approach introduced in the exploration paradigm: rather than looking for the corner bugs, we use model checking techniques to search for mainstream behaviors. Thus, while accurate environment behavior is needed in bug hunting to avoid false positive/negative results, it is not needed when exploring the design. This idea is demonstrated in the case study presented in section 5. Input signals are left free to change by default, and in some cases, this is enough to get a desired trace. However in other cases, input signals need to be modeled in order to get a legal trace. In section 3.2 we describe how control over input signals can be achieved in our system.

3.1   The Visual Specification Formalism

To explore a design, the user needs a way to easily specify a behavior of interest, which forms a *path* through the design. We view a path as an abstraction of a set of traces, demonstrating the same abstract behavior. To specify a behavior of interest, one does not have to describe every signal value in every cycle, but can rather concentrate on the main events he would like to see. The path is composed of a *sequence of phases*, where only important aspects of the behavior are described.

A Phase in a path specification is displayed as a rectangle on the GUI. Each phase consists of two *conditions*:

1. *The Satisfying Condition*: a Boolean expression over design signals. This Boolean expression must hold while the path is in that phase.
   If no condition is given, the default is *true*, which always holds.
2. *The Terminating Condition*: this condition can be either a Boolean expression or a time limit. As a time limit, the user can give either a fixed number of cycles, or cycle bounds.
   When the terminating condition is given as a Boolean expression, the path stays in the current phase until the given Boolean expression holds. It then proceeds to the next phase on the next cycle.
   If a time limit is given as a terminating condition, the path stays in the current phase for the number of cycles indicated by the time limit. A terminating condition must be given for every phase.

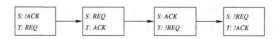

Fig. 1. A Path Specification

As an example, consider the path specification shown in Figure 1. It describes a four-phase-hand-shake protocol, where each phase of the protocol is represented as a phase in the path specification. In each phase, the letter S stands for satisfying, and the letter T stands for terminating. The first phase asks for a (part of) trace where the ACK signal does not rise until the REQ signal asserts. Then the REQ signal should stay steady until ACK responds. It is then the ACK signal which must stay asserted until REQ is deasserted, and finally REQ should not assert again before ACK is deasserted. In this example the terminating condition is always a simple Boolean condition.

The satisfying condition is many times omitted. Phases with terminating condition only, are sometimes called *events*.

The Underlying Language

The underlying language of a path specification is Regular Expressions. The use of regular expression for the specification of temporal properties has become common in contemporary temporal languages (see [6]). The alphabet of the regular language consists of all signals of the design, and boolean combinations of them. We follow the syntax of [6] to represent a regular expression: we use a comma to separate between letters, and square brackets for '*' or '+'. Thus the regular expression $ab * c$ will be written as a,b[*],c. Every phase is translated into a regular expression in a straightforward way:

Let the satisfying condition be h. If a duration condition, $1 \leq l \leq r$, is applied to a satisfying condition h, then the regular expression derived from this phase will be $(h[l] \vee h[l+1] \vee h[l+2] \vee \cdots \vee h[r])$, where $h[l]$ means $\underbrace{h, h, \cdots, h}_{l}$. If the terminating condition is given as a Boolean expression t, then the translation will be $(h \wedge \neg t)[*]$,t.

To translate a sequence of phases to a regular expression, we concatenate all the regular expressions derived from the phases.

The regular expression representing a path is translated to an automaton which is fed into the model checking engine.

To demonstrate how a path specification is translated, consider the following example. The design under test has a state machine "ma(0:3)", with 16 possible values. The designer is interested in seeing the state machine passing through states 4 and 6 and then reaching state 1—not necessarily in consecutive cycles. The way it is expressed is by a graphical path description as shown in Figure 2 below. (For the sake of readability, we use the term ma instead of ma(0:3)):

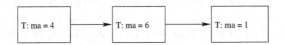

Fig. 2. Simple Path Specification

This path specification is translated into a regular expression as follows

$$ma \neq 4[*], ma = 4, ma \neq 6[*], ma = 6, \ ma \neq 1[*], ma = 1 \qquad (1)$$

The automaton built for formula 1 is given in Figure 3 below, written in the SMV [19] language. In this language, the VAR statement declares a variable and the possible values it can get. The ASSIGN statements assigns the initial and the next state values to the variable. If a set of values is assigned to a variable, it means a non-deterministic choice between those values. A CASE statement is composed of a list of lines, each consists of a Boolean condition and an assignment, separated by a colon. The conditions are evaluated in the order of appearance. The value assigned is that of the first condition to hold.

```
VAR aut: { 0, 1, 2, 3, 4, 5, 6 };
ASSIGN
     init(aut) := { 1, 2 };
     next(aut) :=
     case
          aut = 1 ∧ ma ≠ 4 : { 2, 1 };
          aut = 2 ∧ ma = 4 : { 4, 3 };
          aut = 3 ∧ ma ≠ 6 : { 4, 3 };
          aut = 4 ∧ ma = 6 : { 6, 5 };
          aut = 5 ∧ ma ≠ 1 : { 6, 5 };
          1 : 0;
     esac;
```

Fig. 3. A Non-Deterministic Automaton in the SMV Language

In order to find a trace compliant with the path, we feed the model checker with the design under test and the automaton, together with an $EF(p)$ type formula. The formula for our example is given in Equation 2.

$$\psi = EF((aut = 6) \land (ma = 1)) \tag{2}$$

If ψ is found to hold in the model, the witness trace produced for ψ, will be compliant with the path specification.

3.2   Controlling Input Behavior

In the design exploration approach, the user should be able to produce first traces with minimal effort. Input signals should therefore have a default behavior, to save the effort of modeling each of them. We chose this default to be a "free" behavior, that is, a full non-deterministic behavior. Thus, even with no prior knowledge in formal methods, and with minimal effort, the user is able to generate initial traces. Sometimes, however, traces may exhibit illegal behavior due to the unrestricted behavior of the input signals. We therefore allow several ways of controlling input behavior.

- *Assign a constant value*: this is used mainly to reduce out large data buses which do not affect the design behavior, and thus are not needed in the exploration process.
- *Describe a deterministic behavior (force) through the GUI*: the user can define, using a graphical editor, exactly how a given input signal should behave. This is used to avoid illegal traces. However, it may prove too restrictive in some cases.
- *Assign a predefined state machine behavior*: for common, simple behaviors such as a random pulse, we provide a library of pre-defined state machines, from which the user can choose.

– *Use a non-deterministic HDL for complex behavior*: for the cases where a complex behavior must be modeled, we provide access to a full non-deterministic HDL. This option is very seldom used.

4   Tuning Model Checking to Support Exploration

Although using the same model checking engine, verification and exploration have different needs. The challenge of exploration is to provide the user with as much information as possible on the design under test. This section describes a few features we have added to our model checking engine to better support the exploration needs. We have implemented these features in a BDD-based [8] symbolic model checker. However, implementation in other types of model checkers, (a SAT-based model checker is one example), can also be considered. The algorithmic features we describe include:

– The ability to provide a *maximal partial trace* (4.2), in the case a full trace for the specified path does not exist.
– An algorithm to produce *disjoint multiple traces* (4.3), different from each other for each path. This gives the user more insight about the design.
– An *interactive mode* (4.4) of the model checker, providing the user with the ability to obtain more immediate information about the model.
– The integration with *simulation* (4.5), which, when used for exploration purposes, is important for the success of the concept.

The first three algorithms are based on *invariant on-the-fly verification* ([18, 5]). To keep our paper self-contained, we give this basic algorithm in the next section.

4.1   Basic On-the-Fly Model Checking

The basic invariant on-the-fly model checking and trace generation algorithms are given in Figure 4. We have modified it a bit, to represent the exploration paradigm, where we look for a set of *good* states - representing desired traces, rather than a set of *bad* states indicating a bug, as in verification. We use the term *found* to indicate the set of states representing the invariant. The on-the-fly algorithm saves the *new* sets of states, which are computed in every iteration of reachability analysis, as $S_0 \cdots S_n$ (line 4). This is done to make trace generation more efficient.

4.2   Maximal Partial Trace

When using model checking techniques as a means for design exploration, the user always expects to get a trace as a result of the search. Traditional model checking algorithms will only produce a trace when such exists for the entire path that was specified. In case only part of the specified path exists in the model, no trace will be provided for the user. We show how to produce a maximal *partial*

```
1 reachable = new = initialStates;
2 i = 0;
3 while ((new ≠ ∅)&&(new ∩ found = ∅)) {
4      S_i = new;
5      i = i+1;
6      next = nextStateImage(new);
7      new = next \ reachable;
8      reachable = reachable ∪ next;
9 }
10 if (new = ∅) {
11     print "No trace exists for this path";
12     return;
13 }
14 k = i;
15 print "Trace found on cycle k";
16 good = new ∩ found;
17 while (i¿=0) {
18     Tr_i = choose one state from good;
19     if (i¿0) good=pred(Tr_i)∩S_{i-1};
20     i = i-1;
21 }
22 print "Trace is:" Tr_0 ··· Tr_k;
```

Fig. 4. On-the-fly Model Checking with Trace Generation

trace (in terms of *phases* encountered), when no full trace exists for the given path.

For this purpose, we introduce auxiliary formulas, called *event formulas*, to help determine which events have been encountered at each iteration of the reachability search. An event formula is generated for each event, apart from the final one. We use the special structure of the path specification and the automaton built for it to derive the event formulas.

The automaton derived from a path specification is built in such a way, that a move from one state to another is conditioned by a Boolean condition C. For every state s with condition C, which does not have a self loop, we produce a formula $EF(s \wedge C)$.

For example, consider again the path specification given in Figure 2 and its automaton shown in Figure 3. In addition to the formula $EF((aut = 6) \wedge (ma = 1))$ which specifies the full path, we generate the following formulas:

1. $EF((aut = 2) \wedge (ma = 4))$ and
2. $EF((aut = 4) \wedge (ma = 6))$

These formulas state that *event 1* has been reached and *event 2* has been reached respectively.

The auxiliary formulas are checked on-the-fly, while searching the reachable state space. Thus, when the model checker determines that a full trace does not exist for the specified path, it produces the maximal *partial trace* available in the model. The enhanced algorithm is given in Figure 5 below. The terms $ef_1..ef_n$ represent the set of states of the event formulas.

```
1 reachable = new = initialStates;
2 i = 0; maxe = 0
3 while ((new ≠ ∅)&&(new ∩ found = ∅)) {
4      S_i = new;
5      i = i+1;
6      next = nextStateImage(new);
7      new = next \ reachable;
8      reachable = reachable ∪ next;
9      for (j = n downto maxe+1) do {
10          if (new ∩ ef_j ≠ ∅) {
11              maxe = j; doughnut = i;
12              print "Event "maxe" encountered on cycle "doughnut" "
13              break; (from 'for' loop)
14          }
15      }
16 if (new = ∅ && maxe = 0) {
17      print "No trace exists for this path";
18      return;
19 }
20 else if (new = ∅) {  maxe ¿ 0
21      print "No full trace exists. Producing trace until event "maxe"";
22      found = ef_{maxe}; k = doughnut;
23 }
24 else {
25      k = i-1;
26      print "Trace found on cycle k";
27 }
28 good = S_k ∩ found;
29 while (k¿=0) {
30      Tr_k = choose one state from good;
31      if (k¿0) good=pred(Tr_k)∩S_{k-1};
32      k = k-1;
33 }
34 print "Trace is:" Tr_0 ···Tr_k;
```

Fig. 5. On-the-fly Model Checking, with Partial Trace Generation

Progress Indication. Even when design exploration is applied to relatively small blocks, the search for a trace may take a long time, during which the user has very little information about the progress of the search. In model checkers such as SMV [19] and RuleBase [4], progress information is given in terms of *iteration*, which tells very little to the non-expert user. Information in terms of *events* specified would be of better value to such users.

Lines 9–13 in the Partial Trace algorithm described in Figure 5, show how *event formulas* are checked on-the-fly. When an event is found, the user is notified about it, as shown in line 12.

Taking this one step further, the user is granted the opportunity to interrupt the search, and be presented with the maximal partial trace currently available. Note that a partial trace produced during the search, is not necessarily a prefix of the full trace produced for the given path specification. In fact, it may be the case that the partial trace can not be extended to a full trace.

4.3   Disjoint Multiple Traces

In the exploration paradigm, the user would benefit from being presented with many possible instances of the specified path. Moreover, the produced traces should be made as different from one another as possible, in order to provide the user with as much information as possible. In traditional model checking, a single trace is produced for each specification. In this section we demonstrate how to produce many traces (the number of traces can be specified by the user), while maintaining many variations. Lines 16–22 in Figure 4, give the single trace production algorithm.

The Disjoint Multiple Traces algorithm presented here is heuristic, and therefore is not guaranteed to find disjoint traces. However, our practical experience shows that it almost always does.

The algorithm is based on BDDs [8]. A BDD is a directed acyclic graph (DAG), which is used to represent a Boolean function over a set of variables. In a BDD representation, the order of the variables is fixed. The index of a variable in the fixed order is called its *level*. Each node in the BDD corresponds to a *level* (a variable), and has two outgoing edges *left* and *right*. Given a node corresponding to the variable x, the *left* edge connects to a subgraph representing the function where $x = 0$, and the *right* edge connects to a subgraph representing the function where $x = 1$.

For our algorithm, we define the *distance* between a state s and a set of states P, to be the average of the Hamming distances between s and each of the states in P. The Hamming distance between two vectors (states) $a = (a_1, .., a_n)$ and $b = (b_1, .., b_n)$ is the number of indices in which $a_i \neq b_i$. Given two sets of states Q and P, our algorithm looks for a state $s \in Q$ which is as *far* as possible (has the biggest distance) from P.

Let $S_0, ..., S_k$ be the list of "new" sets, as appear in Figure 4. For each S_i, we keep a BDD P, of all states from S_i, already given in a produced trace. Given a BDD of a set of states Q (A subset of S_i) from which a state should be chosen, we replace line 18 in Figure 4 by choosing a state from Q as *far* as possible form

P, if such a state exists. The heuristic algorithm for finding a *far* state is given in Figure 6.

Briefly, the algorithm works as follows: if $level(Q) < level(P)$, we recursively find a *far* state in the left hand side of Q, and in the right hand side of Q. We then compare their distances from P, and return the farther state, extended with the appropriate value of the current level. If $level(P) < level(Q)$, we recursively find a state in Q which is *far* from the left side of P and a state which is *far* from right side. We return as above. If $level(Q) = level(P)$, we compute $PP = P \to left \vee P \to right$ and recursively find a state in $Q \to left$ and in $Q \to right$ which are *far* from PP. If both sides return zero (no different state was found), we recursively find a state in $Q \to left$ which is *far* from $P \to left$, and a state in $Q \to right$ which is *far* from $Q \to right$. We return as above. We then add the chosen state to P by a disjunction of the BDDs.

The complexity of the algorithm is $O(N^2 * 2^m)$, where N is the size of the BDDs, and m is the number of BDD levels.

4.4   Interactive Design Exploration

The main purpose of this feature is to let the user gain additional information about the design block as quickly as possible. In *interactive mode* the model checker does not terminate after finding the desired traces. It saves all information in memory (list of *new* sets, reachable states set, provided traces etc.), and interactively serves new requests coming from the user, thereby providing the user with new information as desired. The primary types of user requests supported by our experimental exploration system are presented below.

Additional Cycles. This type of request specifies the number, N, of additional cycles required by the user as an extension of the current trace. The algorithm then performs N forward steps from the final state of each previously produced trace. This is possible as the traces and transition relation are stored in the model checker. When performing forward steps, we apply the same algorithm as in section 4.3 to choose the new states different from the previous, and thus more interesting to the user.

Additional Traces. This type of request allows the user to ask for N more traces, different from all the others already produced. Since all previously produced traces for the current path are saved inside the model checker, we simply apply the algorithm given in   4.3 N times to produce the desired traces.

Longer Trace. This type of request allows the user to ask the model checker to search for a longer trace than those already produced. Recall that in an on-the-fly algorithm, we are given an $EF(p)$ type formula, and we search for the first state in which p holds. Thus, the trace produced is the shortest available. In order to provide a longer one, we delete the set of *good* states from the *new*

```
1 function find_diff_state(P, Q) {
2    if (ISLEAF(p) && ISLEAF(q)) {
3       if ((p == ZERO) && (q == ONE))
4          return (one, 1);
5       return (zero, 0);
6    }
7    if ( level(Q) < level(P) ) {
8       (state₀, dist₀) = find_diff_state(P, Q → left);
9       (state₁, dist₁) = find_diff_state(P, Q → right);
10      if ( dist₀ > dist₁ )
11         return ( new_bdd(level(Q), state₀, ZERO), dist₀ );
12      else
13         return ( new_bdd(level(Q), ZERO state₁), dist₁ );
14   }
15 }
16   if ( level(Q) > level(P) ) {
17      (state₀, dist₀) = find_diff_state(P → left, Q);
18      if dist₀ > 0 dist₀ ++;
19      (state₁, dist₁) = find_diff_state(P → right, Q);
20      if dist₁ > 0 dist₁ ++;
21      if ( dist₀ > dist₁ ) {
22         return ( new_bdd(level(P), state₀, ZERO), dist₀ );
23      else
24         return ( new_bdd(level(P), ZERO, state₁), dist₁ );
25      }
26   }
27   if ( level(Q) = level(P) ) {
28      PP = or_bdd(P → left, P → right);
29      (state₀, dist₀) = find_diff_state(PP, Q → left);
30      (state₁, dist₁) = find_diff_state(PP, Q → right);
31      if (dist₀ = 0 and dist₁ = 0) {
32         (state₀, dist₀) = find_diff_state(P → left, Q → left);
33         (state₁, dist₁) = find_diff_state(P → right, Q → right);
34      }
35      if ( dist₀ > dist₁ ) {
36         return ( new_bdd(level(P), state₀, ZERO), dist₀ );
37      else
38         return ( new_bdd(level(P), ZERO, state₁), dist₁ );
39      }
40   }
41 }
```

Fig. 6. Choosing a state in BDD Q which is *far* from all states in BDD P

set in which it was first found, and continue reachability analysis, searching for the next time p holds.

4.5   Reconstruction and Simulation

Contemporary model checking tools apply *reduction* algorithms [4] before model checking search starts. This is done to reduce the size of the model to be actually model-checked, and is an efficient and important step for industrial model checkers. In many cases, this phase may reduce a large portion of the design, leaving the model checker with a much smaller task. The reduction algorithms usually applied are *safe* ones. That is, the reduced variables are indeed redundant, and are not needed for the evaluation of the specification. However, once a trace is produced, the reduced variables are often needed for the analysis of the trace.

Specifically this is true when the tool is used by non-experts, as done in the exploration paradigm.

In order to solve this problem, we need to *reconstruct* the behavior of the reduced variables. To do so, we integrate a *simulator* with the model checker. When a trace is produced, it is first sent together with the original design and environment to the simulator. The simulator uses the values of the signals in the trace to calculate the values of all other signals. Thus, when the trace is presented to the user, all signals values are available and can be viewed.

A very useful feature of the simulation engine underlying our experimental system is that it allows direct manipulation of signal values: once a trace is produced and displayed, the user can edit input variables in the trace, and explore the different scenarios made possible by the introduction of these changes.

5   A Case Study

The exploration approach described in this paper has been implemented in a tool, called PathFinder [7], and has been used by designers for the past two years. In this section we present a short case study, demonstrating how the tool has been used in practice. The block under study is a part of a PCI/Infiniband bridge (see [22,17]). The block, has 96 FlipFlops and 406 input signals, and it is responsible for transferring a packet from the Infiniband bus interface to the PCI bus interface. It stores the packet in an internal buffer, checks a few parameters, then moves it to the PCI bus interface and signals a success by raising an *ACK* signal. The block has a special output signal *ERR*, to indicate detection of error conditions. The input signal *RST* causes the block to reset. In order for the block to function properly, the *RST* signal should be active for a few cycles in the beginning of the run, and then inactive for the rest of the run. A sketch of the block interface is given in Figure 7 below.

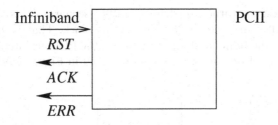

Fig. 7. A Bus Bridge

PathFinder was used on this block at a very early stage of the design cycle, before the simulation environment was ready. The main target of using the tool was to make sure that the block is ready for integration, which means that its basic functionality is working.

The designer defined the proper behavior of the *RST* signal. A special easy-to-use mechanism is provided for this in the tool. He defined the *RST* signal to have the value 1 for the duration of the first cycle, and 0 from the second cycle onwards. The designer had given constant values to the input data lines, (through the GUI) and had left all other inputs free to change on every cycle (this is the default behavior defined by the tool). The whole input setting process took about 15 minutes to complete.

The designer was interested to see under what conditions the *ERR* signal is raised by the design. He defined a single-phased path, with no satisfying condition and with the termination condition *ERR=1*. Since input signals were left free, the designer expected the tool to find those input behaviors, which would lead to an error condition. However, it took PathFinder a few minutes to return with the answer that no such trace exists in the block. That is, the *ERR* signal can never be asserted. To debug this problem, the designer defined a new path, with a more detailed scenario, which should lead the design toward raising the *ERR* signal. This path had four phases, as shown in Fig 8. Since no full path

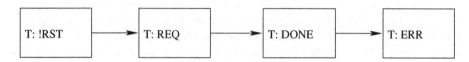

Fig. 8. Searching for an Error Condition

could be found, PathFinder returned a maximal partial path with only the first three phases appearing on it. Using this trace as a basis, the designer examined a few scenarios by graphically changing input values and running the tests on the integrated simulator. It took him about 30 minutes to discover that the code responsible for raising the *ERR* signal, was actually dead code which was never executed.

Next the designer turned to define another scenario. This time he wanted to see how a full transaction is handled by his block. That is, how a packet is transferred from the Infiniband bus interface to the PCI bus interface. He defined a path, consisting of two phases, as demonstrated in Figure 9 below.

Fig. 9. Specifying a Full Transaction

The first phase ended when the *RST* signal deasserts ($\neg RST$ holds), and the second one ended when the *ACK* signal rises. In both phase definitions, only the *terminating* condition was used. (The *satisfying* condition was set to *true* by default) Since *ACK* is only given when the transaction is completed, this simple path description forced Pathfinder to look for a full transaction trace.

It took PathFinder about 20 minutes to return with a set of five multiple traces demonstrating a complete transaction. (The number of traces produced is a parameter controlled by the user) Out of the five multiple traces produced, three were legal transaction traces. The other two were illegal scenarios, caused by a bad choice of input behavior. To learn more, the designer added a third phase, similar to the second one, asking the tool to show a second *ACK*. He was expecting to see a second complete transaction after the first one. However, PathFinder returned with a trace showing signal *ACK* being active for two consecutive cycles at the end of the first transaction. This was a violation of the specification, which, after some debugging effort, was found to be a bug in the code responsible for deasserting the *ACK* signal after a transaction.

PathFinder was used on this block for two days. A total of 6 bugs of a similar nature to the ones described above were discovered and corrected. These bugs were minor ones, and would have been discovered by unit testing in simulation. However, the fact they were discovered so early and so quickly in the verification process, saved a lot of time and effort in the later stage of integration.

6   Conclusion and Future Directions

We have presented the concept of design exploration through model checking techniques. We have given several algorithms and features to support the new concept, searching for ways to improve the facilities provided by the model checking tool, rather than attacking the inherent size problem of these methods. We believe that the exploration flavor of model checking will open up new directions, making model checking accessible to a larger community, and bringing new interest in model checking techniques. While our approach hides most of the difficult parts of model checking, the user must still learn new concepts which are different from those of simulation. The ability to specify events over output and internal signals, and allow the tool to automatically find the right *input* behavior, is a new concept that people need to become accustomed to. The concept of non-determinism is also confusing at first. Thus the deployment of this approach, just like the deployment of traditional bug-hunting model checking, is slow.

We believe the *interactive mode* described in section 4.4 to be a promising method. In order to provide the user with further insight, other options can be developed. For example, allowing the user control over the chosen traces, letting the user direct the choice. (In [9] this is done off-line). Another example is improving the ability to provide a longer trace, beyond the current reachable-states search iterations.

In the future, we plan to address the problem of *regression*. Currently the user must analyze every trace manually to determine if the behavior demonstrated is legal. A way to store and verify expected results in future runs could help extend the use of the exploration tool.

Acknowledgments. We thank Yael Abarbanel-Vinov, Eli Berger, Eli Dichterman and Leonid Gluhovski, for their contribution to the implementation of features described in this paper. We thank Shaul Yifrach and Dan Ramon for providing information for the case study.

References

1. N. Amla, E.A. Emerson, R.P. Kurshan, K.S. Namjoshi. Model Checking Synchronous Timing Diagrams. In *Proc. 3rd International Conference on Formal Methods in Computer-Aided Design (FMCAD)*, LNCS 1954, pages 283–298, 2000.
2. J. Baumgartner, T. Heyman, V. Singhal, and A. Aziz. Model checking the IBM Gigahertz Processor. In *Proc. 11th International Conference on Computer Aided Verification (CAV)*, LNCS 1633, pages 72–83. Springer-Verlag, 1999.
3. J. Baumgartner, A. Tripp, A. Aziz, V. Singhal and F. Andersen. An Abstraction Algorithm for the Verification of Generalized C-slow Designs. In *Proc. of 12th International Conference on Computer Aided Verification (CAV)*, 2000, pp. 5-19.
4. I. Beer, S. Ben-David, C. Eisner, and A. Landver. RuleBase: an industry-oriented formal verification tool. In *Proc. 33rd Design Automation Conference (DAC)*, pages 655–660. Association for Computing Machinery, Inc., June 1996.
5. I. Beer, S. Ben-David, A. Landver, On-The-Fly Model Checking of RCTL Formulas. In *Proc. of 10th International Conference (CAV)*, 1998, pp. 184-194.
6. I. Beer, S. Ben-David, C. Eisner, D. Fisman, A. Gringauze, Y. Rodeh. The Temporal Logic Sugar. In *Proc. of 13th International Conference on Compute Aided verification (CAV)*, LNCS 2102, 2001, pp. 363-367.
7. S. Ben-David, A. Gringauze, B. Sterin, Y. Wolfsthal. Design Exploration Through Model Checking Technical Report H0097, IBM Haifa Research Laboratory.
8. R.E. Bryant, Graph-based algorithms for boolean function manipulation, In *IEEE Transactions on Computers, C-35(8)*, 1986.
9. F. Copty, A. Irron, O. Weissberg, N. Kropp, G. Kamhi. Efficient Debugging in a Formal Verification Environment In *Proc. Correct Hardware Design and Verification Methods (CHARME)* , LNCS 2144, page 275–292, 2001.
10. G.F. De Palma, A.B. Glaser, R.P. Kurshan, G.R. Wesley, Apparatus for defining Properties in Finite-State Machines. *US Patent 6,966,516*, October 1999.
11. Á. Eiríksson. The formal design of 1M-gate ASICs. In *Second International Conference on Formal Methods in Computer-Aided Design (FMCAD)*, LNCS 1522, pages 49–63. Springer-Verlag, 1998.
12. C. Eisner, R. Hoover, W. Nation, K. Nelson, I. Shitsevalov, and K. Valk. A methodology for formal design of hardware control with application to cache coherence protocols. In *Proc. 37th Design Automation Conference (DAC)*, pages 724–729. Association for Computing Machinery, Inc., June 2000.
13. K. Fisler Timing Diagrams: Formalization and Formal Verification, In *Journal of Logic, Language and Information 8(3)*, 1999.
14. A. Goel and W. Lee. Formal verification of an IBM Coreconnect Processor Local Bus arbiter core. In *Proc. 37th Design Automation Conference (DAC)*, pages 196–200. Association for Computing Machinery, Inc., June 2000.

15. E. Gunter and D. Peled. Temporal Debugging for Concurrent Systems. *To appear in TACAS 2002*
16. H. Hardin, Z. Har'El, R.P. Kurshan. COSPAN. In *Proc. of 8th International Conference on Computer Aided Verification (CAV)*, LNCS 1102, 1996, pp. 423-427.
17. P. Interest PCI Local Bus Specification, *PCI Special Interest group, PCI Local Bus Specification, Revision 2.2, December 1995.*
18. D. Long. Model Checking, Abstraction and Compositional Verification. *Ph.D. Thesis*, CMU, 1993.
19. K.L. McMillan. Symbolic Model Checking. *Kluwer Academic Publishers*, 1993.
20. K.L. McMillan. A Methodology for Hardware Verification using Compositional Model-Checking. In *Science of Computer Programming*, 37(1-3):278-309 (2000)
21. K. Ravi, F. Somenzi. Hints to Accelerate Symbolic Traversal. In *Proc of CHARME*, 1999, pp. 250-264.
22. I. SM and T. Association. InfiniBand Architecture Specification. *InfiniBand(SM) Trade Association, InfiniBand Architecture Specification, Release 1.0* October 2000. Available from: http://www.infinibandta.org.
23. B.D. Winters, A.J. Hu. Source-Level Transformations for Improved Formal Verification. In *IEEE International Conference on Computer Design*, 2000.

Mechanical Abstraction of CSP$_Z$ Processes

Alexandre Mota*, Paulo Borba, and Augusto Sampaio

Universidade Federal de Pernambuco
Centro de Informática - CIn
P.O.Box 7851 - Cidade Universitária
50740-540 Recife - PE Brazil
{acm,phmb,acas}@cin.ufpe.br

Abstract. We propose a mechanised strategy to turn an infinite CSP$_Z$ process (formed of CSP and Z constructs) into one suitable for model checking. This strategy integrates two theories which allow us to consider the infiniteness of CSP$_Z$ as two separate problems: data independence for handling the behavioural aspect and abstract interpretation for handling the data structure aspect. A distinguishing feature of our approach to abstract interpretation is the generation of the abstract domains based on a symbolic execution of the process.

1 Introduction

Impressive efforts have been carried out to compact various classes of transition systems while still preserving most properties; currently, even a simple model checker can easily analyse millions of states. However, many systems cannot be analysed either because they are infinite state or are too large. This is normally induced by the use of (infinite or too large) data types on communications and process parameters. Indeed, various techniques have been proposed and are still being carefully studied in order to handle certain classes of such systems: local analysis [15,17], data independence [23,26], symmetry elimination and partial order reduction [10], test automation [28], abstract interpretation [22], integration of model checkers with theorem provers [29,30], etc. Unfortunately, the most powerful techniques still need a non-guided user support for a complete and adequate usage. This support concerns the elaboration of some kind of abstraction such that model checking can be applied successfully; in the current literature—to the best of our knowledge—there is no technique nor strategy to generate such abstractions from the system description itself.

The goal of this paper is to propose a strategy for analysing infinite CSP$_Z$ processes in which user intervention is only needed to aid theorem proving. Therefore, even though the strategy is not fully automatic in general it can be mechanised via model checking and theorem proving integration, which seems to be a promising research direction in formal verification [30]. In particular, this strategy is a combination of data independence and abstract interpretation

---

* This work was financially supported by CNPq grant 143720/98-8.

L.-H. Eriksson and P. Lindsay (Eds.): FME 2002, LNCS 2391, pp. 163–183, 2002.

in a slightly different manner than approaches available in the literature. More specifically, our approach is based on Lazić's work [26] to model checking data independent CSP processes and Wehrheim's work [13,14] to data abstracting CSP_{OZ} [8] (a combination of CSP and Object-Z), although we concentrate on CSP_Z [7,8] (an integration of CSP and Z). The reason to use Wehrheim's approach instead of, for example, the ones proposed in [24,9], is that her approach already uses a CSP algebraic style which is very convenient for using FDR [12]. Wehrheim's work can be seen as a CSP view of other approaches [24,9]. Lazić's work is used on the CSP part to fix a flaw in the work of Wehrheim. This is the reason why we consider the CSP part of a CSP_Z process data independent, while the Z part takes into account the data dependencies.

We show that a data dependent infinite state CSP_Z process can be transformed into a finite CSP_Z process by using generated subtypes on its channel declarations, state, input and output variables, and by rewriting some expressions (the postconditions of the schemas) in order to perform model checking. We present an algorithm for our strategy in which decidable aspects are transferred to the user by means of using theorem provers to answer the algorithm's questions. Currently, the strategy supports model checking of some classical properties, in general, and other properties on special situations. The classical properties readily available are: deadlock and livelock (See [4] for more details).

The major advantage of our approach is that, unlike related work in the literature, we calculate the data abstraction from the process description itself. Notably, the most promising works on this research area assume some kind of data abstraction determined by the user [24,9,29,16]. The success of our strategy is directly related to how much the expansion of the Z part yields infinite regular behaviours [1]. We deal with infinity in the following way: if the composition of schemas originate a *stable behaviour* from a certain state to infinite then we can obtain optimal abstraction. The abstraction is obtained by replacing infinite states for a representative state according to the *stable property*.

Although, in principle, we could employ our strategy to other specification languages, the choice for CSP_Z was based on the way a process is modelled and interpreted. Every CSP_Z process is seen as two independent and complementary parts: a behavioural one—described in CSP—and a data structure based—modelled in Z. The behavioural part is naturally data independent while data dependent aspects are confined to the data structures part. Finally, the data structures part has a very simple form which enables the mechanisation of the strategy to be relatively straightforward.

This paper is organised as follows. The following section presents an overview of CSP_Z through an example; its semantics is informally described to ease the understanding of our data abstraction approach. Section 3 introduces the notion of data independence for CSP processes. The theory of abstract interpretation is briefly described in Section 4. The main contribution of this paper is described in Section 5 where some examples are used for illustrating our approach to abstracting CSP_Z processes, before we present our algorithm for data abstraction. Finally, we present our conclusions including topics for further research.

2   Overview of CSP$_Z$

This section introduces the language CSP$_Z$ [7,8]; a process of the On-Board Computer (OBC) of a Brazilian artificial microsatellite (SACI-1) [11,3] is used for that purpose. The Watch-Dog Timer, or simply *WDT*, is responsible for waiting periodic reset signals that come from another OBC process, the Fault-Tolerant Router (*FTR*). If such a reset signal does not come, the *WDT* sends a recovery signal to the *FTR* asynchronously, to normalise the situation. This procedure is repeated three times; if, after that, the *FTR* still does not respond, then the *WDT* considers the *FTR* faulty, finishing its operation successfully.

CSP$_Z$ is based on the version of CSP presented by Roscoe [4] instead of the original version of Hoare [6]. A CSP$_Z$ specification is enclosed into a spec and end_spec scope with its name following these keywords. The *interface* is the first part of a CSP$_Z$ specification and there it is declared the external channels (keyword chan) and the local (or hidden) ones (keyword lchan). Each list of communicating channels has an associated type: a schema type, or $[v_1 : T_1; \ldots v_n : T_n \mid P]$ where $v_1, \ldots, v_n$ are lists of variables, $T_1, \ldots, T_n$ their respective types, and P is a predicate over $v_1, \ldots, v_n$. Untyped channels are simply events by CSP tradition. Types could be built-in or user-defined types; in the latter case, they might be declared outside the spec and end_spec scope, as illustrated by the following *given-set* and used to build the type of the channel *clockWDT*.

$[CLK]$

The *WDT* interface includes a communicating channel *clockWDT* (it can send or receive *CLK* data via variable *clk*), two external events *reset* and *recover*, and four local events *timeOut*, *noTimeOut*, *failFTR*, and *offWDT*.

spec *WDT*
   chan *clockWDT*: $[clk : CLK]$
   chan *reset*, *recover*
   lchan *timeOut*, *noTimeOut*, *failFTR*, *offWDT*

The concurrent behaviour of a CSP$_Z$ specification is introduced by the keyword main, where other equations can be added to obtain a more structured description: a hierarchy of processes. The equation main describes the *WDT* behaviour in terms of a parallel composition of two other processes, *Signal* and *Verify*, which synchronise in the event *offWDT*. The process *Signal* waits for consecutive *reset* signals (coming from the *FTR* process) or synchronises with *Verify* (through the event *offWDT*) when the *FTR* goes down. The process *Verify* waits for a clock period, then checks whether a *reset* signal arrived at the right period or not via the choice operator ($\Box$). If a *timeOut* occurs then the *WDT* tries to send, at most for three times, a recovery signal to the *FTR*. If the *FTR* is not ready to synchronise in this event, after the third attempt, then *Verify* assumes that the *FTR* is faulty (enabling *failFTR*) and then synchronises with *Signal* (at *offWDT*), in which case both terminate (behaving like SKIP). From the viewpoint of the SACI-1 project, the *WDT* is turned off because it cannot restart (recover) the *FTR* anymore.

$$
\begin{array}{l}
\text{main} = Signal \quad\quad || \quad\quad Verify \\
\quad\quad\quad\quad \{ offWDT \} \\
Signal = (reset \rightarrow Signal \ \Box \ offWDT \rightarrow SKIP) \\
Verify = (clockWDT?clk \rightarrow (noTimeOut \rightarrow Verify \\
\quad\quad\quad\quad\quad\quad\quad\quad \Box \ timeOut \rightarrow (recover \rightarrow Verify \\
\quad\quad\quad\quad\quad\quad\quad\quad\quad\quad\quad \Box \ failFTR \rightarrow offWDT \rightarrow SKIP)))
\end{array}
$$

The Z part complements the main equation by means of a state space and operations defining the state change upon occurrence of each CSP event. The system state (*State*) has simply a declarative part recording the number of cycles the *WDT* tries to recover the *FTR*, and the last clock received. The initialisation schema (*Init*) asserts that the number of cycles begins at zero; prime ($'$) variables characterises the resulting state. The number of cycles belongs to the constant set *LENGTH* (used in the declarative part of the state space).

$$
LENGTH == 0 \,..\, 3 \quad\quad\quad\quad State \ \widehat{=} \ [cycles : LENGTH; \ time : CLK]
$$
$$
Init \ \widehat{=} \ [State' \mid cycles' = 0]
$$

To fix a time out period we introduce the constant *WDTtOut* of type *CLK*. To check whether the current time is a time out, we use the constant relation *WDTP* which expresses when one element of *CLK* is a multiple of another.

$$
\begin{array}{|l}
WDTtOut : CLK \\
WDTP : CLK \leftrightarrow CLK
\end{array}
$$

The following operations are defined as standard Z schemas (with a declaration part and a predicate which constrains the values of the declared variables) whose names originate from the channel names, prefixing the keyword com_. Informally, the meaning of a CSP$_Z$ specification is that, when a CSP event c occurs the respective Z operation com_c is executed, possibly changing the data structures. When a given channel has no associated schema, this means that no change of state occurs. For events with an associated non-empty schema type, the Z schema must have input and/or output variables with corresponding names in order to exchange communicated values between the CSP and the Z parts. Hence, the input variable *clk?* (in the schema com_*clockWDT* below) receives values communicated via the *clockWDT* channel. For schemas where prime variables are omitted, we assume that no modification occurs in the corresponding component; for instance, in the schema com_*reset* below it is implicit that the time component is not modified (*time'* = *time*).

$$
\text{com\_}reset \ \widehat{=} \ [\Delta State \mid cycles' = 0]
$$
$$
\text{com\_}clockWDT \ \widehat{=} \ [\Delta State; \ clk? : CLK \mid time' = clk?]
$$

The precondition of the schema com_*noTimeOut* specifies that the current time is not a multiple of the time out constant (the time out has not yet occurred) by $\neg \ WDTP(time, WDTtOut)$. Its complement is captured by com_*timeOut*.

com_*noTimeOut* $\widehat{=}$ [Ξ*State* | ¬ *WDTP*(*time*, *WDTtOut*)]
com_*timeOut* $\widehat{=}$ [Ξ*State* | *WDTP*(*time*, *WDTtOut*)]

As already explained, the recovery procedure is attempted for 3 times, after which the *WDT* assumes that the *FTR* is faulty. This forces the occurrence of *failFTR* and then turns off the *WDT* process.

com_*recover* $\widehat{=}$ [Δ*State* | *cycles* < 3 ∧ *cycles'* = *cycles* + 1]
com_*failFTR* $\widehat{=}$ [Ξ*State* | *cycles* = 3]

end_spec *WDT*

2.1 Semantics and Refinement

A CSP$_Z$ process is defined as a combination of a CSP and a Z part. Its semantics is given in terms of the semantic models of CSP, that is, traces, failures, and failures-divergences [7,8]. Thus, the Z part has a non-standard semantics (see the standard semantics of Z [20]) given by the standard semantics of CSP.

These semantic models yield different views of a process. The traces model ($\mathcal{T}$) is the simplest; it allows one to observe the possible behaviours of a process. The failures model ($\mathcal{F}$) is more complex: possible (traces) and non-possible (refusals) behaviours can be appreciated. The strongest model is the failures-divergences ($\mathcal{FD}$) model, which also considers divergent behaviours.

Following the CSP tradition, a specification is better than another in terms of the semantic models when it satisfies a (parameterised) refinement relation $\sqsubseteq_M$, where M is one of the three possible models. For example, let P and Q be CSP processes. We say that Q is better than P (in the semantical model M) iff

$$P \sqsubseteq_M Q$$

which means
$\mathcal{T}(Q) \subseteq \mathcal{T}(P)$, for the traces model,
$\mathcal{T}(Q) \subseteq \mathcal{T}(P) \wedge \mathcal{F}(Q) \subseteq \mathcal{F}(P)$, for the failures model, and
$\mathcal{F}(Q) \subseteq \mathcal{F}(P) \wedge \mathcal{D}(Q) \subseteq \mathcal{D}(P)$, for the failures-divergences model.

2.2 A Normal Form for CSP$_Z$ Processes

In [2,3] we show how an arbitrary CSP$_Z$ process can be transformed in a pure CSP process, for the purpose of model checking using FDR. In this approach, a CSP$_Z$ specification is defined as the parallel composition of two CSP processes: the CSP part and the Z one. In the remaining sections we assume that this transformation has already been carried out. Let P be a CSP$_Z$ process with *Interface* = {$a_1, \ldots, a_n$}. The normal form of P, as a pure CSP process, looks like P_{NF} = *main* $\underset{\{a_1, \ldots, a_n\}}{\|}$ Z^{State}, where

$$\text{pre } com\_a_1 \,\&\, a_1 \rightarrow Z^{com\_a_1}(State)$$
$$\square \text{ pre } com\_a_2 \,\&\, a_2 \rightarrow Z^{com\_a_2}(State)$$

$$Z^{State} = \begin{array}{cc} \vdots & \vdots \\ \square \\ \text{pre } com\_a_n \,\&\, a_n \rightarrow Z^{com\_a_n}(State) \end{array}$$

It is worth observing that schemas are transformed into functions[1]. This kind of normal form[2] is turned out to be very useful for our abstraction strategy as further discussed in the remainder of this paper.

3   Data Independence

Informally, a data independent system P [23,26] (with respect to a data type X) is a system where no operations involving values of X can occur; it can only input such values, store them, and compare them for equality. In that case, the behaviour of P is preserved by replacing any concrete data type (with equality) for X (X is a parameter of P). This is precisely defined by Lazić in [26] as:

Definition 1 (Data independence) P *is data independent in a type* X *iff:*

1. *Constants do not appear in P, only variables appear, and*
2. *If operations are used then they must be polymorphic, or*
3. *If comparisons are done then only equality tests can be used, or*
4. *If used, complex functions and predicates must originate from 2 and 3, or*
5. *If replicated operators are used then only nondeterministic choices over X may appear in P.* ◇

The combination of the items in Definition 1 yields different classes of data independent systems. In this section we consider the most simplest class to represent the CSP part of a CSP_Z process. This is done in order to leave the Z part free from (possible) influences originated by the CSP part.

The work of Lazić deals with the refinement relation between two data independent processes by means of the cardinality of their data independent types. The cardinality originates from the items in Definition 1 present in the processes bodies. That is, suppose $P \sqsubseteq_M Q$ has to be checked, for some model M, such that P and Q are infinite state and data independent. Further, consider X the unique data independent type influencing $P \sqsubseteq_M Q$. Then, Lazić guarantees this refinement provided $\#X \geq N$, for some natural N, and according to Definition 1.

These results form the basis to analyse the CSP part of a CSP_Z specification. Definition 2 states the kind of data independence we are focusing.

Definition 2 (Trivially Data Independent) *A trivially data independent CSP process is a data independent process which has no equality tests, no polymorphic operations, and satisfies $\#X \geq 1$ for all data independent type X.* ◇

---

[1] This is presented formally in Section 5.

[2] Indeed, this normal form is a simplified version of the original one (See Mota and Sampaio [3] for further information).

Definition 3 is used to guarantee that the CSP$_Z$ specification we are analysing has the simplest data independent process description for its CSP part.

Definition 3 (Partially Data Independent) *A CSP$_Z$ specification is partially data independent if its CSP part is trivially data independent.*   ◇

As long as the Z part of a CSP$_Z$ specification is normally data dependent, the previous theory cannot be applied to handle it. Hence, a more powerful theory has to be introduced to deal with the Z part. Now, we briefly present the theory of abstract interpretation for treating data dependent questions.

4   Abstract Interpretation

Abstract interpretation is an attractive theory based on the notion of galois connections (or closure operators), and was originally conceived for compiler design [21,22]. Its role is to interpret a program in an abstract domain using abstract operations. Therefore, its main benefit is to obtain useful information about a concrete system by means of its abstract version.

For model checking [10], this approach is used to avoid state explosion by replacing infinite data types by finite ones; in view of this, model checking can be extended to analyse infinite state systems. The drawbacks of this approach are related to how to determine the abstract domains and operations, and the possible loss of precision coming from the choice of abstract domains.

Definition 4 (Galois connection) *Let $\langle A, \sqsubseteq_A \rangle$ and $\langle C, \sqsubseteq_C \rangle$ be lattices. Further, let $\alpha : C \to A$ (the abstraction map or left adjunction) and $\gamma : A \to C$ (the concretisation map or right adjunction) be monotonic functions such that*

- $\forall a : A \bullet \alpha \circ \gamma(a) \sqsubseteq_A a$
- $\forall c : C \bullet c \sqsubseteq_C \gamma \circ \alpha(c)$ *(whereas $c =_C \gamma \circ \alpha(c)$ for a galois insertion)*

then $\langle C, \sqsubseteq_C \rangle \xleftrightarrow[\alpha]{\gamma} \langle A, \sqsubseteq_A \rangle$ represents a galois connection.   ◇

Note that, in the terminology of abstract interpretation, the order $\sqsubseteq$ is defined such that $x \sqsubseteq y$ means x is more precise than y. Hence, $\alpha \circ \gamma(a) \sqsubseteq_A a$ means $\alpha \circ \gamma(a)$ is the best approximation for a and $c \sqsubseteq_C \gamma \circ \alpha(c)$ means the application of $\gamma \circ \alpha$ adds no information to c. The lattice $\langle A, \sqsubseteq_A \rangle$ represents the lattice of properties of the system having $\langle C, \sqsubseteq_C \rangle$ as the usual semantic domain.

In the tradition of abstract interpretation, one has to establish adjunctions such that they form a galois connection (or insertion) and, for all concrete operators, propose abstract versions for them. Moreover, this proposal might be done such that the operators (concrete and abstract) be compatible in some sense; this compatibility originates the notions of soundness (safety) and completeness (optimality) [24,25]. For example, let $f : C \to D$ be a concrete operation defined over the concrete domains C and D. Let an abstract interpretation be specified by the following galois connections $\langle C, \sqsubseteq_C \rangle \xleftrightarrow[\alpha]{\gamma} \langle A, \sqsubseteq_A \rangle$ and $\langle D, \sqsubseteq_D \rangle \xleftrightarrow[\alpha']{\gamma'} \langle B, \sqsubseteq_B \rangle$. In addition, let $f^\star : A \to B$ be the corresponding abstract semantic operation for f. Then, $f^\star$ is sound for f if $\alpha' \circ f \sqsubseteq f^\star \circ \alpha$. Completeness is meant as the natural strengthening of the notion of soundness, requiring its reverse relation to hold. Hence, $f^\star$ is complete for f iff $\alpha' \circ f = f^\star \circ \alpha$.

Now, we present how an abstract interpretation can be defined in terms of CSP_Z elements as well as its integration with the notion of data independence.

5 CSP_Z Data Abstraction

In this section we present what means performing an *ad hoc* CSP_Z data abstraction, in terms of the theory of abstract interpretation.

Let P be a CSP_Z specification and *Interface* be its set of channel names. Abstract a CSP_Z specification P means to find an abstract interpretation for the data domains of channels and state of P, that is, define new domains and new operations for P. Thus, let D be the data domains of state variables and M_c the data domain of channel c ($c \in$ *Interface*) to be abstracted. By convention, messages are split into input (M_c^{in}) and output (M_c^{out}) messages. Recall from Section 2.2 that *com_* operations are transformed into functions with signature.

$\langle\!\langle$ com_c $\rangle\!\rangle : D \times M_c^{in} \to \mathbb{P}(D \times M_c^{out})$

We build abstract *com_* functions in terms of abstract data domains and abstract versions of primitive operations. Thus, let D^A and M_c^A be abstract data domains of variables and channels, and h and r_c be abstraction maps. Recall from Definition 4 that h and r_c are our left adjunctions while the concretisations are simply identity maps, that is, we are employing the concept of galois insertion.

$h : D \to D^A$

$r_c : M_c \to M_c^A$

The communication abstractions (r_c) are only defined over communicating channels; events are not abstracted.

An abstract interpretation $\{\!| \cdot |\!\}$ is defined over abstract domains. Thus, the signature of the abstract versions become.

$\{\!|$ com_c $|\!\} : D^A \times M_c^{in,A} \to \mathbb{P}(D^A \times M_c^{out,A})$

It is worth noting that $\{\!|$ com_c $|\!\}$ is compositional in the sense that, for example, let s, s_1, s_2 be state variables of type sequence then a predicate $s' = s_1 \frown s_2$ (in a *com_* function) is abstracted to $s'^A = s_1^A \frown\!\!\!\!^\sim s_2^A$.

To deal with abstract powerset of data domains we present the most natural extension of the previous abstract functions. Therefore, the functions h and R_c are extended naturally to the powerset of D as follows

$H : \mathbb{P}\,D \to \mathbb{P}\,D^A = \lambda\,\mathbb{D} : \mathbb{P}\,D \bullet \{d^A : D^A \mid d \in \mathbb{D} \wedge d^A = h(d)\}$

$R_c : \mathbb{P}\,M_c \to \mathbb{P}\,M_c^A = \lambda\,\mathbb{M} : \mathbb{P}\,M_c \bullet \{m^A : M_c^A \mid m \in \mathbb{M} \wedge m^A = r_c(m)\}$

Recall from Section 4 that abstract domains and operations might be found such that the new interpretation be optimal abstraction of the original system. In the following we present what that means for CSP_Z.

Definition 5 (Optimal abstraction) *An abstract interpretation $\{\!| \cdot |\!\}$ is optimal according to abstractions h and r_c iff*

$\forall\,d : D;\ m : M \bullet \{\!|$ com_c $|\!\}(h(d), r_c(m)) = (H \times R_c(\langle\!\langle$ com_c(d, m) $\rangle\!\rangle))$ $\diamondsuit$

By convention, the process P^A denotes the abstract version of the process P via abstract interpretation $\{\!| \cdot |\!\}$. The abstract version is built by replacing the channel types for abstract versions (images of r_c) and all $com\_$ functions (that is, replacing inner operations, such as $+$, $^\frown$, $\leq$, etc.) for their abstract versions.

Definition 5 can be seen as a combination between Z data refinement and interface abstraction. Due to the interface abstraction, a renaming must be used to link this result with the theory of CSP process refinement. Therefore, a renaming R based on the abstract communication functions is defined.

Definition 6 (Interface Abstraction) *Let $r_c : M_c \to M_c^A$ be communication abstractions for all channels ($c \in Interface$). Then, the interface abstraction is given by $R = \bigcup_{c \in Interface} \{(m, m^A) : r_c \bullet (c.m, c.m^A)\}$* $\diamond$

The following lemma relates the original and abstract versions of a CSP$_Z$ process. It is a corrected extension[3] of a theorem proposed by Wehrheim [13,14].

Lemma 1 *Let P be a partially data independent CSP$_Z$ specification and P^A its abstract version defined by optimal abstract interpretation $\{\!| \cdot |\!\}$ with interface abstraction given by the renaming R. Then $P[\![R]\!] =_{\mathcal{FD}} P^A$.* $\diamond$

It is worth noting that, in general, Lemma 1 concern only renamed versions of the CSP$_Z$ original processes. Thus, only those properties preserved via renaming might be checked. Wehrheim [13,14] still tries to avoid this limitation via algebraic manipulation but the problem of infinity occurs again. This is exactly why we are primarily concerned with deadlock and livelock analysis.

Example 1 (An Ad Hoc Data Abstraction) *Consider the CSP$_Z$ process*
spec P
    chan $a, b : \mathbb{N}$
    $main = a?x \to b?y \to main$

    $State \mathrel{\widehat{=}} [c : \mathbb{N}]$
    $com\_a \mathrel{\widehat{=}} [\Delta State;\ x? : \mathbb{N} \mid c' = x?]$
    $com\_b \mathrel{\widehat{=}} [\Delta State;\ y? : \mathbb{N} \mid c * y? > 0 \wedge c' = y?]$

end_spec
Now, let $N^A = \{pos, nonPos\}$ be an abstract domain with abstraction maps

$$r_a = r_b = h = \{n : \mathbb{N} \mid n > 0 \bullet n \mapsto pos\} \cup \{n : \mathbb{N} \mid n \leq 0 \bullet n \mapsto nonPos\}$$

The renaming and abstract operator versions are defined as

$R =$
$\{(e^C, e^A) : r_a \bullet (a.e^C, a.e^A)\}$ $s_1 \tilde{*} s_2 = \begin{cases} pos, & s_1 = s_2 = pos \\ nonPos, & otherwise \end{cases}$
$\cup$
$\{(e^C, e^A) : r_a \bullet (b.e^C, b.e^A)\}$ $s_1 \tilde{>} s_2 = \begin{cases} true, & s_1 = pos \wedge s_2 = nonPos \\ false, & otherwise \end{cases}$

---

[3] Please refer to Mota [1] for the proof of Lemma 1

Then, applying r_a, r_b *to the channels,* h *to state variable* c *and constants, and using the abstract operators, we get*

spec P^A
    chan $a, b : N^A$
    $main = a?x \rightarrow b?y \rightarrow main$

    $State^A \cong [c : N^A]$
    $com\_a^A \cong [\Delta State^A; \ x? : N^A \mid c' = x?]$
    $com\_b^A \cong [\Delta State^A; \ y? : N^A \mid c \widetilde{*} y? \widetilde{>} nonPos \wedge c' = y?]$

end_spec   ◇

From Lemma 1 we have $P^A =_{\mathcal{FD}} P[\![R]\!]$. Note that the operator $\widetilde{>}$ is optimal due to the predicate $x > 0$ be more restrict than $x > y$. By using the latter, N^A would be refined to $\{pos, zero, neg\}$ to achieve optimality (See [25] for details).

5.1   Guidelines for CSP$_Z$ Data Abstraction

This section introduces the guidelines for CSP$_Z$ data abstraction. Recall from Section 2.2 that the normal form of a CSP$_Z$ specification has a very simple structure for the Z part. This structure is exactly what eases the search for a data abstraction as described in the following examples.

Initially we present an example taken from Wehrheim's work [13,14], where the data abstraction was proposed by the user. We demonstrate that following our informal strategy we are able to calculate such a data abstraction.

Example 2 *(Infinite Clock) Let* P_{Clock} *be an infinite CSP$_Z$ process given by*

spec P_{Clock}
    chan $tick, tack$
    $main = \square e : \{tick, tack\} \bullet e \rightarrow main$

    $State \cong [n : \mathbb{N}]$ $Init \cong [State' \mid n' = 0]$
    $com\_tick \cong [\Delta State \mid$ $com\_tack \cong [\Delta State \mid$
        $n \bmod 2 = 0 \wedge n' = n + 1]$ $n \bmod 2 = 1 \wedge n' = n + 1]$

end_spec

Set the abstraction data domain to be equal to the concrete one. Set abstraction function h *to be the identity map. Recall from Section 5 that the abstractions* r_{tick} *and* r_{tack} *are not defined since there is no communication. Therefore we already know that we do not need a renaming (interface abstraction). Our first step is very simple: expand (symbolically) the Z part[4] until the set of enabled preconditions in the current state has already occurred in an earlier state. This step yields the LTS of Figure 1. Note that the precondition pre* com_tick, $n \bmod 2 = 0$ *(n is even) is valid in* $n = 0$ *and* $n = 2$. *At this point we perform our second step: try to prove that this repetition is permanent. Let conj be a conjunction of preconditions and comp be a sequential composition as follows*

---

[4] This is relatively simple due to the normal form presented in Section 2.2.

$conj \mathrel{\widehat{=}} pre\, com\_tick \wedge \neg\ pre\, com\_tack$
$comp \mathrel{\widehat{=}} com\_tick \mathbin{\stackrel{\circ}{,}} com\_tack$

Fig. 1. LTS of the Z part of P_{Clock}

Then the general predicate to be proven is

$\forall\, State;\ State' \mid conj \bullet comp \Rightarrow conj'$

This predicate (we call it by stability predicate) can be proven by theorem provers like Z-Eves [19] or ACL2 [18], for example.

Our third step checks the proof status of the stability predicate. If it is valid then the abstraction function h is modified. Further, this validity assures an equivalence relation—under the conjunction of preconditions (the property)— between the states before and after the sequential composition of com_ opera-tions, including the operations inside the schema composition. That is, as long as com_tick $\stackrel{\circ}{,}$ com_tack is stable then the next possible schema operation must be com_tick, and after this the next must be com_tack, and so on. Thus, from the above predicate we build the equivalence relation

$E_{tick} = \{n : \mathbb{N} \mid n \bmod 2 = 0 \bullet n \mapsto n + 2\}^*$
$E_{tack} = \{n : \mathbb{N} \mid n \bmod 2 = 1 \bullet n \mapsto n + 2\}^*$

and, for each partition, we take one element to build the abstraction function. It is worth noting that $n \bmod 2 = 0$ is the essence (simplification) of the property $pre\, com\_tick \wedge \neg\ pre\, com\_tack$ as well as $n \bmod 2 = 1$ is the essence of $\neg\ pre\, com\_tick \wedge pre\, com\_tack$.

$$h(n) = \begin{cases} 0, & 0\ E_{tick}\ n \\ 1, & 1\ E_{tack}\ n \end{cases}$$

That is, the abstraction function is induced by the equivalence relation built. After that, we discard this execution path and try to explore another one, repeating the previous steps. Since our example does not have any other paths to explore, we start the final step which builds the abstract domains and abstract operators. For us, the abstract domain is $A = \{0, 1\}$ (the image of h), and the abstract version of the successor operator is the application of the abstraction ($\alpha = h$) and concretisation ($\gamma = i_A$) functions as follows

$$\{\!\mid \lambda\, x : \mathbb{N} \bullet x + 1 \mid\!\} = \alpha \circ (\lambda\, x : \mathbb{N} \bullet x + 1) \circ \gamma = \lambda\, x^A : A \bullet h(x^A + 1)$$

That is, the abstraction is built by replacing the concrete domains, applying the abstraction function h to the constants, and the concrete operators are abstracted

174 A. Mota, P. Borba, and A. Sampaio

by an application of the abstraction function to the result. It is worth noting that our strategy is done in such a way that we do not have to abstract the preconditions. The reason for this is that our abstract domains are always the subsets of the original types determined from the lattice of the preconditions (repetition of the set of preconditions enabled).

Note that this abstraction is optimal by construction. The absence of communication abstractions (renaming) yields an equivalence under Z data refinement and process refinement, that is, $P_{Clock} \equiv_{\mathcal{FD}} P_{Clock}^{A}$ (see Lemma 1). ◇

It is worth noting that the stability predicate originates from the lattice of the preconditions of the Z part: all preconditions disabled lead to deadlock whereas all preconditions enabled lead to full nondeterminism. This lattice is known as the lattice of properties in the terminology of abstract interpretation [22]. If, during the symbolic execution of the Z part, we achieve a point (trace) such that after it the set of preconditions (a given property in the lattice of preconditions) is always the same, the domain used until that point can be seen as a representative for the future values because they all have the same property.

Example 3 *(A Precise Loop) Let P be a CSP_Z process given as*
spec P
 chan a, b
 main $= a \rightarrow$ main$\Box b \rightarrow$ main

$State \mathrel{\widehat{=}} [c : \mathbb{N}]$	$Init \mathrel{\widehat{=}} [State' \mid c' = 0]$
$com\_a \mathrel{\widehat{=}} [\Delta State \mid$	$com\_b \mathrel{\widehat{=}} [\Delta State \mid$
$c \le 5 \wedge c' = c + 1]$	$c \ge 5 \wedge c' = c + 1]$

end_spec

Start by setting the abstract domain as $\mathbb{N}$ and h to be the identity. After that, we explore the LTS (of the Z part) in a lazy fashion, observing whether the set of valid preconditions repeats. To ease the explanation, observe Figure 2. This figure shows that we need 6 expansions, and respectively 5 stability predicates with status false, in order to get a stable path. Let conj be the property being repeated and comp the sequential composition where this is happening

$$conj \mathrel{\widehat{=}} pre\, com\_b \wedge \neg\, pre\, com\_a$$
$$comp \mathrel{\widehat{=}} com\_b$$

and the general predicate to be proven is

$$\forall State;\ State' \mid conj \bullet comp \Rightarrow conj'$$

From this predicate we achieve the following unique equivalence relation, since the sequential composition is built by only one schema operation.

$$E = \{c : \mathbb{N} \mid c > 5 \bullet c \mapsto c + 1\}^{*}$$

where $c > 5$ is the reduced form for $\neg\, pre\, com\_a \wedge pre\, com\_b$. The abstraction function is built in terms of the least elements of each partition. Then

$$h(c) = \begin{cases} 6, & 6 \; E \; c \\ c, & otherwise \end{cases}$$

which determines the abstraction $A = 0..6$ *and* $\{\!| \; n+1 \; |\!\} = \lambda \, n^A : A \bullet h(n^A + 1)$.
$\Diamond$

Fig. 2. LTS of the Z part of P

5.2 Algorithm

In this section we present the algorithm for CSP$_Z$ data abstraction. It is described in a functional style using pattern matching. The main part of the algorithm concentrates on the function findAbstraction. The other functions are defined modularly as well and called by findAbstraction (See [1] for further details).

From Examples 2 and 3, we can note that the current state, trace, and property must be known. Recall from Section 2 that we can represent all this information using channel names. That is, via channel names we can build a (symbolic) trace (a sequence of channel names), the current state (a sequential schema composition where the schemas are built by prefixing the keyword com_ in front of the channel names) and a property (as a set of channels). For example, suppose a CSP$_Z$ process with interface $\{a, b, c\}$ (without values for ease). Let $\langle a, b, b, c \rangle$ be a trace of this process. The corresponding state is given by

$Init \, \mathbin{_9^9} \, \mathsf{com\_}a \, \mathbin{_9^9} \, \mathsf{com\_}b \, \mathbin{_9^9} \, \mathsf{com\_}b \, \mathbin{_9^9} \, \mathsf{com\_}c$

and, finally, a property could be characterised by the set $\{a, b\}$, which means

$\mathsf{pre\,com\_}a \, \wedge \, \mathsf{pre\,com\_}b \, \wedge \, \neg \, \mathsf{pre\,com\_}c$

that is, if a channel does not belong to the property set, then we take the negation of the precondition of its corresponding com_ schema.

We introduce some short names, frequently used by the functions.

$PCh == \mathbb{P}\,ChanName$	$Label == ChanName$
$AcceptanceSet == PCh$	$Property == PCh$

As traces are sequences of events and the next alternatives as well as the current property can vary with the trace, we define the following structure.

$Path == \mathrm{seq}(AcceptanceSet \times Label \times Property)$

Our first function is findAbstraction; the kernel of our guided data abstraction.

The base case corresponds to the empty structure; that is, no further progress is possible, return the identity map, according to the data domains of the Z part (assume D as the type related to the schema $State$). This identity will be overridden recursively by the abstractions found.

When the $Path$ structure is not empty, the Z part is expanded, according to the elements in $accS_{curr}$. The first branch corresponds to $accS_{curr} = \varnothing$. If this is the case, then the current tuple of the $Path$ structure is discarded and a previous one takes place, recursively (findAbstraction t).

If the current acceptance set is not empty, the function findAbstraction tries a next transition, based on the event chosen to be engaged ($lt_{next} \in accS_{curr}$). A next transition can assume two differing forms:

1. t_{next}: an abstraction can be performed or the next acceptance set is empty;
2. $t_{further}$: no abstraction can be performed.

If $accS_{next} \neq \varnothing$ is verified, then we check if the property repeats[5]. If it repeats, then it calls checkStability. If an abstraction is possible, we calculate a new $Path$ structure—t_{new}—by calling newExploration. Otherwise, a further expansion occurs (findAbstraction $t_{further}$).

```
findAbstraction :: Path → (D → D^A)
findAbstraction ⟨⟩ = i_D
findAbstraction ⟨(accS_curr, lt_curr, prop_curr)⟩ ⌢ t=
  if accS_curr = ∅ then findAbstraction t
  else
    let
      lt_next ∈ accS_curr
      t_next = ⟨(accS_curr \ {lt_next}, lt_next, prop_curr)⟩ ⌢ t
      accS_next =validOpers t_next Interface
      t_further = ⟨(accS_next, τ, accS_next)⟩ ⌢ t_next
    •
      if accS_next ≠ ∅ then
        if ∃ s : ran t_next • π_3(s) = accS_next then  /* Property repeats */
          let
            user =checkStability t_next accS_next
            t_new =newExploration t_next accS_next
          •
            case user of
              optimal : findAbstraction t_new ⊕ optimalAbs t_next accS_next
              none    : findAbstraction t_further
        else findAbstraction t_further
      else findAbstraction t_next
```

Recall from Section 2 that the Z part constrains the CSP part through the preconditions. That is, for a channel c, if the precondition of com_c is valid, then c is ready to engage with the CSP part. Otherwise, c is refused in the Z

---

[5] Note that the predicate $\exists s;\ \mathrm{ran}\ t_{next} \bullet \pi_3(s) = accS_{next}$ uses the function π_3. The function π is simply a projection function, that is, $\pi_3(a, b, c) = c$.

part and consequently in the CSP part too, because they cannot synchronise. The function validOpers has this purpose. It takes a path and an acceptance set as input and returns the set of channels (subset of the interface) which has the precondition valid for the current state (built using buildComp).

```
validOpers :: Path → AcceptanceSet → AcceptanceSet
validOpers t ∅ = ∅
validOpers t accS_curr =
  let
    e ∈ accS_curr
  •
    (if ⟦(buildComp t ∅) ⟹ (pre com_e)′⟧^P = ⟦false⟧^P then ∅
    else {e}) ∪ (validOpers t accS_curr \ {e})
```

The term $\llbracket p \rrbracket^P$ means the semantic interpretation of the predicate p. Hence, generally, the clause $\llbracket (\text{buildComp } t\,\varnothing) \Rightarrow (\text{pre com\_}e)' \rrbracket^P$ needs some theorem proving support. But when all variables have an associated value, it is possible to get the same result by direct application of the current state to the preconditions. Recall from Section 2 that, for a given trace, we have a corresponding Z schema composition. For example, suppose that the trace $\langle a, b, c \rangle$ has occurred, then the state of the system is given by $\text{Init} \,\S\, \text{com\_}a \,\S\, \text{com\_}b \,\S\, \text{com\_}c$. The function buildComp, presented in what follows, has this purpose.

```
buildComp :: Path → Property → SchemaExpr
buildComp ⟨⟩ prop = Init
buildComp ⟨(accS_curr, e, prop_curr)⟩ ⌢ t prop =
  if prop = prop_curr then com_e else (buildComp t prop) ⨾ com_e
```

Recall from Section 5.1 that we define a property to be a conjunction of preconditions. The functions validGuards and invalidGuards, together, build properties.

The function newExploration searches for an unexplored trace. It takes a path structure and a property as input. Associated to the *Path* structure only, we have two possibilities: Either it is empty and we return an empty sequence, or it is not empty and the resulting *Path* structure depends on the given property. The first two branches deal with the current property being equal to the given property. That is, we have found the element of the *Path* structure which is keeping the information concerning the previous repeated property. Here, two cases are checked: either the current tuple must be discarded ($alts_{curr} = \langle \rangle$), or this tuple still has a possible alternative to be considered ($alts_{curr} \neq \langle \rangle$). The last point simply discards the current tuple and considers the rest recursively.

```
newExploration :: Path → Property → Path
newExploration ⟨⟩ prop = ⟨⟩
newExploration ⟨(accS_curr, e, prop_curr)⟩ ⌢ t prop =
  if prop = prop_curr ∧ accS_curr = ∅ then t
  else
    if prop = prop_curr ∧ accS_curr ≠ ∅ then ⟨(accS_curr, e, prop_curr)⟩ ⌢ t
    else newExploration t prop
```

The function checkStability deserves special attention. Its purpose is to transfer the undecidability problem, related to the check for stability, to the user, via application of theorem proving. In this sense, we are integrating model checking with theorem proving; a research direction stated by Pnueli [30]. This function returns a user decision. Obviously, a user for us means some external interaction: a human being, a theorem prover, etc. That is, we can have a predicate which can be proven fully automatic by a theorem prover without a human being intervention. Hence, our strategy can be fully automatic as long as the predicates considered belong to a class of a decidable logic [23,27,18,28,5].

Therefore, before presenting the function checkStability, we introduce the user response using a free-type definition. It can be *optimal*—the abstraction is a total surjective function—or *none*—we must further expand this path.

$$USER ::= optimal \quad – \text{The abstraction is optimal}$$
$$\mid none \quad\quad – \text{We cannot abstract this trace}$$

The function checkStability checks the validity of the predicate $\forall State;\ State' \mid conj \bullet comp \Rightarrow conj'$, where $conj$ captures the stable property (conjunction of valid and invalid preconditions) and $comp$ is a sequential schema composition.

```
checkStability :: Path → Property → USER
checkStability t prop =
   let
      conj = validGuards prop ∧ invalidGuards (Interface \ prop)
      comp = buildComp t prop
      stable = ∀ State; State' | conj • comp ⇒ conj'
   • if [stable]^P = [true]^P then optimal else none
```

The function validGuards yields the conjunction of the valid preconditions.

```
validGuards :: AcceptanceSet ↦ ZPred
validGuards ∅ = true
validGuards accS_curr =
   let e ∈ accS_curr • pre com_e ∧ (validGuards accS_curr \ {e})
```

Complementarily, the function invalidGuards generates the conjunction of the invalid preconditions; those with a negation ($\neg$) in front of each precondition.

```
invalidGuards :: AcceptanceSet ↦ ZPred
invalidGuards ∅ = true
invalidGuards accS_curr =
   let e ∈ accS_curr • ¬ pre com_e ∧ (invalidGuards accS_curr \ {e})
```

If the function checkStability results *optimal*, then we have to produce the expected data abstraction; that is, a (total and surjective) map between a small (finite) set and an infinite one. For instance, consider Example 2. In this example, the trace $\langle tick^0, tack^1, tick^2, tack^3, \ldots \rangle$ is abstracted by $\langle tick^0, tack^1 \rangle^k$ using

$$h(n) = \begin{cases} 0, 0\ E_{tick}\ n \\ 1, 1\ E_{tack}\ n \end{cases}$$

where

$$E_{tick} = \{n : \mathbb{N} \mid n \bmod 2 = 0 \bullet n \mapsto n + 2\}^*$$
$$E_{tack} = \{n : \mathbb{N} \mid n \bmod 2 = 1 \bullet n \mapsto n + 2\}^*$$

Prior to present the function which generates abstraction, we consider some auxiliary functions. First, buildTrace, identical to buildComp, except the response.

---

buildTrace :: $Path \rightarrow Property \rightarrow$ seq $ChanName$
buildTrace $\langle\rangle$ $prop$ = $\langle\rangle$
buildTrace $\langle(accS_{curr}, e, prop_{curr})\rangle \frown t$ $prop$ =
    if $prop = prop_{curr}$ then $\langle e \rangle$ else (buildTrace t $prop$) $\frown \langle e \rangle$

The function cShiftT makes a cyclic shift in a trace; it always shifts the elements to the left. For instance, the call cShiftT $\langle a, b, b, c \rangle$ returns $\langle b, c, a, b \rangle$.

---

cShiftT :: seq $ChanName \rightarrow \mathbb{N} \rightarrow$ seq $ChanName$
cShiftT s 0 = s
cShiftT $\langle e \rangle \frown s$ n = (cShiftT s $(n-1)$) $\frown \langle e \rangle$

Finally, we have buildSeqC; it returns a sequential schema composition from a trace. Or, buildSeqC$\langle a, b, b, c \rangle$ returns com_a $\overset{\circ}{9}$ com_b $\overset{\circ}{9}$ com_b $\overset{\circ}{9}$ com_c.

---

buildSeqC :: seq $ChanName \nrightarrow SchemaExpr$
buildSeqC $\langle e \rangle$ = com_e
buildSeqC $\langle e \rangle \frown s$ = com_e $\overset{\circ}{9}$ (buildSeqC s)

The function optimalAbs generates the abstraction; a mapping between one fixed value, according to the equivalence relations of the periodic property, and their infinite equivalents. Note that the least value refers to the first element of the stable trace. The rest is obtained by sequential composition, since the future sequential compositions repeat indefinitely. And, differently from the Examples 2 and 3, this function builds the abstraction using the Z notation.

---

optimalAbs :: $Path \rightarrow Property \rightarrow (D \rightarrow D^A)$
optimalAbs t $prop$ =
  let
    $stable =$ buildTrace t $prop$
    $1 \leq j \leq \#stable$
    $EqRel(j) = \{[\![\text{buildSeqC}(\text{cShiftT } stable \ (j-1))]\!]^\varepsilon\}$
    $abs_j \in EqRel(j)$
  $\bullet$
    $\bigcup_{i=1}^{\#stable}\{s : EqRel(i) \bullet s \mapsto abs_i\}$

It is worth noting that, unlike the Examples 2 and 3, optimalAbs builds the equivalence relations ($EqRel$) implicitly. The difference is that while in the examples we deal with values directly, in this definition we are working with bindings (association between names and values) provided by the Z language [20].

In what follows, we present the proof of correctness for our algorithm. But first, a previous result is given (See [1] for a detailed proof).

Lemma 2 *(Overhidden Preserved Abstraction) Let P be a CSP_Z process, t and t' be Path structures, and prop be a property of P. If the overhidden*

$$findAbstraction\ t \oplus optimalAbs\ t'\ prop$$

could be applied and terminates successfully then it yields optimal abstraction.◊

Now, the main result of this section can take place.

Theorem 1 *(Optimal Abstraction) Let P be a CSP_Z process. If the function findAbstraction, applied to the Z part of P, terminates then it yields optimal data abstraction.*

Proof. *The proof follows by induction on the size of the Path structure.*

- *Base case ($\langle\rangle$): trivial.*
- *Induction case ($\langle\langle(accS_{curr}, lt_{curr}, prop_{curr})\rangle\rangle \frown t$): by case analysis where $accS_{curr}$, lt_{next}, t_{next}, $t_{further}$, $accS_{next}$, and t_{new} are given as in the algorithm*
  1. *$accS_{curr} = \varnothing$: via induction hypothesis on findAbstraction t.*
  2. *$accS_{curr} \neq \varnothing \wedge accS_{next} \neq \varnothing$: it depends on the analysis of case 4.*
  3. *$accS_{curr} \neq \varnothing \wedge accS_{next} = \varnothing$: in this case, the call findAbstraction t_{next} occurs. As $t_{next} \neq \langle\rangle$, the induction case is considered again. The unique open situation is when the future calls belong to the present situation. Therefore, after m calls we get $accS_{curr} = \varnothing$ which yields optimal data abstraction by 1.*
  4. *$accS_{curr} \neq \varnothing \wedge accS_{next} \neq \varnothing \wedge \exists s : ran\ t_{next} \bullet \pi_3(s) = accS_{next}$: we have*

$$findAbstraction\ t_{new} \oplus optimalAbs\ t_{next}\ accS_{next}$$

  which, by hypothesis and Lemma 2, yields optimal data abstraction.
  5. *$accS_{curr} \neq \varnothing \wedge accS_{next} \neq \varnothing \wedge \neg\ \exists s : ran\ t_{next} \bullet \pi_3(s) = accS_{next}$: as long as the call findAbstraction $t_{further}$ terminates, by hypothesis, then optimal data abstraction is guaranteed by the previous situations.*   ◊

Currently, we have a Haskell prototype[6] for the algorithm. It was integrated to the theorem prover Z-Eves [19]. The function checkStability generates the predicates—to be proven by Z-Eves—and the user controls every step, guiding the approach. Indeed, Examples 2 and 3 were built using the prototype. The Z part is introduced via a functional characterisation of the *com_* operations [2, 3]. Further, when the postcondition of some *com_* operation is nondeterministic or is based on communication two approaches can used to compute the next state: one is based on testing [28] and another on theorem proving [16]. We have employed the testing approach on the WDT because it is less expensive and its nondeterminism is simple. The WDT was submitted to the prototype and we have confirmed our hypothesis stated in [2,3] which assumes that the WDT only needs two clock elements in its CLK given type: one for enabling the schema *com_noTimeOut* and another for *com_timeOut*. The WDT abstraction is optimal with interface abstraction (Please refer to [1] for further details).

---

[6] It is located at http://www.cin.ufpe.br/˜acm/stable.hs

Acknowledgements. We would like to thank Ana Cavalcanti, David Deharb, David Naumann, Jim Woodcock, and He Hifeng for comments on earlier drafts of this paper. We also thank Ranko Lazić and Heike Wehrheim for sending us drafts of their papers.

6   Conclusion

Our original goal was about model checking CSP$_Z$ [2,3]. This effort has presented another difficulty: how to model check infinite state systems since they emerge naturally in CSP$_Z$ specifications. The works of Lazić [26] and Wehrheim [13,14] has been adopted as a basis for this work due to their complementary contributions to our aim. However, both had some kind of limitation: Lazić's work allows only to check data independent refinements, whereas Wehrheim's work leaves the task of proposing abstract domains and operations (the most difficulty part of a data abstraction) to the user. In this sense, we believe that the results reported here contribute in the following way to the works: to our earlier work [2,3] by enabling model checking of infinite CSP$_Z$ processes; to Lazić's work by capturing data dependencies in the Z part of a CSP$_Z$ specification; and to Wehrheim's work by mechanising her non-guided data abstraction technique.

Another result was to find a flaw in some results of Wehrheim's work, based on Lazić's work (See [1] for further details). It is related to the CSP part of a CSP$_Z$ process; Wehrheim's work does not discriminate what CSP elements the CSP part can use. Thus, if equality tests are allowed the CSP part can have stronger dependencies than those of the Z part. This was fixed on Lemma 1 by considering the CSP part to be trivially data independent.

In the direction of mechanisation, our approach is similar to the works of Stahl [16] and Shankar [29]. The main difference is that while they use boolean abstraction (replace predicates and expressions for boolean variables), we use subtype abstraction (replace types for subtypes and abstract operations for operations closed under the subtypes); this choice is crucial to make our work free from user intervention and can yield optimal abstraction, but it offers some limitations if the state variables are strongly coupled; on the other hand, Stahl and Shankar work with weakly coupled variables due to the boolean abstraction strategy, however they need an initial user support and focus on safe abstractions. The normal form of a CSP$_Z$ specification [2,3] has also played an important role in this part of our work by allowing the Z part to be more easily analysed. Both their approach and ours need theorem proving support and follow the research direction of tool and theory integration [30]. Therefore, our work is also an inexperienced research in the direction of data abstraction mechanisation.

For future research we intend to investigate compositional results for optimal abstractions, analyse further properties beyond deadlock and livelock, classify processes according to the predicates they use, and incorporate the abstraction algorithm into our mechanised model checking strategy in order to handle infinite CSP$_Z$ processes with minimum user assistance.

References

1. A.Mota. *Model checking CSP_Z: Techniques to Overcome State Explosion.* PhD thesis, Universidade Federal de Pernambuco, 2002.
2. A.Mota and A.Sampaio. Model-Checking CSP-Z. In *Proceedings of the European Joint Conference on Theory and Practice of Software*, volume 1382 of *LNCS*, pages 205–220. Springer-Verlag, 1998.
3. A.Mota and A.Sampaio. Model-Checking CSP-Z: Strategy, Tool Support and Industrial Application. *Science of Computer Programming*, 40:59–96, 2001.
4. A.W.Roscoe. *The Theory and Practice of Concurrency.* Prentice Hall, 1998.
5. B.Boigelot, S.Rassart, and P.Wolper. On the Expressiveness of Real and Integer Arithmetic Automata (Extended Abstract). *LNCS*, 1443:01–52, 1999.
6. C.A.R.Hoare. *Communicating Sequential Processes.* Prentice-Hall, 1985.
7. C.Fischer. Combining CSP and Z. Technical report, Univ. Oldenburg, 1996.
8. C.Fischer. *Combination and Implementation of Processes and Data: from CSP-OZ to Java.* PhD thesis, Fachbereich Informatik Universität Oldenburg, 2000.
9. C.Loiseaux, S.Graf, J.Sifakis, A.Bouajjani, and S.Bensalem. Property Preserving Abstractions for the Verification of Concurrent Systems. In *Formal Methods in System Design*, volume 6, pages 11–44. Kluwer Academic Publishers, Boston, 1995.
10. E.M.Clarke, O.Grumberg, and D.A.Peled. *Model Checking.* The MIT Press, 1999.
11. J.A.C.F.Neri et al. SACI-1: A cost-effective microssatellite bus for multiple mission payloads. Technical report, Instituto Nacional de Pesquisas Espaciais - INPE, 1995.
12. M.Goldsmith et al. *FDR: User Manual and Tutorial, version 2.77.* Formal Systems (Europe) Ltd, August 2001.
13. H.Wehrheim. Data Abstraction for CSP-OZ. In J.Woodcock and J.Wing, editors, *FM'99 World Congress on Formal Methods.* LNCS 1709, Springer, 1999.
14. H.Wehrheim. Data Abstraction Techniques in the Validation of CSP-OZ Sp. In *Formal Aspects of Computing*, volume 12, pages 147–164, 2000.
15. K.Laster and O.Grumberg. Modular model checking of software. In *Tools and Algorithms for the Construction and Analysis of Systems*, number 1382 in LNCS, pages 20–35, 1998.
16. K.Stahl, K.Baukus, Y.Lakhneich, and M.Steffen. Divide, Abstract, and Model Check. *SPIN*, pages 57–76, 1999.
17. M.Huhn, P.Niebert, and F.Wallner. Verification based on local states. In *Tools and Algorithms for the Construction and Analysis of Systems*, number 1382 in LNCS, pages 36–51, 1998.
18. M.Kaufmann and J.Moore. An Industrial Strength Theorem Prover for a Logic Based on Common Lisp. *IEEE Trans. on Software Engineering*, 23(4):203–213, 1997.
19. M.Saaltink. The Z-Eves System. In *ZUM'97: The Z Formal Specification Notation.* LNCS 1212, Springer, 1997.
20. M.Spivey. *The Z Notation: A Reference Manual.* Prentice-Hall International, 2nd edition, 1992.
21. P.Cousot and R.Cousot. Systematic design of program analysis frameworks. In *Conference Record of the 6th ACM Symp. on Principles of Programming Languages (POPL'79)*, pages 269–282. ACM Press, New York, 1979.
22. P.Cousot and R.Cousot. Abstract interpretation frameworks. *J. Logic. and Comp.*, 2(4):511–547, 1992.
23. P.Wolper. Expressing interesting properties of programs in propositional temporal logic (extended abstract). In *Proc. 13th ACM Symposium on Principles of Programming Languages*, pages 184–193, 1986.

24. R.Cleaveland and J.Riely. Testing-based abstractions for value-passing systems. In J. Parrow B. Jonsson, editor, *CONCUR'94*, volume 836, pages 417–432. Springer-Verlag Berlin, 1994.

25. R.Giacobazzi and F.Ranzato. Making abstract interpretations complete. *Journal of the ACM*, 47(2):361–416, 2000.

26. R.Lazić. *A semantic study of data-independence with applications to the mechanical verification of concurrent systems.* PhD thesis, Oxford University, 1999.

27. S.A.Cook and D.G.Mitchell. Satisfiability Problem: Theory and Applications. In *Discrete Mathematics and Theoretical Computer Science*. AMS, 1997.

28. S.Liu. Verifying Consistency and Validity of Formal Specifications by Testing. In *FM'99 - Formal Methods*, pages 896–914. LNCS 1708, 1999.

29. S.Owre, S.Rajan, J.M.Rushby, N.Shankar, and M.K.Srivas. PVS: Combining Specification, Proof Checking, and Model Checking. In Rajeev Alur and Thomas A. Henzinger, editors, *Computer-Aided Verification, CAV'96*, volume 1102 of *LNCS*, pages 411–414, New Brunswick, NJ, July/August 1996. Springer-Verlag.

30. Y.Kesten, A.Klein, A.Pnueli, and G.Raanan. A Perfecto Verification: Combining Model Checking with Deductive Analysis to Verify Real-Life Software. In J.M.Wing, J.Woodcock and J.Davies, editor, *FM'99-Formal Methods*, volume 1 of *LNCS 1708*, pages 173–194. Springer-Verlag, 1999.

Verifying Erlang Code: A Resource Locker Case-Study

Thomas Arts[1], Clara Benac Earle[2], and John Derrick[2]

[1] Ericsson, Computer Science Laboratory
Box 1505, 125 25 Älvsjö, Sweden
thomas@cslab.ericsson.se
[2] University of Kent, Canterbury
Kent CT2 7NF, United Kingdom
{cb47,jd1}@ukc.ac.uk

Abstract. In this paper we describe an industrial case-study on the development of formally verified code for Ericsson's AXD 301 switch. For the formal verification of Erlang software we have developed a tool to apply model checking to communicating Erlang processes. We make effective use of Erlang's design principles for large software systems to obtain relatively small models of specific Erlang programs. By assuming a correct implementation of the software components and embedding their semantics into our model, we can concentrate on the specific functionality of the components. We constructed a tool to automatically translate the Erlang code to a process algebra with data. Existing tools were used to generate the full state space and to formally verify properties stated in the modal μ-calculus.

As long as the specific functionality of the component has a finite state vector, we can generate a finite state space, even if the state space of the real Erlang system is infinite. In this paper we illustrate this by presenting a case-study based on a piece of software in Ericsson's AXD 301 switch, which implements a distributed resource locker algorithm. Some of the key properties we proved are mutual exclusion and non-starvation for the program.

Keywords: Model checking, formal verification, telecommunication, Erlang, process algebra

1 Introduction

Ericsson's AXD 301 is a high capacity ATM switch [5], used, for example, to implement the backbone network in the UK. The control software for this switch is written in the functional language Erlang [1]. The software consists of over five hundred thousands lines of Erlang code and complete formal verification of such large projects is too ambitious at the moment. However, for some critical parts of the software, it is worth spending some effort to increase trust in the chosen implementation.

L.-H. Eriksson and P. Lindsay (Eds.): FME 2002, LNCS 2391, pp. 184–203, 2002.
© Springer-Verlag Berlin Heidelberg 2002

In Ericsson the software in such large projects is written according to rather strict design principles. For example in the AXD software, a few software components have been specified in the beginning of the project. These components can be seen as higher-order functions for which certain functions have to be given to determine the specific functionality of the component. About eighty percent of the software implements code for this specific functionality of one of these components, the majority of this for the *generic server* component. The generic server is a component that implements a process with a simple state parameter and mechanism to handle messages in a *fifo* message queue. The generic part of the component has been extensively tested and carefully thought through. In other words, if an error occurs in one of the several thousands of server processes, it is assumed to be an error in the specific functionality of that server causing the error.

To help increase trust in the particular implementation, we constructed a tool to translate server processes and their clients into a process algebraic model, such that we can generate all possible communication patterns that occur in the software. The model incorporates data as well, since messages sent between server and clients contain data that influences the behaviour of the protocol. The process architecture of a system is in general not derivable from the Erlang code; information about which process is communicating with a certain process is in principle only visible at runtime. However, the software component to ensure fault tolerance of the system, the so called *supervisor* contains static information about the relation between processes. Again, this component consists of a generic part and a few functions implementing the specific behaviour. By using the code of the specific functions of the supervisor processes, we are able to configure the process algebra models with a fixed (but flexible per translation) number of processes.

The case-study we had at hand implemented an algorithm for resource management. A server process, the so called *locker*, provides access to an arbitrary number of resources, for an arbitrary number of client processes. The clients may either ask for *shared* or *exclusive* access to the resources.

We used our tool, together with two external tools, on the key portions of the locker module as it appears in the AXD 301 switch. The external tools were used to generate the state space, reduce the state space with respect to bisimulation relations and to model check several properties. We successfully verified mutal exclusion and non-starvation for exclusive locks, priority of exclusive locks over shared locks and non-starvation of shared locks in the absence of exclusive requests. Proving the safety properties was rather straightforward, but the non-starvation is normally expressed by a formula with alternating fix points. Therefore, we used hiding and bisimulation to remove irrelevant cycles from the state space, and this allowed a simplified property to be checked.

The paper is organised as follows: we start with a brief explanation of the AXD 301 switch in Sect. 2. Thereafter we explain the software components we focussed on, viz. the *generic server* and *supervisors* in Sect. 3. The actual Erlang code, given in Sect. 4, is built using those components and along with the code we describe the implemented algorithm. The key points of the translation of Erlang into a process algebra model are presented in Sect. 5. This model is used to generate the labeled transition system in which the labels correspond to communication events between Erlang processes. In Sect. 6 we summarize which properties have been proved for the code using model checking in combination with bisimulation reduction. We conclude with some remarks on performance and feasability, and a comparison to other approaches (Sect. 7).

2   Ericsson's AXD 301 Switch

Ericsson's AXD 301 is a high capacity ATM switch, scalable from 10 to 160 GBits/sec [5]. The switch is, for example, used in the core network to connect city telephone exchanges with each other.

From a hardware point of view, the switch consists of a switch core, which is connected on one side to several device processors (that in their turn are connected to devices), and on the other side to an even number of processing units (workstations). The actual number of these processing units depends on the configuration and demanded capacity and ranges from 2 till 32 (see Fig. 1).

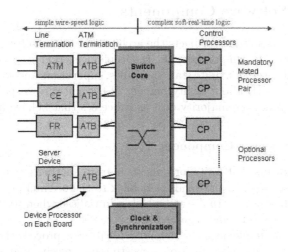

Fig. 1. AXD 301 hardware architecture

The workstations operate in pairs for reasons of fault tolerance; one workstation is assigned to be the *call control (cc)* node and the other the *operation and maintenance (o&m)* node. Simply put, call control deals with establishing connections, and operation and maintenance deals with configuration management, billing and such. Both the *cc* and *o&m* software consists of several applications, which on their turn implement many concurrently operating processes.

Every workstation runs one Erlang node, i.e., a program to execute Erlang byte code implementing several thousands of concurrent Erlang processes. The critical data of these processes is replicated and present on at least two nodes in the system. In case a workstation breaks down, a new Erlang node is started on the pairing workstation and depending on the functionality of the broken node, either the *cc* or the *o&m* applications are started.

The distributed resource locker is necessary when the broken workstation is restarted (or replaced) and available again for operation. A new Erlang node is started at the workstation, and the pairing workstation can leave one of its tasks to the restarted workstation. Typically *o&m* will be moved, since that is easiest to move. Although easiest, this is not without consequences. Every *o&m* application may access several critical resources and while doing so, it might be hazardous to move the application. For that reason the designers of the switch have introduced a classical resource manager, here called a *locker*. Whenever any of the processes in any application needs to perform an operation during which that application cannot be moved, it will request a lock on the application. The lock can be shared by many processes, since they all indicate that the application is to remain at its node. The process that wants to move an application will also request a lock on that application, but an exclusive one. Using this lock, a process is guaranteed to know when it can safely move an application.

3 Erlang Software Components

In Ericsson's large software projects the architecture of the software is described by means of software components, i.e., the implementation is specified by means of communicating servers, finite state machines, supervisors and so. In the control software for the AXD about eighty percent of the software is specified in terms of such components, the majority of it as processes that behave like servers.

3.1 Generic Server Component

A server is a process that waits for a message from another process, computes a certain response message and sends that back to the original process. Normally the server will have an internal state, which is initialised when starting the server and updated whenever a message has been received.

In Erlang one implements a server by creating a process that evaluates a (non-terminating) recursive function consisting of a receive statement in which every incoming message has a response as result.

```
serverloop(State) ->
   receive
     {call,Pid,Message} ->
        Pid ! compute_answer(Message,State),
        serverloop(compute_new_state(Message,State))
   end.
```

Erlang has an asynchronous communication mechanism where any process can send (using the ! operator) a message to any other process of which it happens to know the *process identifier* (the variable `Pid` in the example above). Sending is always possible and non-blocking; the message arrives in the unbounded mailbox of the specified process. The latter process can inspect its mailbox by the `receive` statement. A sequence of patterns can be specified to read specific messages from the mailbox. In the example above the first message in the mailbox which has the form of a tuple is read, where the first argument of the tuple should be the atom `call`, the variable `Pid` is then bound to the second argument of this tuple, and `Message` is bound to its last argument.

Of course, this simple server concept gets decorated with a lot of features in a real implementation. There is a mechanism to delay the response to a message, and some messages simply never expect a reply. Certain special messages for stopping the server, logging events, changing code in a running system and so on, are added as patterns in the receive loop. Debugging information is provided, used during development and testing. All together this makes a server a rather large piece of software and since all these servers have the same structure, it is a big advantage to provide a *generic server* implementation. This generic server has all features of the server, apart from the specific computation of reply message and new state. Put simply, by providing the above functions `compute_answer` and `compute_new_state` a fully functional server is specified with all necessary features for production code.

Reality is a bit more complicated, but not much: when starting a server one provides the name of a module in which the functions for initialisation and call handling are specified. One could see this as the generic server being a higher-order function which takes these specific functions, called *callback functions*, as arguments. The interface of these functions is determined by the generic server implementation. The initialisation function returns the initial state. The function `handle_call` is called with an incoming message, the client process identifier, and state of the server. It returns a tuple either of the form {`reply`,`Message`,`State`}, where the server takes care that this message is replied to the client and that the state is updated, or {`noreply`,`State`} where only a state update takes place. The locker algorithm that we present in this paper is implemented as a callback module of the generic server, thus the locker module implements the above mentioned functions for initialisation and call handling.

Client processes use a uniform way of communicating with the server, enforced by embedding the communication in a function call, viz. `gen_server:call`. This call causes the client to suspend as long as the server has not replied to the message. The generic server adds a unique tag to the message to ensure that clients stay suspended even if other processes send messages to their mailbox.

3.2   Supervisor Component

The assumption made when implementing the switch software is that any Erlang process may unexpectedly die, either because of a hardware failure, or a software error in the code evaluated in the process. The runtime system provides a mechanism to notify selected processes of the fact that a certain other process has vanished; this is realized by a special message that arrives in the mailbox of processes that are specified to monitor the vanished process.

On top of the Erlang primitives to ensure that processes are aware of the existence of other processes, a supervisor process is implemented. This process evaluates a function that creates processes which it will monitor, which we refer to as its children. After creating these processes, it enters a receive loop and waits for a process to die. If that happens, it might either restart the child or use another predefined strategy to recover from the problem.

All the processes in the AXD 301 software are children in a big tree of supervisor processes. Thus, the locker and the clients of the locker also exist somewhere in this tree. In our case-study we implemented a small supervisor tree for only the locker and a number of clients (Fig. 2).

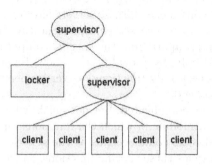

Fig. 2. Supervisor tree for locker and clients

The root of the tree has two children: the locker and another supervisor, which has as children all the client processes. As in the real software, the whole locker application is started by evaluating one expression, which starts building the supervisor tree and makes all processes run.

It is important to realize that we use this supervision tree to start the locker in different configurations. As an argument of the start function for the supervisor we provide the set of resources that the specific clients want to access. The expression `locker_sup:start([{[a],shared},{[a,b],exclusive}])`, for example, would start a supervisor tree with a locker and two clients, one client repeatedly requesting shared access to resource a, the other repeatedly requesting exclusive access to the resources a and b.

4   The Resource Locker Algorithm

In the previous section we described how the locker and client processes are placed in a supervision tree. We also mentioned that the locker is implemented as a callback module for the generic server. In this section we present the actual implementation of the client and locker and we explain the underlying algorithm.

We present a significant part of the actual Erlang code in order to stress that we verify Erlang code and to illustrate the complexity of the kind of code we can deal with. The full case-study contains about 250 lines of code in which many advanced features of Erlang are used[1].

4.1   Code of the Client

The client process is implemented in a simple module, since we have abstracted from all evaluations in clients that do not directly relate to entering and leaving the critical section. The generic server *call* mechanism is used to communicate with the locker.

```
-module(client).

start(Locker,Resources,Type) ->
    {ok,spawn_link(client,loop,[Locker,Resources,Type])}.

loop(Locker,Resources,Type) ->
    gen_server:call(Locker,{request,Resources,Type}),
    gen_server:call(Locker,release),
    loop(Locker,Resources,Type).
```

Between the two synchronous calls for request and release is the so called critical section. In the real implementation some critical code is placed in this critical section, but we have (manually) abstracted from that. The variable Type is either instantiated with shared or exclusive and Resources is bound to a list of resources that the client wants access to.

4.2   Code of the Locker

The code of the locker algorithm is given as a generic server callback module. The state of this server contains a record of type lock for every resource that the locker controls.

```
-module(locker).
-behaviour(gen_server).

-record(lock,{resource,exclusive,shared,pending}).
```

The lock record has four fields: resource for putting the identifier of the resource, exclusive containing the process that is having exclusive access to the resource (or none otherwise), shared containing a list of all processes that are having shared access to the resource, and pending containing a list of pending processes, either waiting for shared or for exclusive access.

---

[1] The code is available at http://www.cs.ukc.ac.uk/people/rpg/cb47/

The supervisor process constructs a list of all resources involved from the starting configuration and passes it to the initialisation of the locker. The locker initialisation function then initialises a `lock` record for every resource in that list. The state of the server is built by taking this list and constructing a tuple together with the lists for all exclusive requests and all shared requests that have not been handled so far.

```
init(Resources) ->
  {ok,{map(fun(Name) ->
              #lock{resource = Name,
                    exclusive = none, shared = [], pending = []}
            end,Resources),[],[]}}.
```

The latter two (initially empty) lists in the state of the server are used by the algorithm to optimize the computations performed when deciding which pending client is the next one that gets access. The first client in the pending list of the `lock` record is not necessarily granted permission to obtain the resource. It may be the case that the same client also waits for another resource, for which another client has higher priority. The priority could be reconstructed by building a graph of dependencies between the clients, but it is much easier to store the order in which the requests arrive.

Whenever a client requests a resource, the function `handle_call` in the locker module is called. This function first checks whether all requested resources are available. If so, it claims the resources by updating the `lock` records. The client receives an acknowledgement and the state of the server is updated accordingly. If the resources are not available, the `lock` records are updated by putting the client in the pending lists of the requested resources. The priority lists are changed, resulting in a new state for the server. No message is sent to the client, which causes the client to be suspended.

```
handle_call({request,Resources,Type},Client,{Locks,Excls,Shared}) ->
  case check_availables(Resources,Type,Locks) of
      true ->
        NewLocks =
          map(fun(Lock) ->
                  claim_lock(Lock,Resources,Type,Client)
              end,Locks),
        {reply, ok, {NewLocks,Excls,Shared}};
      false ->
        NewLocks =
          map(fun(Lock) ->
                  add_pending(Lock,Resources,Type,Client)
              end,Locks),
        case Type of
            exclusive ->
              {noreply, {NewLocks,Excls ++ [Client],Shared}};
            shared ->
```

```
                    {noreply, {NewLocks,Excls,Shared ++ [Client]}}
            end
   end;
```

A client can release all its obtained resources by a simple **release** message, since the identity of the client is sufficient to find out which resources it requested. After removing the client from the fields in the **lock** record, it is checked whether pending processes now have the possibility to access the requested resources. This happens with higher priority for the clients that request exclusive access, than for the clients that request shared access. The algorithm prescribes that clients that requested shared access to a resource but are waiting for access, should be by-passed by a client that requests exclusive access.

```
handle_call(release, Client, {Locks,Exclusives,Shared}) ->
  Locks1 =
    map(fun(Lock) ->
             release_lock(Lock,Client)
          end,Locks),
  {Locks2,NewExclusives} =
    send_reply(exclusive,Locks1,Exclusives,[]),
  {Locks3,NewShared} =
    send_reply(shared,Locks2,Shared,[]),
  {reply,done, {Locks3,NewExclusives,NewShared}}.
```

The function **send_reply** checks for a list of pending clients (either requesting exclusive or shared access) whether they can be granted access. If so, the client receives the acknowledgement that it was waiting for, and the state of the server is updated.

```
send_reply(Type,Locks,[],NewPendings) ->
  {Locks,NewPendings};
send_reply(Type,Locks,[Pending|Pendings],NewPendings) ->
  case all_obtainable(Locks,Type,Pending) of
       true ->
          gen_server:reply(Pending,ok),
          send_reply(Type,
                         map(fun(Lock) ->
                                 promote_pending(Lock,Type,Pending)
                              end,Locks),Pendings,NewPendings);
       false ->
          send_reply(Type,Locks,Pendings,NewPendings ++ [Pending])
  end.
```

The above mentioned Erlang functions in the locker combine message passing and computation. The rest of the function is purely computational and rather straight forward to implement. Here we only show the more interesting aspects.

The function **check_availables** is used to determine whether a new requesting client can immediately be helped. A resource is available for exclusive access if no client holds the resource and no other client is waiting for exclusive access to it. Note that it is not sufficient to only check whether no client accesses the resource at the time, since this could cause a starvation situation. Imagine two resources and three clients, such that client 1 requests resource A, client 2 requests resource B, and thereafter client 3 requests both resources. Client 1 releases and requests resource A again, client 2 releases and requests B again. If this repeatedly continues, client 3 will wait for ever to get access, i.e., client 3 will starve.

	A	B			A	B
access	1			access	1	2
pending				pending	3	3
access	1	2		access	1	
pending				pending	3	3
access	1	2		access	1	2
pending	3	3		pending	3	3
					⋮	
access		2				
pending	3	3				

This scenario indicates that in general one has to pay a price for optimal resource usage: viz. a possible starvation. Therefore, in the implementation it is checked whether a client is waiting for a certain resource. Similar to the exclusive case, for shared access the resource is available if no process holds the resource exclusively, neither is a client waiting for access to it.

The function add_pending simply inserts the client in the pending lists of the resources it is requesting. An optimisation is applied when inserting clients in the pending list: clients requesting exclusive access are mentioned before the ones requesting shared access. This allows a quick check to see if there is a client exclusively waiting for a resource, such a client should then be at the head of the pending list.

The difference between the functions check_available and all_obtainable is that in the latter the clients have already been added to the pending lists of the requested resources and therefore it should be checked that they are at the head of these lists instead of checking that these lists are empty. Moreover, there might be several clients able to get access to their resources after only one release, e.g. resources that were taken exclusively can be shared by several clients and a client that occupied several resources can free those resources for a number of different clients.

5   Translating Erlang into Process Algebra

In order to check that certain properties hold for all possible runs of the program, we automatically translate the Erlang modules into a process algebraic specification. The translation approach means that we do not have to make an efficient state space generation tool ourselves, it also allows us to distinghuish in a formal way communication actions and computation, and allows us to use tools developed for analyzing process algebra's.

The process algebra we used to translate to is μCRL [15], where we in particular used the fact that we can express data in this algebra. Several tools have been developed to support verification of μCRL specifications [9,24]. We mainly used the state space generation tool and experimented with static analysis tools to obtain specifications that resulted in smaller state spaces after generation.

We have experimented with translating the synchronous communication imposed by the *call* primitive of the generic server component directly in a synchronizing pair of actions in μCRL. This results in comfortably small state spaces, much smaller than when we implement a buffer for a server and use both synchronization between client and buffer of the server and synchronization between buffer and server. The latter is, however, necessary if we use the more extended functionality of the generic server, where we also have an asynchronous way of calling the server.

The buffer associated with each process is parameterized by its size and by default unbounded; during the verification process the buffer is bound to a certain size to allow the verifier to experiment with the size. The latter is important, since some errors cause a buffer overflow, which induces a non-terminating generation of the state space. However, if the message queue is bound to a low enough value, the buffer overflow is visible as an action in the state space. We use the knowledge about the generic server component to implement a restricted buffer in μCRL: the generic server uses a *fifo* buffer structure. This is in contrast with a classic Erlang buffer where an arbitrary Erlang process can read messages from the buffer in any order.

Moreover, we add several assertions that, if not fullfilled, cause the Erlang program to crash. These assertions mainly originate from pattern matching in Erlang, which is not as easily expressed in μCRL. As soon as the action `assertion(false)` occurs in the state space, the corresponding Erlang process would have crashed and we obtain for free a path from the initial state to the location where this happens. We provided the possibility to add user defined actions. By annotating the code with dummy function calls, we may add extra actions to the model to allow us to explicitly visualize a certain event. This feature was used, for example, when proving mutual exclusion, as is described in the next section.

Erlang supports higher-order functions, but μCRL does not. Luckily, in practice only a few higher-order alternatives are used, like `map`, `foldl`, `foldr`, *etc.* For the purpose of this locker version we wrote a source to source translation on the Erlang level to replace function occurrences like

```
map(fun(X) -> f(X,Y1,...,Yn) end, Xs)
```

by a call to a new function `map_f(Xs,Y1,...,Yn)` which is defined and added to the code as

```
map_f([],Y1,...,Yn)       -> [];
map_f([X|Xs],Y1,...,Yn) -> [f(X,Y1,...,Yn)| map_f(Xs,Y1,...,Yn)].
```

By using this transformation we automatically get rid of all map functions in the Erlang code.

With some minor tricks the side-effect free part of the Erlang code is rather easily translated into a term rewriting system on data, as necessary in a μCRL model. With respect to the part with side-effects, we are faced with two problems:

1. in μCRL we have to specify exactly which processes start and with which arguments they are started,
2. in μCRL a process is described with all side effects as actions on the top level. Thus, a function with side-effect cannot return a result.

The first problem is tackled by using the supervision tree that describes the Erlang processes that should be started. Using this structure, a translation to μCRL's initial processes is performed automatically. The second problem is solved by analyzing the call graph of functions that contain side-effects, i.e., functions that call the server or handle this call. We implement a stack process comparable to a call-stack when writing a compiler. Given the call graph, we can replace the nested functions with side-effect by functions that send as their last action a message to the stack process to push a value, since returning it is not possible. The stack process implements a simple stack with push and pop operations. A *pop* message is sent to the stack process directly after the point where the nested function has been called. This solution works fine, but, clearly, increases the state space.

With our translation tool for Erlang we can automatically generate μCRL models for Erlang programs like the one presented in Sect. 4. We build such models for a certain configuration in the same way as we start the code in a certain configuration. In Sect. 3.2 we explained how to start the locker process, for example, by evaluating `locker_sup:start([{[a],shared},{[a,b],exclusive}])`. Evaluating the same expression in our tool instead of in the Erlang runtime system, results in a μCRL model[2] for this configuration.

By using the state space generation tool for μCRL, we obtain the full state space, in the form of a labeled transition system (LTS), for the possible runs of the Erlang program. The labels in this state space are syntactically equal to function calls in Erlang that accomplish communication, e.g. `gen_server:call` and `handle_call`. This makes debugging the Erlang program easy when a sequence in the state space is presented as counter example to a certain property.

Once we have obtained the state space, the CÆSAR/ALDÉBARAN toolset [14] is used for verifying properties, as is described in the next section.

---

[2] For completeness one of these automatically generated μCRL models is available at `http://www.cs.ukc.ac.uk/people/rpg/cb47/`

6   Checking Properties with a Model Checker

The verification of safety and liveness properties are crucial in this application and were the key requirements that the AXD 301 development team were interested in. Safety properties include mutual exclusion for exclusive locks and priority of exclusive locks over shared locks. These and other properties have succesfully been verified and here we explain in detail how mutual exclusion (Sect. 6.1) and non-starvation (Sect. 6.2) are proved. The liveness property, non-starvation, is the more difficult of the two.

In order to verify the properties we have used the CÆSAR/ALDÉBARAN toolset which provides a number of tools including an interactive graphical simulator, a tool for visualization of labeled transition systems (LTSs), several tools for computing bisimulations (minimizations and comparisons), and a model checker [14]. Many aspects of the toolset were found useful for exploring the behaviour of the algorithm, but here we concentrate on the model checker.

Model checking (e.g. [7]) is a formal verification technique where a property is checked over a finite state concurrent system. The major advantages of model checking are that it is an automatic technique, and that when the model of the system fails to satisfy a desired propery, the model checker always produces a counter example. These faulty traces provide a priceless insight to understanding the real reason for the failure as well as important clues for fixing the problem.

The logic used to formalize properties is the regular alternation-free μ-calculus which is a fragment of the modal μ-calculus [20,11], a first-order logic with modalities and least and greatest fixed point operators. Logics like *CTL* or *ACTL* allow a direct encoding in the alternation free μ-calculus.

6.1   Mutual Exclusion

To prove mutual exclusion we formulate a property expressing that when a client gets exclusive access to a resource, then no other client can access it before this client releases the resource. In order to simplify checking this we add two actions, use and free, to the Erlang code which are automatically translated into the μCRL specification[3]. As soon as a client process enters its critical section, the use action is applied with the list of resources the client is requesting as an argument.

Before the client sends a release message to the locker process, it performs a free action. In the logic we specify the action in plain text or with regular expressions. However, the formalism does not permit binding a regular expression in one action and using it in another. Therefore, we have to specify mutual exclusion for every resource in our system. We defined a macro to help us improve readability:

$$BETWEEN(\mathsf{a_1},\ \mathsf{a_2},\ \mathsf{a_3}) = [\text{-}^* . \mathsf{a_1} . (\neg \mathsf{a_2})^* . \mathsf{a_3}]\mathit{false}$$

---

[3] The tools allow renaming of labels in the LTS, which could have been used as well.

stating that 'on all possible paths, after an (a_1) action, any (a_3) action must be preceded by an (a_2) action'.

The mutual exclusion property depends on the number of resources. For a system with two resources, A and B, the mutual exclusion property is formalized by

$MUTEX$(A, B) =
$BETWEEN('use(.*A.*, exclusive)', 'free(.*A.*)', 'use(.*A.*,.*)')$ ∧
$BETWEEN('use(.*B.*, exclusive)', 'free(.*B.*)', 'use(.*B.*,.*)')$

Informally the property states that when a client obtains exclusive access to resource A no other client can access it until the first client frees the resource, and the same for resource B.

The mutual exclusion property has been successfully checked for various configurations up to three resources and five clients requesting exclusive or shared access to the resources.

For example, a scenario with five clients requesting exclusive access to three resources where client 1 requests A, client 2 requests B, client 3 requests A, B and C, client 4 requests A and B, and client 5 requests C, contains about 30 thousand states. Building an LTS for this example takes roughly thirteen minutes, while checking the mutual exclusion property takes only nine seconds. A bigger state space of one million states needs one hour to be built and four minutes to be checked for mutual exclusion. Part of the reason that building the LTS takes much more time than checking a property is that we deal with data and that a lot of computation is done inbetween two visible actions (only visible actions correspond to states in the LTS).

As stated in the previous section, model checking is a powerful debugging tool. Imagine that the code of the locker contains the following error: the function check_available is wrongly implemented such that when a client requests a resource there is no check that the resource is being used by another client. Now consider a scenario with two clients, client 1 and client 2, requesting the same resource A. Given the LTS for this scenario and the property $MUTEX$(A), the model checker returns **false** and the counter example as shown in Fig. 3.

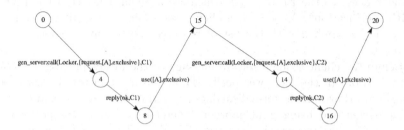

Fig. 3. mutex counterexample

The counter example generated depicts an execution trace of client 1 requesting and obtaining resource A and client 2 requesting and obtaining resource A, that is, both processes enter the critical section and, therefore, mutual exclusion is not preserved. The numbers that appear inside the circles correspond to the numbers of the states as they appear in the complete LTS. By keeping the Erlang code and our μCRL specification as close as possible, this trace helps us easily identify the run in the Erlang program.

Although we only use a small number of clients and resources, this already illustrates the substantive behaviour. Like with testing software, we choose our configurations in such a way that we cover many unique situations, however, in contrast to testing, we explore all possible runs of a certain configuration. Faults that occur when ten clients request sets out of eight resources are most likely found as well in configurations with five clients and four resources.

6.2   Non-starvation

Starvation is the situation where a client that has requested access to resources never receives permission from the locker to access them. Because exclusive access has priority over shared access, the algorithm contains potential starvation for clients requesting shared access to resources that are also exclusively requested. More precisely, the clients requesting exclusive access have priority over all clients that are waiting for shared access, therefore the ones requesting shared access can be withheld from their resources.

Within the use of the software in the AXD at most one client is requesting exclusive access to the resources (the take-over process). In that setting, the starvation of clients requesting shared access cannot occur, as we prove below. The reason is the synchronized communication for the release. As soon as the client requesting exclusive access sends a release to the locker, all waiting shared clients get access to the resources they requested (they share them). Only after this is an acknowledgement sent on the release.

Here we look at more general cases where more than one client is requesting exclusive access to the resources (since this type of scenarios may occur in a more general setting).

Because of the fact that the algorithm contains a certain form of starvation, the property one wants to check for non-starvation has to be specified with care. The following cases have been verified: non-starvation of clients requesting exclusive access and non-starvation of clients requesting shared access in the presence of at most one exclusive request.

Non-starvation for exclusive access. Proving that there is no starvation for the clients requesting exclusive access to the resources turned out to be tricky. This is caused by the fact that there are traces in the LTS that do not correspond to a fair run of the Erlang program.

The Erlang run-time system guarantees that each process obtains a slot of time to execute its code. However, in the LTS there are traces where certain processes do not get any execution time, even though they are enabled along the path. To clarify this, let us consider a scenario with two resources and three clients.

Client 1 requests resource A and obtains access to it, client 2 request resource A and has to wait. Thereafter client 3 requests B, obtains access to it, releases the resource and requests it again. In the LTS there is a clear starvation situation for client 2, viz. infinitely often traversing the cycle that client 3 is responsible for $(4 \to 23 \to 10 \to 24 \to 4 \to \ldots$ in Fig. 4). The above scenario, however, does

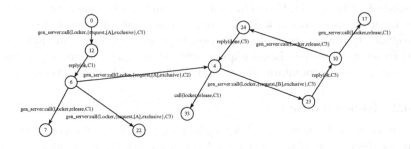

Fig. 4. Unreal starvation of client 2

not reflect the real execution of the program since the Erlang run-time system will schedule client 1 to execute its code. Client 1 will sooner or later release resource A, which causes client 2 to get access to the resource. In the LTS, it is visible that client 2 has the possibility to access resource A, but the unfair cycle of client 3 hides the fact that this will happen. Note, though, that we cannot simply forget about every cycle. If the cycle would be shown with resource A instead of B mentioned, then this would indicate a real starvation.

One could think of a number of solutions to solve the problem of cycles in the LTS that do not correspond to fair infinite computations in the Erlang program. For example, one could explicity model the Erlang run-time scheduler. However, modelling the scheduler is a rather complex solution that would increase the size of the LTS notably. Besides, we would be scheduling the actions in the μCRL code, not in the real Erlang code. Thus we would not be sure that starvation really occurs in the Erlang implementation.

Another possible solution is to encode the unrealistic cycles, i.e., the ones that the real scheduler would exclude, in the property so that they are ignored. In order to do that we need to characterize the unrealistic cycles. An unrealistic cycle corresponds to unfair execution of a number of clients that is *independent* of the client one wants to prove non-starvation for.

In our specific case a client depends on another client when the disjunction of the sets of resources they request is non-empty. Given that one is interested in proving non-starvation of a certain client, then computing the clients that are independent of this client is done by taking the complement of the reflexive, transitive closure of this dependency relation. If we now consider all actions of independent clients to be internal actions (τ actions in process algebra terminology), then non-starvation of the client C we are interested in, could be expressed by the guaranteed occurence of $'reply(ok,C)'$ in any path starting from $'gen\_server:call(.*request.*,C)'$, modulo possible cycles with only τ steps. This can be expressed by the following formula in the μ-calculus, where we allow only finite cycles of actions that are neither τ, nor $'reply(ok,C)'$ actions. Infinite sequences of only τ actions are, however, permitted:

$$[-* . 'gen\_server:call(.*request.*,C)']$$
$$\mu X.(\nu Y.(\langle-\rangle true \ \wedge \ [\neg\tau \ \wedge \ \neg'reply(ok,C)']X \ \wedge \ [\tau]Y)).$$

The disadvantage with the above formula is that it has alternating fixed point operators and hence the model checker cannot verify this property.

The solution is to reduce the state space by use of observational equivalence [23] and a facility to do this is provided by the CÆSAR/ALDÉBARAN toolset. By applying this reduction we replaced actions of independent processes by internal actions, we obtain a model in which pure τ cycles no longer occur. Thus, we removed all unfair cycles.

Modulo observational equivalence, the formula to prove non-starvation becomes much simpler and in particular is alternation-free:

$$NONSTARVATION(C) =$$
$$[-* . 'gen\_server:call(.*request.*,C)']\mu X.(\langle-\rangle true \ \wedge \ [\neg'reply(ok,C)']X)$$

Verification of non-starvation for a configuration of clients and resources is now performed by consecutively selecting a process that requests exclusive access to a set of resources. We manually determine the set of processes that is independent of this process, and then hide the labels of the independent processes The LTS obtained is reduced modulo observational bisimulation, and we can then verify the above given property on the reduced LTS.

In this way we successfully verified non-starvation of the clients requesting exclusive access to resources in several configurations. We also found a counter example, by checking this property for a process that requests shared access to resources in a configuration where two clients ask exclusive access to resource A and a third requests shared access to A. In this case we see that the third client is starving. This is exactly as we expect, since clients demanding exclusive access have priority over clients asking for shared access.

Non-starvation for shared access. Even though clients that request shared access to a resource may potentially starve, as explained above, we can still prove non-starvation of all the clients in the system, provided that at most one client demands exclusive access.

In analogy to the procedure described above, we hide the actions of independent processes and verify $NONSTARVATION(C)$ for every client C in the configuration. As such, the verification is performed successfully.

7 Conclusions

In this paper we describe an approach to verify properties of Erlang code. The approach consists of the following steps. First, the Erlang code is automatically translated to a μCRL specification. Second, a labeled transition system (LTS) is generated from this μCRL specification by using tools from the μCRL toolset. We then code up the property of interest in the alternation-free μ-calculus, and the LTS is checked against this property using the CÆSAR/ALDÉBARAN toolset. For some properties we transform the LTS (e.g., using hiding for non-starvation) so that we can model check with a simple formulation of the property of interest (e.g., one without alternating fixed points).

The case-study we have at hand, a critical part of the AXD 301 software consisting of about 250 lines of Erlang code, implements a resource locking problem for which we prove the obvious properties, viz. mutual exclusion and non-starvation. Mutual exclusion algorithms have been studied before (e.g. [10, 19,21,22]) and these algorithms have been proved correct. Automatically proving the same properties on a slightly different algorithm implemented in a real programming language, however, lifts formal methods from an academic exercise to industrial practice.

Similar projects for different programming languages exist, such as the verification on Java code [8,16] using the specification language Promela and LTL model checker SPIN [17]. The difference with those approaches is that we make extensive use of components on top of the language primitives, therewith obtaining smaller state spaces for similar problems. Moreover, the underlying logics for the model checkers differ, which makes different properties expressible in both approaches.

For Erlang there are also other relevant verification tools developed, e.g., a theorem prover with Erlang semantics build into it [3,13] and the model checker of Huch [18]. Huch's model checker works on Erlang code directly and provides the possibility to verify LTL properties.

The main difference between Huch's approach and the approach we sketch in this paper, is that Huch uses abstract interpretation to guarantee small (finite) state spaces. In Huch's approach all data is abstracted to a small, fixed set and tests on the data are often translated to non-deterministic choices. This approach is not suitable for our situation, since a non-deterministic choice whether a resource is available or not will result in error messages that do not reflect reality. That is, the properties we wish to verify are very data dependent and thus this particular approach to abstract interpretation will not work here.

The Erlang theorem prover can be used to prove similar properties, in particular if one uses the extra layer of semantics for software components added to the proof rules [4]. However, such a proof has to be provided manually, in contrast to more automatic approach we have explained here [4]. However, an advantage of the theorem prover is that one can reason about sets of configurations at once, and not fix the number of clients and resources per attempt.

---

[4] However, tactics can increase the degree of automation for the theorem prover

The translation of Erlang into μCRL is performed automatically. Our tool can deal with a large enough part of the language to make it applicable for serious examples. The tool computing the state spaces for μCRL models [9] is very well developed and stable. However, despite the many optimisations, it takes a few minutes up to hours to generate a state space. Whenever the model is obtained, model checking with the CÆSAR/ALDÉBARAN toolset [14] takes a few seconds up to a few minutes. Thus, the generation of the state space is rather slow compared to verifying it, which is partly due to the computation on the complex data structures we have in our algorithm. In particular, in the case when the property does not hold, creating the whole state space is often unnecessary: a counter-example could be provided without having all states available. A collaboration between both providers of the external tools recently resulted in an on-the-fly model checker to overcome this inconvenience. At the same time a distributed state space generation and model checking tool are being built as cooperation between CWI and Aachen University [6]. With such a tool, a cluster of machines can be used to quickly analyse rather large state spaces. Experiments showed the generation of an LTS with 20 million states in a few hours. We have not found serious performance problems and by these new developments we expect to push them forward even more.

Formal verification of Erlang programs is slowly becomming practically possible, particularly the development of new programs [2]. We plan to extend our translation tool to cover a few more components and to deal with fault tolerance. At the moment, crashing and restarting of processes is not considered inside the μCRL model, so that properties about the fault tolerance behaviour cannot be expressed. In the near future we plan to verify more software and construct a library of verified Erlang programs that can be used within Ericsson products.

Acknowledgements. We thank Ulf Wiger from Ericsson for providing us with the case-study and clarifying the use of this code. Specially helpful were the tool development teams at INRIA Rhône-Alpes and CWI with their support and advices, and Lars-Åke Fredlund and Dilian Gurov from SICS with their contribution in the discussions. We thank Howard Bowman from the University of Kent for useful explanations.

References

[1]   J.L. Armstrong, S.R. Virding, M.C. Williams, and C. Wikström. *Concurrent Programming in Erlang*. Prentice Hall International, 2nd edition, 1996.

[2]   T. Arts and C. Benac Earle. Development of a verified distributed resource locker, In Proc. of FMICS, Paris, July 2001.

[3]   T. Arts, M. Dam, L-Å. Fredlund, and D. Gurov. System Description: Verification of Distributed Erlang Programs. In *Proc. of CADE'98*, LNAI 1421, p. 38–42, Springer-Verlag, Berlin, 1998.

[4]   T. Arts and T. Noll. Verifying Generic Erlang Client-Server Implementations. In *Proc. of IFL2000*, LNCS 2011, p. 37–53, Springer Verlag, Berlin, 2000.

[5]   S. Blau and J. Rooth. AXD 301 – A new Generation ATM Switching System. *Ericsson Review*, no 1, 1998.

[6]   B. Bollig, M. Leucker, and M. Weber. Local Parallel Model Checking for the Alternation Free μ-Calculus. tech. rep. AIB-04-2001, RWTH Aachen, 2001.

[7]   E.M. Clarke, O. Grumberg, D. Peled. Model Checking, MIT Press, December 1999.

[8]   J. Corbett, M. Dwyer, L. Hatcliff. Bandera: A Source-level Interface for Model Checking Java Programs. In *Teaching and Research Demos at ICSE'00*, Limerick, Ireland, 4-11 June, 2000.

[9]   CWI. http://www.cwi.nl/~mcrl. A *Language and Tool Set to Study Communicating Processes with Data*, February 1999.

[10]   E. W. Dijkstra. Solution of a Problem in Concurrent Programming Control. In *Comm. ACM*, 8/9, 1965.

[11]   E.A. Emerson and C-L. Lei. Efficient Model Checking in Fragments of the Propositional Mu-Calculus, In *Proc. of the 1st LICS*, p. 267-278, 1986.

[12]   Open Source Erlang. http://www.erlang.org, 1999.

[13]   L-Å. Fredlund, et. al. A Tool for Verifying Software Written in Erlang, To appear in: *STTT*, 2002.

[14]   J.-C. Fernandez, H. Garavel, A. Kerbrat, R. Mateescu, L. Mounier, and M. Sighireau. CADP (CÆSAR/ALDÉBARAN development package): A protocol validation and verification toolbox. In *Proc. of CAV*, LNCS 1102, p. 437–440, Springer-Verlag, Berlin, 1996.

[15]   J. F. Groote, The syntax and semantics of timed μCRL. Technical Report SEN-R9709, CWI, June 1997. Available from http://www.cwi.nl.

[16]   K. Havelund and T. Pressburger, Model checking JAVA programs using JAVA PathFinder. *STTT*, Vol 2, Nr 4, pp. 366–381, March 2000.

[17]   G. Holzmann, *The Design and Validation of Computer Protocols*. Edgewood Cliffs, MA: Pretence Hall, 1991.

[18]   F. Huch, Verification of Erlang Programs using Abstract Interpretation and Model Checking. In *Proc. of ICFP'99*, Sept. 1999.

[19]   D. E. Knuth. Additional Comments on a Problem in Concurrent Programming Control. In *Comm. ACM*, 9/5, 1966.

[20]   D. Kozen. Results on the propositional μ-calculus. *TCS*, **27**:333-354, 1983.

[21]   L. Lamport. The Mutual Exclusion Problem Part II - Statement and Solutions. In *Journal of the ACM*, 33/2, 1986.

[22]   N. A. Lynch. *Distributed Algorithms*. Morgan Kaufmann Publishers, Inc. San Francisco, California, 1996.

[23]   R. Milner. A Calculus of Communicating Systems, Springer 1980.

[24]   A. G. Wouters. Manual for the μCRL tool set (version 2.8.2). Tech. Rep. SEN-R0130, CWI, Amsterdam, 2001.

Towards an Integrated Model Checker for Railway Signalling Data

Michael Huber[1] and Steve King[2]

[1] Siemens Transportation Systems*** , Industriestrasse 42, CH-8304 Wallisellen,
Switzerland
michael.mh.huber@siemens.com
[2] The University of York, Dept of Computer Science, York YO10 5DD, UK
king@cs.york.ac.uk

Abstract. Geographic Data for Solid State Interlocking (SSI) systems
detail site-specific behaviour of the railway interlocking. This report
demonstrates how five vital safety properties of such data can be verified
automatically using model checking. A prototype of a model checker for
Geographic Data has been implemented by replacing the parser and compiler of NuSMV. The resulting tool, gdlSMV, directly reads Geographic
Data and builds a corresponding representation on which model checking
is performed using NuSMV's symbolic model checking algorithms.

Because of the large number of elements in a typical track layout controlled by an SSI system, a number of optimisations had to be implemented in order to be able to verify the corresponding data sets.

We outline how most of the model checking can be hidden from the user,
providing a simple interface that directly refers to the data being verified.

Keywords: Data verification, model checking, hidden formal methods.

1 Introduction

The basic purpose of railway interlockings is to provide trains with safe routes
to their destinations. A route can be any part of track between two signals. The
first signal, often referred to as the entry signal, allows a train to proceed once
the route is locked. This means that all points have been moved and locked
to the required position, and protections such as gates at level-crossings are
appropriately deployed. By locking all elements necessary for safely passing a
route before opening the entry signal, the interlocking makes sure that no two
routes with conflicting requirements will be allowed at the same time [1].

The Solid State Interlocking (SSI) system is a modular computer interlocking of
the first generation [5]. It consists of interlocking modules which communicate
with signals, points and track circuits via track-side data links. In that way, each
SSI module can control an area with up to 40 signals and about 40 points [9].

*** The first author joined Siemens after the work reported in this paper had been
completed. Siemens did not take part in this research.

L.-H. Eriksson and P. Lindsay (Eds.): FME 2002, LNCS 2391, pp. 204–223, 2002.
© Springer-Verlag Berlin Heidelberg 2002

For larger control areas, several SSI modules can be grouped and operated from a single control panel.

Whether it is safe to set a route depends on the site-specific track layout. Therefore, the generic SSI program needs to rely on configuration data specifying the conditions under which routes can be set for the specific track layout controlled by the installation. Therefore, each SSI interlocking module keeps a database with the necessary geographic information, which is referred to as Geographic Data.

Errors in the Geographic Data could lead to conflicting routes being set at the same time, which would allow trains to proceed to the same track segment. Other data errors could allow points to be moved while a train is passing over them, which could lead to derailment of the train. Therefore, Geographic Data are safety-critical. For each installation, the data set has to be verified carefully. The aim of the work reported here is to provide a data verification tool based on model checking, which is both efficient enough to verify full Geographic Data sets, and easy to use for signal engineers without special knowledge of formal verification techniques. In order to achieve the latter, one of the design goals was to hide the model checking from the user, and to present him with a simple interface.

The rest of this paper starts with a section on Geographic Data and its verification. Then the model checker for Geographic Data, which has been developed based on the NuSMV [2] system, is described and the safety properties to be verified are introduced. We then set out how both the efficiency and the usability of the resulting model checker have been improved. Finally, the results are compared to previous work and conclusions are drawn.

2   SSI's Geographic Data

2.1   Geographic Data Specifying Routes

There are three types of data sets specifying how routes can be set and released:

Panel Route Request (PRR) data define the conditions under which route requests can be granted, and the actions necessary in order to lock the route.

Points Free to Move (PFM) data specify the conditions under which points are allowed to be moved from one position to the other.

Sub-Route Release (SRD) data define the conditions under which sub-routes which have been locked for a route can be released again.

The following subsections present brief descriptions of a slightly simplified version of these data. [12] contains more detailed definitions.

PRR Data. PRR data define the response of the interlocking to route requests issued by the signalman. The following data relates to the track layout shown in Fig. 1. The highlighted part is the route from signal S10 to signal S14, for which the PRR data is shown below:

```
*QR10B if   R10B a, P201 cfn, UAB-BC f, UAC-AB f
        then R10B s, P201 cn,  UAB-CB 1, UAC-BA 1
```

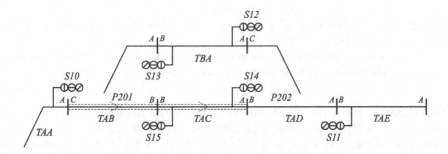

Fig. 1. Route R10B from signal S10 to S14

The data for the request to set route R10B above starts with the label *QR10B. This is recognised as a unique identifier for the route setting data (*Q) for route R10B (R10B). This is followed by the conditions under which the route may be set, indicated by the key word if. In this case, the conditions are as follows:

R10B a   Route R10B is available, i.e. not barred from being set;

P201 cfn   Point P201 is either already in its normal position, or it is free to go there;

UAB-BC f   Sub-route UAB-BC[1]is free; and

UAC-AB f   Sub-route UAC-AB is free — these last two conditions ensure that no route in the opposite direction is set over any part of the route currently requested.

If these conditions are met, than the route can be set. The necessary steps for that are specified after the key word **then**. In the example, they are as follows:

R10B s   The status of route R10B is 'set'.

P201 cn   Point P201 is moved to its normal position.

UAB-CB 1   Sub-route UAB-CB is locked.

UAC-BA 1   Sub-route UAC-BA is locked.

PFM Data. In the PRR data described above, the acronyms cfn and cfr refer to points being free to move to their normal position, or their reverse position respectively. The conditions under which points are free to move are defined in the PFM data . An example for point P201 is shown below.

```
*P201N  TAB c, UAB-AC f, UAB-CA f
*P201R  TAB c, UAB-BC f, UAB-CB f
```

---

[1] The names of subroutes start with the same identifier as the track-circuit to which they are associated, except for the first letter which is T for track-circuits but U for sub-routes. The two characters following the dash give the direction of the sub-route.

The labels for PFM data contain the identifier of the point for which the data applies, and N or R depending on whether the conditions are for moving to the normal or reverse position. Therefore, the statement starting with *P201N above gives the condition under which point P201 is free to move to its normal position:

TAB c   Track-circuit TAB is clear.
UAB-AC f,   The two sub-routes over the reverse branch of the point are
UAB-CA f   free.

In other words, point P201 can move to its normal position if there is no train occupying the point and if no route is set over the reverse position of the point.

SRD Data. PRR and PFM data contain all the information necessary for setting routes. SRD data are responsible for freeing the individual sub-routes locked by a route as soon as it is safe to do so. SRD data are periodically checked, unlike PRR and PFM data which are executed on request.

```
UAB-CB f    if TAB c, R10B xs
UAC-BA f    if TAC c, UAB-CB f
```

The first sub-route of the route can be released as soon as

TAB c   Track-circuit TAB is clear, and
R10B xs   Route R10B is unset.

Following sub-routes depend on the release of their predecessors, therefore the second sub-route can be released when

TAC c   Track-circuit TAC clear is, and
UAB-CB f   the previous sub-route UAB-CB is free, i.e. it has already been
                 released.

2.2   Verification of Geographic Data

The Geographic Data specifying when and how routes are locked, and when sub-routes are allowed to be released again, are safety-critical. An error in the data could mean that conflicting routes are allowed to be set at the same time, which would allow trains to proceed on conflicting paths. Furthermore, an error in PFM data could allow points to move under a passing train.

For example, route R11A in Fig. 2 conflicts with route R10B shown earlier in Fig. 1, as both routes set at the same time would allow two trains from opposite directions to proceed to the same track segment, namely TAC. However, a simple mistake in the PRR data can allow these two routes to be set at the same time. In the data shown below, sub-route UAC is checked in the wrong direction for route R10B, i.e. UAC-*BA* is checked instead of the opposing sub-route UAC-*AB* (last statement in the first line):

```
*QR10B if R10B a, P201 cfn, UAB-BC f, UAC-BA f
       then R10B s, P201 cn, UAB-CB 1, UAC-BA 1
*QR11A if R11A a, P202 cfn, UAD-BA f, UAC-BA f
       then R11A s, P202 cn, UAD-AB 1, UAC-AB 1
```

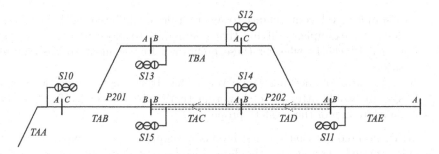

Fig. 2. Route R11A from signal S11 to S15

Mistakes like this one are sufficient to allow conflicting routes to be set at the same time, which could have catastrophic consequences. Therefore, Geographic Data have to be verified carefully before they can become operational on an installation. Currently, this verification is mostly done manually [16]. There are two main verification steps:

Checking of Geographic Data is carried out after all the data have been prepared. An independent signal engineer who has not been involved in the preparation of the data inspects print-outs of the complete data and verifies them against design information.

Testing involves actually running a simulated interlocking with the checked data. A third not previously involved engineer carries out the tests. In a first stage, correspondence between the simulated states of trackside equipment and the display is systematically tested. After that, it is tested whether signalling principles are correctly followed. Extensive tests are carried out to gain confidence in the data. For example, attempts are made to set all possible opposing and conflicting routes for each route in order to confirm that this is not possible.

Finally, an on-site test on the complete installation checks for timing problems and for interoperation with neighbouring interlockings. Task and error analyses of the SSI data design process have been carried out ([16,17]). It has been reported that the bulk of errors detected shifts from checking to testing with increasing complexity of the data: in simple schemes most errors are detected early in the checking phase, but in more complex data sets the majority of problems are discovered during testing. Furthermore, some categories of errors were particularly resistant to the checking phase. Most problems with opposing subroutes, for example, slipped through the checking phase and were only detected by testing [17].

2.3 Automated Verification of Geographic Data

As manual verification of Geographic Data is time-consuming and demanding, the potential for automation has been assessed earlier. [6] noted that there are two levels at which automated data checking could be applied:

- At a simpler level, conformance to general rules could be checked. This would include, for example, verifying that commands to move points are always preceded by checks whether these points are free to move to the required positions.
- A higher level of checking would verify that basic safety properties always hold. This would attempt to show that there exists no series of inputs that can violate any of these safety properties.

[6] further pointed out that the first level of checking is to some extent similar to the rules applied when writing the data. Therefore, it is susceptible to common mode errors: the errors that are likely to be made in the data preparation are at the same time unlikely to be detected by that checking approach. The paper concluded that the second approach "is potentially the best means of detecting any unexpected side-effects of data errors which cannot be guaranteed to be found by testing" [6, p 62].

In order to obtain such an extensive verification of safety properties, model checking has been deployed in previous work. [11] modelled Geographic Data data with CCS, and the Concurrency Workbench (CWB) was used for model checking. However, because of CWB's explicit representation of the modelled system as a graph, it was found to be unsuitable for large scale applications. [14] obtained better results by using CSP for modelling the data and FDR2 for model checking it. This work also describes a formal translation from SSI data to CSP. [7] developed a tool for the automated translation from Geographic Data to machine readable CSP as input to the FDR2 model checker. [13] investigated both the use of CSP and SMV for the verification of Geographic Data. Emphasis was set on devising a library of general SMV modules that could be used for any railway network described by Geographic Data.

The work described here builds on the experience gained from [13]. The goal was to build a tool for the verification of five vital safety properties for locking and releasing routes. The tool should be efficient enough to handle Geographic Data sets of realistic sizes. Furthermore, model checking technicalities should be hidden from the user as far as possible, in order to allow signal engineers without special knowledge in model checking to work with the tool.

3   gdlSMV: A Symbolic Model Checker for Geographic Data

For reasons of both efficiency and usability, it was decided not to translate Geographic Data to an SMV input script, but to integrate a Geographic Data parser with an SMV model checker. In that way, Geographic Data input is translated directly to Ordered Binary Decision Diagrams (OBDDs), which are the model checker's internal representation. It was assumed that abstractions and optimisations would be easier to apply at the OBDD level. Furthermore, an integrated tool that reads Geographic Data and produces verification output directly without the need for an intermediate SMV representation can be better tailored to the user's needs concerning the interface.

3.1   Adapting NuSMV for the Verification of Geographic Data

Fig. 3 shows the basic concept of adapting an existing SMV model checker for the verification of Geographic Data. Instead of SMV scripts, the inputs are Geographic Data files. Therefore, the parser and compiler of the model checker are replaced. Furthermore, optimisations are performed on the OBDD representation. As the basis model checker to be adapted, NuSMV [2] has been chosen.

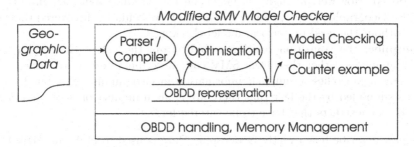

Fig. 3. NuSMV's parser and compiler are replaced in order to obtain a model checker which directly reads Geographic Data. This makes it possible to perform optimisations on the internal OBDD representation

NuSMV is a modular and well-documented re-implementation of the SMV system [10]. In the design of NuSMV, it is explicitly acknowledged that the SMV input language is not optimal for all applications. Therefore, NuSMV provides a clear distinction between the SMV input front end and the model checking algorithms: only the parser, instantiation, encoder, semantic checking and parts of the compiler are dependent on the format of the model description, i.e. the SMV language. The actual model checking, the computation of fairness constraints, and the generation of counter examples operate on the OBDD representation of the system and therefore independent of the initial input format. Also the kernel providing OBDD handling routines and memory management functions, and the user interfaces are, with minor exceptions, independent.

Converting NuSMV with its SMV input format to gdlSMV which directly reads Geographic Data files necessitated the following changes:

Parser: a new parser has been written for reading Geographic Data files and storing their content in an appropriate form. However, parts of the original NuSMV parser are still necessary, as it is also used to parse CTL formulas, which are still required in gdlSMV.

Instantiation: this module is obsolete in gdlSMV, as there are no hierarchical definitions or module declarations. There is, however, information necessary to build the transition relation which is not explicitly declared in Geographic Data. For example, there is no variable declaration in Geographic Data, nor are initial states specified. Therefore, the instantiation module of NuSMV has been replaced with a set of functions that extract implicit information from Geographic Data and store it in an adequate way for use in later stages.

Encoder: all variables in Geographic Data have to be encoded in the same way that variables in SMV scripts are encoded by NuSMV. However, the variables in Geographic Data are of a small number of pre-defined types; there is no need to deal with type declarations. That means variable encoding in gdlSMV is static and much simpler than in NuSMV.

Semantic checking: the semantic checks performed in NuSMV for SMV scripts are obsolete. Therefore semantic checking has, for now, been abandoned. However, it might be beneficial to introduce some semantic checks for Geographic Data, as some classes of errors could be discovered that way, without the need to perform model checking.

Compiler: the transition relation is built from the list of Geographic Data statements rather than from SMV code describing next state assignments. This again relies on implicit information in Geographic Data, but the task is simplified by the fact that there are a small number of basic Geographic Data constructs that have to be catered for.

We now describe how exactly Geographic Data is used to build an OBDD representation of a corresponding finite state machine.

3.2   Modelling the Operations Specified by Geographic Data

The three parts of the finite state machine for performing model checking, i.e. the initial states, the transition relation, and the fairness constraints are built as follows:

Initial States. gdlSMV considers four types of variables, namely points, track-circuits, routes, and sub-routes. The set of initial states is defined as:

- points are either controlled normal or controlled reverse,
- track-circuits are either clear or occupied,
- all routes are unset, and
- all sub-routes are free.

This results in a set of 2^{p+t} initial states, where p and t are the numbers of points and track-circuits respectively. These initial states differ slightly from the initial state of a real Solid State Interlocking when it is reset. However, since the modelled initial states are less restrictive than what is possible in practice, it is safe to use this initialisation (see [8] for details).

Transition Relation. In NuSMV, both synchronous and asynchronous systems can be modelled. In synchronous systems, all variables change their value at the same time. Each transition evaluates all expressions for the new values of all variables depending on the present values. In asynchronous systems, there are a number of processes. In each process, one or several variables can change their state. For each individual transition, one process is chosen non-deterministically and its variables updated according to the specified transitions. All other variables not changed by that process retain their previous value. This second behaviour is what is needed for gdlSMV: each PRR and SRD statement from the Geographic Data is modelled as a process. Therefore, at any time at most one statement will be executed. However, if in this statement several variables change their value, then this is done synchronously as all variables belong to the same process. Such a behaviour closely resembles SSI, as in SSI at most one Geographic Data statement can be executed at any time, and all the variables affected by a statement are updated in one atomic operation.

SRD statements. The SRD statements specify the conditions under which a sub-route can be released, and they easily translate to corresponding transition expressions, as shown below.[2]

```
UAB-CB f   if TAB c, R10B xs       IF(TAB = c AND R10B = xs) THEN
                                      UAB-CB':=f
                                   ELSE
                                      UAB-CB':=UAB-CB
```

As there are individual SRD statements for all sub-routes, there is always exactly one variable that can change its value in an SRD transition. Each SRD statement is modelled as a process that can be executed at any time. The ELSE clause needs to state explicitly that the variable does not change, as a variable that is not mentioned in a transition can take any value.

PRR and PFM statements. PFM statements just represent conditions under which points are free to move. They do not themselves represent transitions, but the PFM conditions will be incorporated in the transitions constructed from PRR statements. The PFM and PRR statements

```
/ Points free to move (PFM)
*P201N    TAB c, UAB-AC f, UAB-CA f

/ Panel Route Request (PRR)
*QR10B if   P201 cfn, UAB-BC f, UAC-AB f
        then P201 cn, R10B s, UAB-CB 1, UAC-BA 1
```

translate to the following transition:

```
IF((P201 = cn OR (TAB = c AND UAB-AC = f AND UAB-CA = f)) AND
   UAB-BC = f AND UAC-AB = f) THEN
   P201':=cn;   R10B':=s;    UAB-CB':=1;      UAC-BA':=1;
ELSE
   P201':=P201; R10B':=R10B; UAB-CB':=UAB-CB; UAC-BA':=UAC-BA
```

As described in section 2.1, the expression P201 cfn in the PRR statement is an implicit reference to the PFM statement. The attribute cfn requires that P201 is

---

[2] Dashed variable names (UAB-CB') indicate the next state as opposed to the current state (UAB-CB).

either in controlled normal, or that it is free to go to controlled normal. Whether the latter is the case is specified in the PFM statement *P201N, which sets out the condition under which P201 might change to normal. In the pseudo-code for the transition above, it can be seen that the PFM condition has been integrated in the condition of the PRR statement. Each PRR statement is extended in that way with the corresponding PFM statement(s), and for each PRR statement a process is created.

Track-circuits. Finally, the behaviour of track-circuits is modelled by allowing them to change their states at any time. For reasons of efficiency, this is not implemented as a further transition, but it is dealt with in the frame axiom. Letting track-circuits change their states unconditionally at any time is an unrealistic behaviour, as it represents trains jumping across the track layout. However, as [11] has shown, if setting routes and releasing sub-routes is safe with this behaviour than it is also safe with the more orderly behaviour of real trains.

Fairness Constraints. Presently, there are no fairness constraints generated, as they are not necessary for checking our safety properties (see [8] for details).

3.3   Verifying Safety Properties

[14] lists the following safety properties that could potentially be violated by errors in Geographic Data:

(i)   At any time, at most one sub-route over a given track-circuit is locked.
(ii)   Whenever a sub-route over a point is locked, the point is in alignment with that sub-route.
(iii) Whenever a route is set, all its sub-routes are locked.[3]
(iv)   If a sub-route is locked for a route, then all sub-routes ahead of it on that route are also locked.
(v)   It is never the case that points are moved while the corresponding track-circuit is occupied.

Assuming that trains obey signals and therefore only enter routes that are locked for them, properties (i), (iii) and (iv) guarantee that there is never more than one train on the same track segment. This is achieved by safe handling of the sub-routes (i), and by verifying that routes are properly composed of their sub-routes (iii), (iv). Property (ii) assures that trains never pass over points that are in the wrong position. Finally, (v) makes sure that points are prevented from moving while trains are passing over them.

These five properties can easily be translated to CTL specifications which can be verified with gdlSMV:

---

[3] Note that the first sub-route of a route can not be released before the route is unset. Then the sub-routes are released in sequence, as it is safe to do so.

(i) *At most one sub-route over the same track-circuit is locked at any time.*

```
AG !(UAA-AB = 1 & UAA-BA = 1)
```

i.e. it is never the case (`AG !`: in all reachable states it is not true) that both UAA-AB and UAA-BA are locked. For each track-circuit, there is a CTL expression required, stating that any two of the sub-routes over that circuit can not be locked at the same time. There can be more than two sub-routes over the same track-circuit, in which case the property expands.

(ii) *Whenever a sub-route over a set of points is locked, then the points are in alignment with that sub-route.*

```
AG ((UAB-AC = 1 | UAB-CA = 1) -> P201 = cr)
AG ((UAB-BC = 1 | UAB-CB = 1) -> P201 = cn)
```

i.e. whenever a sub-route over the reverse position of point P201 is locked, then P201 is in that position, and when a sub-route over the normal position is locked, it is in the normal position.

(iii) *Whenever a route is set, all its sub-routes are locked*

```
AG ((R13  = s) -> (UAA-AB = 1 & UAB-AC = 1 & UAK-AB = 1))
```

i.e. it is always the case that when route R13 is set, all its sub-routes UAA-AB, UAB-AC, and UAK-AB are locked.

(iv) *Sub-routes are released in correct order*

```
AG ((R13  = s) -> (!E[UAB-AC = 1 U UAA-AB = f] &
                   !E[UAA-AB = 1 U UAK-AB = f]))
```

i.e. from any state where route R13 is set, there exists no path along which UAB-AC remains locked until UAA-AB is free, nor exists a path along which UAA-AB remains locked until UAK-AB is free. By asserting that no sub-route can be freed as long as its immediate predecessor is still locked, this property enforces the sub-routes to be released in correct order.

(v) *Occupied points never move*

```
AG (TAB = o -> ((P201 = cr -> AX P201 = cr) &
                (P201 = cn -> AX P201 = cn)))
```

i.e. in any state where track-circuit TAB is occupied, if point P201 is in its reverse position in that state then it will remain so in all next states. Correspondingly, if it is in its normal position it will remain there in all next states. It is sufficient to consider next states only: if the track-circuit is still occupied in that next state, then the property applies again for all next states reachable from that state, and so on as long as TAB is occupied.

Such CTL specifications need to be generated and verified for all track-circuits, points and routes in a set of Geographic Data. See section 4.2 on how these CTL expressions can be hidden from the user.

4 Improving Efficiency and Usability

4.1 Efficiency

Before gdlSMV was tested on a large data set, some optimisations were implemented in order to reduce run-time. The results were tested on a small data set called "OpenAlvey" (Data from [11]).

Variable ordering [13] pointed out that the order of the variables for constructing the OBDDs representing SSI data can have a huge impact on run-time requirements. It has therefore been attempted to extract a satisfactory variable ordering from the data. Generally, it seems that orderings where related variables are kept close together tend to yield good results [4]. In SSI data, variables occurring in the same statement clearly are related. Therefore, it was expected that ordering the variables as they are found in a traversal of the data should yield satisfactory results. Experimenting with all possible permutations, the order PRR - SRD - PFM obtained the best results. Within each data block, the individual statements are examined in the order in which they occur in the source file. The quality of the results obtained therefore depends on the order of the statements. However, as this order is not usually random but follows a geographical logic, the obtained result is satisfactory.

Modified frame axiom.[4] Initially, there was a separate transition in which track-circuits could change their state, and routes which are set could become unset. However, this leads to unnecessary iterations in reachability analysis, and it makes the representation of intermediate sets of states found needlessly complicated. In the case of track-circuits which can change their states unconditionally at any time, it is clear that for each reachable state, the same state with any possible combination of track-circuits being occupied and clear is also reachable. However, if track-circuits need an explicit transition to change their state, then there are intermediate results which specify in detail that certain track-circuits must be clear and others occupied — only to find in the next iteration that all other permutations are also permitted. Similar situations occur for routes which would be explicitly specified to be set, while whenever a state with a route set is reachable, the same state with that route no longer set is also reachable.

Moving the specification of the behaviour of track-circuits and the un-setting of routes to the frame reduced both the number of iterations necessary in reachability analysis, and the size of the representation of intermediate sets of states found after each iteration. For the track-circuits, describing their behaviour in the frame axiom is particularly easy as they are simply not mentioned. This allows them to take any value. Technically, they will not be mentioned in the OBDD representing the set of states after each transition,

---

[4] The frame axiom is the expression specifying what does *not* change in a transition. For each transition, it explicitly assigns present state to next state for all variables not affected by the transition.

therefore reducing the size of that OBDD and allowing the variables to take either of their values. As for routes, as soon as they are set they will disappear from the expression describing that state, as whenever a route is set the same state with that route unset is also reachable.

Compared to the version with a separate transition, the modification to the frame axiom significantly decreased run-time (by almost 90% for a simple data set).

Expanded set of initial states. At first, all points had been initialised to their normal position. However, this implied that many reachable states were only found after a relatively large number of iterations. Consider the state where no routes are set, all sub-routes are free, and all points are reverse. Except for the position of the points, this is the same state as the initial state. Nevertheless, it can only be reached after routes have been set which change the points to reverse, and after these routes have been unset and all sub-routes released again. Throughout the necessary iterations to reach that state, the OBDD describing the set of states reached so far has to exclude states which have not yet been found. Therefore, the size of that OBDD is likely to be large.

The set of initial states has therefore been expanded to include all possible combinations of point positions. Apart from placing no unnecessary restrictions on the initial states, this leads to a greater number of states being found in earlier iterations, and it can reduce the size of the OBDDs representing the sets of states found after each iteration.

For the small data example, the above change reduced run-time by almost 50%. As the impact of the optimisation depends on the number of points in a scheme and the complexity of routes leading over these points, it is assumed that its benefits are even bigger on larger data sets.

The optimisations described so far have reduced the verification time for a small data example from around 10 minutes to around 7 seconds — slightly faster than a model for the same data written in SMV verified by the original NuSMV, which included the optimisation of the initial set, and had been run with the same variable ordering. However, when a larger data set (Leamington Spa railway station) was made available for tests, an as-yet-unexpected problem occurred. With 64 route requests, 98 sub-routes, 15 points and 35 signals, Leamington Spa is a fairly large scheme. 223 binary variables are necessary to model it, spanning a space of $1.3 \cdot 10^{67}$ states, $4.7 \cdot 10^{27}$ of which are reachable. While reachability analysis in a state space of such dimensions was expected to take much longer than it did for the small data example used so far (64 binary variables; $2.8 \cdot 10^9$ reachable states out of a total of $1.8 \cdot 10^{19}$), no thought had been given to the fact that memory usage too could become a problem. However, the first verification attempt of Leamington Spa used up all 256M of RAM after just over an hour, and in a few more hours it also exhausted the 306M of available swap memory. By that time, it had completed only the first five iterations of reachability analysis. While run-time optimisation remained a goal, memory usage become the dominating concern. The following optimisations were then introduced:

Disjunctive partitioning. While early tests had not suggested disjunctive partitioning to be more efficient than a monolithic representation of the transition relation, its implementation in gdlSMV led to a remarkable reduction in memory usage. In a simplified version of Leamington Spa with 139 binary variables, maximum memory usage could be reduced from 160M to 95M, and run-time from 2 hours 40 minutes to 1 hour 55 minutes.

Dynamic variable re-ordering. The importance of a suitable variable ordering has been mentioned before. However, a variable ordering which allows for representing the transition relation in a compact form does not necessarily also result in optimal representations of the set of states found after each iteration in reachability analysis. Since, in general, different variable orderings are optimal for different stages in model checking, NuSMV offers dynamic variable re-ordering (as do other model checkers). In NuSMV, as soon as dynamic variable re-ordering is enabled it will be applied to find a compact representation of the OBDDs currently in use. According to their size, a limit is set for memory usage. As soon as this limit is reached, the re-ordering process is started again, and a new memory limit is set. As the model checking part of NuSMV has not been changed in any way in gdlSMV, the option for dynamic re-ordering is also available in gdlSMV. Enabling it not only greatly reduces the amount of memory required, but also decreases run-time. Although almost half of the verification time for Leamington Spa is spent re-ordering variables, the total run-time is still much lower than without re-ordering, because operations on compact OBDDs are much faster than on large OBDDs.

Although the above measures did decrease both run-time and memory usage, they were still not sufficient to reduce resource requirements to an acceptable level for the full verification of Leamington Spa. On smaller examples it could be seen that the first few iterations run fairly quickly, as do the last iterations. Both the OBDD size of the set of reachable states found and run-time requirements drastically increase in the middle iterations. As this is a common problem in model checking, it was expected that there is previous work addressing it. [3], although concerned with hardware verification, provided the vital clue. It suggested decomposing complex hardware circuits into loosely coupled modules. Then, instead of performing a breadth-first search with the whole transition relation, an initial search is restricted to one of these modules. As before, this search will have peak resource requirements in its middle iterations, but as it is restricted to a smaller state space, that peak will be smaller. Such local searches are carried out individually for all modules. However, these searches will not initially find all reachable states if modules depend on each other. Therefore, the reachability analysis for all modules has to be repeated with the states found in the previous searches of the individual modules until no new states are found anymore. This results in more iterations being required to find all reachable states, but in small peak sizes of the intermediate OBDDs.

Splitting the transition relation. The principle described in [3] and outlined above has been incorporated in gdlSMV by splitting the disjunctively partitioned transition relation into two parts, one containing all transitions for route setting, and one containing all sub-route release transitions. The route setting transitions are applied iteratively, first to the initial states, and then to the set of reachable states found previously. The latter is repeated until no new states are found anymore: all combinations of routes that can be set from the initial states are found. Now the sub-route releasing data are applied iteratively, again until no new states are found anymore. After that the route setting transitions have to be applied again, as there are reachable states where a route can be set after a previous route has been partially released. Therefore, iterating over route setting and sub-route releasing transitions is repeated until the set of reachable states remains constant.

For the simplified data of Leamington Spa, splitting the transition relation in the above manner reduced run-time from about an hour (with all the previous optimisations including dynamic re-ordering) to under 10 minutes, and memory usage from 31M to 10M. For the first time it now became possible to complete reachability analysis for the original Leamington Spa data. However, this still took more than 70 hours and up to 360M of RAM. Further improvement was clearly needed. As splitting of the transition relation had been successful, it was an obvious choice to apply the same technique again:

Second splitting of the transition relation. There is no second partitioning as obvious as separating route setting from sub-route releasing. However, there are two more classes in which data can easily be grouped, namely whether the route or sub-route they apply to are in up- or in down-direction. The naming convention set out in [15] ensures that the direction of sub-routes can be determined by the last two characters of their name: if these characters are in alphabetical order, the sub-route is in down direction, otherwise up. Therefore, sub-route release data can be immediately grouped by the corresponding direction using the name of the sub-route concerned. For route setting data, the name of the first sub-route to be locked is used. Combined with the previous splitting, this results in four categories of transitions: route setting for up direction, sub-route releasing for up direction, route setting for down direction, and sub-route releasing for down direction. As before, reachability analysis is done over these groups of statements individually, and all four sub-analyses are repeated until the full reachable state space is explored.

This final version reduced run-time of reachability analysis for Leamington Spa to 9 hours, and peak memory during that time to below 70M. Fig. 4 summarises data for the verification of the simplified data set for Leamington Spa with three versions of gdlSMV: without splitting the transition relation for reachability analysis, all reachable states are found in 54 iterations. However, the second graph shows that intermediate OBDDs are of large size, and the iterations on these large OBDDs are very slow, as can be seen on the third graph. For the first splitting of the transition relation, the top graph clearly shows how reachable states are now found stepwise (first with route setting, then sub-route release,

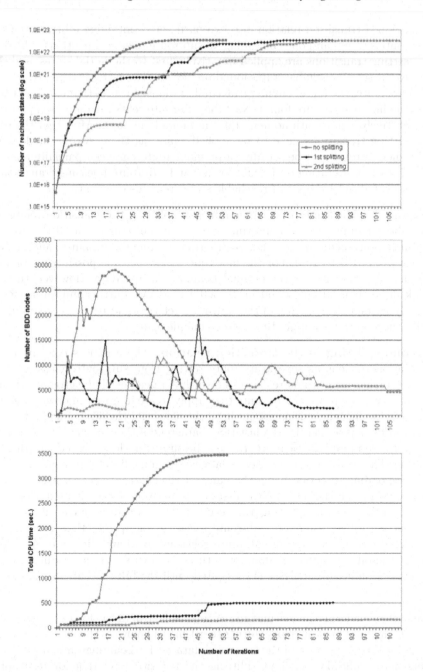

Fig. 4. From top to bottom: number of states found, size of the OBDD representing the set of these states, and total execution time after each iteration of reachability analysis. The three data series are for the original transition relation; with transitions split into route setting and sub-route release; and with additional splitting according to the direction.

next route setting again, and so on). Although the total number of iterations necessary to find all reachable states grew to 87, OBDD sizes have been reduced resulting in individual iterations executing much faster. Finally, the second splitting of both route setting and sub-route releasing transitions according to direction further decreases peak OBDD size and run-time, although it increases the number of iterations to 108. Concerning the OBDD size, it is important to take into account that computations during reachability analysis combine two OBDDs. The complexity of these operations is proportional to the product of the sizes of the two OBDDs. After each iteration, there is an operation on the OBDDs representing the previous and the current set of reachable states in order to determine whether still new states were found, or whether the search can be terminated. Therefore, runtime is a function of OBDD size squared. Seemingly modest reductions of OBDD sizes, as shown in the middle graph in Fig. 4, can considerably improve run-time, as well as memory requirements while the operations take place.

4.2   Usability

Although the current version of gdlSMV still refers to model checking in many places, the potential to hide the underlying technique in gdlSMV clearly exists. In particular, the following improvements could be implemented easily:

Hiding CTL. In the current version of gdlSMV, the specific instantiation of the safety properties for a given data set have to be expressed in CTL. As the structures of these properties follow simple principles, it would be easily possible to generate them automatically. Simple lists of sub-routes for each track-circuit; routes with their sub-routes in correct order; and points with corresponding track-circuit and sub-routes for each branch would be sufficient as input. Such data could be extracted from design specifications.

Managing counter-examples. There are exceptional circumstances when it is permitted to violate a safety property. For example, opposing routes might be set for shunting. In such situations, the question is no longer whether there exists a state that violates a property, but whether there is such a state other than the permitted exceptions. Currently gdlSMV would just report the property to be violated and would produce one arbitrary counter-example. If this example is a permitted exception, then this result is not satisfactory in that it does not specify whether there are other, unintended violations besides it. For that reason, it would be necessary to verify whether there is a counter-example which does not incorporate the permitted violation. This could be implemented by repeating the backward search from states that violate the safety property with a modified transition relation from which the transitions causing the permitted exceptions are excluded. If this search still leads back to an initial state, then another unintended violation is found and a counter example for it can be generated.

Further improvements to gdlSMV's usability could include the provision of additional information relating results back to the SSI data, such as line numbers in the source file when referring to route requests and sub-route release transitions.

5   Evaluation and Conclusions

Our aim was to develop an integrated verification tool for Geographic Data, which is efficient enough for verifying large data sets, and easy to use by signal engineers who are not experts in the underlying model checking techniques. Compared to previous work, it seems that we made important steps in this direction.

As mentioned earlier, there are two main previous works on model checking SSI data. [11] used CCS for the verification of SSI data. However, as the corresponding model checker in the Concurrency Workbench uses an explicit internal representation of the state transition graph, it was impossible to use it for other than very small data examples. An optimised version using HOL has been tested with data for Leamington Spa. However, no full verification has been carried out. It is understood that the correctness of individual statements has been proved. For the most complex route request, this took almost half an hour. Therefore, a full verification would be unlikely to be more efficient than what has been achieved with gdlSMV. Furthermore, [11] does not mention any attempt to develop the verification techniques towards a tool that could be used in the SSI data production process.

In contrast, [14] did suggest the integration of work on translating Geographic Data to CSP and model checking it, with FDR2 in an automated SSI verification tool [7]. The approach differs from gdlSMV in that it does not construct the full model but only extracts data relevant to the property currently verified. No indication is given of the efficiency of a full verification for the small data set "OpenAlvey", except that checking individual properties is said to complete 'in a matter of seconds'. Compared to these results, the full verification of the five safety properties for all elements in the OpenAlvey in under 1.6 seconds, and the ability to fully verify a scheme as complex as Leamington Spa in gdlSMV seem a considerable improvement.

These results suggest two main conclusions in the wider context of verifying configuration data, and for the application of model checking in general.

Verifying Configuration Data. Model checking has seen successful applications in the verification of hardware designs. Although previous work on model checking configuration data exists, it seems not yet to be in industrial use.

One reason for the success of model checking in hardware verification is that properties of particular types of hardware verification problems often allow for specific optimisation techniques to increase efficiency of model checking. The verification of SSI data in this work has followed the same pattern in that it applied optimisations which are particularly suited to the general characteristics of SSI data. Consider, for example, the fact that from any state, a large number of states are reachable in one transition, and any other state is reachable in a relatively small number of transitions. Whereas the latter is an advantage in reachability analysis as it limits the number of iterations necessary to find all states, the former is a problem as it leads to complicated representations of the intermediate set of states found during reachability analysis. This characteristic is the reason for the success of splitting the transition relation during reachability analysis, as the increased number of iterations necessary is still small whereas the sizes of intermediate sets are drastically reduced. Systems with a different characteristic could not equally benefit from the technique — in contrast, it might even have adverse effects on some systems.

Since configuration data such as Geographic Data can be expected to have general characteristics which hold for all data sets of that specific type, it is likely that techniques can be found which result in efficient model checking for these particular types of systems. Therefore, as was the case in this work, many encouraging results from hardware verification could potentially be applied to model checking configuration data.

Purpose-Built Model Checkers. As mentioned earlier, essential improvements to gdlSMV's efficiency required direct access to the internal representation of the transition relation. The decision to integrate translation from Geographic Data with the model checker, rather than building a separate translator which would generate an SMV input script, has made it possible to apply these improvements. Furthermore, the same decision opened opportunities for considerable improvements to the tool's usability, as the format of input and output to the model checker can be adapted as required. The model checking technique can be hidden from the user to a great extent

NuSMV has proven to be well-documented, and replacing its parser and compiler has been relatively easy, as its architecture clearly separates them from the actual model checking modules.

The results achieved with gdlSMV suggest that moderate efforts allow an open model checker such as NuSMV to be turned into a purpose-built adaptation for a particular input format. In contrast to translating the verification input to a standard model checking language such as SMV, purpose-built model-checkers have two main advantages:

- Access to internal representations allows for specific optimisations appropriate for the general structure of the systems to be verified. Although recent model checkers do provide techniques to increase their efficiency, some relatively simple and powerful techniques such as splitting of the transition relation for reachability analysis in gdlSMV are not applicable without direct access to the internal representation of the transition relation.
- Both input of verification properties and output of results and counterexamples can be tailored to the application area if the model checker itself is modified. Modest efforts in this area can significantly improve usability.

For these reasons, it is suggested that purpose-built model checkers should be considered for areas where an efficient, self-contained and usable tool for the verification of inputs with particular characteristics is required.

References

1. Bailey, C. (ed.): European Railway Signalling. Institution of Railway Signal Engineers. A & C Black, London (1995)
2. Cimatti, A., Clarke, E., Giunchiglia, F. and Roveri, M.: NuSMV: a new Symbolic Model Checker. Springer: International Journal on Software Tools for Technology Transfer, Volume 2 Issue 4, pp410–425 (2000)
3. Cabodi, G., Camurati, P. and Quer, S.: Reachability analysis of large circuits using disjunctive partitioning and partial iterative squaring. Elsevier: Journal of Systems Architecture, Volume 47, Issue 2, pp163–179 (February 2001)
4. Clarke, M.E., Grumberg, O. and Peled, D.A.: Model Checking. MIT Press (1999, 2nd printing 2000)
5. Cribbens, A.H.: Solid State Interlocking (SSI): an Integrated Electronic Signalling System for Mainline Railways. IEE Proceedings, Part B: Electric Power Applications, Volume 134, Issue 3, pp148–158. IEE (1987)
6. Cribbens, A.H. and Mitchell, I.H.: The Application of Advanced Computing Techniques to the Generation and Checking of SSI Data. Institution of Railway Signal Engineers. IRSE Proceedings, Volume 1991/92, pp 54–64 (1991)
7. Gurukumba, T.: From GDL to CSP: towards the full formal verification of solid state interlockings. Oxford University, MSc dissertation (1998)
8. Huber, M.: Towards an Industrially Applicable Model Checker for Railway Signalling Data. York University, MSc Dissertation, Department of Computer Science (2001)
9. Leach, M. (ed.): Railway Control Systems. Institution of Railway Signal Engineers. A & C Black, London (1991, Reprint 1993)
10. McMillan, K.L.: Symbolic Model Checking. Carnegie Mellon University, PhD thesis CMU-CS-92-131 (1992)
11. Morley, M.J.: Safety Assurance in Interlocking Design. Edinburgh University, PhD thesis ECS-LFCS-96-348 (1996)
12. Morley, M.J.: Semantics of Geographic Data Languages. In Proceedings of the 1st FMERail Workshop; Breukelen, Netherlands (June 1998)
13. Raili, E.L.: The Verification of the Design of Railway Networks. York University, MSc Dissertation, Department of Computer Science (1996)
14. Simpson, A.: Model Checking for Interlocking Safety. In Proceedings of the 2nd FMERail Workshop, Canary Wharf, London (October 1998)
15. SSI 8003: SSI Applications Manual. London: Railtrack, Head of Corporate Standards, electronic copy (February 1999)
16. Westerman, S.J., Shryane, N.M., and Sauer, J.: Task Analysis of the Solid State Interlocking Design Process. Human Factors in the Design of Safety Critical Systems project, Work package 1.1, Report No. SCS-01. University of Hull, Department of Psychology (April 1994)
17. Westerman, S.J., Shryane, N.M., Crawshaw, C.M. and Hockey, G.R.J.: Error Analysis of the Solid State Interlocking Design Process. Human Factors in the Design of Safety Critical Systems project, Work package 1.2, Report No. SCS-04. University of Hull, Department of Psychology (June 1995)

Correctness by Construction: Integrating Formality into a Commercial Development Process

Anthony Hall

Praxis Critical Systems Limited,
20 Manvers Street,
Bath BA1 1PX, U.K.
+44 1225 466991
anthony.hall@praxis-cs.co.uk

Abstract. This paper describes a successful project where we used formal methods as an integral part of the development process for a system intended to meet ITSEC E6 requirements. The system runs on commercially available hardware and uses common COTS software. We found that using formal methods in this way gave benefits in accuracy and testability of the software, reduced the number of errors in the delivered product and was a cost-effective way of developing high integrity software. Our experience contradicts the belief that formal methods are impractical, or that they should be treated as an overhead activity, outside the main stream of development. The paper explains how formal methods were used and what their benefits were. It shows how formality was integrated into the process. It discusses the use of different formal techniques appropriate for different aspects of the design and the integration of formal with non-formal methods.

1 Background

Praxis Critical Systems Ltd developed the Certification Authority (CA) for the MULTOS [1] smart card scheme on behalf of Mondex International. The purpose of the CA is to provide the necessary information to initialise cards, and to sign the certificates that allow applications to be loaded and deleted from MULTOS cards.

The CA is a distributed multiprocessor system for which the main requirements were security and throughput. It was required to be developed to the E6 process and standards, since previous experience had shown that this process forced a rigorous development which helped clarify requirements and meant there were no late surprises in testing. Thus the process was important even though the product did not actually go through evaluation. To meet the development budget and timescale it was infeasible to build the system entirely from scratch and so use of commercial off-the shelf (COTS) hardware and infrastructure software was mandatory.

An overview of the development approach and some results from the project can be found in a more general paper [7]. The present paper concentrates on the use of formal methods within the project.

L.-H. Eriksson and P. Lindsay (Eds.): FME 2002, LNCS 2391, pp. 224-233, 2002.
© Springer-Verlag Berlin Heidelberg 2002

2 The Development Approach

2.1 Overview

The development was a single process in which the formal and semi-formal deliverables were fully integrated. Figure 1 shows the overall set of deliverables from the development process, grouped into the main process steps. Formal deliverables are shown with heavy borders.

2.2 Requirements

We used REVEAL®, Praxis' well-tried requirements engineering method [6], to establish functional, security and performance requirements, including the threat analysis and informal security policy. In addition we developed a Formal Security Policy Model (FSPM) which is discussed in detail below.

2.3 Specification and Architecture

Of the three deliverables from this phase, one, the formal top level specification (FTLS), used mathematical notation.

The user interface specification was a relatively formal document in that it defined the complete look and feel of the UI. We started by working with the system operators to prototype a user interface, which would be acceptable and reasonably secure in the rather difficult physical conditions of the CA. We then wrote a complete definition of the user interface using screen shots to define the appearance and state transition tables to define the behaviour.

The high level design covered several aspects of the system's structure including:

1. distribution across machines and processes;
2. database structure and protection mechanisms;
3. mechanisms to be used for transactions and inter-machine and inter-process communications.

Writing a formal high level design is not a well-understood topic, unlike writing a formal functional description. There are many different aspects to a design, and there are several problems in using formality:

1. No single notation covers all aspects. A formal design will at best need a mixture of notations.
2. Some aspects, such as distribution, do not have an appropriate formal notation at all.
3. Even where different aspects can be described formally, care is needed to relate the different formal notations.
4. The relationship between the formal design and the FTLS is not well understood: current techniques of refinement are not powerful enough for systems of this complexity.

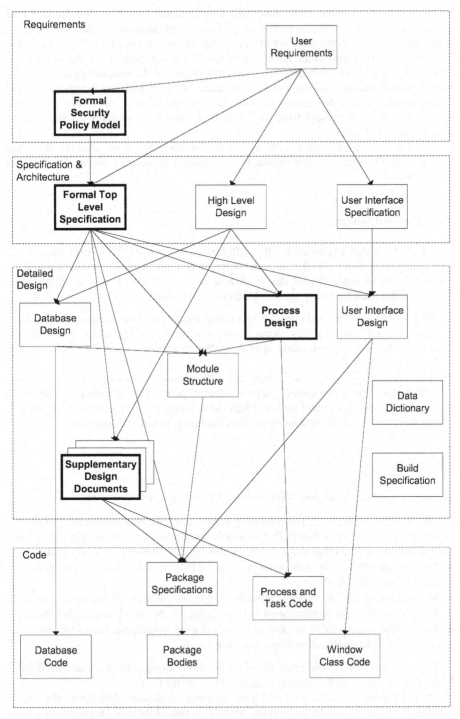

Fig. 1. Development Deliverables

The last point is particularly important. Conventional formal refinement in VDM or Z assumes that the structure of the design matches the structure of the specification, in the sense that it has the same set of operations. However, because of separation into processes, layering and other design techniques, the components of the design are structurally completely different from the components of the specification. Notations like B, which include programming constructs, can deal with some aspects of this restructuring but not, for example, with decomposition into concurrent processes. Overall we don't at present have any industrial-strength techniques for this sort of refinement in the large.

We therefore used semi-formal notations for the high level design. We then supplemented the semi-formal design by two formal techniques during the Detailed Design phase

2.4   Detailed Design

The detailed design expanded on the different aspects of the high level design. As with the HLD, most of the aspects were described in appropriate non-formal notations. For example the UI design described the window classes as simple state machines. We used formality for two kinds of deliverable:

1. Some of the modules had complex or critical behaviour. For example, the modules that managed low-level key storage were obviously highly critical and also had complex behaviour particularly at start up. We therefore specified the behaviour of these modules in Z.
2. We were very concerned about the concurrent behaviour of the system. Distributing the functionality across several processes on different machines introduces complexity and makes it hard to demonstrate correctness of the design. We therefore specified and analysed the concurrent behaviour formally.

2.5   Code

We used a mixture of languages for coding different parts of the system:

- The security-enforcing kernel of the system is implemented in SPARK Ada [2]— an annotated subset of Ada95 that is widely used in safety-critical systems, but has particular properties that make it suitable for the development of secure systems.
- The infrastructure of the system (e.g. RPC mechanisms, concurrency) is implemented in Ada95.
- The architecture of the system carefully avoids any security-related functionality in the GUI, so this was implemented in C++, using Microsoft's Foundation Classes.
- Some small parts, such as device drivers for cryptographic hardware, and one standard cryptographic algorithm, were used as-is.

We used automatic static analysis where possible, using tools such as the SPARK Examiner for Ada, and BoundsChecker and PC-Lint for C++.

From a formal methods point of view, the most significant choice was the use of SPARK for critical parts of the system. SPARK is one of the few languages that have a formal definition and thus meets the ITSEC requirement that the language "unambiguously define the meaning of all statements". Furthermore use of SPARK allowed us to prove automatically some key properties of the code, such as freedom from data flow errors.

For more discussion of SPARK and the choice of languages in this project, see [7].

2.6   Testing

All our testing was top-down, as far as possible at the system level. Tests were systematically derived from the formal specifications and UI specifications. This systematic process coupled with the formality of the specification guaranteed a level of functional coverage. We measured code coverage and filled code coverage gaps with supplementary tests.

3   The Formal Deliverables

3.1   Formal Security Policy Model

The user requirements included an informal security policy, which identified assets, threats and countermeasures. We formalised a subset of the whole policy. Of the 45 items in the informal policy, 28 were technical as opposed to physical or procedural. Of these, 23 items related to the system viewed as a black box, whereas 5 were concerned with internal design and implementation details. We formalised these 23 items.

We used Z to express the formal model. We based our approach on CESG's Manual "F" [5] but simplified the method described there. The FSPM consisted of three parts:

1. A general model of a system.
   We model any system as a state plus a set of operations. This is a simplification of the Manual "F" model of a state plus transition relation.
2. A model of a CA system.
   This is a specialisation of the general model of a system with some mapping between system state and real-world concepts such as users, sensitive data and so on.
3. A definition of a secure CA system.
   Each formalisable clause in the security policy is turned into a predicate that constrains the CA system in some way. The overall definition of a secure CA system is one where all the constraints are satisfied.

There were four different kinds of clause in the informal security policy, and each kind gave rise to a different kind of predicate in the FSPM.

1. Two of the clauses constrained the overall state of the system. Each of these became a state invariant in the formal model.
2. Eight clauses required the CA to perform some function (for example, authentication). Each of these was expressed in the formal model as a predicate of the form:

$\exists\, op : Operation \bullet property(op)$

That is, there must exist an operation op with a particular property.

3. Sixteen clauses were constraints applicable to every operation in the system (for example, that they were only to be performed by authorised users). Each of these was expressed in the form:

$\forall o : opExecutions \mid applicable(o) \bullet property(o)$

That is, during any operation execution where the clause is applicable, the property must hold.

4. One clause was an information separation clause. We expressed this in the form:

$\forall op : Operation \bullet start_1 \sim start_2 \Rightarrow end_1 \sim end_2$

That is, for every operation if the starting states are indistinguishable from a particular point of view, then the final states should also be indistinguishable from that point of view.

The fact that only one out of the 25 clauses was about information separation is interesting because information separation is harder to express in Z than other properties, and that fact has led to suggestions that languages like CSP are more appropriate for expressing security properties. Indeed our formulation of the property is actually slightly stronger than is strictly necessary (we have essentially oversimplified the unwinding of all execution sequences). However it seems clear in this case at least that the benefit of using Z for the other 24 clauses, all of which are straightforward to express in Z, may outweigh its awkwardness in expressing information separation.

3.2   The Formal Top Level Specification

The FTLS is a complete description of the behaviour of the CA at a particular level of abstraction. It is complemented by a user interface specification that gives a more concrete description of the appearance of the system.

The FTLS is a fairly conventional Z specification. However, it contains some special features to allow checking against the FSPM. Whereas in conventional Z an operation is specified by one or perhaps two schemas, in the FTLS we used a number of different schemas to capture different security-relevant aspects of the operation.

1. We used separate schemas to define the inputs, displayed information and outputs of each operation. This allowed us to trace clearly to FSPM restrictions on what is displayed and how outputs are protected.
2. We used separate schemas to define when an operation was available and when it was valid. This is not directly a security issue but it allows us to distinguish those errors which are prevented by the user interface (for example by making certain options unavailable) and those which are checked once the operation has been confirmed and thus cause error messages to be displayed. In fact both kinds of condition must be checked in a secure way and since the user interface is insecure, some of its checks are repeated in the secure parts of the system.
3. We used an elaborate modelling of errors to satisfy the requirement that all errors be reported, whereas commonly Z specifications of error behaviour are under-determined.

3.3   Formal Module Specification

We specified critical modules in conventional Z. Since these modules were internal to the system, issues such as what was displayed were not relevant, so we did not need the elaborate structure we had used for the FTLS.

The state specifications of these specifications were of course quite close to the actual machine state, and often the operation specifications used connectives such as sequential composition rather than the conceptually simpler logical connectives. We found, nevertheless, that the mathematical abstraction of this state, and the relative simplicity of Z operation specifications compared with implementations, was extremely useful in clarifying the exact behaviour of the modules.

3.4   Process Design

The CSP design was carried out at two levels: first we investigated the overall distribution across machines and major processes within machines. Then we checked the more detailed design of selected major processes.

For the top level design, we matched the CSP to the Z FTLS by mapping sets of Z operations into CSP actions. We also introduced actions to represent inter-process communications. This CSP model allowed us to carry out two kinds of check:

1. We checked that the overall system was deadlock-free.
2. We checked that an important security property was satisfied by the process design.

We checked that these properties were preserved even in the face of machine or software failure.

These checks were carried out automatically, by using the FDR tool from Formal Systems Europe. In order to use the tool we had to simplify the model by reducing the number of instances of identical processes, and we justified this reduction manually rather than by automatic checking.

We were able to find significant flaws in our first design by expressing it in CSP and checking its properties, and we have much greater confidence in the final design as a result.

At the second level we carried out detailed design of the processes on each machine. We then tried to prove that these were refinements of our high level design. Unfortunately it was not always possible to carry out these checks using the tool, because the processes were too big. However, we did increase our confidence in the lower level design by formalising it. Furthermore it was then extremely straightforward to implement the design using Ada 95 tasks and protected objects. We devised a set of rules for systematically translating CSP constructs into code. This was very successful and yielded code which worked first time, a rare experience among concurrent programmers.

4 Relationships between Deliverables

4.1 Tracing

We used requirements tracing to record the relationships between different levels of requirements, specification and design. This gave us a syntactic link between, for example, a piece of Z specification and the requirement that it helps to meet and the parts of the design that implement it. Simple tracing links of this sort do not carry any semantic information, although it is possible to enrich them to give more information about the way in which later deliverables satisfy earlier ones [6].

4.2 Relating Formal Deliverables

There are two kinds of relationship between the formal deliverables. There is a refinement relation between later deliverables and earlier ones: for example the FTLS should refine the FSPM. There is a more complex relationship between formal deliverables that cover different aspects of the system, for example between the FTLS and the process design.

We did not formalise these relationships. For example we did not carry out a refinement proof of the FTLS against the FSPM, although we did structure the FTLS to make informal checking of some aspects of the refinement straightforward.

Although we did not formalise the relationship between the FTLS and the process design, we did consider the nature of this relationship carefully.

It is sometimes suggested that in order to use different formal notations together, one must find a common semantic base that embraces both notations. However, the whole purpose of using different notations is to express different aspects of the system. One should expect, therefore, that there are aspects that are expressible in one notation but not in another. For example, Z allows us to express complex data structures while CSP allows us to talk about failures and divergences, which are inexpressible in Z (or, more strictly, in Z specifications using the established strategy).

On the other hand, clearly we need to find some link between the different notations; otherwise we are simply describing different systems. Our approach, therefore, is to define some intersection between the notations rather than trying to find their union.

In this case we chose actions as the intersection between CSP and Z. Roughly speaking, a CSP action is the same as an operation in Z.

More precisely, the link between our process design and our Z specification involved two steps. First, we mapped sets of similar operations into CSP actions. Similarity, for this purpose, meant that the operations had the same security properties. For example there was a set of those actions that were both *security-critical* and *user-activated*: although these did very different things functionally, from a security point of view they all used the same processing path.

Having identified the significant sets of actions, we then broke them down to operations of the various processes in the system. These operations did not have Z specifications (since we did not do a complete Z specification of all modules below the FTLS) but they did correspond to sets of operations in the code. This second step is in fact a form of refinement.

4.3   Relating Formal and Informal Deliverables

There was a very strong, but informal, relationship between the FTLS and the UIS. Every operation in the FTLS had a corresponding specification in the UIS. The UIS defined the lexical and syntactic levels of the operation, while the FTLS defined its semantics. Usually the UIS was finer-grained than the FTLS: for example an operation which appears atomic in the Z might involve several actions by the user to select values or type in text.

Most modules did not have formal specifications. In many cases, however, the module directly implemented a substantial part of the operation defined in the FTLS, so the tracing to the FTLS gave an "almost formal" definition of the module's behaviour. Where the module did have a low level Z specification, there was a direct correspondence between the operations of the module and those defined in the Z. We could have achieved even greater rigour by translating the Z into SPARK pre- and post-condition annotations. However, we did not feel that this gave us enough extra benefit to be worthwhile. The main reason was that the concrete state was usually more complex than the abstract state in the Z, but the relationship was very straightforward. The translation would therefore have been tedious but not very valuable.

The low-level CSP processes translated very directly into Ada tasks and calls to protected objects. This relationship, although again informal, is quite straightforward.

5   Conclusions

It is clear that the use of formal methods in a development of this sort is practical. Furthermore it is our experience in this and other projects that well-considered use of formal methods is beneficial whether or not there is any regulatory requirement for it.

Specifically, our use of Z for the formal security policy model and for the formal functional specification helped produce an indisputable specification of functionality, which was the authority for all future development, testing and change control.

At the design level, we extended this formality by using Z, CSP and SPARK. This was also beneficial. However, not all aspects of design can be formalised and it is necessary to have clear relationships between formal and informal parts of the design.

The development has been successful. The number of faults in the system is low compared with systems developed using less formal approaches. The delivered system satisfies ist users, performs well and is highly reliable in use. Productivity is within normal commercial range for systems of this type: formal methods do not add to the cost of the project. Furthermore, the benefits continue into the maintenance phase. The CA is now maintained by Mondex, and they endorse the advantages of a formal specification for maintenance, since it makes the specification of changes less ambiguous and greatly improves the chances of identifying side effects of a change on other parts of the system.

However, we must include two caveats. The first is that our use of formality did not extend to the use of proof, although in other contexts [3] we have used proof at both specification and code level successfully. The second is that the product has not in fact been evaluated against ITSEC E6, so that our view of whether we actually achieved E6 levels of assurance remains conjecture. Nevertheless, we are convinced that the rigour of E6 and in particular ist emphasis on formality is beneficial for high integrity projects.

Acknowledgements. The author would like to thank John Beric of Mondex International for his permission to publish this paper.

References

1. See www.multos.com
2. Barnes, J., *High Integrity Ada - The SPARK Approach.* Addison Wesley, 1997. See also www.sparkada.com
3. Steve King, Jonathan Hammond, Rod Chapman and Andy Pryor *Is Proof More Cost-Effective Than Testing?*, IEEE Transactions on Software Engineering, Vol 26 No 8, pp675–686 (August 2000).
4. Information Technology Security Evaluation Criteria (ITSEC), Provisional Harmonised Criteria, Version 1.2, June 1991.
5. CESG Computer Security Manual 'F' – A Formal Development Method for High Assurance Systems, Communications Electronics Security Group, 1995.
6. Jonathan Hammond, Rosamund Rawlings and Anthony Hall, *Will it Work?* Proceedings of RE'01, 5th International Symposium on Requirements Engineering August 2001.
7. Anthony Hall and Roderick Chapman, *Correctness by Construction: Developing a Commercial Secure System*, IEEE Software, Jan/Feb 2002, pp18 – 25.

VAlloy – Virtual Functions Meet a Relational Language

Darko Marinov and Sarfraz Khurshid

MIT Laboratory for Computer Science
200 Technology Square
Cambridge, MA 02139 USA
{marinov,khurshid}@lcs.mit.edu

Abstract. We propose VAlloy, a veneer onto the first order, relational language Alloy. Alloy is suitable for modeling structural properties of object-oriented software. However, Alloy lacks support for dynamic dispatch, i.e., function invocation based on actual parameter types. VAlloy introduces virtual functions in Alloy, which enables intuitive modeling of inheritance. Models in VAlloy are automatically translated into Alloy and can be automatically checked using the existing Alloy Analyzer. We illustrate the use of VAlloy by modeling object equality, such as in Java. We also give specifications for a part of the Java Collections Framework.

1 Introduction

Object-oriented design and object-oriented programming have become predominant software methodologies. An essential feature of object-oriented languages is *inheritance*. It allows a (sub)class to inherit variables and methods from superclasses. Some languages, such as Java, only support single inheritance for classes.

Subclasses can *override* some methods, changing the behavior inherited from superclasses. We use C++ term *virtual functions* to refer to methods that can be overridden. Virtual functions are *dynamically dispatched*—the actual function to invoke is selected based on the dynamic types of parameters. Java only supports single dynamic dispatch, i.e., the function is selected based only on the type of the *receiver* object.

Alloy [9] is a first order, declarative language based on relations. Alloy is suitable for specifying structural properties of software. Alloy *specifications* can be analyzed automatically using the Alloy Analyzer (AA) [8]. Given a finite *scope* for a specification, AA translates it into a propositional formula and uses SAT solving technology to generate *instances* that satisfy the properties expressed in the specification.

Alloy supports some features of object-oriented design. However, Alloy does not have built in support for dynamic dispatch. Recently, Jackson and Fekete [7] presented an approach for modeling parts of Java in Alloy, pointing out that modeling "the notion of equality is problematic".

L.-H. Eriksson and P. Lindsay (Eds.): FME 2002, LNCS 2391, pp. 234–251, 2002.
© Springer-Verlag Berlin Heidelberg 2002

In Java, the `equals` method, which allows comparing object values, as opposed to using the '`==`' operator, which compares object identities, is overridden in majority of classes. Good programming methodology suggests that `equals` be overridden in all immutable classes [14]. This method is pervasively used, for example in the Java Collections Framework [22] for comparing elements of collections. Any `equals` method must satisfy a set of properties, such as implementing an equivalence relation; otherwise, the collections do not behave as expected. However, getting `equals` methods right is surprisingly hard.

We present VAlloy, a veneer onto Alloy that enables intuitive modeling of dynamic dispatch. VAlloy introduces in Alloy virtual functions and related inheritance constructs. We give VAlloy a formal semantics through a translation to Alloy. The translation is similar to compilation of object-oriented languages, involving creation of virtual function tables. Since VAlloy models can be automatically translated to Alloy, they can also be automatically analyzed using the existing AA.

Having an easy way to model dynamic dispatch is important for several reasons. First, it enables automatic analysis of models of overridden methods. Second, it allows modeling comparisons based on object values and developing specifications for collections that use these comparisons, such as Java collections. Third, such specifications can be used to test the actual implementations, for example using the TestEra framework [16].

The rest of this paper is organized as follows. Section 2 gives an example that illustrates the key constructs of VAlloy. Section 3 defines a semantics for VAlloy through a translation to Alloy. Section 4 presents VAlloy specifications that partially model Java-like collections. Section 5 discusses some extensions to the key constructs of VAlloy. Section 6 reviews related work, and Section 7 presents our conclusions. The Appendix describes the basics of Alloy and the Alloy Analyzer.

2 Example

We illustrate VAlloy by modeling and analyzing an (in)correct overriding of the `equals` method in Java. We first develop an Alloy specification that contains only one `equals` method, and then describe challenges that arise in modeling method overriding. Finally, we present how VAlloy tackles these challenges.

2.1 Modeling `Equals` in Alloy

Consider the following `equals` method that appears in `java.awt.Dimension` in the standard Java libraries [22]:

```
class Dimension {
    int width;
    int height;
    public boolean equals(Object obj) {
        if (!(obj instanceof Dimension))
            return false;
        Dimension d = (Dimension)obj;
```

```
        return (width == d.width) && (height == d.height);
    }
}
```

We develop in Alloy (not yet VAlloy) a specification for the above method. An Alloy specification consists of a sequence of paragraphs that either introduce an *uninterpreted type* or express constraints over the types. We start with the following declarations:

```
sig Object {}                    // java.lang.Object
sig Dimension extends Object {   // java.awt.Dimension
  width: Integer,
  height: Integer
}
```

Each *signature*, introduced by the keyword `sig`, denotes a set of atomic individuals. In this specification, atoms in `sig Object` model Java objects. The signature `Dimension` is declared it to be a subset of `Object`. Alloy subsets model Java subclassing with typing rules being as follows.

Signatures declared without `extends` are *basic* signatures. Basic signatures are disjoint from one another and represent Alloy types. Subsets do not introduce new Alloy types. The type of an atom is the basic signature it belongs to; all atoms in the above specification, including those in `Dimension`, have Alloy type `Object`. We can reconstruct Java type, i.e., class, of modeled Java objects based on their (sub)set membership.

Fields `width` and `height` introduce relations between `Dimension` atoms and `Integer` atoms, where `Integer` is predefined in Alloy. More precisely, each field introduces a function that maps `Dimension` atoms to `Integer` atoms.

We next add to the specification a model of the above `equals` method:

```
fun Dimension::equals(obj: Object) {
  obj in Dimension              // instanceof
  this.width = obj.width && this.height = obj.height
}
```

The Alloy *function* `equals` records constraints that can be invoked elsewhere in the specification. This function has two arguments: `obj` and the implicit `this` argument, introduced with '`::`'. The function body constrains `obj` to be an atom of `Dimension`, effectively modeling Java's `instanceof`. This constraint is conjoined with the other that requires the fields to be the same. However, the above declaration does not constrain `this` to be an atom of `Dimension`; the declaration is equivalent to `fun Object::equals(obj: Object)`.

We next use the Alloy Analyzer (AA) to automatically check properties of the above specification. Each `equals` method should satisfy a set of properties: implement an equivalence relation and be consistent with `hashCode` [22]. The following Alloy assertion requires the function `equals`, which models the method `equals`, to be an equivalence relation:

```
assert equalsIsEquivalence {
  all o: Object |            // reflexivity
    o..equals(o)
  all o1, o2: Object |       // symmetry
    o1..equals(o2) => o2..equals(o1)
  all o1, o2, o3: Object |   // transitivity
    o1..equals(o2) && o2..equals(o3) => o1..equals(o3)
}
```

The operator '..' invokes Alloy functions (using static resolution). AA checks the above assertion and reports that there are no counterexamples.

2.2 Overriding

Consider `Dimension3D`, a subclass of `java.awt.Dimension` that adds a field `depth` and overrides `equals`:

```
class Dimension3D extends java.awt.Dimension {
    int depth;
    boolean equals(Object obj) {
        if (!(obj instanceof Dimension3D))
            return false;
        Dimension3D d = (Dimension3D)obj;
        return super.equals(obj) && depth = d.depth;
    }
}
```

In order to check the `equals` method in `Dimension3D`, we would like to add the following to the Alloy specification presented so far:

```
sig Dimension3D extends Dimension {
  depth: Integer
}
// duplicate function names are NOT allowed in Alloy
fun Dimension3D::equals(obj: Object) {
  obj in Dimension3D
  // super.equals needs to be inlined because
  // there is no built in support for super
  this.width = obj.width && this.height = obj.height
  this.depth = obj.depth
}
```

However, this does not produce the intended model of overriding. In fact, this is not even a legal Alloy specification—each Alloy specification must have unique function names.[1] We could try renaming one of the `equals` functions, but it does not directly solve the problem of modeling overriding. Namely, the invocations `o..equals(o')` should choose the function based on the Java type/class of o. Since Alloy has no built in support for dynamic dispatch, we would need to model it manually for each function. Instead, we propose that it be done automatically.

2.3 Modeling `Equals` in VAlloy

VAlloy introduces a natural way to model dynamic dispatch in Alloy. The following VAlloy specification models the above Java classes:

```
class Object {}
virtual fun Object::equals(obj: Object) { this = obj }

class Dimension {
  width: Integer,
  height: Integer
}
virtual fun Dimension::equals(obj: Object) {
  obj in Dimension
  this.width = obj.width && this.height = obj.height
}
```

---

[1] That is why we do not initially add `equals` function for `Object`.

```
class Dimension3D extends Dimension {
  depth: Integer
}
virtual fun Dimension3D::equals(obj: Object) {
  obj in Dimension3D
  super..equals(obj) && this.depth = obj.depth
}
```

The **class** declaration in VAlloy corresponds to the Alloy declaration **disj sig**, where **disj** indicates that the declared subset is disjoint from other **disj** subsets of its parent set. As in Java, VAlloy classes by default extend **Object**.

The **virtual** function modifier[2] is the main VAlloy extension to Alloy. This modifier declares a function that is dynamically dispatched at invocation, based on the VAlloy class of the receiver. VAlloy allows virtual functions to have the same name. The above example also shows the keyword **super** that VAlloy provides for modeling **super** as found in Java.

2.4   Checking VAlloy Specifications

Every VAlloy specification can be automatically translated into an Alloy specification. Section 3 presents the translation and the resulting Alloy specification for our running example.[3]

We use AA to automatically check the above assertion **equalsIsEquivalence**. Note that the invocations in the assertion do not need to change; the translation properly models dynamic dispatch. AA generates a counterexample[4]:

```
Object_2: Dimension3D {
  width = 0,
  height = 1,
  depth = 2
}
Object_1: Dimension {
  width = 0,
  height = 1
}
```

These two objects violate the symmetry property: `Object_1..equals(Object_2)`, but *not* `Object_2..equals(Object_1)`. This is because **equals** of **Dimension** is oblivious of the field **depth** declared in **Dimension3D**. This counterexample shows that it is hard to extend the **java.awt.Dimension** class and preserve the properties of **equals**.

A way to provide an overridable implementation of **equals** in Java is to use the **getClass** method instead of the **instanceof** primitive [18]. In the running example, it requires changing **equals** of **java.awt.Dimension** to use the expression `obj.getClass() == this.getClass()` instead of `obj instanceof Dimension`. A similar change should be made in **Dimension3D**, unless it is declared **final**, and therefore cannot be extended.

---

[2] VAlloy borrows the modifier name from C++.

[3] We have not yet implemented the translation; we perform it manually.

[4] AA took 5 seconds (including its boot-up time) using a scope of 3 atoms in each basic signature on a Pentium III 700 MHz with 256MB RAM.

Modeling this change in VAlloy is straightforward: change `obj in Dimension` with `obj..getClass() = this..getClass()` in the function `Dimension::equals`. VAlloy provides the function `getClass` that models the `final` method `getClass` from the class `java.lang.Object`. We translate the changed VAlloy specification into Alloy and again use AA to check the equivalence assertion. This time AA reports that there are no counterexamples.

3   VAlloy

This section presents VAlloy as an extension to Alloy. We define a formal semantics for VAlloy by giving a translation of VAlloy specifications to Alloy specifications. Details of Alloy semantics can be found in [9].

VAlloy adds the following to Alloy:

- `virtual` function modifier that declares a function whose invocation depends on the class of the receiver;
- `class` declaration that introduces VAlloy classes;
- `super` keyword that directly correspond to Java;
- `getClass` function that corresponds to the `getClass` method of the class `java.lang.Object`.

These constructs are syntactically added to Alloy in the obvious way.

3.1   Translation Example

We give a semantics to the new constructs through a translation into Alloy. The translation algorithm operates in six steps, which we first describe through examples. Figures 1 and 2 show the Java code and VAlloy specification from Section 2. For this example, the translation proceeds as follows.

Step 1. Compute the hierarchy of `class` declarations:

```
Object
+-- Dimension
     +-- Dimension3D
```

Step 2. Construct `sig Class` and `sig Object` based on the above hierarchy:

```
sig Class { ext: option Class }
static part sig Object_Class, Dimension_Class,
              Dimension3D_Class extends Class {}
fact Hierarchy {
  no Object_Class.ext
    Dimension_Class.ext = Object_Class
      Dimension3D_Class.ext = Dimension_Class
}
sig Object { class: Class }
fact ObjectClasses {
  (Object - Dimension).class = Object_Class
    (Dimension - Dimension3D).class = Dimension_Class
      Dimension3D.class = Dimension3D_Class
}
fun Object::getClass(): Class { result = this.class }
```

```
class Object {
    boolean equals(obj: Object) {
        return this == obj;
    }
}
class Dimension {
    int width;
    int height;
    boolean equals(obj: Object) {
        if (obj.getClass() != this.getClass())
            return false;
        Dimension d = (Dimension)obj;
        return width == d.width &&
               height == d.height;
    }
}
class Dimension3D extends Dimension {
    int depth;
    boolean equals(obj: Object) {
        if (obj.getClass() != this.getClass())
            return false;
        Dimension3d d = (Dimension3d)obj;
        return super.equals(obj) &&
               depth == d.depth;
    }
}
```

Fig. 1. Java code

```
class Object {}
virtual fun Object::equals(obj: Object) {
    this = obj
}

class Dimension {
    width: Integer,
    height: Integer
}
virtual fun Dimension::equals(obj: Object) {
    obj..getClass() = this..getClass()
    this.width = obj.width
    this.height = obj.height
}
class Dimension3D extends Dimension {
    depth: Integer
}
virtual fun Dimension3D::equals(obj: Object) {
    obj..getClass() = this..getClass()
    super..equals(obj)
    this.depth = obj.depth
}

assert equalsIsEquivalence {
    all o: Object |              // reflexivity
        o..equals(o)
    all o1, o2: Object |         // symmetry
        o1..equals(o2) => o2..equals(o1)
    all o1, o2, o3: Object |     // transitivity
        o1..equals(o2) && o2..equals(o3) =>
        o1..equals(o3)
}
```

Fig. 2. VAlloy specification

```
sig Class { ext: option Class }
static part sig
    Object_Class, Dimension_Class,
    Dimension3D_Class extends Class {}
fact Hierarchy {
    no Object_Class.ext
    Dimension_Class.ext = Object_Class
        Dimension3D_Class.ext = Dimension_Class
}
sig Object { class: Class }
fact ObjectClasses {
    (Object - Dimension).class = Object_Class
    (Dimension - Dimension3D).class =
        Dimension_Class
    Dimension3D.class = Dimension3D_Class
}
fun Object::getClass(): Class {
    result = this.class
}
fun Object::equals(obj: Object) {
    this.class = Object_Class =>
    this..Object_equals(obj)
        this.class = Dimension_Class =>
        this..Dimension_equals(obj)
            this.class = Dimension3D_Class =>
            this..Dimension3D_equals(obj)
}

fun Object::Object_equals(obj: Object) {
    this = obj
}

disj sig Dimension extends Object {
    width: Integer,
    height: Integer
}
fun Object::Dimension_equals(obj: Object) {
    obj..getClass() = this..getClass()
    this.width = obj.width
    this.height = obj.height
}

disj sig Dimension3D extends Dimension {
    depth: Integer
}
fun Object::Dimension3D_equals(obj: Object) {
    obj..getClass() = this..getClass()
    this..Dimension_equals(obj)
    this.depth = obj.depth
}

assert equalsIsEquivalence {
    all o: Object |              // reflexivity
        o..equals(o)
    all o1, o2: Object |         // symmetry
        o1..equals(o2) => o2..equals(o1)
    all o1, o2, o3: Object |     // transitivity
        o1..equals(o2) && o2..equals(o3) =>
        o1..equals(o3)
}
```

Fig. 3. Translated Alloy specification

Atoms in `Class` and the *fact* `Hierarchy` represent the VAlloy `class` declarations. (A `fact` in Alloy expresses constraints that must hold for all instances of the specification.) For each atom `c` in `Class`, `c.ext` gives the `Class` atom that corresponds to the superclass of `c`.[5] The keyword `static` constrains each of the declared subsets to contain exactly one atom, and the keyword `part` declares a partition—the subsets are disjoint and their union is the whole set.

For each atom `o` in `Object`, `o.class` gives the corresponding `Class` atom. This correspondence is set with `fact ObjectClasses` based on the VAlloy `class` hierarchy. (The '-' operator denotes set difference in Alloy.) This translation step also introduces the function `getClass`.

Step 3. Change `class` declarations into `disj sig` declarations, adding `extends Object` where required:

```
disj sig Dimension extends Object { ... }
disj sig Dimension3D extends Dimension { ... }
```

This step does not change field declarations.[6]

Step 4. Rename each virtual function so that all functions in the specification have unique names:

```
fun Object::Object_equals(obj: Object) { this = obj }
fun Object::Dimension_equals(obj: Object) { ... }
fun Object::Dimension3D_equals(obj: Object) { ... }
```

This step also removes the modifier `virtual`, translating dynamically dispatched VAlloy functions into statically dispatched Alloy functions.

Step 5. Add, for each overridden function name, a *dispatching* function, i.e., a new Alloy function that models dynamic dispatch:

```
fun Object::equals(obj: Object) {
  this.class = Object_Class =>
  this..Object_equals(obj)
    this.class = Dimension_Class =>
    this..Dimension_equals(obj)
      this.class = Dimension3D_Class =>
      this..Dimension3D_equals(obj)
}
```

This step is the crux of the translation. It allows function invocations in VAlloy to be written in the usual Alloy notation, but it models dynamic dispatch semantics—the actual function is selected based on the class of the receiver.

Step 6. Replace each invocation on `super` with an invocation to the corresponding, previously renamed, static function:

```
fun Object::Dimension3D_equals(obj: Object) {
  obj..getClass() = this..getClass()
  this..Dimension_equals(obj) && this.depth = obj.depth
}
```

---

[5] For simplicity, we only present single inheritance, where the hierarchy can only be a tree. In multiple inheritance, each class can have a set of superclasses.

[6] For simplicity, we do not present modeling `null`, which would require slightly changing field declarations.

This completes the translation. Figure 3 shows the full resulting Alloy specification. Note that the translation does not change the assertion; the invocations o..equals(o') remain written in the most intuitive manner, but they have dynamic dispatch semantics.

3.2 General `Class` Hierarchy

To illustrate the general translation of `class` hierarchy, consider the following excerpt from a VAlloy specification:

```
class O {}              virtual fun O::hC() { /*O*/ }
  class C extends O {}     virtual fun C::hC() { /*C*/ }
    class C1 extends C {} // C1 does not define fun hC
    class C2 extends C {} virtual fun C2::hC() { /*C2*/ }
  class D extends O {}     // D does not define fun hC
    class D1 extends D {} virtual fun D1::hC() { /*D1*/ }
```

For this hierarchy, the translation generates the following `sig Class` and `sig Object`:

```
sig Class { ext: option Class }
static part sig O_Class, C_Class, C1_Class, C2_Class,
                D_Class, D1_Class extends Class {}
fact Hierarchy {
  no O_Class.ext
    C_Class.ext = O_Class
      C1_Class.ext = C_Class
      C2_Class.ext = C_Class
    D_Class.ext = O_Class
      D1_Class.ext = D_Class
}
sig Object { class: Class }
fact ObjectClasses {
  (O - C - D).class = O_Class
    (C - C1 - C2).class = C_Class
      C1.class = C1_Class
      C2.class = C2_Class
    (D - D1).class = D_Class
      D1.class = D1_Class
}
```

For the function `hC`, the translation generates the following Alloy functions:

```
fun O::O_hC() { /*O*/ }
fun O::C_hC() { /*C*/ }
// there is no O::C1_hC()
fun O::C2_hC() { /*C2*/ }
// there is no O::D_hC()
fun O::D1_hC() { /*D1*/ }
fun O::hC() {
  this.class = O_Class => this..O_hC()
    this.class = C_Class => this..C_hC()
      this.class = C1_Class => this..C_hC() /* not C1 */
      this.class = C2_Class => this..C2_hC()
    this.class = D_Class => this..O_hC() /* not D */
      this.class = D1_Class => this..D1_hC()
}
```

3.3 Summary

To summarize, the translation from VAlloy to Alloy proceeds in the following six steps:

1. Compute the hierarchy of `class` declarations.
2. Construct `sig Class` and `sig Object`.
3. Change `class` into `disj sig` declarations.
4. Rename uniquely each virtual function.
5. Add dispatching functions.
6. Replace `super` with an appropriate static invocation.

4   Collections

This section presents VAlloy models for some collection classes. Our main focus is comparison based on object values. We ignore the orthogonal issue of modeling state, i.e., sharing and object interactions. An approach for modeling state in Alloy is discussed in [7], and we can apply the same approach to VAlloy.

We first present a specification for sets and then reuse it to specify maps. Finally, using a tree-based implementation of sets, we show how properties of abstract data types can be expressed in VAlloy.

4.1   Sets

We develop a VAlloy specification for sets whose membership is based on object values, not object identities. As in Java, elements of the sets are objects of classes that (in)directly extend `Object` and potentially override `equals`.

We first declare a VAlloy class for sets:

```
class Set { s: set Object }
```

For each atom `a` in `Set`, `a.s` is the (Alloy) set of objects in the (modeled) set `a`. To constrain set membership to be based on object values, we introduce the following `fact`:

```
fact SetIsBasedOnEquals {
  all a: Set | all disj e1, e2: a.s | !e1..equals(e2)
}
```

This `fact` requires distinct elements in each set to be not equal with respect to `equals`. For example, this rules out the set `a` such that `a.s={d1,d2}`, where `d1` and `d2` are distinct atoms (i.e., `d1!=d2`) of `Dimension`, but `d1.width=3`, `d1.height=8` and also `d2.width=3`, `d2.height=8`, which makes `d1..equals(d2)`. Note that `a.s` is a valid Alloy set.

It is now easy to specify some set functions from the `java.util.Set` interface:

```
virtual fun Set::contains(o: Object) {
  some e: this.s | o..equals(e)
}
virtual fun Set::add(o: Object): Set {
  this.s..contains(o) =>
    result.s = this.s,
    result.s = this.s + o
}
virtual fun Set::remove(o: Object): Set {
  result.s = this.s - { e: this.s | e..equals(o) }
}
virtual fun Set::isEmpty() { no this.s }
```

```
virtual fun Set::clear(): Set { no result.s }
virtual fun Set::size(): Integer { result = #this.s }
virtual fun Set::subset(a: Set) {
  all e: this.s | a..contains(e)
}
virtual fun Set::equals(o: Object) {
  o in Set
  o..size() = this..size()
  o..subset(this)
}
```

The most interesting function is **equals**, which compares two sets for equality. It checks that both sets have the same number of elements and that **o** is a subset (based on **equals**) of **this**. The function **remove** uses set comprehension to specify an object's removal from a set.

The above VAlloy specification closely models **java.util.Set**. The main difference is that this specification is written in a functional style and does not model state modifications. As mentioned, state can be modeled using the approach from [7], which also presents a way to handle iterators. Therefore, we do not model "bulk operations" on sets, such as **addAll**, based on iterators. Instead, we present an analogous function for set union:

```
virtual fun Set::union(a: Set): Set {
  this..subset(result)
  a..subset(result)
  all e: result.s | this..contains(e) || a..contains(e)
}
```

Note that the use of **contains** (and **subset** based on **contains**), which is based on **equals**, enables specifying **union** in a direct way.

4.2   Maps

We next develop a partial VAlloy specification for maps, such as **java.util.Map**, that compare keys based on **equals**. In this specification, we reuse the **class Set** defined above to automatically constrain the set of keys:

```
class Map {
  keys: Set
  map: keys.s ->! Object
}
```

We model the mapping from keys to values using an Alloy relation **map**; the *multiplicity marking* '!' indicates that for each key, there is exactly one **Object**. For each atom **a** in **class Map**, **a.map** is the actual mapping. For a key **k**, **a.map[k]** gives the value that **k** is mapped to in map **a**.

We next model the essential map functions:

```
virtual fun Map::get(key: Object): Object {
  this.keys..contains(key) => result = this.map[key]
}
virtual fun Map::put(key: Object, value: Object): Map {
  result.keys = (this.key - { e: this.keys | e..equals(key) }) + key,
  result.map = (this.map - { e: this.keys | e..equals(key) }->Object) + key->value
}
```

The function **get** returns the value that **key** is mapped to, if such a key exists in the map; otherwise, the behavior of **get** is unspecified. (Since Alloy is a relational language, non-determinism comes for free.) We can constrain **get** to be deterministic, e.g., to return an explicit **Null** object, if the key is not in the map.

4.3   Trees

We next use a tree-based implementation of sets to illustrate how properties of abstract data types can be expressed in VAlloy. Consider the following declaration for binary trees:

```
class Tree { root: Node }
class Node {
  left: Node,
  right: Node,
  data: Object
}
```

Suppose that these VAlloy trees model a Java implementation of sets based on `equals`. We can state the *abstraction function* [14] for these trees in VAlloy:

```
fun Tree::abstractionFunction(): Set {
  result.s = this.root.*(left+right).data
}
```

The '*' operator is reflexive transitive closure, and `root.*(left+right)` denotes an (Alloy) set of all `Node`s reachable from the `root`. The set of `Object`s from those nodes is obtained accessing `data`, and the abstraction function constrains this Alloy set to be a `Set`.

We also use VAlloy to state *representation invariant* [14] for these trees. Assume that they have the following structural constraints: root nodes are sentinels (and thus never `null`) and leaf nodes point to themselves. The following `repOk` predicate characterizes the representation invariants for a tree:

```
fun Tree::repOk() {
  // no node points to root
  no this.root.~(left+right)
  // acyclic (with self loops for leafs)
  all n: this.root.*(left+right) {
    n.left = n || n !in n.left.*(left+right)
    n.right = n || n !in n.right.*(left+right)
  }
  // no duplicates w.r.t equals()
  some a: Set | a = this..abstractionFunction()
}
```

(The '~' operator denotes transpose of a binary Alloy relation.) Beside the structural invariants, a valid tree is required to be a concrete representation of some `Set`. Note how the `equals` constraints from the abstract representation, `Set`, propagate to the concrete representation, `Tree`.

5   Extensions

VAlloy presents our first step toward modeling in Alloy advanced constructs from object-oriented languages. The main focus has been on method overriding in Java. We have therefore designed VAlloy to support subclasses that can arbitrarily change behavior of inherited methods.

Our approach can easily be extended to support intuitive modeling of multiple inheritance, such as in C++, and multi-method dispatch, such as in Cecil. Support for method overloading can clearly be added through a simple syntactic manipulation. We omitted support for Java's interfaces, keeping in line with

Alloy's "micromodularity" philosophy of being a lightweight language amenable to fully automatic analysis. Similarly, we do not consider encapsulation.

We have recently developed some recipes to model in Alloy several other common imperative programming constructs like mutation, statement sequencing, object allocation, local variables, and recursion. We have used these recipes to design AAL [12], an annotation language based on Alloy for Java programs. AAL offers both fully automatic compile-time analysis using the Alloy Analyzer and dynamic analysis through generation of run-time assertions.

We would like to develop further recipes, for example, for modeling in Alloy the exceptional behavior of methods. Having exceptions would also allow modeling arrays with bound checking. We are also considering adding support for modeling multi-threading.

To explore practical value of VAlloy, we intend to implement the translation and use VAlloy in connection with some existing frameworks. Daikon [3] is a tool for dynamically detecting likely program invariants; we are considering to use it to detect (partial) VAlloy specifications of Java classes. TestEra [16] is a framework for automated test generation and correctness evaluation of Java classes; we are considering to use VAlloy specifications for TestEra.

6   Related Work

Recently, Jackson and Fekete [7] proposed an approach for modeling in Alloy object interactions, like those in Java. Their approach models heap using explicit references and captures properties of object sharing and aliasing. However, the approach does not handle inheritance in the presence of method overriding and dynamic dispatch. Their approach is orthogonal to our handling of virtual functions; we are planning to combine these two approaches.

Alloy has been used to check properties of programs that manipulate dynamic data structures. Jackson and Vaziri [10] developed a technique for analyzing bounded segments of procedures that manipulate linked lists. Their technique automatically builds an Alloy model of computation and checks it against a specification. They consider a small subset of Java, without dynamic dispatch.

We developed TestEra [16], a framework for automated testing of Java programs. In TestEra, specifications are written in Alloy and the Alloy Analyzer is used to provide automatic test case generation and correctness evaluation of programs. Writing specifications for Java collections, which use comparisons based on object values, requires modeling the equals method in Alloy. This led us to tackle modeling general Java-like inheritance in Alloy. VAlloy presents some ideas toward that goal.

The Java Modeling Language (JML) [13] is a popular specification language for Java. JML assertions use Java syntax and semantics, with some additional constructs, most notably for quantification. Leveraging on Java, JML specifications can obviously express dynamic dispatch. However, JML lacks static tools for automatic verification of such specifications.

The LOOP project [23] models inheritance in higher order logic to reason about Java classes. Java classes and their JML specifications are compiled into logical theories in higher order logic. A theorem prover is used to verify the desired properties. This framework has been used to verify that the methods of `java.util.Vector` maintain the safety property that the actual size of a vector is less than or equal to its capacity [4].

Object-oriented paradigm has been integrated into many existing languages, typically to make reuse easier. For example, Object-Z [20] extends the Z specification language [21], which enables building specifications in an object-oriented style. Object-Z retains the syntax and semantics of Z, adding new constructs. The major new construct is the class schema that captures the object-oriented notion of a class.. Object-Z allows inheritance to be modeled, but it lacks tool support for automatically analyzing specifications.

Objects and inheritance have also been added to declarative languages. For example, Prolog++ [17] extends Prolog. OOLP+ [2] aims to integrate object-oriented paradigm with logic programming by translating OOLP+ code into Prolog without meta-interpretation.

Keidar et al. [11] add inheritance to the IOA language [15] for modeling state machines, which enables reusing simulation proofs between state machines. This approach allows only a limited form of inheritance, subclassing for extension: subclasses can add new methods and *specialize* inherited methods, but they cannot override those inherited methods, changing their behavior arbitrarily. VAlloy allows subclasses to arbitrarily change the behavior of inherited methods.

7 Conclusions

We described VAlloy, a veneer onto the first order, relational language Alloy. All function invocations in Alloy are static; Alloy has no direct support for dynamic dispatch. VAlloy introduces virtual functions in Alloy, which enables intuitive modeling of inheritance, such as that of Java. We illustrated the use of VAlloy by modeling a small part of the Java Collections Framework.

We defined a formal semantics for VAlloy through a translation to Alloy. VAlloy models can be automatically translated into Alloy. The translation is similar to building virtual function tables for object-oriented languages and can benefit from optimizations based on class hierarchy. The translated specifications can be automatically checked using the existing Alloy Analyzer. We believe that VAlloy can be effectively used for specification and checking of Java classes.

Acknowledgments. We would like to thank Manu Sridharan and Ang-Chih Kao for comments on an earlier draft of this paper. This work was funded in part by ITR grant #0086154 from the National Science Foundation.

References

1. J. Crawford, M. Ginsberg, E. Luks, and A. Roy. Symmetry-breaking predicates for search problems. In *Proc. Fifth International Conference on Principles of Knowledge Representation and Reasoning*, 1996.
2. Mukesh Dalal and Dipayan Gangopahyay. OOLP: A translation approach to object-oriented logic programming. In *Proc. First International Conference on Deductive and Object-Oriented Databases (DOOD-89)*, pages 555–568, Kyoto, Japan, December 1989.
3. Michael D. Ernst. *Dynamically Discovering Likely Program Invariants*. PhD thesis, University of Washington Department of Computer Science and Engineering, Seattle, Washington, August 2000.
4. Marieke Huisman, Bart Jacobs, and Joachim van den Berg. A case study in class library verification: Java's Vector class. *Software Tools for Technology Transfer*, 2001.
5. Daniel Jackson. Micromodels of software: Modelling and analysis with Alloy, 2001. Available online: http://sdg.lcs.mit.edu/alloy/book.pdf.
6. Daniel Jackson. Alloy: A lightweight object modeling notation. *ACM Transactions on Software Engineering and Methodology*, 2002. (to appear).
7. Daniel Jackson and Alan Fekete. Lightweight analysis of object interactions. In *Proc. Fourth International Symposium on Theoretical Aspects of Computer Software*, Sendai, Japan, October 2001.
8. Daniel Jackson, Ian Schechter, and Ilya Shlyakhter. ALCOA: The Alloy constraint analyzer. In *Proc. 22nd International Conference on Software Engineering (ICSE)*, Limerick, Ireland, June 2000.
9. Daniel Jackson, Ilya Shlyakhter, and Manu Sridharan. A micromodularity mechanism. In *Proc. 9th ACM SIGSOFT Symposium on the Foundations of Software Engineering (FSE)*, Vienna, Austria, September 2001.
10. Daniel Jackson and Mandana Vaziri. Finding bugs with a constraint solver. In *Proc. International Symposium on Software Testing and Analysis (ISSTA)*, Portland, OR, August 2000.
11. Idit Keidar, Roger Khazan, Nancy Lynch, and Alex Shvartsman. An inheritance-based technique for building simulation proofs incrementally. In *Proc. 22nd International Conference on Software Engineering (ICSE)*, pages 478–487, Limerick, Ireland, June 2000.
12. Sarfraz Khurshid, Darko Marinov, and Daniel Jackson. An analyzable annotation language. In *Proc. ACM SIGPLAN 2002 Conference on Object-Oriented Programming Systems, Languages and Applications (OOPSLA)*, Seattle, WA, Nov 2002.
13. Gary T. Leavens, Albert L. Baker, and Clyde Ruby. Preliminary design of JML: A behavioral interface specification language for Java. Technical Report TR 98-06i, Department of Computer Science, Iowa State University, June 1998. (last revision: Aug 2001).
14. Barbara Liskov. *Program Development in Java: Abstraction, Specification, and Object-Oriented Design*. Addison-Wesley, 2000.
15. Nancy Lynch. *Distributed Algorithms*. Morgan Kaufmann Publishers, 1996.
16. Darko Marinov and Sarfraz Khurshid. TestEra: A novel framework for automated testing of Java programs. In *Proc. 16th IEEE International Conference on Automated Software Engineering (ASE)*, San Diego, CA, November 2001.
17. Chris Moss. *Prolog++ The Power of Object-Oriented and Logic Programming*. Addison-Wesley, 1994.

18. Mark Roulo. How to avoid traps and correctly override methods from `java.lang.Object`.
    http://www.javaworld.com/javaworld/jw-01-1999/jw-01-object.html.
19. Ilya Shlyakhter. Generating effective symmetry-breaking predicates for search problems. In *Proc. Workshop on Theory and Applications of Satisfiability Testing*, June 2001.
20. G. Smith. *The Object-Z Specification Language*. Kluwer Academic Publishers, 2000.
21. J. M. Spivey. *The Z Notation: A Reference Manual*. Prentice Hall, second edition, 1992.
22. Sun Microsystems. *Java 2 Platform, Standard Edition, v1.3.1 API Specification*. http://java.sun.com/j2se/1.3/docs/api/.
23. Joachim van den Berg and Bart Jacobs. The LOOP compiler for Java and JML. In *Proc. Tools and Algorithms for the Construction and Analysis of Software (TACAS), (Springer LNCS 2031, 2001)*, pages 299–312, Genoa, Italy, April 2001.

A   Alloy

In this section we describe the basics of the Alloy specification language and the Alloy Analyzer; details can be found in [5,6,8]. Alloy is a strongly typed language that assumes a universe of atoms partitioned into subsets, each of which is associated with a basic type. An Alloy model is a sequence of paragraphs that can be of two kinds: signatures, used for construction of new types, and a variety of formula paragraphs, used to record constraints.

A.1   Signature Paragraphs

A signature paragraph introduces a basic type and a collection of relations (that are called *fields*) in it along with the types of the fields and constraints on their values. For example,

```
sig Class{
    ext: option Class
}
```

introduces `Class` as an uninterpreted type (or a set of atoms). The field declaration for `ext` introduces a relation from `Class` to `Class`. This relation is a partial function as indicated by the keyword `option`: for each atom c of `Class`, c.`ext` is either an atom of `Class` or the empty set. In a field declartion, the keyword `set` can be used to declare an arbitrary relation; ommiting a keyword declares a total function.

A signature may inherit fields and constraints from another signature. For example,

```
static part sig Object_Class, Dimension_Class, Dimension3D_Class extends Class {}
```

declares `Object_Class`, `Dimension_Class`, and `Dimension3D_Class` to be subsets of `Class` and inherit the field `ext`. The keyword `part` declares these subsets to be disjoint and their union to be `Class`; `disj` declares disjoint subsets. In a signature declartion, the keyword `static` specifies the declared signature(s) to (each) contain exactly one element.

A.2 Formula Paragraphs

Formula paragraphs are formed from Alloy expressions.

Relational expressions. The value of any expression in Alloy is always a relation—that is a collection of tuples of atoms. Each element of such a tuple is atomic and belongs to some basic type. A relation may have any arity greater than one. Relations are typed. Sets can be viewed as unary relations.

Relations can be combined with a variety of operators to form expressions. The standard set operators—union (+), intersection (&), and difference (-)—combine two relations of the same type, viewed as sets of tuples. The dot operator is relational composition. When p is a unary relation (i.e., a set) and q is a binary relation, p.q is standard composition; p.q can alternatively be written as q[p], but with lower precedence. The unary operators ~ (transpose), ^ (transitive closure), and * (reflexive transitive closure) have their standard interpretation and can only be applied to binary relations.

Formulas and declarations. Expression quantifiers turn an expression into a formula. The formula no e is true when e denotes a relation containing no tuples. Similarly, some e, sole e, and one e are true when e has some, at most one, and exactly one tuple respectively. Formulas can also be made with relational comparison operators: subset (written : or in), equality (=) and their negations (!:, !in, !=). So e1:e2 is true when every tuple in (the relation denoted by the expression) e1 is also a tuple of e2. Alloy provides the standard logical operators: && (conjunction), || (disjunction), => (implication), and ! (negation); a sequence of formulas within curly braces is implicitly conjoined.

A *declaration* is a formula v op e consisting of a variable v, a comparison operator op, and an arbitrary expression e. Quantified formulas consist of a quantifier, a comma separated list of declarations, and a formula. In addition to the universal and existential quantifiers all and some, there is sole (at most one) and one (exactly one). In a declaration, part specifies partition and disj specifies disjointness; they have their usual meaning.

A set marking is one of the keywords scalar, set or option, prefixing the expression. The keyword scalar adds the side condition that the variable denotes a relation containing a single tuple; set says it may contain any number of tuples; option says it contains at most one tuple. The default marking is set, except when the comparison operator is the colon(:) or negated colon (!:), and the expression on the right is unary, in which case it is scalar.

A relation marking is one of the symbols !, ?, and + read *exactly one, at most one*, and *one or more* respectively. These markings are applied to the left and right of an arrow operator. Suppose a relation r is declared as

```
r : e1 m -> n e2
```

where m and n are relation markings. The markings are interpreted as imposing a side condition on r saying that for each tuple t_1 in e1, there are n tuples t_2 in e2 such that t_1t_2 appears in r, and for each tuple t_2 in e2, there are m tuples t_1 such that t_1t_2 appears in r.

The declaration

```
disj v1,v2,... : e
```

is equivalent to a declaration for each of the variables v1,v2,..., with an additional constraint that the relations denoted by the variables are disjoint (i.e., share no tuple); the declaration part additionally makes their union e.

A.3 Functions, Facts, and Assertions

A function (fun) is a parametrized formula that can be "applied" elsewhere. A fact is a formula that takes no arguments and need not be invoked explicitly; it is always true. An assertion (assert) is a formula whose correctness needs to be checked, assuming the facts in the model.

A.4 Alloy Analyzer

The Alloy Analyzer [8] (AA) is an automatic tool for analyzing models created in Alloy. Given a formula and a *scope*—a bound on the number of atoms in the universe—AA determines whether there exists a model of the formula (that is, an assignment of values to the sets and relations that makes the formula true) that uses no more atoms than the scope permits, and if so, returns it. Since first order logic is undecidable, AA limits its analysis to a finite scope.

AA's analysis [8] is based on a translation to a boolean satisfaction problem, and gains its power by exploiting state-of-the-art SAT solvers.

AA provides two kinds of analysis: *simulation* in which the consistency of a fact or function is demonstrated by generating a snapshot showing its invocation, and *checking*, in which a consequence of the specification is tested by attempting to generate a counterexample.

AA can enumerate all possible instances of an Alloy model. AA adapts the symmetry-breaking predicates of Crawford et al. [1] to provide the functionality of reducing the total number of instances generated—the original boolean formula is conjugated with additional clauses in order to produce only a few instances from each isomorphism class [19].

Verification Using Test Generation Techniques

Vlad Rusu

IRISA/INRIA, Rennes, France
rusu@irisa.fr

Abstract. Applying formal methods to testing has recently become a popular research topic. In this paper we explore the opposite approach, namely, applying testing techniques to formal verification. The idea is to use symbolic test generation to extract subgraphs (called *components*) from a specification and to perform the verification on the components rather than on the whole system. This may considerably reduce the verification effort and, under reasonable sufficient conditions, a safety property verified on a component also holds on the whole specification. We demonstrate the approach by verifying an electronic purse system using our symbolic test generation tool STG and the PVS theorem prover.

Keywords: Formal verification, conformance testing, electronic purse.

1 Introduction

Formal verification and testing are two complementary approaches for ensuring that computer systems operate correctly. In verification, a formal specification of the system is proved correct with respect to some higher-level requirements. In testing, sample runs are executed and an oracle decides whether an error was detected. In *conformance* testing [18,26] the external, observable traces of a black-box implementation of the system are tested for conformance with respect to a formal specification, and the oracle and sample runs are automatically computed from the specification. Test generation tools [4,20] for conformance testing have been developed based on enumerative model-checking algorithms. As specifications are usually large (typically, extended state machines with tens of variables and hundreds of transitions) the enumerative algorithms suffer from the state-explosion problem. Recently, symbolic test generation techniques [23] have been proposed to tackle this problem.

For conformance testing to produce trustworthy results, i.e., to be exempt of false positives and false negatives, it is essential that that the formal specification of the system meets its requirements. Otherwise, the following undesirable scenario can happen. Assume that we (an independent third-party testing laboratory) have to test the conformance of a black-box implementation $\mathcal{I}$ of a system developed by a software company, with respect to a standard provided by a normalization body. The standard includes a large state machine $\mathcal{S}$ and some requirements P describing what $\mathcal{S}$ is supposed to do. Assume that the implementation $\mathcal{I}$ does satisfy P, but, because of an error, the formal specification $\mathcal{S}$

L.-H. Eriksson and P. Lindsay (Eds.): FME 2002, LNCS 2391, pp. 252–271, 2002.

does not. Then, conformance testing may reveal that $\mathcal{I}$ does not conform to $\mathcal{S}$. But, in conformance testing, the specification is assumed to be correct, thus, we may wrongly blame the error on the implementation (and on its developers)!

Hence, an error in the specification can produce a false negative. A similar scenario may lead to false positive verdicts, in which case actual errors in the implementation are missed. To avoid these problems the specification should first be formally verified before test cases are generated from it.

However, verifying a large extended state-machine specification is difficult and is rarely done in practice. In this paper we propose an approach to integrate the verification and test generation efforts in one common task. Specifically, we use symbolic test generation techniques to compute a set of *components* (subgraphs) of the specification $\mathcal{S}$, and verify the requirements on the components only. Once verified, the components constitute sound test cases: if a test case discovers a difference between $\mathcal{S}$ and $\mathcal{I}$ with respect to a verified requirement, it can only be the implementation's fault. Moreover, we provide reasonable sufficient conditions under which a requirement verified on the components also holds on the whole specification as well. This may considerably reduce the verification effort as components are typically much smaller than the whole specification.

We use the STG symbolic test generation tool [9] for extracting components, the PVS theorem prover [21] for verifying them, and demonstrate the approach on the CEPS (Common Electronic Purse System) specification [7]. The properties verified are invariants involving existential and universal quantifiers over unbounded domains, and the specification is an infinite-state, extended state machine with about forty variables of complex record and parametric-size array types, and about one hundred transitions. By contrast, the components extracted with STG have less than ten transitions each and affect only a subset of the variables. This is small enough to be dealt with efficiently using theorem proving. Because of the infinite-state nature of the system and properties, an approach based exclusively on model checking [2,17,10] cannot solve this problem.

For most of the requirements we have used a straightforward invariant-strengthening approach, which consists in strengthening the invariant under proof using information obtained from the subgoals left unproved by PVS until it becomes inductive. However, for one of the requirements this did not work so easily, which made it a more challenging theorem-proving exercise. This is because an essential part of the invariant under proof holds only in some particular place, and no simple syntactical variant of it holds elsewhere. Auxiliary invariants had to be discovered, which involve finite sets that have been encoded using the finite-sets library for PVS. Proving these auxiliary invariants required to make a quite intensive use of the lemmas provided in the library. It was useful for the success of this verification task that we could extract (using STG) components with just a few transitions each.

The rest of the paper is organized as follows. In Section 2 we present the basics of conformance testing and symbolic test generation using a simple example. In Section 3 the verification of invariants with PVS is presented. In Section 4 we present the results that allow to reduce the correctness of a specification to that of one or several of its components. In Section 5 we describe the experiment with the CEPS case study, and we conclude in Section 6. The CEPS specification, the components extracted with STG, their translation to PVS, and the PVS proofs are available at http://www.irisa.fr/vertecs/Equipe/Rusu/FME02/.[1]

2   Symbolic Test Generation

Symbolic test generation is a program-synthesis problem. Starting from the formal *specification* of a system under test and from a test *purpose* describing a set of behaviours to be tested, compute a reactive program (the *test case*) which 1. attempts to control a black-box *implementation* of the system towards satisfying the test purpose and 2. observes the external traces of the implementation for detecting non-conformances between implementation and specification.

A complete set of formal definitions can be found in [23]. Here, we present the main concepts intuitively, by means of a simple example. The model used is a variant of the Lynch and Tuttle I/O automata, called IOSTS (Input-Output Symbolic Transition Systems)[2].

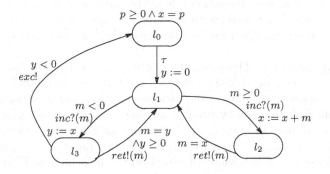

Fig. 1. Example of IOSTS $\mathcal{S}$

The IOSTS Model. Figure 1 depicts an IOSTS with four *locations* l_0, l_1, l_2, l_3, where l_0 is the *initial location*. The IOSTS has several *transitions* between locations, which are labeled with an *action* that can be an *input*, an *output*, or an *internal* action. By convention, the name of an input (resp. output) action ends with a ? (resp. !). For example, the IOSTS in Figure 1 has one input action

---

[1] PVS and STG are available free of charge at URL http://pvs.csl.sri.com and, respectively, at URL http://http://www.irisa.fr/vertecs/Equipe/Rusu/stg.

[2] The main difference with I/O automata concerns the input-completeness condition, which is not required in IOSTS. Another difference concerns the separation of symbolic data into variables, parameters, and messages, each playing a specific role.

inc?, two outputs *ret!*, *exc!*, and one internal action τ. Input and output actions may carry *messages*, which, together with *variables* and *parameters* are the three distinct kinds of *data* the system manipulates (the difference between them is explained below). The data can be of any type, including boolean, integer, record, and array of fixed or parametric size. For example, the IOSTS in Figure 1 has two variables x, y, one parameter p, and one message m, all of integer type.

Each transition is also decorated with a *guard* and a set of parallel *assignments* that may involve any of the variables and parameters, but only those messages carried by that transition's action. It is assumed that all operations in guards and assignments are type-correct, e.g., all guards have the type boolean, and only expressions of integer type may be assigned to integer variables. For example, the transition with origin l_1 and destination l_2 has guard $m \geq 0$, action *inc?* carrying message m, and assignment $x := x + m$.

Variables, parameters and messages. Intuitively, variables are data to compute with (e.g., loop counters), parameters are symbolic constants, and messages are used to communicate with the environment. Messages are the only data visible from outside. The value of a variable stays the same between two assignments, and the value of a parameter is never modified. The value of a message is only relevant when firing a transition labeled by an action that carries the message: after the transition is fired the value of the message is lost, thus, to be memorized it has to be assigned to a variable by one of the transition's assignments.

Informal semantics. The predicate $p \geq 0 \wedge x = p$ near the initial location l_0 (Fig. 1) is called the *initial condition*. A *behaviour* of an IOSTS starts in the initial location with values of the variables and parameters satisfying the initial condition, and proceeds by firing transitions, updating the variables according to the guards and assignments of the transitions fired, and exchanging messages with the environment through the corresponding input and output actions.

For example, a behaviour of the IOSTS represented in Figure 1 starts in location l_0 with some positive value for p and the same value for x, fires the transition labeled by the τ internal action, assigns variable y to 0, and reaches location l_1. Then, when an *inc?* input action carrying a message m occurs from the environment the variable x is increased by the value of m, and the control is now in location l_2. Next, the IOSTS performs the *ret!* output action, which fires the transition with origin l_2 and destination l_1. The value of message m is "chosen" to satisfy the guard of that transition, i.e., $m = x$. That is, the value of x is sent to the environment by the *ret!* output action carrying message m.

Formal semantics. More formally, a *state* is a pair $\langle l, v \rangle$ where l is a location and v is a valuation for the variables and the parameters. An *initial state* is a state $\langle l_0, v_0 \rangle$ such that l_0 is the initial location and v_0 satisfies the initial condition. A *valued action* is a pair $\langle a, w \rangle$ where a is an action and w is a valuation for the message(s) carried by the action. Note that the values of messages are not contained in the states, but in the valued actions. For convenience, we consider that internal actions are valued actions carrying a tuple of values of length 0. The *transition relation* ρ is the set of triples $\langle s, \alpha, s' \rangle$ where $s = \langle l, v \rangle$, $s' = \langle l', v' \rangle$ are states and $\alpha = \langle a, w \rangle$ is a valued action such that values of variables, parameters and actions defined by v, w satisfy the guard of the transition t labeled a from l to l', and the valuation v' is obtained from v, w by the assignments of transition t.

Definition 1 (behaviour). *A behaviour is a sequence of alternating states and valued actions* $\beta : \quad s_1 \alpha_1 s_2 \alpha_2 \cdots \alpha_{n-1} s_n$ *such that s_1 is an initial state and such that for $i = 1, \ldots, n-1$, the triple $\langle s_i, \alpha_i, s_{i+1} \rangle$ is in the transition relation ρ.*

A run is the subsequence of a behaviour obtained by removing all the actions:

Definition 2 (run). *Given a behaviour $\beta : \quad \alpha_1 s_2 \alpha_2 \cdots \alpha_{n-1} s_n$, the run of β is the subsequence $\rho : \quad s_1 s_2 \cdots s_n$ of β containing only the states of the sequence.*

A trace is the subsequence of a behaviour containing only what is externally visible, that is, states and internal actions are removed form the sequence:

Definition 3 (trace). *The* trace *of a behaviour β is the subsequence $\sigma :$ $\alpha_{i_1} \ldots \alpha_{i_k}$ of β containing only the valued inputs and valued outputs of β.*

Conformance Relation. This is what is being tested for in conformance testing. There are several variants (see, e.g., [26]) of this relation, based on interpretations of the standard [18]. We formalize such a relation between two IOSTS.

First, for β a behaviour of an IOSTS $\mathcal{I}$ and ρ a run (respectively, σ a trace) of β, we say β is a *witness* of ρ (resp. σ). We denote by $\mathcal{I}\, after\, \beta$ the last state of β, and, for a trace σ, by $\mathcal{I}\, after\, \sigma$ the set of states $\{\mathcal{I}\, after\, \beta | \beta$ is a witness of $\sigma\}$. That is, $\mathcal{I}\, after\, \sigma$ is the set of states in which the IOSTS $\mathcal{I}$ may be after the observable trace σ. Because of internal actions that are hidden in the trace, a black-box $\mathcal{I}$ may be in any of those states, but the exact one is not known.

Next, for a state $s = \langle l, v \rangle$, we denote by $out(s)$ the set of valued outputs $\langle a, w \rangle$ for which there exists a transition t of the IOSTS with origin l whose guard evaluates to *true* when the variables and parameters evaluate according to v and the messages evaluate according to w. For S a set of states, we let $out(S) = \{out(s) | s \in S\}$. That is, $out(S)$ is the set of valued outputs that the IOSTS can emit when it is in a state from the set S.

Finally, let $traces(\mathcal{I})$ denote the set of traces of the IOSTS $\mathcal{I}$ and, for two IOSTS $\mathcal{I}, \mathcal{S}$ and each trace $\sigma \in traces(\mathcal{S}) \setminus traces(\mathcal{I})$, we define $out(\mathcal{I}\, after\, \sigma)$ to be the empty set. These notations allow to introduce the following definition:

Definition 4 (conformance). *Given $\mathcal{I}, \mathcal{S}$ two IOSTS, we say $\mathcal{I}$ conforms to $\mathcal{S}$ if, for each trace $\sigma \in traces(\mathcal{S})$: $out(\mathcal{I}\, after\, \sigma) \subseteq out(\mathcal{S}\, after\, \sigma)$.*

That is, after every observable sequence of valued actions of the IOSTS $\mathcal{S}$, which plays the role of the *specification*, the next possible valued outputs observed on the *black-box implementation* $\mathcal{I}$ are among those allowed by the specification.

Example 1. Consider the IOSTS $\mathcal{S}$ depicted in Figure 1 and $\mathcal{I}$ depicted in Figure 2. Then, $\mathcal{I}$ does not conform to $\mathcal{S}$ because, after an *inc?* input carrying a negative value m, $\mathcal{S}$ cannot emit the *exc!* output: the guard $y < 0$ does not allow it. If this guard is changed to $y \geq 0$ then $\mathcal{I}$ conform to the new specification.

$$m < 0$$
$$inc?(m)$$

$$exc!$$

Fig. 2. IOSTS $\mathcal{I}$: model for the Implementation

Test Generation. In practice, following the recommendation [18] test cases are generated using a specification (e.g., the IOSTS depicted in Figure 1) and a *purpose*. A purpose is another IOSTS that gives an abstract description of a part of the system that will be tested. For example, Figure 3 depicts a purpose that accepts behaviours where the *exc!* action occurs. Note that it is not necessary to give all the details, e.g., behaviours of the specification after which the *exc!* action occurs. These are automatically computed by the symbolic test generation algorithm [23] by means of a product operation between the specification and purpose IOSTS. Here, we decide that we are not interested in the "right half" of the specification depicted in Figure 1, and the corresponding behaviours are rejected by the purpose. Thus, the purpose targets (accepts) the behaviours of the specification in Figure 1 that end with the *exc!* action, excepting those during which an *inc?* action carrying a positive value occurs.

For symbolic test generation we have developed the STG tool [9]. The resulting IOSTS test case is automatically translated into C++, which can then be linked with and executed on a running implementation. This produces *verdicts* about the conformance between implementation and specification. In particular, a *Fail* verdict means that an error (a non-conformance) was detected, and a *Pass* verdict means that the purpose was satisfied and no errors were detected. For example, the test case generated from the specification in Figure 1 and purpose in Figure 3 is represented (slightly simplified) in Figure 4. Note that the inputs of the specification are outputs of the test case and reciprocally. Note also that the transition labeled $y < 0$ is never fireable, thus, the *Pass* location is not reachable.

That is, the purpose cannot be satisfied, but we still obtain valuable information when the *Fail* location is reached, i.e., a non-conformance is detected.

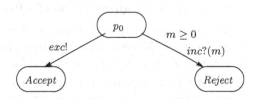

Fig. 3. Sample Purpose

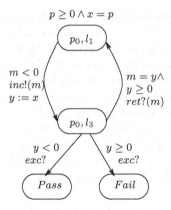

Fig. 4. Sample Test Case $\mathcal{TC}$

Running the Test. The IOSTS $\mathcal{TC}$ in Figure 4 can be employed to test, e.g., an implementation $\mathcal{I}$ whose model is shown in Figure 2 for conformance to the specification $\mathcal{S}$ given in Figure 1. By executing $\mathcal{TC}$ on $\mathcal{I}$ the *Fail* location is reached and a *Fail* verdict is given, meaning that $\mathcal{I}$ does not conform to $\mathcal{S}$.

Now, assume that the IOSTS $\mathcal{S}$ is the specification of a system that (among other requirements) should satisfy the property P: an *exc*! action never occurs. The specification $\mathcal{S}$ depicted in Figure 1 does satisfy this requirement. However, if the guard $y < 0$ on the transition from l_3 to l_0 is mistyped $y \geq 0$, the resulting specification $\mathcal{S}'$ does not. Then, the test case $\mathcal{TC}'$ obtained from the specification $\mathcal{S}'$ also contains the erroneous guard, and, as a consequence, the implementation $\mathcal{I}$ (which does not meet the requirement P) passes the test $\mathcal{TC}'$.

Because of the error in the specification, an error in the implementation goes undetected. For large specifications it is not unreasonable to suppose that such errors may happen, and the above example (or the dual scenario presented in Section 1) demonstrates the need to verify specifications prior to test generation.

3   Verifying Invariants of IOSTS Using PVS

In this section we describe the PVS theorem prover [21], the encoding of IOSTS into PVS, and the invariant-strengthening technique for proving invariants.

PVS. The PVS system consists of an input language, a typechecker, and an interactive prover. The input language is typed higher-order logic with a rich type system including simple types such as booleans, enumerations, integers, and records, and more complex function types, subtypes, dependent types, and abstract datatypes. Having such an expressive language makes it easy to specify, e.g., concurrent programs in a natural way, very close to a programming language. The drawback is that typechecking the input language is undecidable. Actually, PVS transforms this apparent weakness into an actual strength, because whenever the typechecker cannot decide whether an expression is type-correct it generates a TCC (type-correctness condition). PVS declares unsound a theory where some TCCs are left unproved. Most can be discharged automatically, and those that cannot often point to subtle errors in the specification.

A PVS *proof* is a tree, the root of which is the theorem being proved. The leaves of the tree are called *pending subgoals*. A proof proceeds as a sequence of commands, each of which transforms the proof tree by either proving a pending subgoal or by replacing a pending subgoal by a new set of pending subgoals. There are many proof commands, from propositional and first-order logic commands, to decision procedures and heuristic quantifier instantiation, all of which can be combined into high-level, user-defined proof strategies.

Inductive and non-inductive invariants. A state predicate φ is *inductive* if it holds initially and, for every state s, if φ holds at s then φ also holds at all successors s' of s through the transition relation. A state predicate is an *invariant* if it holds at every state of every run. For example, in the IOSTS $\mathcal{S}$ represented in Figure 1, it is not hard to check that the predicate $x \geq 0$ is inductive. Indeed, it is true initially, and from any state satisfying $x \geq 0$, each transition leads to a state satisfying the predicate. Any inductive predicate is also an invariant, but the converse is not true: for example, consider the predicate $pc = l_3 \supset y \geq 0$ (that is, whenever control is at location l_3, y is positive). We can prove in a variety of ways that this predicate is an invariant, but it is not inductive: by knowing only that it is true before transition labeled $inc?$ from l_1 to l_3, it cannot be inferred that it is still true after the transition. To prove this we need additional information, which can be obtained by *invariant strengthening*. Here, the additional information required is that $x \geq 0$ is an invariant.

IOSTS in PVS. Figure 5 shows a fragment of a PVS theory for the IOSTS in Figure 1. First, the *actions* of the IOSTS are encoded into the `Action` abstract datatype. Note that actions can carry messages, e.g., `inc(m)` carries the integer message `m`. Then, the `Location` enumerated type, and the `State` record type are declared. The `initial` state predicate and the the the transition relation `trans` closely follow the description of the IOSTS. For example, the second disjunct of the transition relation says that if control in the state `s` is at location `l1` and `a` is an `inc` action carrying a positive message `m(a)`, then the next state `s_` is just like `s` except for the changes made by the `WITH` record modifier, i.e., the `x` field of `s_` is increased by the value of `m(a)`, and the control is now in `l2`.

Invariant strengthening. To perform invariant-strengthening in PVS a specific strategy attempts to prove that the goal is inductive. If this is the case the strategy succeeds and the proof is done. Otherwise, the same strategy tries to prove that the conjunction of the initial goal with the subgoals left unproved at the previous step is inductive. The process can be iterated until an inductive invariant is obtained. This is not guaranteed to terminate, because the problem of proving invariants of general extended state machines is undecidable.

```
Action : DATATYPE
BEGIN
tau : tau?
inc(m: int) : inc?
ret(m: int) : ret?
exc: exc?
END Action

Location : TYPE = {10,11,12,13}
State : TYPE = [# pc: Location, x,y : int #]
p : nat
initial(s:State) : bool = (s'pc = 10 AND s'x = p)

trans(s:State, a: Action, s_ : State) : bool =
    (s'pc=10 AND tau?(a) AND s_=s WITH[pc := 11, y := 0])
OR (s'pc=11 AND inc?(a) AND m(a) >= 0 AND s_=s WITH[x:=s'x+m(a),pc := 12])
OR(s'pc=11 AND inc?(a) AND m(a) < 0 AND s_=s WITH[y := s'x, pc := 13])
OR (s'pc=12 AND ret?(a) AND m(a)=s'x AND s_=s WITH[pc := 11])
OR (s'pc=13 AND ret?(a) AND m(a)=s'y AND s'y >= 0 AND s_=s WITH[pc := 11])
OR (s'pc=13 AND exc?(a)  AND s'y < 0 AND s_=s WITH[pc := 11])
```

Fig. 5. Encoding the IOSTS S (Figure 1) in PVS

However, the user can often detect infinite patterns of behavior and formulate a predicate which is not just the pre-condition of a predicate by one transition, but the fixpoint of an infinite sequence of such operations. For simple systems such as the one described above or for academic case studies such as [15,22] this is often enough. For larger case studies such as the Common Electronic Purse System [7] the effort of performing invariant strengthening becomes prohibitive.

4   Verification by Components

In this section we show how to reduce the verification of an IOSTS specification to the verification of a number of its *components*, which are particular subgraphs of the specification. We present sufficient conditions under which a safety property verified on a component also holds on the whole specification. The components are computed using the test generation mechanism described in Section 2 and verified using PVS and invariant strengthening (cf. Section 3).

In the next section we combine all these ingredients to perform a larger case study, the Common Electronic Purse System [7].

Definition 5 (control graph). *Given a IOSTS S, let L be the set of locations of S and $\mathcal{T}$ the set of its transitions. The control graph $G(S)$ is the labeled graph $(L, \mathcal{T})$, where every edge in $\mathcal{T}$ is labeled by the guard, action, and assignments of the corresponding transition of S.*

For convenience, we call the nodes of $G(S)$ *locations* and the edges *transitions*. Intuitively, a *component* is a part of a larger system that can be called and returns in the same control point (the *root*), and may terminate with an exception. A component can also be seen as a part of the system that performs some specific function, for example, in an information system there may be a component for inserting new elements in a database, another to query the database, and a third component to log all operations. It is reasonable to suppose that the control flow of such a function starts and returns in the same control node (unless an exception is raised) and is strongly connected as imposed by Definition 6.

Definition 6 (component). *Given an IOSTS S and l a location of S, let T be the set of transitions of S with origin l, let $t \in T$ be a transition in this set, and let T' be a set of transitions of S such that $T \cap T' = \emptyset$.*

The component of S with entry t and exceptions T' is the maximal strongly connected component of the graph $(L, T \setminus ((T \setminus \{t\}) \cup T'))$ containing t. The origin l of transition t is called the root of component F.

Example 2. For the IOSTS represented in Figure 1, let $t_{i,j}$ denote the transition between locations i and j (for $i, j \in \{0, 1, 2, 3\}$). Then, the component F_1 with entry $t_{1,3}$ and exception set $\{t_{3,0}\}$ consists of locations l_1, l_3 and the transitions $t_{1,3}$, $t_{3,1}$ between them. The component F_2 with entry $t_{1,2}$ and empty exception set consists of locations l_1, l_2 and the transitions $t_{1,2}$, $t_{2,1}$ between them.

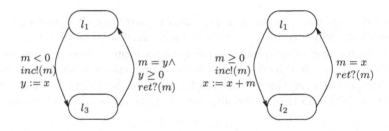

Fig. 6. Components F_1 (left) and F_2 (right)

Definition 7 (defined and used variables). *Let S be an IOSTS. A transition t of S uses a variable, parameter, or message v if v is present in the guard of t, or in the right hand-side of an assignment of t, or in the left-hand side of an assignment of t within the index of an array. Transition t defines a variable v if v appears in t in the left-hand side of an assignment except in an array index.*

Example 3. A transition with guard $x > 3$ and assignments $x := x + 1$ and $A[i] := 3$ defines the variables A and x, and uses the variables i and x.

Definition 8 (variables, parameters of a component). *Given F a component of an IOSTS S, the variables and parameters of S that are defined (used) by the transitions of F are said to be defined (resp. used) by F. The variables that are defined only by transitions of F are said to be exclusively defined by F.*

Example 4. For the IOSTS represented in Figure 1, consider the components F_1, F_2 from Example 2. Component F_1 uses variable x and defines variable y, but y is not exclusively defined by F_1 as it is also defined by transition $t_{0,1}$. On the other hand, the variable x is exclusively defined by the component F_2.

A component is *rooted* if the only way to enter from outside is through its root:

Definition 9 (rooted component). *Let F be a component of an IOSTS S. A transition t of S whose origin is not a location of F and whose destination is a location of F is said to enter the component F. We say F is rooted if every transition that enters F has the root l of F as its destination.*

Example 5. Both components F_1 and F_2 defined in Example 2 are rooted.

A component is not an IOSTS by itself, but it can be transformed into an IOSTS by giving it an initial condition and taking its root as the initial location.

Definition 10 (IOSTS obtained from component and initial condition). *Given a component F of an IOSTS S and a predicate Q on the variables and parameters of F, we denote by $iosts(F, Q)$ the IOSTS whose graph is the graph of F, whose initial location is the root of F, and whose initial condition is Q.*

Example 6. Let $Q_1 : x \geq 0$. The component F_2 of Example 2 can be transformed into the IOSTS $iosts(F_2, Q_1)$ with initial location l_1 and initial condition Q_1.

In the rest of this section we state and prove two propositions, which provide sufficient conditions under which an invariant proved on a component also holds on the whole specification. *Proposition 1* deals with the case of properties that may only involve data which is not modified outside the component (i.e., syntactically, the formula expressing the property contains only parameters and variables exclusively defined in the component in the sense of Definition 8).

This is not enough, in general, and *Proposition 2* provides another set of sufficient conditions, which cover the case of properties that may also involve variables defined outside the component, provided a global invariant on the variables is known to hold. We use the notations $S \models \Box Q$ for "The predicate Q is an invariant of the system S" and $S \models Q$ for "Q holds in the initial states of S".

Proposition 1. *Let F be a rooted component of an IOSTS S, let V' be the set of variables that are exclusively defined by F, and P' be the set of parameters used by F. Let Q be a property involving only variables and parameters in $V' \cup P'$, such that $S \models Q$ and $iosts(F, Q) \models \Box Q$. Then, $S \models \Box Q$ also holds.*

Proof. Assume $S \not\models \Box Q$. This means there exists a run ρ of S and a state s' on ρ such that s' violates Q. We assume s' is the first state on ρ where Q is violated, and let s be its immediate predecessor on the sequence ρ (s exists because Q holds at least in the initial states of S). Thus, there exists a transition t of S that is taken by ρ for going from s to s'. Since the truth value of Q changes when this transition is taken, this means some variable involved in Q is modified by t (remember that parameters cannot be modified). Since the only variables involved in Q are among the variables V' exclusively defined by F, t must be a transition of F. Hence, the run ρ can be split in two subsequences, $\rho = \rho_1 \cdot \rho_2$:

ρ_1 is the prefix of ρ from the initial location of S to the last time it enters F,
ρ_2 is the suffix of ρ from the last time it has entered F, to the faulty state s'.

Since F is rooted, the only way ρ can (re-)enter F is through the root of F, by taking the entry transition t_0 of F. We now prove (1) that the first state s_0 of ρ_2 satisfies the initial condition Q of $iosts(F, Q)$. But we have shown that transition t leading from s to s' is a transition of F (s' is the first state on ρ where Q is violated). Thus, every state before s' on this run, in particular, the first state s_0 of ρ_2, satisfies Q, and (1) is proved. Thus, after the run ρ_1, it is possible to execute the sequence ρ_2 and to reach the faulty state s'. Hence, the sequence ρ_2 can also be executed as a run in $iosts(F, Q)$. This means that s', the last state of ρ_2, is reachable in $iosts(F, Q)$, and since Q is an invariant of $iosts(F, Q)$, the predicate Q holds in s'. We have reached a contradiction: the proof is done.

Below is an example of how *Proposition 1* can be used to prove an invariant.

Example 7. Consider the component F_2 defined in Example 2. This component exclusively defines variable x. The predicate $Q_1 : x \geq 0$ is inductive on $iosts(F_2, Q_1)$, thus, it is an an invariant of $iosts(F_2, Q_1)$. Thus, we can apply *Proposition 1* to show that Q_1 is an invariant of the whole IOSTS S of Figure 1.

We now present another technique for reducing the proof of invariant properties from larger to smaller IOSTS, which cover the case of local properties that may involve variables defined outside a component, provided a global invariant on the variables is known to hold. For l_0 a location of an IOSTS, we denote by $pc = l_0$ the predicate that characterizes all states $s = \langle l, v \rangle$ such that $l = l_0$ and v is an arbitrary valuation of the variables and parameters of the IOSTS.

Definition 11 (predicate local to a component). *A predicate Q is local to component F if Q is of the form $pc = l \supset Q'$, where l is a location of F, and Q' is a predicate involving only variables and parameters defined or used by F.*

Example 8. Let F_1 denote the component previously defined in Example 2. Then, the properties $pc = l_3 \supset y \geq 0$ and $pc = l_1 \supset y \geq 0$ are local to F_1. The predicate $pc = l_0 \supset x \geq 0$ is not local to F_1 because l_0 is not a location of F_1.

Proposition 2. *Let F be a rooted component of IOSTS S. Assume that for some predicate Q' we have proved that Q' is an invariant of S. Then, for any local property Q, if $iosts(F, Q') \models \Box Q$ holds, then $S \models \Box Q$ also holds.*

Proof. Assume $S \not\models \Box Q$. This means there exists a run ρ of S and a state $s = \langle l, v \rangle$ on ρ such that s violates Q. Since Q is a local property of F, this means that that the location l of s is a location of F. Then, just as in the proof of *Proposition 1*, the run ρ can be split in two subsequences, $\rho = \rho_1 \cdot \rho_2$:

ρ_1 is the prefix of ρ from the initial location of S to the last time it enters F,
ρ_2 is the suffix of ρ from the last time it has entered F, to the faulty state s.

We now show (1) that the first state s_0 of ρ_2 satisfies the initial condition Q' of $iosts(F, Q')$. By hypothesis, we have $\mathcal{S} \models \Box Q'$, and s_0 is a reachable state in $\mathcal{S}$, thus, this state satisfies Q', and (1) is proved. Hence, from the state s_0 it is possible to execute the sequence ρ_2 and to reach s. This means that s is reachable in $iosts(F, Q')$, and, by $iosts(F, Q') \models \Box Q$, s must satisfy Q, and we have obtained a contradiction: the proof is done.

Example 9. We show on a simple example how Propositions 1 and 2 can be used together to prove invariants of the IOSTS $\mathcal{S}$ represented in Figure 1, by reducing them to invariants of the components F_1 and F_2 of $\mathcal{S}$ (cf. Example 2). Suppose we want to prove that in $\mathcal{S}$ the exception *exc!* never occurs. For this, we have to prove that the guard $y < 0$ of transition $t_{3,1}$ is always *false* in location l_3, that is, we have to prove $\mathcal{S} \models \Box(pc = l_3 \supset y \geq 0)$. Let Q_2 denote the predicate $pc = l_3 \supset y \geq 0$. Then, Q_2 is a predicate local to component F_1 (cf. Definition 11). We want to apply *Proposition 2* to prove $\mathcal{S} \models \Box Q_2$. For this, we need a predicate Q_1 such that (1) $\mathcal{S} \models \Box Q_1$ and (2) $iosts(F_1, Q_1) \models \Box Q_2$. We have already seen in Example 7 that, by taking $Q_1 : x \geq 0$ and using *Proposition 1*, we obtain $\mathcal{S} \models \Box Q_1$. Then, it is not hard to show that $iosts(F_1, Q_1) \models \Box Q_2$ holds as well (Q_2 is inductive over $iosts(F_1, Q_1)$). Thus, requirements (1) and (2) hold, and the proof of $\mathcal{S} \models \Box(pc = l_3 \supset y \geq 0)$ is done.

Components can be selected using symbolic test generation (cf. Section 2). For example, the purpose represented in Figure 3 selects, from the specification depicted in Figure 1, the test case shown in Figure 4. Except for the verdict locations *Pass* and *Fail* (and the names of the other locations, which are irrelevant details) the test case is identical to the component F_1 depicted in Figure 6.

In the next section we apply these mechanisms to prove properties of an electronic purse system. As a result, the components on which we actually have to perform the interactive proofs are about ten times smaller than the specification of the whole system.

5   Case Study: An Electronic Purse System

The CEPS (Common Electronic Purse System) [7] is a standard for creating multi-currency smart-card electronic purse systems. An electronic purse has a number of *slots*, each of which corresponds to a currency and its respective balance. The CEPS specifies, among others, functions that create, modify, or query the slots. In previous work [8] on test generation and execution with the STG tool we have built a detailed model of a significant portion of the CEPS as an IOSTS with 40 variables of complex record and array types and 92 transitions.

In particular, the slot type is a record, and the slots are contained in an array of slots of parametric size. Each function corresponds to a component in the sense of Definition 6, i.e., it starts in a given location, performs its computation, then terminates either normally by returning to the same location, or abnormally by an exception.

```
create_update: THEOREM
  invariant(LAMBDA (s: State):
         s'pc = CepInit_P1 IMPLIES
         FORALL (i,j: below(pSlotCount)):
           s'vSlots(i)'InUse AND s'vSlots(j)'inUse AND i/=j IMPLIES
           s'vSlots(i)'Currency /= s'vSlots(j)'Currency)
```

Fig. 7. PVS Invariant for Properties of Create/Update Function

Here, we use STG together with the PVS theorem prover and the results from Section 4 to verify the functions for the creation, updating, and query of slots. We merely outline the approach followed to prove the first two operations, and give some details for the substantially more involved verification of the third.

Create/Update Slots. For this function, the requirements [7] are that all used slots contain different currencies. We have to prove the PVS theorem represented in Figure 7. Instead of attempting to prove the **create_update** invariant on the whole specification, we first prove it on the component of the CEPS dedicated to creating and updating slots, and then use *Proposition 1* to show that it holds on the whole specification. To select the Create/Update component we use STG with the purpose represented in Figure 8. The resulting component has 8 transitions[3]. (Guards and assignments are unfortunately too small to read).

The component is then translated to PVS along the lines of what was described in Section 3 . The translation is automatic, except for the initial condition that has to be added to transform the component into an IOSTS (Definition 10) suitable of use with *Proposition 1*.

We choose as initial condition the property that all used slots contain different currencies. We prove the **create_update** invariant on the resulting IOSTS by attempting to prove that it is inductive. Here, this is not the case, but by examining the subgoals left unproved by PVS it was quite straightforward to figure out the relevant auxiliary invariants. Four invariants were proved, three of which are trivially inductive. The fourth one is a small syntactical modification of the **create_update** invariant. Then, using *Proposition 1* we show that **create_update** also holds globally.

Query. We proceed with proving the CEPS requirements regarding the query of all slots in sequence, for which [7] requires that the slots can be returned in any order provided that each used slot is reported exactly once. In other words, our IOSTS specification of the CEPS regards as being conformant any implementation that chooses any particular order for reporting the used slots. Clearly, some kind of non-deterministic assignment for the "next" values of variables was needed to obtain an arbitrary ordering. For reasons that go beyond the scope

---

[3] Figure 8 is generated by STG using the DOTTY graph visualizer from AT&T.

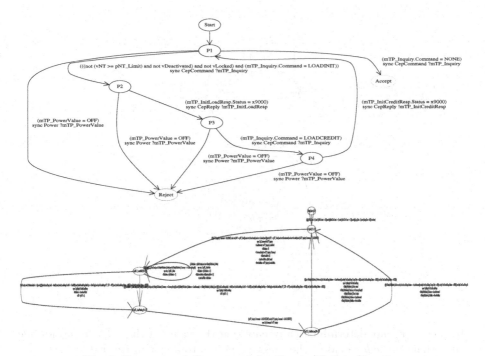

Fig. 8. Purpose and Component for Create/Update Function.

of this paper we do not allow such assignments in IOSTS, but we can use the observable non-determinism of input and outputs, and messages.

To extract the query component we use a purpose (not shown here). The result, simplified for better understanding, is shown in Figure 9.

The slots are encoded in *vSlots*, a parametric-size array of length *pSlotCount*. Each slot in the array has many fields, but for this component only two matter: the *currency* field and the Boolean *inUse* field. The query is initiated by the terminal requesting information about a "first" slot, using the SLOT_INQUIRY? input. Then, an initialization process is performed by the two transitions looping on the **CepSlotInquirySequence** location, for which *vSlotIndex* serves as a loop counter. The number of *unused* slots is recorded in the *vSlotsReported* variable, and the positions in the *vSlots* array where the unused slots stand are recorded by setting to *true* the corresponding cell in the *slotsReported* array.

When the initialization is done (i.e., when *vSlotIndex* has reached the value *pSlotCount*) the control goes to the **CepSIQ_Reply** location by an internal action, and then directly to the **CepSIQ_Ready** location by performing a SLOT_REPORT! output with a *mSlotInfo* message. Here, several things happen.

First, the transition may only be taken if *vSlotsReported < pSlotCount* holds, that is, if there is still something to report. As the unused slots were reported in the previous initialization phase, this means that the transition will be taken if there still is some *used* slot to report (which is exactly what it is supposed to do).

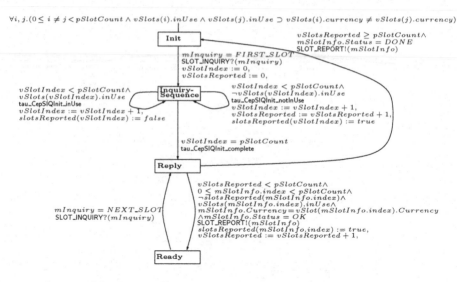

Fig. 9. Query Component

It does so by nondeterministically choosing the value of the *mSlotInfo* message such that the *index* field of the message points to a slot in the *vSlots* array not previously reported. The whole message, containing the currency and several other fields is sent to the environment. The *vSlotsReported* and *slotsReported* variables are updated, and the message is recorded in a new cell of the *report* array, a specification variable used to formalize the requirements for the component (cf. Figure 10). Then, the terminal may ask for a next unreported slot, and if there is one the card reports it, otherwise, it goes back to the initial location.

There are also exceptional behaviours, but these have been ruled out when the component was selected and are irrelevant to the truth of its requirements, which are expressed by the PVS invariants in Figure 10.

To transform the component into an IOSTS, an initial condition saying that initially all used slots contain different currencies is added to it. We first prove the invariants on the PVS translation of the IOSTS and then, using *Proposition 2* we show that the invariants in Figure 10 hold on the whole specification as well.

The `allslots1` invariant in Figure 10 specifies that all cells in the *report* array correspond to different slots. The second invariant `allslots2` specifies that each slot in the *vSlots* array, i.e., the actual slots on the card, is present in the *report* array. Together, they formally encode the requirements for the Query function.

To prove the `allslots1` invariant we follow the basic invariant-strengthening scheme already described in the Create/Update section. Four auxiliary invariants had to be proved, two of which are small syntactical modifications of the original property, while the two others are trivial inductive invariants.

However, this simple approach does not work for proving the `allslots2` invariant. This is because the `allslots2` property is of the form ($pc = CepInit \wedge$

```
%%% at the end, all reported slots are different
allslots1: THEOREM
   invariant(LAMBDA (s: State):
               s'pc = CepInit_P1 AND s'vSlotsReported = pSlotCount IMPLIES
                (FORALL (i, j: below(s'reportSize)): i /= j IMPLIES
                        s'report(i)'currency /= s'report(j)'currency))~\cite{ors95}

%%% at the end, all used slots have been reported
allslots2: THEOREM
   invariant(LAMBDA (s: State):
               s'pc = CepInit_P1 AND s'vSlotsReported = pSlotCount IMPLIES
                (FORALL (i: below(pSlotCount)):  vSlots(i)'InUse IMPLIES
                   (EXISTS (j: below(s'reportSize)):
                        s'report(j)'currency = vSlots(i)'currency)))
```

Fig. 10. PVS Invariants for Properties of Query Function

$vSlotsReported = pSlotCount) \supset Q$, and Q, which states that every used slot is reported, holds only at the end, i.e., when all slots have been reported. Moreover, no small syntactical modification of it holds "during" the reporting process to make a convenient auxiliary invariant. The reason for this difficulty is precisely the fact that the slots have been reported in an arbitrary order.

Thus, we have to reformulate the `allslots2` invariant. A convenient way to do it is to use finite sets, i.e., write the `allslots2_aux` property stating that when the reporting process is done, the used slots are a subset of the reported slots. The main steps of the proof of `allslots2_aux` are:

1. prove that the opposite inclusion holds *during the reporting process*, i.e., that the reported slots are a subset of the used slots
2. at the end of the reporting process, the cardinals of the two sets are equal.

We also use the fact that two sets are equal if one is a subset of the other and they have the same cardinal. Properties 1. and 2. had to be strengthened to become inductive. Twelve auxiliary predicates were proved, which took one week to a moderately experienced PVS user, who became more experienced in the process.

One difficulty that we have encountered when proving invariants on finite sets is the rather large number of type-correctness conditions (a few dozens) that PVS generates to ensure, e.g., that the sets in question are indeed finite. Most are trivial, but a few non-trivial ones that would appear over and over again had to be factored using PVS judgements (a mechanism to reduce the number of TCCs, which was quite useful in this circumstance). Another difficulty is that, even if a transition does not modify a set it still requires a proof, e.g., expanding definitions and repeatedly using apparently trivial lemmas from the finite-sets library of PVS. We had to enrich the library with some more lemmas, e.g., the image of a finite set through a function is a finite set, and there exists a bijective inverse for every injective function. Such is the nature of theorem proving.

Hence, it was essential that STG allowed us to select components with a relatively small number of transitions. This concludes the description of the case study.

6   Conclusion, Related Work, and Future Work

Safety-critical systems have to satisfy strict, formal requirements. Verification consists in proving that a formal specification of the system satisfies the requirements, while conformance testing consists in comparing a running implementation of the system with respect to its formal specification. Both approaches are useful to ensure that the final, running system operates correctly. In this paper we propose an approach to factor the verification and test generation efforts into one common task. Using test generation techniques we extract from the specification the components that are relevant to the requirements. We verify the requirements on the components and, if some reasonable sufficient conditions hold, we can conclude that the whole specification also satisfies the requirements. By construction, the extracted components constitute sound symbolic test cases.

We use the STG tool for extracting components and the PVS theorem prover to verify them, and demonstrate the approach on an electronic purse system.

Comparison with Related Work. There are many ways in which a specification can be simplified or annotated to make it amenable to verification. Among the promising are abstraction [15,13,12,24,5,3,16], invariant generation [6,11], and slicing [28,25,14]. Once an adequate abstraction mapping (respectively, adequate invariants, or an adequate slicing criterion) is found, computing the abstract (resp. annotated, resp. sliced) system is fully automatic, and the verification is automatic, too. Here, adequate means that the property of interest holds on the simplified system.

Our approach is similar in that the user has to provide an adequate *purpose* to select the relevant component of the specification, and then the component is computed automatically. However, the verification still needs to be done with a theorem prover. (Using an interactive theorem prover is not mandatory; here, it was imposed by the infinite-state nature of the problem.) On the other hand, slicing and abstraction are sometimes too conservative. Our approach can be more precise: by writing a detailed purpose the user can select precisely the part of the system relevant for a given property. A purpose with an adequate level of detail can usually be found by trial and error.

Conformance testing is by no means the only formal approach to testing, nor is it the only one that has benefited from results in formal verification. The literature on the subject is vast and the approaches far too numerous for comprehensive citation. Among those known to us are [1,27] as well as the contributions to the Formal Approaches to Software Testing workshop, a satellite event of the CONCUR conference (see http://fmt.cs.utwente.nl/conferences/fates).

Finally, in the smart-card validation area, the Verificard European project (see http://www.verificard.org) aims at verifying JavaCard software using a variety of means including model checking, theorem proving, and abstractions.

Future Work. The main direction for future work is aimed at better automation. Invariant-generation techniques such as [6,11,5] may automatically suggest some auxiliary invariants. Adequate abstractions may reduce the state-space from infinite to finite while preserving the properties of interest. Preliminary results about data-independent arrays [19] might make some of the properties of the CEPS amenable to model checking. Finally, the precision of STG for selecting components can also be improved, in particular, by using a language with a built-in notions of component such as Java or NTIF from Inria Rhône-Alpes.

Acknowledgments. Duncan Clarke has implemented most of the STG tool and wrote the IOSTS specification of the CEPS previously used in [8]. John Rushby has signaled several recent papers [3,16,11] on automated abstraction and invariant generation that show significant progress in the area.

References

1. P. Ammann and P. Black. Abstracting formal specifications to generate software tests via model checking. In *Digital Avionics Systems Conference, DASC'99.* Also a National Institute of Research and Technology research report, NIST-IR 6405.
2. J.R. Burch, E.M. Clarke, K.L. McMillan, D.L. Dill and J. Hwang. Symbolic model checking: 10^{20} states and beyond. *Information and Computation*, 98(2):142-170, 1992.
3. T. Ball, R. Majumdar, T. Millstein, and S.K. Ramajani. Automatic predicate abstraction of C programs. *ACM SIGPLAN Conference on Programming Language Design and Implementation, PLDI'01*, pages 203–213.
4. A. Belinfante, J. Feenstra, R. de Vries, J. Tretmans, N. Goga, L. Feijs, and S. Mauw. Formal test automation: a simple experiment. *Int. Workshop on the Testing of Communicating Systems, IWTCS'99*, pages 179–196.
5. S. Bensalem, V. Ganesh, Y. Lakhnech, C. Munoz, S. Owre, H. Rueß, J. Rushby, V. Rusu, H. Saïdi, N. Shankar, E. Singerman, and A. Tiwari. An overview of SAL. *LFM 2000: NASA Langley Formal Methods Workshop, LFM'00*, pages 187–196.
6. S. Bensalem and Y. Lakhnech. Automatic generation of invariants. *Formal Methods in System Design*, 15(1):75–92, 1999.
7. CEPS: Common Electronic Purse System. Available at http://www.cepsco.org.
8. D. Clarke, T. Jéron, V. Rusu, and E. Zinovieva. Automated test and oracle generation for smart-card applications. *Conference on Research in Smart Cards, eSmart'01*, pages 58–70. LNCS 2140.
9. D. Clarke, T. Jéron, V. Rusu, and E. Zinovieva. STG: a Symbolic Test Generation tool. *Tools and Algorithms for the Construction and Analysis of Systems (TACAS'02)*, pages 470–475. LNCS 2280.
10. J-C. Fernandez, H. Garavel, A. Kerbrat, R. Mateescu, L. Mounier, and M. Sighireanu. CADP: A protocol validation and verification toolbox. *Computer-Aided Verification, CAV'96*. LNCS 1102.
11. C. Flanagan and S. Qadeer. Predicate Abstraction for Software Verification. To appear in *Principles of Program Design, POPL'02*.
12. S. Graf and H. Saïdi. Construction of abstract state graphs with PVS. *Computer Aided Verification, CAV'97*, pages 72–83. LNCS 1254.
13. N. Halbwachs, Y.E. Proy, and P. Roumanoff. Verification of real-time systems using linear relation analysis. *Formal Methods in System Design*, 11(2):157–185, 1997.

14. J. Hatcliff and M. Dwyer, Using the Bandera tool set to model-check properties of concurrent Java software. *Concurrency Theory, CONCUR'01*, pages 39–59. LNCS 2154.
15. K. Havelund and N. Shankar. Experiments in theorem proving and model checking for protocol verification. *Formal Methods Europe, FME'96*, pages 662–681. LNCS 1051.
16. T.A. Henzinger, R. Jhala, R. Majumdar, and G. Sutre. Lazy Abstraction. To appear in *Principles of Program Design, POPL'02*.
17. G.J. Holzmann. *Design and validation of communication protocols*. Prentice Hall, 1991.
18. ISO/IEC. International Standard 9646, OSI-Open Systems Interconnection, Information Technology - Conformance Testing Methodology and Framework, 1992.
19. R.S Lazić, T.C. Newcomb, and A.W. Roscoe. On model checking data-independent systems with arrays without reset. Oxford University Computing Laboratory, Research Report RR-02-02.
20. T. Jéron and P. Morel. Test generation derived from model-checking. *Computer-Aided Verification, CAV'99*, pages 108-122. LNCS 1633.
21. S. Owre, J. Rusby, N. Shankar, and F. von Henke. Formal verification of fault-tolerant architectures: Prolegomena to the design of PVS. *IEEE Transactions on Software Engineering*, 21(2): 107-125, 1995.
22. V. Rusu. Verifying a sliding-window protocol using PVS. In *Formal Techniques for Networked and Distributed Systems, FORTE'01*, pages 251–266. Kluwer Academic Publishers, 2001.
23. V. Rusu, L. du Bousquet, and T. Jéron. An approach to symbolic test generation. *Conference on Integrating Formal Methods (IFM'00)*, pages 338–357. LNCS 1945.
24. H. Saïdi and N. Shankar. Abstract and model check while you prove. *Computer-Aided Verification, CAV'99*, pages 443-454. LNCS 1633.
25. F. Tip. A survey of program slicing techniques. Technical Report CS-R9438, Centrum voor Wiskunde en InformatIca, 1994.
26. J. Tretmans. Testing concurrent systems: A formal approach. *Concurrency Theory, CONCUR'99*, pages 46–65. LNCS 1664.
27. L. Van Aertryck, M. Benveniste, and D. Le Metayer. CASTING: a formally based software test generation method. In *IEEE International Conference on Formal Engineering Methods (ICFEM'97)*, 1997.
28. M. Weiser. Program slicing. *IEEE Transactions on Software Engineering*, 10(4):352-357, 1984.

Formal Specification and Static Checking of Gemplus' Electronic Purse Using ESC/Java

Néstor Cataño and Marieke Huisman

INRIA Sophia-Antipolis, France
{Nestor.Catano, Marieke.Huisman}@sophia.inria.fr

Abstract. This paper presents a case study in formal specification of smart card programs, using ESC/Java. It discusses an electronic purse application, provided by Gemplus, that we have annotated with functional specifications (*i.e.* pre- and postconditions, modifies clauses and class invariants), that are as detailed as possible. The specification is based on the informal documentation of the application. Using ESC/Java, the implementation has been checked *w.r.t.* the specification. This revealed several errors or possibilities for improvement in the source code (*e.g.* removing unnecessary tests).

Our paper shows that a relatively lightweight use of formal specification techniques can already have a serious impact on the quality of a program and its documentation. Furthermore, we also present some ideas on how ESC/Java could be further improved, both *w.r.t.* specification and verification.

Keywords: static checking, specification, ESC/Java, Java, smart cards.

1 Introduction

Background. When developing a large software application, a significant part of the work is spent on writing clear and concise documentation. This documentation serves several purposes. First of all, it helps the developers of the application to do maintenance, as the documentation helps to understand the implementation decisions taken by a colleague, but also to understand ones own decisions after a certain period of time. Further, software documentation also is useful when somebody else builds a new application, using features provided by the application at hand.

However, such program documentation is only useful if it correctly describes the implementation, thus one would like to have some trust in its appropriateness. A way to achieve this is to write a formal specification, *i.e.* a description of the program behaviour in logic, and then prove the correctness of the implementation *w.r.t.* this specification, but this is difficult (as it requires a good understanding of the semantics underlying the specification and programming language), and labour-intensive (see *e.g.* [9,2] for examples of full program verification). Thus, although it is feasible to do formal specification and verification, the benefits in general do not outweigh the costs.

L.-H. Eriksson and P. Lindsay (Eds.): FME 2002, LNCS 2391, pp. 272–289, 2002.

Recently, several projects have started developments to overcome these problems. First of all, to encourage application developers to write formal specifications, specifications are written in a language that is close to the language in which the specified programs are written: the specification languages reuses the expression syntax of the programming language. The assertions that can be written in an Eiffel program [15] are a first example of such a specification style, and recently several annotation languages for Java have been proposed, following the same strategy: JML [11], ESC/Java [6], and the Jass annotation language [10]. For JML and ESC/Java, effort has been put into making these specification languages converge [5], so that the respective tools can be used for both languages. Typical for these languages is that expressions are written as Java expressions, extended with some specification-specific constructs.

Secondly, together with the ESC/Java language, a static checker has been developed [6], which can be used to check automatically simple, but useful properties. This static checker tries to check that a program satisfies its annotations, by using a dedicated, automatic theorem prover. This automatic theorem prover has been fine-tuned to find common programming problems like `Nullpointer-Exceptions`, and `ArrayIndexOutOfBoundExceptions`, but it also can be used to check other annotations. If the theorem prover cannot establish that a certain specification is satisfied, ESC/Java issues a warning. Such a warning does not necessarily mean that the program is wrong, as the ESC/Java approach is neither sound, nor complete. When designing the tool, a compromise has been made between soundness, completeness, and efficiency. The result is an efficient, automatic checker, that can increase the confidence in the correctness of programs, and that finds many common programming errors. However, if one wishes to establish formally the correctness of a complicated algorithm, other (possibly interactive) verification techniques have to be used, as advocated in *e.g.* the LOOP project [13] or the Jive project [16]. But even for such complex algorithms it pays to use ESC/Java first, in order to find quickly and automatically a first approximation of the errors in the algorithm and/or specification, before diving into the complete formal verification.

This paper. To demonstrate the usefulness of this approach, this paper describes the ESC/Java annotation of a smart card application. This case study shows that annotating programs with ESC/Java specifications can be helpful to create quickly clear, concise and unambiguous documentation for a software application, which is in correspondence with the implementation. The original source code of the case study – which implements an electronic purse – comes from Gemplus [8]. In this paper we discuss the annotations of the source code, and several possibilities for improvement that we encountered. The result of this work does not give a fully verified specification, but it gives a reasonable description of the electronic purse implementation, which could serve as a basis for further formal verification, *e.g.* by using the LOOP compiler.

The main contribution of this paper is that it shows that by making lightweight use of formal verification techniques, as provided by ESC/Java, it is feasible (i) to write a formal specification of an application, and (ii) to have the implementation checked *w.r.t.* the specification so as to increase confidence in the correctness of the implementation. When specifying the purse we have found several (simple) properties which are informally documented, but are not satisfied by the implementation. It is straightforward to formally specify these properties and ESC/Java immediately finds the places where these properties are not preserved in the implementation.

Furthermore, to the best of our knowledge this case study is one of the first larger case studies using ESC/Java, and we found several points for improvement in the static checker and its specification language. This leads us to a wish list on improvements in the specification language and to the development of a checker for so-called modifies clauses. This checker will be described in a separate paper [4].

The rest of this paper is organised as follows. Section 2 describes the general outline of the case study. Section 3 gives a brief introduction into the static checker ESC/Java. Section 4 describes the annotations of the purse in general, and discusses several aspects of the specification in more detail. Section 5 comments on the use of ESC/Java and gives suggestions for improvement. Finally, Section 6 gives conclusions and presents future work.

2   General Outline of the Electronic Purse

The electronic purse is a JavaCard application, published as an advanced smart card programming case study by Gemplus [8]. A JavaCard smart card is capable of running programs developed in JavaCard [18], a dialect of standard Java. JavaCard does not provide concepts such as dynamic class loading, security management, multi-threading and synchronisation, object cloning and large primitive date types (float, double, long and char). JavaCard applications are called *applets*. The electronic purse applet provides the ability to perform banking operations to the card holder. Typical operations are credit, debit, and currency changes.

The *debit* operation. Debit operations which involve an amount greater than maxDebitWOPIN are protected by a pin code. During one session, a user can do several of these transactions by presenting his pin code only once. To protect the card against attacks, the number of transactions that can be performed without presenting a pin code is limited to maxTransactionWOPIN.

The *credit* operation. If the balance on the card is not sufficient to execute a certain debit operation, the balance can be increased by performing a credit operation. To do this, the point of sale terminal asks the bank of the card holder for credit permission. If the permission is obtained, the account is credited and a confirmation is sent to the bank.

The *currency change* operation. The balance of the purse is expressed in a certain currency. When the card holder travels, the current currency can be changed. In order to do this, the terminal requests a new exchange rate and a certificate from the bank. The purse verifies that the bank is really the expected bank and validates the exchange rate. After changing the balance value, the purse must modify all variables related to the currency.

The purse applet interacts with so-called *loyalty applets* (implementing *e.g.* a frequent flyer program) that may be present on the card. Within the loyalty applet, the card holder gets loyalty points having made certain purchases, and these points can be used later to make other purchases. Further, a *card issuer applet* should be available on the card, which can initialise the purse. Finally, the purse applet also communicates with the *point of sale terminal*.

The purse application consists of three packages: utils, purse and pacap-interfaces. The utils package implements basic classes such as Annee (year), Mois (month) Jour (day) and Decimal (floating point numbers). The pacap-interfaces package declares shareable interfaces which enable the purse applet to communicate with *e.g.* the loyalty applets on the card. The purse package is the core of the purse application. It contains the class PurseApplet, which manages the operations related with installation, selection and deselection of the applet, and which communicates with the point of sale terminal. The basic purse functionalities are implemented in the class Purse. This class performs the communication with the loyalty applets, using the interfaces described in the pacapinterfaces package. Also, this class keeps track of the balance of the purse, the transactions done by the purse (stored as a TransactionRecord), the different currency changes that have taken place (in an ExchangeRecord) and the different loyalty programs that the card holder is subscribed to (in a LoyaltiesTable).

Certain operations can only be performed by a restricted set of users, *e.g.* because a pin code is needed. The class AccessCondition defines the different access conditions, and the class AccessControl binds the access conditions to the operations. So, when a card holder intends to perform a certain operation, the purse application will check that the card holder has the appropriate permissions. The class Currencies stores the different currencies used by the purse application. Finally, the purse application contains several classes implementing cryptographic concepts, namely, PacapCertificate, PacapCipher, PacapKey, PacapRandom, PacapSecureMessaging and PacapSignature. These classes are not studied in full detail in this case study.

3 Static Checking of Java Programs

ESC/Java is a verification tool developed at Compaq SRC, which permits a user to find common errors in Java programs. The basic idea is that a user specifies the desired behaviour of a class and its methods and the ESC/Java tool checks whether the implementation satisfies the specification. If it cannot establish this, it issues a warning. As explained above, such a warning does not necessarily mean that there is an error, as ESC/Java is neither sound, nor complete.

The specifications are given as *pre-* and *postconditions* of methods and as *class invariants*. The specifications are written as special Java comments, thus they do not change the annotated program. The properties are specified as Java expressions, enriched with several specification-specific constructs. Here, we present some ESC/Java specification constructs, together with an example of their use. Their full description can be found in [12].

3.1 ESC/Java Pragmas to Specify Method and Class Behaviour

- `requires` P. This pragma specifies a method precondition P. When ESC/Java checks the body of the method, it assumes that P holds initially, but when ESC/Java checks a method call, it will issue a warning if it can not establish that P holds at the call site.
- `ensures` Q. This pragma specifies a method postcondition Q. The postcondition is supposed to hold if the method terminates normally, *i.e.* without throwing an exception.
- `exsures` (E) R. This pragma specifies a exceptional condition. This condition is supposed to hold if the method finishes abruptly and if the exception e that is thrown is a subclass of E.
- `modifies` L. This pragma specifies that a method *may* modify the state components listed in L, where these state components are variable names, field or array accesses and array range expressions (denoting the elements within an array). Within a method body, the method parameters and the local variables always may be modified. When checking a method call, ESC/Java assumes that only the state components denoted by the modifies clauses may have been changed, but it does not check the correctness of the modifies clause.
- `assert` P. This pragma states that the property P should be true whenever control reaches this program point.
- `invariant` I. This pragma specifies a class invariant, *i.e.* the property I has to be established by the constructor of the class and it has to be preserved by all the methods in the class.

3.2 Specification Expressions

- `==>` is the logical implication. So, P `==>` Q is true if and only if P is false or Q is true, where P and Q are specification expressions of `boolean` type. Further, `<==>` denotes logical equivalence and `<=!=>` specifies non-equivalence.
- `(\forall T V; E)` and `(\exists T V; E)` are quantifier expressions of type `boolean`. The first one denotes that E is true for all substitutions of values of type T for the bound variable V. The second one denotes that E is true for at least one substitution of a value of type T for the bound variable V.
- `\old(E)` is used within a postcondition, where it denotes the value of E in the pre-state of the method invocation.
- `\result` represents the value returned by a non-void method. It can only be used within an `ensures` clause.

```
/*@
  modifies nbData, data[nbData];
  ensures (\old(nbData) < MAX_DATA) ?
            (nbData == \old(nbData) + 1 && data[\old(nbData)] == cur) :
            (nbData == \old(nbData));
*/
void addCurrency(byte cur){
   if(nbData < MAX_DATA) {
      data[nbData] = cur ;
      nbData++ ;
   }
}
```

Fig. 1. Example ESC/Java specification

Fig. 1 shows a typical annotation example using ESC/Java. This example comes from the specification of the electronic purse [3]. The addCurrency method belongs to the class Currencies. This class stores all currencies supported by the purse application. The method addCurrency adds a new currency to the list of valid currencies. This list is represented by the array data. The modifies clause declared in the method's header specifies that this method may modify nbData and data in the position nbData[1]. The postcondition of the method addCurrency – written as ensures clause – expresses that if nbData has not yet reached the threshold value MAX_DATA, nbData will increase its value by one and the value of the formal parameter cur will be assigned to data[\old(nbData)], otherwise nbData remains unchanged. Inside the postcondition, the expression \old(nbData) refers to the value of nbData before the method invocation.

4   Specification of the Electronic Purse

4.1   The General Specification Approach

ESC/Java forces one to start writing specifications for the classes that are 'used' by many other classes, either because they are used as components or because they are inherited from. In the electronic purse case study most classes inherit directly from classes as *e.g.* Object, Exception or – in the case of interfaces – Shareable, so the inheritance structure is not very complex. Therefore, we started by specifying classes that provide basic (and general) features, *e.g.* those in the utils package, that are used by the classes in the purse package. The specifications for these basic classes form the basis for the specification of the

---

[1] More precisely, it specifies that the method body only may modify these instance variables and the local variables and formal parameters of the method.

more application-specific classes, so it is important that they are sufficiently detailed.

For every method, we specify the precondition (as a **requires** clause in ESC/Java), the postcondition (**ensures**), the modifies clause (**modifies**), and the exceptional postcondition (**exsures**). ESC/Java does not have a keyword to specify that a method may not modify any variables, but this is implied by the absence of a modifies clause. To make our specifications explicit about this, in such a case we added a comment **modifies** \nothing; – as in JML [11]. Further, ESC/Java requires that every exception that is mentioned in the exceptional postcondition is also mentioned in the **throws** clause of the method. To avoid having to add **throws** clauses to every method, in many cases we chose to have the assertion **exsures (Exception) false;** – meaning that no exception will be thrown – as a comment, without having it checked by ESC/Java. However, everywhere where there can be any doubt about the correctness of the **exsures** clause, we add the **throws** clauses and have it checked by ESC/Java.

When writing method specifications, two different styles can be used: either a precondition is given which ensures that no exceptions will be thrown, or one specifies a light precondition (*e.g.* true), and an exceptional postcondition which describes under which conditions an exception will be thrown. For example, given the left specification, one has to show that P is satisfied before the method is called, and then it is guaranteed that the method cannot produce an exception, while the right hand specification makes no requirements on the method call, but specifies that if an exception occurs, this is because P did not hold in the pre-state.

```
/*@ modifies M;              /*@ modifies M;
      requires P;                  requires true;
      ensures Q;                   ensures Q;
      exsures (E) false;           exsures (E) !\old(P);
*/                            */
void m() {                    void m () {
 ...                           ...
}                             }
```

In our specifications, we usually follow the first approach, unless the informal documentation clearly suggests that the second approach is intended.

Further, we specify appropriate class invariants for each class, typically restricting the set of legal values for the instance variables. In some cases, the class invariant immediately follows from the informal documentation (*e.g.* the documentation in class **Decimal** states: **the decimal part must be done in the interval [000,999]** [8]) and in other cases the appropriate class invariant follows from closer inspection of the code, *e.g.* a variable is never **null**. Section 4.2 discusses the specification of class invariants in more detail.

Sometimes discrepancies between the informal documentation and the implementation occur. In general we try to follow the informal documentation, and we correct the implementation where necessary (and document these changes).

In several cases we consulted the case study developers at Gemplus, to get a better understanding which behaviour was actually intended.

In the case study, several functions from the JavaCard API [17] are used. When we specify methods using API functionalities, we use the API specification as constructed by Erik Poll and Hans Meijer (see [7,14]). In the classes `Purse` and `PurseApplet`, several classes are used that we do not have access to. To overcome this problem, we construct specification files, declaring the methods and fields that we need, but without making any assumptions about their behaviour.

Our aim is to give a functional specification of the behaviour of the purse. However, we did not study the algorithms to manage secret keys, and therefore we only give a lightweight specification (*i.e.* specifying the precondition and modifies clauses, but no postcondition) of the classes dealing with key generation and certification. This enables us to write and check the specifications of the classes `Purse` and `PurseApplet`. How to specify and verify cryptographic algorithms is a topic of future research.

We aim at giving specifications which describe the behaviour of the application as complete as possible. As ESC/Java is not complete, it will sometimes produce a warning for a correct specification. Typically, if a complex control structure occurs in a method (*e.g.* loops in which method calls are made) ESC/Java is unable to establish complicated postconditions. However, in the case study at hand such complex control structures are not very frequent and ESC/Java is able to check most of the specifications without any problems. If one wishes to certify these methods, other verification techniques, as advocated *e.g.* in the LOOP project [13], should be used. As an example of such a verification, the addition and multiplication methods of class `Decimal` have been verified within the LOOP project [2]. In the final version of the specifications, the only remaining warnings are caused by ESC/Java's incompleteness. When we encountered other warnings during the specification and checking process, we adapted the implementation or specification appropriately.

At [3] the full annotated version of the purse case study can be found. In the code it is documented which postconditions cannot be established by ESC/Java. It is also documented which changes we have had to make to the code.

4.2   Interesting Aspects of the Specification

Below, several interesting aspects of the specification are discussed in more detail. First we elaborate on some implementation errors that we found in the purse application. Then we discuss the specification of class invariants, and how this can help to simplify the code. Finally, we discuss miscellaneous aspects of the case study, and present some possible improvements. The problems that we have found probably also would have been found by doing thorough testing, but using theorem proving techniques one is sure not to forget some cases, without having to put much effort in developing test scenarios. Also, writing the formal specifications forces one to think very precisely about the intended behaviour of programs, which helps in finding errors.

```
/*@
  requires d != null;
  ensures \result == (intPart>d.intPart ||
                     (intPart == d.intPart &&
                      (decPart == d.decPart||decPart > d.decPart)));
*/
public boolean isGreaterEqualThan(Decimal d){
  boolean resu = false ;
  if(intPart>d.getIntPart()) resu = true ;
  else if(intPart<d.getIntPart()) resu = false ;
  else if(intPart==d.getIntPart()){
    if((decPart>d.getDecPart()) || (decPart>d.getDecPart())) resu=true ;
    else if(decPart<d.getDecPart()) resu = false ;
  }
  return resu ;
}
```

Fig. 2. Method isGreaterEqualThan

Implementation mistakes. This section presents some examples of common programming errors, and how we found them using ESC/Java.

The method isGreaterEqualThan. The class Decimal represents a floating point number composed of a decimal part and an integer part, denoted by instance variables decPart and intPart, respectively. The method isGreaterEqualThan (see Fig. 2) belongs to this class and, as suggested by its name and the informal documentation, it is supposed to decide whether the decimal represented by this is greater or equal than the decimal represented by parameter d. This behaviour is specified in the method specification.

However, after running ESC/Java on this asserted method, a warning is issued, suggesting that the postcondition might not hold. Inspection of the code reveals a *"copy paste"* error in the fourth if statement, where the condition decPart > d.getDecPart() is tested twice, on both side of an || (or) operator. Replacing the whole expression by decPart >= d.getDecPart() would solve the problem, although it would probably be better to rewrite the method in such a way that it simply tests the condition as expressed in the postcondition.

Final modifiers. The class Annee represents a *year*. It declares two static variables called MIN and MAX, which represent the minimum and maximum year allowed by the application. Its declarations are as follows:

```
public static byte MIN = (byte)99 ;
public static byte MAX = (byte)127 ;
```

The class Annee also defines a method check, which is used to determine whether a value is between MIN and MAX. The class Date has three instance

```
/*@
  modifies jour, mois, annee;
  requires j >= Jour.MIN  && j <= Jour.MAX;
  requires m >= Mois.MIN  && m <= Mois.MAX;
  requires a >= Annee.MIN && a <= Annee.MAX;
  ensures jour == j && annee == a && mois == m;
*/
public void setDate(byte j, byte m, byte a) throws DateException{...}
```

Fig. 3. Fragment of class `Date`

variables, representing the components of a date: `jour` (day), `mois` (month), and `annee` (year). The method `setDate` (see Fig. 3) in this class assigns its arguments to these instance variables, provided they are in a valid interval (see the `requires` pragma). Surprisingly, ESC/Java complains when it finds a statement such as `date.setDate((byte)1, (byte)1, (byte)110);` (where date is a instance of class `Date`). The warning message states that the the third precondition of this call might not hold, even though 110 is between 99 and 127.

The problem is caused by the erroneous declaration of the variables `MIN` and `MAX` in class `Annee`. Since these variables are not declared `final`[2], their values can be changed at runtime by a direct assignment (as they are declared public), and thus ESC/Java warns correctly that the precondition of `setDate` might not be satisfied.

Class invariants. Typically, invariants are used to restrict the state space of a class, *i.e.* the set of allowed values for its instance variables. The most common example is an invariant which states that a reference may never be a null pointer, *e.g.* the variable `purse`, as declared in the class `PurseApplet` should never be null.

```
//@ invariant purse != null;
```

Another common example of an invariant is to restrict the possible values of a numeric variable to a certain range. As remarked above, the class `Decimal` says that the value of the decimal fraction part must be between 0 and 999. Inspection of the code reveals that the integer part of the decimal number is supposed to be a positive short, and combining this gives the following class invariant:[3]

---

[2] According to the Java semantics, final variables may only be assigned to when they are initialised, and afterwards they remain constant.

[3] `MAX_DECIMAL_NUMBER` is equivalent to the maximal value of a short and the clause `intPart <= MAX_DECIMAL_NUMBER` of the invariant will thus be ensured by the type of the variable. We chose to state this explicitly for clarity of specification.

```
/*@
  invariant decPart >= 0 && decPart < PRECISION ;
  invariant intPart >= 0 && intPart <= MAX_DECIMAL_NUMBER;
*/
```

Another way to use class invariants, is to improve the simulation of enumeration types, which are not available in Java(Card). To simulate them, typically several constants with suggestive names are defined and a variable is silently assumed to contain always one of these values. This implicit assumption can be made explicit by specifying invariants. For example, the class `Transaction` contains the following declarations.

```
public static final byte INDETERMINE      = (byte)0;
public static final byte TYPE_CREDIT       = (byte)50;
public static final byte TYPE_DEBIT     = (byte)51;

/* the transaction type: debit or credit*/
/*@ spec_public*/ private byte type;
```

The documentation above suggests that the variable `type` always should have a value `TYPE_CREDIT` or `TYPE_DEBIT`. However, in the code (in the method `reset()`), an assignment `type = INDETERMINE;` occurs, suggesting that this is also a correct value for `type`. Having a specification which states the allowed values for this variable avoids all confusion[4].

```
/*@ invariant type == INDETERMINE ||
              type == TYPE_CREDIT ||
              type == TYPE_DEBIT;
*/
```

Invariants of this kind often occur in the specification of the electronic purse. It is easy to specify them, and useful as well, as there are examples in the electronic purse where such implicitly assumed invariants are violated. For example, the class `AccessCondition` declares constants to state the different access conditions for the actions in the purse. Following [1], variables that denote access conditions should be restricted as follows.

```
/*@ invariant condition == FREE ||
              condition == LOCKED ||
              condition == SECRET_CODE ||
              condition == SECURE_MESSAGING ||
              condition == (SECRET_CODE | SECURE_MESSAGING);
*/
```

However, in the constructor of this class, the variable `condition` is set to 0, which breaks this invariant[5]. Correcting this and maintaining the invariant also

---

[4] However, notice that this does not give type safety, in contrast to real enumeration types.

[5] As none of these constants is equal to 0.

allows to improve other parts of the implementation in this class. For example, in the method `verify()`, the following statement occurs:

```
switch(condition) {
  case FREE: ...
  case SECRET_CODE: ...
  case SECURE_MESSAGING: ...
  case SECRET_CODE | SECURE_MESSAGING: ...
  case LOCKED: ...
  default: //@ assert false;
          t = AccessConditionException.CONDITION_COURANTE_INVALIDE;
          AccessConditionException.throwIt(t);
}
```

Because of the invariant we know that the default case will never be reached (as signalled by the `//@ assert false;` annotation, which states that false should hold, every time this program point is reached), and thus that the exception never will be thrown. Therefore the default case can be removed from the code.

Similar cases occur frequently with `try-catch` statements. An operation is executed within a `try`, but as the class invariants assure that the operation never will throw an exception, the `catch` clause will never be executed. In the specification, we have annotated these cases with `//@ assert false;`. We think that the removal of this "dead code" can improve the readability of the class and, importantly for smart cards, it reduces the size of the byte code.

Miscellaneous aspects of the specification. There are many other aspects of the specification that are worth mentioning. Here we mention some.

- As explained above, in the class `Decimal`, two shorts are maintained denoting the integer and the decimal part (`intPart` and `decPart`, respectively) of a decimal number. The integer part ranges between 0 and `MAX_DECIMAL_NUMBER` (which is 32767, the maximal value for shorts). It is left unspecified whether numbers such as `MAX_DECIMAL_NUMBER.999` are allowed. However, a method `round()` is defined, which according to the documentation returns a decimal number with `decPart` set to 0 and `intPart` set to the closest integer value. An obvious specification of this method reads as follows:

```
/*@
  modifies intPart, decPart;
  ensures decPart == 0;
  ensures intPart == (\old(decPart) >= (PRECISION/2) ?
                     (short)(\old(intPart) + 1) :
                     (short)(\old(intPart)))
*/
public Decimal round(){ ... }
```

But, as pointed out by ESC/Java, an implementation of this specification breaks the class invariant `intPart >= 0`. The counterexample that is produced has `intPart` set to `MAX_DECIMAL_NUMBER` and `decPart` *e.g.* to 999. Possible solutions are to specify explicitly the outcome of `round()` in the case that `intPart == MAX_DECIMAL_NUMBER`, or to restrict the set of valid decimal numbers by further strengthening of the class invariant through addition of the following clause:

```
//@ invariant intPart == MAX_DECIMAL_NUMBER ==> decPart == 0;
```

We chose this last solution.

– Among the developers of the electronic purse application there apparently have been different ideas about the implementation of the class `Decimal` (which could have been avoided if the class invariants immediately would have been specified explicitly in the class). The implementation of several `setValue(...)` methods reveal that `intPart` is assumed to be greater or equal than 0, but on the other hand there are methods `isNegatif()` and `isPositif()`, which test whether a decimal value is negative or positive, respectively. As we specify[6] that `intPart` should be greater or equal than 0 these methods become obsolete. We can show this by specifying that their results can be predicted, *e.g.* `isNegatif()` we specify as follows:

```
/*@
  ensures \result == false;
*/
public boolean isNegatif(){ ... }
```

– Two classes, `TransactionRecord` and `ExchangeRecord` implement a cyclic table (of `Transactions` and `ExchangeSessions` (currency changes), respectively). These implementations are clearly copied from each other, but this is nowhere documented. Also the fact that a cyclic data structure is implemented is not clearly documented. Class `TransactionRecord` contains a single remark that it is implemented as a cyclic table, and in class `ExchangeRecord` this is only stated in the documentation of a private method. Also, no specification of the operations on the cyclic data structure are given. As a result, in class `ExchangeRecord`, part of the code that is crucial for its behaviour has been commented out by other developers of the electronic purse. Having a formal specification would probably have been helpful to explain the complexity of the implementation to the other developers, and the "wrong correction" would have been signaled earlier[7].

Finally, when writing the formal specifications of the cyclic tables, we found an error in the implementation. When a delete operation is called for an element that is not in the range of the table, the operation nevertheless will be executed and as a side-effect it will corrupt the table by erroneously moving its first element outside the range of the table.

---

[6] *cf.* our email exchange with H. Martin, Gemplus.

[7] Of course, having a general implementation of a cyclic table and instantiating this for the different kinds of data would have been even more elegant.

```
/*@
  modifies \fields_of(this), \fields_of(date), \fields_of(heure),
           id[*], terminalTC[*], terminalSN[*];
  requires es != null ;
  requires es.id != terminalTC & es.id != terminalSN &
           es.terminalTC != terminalSN;
  ensures this.equal(es);
  exsures (TransactionException e)
             e._reason == TransactionException.BUFFER_FULL
             && JCSystem._transactionDepth == 1;
  exsures (NullPointerException) false;
  exsures (ArrayIndexOutOfBoundsException) false;
*/
void clone(ExchangeSession es) { ...
}
```

Fig. 4. Specification of `clone` in `ExchangeSession` in ideal ESC/Java

5   On the Use of ESC/Java

We find ESC/Java a useful tool, which is pleasant to work with, but nevertheless we have some suggestions for improvements, both for the specification language and for the checker.

Concerning the specification language, we feel that certain specification constructs that are available in JML [11] should be provided in ESC/Java as well, in order to be able to write clear and concise specifications.

First of all, it would be convenient to have some extra specification constructs for modifies clauses, e.g. \fields_of(E), to denote all the fields of an object, and \nothing. This could easily be implemented as syntactic sugar, in particular modifies \nothing.

Another improvement that would be easy to implement, would be to enable the specification of runtime exceptions in **exsures** clauses, without mentioning them explicitly in the **throws** clause of the method.

Also we feel that having some extra quantifiers, such as \min, \max, and \choose could be useful to increase expressiveness of the specification language. However, to implement this would require an extension of the theorem prover underlying ESC/Java, so that it also can deal with these language constructs.

Finally, we would like to be able to use method names in specifications, as is allowed in JML for so-called *pure* methods, *i.e.* methods without side-effects, but this would require a major change to ESC/Java.

Fig. 4 shows as an example the specification of the method `clone()` in class `ExchangeSession` the way we would prefer it (see [3] for the ESC/Java specification as it is). We only specify that all the fields of the current class may be modified, without explicitly mentioning them. As the fields of the component classes date and heure may be modified as well, we mention this explicitly. Similarly, we mention explicitly that the elements in the arrays id, terminalTC and terminalSN may be modified[8]. Further, instead of having postconditions stating that all the fields are ensured to be equal to the corresponding fields of es, this is denoted by writing this.equal(es), where equal is overwritten appropriately in ExchangeSession.

With respect to the verification that is done by ESC/Java, we found that it is unfortunate that ESC/Java does not try to check the modifies clauses, because an incorrect modifies clause can influence the acceptance of other specifications. For example, suppose one has the following (annotated) methods:

```
/*@ modifies x;
    ensures x == 3;
*/
void m() { x = 3;
           n (); }


void n() { x = 4; }
```

Remember that a method without any modifies clause is assumed to modify only freshly allocated memory, if any [12]. The specification for method m() is thus accepted by ESC/Java, although it is incorrect. When annotating existing programs, as we did, it is easy to forget to mention that a variable may be modified, and we felt the need to overcome this problem. Therefore, we have implemented a static checker for modifies clauses. In the tradition of ESC/Java, this checker is designed to be efficient, but it is neither sound, nor complete. It does a syntactic analysis of the annotated program to recognise the various assignment statements and then checks whether the variables that are the "destination" of an assignment are appropriately specified in the corresponding modifies clauses. This checker will be described in more detail in a separate paper [4].

Finally, we feel that it would be an important improvement if the ESC/Java theorem prover would deal more precisely with arithmetic operations (also on bytes and shorts). For example, the current version of ESC/Java issues a warning for the following specification.

```
/*@ requires b == (byte)4 & d == (byte)8;
    ensures \result >= 0;
*/
byte m(byte d) {return (byte)(b | d);}
```

We found that almost all spurious warnings that are produced by ESC/Java are caused by arithmetic operations[9] and it would be a significant improvement if less of these warnings would be generated.

---

[8] In JML this whole modifies clause also can be written as \fields_of(\reach(this)), which would probably also be useful in many cases, but has a more complex semantics.

[9] Warnings about loops are not considered to be spurious, as they are inherent to how ESC/Java works.

6   Conclusions

We have presented a case study in formal specification of smart card programs, using ESC/Java. We have taken an electronic purse application and annotated it with a functional specification, describing its behaviour, basing ourselves on the informal documentation of the application. We have checked the implementation *w.r.t.* the specification, using ESC/Java, thereby revealing several errors in the implementation. Using ESC/Java we were also able to find that some parts of the program will never be reached, thus allowing reduction of the code size – which is important for smart card applications.

The whole case study consists of 42 classes and 432 kB in total (736 kB with annotations). It has taken approximately three months to write the complete specifications. Most of the specifications are written by the first author, who beforehand did not have any experience with ESC/Java, or with writing formal specifications in general. The second author – who had experience in writing formal specifications, but not with ESC/Java – supervised the work and made suggestions to extend the specifications. Of the time spend on writing the specifications, approximately one third was used on getting to know ESC/Java, and understanding the electronic purse application, the remaining time was used on writing and checking the actual specifications.

The errors that we found in general are not very intricate, they could have been found by careful code-inspection or testing. But, writing the formal specification (for existing code) forces one to do code-inspection, and having the theorem prover ensures that all cases are considered, when checking the specification, without having to put effort in writing appropriate test scenarios.

The specifications that we have constructed for the electronic purse application are not very complex, but describe the functional behaviour of methods as precisely as possible. Nevertheless, we found errors in the code, and we would like to emphasise that even simple formal verification can help significantly to increase confidence in a program. In particular, explicitly specifying class invariants – which are often implicitly assumed by the program – turns out to be very useful.

Future work. We plan to work in the field of specification languages for Java: how to improve them, and how to develop appropriate verification techniques for them. In particular, we will focus on the following points.

– We plan to develop a full smart card application from scratch, with annotations. We are interested whether this will affect the quality of the specification and/or the program. Also we would like to know how easy it is to construct the specifications at the same time as developing the code. We would like to evaluate the tradeoff between usability – because one gets immediate feedback on an implementation – and the extra time that is spend on keeping the specification up-to-date.

- Future versions of JavaCard will probably allow multi-threading. Therefore we plan to study how ESC/Java (and JML) can be used to specify (and check) concurrent programs.
- Related with this is an extension of JML with temporal logic. Currently we are studying how to integrate temporal logic in the specification language [19], future work will be to study appropriate verification techniques.
- Most loop structures that are used in typical smart card programs are very restricted and it is relatively easy to show their termination. We plan to develop an automatic verification technique for termination of loops in the tradition of ESC/Java, covering the most common cases.
- We skipped the cryptographic aspects of the application at hand. It is future work to see whether ESC/Java (or JML) is useful to specify such algorithms more precisely, and to develop appropriate (automatic) verification techniques.

Acknowledgements. We thank Erik Poll, Dilian Gurov and Arnd Poetzsch-Heffter for useful feedback on the specifications and on earlier versions of this paper. Also we would like to thank Rustan Leino and his team for their help with ESC/Java.

References

1. E. Bretagne, A. El Marouani, P.Girard, and J.-L. Lanet. Pacap purse and loyalty specification. Technical Report V 0.4, Gemplus, 2000.
2. C. Breunesse, B. Jacobs, and J. van den Berg. Specifying and Verifying a Decimal Representation in Java for Smart Cards. In *Algebraic Methodology And Software Technology (AMAST '02)*, LNCS. Springer, 2002. To appear.
3. N. Cataño and M. Huisman. Annotated files Electronic Purse case study, 2001. http://www-sop.inria.fr/lemme/verificard/electronic_purse.
4. N. Cataño and M. Huisman. A static checker for JML's *assignable* clause, 2002. Manuscript.
5. Differences between Esc/Java and JML, 2000. Comes with JML distribution, in file esc-jml-diffs.txt.
6. Extended static checking for Java. http://research.compaq.com/SRC/esc/.
7. ESC/Java specifications for the JavaCard API. http://www.cs.kun.nl/~erikpoll/publications/jc211_specs.html.
8. Gemplus. Applet benchmark kit. http://www.gemplus.com/smart/r_d/publications/case-study/.
9. M. Huisman, B. Jacobs, and J. van den Berg. A Case Study in Class Library Verification: Java's Vector Class. *Software Tools for Technology Transfer*, 3/3:332–352, 2001.
10. The JASS project. http://semantik.informatik.uni-oldenburg.de/~jass/.
11. G.T. Leavens, A.L. Baker, and C. Ruby. Preliminary Design of JML: a Behavioral Interface Specification Language for Java. Technical Report 98-06, Iowa State University, Department of Computer Science, 2000.
12. K.R.M. Leino, G. Nelson, and J.B. Saxe. ESC/Java user's manual. Technical Report SRC 2000-002, Compaq System Research Center, 2000.

13. The LOOP project. `http://www.cs.kun.nl/~bart/LOOP/`.
14. H. Meijer and E. Poll. Towards a Full Formal Specification of the Java Card API. In I. Attali and T. Jensen, editors, *Smart Card Programming and Security (E-smart 2001)*, number 2140 in LNCS, pages 165–178. Springer, 2001.
15. B. Meyer. *Object-Oriented Software Construction*. Prentice Hall, 2nd rev. edition, 1997.
16. J. Meyer and A. Poetzsch-Heffter. An architecture of interactive program provers. In S. Graf and M. Schwartzbach, editors, *Tools and Algorithms for the Construction and Analysis of Systems (TACAS 2000)*, number 1785 in LNCS, pages 63–77. Springer, 2000.
17. Sun Microsystems, Inc. Java Card 2.1. Platform Application Programming Interface (API) Specification. `http://java.sun.com/products/javacard/htmldoc/`.
18. Sun Microsystems, Inc. JavaCard Technology.
    `http://java.sun.com/products/javacard/`.
19. K. Trentelman and M. Huisman. Extending JML Specifications with Temporal Logic. In *Algebraic Methodology And Software Technology (AMAST '02)*, LNCS. Springer, 2002. To appear.

Development of an Embedded Verifier for Java Card Byte Code Using Formal Methods

Ludovic Casset

Gemplus Research Laboratory
Av du Pic de Bretagne,
13881 Gémenos cedex BP 100
phone:+33(0)4 42 36 40 98
fax:+33(0)4 42 36 55 55
ludovic.casset@gemplus.com

Abstract. The Java security policy is implemented using security components such as a Java Virtual Machine (JVM), API, verifier, and a loader. It is of prime importance to ensure that these components are implemented in accordance with their specifications. Formal methods can be used to bring the mathematical proof that their implementation corresponds to their specification. In this paper, we introduce the formal development of a complete byte code verifier for Java Card and its on-card integration. In particular, we aim to focus on the model and the proof of the complete type verifier for the Java Card language. The global architecture of the verification process implemented in this real industrial case study is described and the detailed specification of the type verifier is discusses as well as its proof. Moreover, this paper presents a comparison between formal and traditional development, summing up the pros and cons of using formal methods in industry.

Keywords: Byte Code Verification, Formal Methods, B Method

1. Introduction

Smart cards have an established reputation for securing data in information systems. These cards lock and protect their contents (data or applications). The strong security of smart cards is linked to their design. All functions are built into a single component: CPU, communication, data and applications. This all fits into 25 square millimeters. *Open* smart cards let you download code onto cards after their issuance (postissuance). They acquire new functions over their lifetime as new applications are uploaded. There is, however, no reason to believe that the uploaded code has been developed using a methodology that ensures its innocuousness. One of the main issues when deploying these applications is to guarantee to the customer that these applications will be safe i.e., that their execution will not jeopardise the smart card's integrity or confidentiality. The Java security policy defines acceptable behaviour for a program and the properties that such a program must respect. For example, it must not be possible to turn an integer into an object reference since Java is a type-safe language.

L.-H. Eriksson and P. Lindsay (Eds.): FME 2002, LNCS 2391, pp. 290-309, 2002.

A key point of this security policy is the byte code verifier. The aim of a byte code verifier is to statically ensure that the control flow and the data flow do not generate errors. Moreover, in order to perform these verifications, one has to ensure the syntactical correctness of a file sent to the verifier. Correct construction of this file is of prime importance to the security of the system. Formal methods provide the mathematical proof that the implementation corresponds to the specification. We have modelled and implemented a byte code verifier on the full Java Card language, excepting *jsr* and *ret* instructions (they concern subroutines). We show that the implementation is compatible with the constrained context of the smart card and lastly we discuss results. Moreover, formal development is compared to traditional development with an assessment of pros and cons of formal methods in an industrial context.

This paper presents the results of one case study of the Matisse[1] project. This project aims to propose methodologies, tools and techniques focusing on the use of formal methods in industrial contexts. The case study described below concerns the formal specifications and implementation of a Java Card byte code verifier. The formal development was integrated on-card, and we focused on the description and the discussion on the model of the type verifier, and this is the most difficult part of the verification process.

The remainder of this paper is organised as follow. Section 2 explains the aims of the B method, section 3 focuses on the principles of byte code verification and the Java Card context. Section 4 emphasises the model for the byte code verifier. Section 5 provides some quantitative indicators about the development and section 6 is the conclusion.

2. The B Method

The B method is a model-oriented formal method based on first-order logic, set theory and generalised guarded substitutions. It is fully described in [1]. This method encompasses the entire development process, from the specification down to the implementation. Code can be automatically generated from the implementation.

The primary component of a B model is the *abstract machine*. A B specification is made of one or more abstract machines. An abstract machine encapsulates data, properties and operations that apply to that data. In a sense, abstract machines are conceptually similar to modules or packages.

There are three main parts in an abstract machine:

- **The variables** describe the state of the machine. They can be sets or elements of a set. Those sets include natural numbers, integers and user-defined sets. B distinguishes between *abstract variables*, used for specification purpose only, and *concrete variables* which correspond to variables in the generated code,
- **The invariant** expresses the properties enforced by the machine. It consists of a predicate expressed on the variables, and it must always hold. It is also used to assign a type to each variable,

---

[1] European IST Project MATISSE number *IST-1999-11435*.

- **The operations** provide a way to access and modify the variables of the machine. They usually contain a *precondition*, which is a predicate that must be true when the operation is called.

Abstract machines are gradually turned into implementations using the *refinement* mechanism. Refinement lets us add specification details to an abstract machine, while preserving its properties. Informally, refining an abstract machine consists in replacing the machine by another machine that has the same interface and that preserves the correctness of the abstraction. A special invariant, called the *gluing invariant* is used to describe the relationship between the state of the abstract machine and its refinement.

Finally, *implementations* correspond to the last refinement step of an abstract machine. They must be specified in a subset of B called B0, matching classical imperative language, and used to generate code.

An important point with the B method is that every step can and should be proved. Each specification has an associated set of *proof obligations* corresponding to proofs that must be demonstrated in order to ensure the consistency of the specification.

3. Byte Code Verification

The byte code verification aims to enforce static constraints on downloaded byte code. Those constraints ensure that the byte code can be safely executed by the virtual machine, and cannot bypass the higher-level security mechanisms. The byte code verification is informally described in [9]. It consists in a static analysis of the downloaded applet ensuring that the downloaded applet file is a valid file, there is no stack overflow or underflow, the execution flow is confined to valid byte code, each instruction argument is of the correct type and method calls are performed in accordance with their visibility attributes (public, protected, etc...).

The first point corresponds to the structural verification, and the next points are performed by the type verification. The next subsections describe in detail the properties ensured by the verifications. Even if this paper focuses on the model and the implementation of the type verifier, we describe the entire verification process used in the case study.

3.1. The Structural Verification

Structural verification consists in ensuring that the downloaded file is valid. Which is to say, it must describe java classes and byte code, and the information contained in the file must be consistent. For example, this verifier makes sure that all structures have the appropriate size and that required components do indeed exist. These tests ensure that the downloaded file cannot be misinterpreted by the verifier or by the virtual machine.

Apart from the purely structural verification of the binary format, tests focusing on the file contents are also carried out. These tests ensure that there are no cycles in the inheritance hierarchy, or that no final methods are overridden.

In the case of Java Card, the structural tests are more complex than those for Java, since the CAP file format used to store Java Card packages was designed for simple installation and minimum linking. Most references to other components are actually given as offsets in the component.

A CAP file consists of several components with specific information from the Java Card package. For instance, the Method component contains the byte code of the methods, and the Class component information on classes such as references to their super classes or declared methods.

Therefore in the case of Java Card, we distinguish internal structural verifications from external structural verifications. The internal verifications correspond to the verifications that can be performed on a component basis. Example verification consists in making sure that the super classes occur first in the class component.

External verifications are tests ensuring the consistency between components or external packages. For example, one of those tests consists in checking that the methods declared in the Class component correspond to existing methods in the Method component.

3.2. The Type Verification

This verification is performed on a method basis, and must be done for each method present in the package.

The type checking part ensures that no disallowed type conversions are performed. For example, an integer cannot be converted into an object reference, downcasting can only be performed using the checkcast instruction, and arguments provided to methods have to be of compatible types.

As the type of the local variables is not explicitly stored in the byte code, it is needed to retrieve the type of those variables by analyzing the byte code. This part of the verification is the most complex, and is demanding on both time and memory. It requires that the type of each variable and stack element be computed for each instruction and each execution path.

```
static void m(boolean b) {
      if(b) {
            int i = 1;
      } else {
            Object tmp = new Object();
      }
      int j = 2;
}
```

Fig. 1. A sample Java method

In order to make such verification possible, the verification is quite conservative about which programs will be accepted. Only programs where the type of each element in the stack and local variable is the same whatever path has been taken to reach an instruction are accepted. This also requires that the size of the stack be the same for each instruction for each path that can reach this instruction.

Fig. 1 shows a sample Java method. The corresponding byte code instructions and types inferred by the verifier are given in Fig. 2. In this example, depending on the value of the Boolean b, an integer or an object is pushed onto the stack and then stored in the local variable v0. In both cases, a second integer is pushed onto the stack and stored in the local variable v0. This lets us study the typing evolution of the stack and more precisely of the local variable v0 which can contain either an integer or an object. The goal of the type verifier is to ensure that each branch is correct by determining the type of each stack element and each local variable at any point of the program. Fig. 2 indicates the typing value of each element, at each point in the program.

3.3. Adaptation to Embedded Devices

Performing full byte code verification requires large amount of computing power and memory. So different systems have been proposed to allow verification to be performed on highly constrained devices such as smart cards. Those systems rely on an external pre-treatment of the applet to verify. As the type verification is the most resource consuming part of the verification, they aim to simplify the verification algorithm.
Two approaches are usually used: Byte code normalisation and proof carrying code (PCC) or similar techniques. The next subsection introduces those techniques. The proof carrying code technique will be discussed more in detail, since this is the approach that has been developed for the type verifier.

Byte code normalisation
Byte code normalisation is the approach used by Trusted Logic's smart card verifier [7]. It consists in normalising the verified applet so that it is simpler to verify. More exactly, the applet is modified so that:
- Each variable has one and only one type.
- The stack is empty at branch destinations.

This greatly reduces the memory requirements, since the verifier does not have to keep typing information for each instruction, but only for each variable in the verified method. The computing requirements are also reduced, since only a simplified fixed point computation has to be performed. However, as the code is modified, its size and memory requirements can theoretically increase.

Lightweight byte code verification
Introduced by Necula and Lee [10], the PCC techniques consist in adding a proof of the program safety to the program. This proof can be generated by the code producer, and the code is transmitted along with its safety proof. The code receiver can then verify the proof in order to ensure the program safety. As checking the proof is simpler than generating it, the verification process can be performed by a constrained device.
An adaptation of this technique to Java has been proposed by Rose [16] and is now used by Sun's KVM [18]. In this context, the "proof" represents additional type information corresponding to the content of local variables and stack element for the branch targets. Fig. 2 depicts the contents of the proof for the previous example

method. Those typing information correspond to the result of the fixed point computation performed by a full verifier. In this case, the verification process consists in a linear pass that checks the validity of this typing information with respect to the verified code. In our example, we note that the proof only concerns elements that are a jump target (**endif** and **else**). The types of these elements are extracted from the full type computation. Moreover, in this example, it only concerns the local variable v0, the stack and the other local variables are empty for jump target.

Compared to byte code normalisation, lightweight verification requires removing the `jsr` and `ret` instructions from the byte code, and needs temporary storage in EEPROM memory for storing the type information. However, lightweight verification performs the verification as a linear pass throughout the code, and leaves the code unmodified.

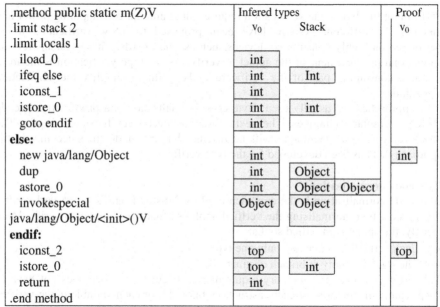

.method public static m(Z)V	Infered types			Proof
.limit stack 2	v_0	Stack		v_0
.limit locals 1				
iload_0	int			
ifeq else	int	Int		
iconst_1	int			
istore_0	int	int		
goto endif	int			
else:				
new java/lang/Object	int			int
dup	int	Object		
astore_0	int	Object	Object	
invokespecial java/lang/Object/<init>()V	Object	Object		
endif:				
iconst_2	top			top
istore_0	top	int		
return	int			
.end method				

Fig. 2. A sample Java bytecode method and its associated proof and type information

3.4 Formal Studies on Byte Code Verification

A lot of formal work has been done on Java byte code verification. Most of those studies focus on the type verification part of the algorithms.

One of the most complete formal models of the Java virtual machine is given by Qian [14]. He considers a large subset of the byte code and aims at proving the runtime correctness from its static typing. Then, he proposes the proof of a verifier that can be deducted from the specifications of the virtual machine. In a more recent work [5] the authors also propose a correct implementation of almost all aspects of the Java byte code verifier. They view the verification problem as a data flow analysis, and aims to formally describe the specification to extract the corresponding code using the Specware tool.

In the Bali project, Push [12] proves a part of the JVM using the Isabelle/HOL[2] prover. Using Qian's work [14], she gives the verifier specification and then proves its correctness. She also defines a subset of Java, μjava [13] and aims to prove properties. More precisely, they formalise the type system and the semantics of this language using the Isabelle theorem prover. In more recent work [11], Nipkow has introduced the formal specification of the Java byte code verifier in Isabelle. The idea is to come up with the generic proof of the algorithm and then to instantiate it with a particular JVM.

Roses' verification scheme has been proven safe using the Isabelle theorem prover by Nipkow [6], and a similar scheme for a Smart Card specific language has been proved correct using B in [15].

Work prior to the one described in this article has also been performed using the B method on the formalisation of a simple verifier [3], and its implementation [4]. Similar work has been done by Bertot [2] using Coq's[3] theorem prover. He proves the correctness of the verification algorithm and generates an implementation using Coq's extraction mechanism.

4. Modeling a Type Verifier in B

In this section, the modelling of the type verifier is described. We focus on how the architecture was chosen and on the benefits of using formal methods in developing a

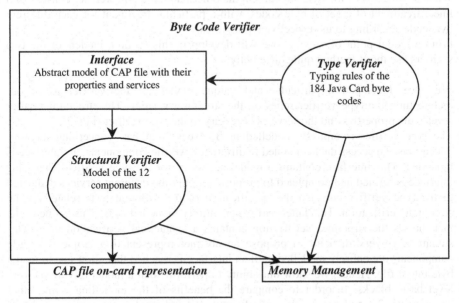

Fig. 3. The Byte Code Verifier Architecture

---

[2] Isabelle web site, http://www.cl.cam.ac.uk/Research/HVG/Isabelle/index.html
[3] Coq's Proof Assistant web site, http://coq.inria.fr

byte code verifier. Moreover, Fig. 3 indicates that the type verifier is only a part of a complete verifier. In our model, the type verifier relies on services expressed in its interface. It also defines and implements the typing behaviour of the Java Card language, byte-code-by-byte-code. The interface between the structural and the type verifiers constitutes the abstraction of the CAP file. This abstraction is refined in the structural verifier where each component of the CAP file is modelled. Moreover, in the structural verifier, tests indicating that the data received by the smart card represent a CAP file are also implemented.

In this paper, and more precisely in this section, we propose to go deeper into the model of the type verifier and leave aside the structural verifier. The first subsection redefines the type verifier in the general verification scheme. Then, next subsections focus on the type verifier.

4.1 The Type Verifier: A Part of a Complete Verifier

As described in section 3, a byte code verifier includes two distinct parts: a structural verifier and a type verifier. These two parts have distinct aspects:

From a purely functional point of view, these parts are the two successive steps of the verification process that can be easily separated,

From an algorithmic point of view, the structural verifier is split into twelve different components that can be modelled separately. Those components correspond to the twelve components defined in the CAP file format. Each component requires a syntactic analysis of the byte stream. On the other hand, the type verifier consists of a linear treatment of a set of byte codes, with a particular treatment for each different byte code according to its respective typing rules.

From a model point of view, as we will develop in this section, models of the two verifiers use the B method quite differently.

We have developed a particular and unique model for the verifier as in our architecture, the type verifier relies on the structural verifier. The structural verifier reveals the properties and the services necessary to the type verifier (Fig. 3).

The type verifier is entirely modelled in B, except that part concerning memory allocations. To access data contained in different CAP file components, an interface is modelled. This interface contains a model necessary for the type verifier. Then, this interface is refined and completed to propose not only the different services dedicated to the type verifier but also the specification of the different tests related to the structural verification. This latter part is not entirely modelled in B. This is due to the fact that as the structural verification contains a syntactical verification of a bytes stream, it is very difficult to propose an abstract representation. Some CAP file components are entirely modelled until an interface is reached that allows us to read a byte into a file. Hence, we show our ability to perform such a model relying on low-level basic blocks. In order to compare the benefits of the modelling, some other components (2 out of 11), are not entirely modelled and are directly implemented in C code. However, all the external tests are modelled in B. These models follow the same refinement scheme as the one used for the type verifier. In the next subsections, such a scheme is described.

4.2 The Type Verifier Model

The aim of the type verifier is to ensure that the typing rules specified by the Java Card language are always respected for each execution of the code. Moreover, it ensures that there is no stack overflow nor underflow during the code runtime. It also ensures the memory confinement. In the specific case of our development, it was decided to include the verification of the *Reference Location* component. In fact, the type verification and the *Reference Location* verification can be simultaneously performed as they both require an analysis of the byte code.

The type verification, according to Sun Specification [17] can be performed method-by-method. For each method, the byte code can be linearly verified thanks to the PCC technique, as described in section 3. Hence, the type verifier complexity increases in linear proportion to the size of the code to verify; although the type verification's search for information within the CAP file can be complex.

The type verifier is entirely modelled in B. It is composed of an abstract model refined by a concrete model. The abstract model contains the high-level loops, *i.e.* a loop over the methods and then a loop through the byte code of a given method, and the complete specification of all tests that have to be performed on each different byte codes. The concrete model implements the abstract one. In particular it relies on services proposed by the structural verifier and on basic machines that model the volatile memory (RAM) which lets us create temporary variables and tables mandatory to the verification.

Abstract model

The highest level abstract machine, which defines its interface, remains very simple as it only proposes a single operation returning a Boolean, true if the verification is a success, otherwise it is false. This operation is then implemented by two overlapped loops that call the operation specifying the test related to the byte code instruction being checked. This is summarised by the architecture depicted in Fig. 4.

The *tyv_type_verifier* machine contains a single operation returning a Boolean. This operation is implemented by a loop for all the methods contained in the file to be checked. It is easy to perform since all methods in Java Card are contained in the *Method* Component [17]. The loop calls an operation of the *tyv_method_verifier* machine that also returns a Boolean. This latter operation is implemented by a second loop over all the instructions of the method being checked. Finally, the second loop calls an operation of the *tyv_bytecode_verifier* machine. This last operation is implemented by a case by case treatment depending the nature of the instruction being checked. In Java Card, there is 184 different byte codes. Hence, there are 184 different cases. In fact, for each different case, a specific operation is called. These operations are basically described in *tyv_bytecodes* and completely described in its refinement. In this way, the eight abstract machines including four machines, 3 implementations and one refinement contribute to constitute the abstract model of the type verifier. This specification part consists of few properties and the proof process is used mainly to ensure that loops terminate and that the types of the variables are correct. This model is relatively complex: the *tyv_bytecodes_r* refinement by itself is of 5000 lines of B distributed for 90 different operations.

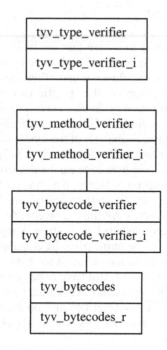

Fig. 4. Abstract model architecture of the type verifier

Concrete model

The concrete model implements the above-mentioned abstract model. Therefore, it lets us to obtain the proof ensuring the correctness of the implementation. The implementation relies on services allowing to access information contained in the CAP file. These services are described in an abstract machine used as an interface. This interface contains the variables and the services used by the type verifier. The main interest of this interface is to propose sufficient properties and services to define and implement a type verifier. We can then admit that this interface represents a first draft of what should be a structural verifier. The only part that the type verifier relies on and that is not entirely modelled in B is the dynamic memory allocation. In fact, this part is developed using basic machines: a basic machine consists in defining the specification in B and directly providing its implementation in C. Hence, there is no proof ensuring the correctness of the implementation compared to its formal specification. The reason why this part is not developed in B is that the size of the stack is not static and moreover, it depends on the method being checked. Therefore one needs to propose a dynamic allocation mechanism to build array in memory.

The remainder of the concrete model construction is classical. It is composed of the structural refinement, with the refinement of the SELECT clauses by IF statement. In this first part, loops are introduced to perform compatibility tests for method signatures or for types of the stack. These refinements end on simple update operations on sequences (for the loop) or on partial functions (for local variables). In a second step, this abstract data is finally refined to obtain the final mapping with a memory pointer.

In a partial conclusion, it seems very interesting to use B method in the type verifier context as, from an abstract model we construct a concrete one containing more than 25 machines. Moreover, half of these 25 machines are implementations. The proof of this concrete model ensures us of its validity among the abstract model which is the straight translation of the informal specification.

4.3 B Architecture of the Interface

The interface defined by the type verifier ensures that both verifiers can really work together. The interface, as described in the previous section appears to be the basis for the structural verifier which implements this interface.

The structural verifier architecture is, from our experience, not really conventional, in particular for the use we propose of the INITIALIZATION clause. The interface between the type and the structural verifier is in reality an abstract machine containing variables and properties over these variables. These latter properties are used by the type verifier to ensure its correctness. However, these properties are not initially ensured. In fact, the structural verifier needs to perform some tests in order to make sure that all the specified properties are enforced. The internal tests of each component are largely responsible for ensuring these properties. The first solution is to guard each property by the fact that the component ensuring the concerned property has been structurally verified. If the type verifier has as a precondition the fact that all components have been successfully verified, it can now use the properties. However, we have not chosen this solution because there is a major drawback: It complicates the proof by replacing all properties P by *(component_x_verified = TRUE => P)*, which is really heavy to handle whit the proof process.

The solution (Fig. 5) that we have set up uses the INITIALIZATION clause of the interface abstract machine. In this INITIALIZATION clause, we call each component internal verification operation. Hence, one ensures that at the initialisation step, in fact after the syntactic verification of all files concerned by the verification, the type verifier, and also the external structural tests, can rely on properties established. In order to allow an abnormal verification termination, in fact if an error is encountered, a special operation is defined, called Fatal_Error. When an error is raised by the structural verifier, this operation is called. The consequence is that the verification is stopped and an error code is returned. This ensures that the type verifier is executed only if the structural verifier has successfully accomplished its task. Note that, we develop a prototype. Hence, we need to know why the verifier has stopped. In normal use, a verifier must only return true or false.

```
MACHINE Interface
VARIABLES
   V, C1_verified
INVARIANT  P &
   C1_verified = TRUE
INITIALISATION
   V : (P)
OPERATIONS
     read_V = …
END
```

```
MACHINE Component1
VARIABLES
   V, C1_verified
INVARIANT
   C1_verified = TRUE
   => P
INITIALISATION
   V : (Typing) ||
   C1_verified :=FALSE
OPERATIONS
res ← C1_verifs =
   V,
   C1_verified : (
   Invariant &
   res = C1_verified);

read_V =
PRE
   C1_verified = TRUE
THEN … END

END
```

```
IMPLEMENTATION
   Interface_i
REFINES Interface
IMPORTS Component1
INITIALISATION
   res ← C1_verifs ;
   IF res = FALSE
   THEN
      Fatal_error
   END

PROMOTES
 read_V

END
```

Fig. 5. Interface specification

4.4 Detailed Specification

In this subsection, we introduce an example of the detailed specification of a bytecode
: aaload. We first present its informal specification as it is described by Sun in
[17]. We then provide our verifier informal specification, extracted from the previous
one, and finally the B model of the operation which checks types when an aaload is
encountered.

The aaload bytecode is used to obtain a reference from an array of reference, the
stack contains the reference on the array and the index, representing the location of
the reference in the array. After the execution of aaload, the stack contains the
reference found in the array at the index.

4.4.1 Sun VM Specification

We have to extract from the Sun virtual machine specification, the part concerning type verification. Within the Sun specification the type verification and the dynamic behaviour of the VM are melted. In this example (Fig.6), in the *Description* paragraph, the two first sentences describe type verification and the two last sentences describe the dynamic VM execution. The *Stack* paragraph describes the stack evolution. The *Exceptions* paragraph is not really useful, one just has to know that this bytecode can throw exceptions.

Aaload
Load reference from array
Stack
..., *arrayref, index* .
..., *value*
Description
The *arrayref* must be of type reference and must refer to an array whose components are of type reference. The *index* must be of type short. Both *arrayref* and *index* are popped from the operand stack. The reference *value* in the component of the array at *index* is retrieved and pushed onto the top of the operand stack.
Runtime Exceptions
If *arrayref* is null, *aaload* throws a NullPointerException. Otherwise, if *index* is not within the bounds of the array referenced by *arrayref*, the *aaload* instruction throws an ArrayIndexOutOfBoundsException

---

Fig. 6. Aaload specification from Sun

Informal type verifier specification
Our informal specification (Fig.7) is usually an extraction of the static part of the defensive machine. The evolution of the stack and/or local variables in term of type is given first, then the pre-modification tests describe the test to be performed before modify the stack and/or the local variables. Modification of the stack and/or local variables are then given. The tests that have to be performed after the modification are described in the post modification test.
For this bytecode, two cases are distinguished. The normal case where the reference on the array is not null and the second one when it is null. The type verifier can distinguish between null reference and non null, since null is described with a special type in the lattice. The lattice concerned here is the lattice of the Java Card types as described in [8]. In the Sun specification, the second case is described in the Exception because in this case, at runtime, an exception is produced. We have chosen to model this case as a normal case, where a null reference is pushed onto the stack.
This example shows that we have had to explain some tricky points of the specification and that its has been really useful to write this informal specification before beginning the formalisation, the formalisation is usually a translation of this text.

---

aaload

[..., refarray class, short] => [..., ref class]
[..., null, short] => [..., null]

Pre-modification tests:
1. The stack must contain at least two elements
2. The two topmost elements of the stack have to be of types compatibles with refarray class and short.

Modifications:
The two topmost elements of the stack are removed. If the second element was a refarray type, then a reference of the same class is pushed onto the stack. Otherwise a type null is pushed.

Post-modification tests:
None

Throws
• NullPointerException
• ArrayOutOfBoundException
• SecurityException

Fig. 7. Informal specification for aaload verification

Formal specification
The next figure (Fig.8) depicts the B operation describing the verifier's behaviour when it is checking an aaload byte code. The different cases are translated with a SELECT clause. This clause allows us to specify action guarded by condition. In this case, all the SELECT are deterministic and the global specification is deterministic.

The operation returns a result, a value is given to the variable containing the result in each branch and the stack is modified in the two correct branches (two elements are popped and one is pushed).

We have three cases, the first two where the byte code is accepted, the last one where it is refused. The first lines of the conditions are exactly the translation of the informal specification, the stack is modelled by a sequence of type, the operator *size, last, front* are defined in the B language with the usual semantics.

Further explanation is needed for two items within this example:

−   The two correct cases contain an additional condition which makes sure that the current pc is in an exception handler. If so, we have to make sure the local variables are compatible with the descriptor associated with the label and also that there are no non-initialised references in the local variables. This must be done for all proof labels of a given handler.

−   This test is factored out at the beginning of the informal specifications.

−   The second item concerns the class information associated with a reference, as the class information is the same for the *refarray* than for the *ref*, we do not have to pop it just to push it.

```
bb ← verify_aaload =
BEGIN
  SELECT
        2 ≤ size(stack) ∧
        last(stack) = c_short ∧
        last(front(stack)) = c_refarray ∧
        (pc ∈ dom(exception_handler)
        ⇒
        ∀label.(label ∈ exception_handler(pc)
            ⇒ COMPATIBLE(loc_var, loc_var_descriptor(label))) ∧
        c_uref ∉ ran(loc_var))
  THEN
        bb   := TRUE ∥
        stack := front(front(stack)) ← c_ref
  WHEN
        2 ≤ size(stack) ∧
        last(stack) = c_short ∧
        last(front(stack)) = c_null ∧
        (pc ∈ dom(exception_handler)
        ⇒
        ∀label.(label ∈ exception_handler(pc)
            ⇒ COMPATIBLE(loc_var, loc_var_descriptor(label))) ∧
        c_uref ∉ ran(loc_var))
  THEN
        bb   := TRUE ∥
        stack := front(front(stack)) ←c_null
  ELSE
        bb := FALSE
  END
END
```

Fig. 8. Formal specification for aaload verification

5. Metrics on the Byte Code Verifier and Its Development

In this section, we provide metrics about the formal development of the byte code verifier.

Table 1 synthesises metrics related to the development. In particular, we can note that the structural verifier is bigger than the type verifier. The reason is that the structural verifier contains a lot of tests which require specifications and implementation for each. The type verifier can be seen as a single machine including the typing rules enforced by Java Card. Moreover, the structural verifier contains services on which the type verifier relies. This explains the difference in the number of components as services are organised in different sets.

There are two other results that are remarkable: the first one concerns the number of generated Proof Obligations (POs). The results shows that the type verifier generates many more POs than the structural verifier. The reason is that there are many more properties in the type verifier than in the structural verifier.

The second results concern the number of C code lines. This number is far smaller than that the of corresponding B code. The reason is that in the code translation, only implementations are taken into account. Moreover, INVARIANT clauses within implementations are not translated. This drastically reduces the number of lines translated from B to C.

Table 1. Metrics on the formal development of the byte code verifier

	Structural Verifier	Type Verifier	Total
Number of lines of B	35000	20000	55000
Number of components	116	34	150
Number of generated POs	11700	18600	30300
POs automatically proved (%)	81 %	72 %	75 %
Project status	90 %	99.9%	95 %
Number of Basic machines	6	0	6
Number of lines of C code	7540	4250	11790
Workload (men months)	8	4	12

One goal of the Matisse project is to compare formal and traditional developments in order to show the benefits and the drawbacks of using formal techniques in industry. For this reason, two developments were completed concerning only the type verifier: one used formal techniques and the other used traditional techniques. Each development was done by a different person. They both had the same starting point, i.e. an internal document emphasising the requirements of a Java Card type verifier, written in natural language. For each development, we provided a test phase. This step allowed us to check the correspondence between the informal requirements and the code embedded into the smart card. The following tables describe the elements of the comparison.

Table 3 summarises the number of errors found and the step of the development where they were found. The first conclusion from this comparison is that the formal development produces fewer errors than the traditional development: 56 errors compared to 95. Moreover, only 14 errors were found during the testing step. This is in accordance with the fact that only one week was used to perform the test of the verifier. Compared to the 95 errors of the conventional development and the 3 weeks of testing, there is a significant difference. Unfortunately for the formal development, the proof is very long and costly. However, we believe that this can be decreased thanks to Atelier B improvements and to the development of particular rules and proof tactics. If we manage to capitalise on experience gained in initial developments, we should decrease the time needed by the proof. Moreover, by proposing a methodology adapted to the smart card, the development time required to build models can also be decreased. Using formal methods could then be a real advantage as it is no more costly than conventional development while providing high-quality code.

Table 2. Comparing number of errors for formal and conventional development

	Formal development	Conventional development
Number of errors discovered by reading	13	24
Number of errors discovered by proof	29	Not applicable
Number of errors discovered by testing related to the type verifier	14	71
Total Number of errors	56	95

Finally, if the number of errors discovered by reviewing for the formal development is smaller than for the conventional one that is because the modelling activity requires a good understanding of the informal specification and a lot of work required by the refinement method. Errors still exist but the modelling activity helps to clarify the specification by going deeper into the meanings of the specification and thus, reduces the risk of introducing errors. Table 2 helps us to state that the code produced through a formal process contains fewer errors which indicates a better quality in terms of compliance with the original requirements.

Table 3. Comparing development time for formal and conventional development

	Formal development	Conventional development
Main development (weeks)	12	12
Proof activity (weeks)	6	Not applicable
Testing (weeks)	1	3
Integration (weeks)	1	2
Number of weeks for the development	20	17

One of the main results of this case study and of this comparison is that it does not appear unreasonable to use formal methods to develop parts of a smart card operating system (Table 3). Moreover, even if in this study the time needed for the formal development is greater than that for a conventional development, it is only a difference of three weeks. With a strong involvement in tool improvement and in methodologies, it is possible to be competitive using formal methods. We demonstrate the possibility and the feasibility of developing parts of the operating system or parts of the Java Card Virtual Machine. Finally, we have also shown that we can control the development time of the formal verifier. Thus, with this experiment, it is now possible to be more accurate about the time required for a given development. Finally, Table 3 allows us to conclude that it is possible to develop a realistic application with an acceptable overhead, i.e., one induced by using formal method is acceptable compared to a conventional development. This conclusion takes into account the fact that the tools and the methodologies are not yet optimised for the smart cards. Hence, we expect to reduce in particular the cost of the proof activity, by developing tools and proof rules to speed up the proof process. Experience gained in the first formal developments should improve our knowledge and speed up future developments.

The last comparison that we can make concerns the efficiency of the produced code, both in terms of the size of the code and in terms of time required to verify an applet. Table 4 and Table 5 contain the results of the comparison. The first comment is that the code obtained and translated from the B is acceptable. Concerning the type verifier, we note that the two sizes are similar. This table also shows that the RAM usage is acceptable for a verification algorithm. Note that there is a large range of RAM usage for the conventional verifier as RAM usage is adaptable for this verifier. We also provide the size of the structural verifier but we cannot compare it as it has not been developed yet for the conventional part. The difference that we can note on the total size regarding the other sizes is that in the total size, we include libraries and APIs necessary for both verifiers inside the card. It includes notably the loader, the memory management and the communication.

Table 4. Comparing code size for both developments

	Formal development	Conventional development
Type verifier ROM size (kb)	18	16
Structural Verifier ROM size (kb)	24	Not Yet Implemented
Total ROM size (kb)	45	24
RAM usage (bytes)	140	128-756
Applet code overhead (%)	10-20	0

Table 5 proposes a comparison of execution time for a set of applets. Note that the two implementations, the formal and the conventional ones, are not actually done on the same chip. The formal verifier is implemented on an ATMEL SC 6464 C and the conventional one on an ATMEL SC 3232. The main difference between those two chips is the free memory size (greater in the case of the formal development). Note also that the conventional verifier does not include a structural verifier. Hence, we cannot compare the time for this particular part. However, we provide the information in order to compare the structural verifier's complexity with that of the type verifier.

The main observation about the execution time is that the conventional type verifier is twice as fast as the formal one. There can be several reasons to explain this difference. The first is the difference of memory management between the two developments. The conventional one uses a pointer to access to the memory. In the formal one, the pointer is a translation from the one in B. Therefore, each time we access the memory, there is a translation which costs some time in the execution. Another reason is that the developments were done to optimise the size of the code, not its efficiency. So, when the code is compiled, the compilation directives that are used aimed to optimise the size. The conventional development already takes into account some efficiency optimisations that the formal one does not. Hence the difference of execution time. We have performed some optimisations on the memory management of the formal type verifier. The obtained results show that, with these optimisations, the execution times on the different applets are now similar.

We think that Table 4 and Table 5 help us conclude that the code generated with the C code translator from the formal implementation fits the smart card constraints.

Table 5. Comparing verification time for a set of example applets

	Formal development			Conventional development	
	Type (ms)	Time	Type Time after optimisation(ms)	Type Time(ms)	
Wallet	811		460	318	
Utils	2794		1422	1463	
Pacap Interface	241		110	61	
Tic Tac Toe	3555		1372	1102	

So, this comparison is encouraging for future formal developments. Of course the data collected concern only a single development. To be more accurate, this kind of comparison should be repeated on other applications. But, this is a realistic application and we think that the comparison is reasonable. Developing methodologies to integrate formal methods into the software development cycle and improving tools to ease and speed up the modelling and the proof activities are possible and may open a new era for software development.

6. Conclusion

In this paper, we have presented the formal development of an embedded byte-code verifier for Java Card, and compared it with a similar development using classical techniques.

This experiment shows that applying formal methods for developing industrial applications is possible, even in a constrained context such as smart cards. It also provides an estimation of the development overhead introduced by the use of formal techniques. Moreover, the code generated from the formal models has been translated into C and then integrated into a smart card as the first complete byte code verifier prototype for the Java Card language

Although the workload overhead cannot be neglected, it appears to be small enough to be offset by the increased confidence gained in the development. This is especially important for critical environments where security or safety is a requirement. In fact, we gain confidence in the obtained code, and the byte code verifier prototype can be used as reference implementation for further development.

It also results from this experiment that all the parts of a program do not benefit equally from formal modelling. For example, some low-level modules of the structural verifier were entirely developed with B, requiring significant proof efforts. However, they expose the same kind of bugs as similar parts developed directly in C.

So, those modules could have been developed classically without reducing the confidence in the code.

It seems that efficiently applying formal methods will require trade-offs, by identifying which parts of the development require formal development and which parts would incur overhead without providing significant benefits.

References

[1]   J.R. Abrial, *The B Book, Assigning Programs to Meanings*, Cambridge University Press, 1996.

[2]   Y. Bertot, *A Coq formalization of a Type Checker for Object Initialization in the Java Virtual Machine*, Research Report, INRIA Sophia Antipolis, 2001.

[3]   L. Casset, J.-L. Lanet, *A Formal Specification of the Java Byte Code Semantics using the B method*, Proceedings of the ECOOP'99 workshop on Formal Techniques for Java Programs, Lisbon, June 1999.

[4]   L. Casset, *Formal Implementation of a Verification Algorithm Using the B Method*, Proceedings of AFADL01, Nancy, France, June 2001

[5]   A. Coglio, Z. Qian and A. Goldberg, *Towards a Provably-correct Implementation of the JVM Bytecode Verifier*, In Proc. DARPA Information Survivability Conference and Exposition (DISCEX'00), Vol. 2, pages 403-410, IEEE Computer Society, 2000.

[6]   G. Klein, T. Nipkow, *Verified Lightweight Bytecode Verification*, in ECOOP 2000 Workshop on Formal Techniques for Java Programs, pp. 35-42, Cannes, June 2000.

[7]   X. Leroy, *On-Card Byte Code Verification for Java Card*, Proceedings of e-Smart, Cannes, France, September 2001.

[8]   X. Leroy, *Bytecode Verification on Java smart Cards*, to appear in Software Practice and Experience, 2002.

[9]   T. Lindholm, F. Yellin, *The Java Virtual Machine Specification*, Addison Wesley, 1996

[10] G. Necula, P. Lee, Proof-Carrying Code, in 24th ACM SIGPLAN-SIGACT Symposium on Principles of Programming Languages, pp. 106-119, Paris, France, 1997. http://www-nt.cs.berkeley.edu/home/necula/public_html/popl97.ps.gz

[11] T. Nipkow, *Verified Byte code Verifiers*, Fakultät für Informatik, Technische Universität München, 2000. http://www.in.tum.de/~nipkow

[12] C. Pusch, *Proving the Soundness of a Java Bytecode Verifier in Isabelle/HOL*, In OOPSLA'98 Workshop Formal Underpinnings of Java, 1998.

[13] C. Pusch, T. Nipkow, D. von Oheimb, *microJava: Embedding a Programming Language in a Theorem Prover*. In Foundations of Secure Computation, IOS Press, 2000.

[14] Z. Qian, *A Formal Specification of Java Virtual Machine Instructions for Objects, Methods and Subroutines*. In Jim Alves-Foss, editor, *Formal Syntax and Semantics of Java*, volume 1523 of *Lecture Notes in Computer Science*, pages 271-312. Springer, 1999.

[15] A. Requet, L. Casset, G. Grimaud, Application of the B Formal Method to the Proof of a Type Verification Algorithm, HASE 2000, Albuquerque, November 2000.

[16] E. Rose, K. H. Rose, Lightweight Bytecode Verification, in Formal Underpinnings of Java, OOPSLA'98 Workshop, Vancouver, Canada, October. 1998. http://www-dse.doc.ic.ac.uk/~sue/oopsla/rose.f.ps

[17] *Java Card 2.1.1 Virtual Machine Specification*, Sun Microsystem, 2000.

[18] *Connected, Limited Device Configuration*, Specification 1.0a, Java 2 Platform Micro Edition, Sun Microsystems, 2000.

Deriving Cryptographically Sound Implementations Using Composition and Formally Verified Bisimulation

Michael Backes[1], Christian Jacobi[2], and Birgit Pfitzmann[3]

[1] Saarland University, Saarbrücken, Germany
mbackes@cs.uni-sb.de
[2] IBM Deutschland Entwicklung GmbH, Processor Development 2, Böblingen, Germany
cjacobi@de.ibm.com
[3] IBM Zurich Research Laboratory, Rüschlikon, Switzerland
bpf@zurich.ibm.com

Abstract. We consider abstract specifications of cryptographic protocols which are both suitable for formal verification and maintain a sound cryptographic semantics. In this paper, we present the first abstract specification for ordered secure message transmission in reactive systems based on the recently published model of Pfitzmann and Waidner. We use their composition theorem to derive a possible implementation whose correctness additionally involves a classical bisimulation, which we formally verify using the theorem prover PVS. The example serves as the first important case study which shows that this approach is applicable in practice, and it is the first example that combines tool-supported formal proof techniques with the rigorous proofs of cryptography.

Keywords: security, cryptography, formal verification, PVS, simulatability

1 Introduction

Nowadays, security proofs are getting more and more attention both in theory and practice. Some years ago, this field of research only focused on certain cryptographic primitives such as encryption and digital signature schemes. In current research, larger systems like secure channels or fair exchange protocols are to be verified. The main goal researchers are ultimately aiming at is to verify really large systems like whole e-commerce architectures.

If we turn our attention to what already has been done, we can distinguish between two main approaches that unfortunately seem to be rather disjoint. One approach mainly considers the cryptographic aspects of protocols aiming at complete and mathematically rigorous proofs with respect to cryptographic definitions. The other one involves formal methods, so protocols should be verified using formal proof systems or these proofs should even be generated automatically by theorem provers. Usually, these proofs are much trustworthier than hand-made proofs, especially if we consider large protocols using many single steps. The main problem of this approach lies in the necessary abstraction of cryptographic details. This abstraction cannot be completely avoided, since formal methods cannot handle probabilistic behaviours so far, so usually perfect cryptography is assumed (following the approach of Dolev and Yao [4]) in order to make

L.-H. Eriksson and P. Lindsay (Eds.): FME 2002, LNCS 2391, pp. 310–329, 2002.
© Springer-Verlag Berlin Heidelberg 2002

machine-aided verification possible. However, these abstractions are unfaithful, since no secure implementation is known so far.

Comparing both approaches, we can see that cryptographic proofs are more meaningful in the sense of security but they also have one main disadvantage: cryptographic proofs usually are very long and error-prone even for very small examples like encryption schemes, and moreover have to be done be hand so far. Hence, it seems rather impossible to verify large systems like whole e-commerce architectures by now.

Our approach tries to combine the best of both worlds: We aim at proofs that allow abstractions and the use of verification tools but nevertheless keep a sound cryptographic semantics. For this, we split our system into two layers, the lower one containing cryptographic systems, the higher one hiding all cryptographic details enabling tool-supported proofs. Secure composition with respect to these layers has already been shown by Pfitzmann and Waidner in [16], so if we consider a large system and replace a verified abstract subsystem with a cryptographic implementation, we again obtain a secure system if the implementation is proven to be at least as secure as its abstract counterpart.

In this paper we present the first abstract specification for ordered secure message transmission, and we derive a possible implementation serving as the first example of a concrete and secure system derived using the composition theorem from [16]. Moreover, the crucial part of this security proof involves a bisimulation, which we formally verify using the theorem prover PVS [13] yielding a trustworthy proof. Our implementation is based on the scheme for standard secure message transmission presented in [16], but we put a system on top of it to prevent message reordering.

Outline. We recapitulate the underlying model of reactive systems in asynchronous networks in Section 2. Furthermore we briefly review how to express typical trust models and what secure composition of systems means. Sections 3, 4 and 5 contain the main work. In Section 3 we present an abstract specification for ordered secure message transmission, and a possible implementation derived using the composition theorem. In Section 4 we accomplish some preparatory work for proving the security of the implementation, which is performed in Section 5 using the theorem prover PVS. Section 6 summarizes and gives an outlook on future work.

Related Literature. One main goal in the verification of cryptographic protocols is to retain a sound cryptographic semantics and nevertheless provide abstract interfaces in order to make machine-aided verification possible. This goal is pursued by several researchers: our specification for ordered secure message transmission is based on a model recently introduced by Pfitzmann and Waidner [16], which we believe to be really close to this goal. Another possible way to achieve this goal has been presented in [7,8]: actual cryptography and security is directly expressed and verified using a formal language (π-calculus), but their approach does neither offer any abstractions nor abstract interfaces that enable tool support. [11] has quite a similar motivation to our underlying model, but it is restricted to the usual equational specifications of cryptographic primitives, the Dolev-Yao model [4], and the semantics is not probabilistic. Moreover, [11] only considers passive adversaries and a restricted class of users, referred to as "environment". So the abstraction from cryptography is not faithful. This applies also to other formal-methods papers about security, e.g., [9,17,1,14,5]: they are based on intuitive but unfaithful abstractions, i.e., no secure cryptographic implementation is known. In [2], it is shown that a slight variation of the Dolev-Yao model is cryptographically faithful specifically for symmetric encryption, but only under passive attacks.

As to secure message transmission, several specifications have been proposed, but they are either specific for one concrete protocol or lack abstraction [7]. So far, no model for ordered secure message transmission has been published. Thus, we present the first completely abstract specification and a possible implementation for secure message transmission that prevents message reordering. We furthermore showed that the composition theorem of [16] is in fact applicable in practice. Moreover, our proof contains machine-aided verification, so this paper is the first one that uses formal verification of cryptographic protocols while retaining a sound semantics with respect to the underlying cryptographic primitives.

2   Reactive Systems in Asynchronous Networks

In this section we briefly recapitulate the model for reactive systems in asynchronous networks as introduced in [16]. All details not necessary for understanding are omitted, they can be found in [16]. Machines are represented by probabilistic state-transition machines, similar to probabilistic I/O automata [10]. For complexity we consider every automaton to be implemented as a probabilistic Turing machine; complexity is measured in the length of its initial state, i.e., the initial worktape content (often a security parameter k in unary representation).

2.1   General System Model and Simulatability

Systems are mainly compositions of several machines. Usually we consider real systems that are built by a set $\hat{M}$ of machines $\{M_1, \dots, M_n\}$, and ideal systems built by one machine $\{TH\}$.

Communication between different machines is done via ports. Inspired by the CSP notation [6], we write output and input ports as p! and p? respectively. The ports of a machine M are denoted by ports(M). Connections are defined implicitly by naming convention, that is port p! sends messages to p?. To achieve asynchronous timing, a message is not directly sent to its recipient, but it is first stored in a special machine $\tilde{p}$ called a buffer and waits to be scheduled. If a machine wants to schedule the i-th message of buffer $\tilde{p}$ (this machine must have the unique clock out-port $p^{\triangleleft}!$) it simply sends i at $p^{\triangleleft}!$. The i-th message is then scheduled by the buffer and removed from its internal list. Usually buffers are scheduled by the adversary, but it is sometimes useful to let other machines schedule certain buffers. This is done by the mentioned clock out-port $p^{\triangleleft}!$.

A *collection* C of machines is a finite set of machines with pairwise different machine names and disjoint sets of ports. The *completion* $[C]$ of a collection C is the union of all machines of C and the buffers needed for every connection.

A *structure* is a pair $(\hat{M}, S)$, where $\hat{M}$ is a collection of machines and $S \subseteq \text{free}([\hat{M}])$, the so called *specified ports*, are a subset of the free[1] ports in $[\hat{M}]$. Roughly, the ports

---

[1] A port is called *free* if its corresponding port is not in the collection. These ports will be connected to the users and the adversary.

S guarantee specific services to the honest users. We always describe specified ports by their complements S^c, i.e., the ports honest users should have. A structure can be completed to a *configuration* by adding machines H and A modeling honest users and the adversary. The machine H is restricted to the specified ports S, A connects to the remaining free ports of the structure and both machines can interact. If we now consider a set of structures, we obtain a *system Sys*.

Scheduling of machines is done sequentially, so we have exactly one active machine M at any time. If this machine has clock-out ports, it is allowed to select the next message to be scheduled as explained above. If that message exists, it is delivered by the buffer and the unique receiving machine is the next active machine. If M tries to schedule multiple messages, only one is taken, and if it schedules none or the message does not exist, a designated master scheduler is scheduled.

Altogether we obtain a probability space of runs (sometimes called *traces* or *executions*) of a configuration *conf* for each security parameter k. If we restrict these runs to a set $\hat{M}$ of machines, we obtain the *view* of $\hat{M}$; this is a random variable denoted by $view_{conf,k}(\hat{M})$.

An important security concept is *simulatability*. Essentially it means that whatever might happen to an honest user H in a real system Sys_{real} can also happen to the same honest user in an ideal System Sys_{id}. Formally speaking, for every configuration $conf_1$ of Sys_{real} there is a configuration $conf_2$ of Sys_{id} yielding indistinguishable views for the same H in both systems [18]. We write this $Sys_{real} \geq_{sec} Sys_{id}$ and say that Sys_{real} is *at least as secure as* Sys_{id}; indistinguishability of the views of H is denoted by $view_{conf_1}(H) \approx view_{conf_2}(H)$. Usually, only certain "corresponding" structures $(\hat{M}_1, S_1)$ of Sys_{real} and $(\hat{M}_2, S_2)$ of Sys_{id} are compared, in particular we require $S_1 = S_2$. In general, a mapping f may denote this correspondence and one writes $\geq_{sec}^{f}$, but if the requirement $S_1 = S_2$ gives a unique one-to-one correspondence, we call the mapping canonical and omit it. This is the case in all our examples.

An important feature of the system model is transitivity of $\geq_{sec}$, i.e., the preconditions $Sys_1 \geq_{sec} Sys_2$ and $Sys_2 \geq_{sec} Sys_3$ together imply $Sys_1 \geq_{sec} Sys_3$ [16].

2.2 Standard Cryptographic Systems

We now turn our attention to the specific class of standard cryptographic systems with static adversaries. In real life, every user u usually has exactly one machine M_u, which is correct if and only if its user is honest. The machine M_u has special ports $in_u?$ and $out_u!$, which are specified ports of the system and connect to the user u. A standard cryptographic system Sys can now be derived by a *trust model*, which consists of an access structure $\mathcal{ACC}$ and a channel model χ. $\mathcal{ACC}$ is a set of subsets $\mathcal{H}$ of $\{1, \ldots, n\}$ and denotes the possible sets of correct machines. The channel model classifies every connection as secure (private and authentic), authenticated or insecure. In the given model these changes can easily be done via port renaming [16]. Thus, for each set $\mathcal{H}$ and a fixed channel model, we obtain a modified machine $M_{u,\mathcal{H}}$ for every machine M_u with $u \in \mathcal{H}$. These machines form the structure for the set $\mathcal{H}$; the remaining machines are considered part of the adversary.

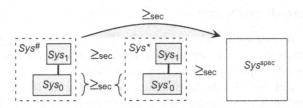

Fig. 1. Composition of Systems.

Ideal systems are typically of the form $Sys_{id} = \{(\{TH_{\mathcal{H}}\}, S_{\mathcal{H}}) \mid \mathcal{H} \in \mathcal{ACC}\}$ with the same sets $S_{\mathcal{H}}$ as in the corresponding real system Sys_{real}, i.e., each structure consists of only *one* machine that we usually refer to as *trusted host* $TH_{\mathcal{H}}$, or TH for short.

2.3   Composition

We conclude this section with a briefly review of what has already been proven about composition of reactive systems. Assume that we have already proven that a system Sys_0 is at least as secure as another system Sys_0'. Typically Sys_0 is a real system whereas Sys_0' is an ideal specification of the real system. If we now consider larger protocols that use Sys_0' as an ideal primitive we would like to securely replace it with Sys_0. In practice this means that we replace the specification of a system with its implementation yielding a concrete system.

Usually, replacing means that we have another system Sys_1 using Sys_0'; we call this composition Sys^*. We now want to replace Sys_0' with Sys_0 inside of Sys^* which gives a composition $Sys^\#$. Typically $Sys^\#$ is a completely real system whereas Sys^* is at least partly ideal. This is illustrated in the left and middle part of Figure 1. The composition theorem now states that this replacement maintains security, i.e., $Sys^\#$ is at least as secure as Sys^* (see [16] for details).

However, typically a specification of the overall system should not prescribe that the implementation must have two subsystems; e.g., in specifying a payment system, it should be irrelevant whether the implementation uses secure message transmission as a subsystem. Hence, the overall specification is typically monolithic, cf. Sys^{spec} in Figure 1. Moreover, such specifications are well-suited for formal verification, because single machines are usually much easier to validate. Our specification in Section 3 is of this kind.

3   Secure Message Transmission in Correct Order

In this section an abstract specification for *ordered secure message transmission* is presented, so neither reordering the messages in transit nor replay attacks are possible for the adversary. Furthermore, a concrete implementation for this specification is presented according to the composition approach from Section 2.3.

3.1   The Abstract Specification

Our specification is a typical ideal system $Sys^{spec} = \{(\mathsf{TH'}_{\mathcal{H}}, S_{\mathcal{H}}) | \mathcal{H} \in \mathcal{ACC}\}$ as described in Section 2.2 where any number of participants may be dishonest. We start with an intuitive description of how the scheme works.

The ideal machine $\mathsf{TH'}_{\mathcal{H}}$ models initialization, sending and receiving of messages. A user u can initialize communications with other users by inputting a command of the form (snd_init) to the port $\mathsf{in}_u?$ of $\mathsf{TH'}_{\mathcal{H}}$. In the real world, initialization corresponds to key generation and authenticated key exchange. Sending a message to a user v is triggered by a command (send, m, v). If v is honest, the message is stored in an internal array $deliver^{spec}_{u,v}$ of $\mathsf{TH'}_{\mathcal{H}}$ together with a counter indicating the number of the message. After that, the information (send_blindly, i, l, v) is output to the adversary, where l and i denote the length of the message m and its position in the array, respectively. This models that a real-world adversary may see that a message is sent and may even see its length. We speak of tolerable imperfections that are explicitly given to the adversary. Because of the asynchronous timing model, $\mathsf{TH'}_{\mathcal{H}}$ has to wait for a special term (receive_blindly, v, i) or (rec_init, u) sent by the adversary, signaling that the ith message in $deliver^{spec}_{u,v}$ should be delivered to v or that a connection between u and v should be established, respectively. In the first case, $\mathsf{TH'}_{\mathcal{H}}$ reads $(m, j) := deliver^{spec}_{u,v}[i]$ and checks whether $j \geq msg\_out^{spec}_{u,v}$ holds for a message counter $msg\_out^{spec}_{u,v}$. This test prevents replay and message reordering. If the test is successful the message is delivered and the counter is set to $j + 1$. Otherwise, $\mathsf{TH'}_{\mathcal{H}}$ outputs nothing. The user v receives inputs (receive, u, m) and (rec_init, u), respectively.

If v is dishonest, $\mathsf{TH'}_{\mathcal{H}}$ simply outputs (send, m, v) to the adversary. The adversary can also send a message m to a user u by inputting a command (receive, v, m) to the port from_adv$_u?$ of $\mathsf{TH'}_{\mathcal{H}}$ for a corrupted user v. Finally, he can stop the machine of any user by sending a command (stop) to $\mathsf{TH'}_{\mathcal{H}}$; this corresponds to exceeding the machine's runtime bounds in the real world.

The length of each message and the number of messages each user may send and receive is bounded by $L(k), s_1(k)$ and $s_2(k)$, respectively, for polynomials L, s_1, s_2, and the security parameter k. We furthermore distinguish the *standard ordered system* and the *perfect ordered system*. The standard ordered system only prevents message reordering, but the adversary can still leave out messages. In the perfect ordered system, the adversary can only deliver messages between honest users in exactly the sequence they have been sent. We now give the formal specification of the systems.

Scheme 1 (Specification for Ordered Secure Message Transmission) Let $n \in \mathbb{N}$ and polynomials $L, s_1, s_2 \in \mathbb{N}[x]$ be given, and let Σ denote the message alphabet, len the length of strings, and $\downarrow$ an undefined value. Let $\mathcal{M} := \{1, \ldots, n\}$ denote the set of possible participants, and let the access structure $\mathcal{ACC}$ be the powerset of $\mathcal{M}$. Our specification for ordered secure message transmission is a standard ideal system

$$Sys^{msg\_ord,spec}_{n,L,s_1,s_2} = \{(\{\mathsf{TH'}_{\mathcal{H}}\}, S_{\mathcal{H}}) \mid \mathcal{H} \subseteq \mathcal{M}\}$$

with $S^c_{\mathcal{H}} := \{\mathsf{in}_u!, \mathsf{out}_u?, \mathsf{in}_u^{\triangleleft}! \mid u \in \mathcal{H}\}$ and $\mathsf{TH'}_{\mathcal{H}}$ defined as follows. When $\mathcal{H}$ is clear from the context, let $\mathcal{A} := \mathcal{M} \setminus \mathcal{H}$ denote the indices of corrupted machines.

The ports of the machine $\mathsf{TH}'_{\mathcal{H}}$ are $\{\mathsf{in}_u?, \mathsf{out}_u!, \mathsf{out}_u{}^{\triangleleft}! \mid u \in \mathcal{H}\} \cup \{\mathsf{from\_adv}_u?, \mathsf{to\_adv}_u!, \mathsf{to\_adv}_u{}^{\triangleleft}! \mid u \in \mathcal{H}\}$. Internally, $\mathsf{TH}'_{\mathcal{H}}$ maintains seven arrays:

- $(init_{u,v}^{\mathsf{spec}})_{u,v \in \mathcal{M}}$ over $\{0, 1\}$ for modeling initialization of users,
- $(sc\_in_{u,v}^{\mathsf{spec}})_{u \in \mathcal{H}, v \in \mathcal{M}}$ over $\{0, \dots, s_1(k)\}$ for counting how often $\mathsf{TH}'_{\mathcal{H}}$ has been switched by user u using messages intended for v,
- $(msg\_out_{u,v}^{\mathsf{spec}})_{u,v \in \mathcal{H}}$ over $\{0, \dots, s_2(k)\}$ for storing the number of the next expected message (cf. the description above),
- $(sc\_out_{u,v}^{\mathsf{spec}})_{u \in \mathcal{M}, v \in \mathcal{H}}$ over $\{0, \dots, s_2(k)\}$ for counting how often $\mathsf{TH}'_{\mathcal{H}}$ has been switched by the adversary for delivering a message from user u to user v,
- $(msg\_in_{u,v}^{\mathsf{spec}})_{u \in \mathcal{H}, v \in \mathcal{M}}$ over $\{0, \dots, s_1(k)\}$ for counting the incoming messages from u intended for v,
- $(stopped_u^{\mathsf{spec}})_{u \in \mathcal{H}}$ over $\{0, 1\}$ for storing whether the machine of user u has already been stopped, i.e., reached its runtime bounds,
- $(deliver_{u,v}^{\mathsf{spec}})_{u,v \in \mathcal{H}}$ of lists for storing the actual messages.

The first six arrays are initialized with 0 everywhere, except that $msg\_out_{u,v}^{\mathsf{spec}}$ is initialized with 1 everywhere. The last array should be initialized with empty lists everywhere. Roughly, the five arrays $init_{u,v}^{\mathsf{spec}}$, $msg\_out_{u,v}^{\mathsf{spec}}$, $msg\_in_{u,v}^{\mathsf{spec}}$, $stopped^{\mathsf{spec}}$, and $deliver_{u,v}^{\mathsf{spec}}$ ensure functional correctness, whereas the arrays $sc\_in_{u,v}^{\mathsf{spec}}$ and $sc\_out_{u,v}^{\mathsf{spec}}$ help to make the system polynomial-time: the machine $\mathsf{TH}'_{\mathcal{H}}$ ignores certain inputs as soon as these counters reach the given bounds $s_1(k)$ or $s_2(k)$, respectively. The state-transition function of $\mathsf{TH}'_{\mathcal{H}}$ is defined by the following rules, written in a pseudo-code language. For the sake of readability, we exemplarily annotate the "Send initialization" transition, i.e., the key generation in the real world.

- **Send initialization:** Assume that the user u wants to generate its encryption and signature keys and distribute the corresponding public keys over authenticated channels. He can do so by sending a command (snd_init) to $\mathsf{TH}'_{\mathcal{H}}$. Now, the system checks that the user has not already reached his message bound (which is quite improbable in this case unless he tried to send trash all the time), that the machine itself has not reached its runtime bound, and that no key generation of this user has already occurred in the past. These three checks correspond to $sc\_in_{u,v}^{\mathsf{spec}} < s_1(k)$ for all $v \in \mathcal{M}$, $stopped_u^{\mathsf{spec}} = 0$, and $init_{u,u}^{\mathsf{spec}} = 0$, respectively. If at least the check of the message bound (i.e., $sc\_in_{u,v}^{\mathsf{spec}} < s_1(k)$) holds, the counter $sc\_in_{u,v}^{\mathsf{spec}}$ is increased. If all three checks hold, the keys are distributed over authenticated channels, modeled by an output (snd_init) to the adversary which either can schedule them immediately, later or even leave them on the channels forever. In our pseudo-code language this is expressed as follows:

  On input (snd_init) at $\mathsf{in}_u?$: If $sc\_in_{u,v}^{\mathsf{spec}} < s_1(k)$ for all $v \in \mathcal{M}$, set $sc\_in_{u,v}^{\mathsf{spec}} := sc\_in_{u,v}^{\mathsf{spec}} + 1$ for all $v \in \mathcal{M}$, otherwise do nothing. If the test holds check $stopped_u^{\mathsf{spec}} = 0$ and $init_{u,u}^{\mathsf{spec}} = 0$. In this case set $init_{u,u}^{\mathsf{spec}} := 1$ and output (snd_init) at $\mathsf{to\_adv}_u!$, 1 at $\mathsf{to\_adv}_u{}^{\triangleleft}!$.

  The following parts should now be understood similarly:

- **Receive initialization:** On input (rec_init, u) at $from\_adv_v$? with $u \in \mathcal{M}, v \in \mathcal{H}$: If $stopped_v^{\text{spec}} = 0$, $init_{u,v}^{\text{spec}} = 0$, and $[u \in \mathcal{H} \Rightarrow init_{u,u}^{\text{spec}} = 1]$, set $init_{u,v}^{\text{spec}} := 1$. If $sc\_out_{u,v}^{\text{spec}} < s_2(k)$ set $sc\_out_{u,v}^{\text{spec}} := sc\_out_{u,v}^{\text{spec}} + 1$, output (rec_init, u) at $out_v!$, 1 at $out_v^{\triangleleft}!$.

- **Send:** On input $(send, m, v)$ at in_u?: If $sc\_in_{u,v}^{\text{spec}} < s_1(k)$ and $stopped_u^{\text{spec}} = 0$, set $sc\_in_{u,v}^{\text{spec}} := sc\_in_{u,v}^{\text{spec}} + 1$, otherwise do nothing. If $m \in \Sigma^+$, $l := \text{len}(m) \leq L(k)$, $v \in \mathcal{M} \setminus \{u\}$, $init_{u,u}^{\text{spec}} = 1$ and $init_{v,u}^{\text{spec}} = 1$ holds: If $v \in \mathcal{A}$ then $\{$ set $msg\_in_{u,v}^{\text{spec}} := msg\_in_{u,v}^{\text{spec}} + 1$ and output $(send, (m, msg\_in_{u,v}^{\text{spec}}), v)$ at $to\_adv_u!$, 1 at $to\_adv_u^{\triangleleft}!$ $\}$ else $\{$set $i := \text{size}(deliver_{u,v}^{\text{spec}}) + 1$, $msg\_in_{u,v}^{\text{spec}} := msg\_in_{u,v}^{\text{spec}} + 1$, $deliver_{u,v}^{\text{spec}}[i] := (m, msg\_in_{u,v}^{\text{spec}})$ and output $(send\_blindy, i, l, v)$ at $to\_adv_u!$, 1 at $to\_adv_u^{\triangleleft}!$ $\}$.

- **Receive from honest party** u: On input $(receive\_blindly, u, i)$ at $from\_adv_v$? with $u, v \in \mathcal{H}$: If $stopped_v^{\text{spec}} = 0$, $init_{v,v}^{\text{spec}} = 1$, $init_{u,v}^{\text{spec}} = 1$, $sc\_out_{u,v}^{\text{spec}} < s_2(k)$ and $(m, j) := deliver_{u,v}^{\text{spec}}[i] \neq \downarrow$, check $j \geq msg\_out_{u,v}^{\text{spec}}$ ($j = msg\_out_{u,v}^{\text{spec}}$ in the perfect ordered system). If this holds set $sc\_out_{u,v}^{\text{spec}} := sc\_out_{u,v}^{\text{spec}} + 1$, $msg\_out_{u,v}^{\text{spec}} := j + 1$ and output $(receive, u, m)$ at $out_v!$, 1 at $out_v^{\triangleleft}!$.

- **Receive from dishonest party** u: On input $(receive, u, m)$ at $from\_adv_v$? with $u \in \mathcal{A}, m \in \Sigma^+, \text{len}(m) \leq L(k)$ and $v \in \mathcal{H}$: If $stopped_v^{\text{spec}} = 0$, $init_{v,v}^{\text{spec}} = 1$, $init_{u,v}^{\text{spec}} = 1$ and $sc\_out_{u,v}^{\text{spec}} < s_2(k)$, set $sc\_out_{u,v}^{\text{spec}} := sc\_out_{u,v}^{\text{spec}} + 1$ and output $(receive, u, m)$ at $out_v!$, 1 at $out_v^{\triangleleft}!$.

- **Stop:** On input $(stop)$ at $from\_adv_u$? with $u \in \mathcal{H}$: If $stopped_u^{\text{spec}} = 0$, set $stopped_u^{\text{spec}} := 1$ and output $(stop)$ at $out_u!$, 1 at $out_u^{\triangleleft}!$.

Finally, if $\mathsf{TH}'_\mathcal{H}$ receives an input at a port in_u? which is not comprised by the above six transitions (i.e., the user sends some kind of trash), it increases the counter $sc\_in_{u,v}^{\text{spec}}$ for all $v \in \mathcal{M}$. Similarly, if $\mathsf{TH}'_\mathcal{H}$ receives such an input at a port $from\_adv_v$? it increases every counter $sc\_out_{u,v}^{\text{spec}}$ for $u \in \mathcal{M}$. $\diamond$

Thus, at least one counter $sc\_in_{u,v}^{\text{spec}}$ or $sc\_out_{u,v}^{\text{spec}}$ is increased in each transition of $\mathsf{TH}'_\mathcal{H}$, and each transition can obviously be realized in polynomial-time, so the machine $\mathsf{TH}'_\mathcal{H}$ is polynomial-time.

$Sys_{n,L,s_1,s_2}^{\text{msg\_ord,spec}}$ is as abstract as we hoped for. It is deterministic without containing any cryptographic objects. Furthermore it is simple, so that its state-transition function can easily by expressed in formal languages, e.g., in PVS. In the following we simply write $Sys^{\text{msg\_ord,spec}}$ instead of $Sys_{n,L,s_1,s_2}^{\text{msg\_ord,spec}}$ if the parameters n, L, s_1, s_2 are not necessary for understanding.

3.2   The Split Ideal System

This section contains the first step for deriving a real system that is as secure as Scheme 1. If we take a look at Figure 1, the system $Sys^{\text{msg\_ord,spec}}$ plays the role of the monolithic specification Sys^{spec}. We now "split" our specification into a system Sys^* such that $Sys^* \geq_{\text{sec}} Sys^{\text{spec}}$ holds. Sys^* is the combination of two systems Sys_0' and Sys_1. Finally, we replace Sys_0' with Sys_0 using the composition theorem and obtain a real system that still fulfills our requirements.

The systems Sys_0' and Sys_0 are the ideal and real systems for secure message transmission presented in [16]. Sys_1 filters messages that are out of order; we define it next, see also Figure 2.

Scheme 2 (Filtering System Sys_1) Let $n, L, s_1, s_2, \mathcal{M}$ be given as in Scheme 1. Furthermore let a polynomial $L_1 := L + c(k)$ be given; the value of $c(k)$ is explained below. Sys_1 is now defined as

$$Sys_1 = \{(\hat{M}_\mathcal{H}', S_\mathcal{H}) \mid \mathcal{H} \subseteq \mathcal{M}\},$$

where $\hat{M}_\mathcal{H}' = \{\mathsf{M}_u' \mid u \in \mathcal{H}\}$ and $\mathsf{ports}(\mathsf{M}_u') = \{\mathsf{in}_u?, \mathsf{out}_u!, \mathsf{out}_u^{\triangleleft}!\}$ $\cup \{\mathsf{in}_u'!, \mathsf{out}_u'?, \mathsf{in}_u'^{\triangleleft}!\}$. All free ports of $[\hat{M}_\mathcal{H}']$ are specified, i.e., $S_\mathcal{H}$ consists of all ports corresponding to $\mathsf{ports}(\hat{M}_\mathcal{H}')$. Internally, the machine M_u' maintains two arrays $(msg\_in_{u,v}^{\mathsf{id}})_{v \in \mathcal{M}}$, $(sc\_in_{u,v}^{\mathsf{id}})_{v \in \mathcal{M}}$ over $\{0, \dots, s_1(k)\}$ and two arrays $(msg\_out_{v,u}^{\mathsf{id}})_{v \in \mathcal{M}}$, $(sc\_out_{v,u}^{\mathsf{id}})_{v \in \mathcal{M}}$ over $\{0, \dots, s_2(k)\}$. All four arrays are initialized with 0 everywhere. Moreover, it contains a flag $(stopped_u^{\mathsf{id}})$ over $\{0, 1\}$ initialized with 0. We assume that encoding of tuples has the following straightforward length property: $\mathsf{len}((m, num)) = \mathsf{len}(m) + c(k)$ for every $num \in \{0, \dots, \max\{s_1(k), s_2(k)\}\}$ and an arbitrary function c, i.e., $\mathsf{len}(num)$ is constant for each fixed security parameter k. This condition can easily be achieved by padding all values num to a fixed size $\geq \mathsf{len}(\max\{s_1(k), s_2(k)\})$. The behaviour of M_u' is defined as follows.

- **Send initialization:** On input (snd_init) at $\mathsf{in}_u?$: If $sc\_in_{u,v}^{\mathsf{id}} < s_1(k)$ for every $v \in \mathcal{M}$, set $sc\_in_{u,v}^{\mathsf{id}} := sc\_in_{u,v}^{\mathsf{id}} + 1$ for every $v \in \mathcal{M}$. If $stopped_u^{\mathsf{id}} = 0$ then output (snd_init) at $\mathsf{in}_u'!$, 1 at $\mathsf{in}_u'^{\triangleleft}!$.
- **Receive initialization:** On input (rec_init, v) at $\mathsf{out}_u'?$: If $stopped_u^{\mathsf{id}} = 0$ and $sc\_out_{v,u}^{\mathsf{id}} < s_2(k)$, set $sc\_out_{v,u}^{\mathsf{id}} := sc\_out_{v,u}^{\mathsf{id}} + 1$ and output (rec_init, v) at $\mathsf{out}_u!$, 1 at $\mathsf{out}_u^{\triangleleft}!$.
- **Send:** On input (send, m, v) at $\mathsf{in}_u?$: If $stopped_u^{\mathsf{id}} = 0$ and $sc\_in_{u,v}^{\mathsf{id}} < s_1(k)$, set $sc\_in_{u,v}^{\mathsf{id}} := sc\_in_{u,v}^{\mathsf{id}} + 1$, $msg\_in_{u,v}^{\mathsf{id}} := msg\_in_{u,v}^{\mathsf{id}} + 1$ and output (send, $(m, msg\_in_{u,v}^{\mathsf{id}}), v$) at $\mathsf{in}_u'!$, 1 at $\mathsf{in}_u'^{\triangleleft}!$.
- **Receive:** On input (receive, v, m') at $\mathsf{out}_u'?$: If $stopped_u^{\mathsf{id}} = 0$ and $sc\_out_{v,u}^{\mathsf{id}} < s_2(k)$, set $sc\_out_{v,u}^{\mathsf{id}} := sc\_out_{v,u}^{\mathsf{id}} + 1$, otherwise do nothing. If the test was true, decompose the message m' into (m, num). If $num \geq msg\_out_{v,u}^{\mathsf{id}}$ (or $num = msg\_out_{v,u}^{\mathsf{id}}$ in the perfect ordered system), $msg\_out_{v,u}^{\mathsf{id}} := num + 1$ and output (receive, v, m) at $\mathsf{out}_u!$, 1 at $\mathsf{out}_u^{\triangleleft}!$.
- **Stop:** On input (stop) at $\mathsf{out}_u'?$: If $stopped_u^{\mathsf{id}} = 0$, set $stopped_u^{\mathsf{id}} := 1$ and output (stop) at $\mathsf{out}_u!$, 1 at $\mathsf{out}_u^{\triangleleft}!$.

Finally, if M_u' receives an input at a port $\mathsf{in}_u?$ which is not comprised by the above five transitions, it increases the counter $sc\_in_{u,v}^{\mathsf{spec}}$ for all $v \in \mathcal{M}$. Similarly, if M_u' receives such an input at port $\mathsf{out}_u'?$ it increases every counter $sc\_out_{v,u}^{\mathsf{spec}}$ for $v \in \mathcal{M}$. $\Diamond$

Obviously, Sys_0' is polynomial-time for the same reason as $\mathsf{TH}_\mathcal{H}'$.

As described above, the system Sys_0 is the ideal system for secure message transmission of [16]. We now describe it in full because we need it for our security proof in Sections 4 and 5. We made a few adaptations, which do not invalidate the proof.

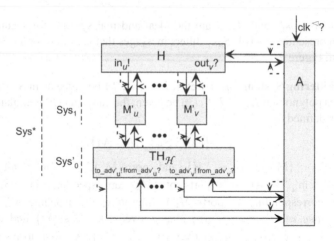

Fig. 2. The Split Ideal System.

Scheme 3 (Ideal System for Unordered Secure Message Transmission) Let $n, L_1, \mathcal{M}$ be given as above. $\mathcal{ACC}$ is the powerset of $\mathcal{M}$. Then

$$Sys'_0 := \{(\{\mathsf{TH}_\mathcal{H}\}, S_\mathcal{H}) \mid \mathcal{H} \subseteq \mathcal{M}\}$$

with $S_\mathcal{H}^c := \{in'_u!, out'_u?, in'_u{}^{\triangleleft}! \mid u \in \mathcal{H}\}$ and $\mathsf{TH}_\mathcal{H}$ defined as follows. The ports of $\mathsf{TH}_\mathcal{H}$ are $\{in'_u?, out'_u!, out'_u{}^{\triangleleft}!, from\_adv'_u?, to\_adv'_u!, to\_adv'_u{}^{\triangleleft}! \mid u \in \mathcal{H}\}$. $\mathsf{TH}_\mathcal{H}$ maintains arrays $(init^*_{u,v})_{u,v \in \mathcal{M}}$ and $(stopped^*_u)_{u \in \mathcal{H}}$ over $\{0, 1\}$, both initialized with 0 everywhere, and an array $(deliver^*_{u,v})_{u,v \in \mathcal{H}}$ of lists, all initially empty. The state-transition function of $\mathsf{TH}_\mathcal{H}$ is defined by the following rules:

- **Send initialization.** On input (snd_init) at $in'_u?$: If $stopped^*_u = 0$ and $init^*_{u,u} = 0$, set $init^*_{u,u} := 1$ and output (snd_init) at $to\_adv'_u!$, 1 at $to\_adv'_u{}^{\triangleleft}!$.
- **Receive initialization.** On input (rec_init, u) at $from\_adv'_v?$ with $u \in \mathcal{M}, v \in \mathcal{H}$: If $stopped^*_v = 0$ and $init^*_{u,v} = 0$ and $[u \in \mathcal{H} \Rightarrow init^*_{u,u} = 1]$, set $init^*_{u,v} := 1$ and output (rec_init, u) at $out'_v!$, 1 at $out'_v{}^{\triangleleft}!$.
- **Send.** On input (send, m, v) at $in'_u?$ with $m \in \Sigma^+$, $l := len(m) \leq L_1(k)$, and $v \in \mathcal{M} \setminus \{u\}$: If $stopped^*_u = 0$, $init^*_{u,u} = 1$, and $init^*_{v,u} = 1$: If $v \in \mathcal{A}$ then { output (send, m, v) at $to\_adv'_u!$, 1 at $to\_adv'_u{}^{\triangleleft}!$ }, else {$i := size(deliver^*_{u,v}) + 1$; $deliver^*_{u,v}[i] := m$; output (send_blindly, i, l, v) at $to\_adv'_u!$, 1 at $to\_adv'_u{}^{\triangleleft}!$ }.
- **Receive from honest party u.** On input (receive_blindly, u, i) at $from\_adv'_v?$ with $u, v \in \mathcal{H}$: If $stopped^*_v = 0$, $init^*_{v,v} = 1$, $init^*_{u,v} = 1$, and $m := deliver^*_{u,v}[i] \neq \downarrow$, then output (receive, u, m) at $out'_v!$, 1 at $out'_v{}^{\triangleleft}!$.
- **Receive from dishonest party u.** On input (receive, u, m) at $from\_adv'_v?$ with $u \in \mathcal{A}$, $m \in \Sigma^+$, $len(m) \leq L_1(k)$, and $v \in \mathcal{H}$: If $stopped^*_v = 0$, $init^*_{v,v} = 1$ and $init^*_{u,v} = 1$, then output (receive, u, m) at $out'_v!$, 1 at $out'_v{}^{\triangleleft}!$.
- **Stop.** On input (stop) at $from\_adv'_u?$ with $u \in \mathcal{H}$, set $stopped^*_u = 1$ and output (stop) at $out'_u!$, 1 at $out'_u{}^{\triangleleft}!$.

$\diamond$

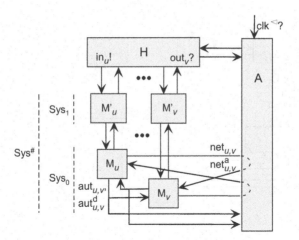

Fig. 3. Sketch of the Real System for Ordered Secure Message Transmission.

If we now combine the two systems Sys'_0 and Sys_1 in the "canonical" way, i.e., we combine those structures with the same index $\mathcal{H}$, we obtain the system Sys^*, which we call split ideal system (Figure 2). Finally, we define all connections $\{out'_u!, out'_u?\}$ and $\{in'_u!, in'_u?\}$ of Sys^* to be secure, because they correspond to local subroutine calls.

3.3 The Real System

Our real system $Sys^\#$ is derived be replacing Sys'_0 with Sys_0. For understanding it is sufficient to give a brief review of Sys_0 from [16]. It is a standard cryptographic system of the form $Sys_0 = \{(\hat{M}_{\mathcal{H}}, S_{\mathcal{H}}) \mid \mathcal{H} \in \mathcal{ACC}\}$, see Figure 3, where $\hat{M}_{\mathcal{H}} = \{M_u \mid u \in \mathcal{H}\}$ and $\mathcal{ACC}$ is the powerset of $\mathcal{M}$, i.e., any subset of participants may be dishonest. It uses asymmetric encryption and digital signatures as cryptographic primitives. A user u can let his machine create signature and encryption keys that are sent to other users over authenticated channels. Messages sent from user u to user v are signed and encrypted by M_u and sent to M_v over an insecure channel, representing a real network. The adversary can schedule the communication between correct machines[2] and send arbitrary messages m to arbitrary users.

We now build the combination of Sys_1 and Sys_0 in the canonical way, which yields a new system $Sys^\#$ that we refer to as real ordered system.

4   Proving Security of the Real Ordered System

We now start to prove that the real ordered system is at least as secure as the specification. This is captured by the following theorem.

Theorem 1. *(Security of Real Ordered Secure Message Transmission)* For all $n \in \mathbb{N}$ and $s_1, s_2, L \in \mathbb{N}[x]$, $Sys^\# \geq_{\text{sec}}^{\text{poly}} Sys^{\text{spec}}$ holds (for the canonical mapping), provided

---

[2] He can therefore replay messages and also change their order. This is prevented in our scheme by the additional filtering system Sys_1.

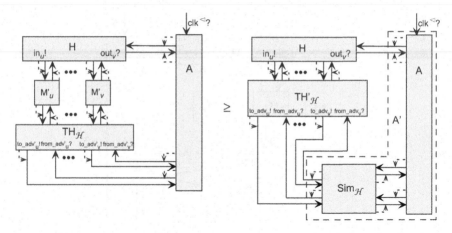

Fig. 4. Proof Overview of $Sys^* \geq_{\text{sec}}^{\text{perf}} Sys^{\text{spec}}$.

the signature and encryption schemes used are secure. This holds with blackbox simu-latability.[3] □

Our proof contains the already described four steps, illustrated in Figure 1. First, [16] contains the result $Sys_0 \geq_{\text{sec}} Sys_0'$. Secondly, the composition theorem (cf. Section 2.3) yields the relation $Sys^{\#} \geq_{\text{sec}} Sys^*$. The only remaining task is to check that its pre-conditions are fulfilled, which is straightforward since we showed that the system Sys_1 is polynomial-time. If we have proven $Sys^* \geq_{\text{sec}} Sys^{\text{spec}}$, then $Sys^{\#} \geq_{\text{sec}} Sys^{\text{spec}}$ follows from the transitivity lemma, cf. Section 2.1. Thus, we only have to prove $Sys^* \geq_{\text{sec}}^{\text{poly}} Sys^{\text{spec}}$. We will even prove the perfect case $Sys^* \geq_{\text{sec}}^{\text{perf}} Sys^{\text{spec}}$.

Lemma 1. *For all $n \in \mathbb{N}$ and $s_1, s_2, L \in \mathbb{N}[x]$, $Sys^* \geq_{\text{sec}}^{\text{perf}} Sys^{\text{spec}}$ holds (for the canonical mapping), and with blackbox simulatability.* □

In order to prove this, we assume a configuration $conf_{\text{si}} := (\{\text{TH}_{\mathcal{H}}\} \cup \hat{M}_u', S_{\mathcal{H}}, \text{H}, \text{A})$ of Sys^* with $\hat{M}_u' = \{\text{M}_u' \mid u \in \mathcal{H}\}$ to be given, which we call split-ideal configuration. We then have to show that there exists a configuration $conf_{\text{sp}} := (\{\text{TH}'_{\mathcal{H}}\}, S_{\mathcal{H}}, \text{H}, \text{A}')$ of Sys^{spec}, called specification configuration, yielding indistinguishable views for the honest user H .

The adversary A' consists of two machines: a so-called simulator $\text{Sim}_{\mathcal{H}}$, which we define in the following, and the original adversary A. This is exactly the notion of blackbox simulatability. These configurations are shown in Figure 4.

Definition of the Simulator $\text{Sim}_{\mathcal{H}}$. The Simulator $\text{Sim}_{\mathcal{H}}$ is placed between the trusted host $\text{TH}'_{\mathcal{H}}$ and the adversary A, see Figure 4. Its ports are given by $\{\text{to\_adv}_u?, \text{from\_adv}_u!, \text{from\_adv}_u^{\triangleleft}! \mid u \in \mathcal{H}\} \cup \{\text{from\_adv}_u'?, \text{to\_adv}_u'!, \text{to\_adv}_u'^{\triangleleft}! \mid u \in \mathcal{H}\}$. The first set contains the ports connected to $\text{TH}'_{\mathcal{H}}$, the ports of the second set are for communication with the adversary. Internally, $\text{Sim}_{\mathcal{H}}$ maintains two arrays $(init_{u,v}^{\text{sim}})_{u,v \in \mathcal{M}}$, $(stopped_u^{\text{sim}})_{u \in \mathcal{H}}$ over $\{0,1\}$, an array $(msg\_out_{u,v}^{\text{sim}})_{u \in \mathcal{A}, v \in \mathcal{H}}$

---

[3] See [16] for further details on valid and canonical mappings and different kinds of simulatability.

over $\{0, \ldots, s_1(k)\}$, and an array $(sc\_out^{\text{sim}}_{u,v})_{u \in \mathcal{M}, v \in \mathcal{H}}$ over $\{0, \ldots, s_2(k)\}$. All four arrays are initialized with 0 everywhere. They match the arrays in the ideal system, except that $msg\_out^{\text{sim}}_{u,v}$ corresponds to $msg\_out^{\text{id}}_{u,v}$ of M'_v for dishonest v only. We now define the behaviour of the simulator. In most cases $\text{Sim}_{\mathcal{H}}$ simply forwards inputs to their corresponding outputs, modifying some internal values.

- **Send initialization:** Upon input (snd_init) at to_adv$_u$?, $\text{Sim}_{\mathcal{H}}$ sets $init^{\text{sim}}_{u,u} := 1$ and outputs (snd_init) at to_adv$'_u$!, 1 at to_adv$'_u{}^{\triangleleft}$!.
- **Receive initialization:** Upon input (rec_init, u) at from_adv$'_v$?: If $stopped^{\text{sim}}_u = 0$ and $init^{\text{sim}}_{u,v} = 0$ and $[u \in \mathcal{H} \implies init^{\text{sim}}_{u,u} = 1]$ $\text{Sim}_{\mathcal{H}}$ sets $init^{\text{sim}}_{u,v} := 1$. If additionally $sc\_out^{\text{sim}}_{u,v} < s_2(k)$ holds, it sets $sc\_out^{\text{sim}}_{u,v} := sc\_out^{\text{sim}}_{u,v} + 1$ and outputs (rec_init, u) at from_adv$_v$!, 1 at from_adv$_v{}^{\triangleleft}$!.
- **Send:** Upon input (send_blindy, i, l', v) at to_adv$_u$?, $\text{Sim}_{\mathcal{H}}$ determines $l := l' + c(k)$ and outputs (send_blindy, i, l, v) at to_adv$'_u$!, 1 at to_adv$'_u{}^{\triangleleft}$!.
  Upon input (send, m, v) at to_adv$_u$?, $\text{Sim}_{\mathcal{H}}$ simply forwards the input to to_adv$'_u$! and schedules it.
- **Receive from honest party** u: Upon input (receive_blindly, u, i) at from_adv$'_v$?, $\text{Sim}_{\mathcal{H}}$ forwards this input to port from_adv$_v$! and schedules it.
- **Receive from dishonest party** u: Upon input (receive, u, m') at from_adv$'_v$? with $u \in \mathcal{A}$, $\text{Sim}_{\mathcal{H}}$ decomposes $m' = (m, num)$: If $stopped^{\text{sim}}_v = 0$, $init^{\text{sim}}_{v,v} = 1$, $init^{\text{sim}}_{u,v} = 1$, $len(m') \leq L_1(k)$, $num \geq msg\_out^{\text{sim}}_{u,v}$ ($num = msg\_out^{\text{sim}}_{u,v}$ in the perfect ordered system) and $sc\_out^{\text{sim}}_{u,v} < s_2(k)$, set $msg\_out^{\text{sim}}_{u,v} := num + 1$, $sc\_out^{\text{sim}}_{u,v} := sc\_out^{\text{sim}}_{u,v} + 1$ and output (receive, u, m) at from_adv$_v$!, 1 at from_adv$_v{}^{\triangleleft}$!.
- **Stop:** On input (stop) at from_adv$'_u$?: If $stopped^{\text{sim}}_u = 0$, $\text{Sim}_{\mathcal{H}}$ sets $stopped^{\text{sim}}_u := 1$ and outputs (stop) at from_adv$_u$!, 1 at from_adv$_u{}^{\triangleleft}$!.

What the simulator does is recalculating the length of message m into $len((m, num))$ to achieve indistinguishability. Furthermore it decomposes messages sent by the adversary, maybe sorting them out, in order to achieve identical outputs in both systems. Now the overall adversary A' is defined by combining A and $\text{Sim}_{\mathcal{H}}$.

Now the ultimate goal is to show that the collections $\hat{M}_* := \{\text{TH}_{\mathcal{H}}\} \cup \{M_u \mid u \in \mathcal{H}\}$ and $\hat{M}_{\text{spec}} := \{\text{TH}'_{\mathcal{H}}, \text{Sim}_{\mathcal{H}}\}$ have the same input-output behaviour, i.e., if they obtain the same inputs they produce the same outputs. We do so by proving a classical deterministic bisimulation, i.e., we define a relation ϕ on the states of the two collections and show that ϕ is maintained in every step of every trace and that the outputs of both systems are always equal. This is exactly the procedure we will perform using the theorem prover PVS.

Definition 1. *(Deterministic Bisimulation) Let two arbitrary collections $\hat{M}_1$ and $\hat{M}_2$ of deterministic machines with identical sets of free ports be given, i.e., free($[\hat{M}_1]$) = free($[\hat{M}_2]$). A deterministic bisimulation between these two collections is a binary relation ϕ on the states of $\hat{M}_1$ and $\hat{M}_2$ such that the following holds.*

- *The initial states of $\hat{M}_1$ and $\hat{M}_2$ satisfy the relation ϕ.*
- *The transition functions δ_1 and δ_2 of $\hat{M}_1$ and $\hat{M}_2$ preserve the relation ϕ and produce identical outputs. I.e., let S_1 and S_2 be two states of $\hat{M}_1$ and $\hat{M}_2$, respectively, with $(S_1, S_2) \in \phi$, let $\mathcal{I}$ be an arbitrary overall input of $\hat{M}_1$ and $\hat{M}_2$, and let $(S'_1, \mathcal{O}_1) := \delta_1(S_1, \mathcal{I})$ and $(S'_2, \mathcal{O}_2) := \delta_2(S_2, \mathcal{I})$. Then we have $(S'_1, S'_2) \in \phi$ and $\mathcal{O}_1 = \mathcal{O}_2$.*

We call two collections $\hat{M}_1$ and $\hat{M}_2$ bisimilar if there exists a bisimulation between them. $\diamond$

We will apply this definition to composed transition functions of each of the two collections $\hat{M}_*$ and $\hat{M}_{\text{spec}}$, i.e., the overall transition from an external input (from H or A) to an external output (to H or A). It is quite easy to see that a deterministic bisimulation in this sense implies perfect indistinguishability of the view of H, cf. Figure 4, and even of the joint view of H and the original adversary A. Assume for contradiction that these views are not identical. Thus, there exists a first time where they can be distinguished. This difference has to be produced by the collections. Since we defined this to be the first different step, the prior input of both collections is identical. But thus, both collections also produce identical outputs because they are bisimilar. This yields the desired contradiction.

The next section describes how the machines are expressed in the formal syntax of PVS and partly explains the bisimulation proof.

It is worth mentioning that we used standard paper-and-pencil proofs before we decided to use a formal proof system to validate the desired bisimulation. However, these proofs have turned out to be very error-prone since they are straightforward on the one hand, but long and tedious on the other, so they are mainly vulnerable to slow-down of concentration. During our formal verification, we in fact found several errors in both our machines and our proofs, which were quite obvious afterwards, but had not been found before. We decided to put the whole paper-and-pencil proof in the web[4], so readers can make up their own minds.

5   Formal Verification of the Bisimulation

5.1   Defining the Machines in PVS

In this section, we describe how Lemma 1 is formally verified in the theorem proving system PVS [13]. As we already showed in the previous section, it is sufficient to prove that the two collections $\hat{M}_*$ and $\hat{M}_{\text{spec}}$ are contained in a deterministic bisimulation. In order to do so, we first describe how the machines are formalized in PVS. Since the formal machine descriptions are too large to be given here completely, we use the machine $\text{TH}'_{\mathcal{H}}$ as an example. The complete machine descriptions and the proof are available online[4].

We denote the number of participating machines by N, and for a given subset $\mathcal{H} \in \mathcal{ACC}$, we denote the number of honest users by $M := \#\mathcal{H}$. As defined in Scheme 1, the machine $\text{TH}'_{\mathcal{H}}$ has $2M$ input ports $\{\text{in}_u?, \text{from\_adv}_u? \mid u \in \mathcal{H}\}$. In

---

[4] http://www-krypt.cs.uni-sb.de/~mbackes/PVS/FME2002/

PVS, we number these input ports $1, \ldots, 2M$, where we identify $1, \ldots, M$ with the user ports and $M + 1, \ldots, 2M$ with the adversary ports. Similarly, $\mathsf{TH}'_{\mathcal{H}}$ has output ports $\{\mathsf{out}_u!, \mathsf{to\_adv}_u! \mid u \in \mathcal{H}\}$, which also are numbered $1, \ldots, 2M$. In PVS, we define the following types to denote machines, honest users, and ports:

```
MACH:     TYPE = subrange(1,N)      %% machines
USERS:    TYPE = subrange(1,M)      %% honest users
PORTS:    TYPE = subrange(1,2*M)    %% port numbers
```

The subrange(i,j) type is a PVS built-in type denoting the integers $i, \ldots, j$. We further define a type STRING to represent messages.

In Scheme 1, the different possible inputs to machine $\mathsf{TH}'_{\mathcal{H}}$ are listed, e.g., $(\mathsf{snd\_init}), (\mathsf{rec\_init}, u), \ldots$ In PVS, the type of input ports is defined using a PVS abstract datatype [12]. The prefix m1i in the following stands for "inputs of machine 1", which is $\mathsf{TH}'_{\mathcal{H}}$, and is used to distinguish between inputs and outputs of the different machines.

```
m1_in_port: DATATYPE
BEGIN
  m1i_snd_init:                                m1i_snd_init?
  m1i_rec_init(u: MACH):                       m1i_rec_init?
  m1i_send(m: STRING, v: MACH):                m1i_send?
  m1i_receive_blindly(u: USERS, i: posnat):    m1i_receive_blindly?
  m1i_receive(u: MACH, m: STRING):             m1i_receive?
  m1i_stop:                                    m1i_stop?
END m1_in_port
```

This defines an abstract datatype with *constructors* m1i_snd_init, m1i_rec_init etc. For example, for given u, i, m1i_receive_blindly(u,i) constructs an instance of the above datatype, which we identify with $(\mathsf{receive\_blindly}, u, i)$. Given an instance p of this datatype, we can use the *recognizers* on the right side of the definition to distinguish between the different forms. For example, m1i_receive_blindly?(p) checks whether the instance p of the m1i_in_port datatype was constructed from the m1i_receive_blindly constructor. If it was, the components u and i can be restored using the *accessor functions* $u(\cdot)$ and $i(\cdot)$; for example, $u(p)$ returns the u component of p. The accessor functions may be overloaded for different constructors (e.g., u is overloaded in m1i_rec_init, m1i_receive_blindly and m1i_receive).

The machine $\mathsf{TH}'_{\mathcal{H}}$ performs a step iff exactly one of the input ports is active. In this case, we call the input *ok*, otherwise *garbage*. Because of our underlying scheduling definition, an input with several active input ports cannot occur so *garbage* naturally correspond to an all-empty input. The type of the complete inputs to $\mathsf{TH}'_{\mathcal{H}}$ comprising all $2M$ input ports is therefore either garbage, or the number u of the active port together with the input p on port u. This is formalized in the following PVS datatype:

```
M1_INP: DATATYPE
BEGIN
  m1i_garbage:                     m1i_garbage?
  m1i_ok(u: PORTS, p: m1_in_port): m1i_ok?
END M1_INP
```

Similar datatypes m1_out_port and M1_OUT are defined to denote the type of individual outputs, and the type of the complete output of $\mathsf{TH}'_{\mathcal{H}}$, respectively.

Next we define the state type of $\mathsf{TH}'_{\mathcal{H}}$. As defined in Scheme 1, this state consists of seven one- or two-dimensional arrays. In PVS, arrays are modeled as functions mapping the indices to the contents of the array. For example [MACH,USERS -> nat] defines a two-dimensional array of natural numbers, where the first index ranges over $\mathcal{M}$, and the second ranges over $\mathcal{H}$. The state type of $\mathsf{TH}'_{\mathcal{H}}$ is defined as a record of such arrays. There is only one small exception: the array $deliver^{\mathrm{spec}}_{u,v}$ stores lists of tuples (m, i) (e.g., see the "Send" transition), where m is a string and $i \in \mathbb{N}$. It is convenient in PVS to decompose this array of lists of tuples into two arrays of lists, where the first array $deliver^{\mathrm{spec}}_{u,v}$ stores lists of messages m, and the second array $deliv\_i^{\mathrm{spec}}_{u,v}$ stores lists of naturals i. Altogether, this yields a state type of eight arrays:

```
M1_STATE: TYPE = [# init_spec: [MACH,MACH -> bool],
                    sc_in_spec: [USERS,MACH -> nat],
                    msg_in_spec: [USERS,MACH -> nat],
                    msg_out_spec: [USERS,USERS -> posnat],
                    sc_out_spec: [MACH,USERS -> nat],
                    deliver_spec: [USERS,USERS -> list[STRING]],
                    deliv_i_spec: [USERS,USERS -> list[posnat]],
                    stopped_spec: [USERS -> bool] #]
```

The initial state m1_init is defined as a constant of type M1_STATE:

```
M1_init: M1_STATE = (#
  init_spec := LAMBDA (w1,w2: MACH): FALSE,
  ...
  deliv_i_spec := LAMBDA (u1,u2: USERS): null,
  stopped_spec := LAMBDA (u1: USERS): FALSE #)
```

The constructor null denotes the empty list. In the definition of machine $\mathsf{TH}'_{\mathcal{H}}$, $sc\_in^{\mathrm{spec}}_{u,v}$ is incremented for all machines v during the "Send initialization" part. This is encapsulated in the following PVS function:

```
incr_sc_in_spec(S: M1_STATE, u: USERS): M1_STATE =
    S WITH [ 'sc_in_spec := LAMBDA (w: USERS, v: MACH):
             IF w=u THEN S'sc_in_spec(w,v)+1 ELSE
                          S'sc_in_spec(w,v) ENDIF ];
```

The WITH construct leaves the record S unchanged except for the sc_in_spec component, which is replaced by the λ-expression. The machine $\mathsf{TH}'_{\mathcal{H}}$ is now formalized in PVS as a next-state/output function mapping current state and inputs to the next state and outputs. We exemplarily give the first few lines of the PVS code:

```
M1_ns(S: M1_STATE, I: M1_INP): [# ns: M1_STATE, O: M1_OUT #] =
  IF m1i_garbage?(I) THEN
    (# ns:=S, O:=m1o_garbage #)
      %% do not change the state, output nothing
  ELSE
    LET ua1=ua(I), p=p(I) IN
      %% ua1 is the active port number,
      %% p is the input on this port
```

```
IF ua1<=M AND m1i_snd_init?(p) THEN
  %% we have a send-init on a user port (<=M);
  IF (FORALL w1: S'sc_in_spec(ua1,w1)<s1k) THEN
    IF S'init_spec(ua1,ua1) OR S'stopped_spec(ua1) THEN
      (# ns:=incr_sc_in_spec(S,ua1),O:=m1o_garbage #)
      %% increment sc_in_spec, but do not send any output
    ELSE
      (# ns:=incr_sc_in_spec(S,ua1)
        WITH [ 'init_spec(ua1,ua1) := TRUE ],
      O := m1o_ok(M+ua1, m1o_snd_init) #)
      %% increment sc_in_spec, set init_spec(ua1,ua1):=true
      %% send m1o_snd_init to adversary port M+ua1
    ENDIF
  ELSE %% otherwise do nothing
    (# ns:=S, O:=m1o_garbage #)
  ENDIF
ELSIF ua1>M AND m1i_rec_init?(p) THEN
  ...
```

In a similar way we have formalized the machines $\mathsf{TH}_{\mathcal{H}}$, $\{\mathsf{M}'_u \mid u \in \mathcal{H}\}$, and $\mathsf{Sim}_{\mathcal{H}}$. The M machines M'_u in the left part of Figure 4 have been combined into a single machine in PVS; however, this is only syntactic and does not change the semantics. The combination of the machines $\mathsf{TH}_{\mathcal{H}}$ and $\{\mathsf{M}'_u \mid u \in \mathcal{H}\}$ respectively $\mathsf{TH}'_{\mathcal{H}}$ and $\mathsf{Sim}_{\mathcal{H}}$ is straightforward by composition of the corresponding state transition functions: An input from H is always first handled by a machine M'_u and $\mathsf{TH}'_{\mathcal{H}}$, and then by $\mathsf{TH}_{\mathcal{H}}$ and $\mathsf{Sim}_{\mathcal{H}}$, respectively, and vice versa. This saves us from implementing the full asynchronous scheduling algorithm in PVS for this example.

The only non-trivial choice we have made in the transliteration of the machines to PVS is the type of the input- and output-ports. In a previous attempt, we did not use the abstract datatype definition of M1_INP, but defined M1_INP as an array of $2M$ individual input ports; in order to model non-active ports, we added an m1i_inactive form to the input port type m1i_in_port. An input from M1_INP was defined to be *ok* iff exactly one of the ports is different from m1i_inactive. This obviously models the same valid inputs as the definition of M1_INP above. The problem with the array definition is that extracting the active port number u involves an application of the choice-function ε in order to choose the index u of the array for which the port is active. The application of the choice-function considerably complicates the proofs in PVS, since the definition of ε is not constructive in PVS. In contrast, in the definition using the abstract datatype, the active port number u can be constructively extracted from the input by applying the accessor function of the abstract datatype. Due to constructiveness, the proofs in PVS become much simpler. This problem in the port definition also applies to the output ports of the machines.

The rest of the transliteration of the machine definitions to PVS is straightforward. In the following, we revert to standard mathematical notation for the sake of brevity and readability. However, it should be noted once more that all the definitions and claims in this section have been formalized and verified in PVS.

5.2   Proving the Bisimulation

In order to prove Lemma 1, we prove the following predicates to be invariants of the collections $\hat{M}_*$ and $\hat{M}_{\mathsf{spec}}$ when they obtain the same inputs.

- $stopped^* = stopped^{\mathsf{id}} = stopped^{\mathsf{sim}} = stopped^{\mathsf{spec}}$.
  Note that we compare whole arrays in this predicate, i.e., we make use of the higher-order capabilities of PVS. One could also write $\forall u : stopped_u^* = stopped_u^{\mathsf{id}} = \ldots$, but the equality of the whole arrays is more concise and easier to use in the proofs.
- $sc\_in^{\mathsf{id}} = sc\_in^{\mathsf{spec}}$.
- $init^* = init^{\mathsf{sim}} = init^{\mathsf{spec}}$.
- $msg\_in^{\mathsf{id}} = msg\_in^{\mathsf{spec}}$.
- $\forall u, v \in \mathcal{H} : length(deliver_{u,v}^*) = length(deliv\_i_{u,v}^*)$.
  $length$ is the PVS function delivering the length of lists. We use the quantified form of the invariant here instead of the higher-order form, since otherwise we would have to 'lift' the $length$ function to arrays of lists.
- $\forall u, v \in \mathcal{H} : length(deliver_{u,v}^{\mathsf{spec}}) = length(deliv\_i_{u,v}^{\mathsf{spec}})$.
- $deliver^* = deliver^{\mathsf{spec}}$ and $deliv\_i^* = deliv\_i^{\mathsf{spec}}$.
- $sc\_out^{\mathsf{id}} = sc\_out^{\mathsf{spec}}$.
- $\forall w \in \mathcal{M}, u \in \mathcal{H} : sc\_out_{w,u}^{\mathsf{sim}} \leq sc\_out_{w,u}^{\mathsf{spec}}$.
  Again we use the quantified form, since otherwise we had to lift "$\leq$" to arrays.
- $\forall w \in \mathcal{M}, u \in \mathcal{H} : ((w \in \mathcal{H} \implies msg\_out_{w,u}^{\mathsf{id}} = msg\_out_{w,u}^{\mathsf{spec}})$ and $(w \in \mathcal{A} \wedge sc\_out_{w,u}^{\mathsf{id}} < s_2(k) \implies msg\_out_{w,u}^{\mathsf{id}} = msg\_out_{w,u}^{\mathsf{sim}}))$.

Each of the 10 invariants is formalized as a predicate $\phi_i(S_{\mathsf{si}}, S_{\mathsf{sp}})$ on the current states of the two collections $\hat{M}_*$ and $\hat{M}_{\mathsf{spec}}$. The conjunction of all the ϕ_i yields the bisimulation relation ϕ. Let δ_{si} and δ_{sp} denote the overall transition function of the machine collections $\hat{M}_*$ and $\hat{M}_{\mathsf{spec}}$, respectively. The following theorem asserts that the invariants indeed are invariants of these collections:

Theorem 2. *Let S_{si} and S_{sp} be states of the two collections $\hat{M}_*$ and $\hat{M}_{\mathsf{spec}}$ such that all invariants $\phi_i(S_{\mathsf{si}}, S_{\mathsf{sp}})$, $1 \leq i \leq 10$ hold. The transition functions $\delta_{\mathsf{si}}, \delta_{\mathsf{sp}}$ preserve the invariants, i.e., for an arbitrary overall input $\mathcal{I}$ of $\hat{M}_*$ and $\hat{M}_{\mathsf{spec}}$ we have*

$$\phi_i(S_{\mathsf{si}}', S_{\mathsf{sp}}') \; \forall i, 1 \leq i \leq 10$$

with $(S_{\mathsf{si}}', \mathcal{O}_{\mathsf{si}}) := \delta_{\mathsf{si}}(S_{\mathsf{si}}, \mathcal{I})$ and $(S_{\mathsf{sp}}', \mathcal{O}_{\mathsf{sp}}) := \delta_{\mathsf{sp}}(S_{\mathsf{sp}}, \mathcal{I})$. Furthermore, the initial states $initial_{\mathsf{si}}$ and $initial_{\mathsf{sp}}$ satisfy all 10 invariants.   □

In PVS, this theorem is split into 10 lemmas, one for each invariant. Using the invariants ϕ_i, we prove the following theorem:

Theorem 3. *Let S_{si} and S_{sp} be states satisfying all invariants $\phi_i(S_{\mathsf{si}}, S_{\mathsf{sp}})$, $1 \leq i \leq 10$, and let $\mathcal{I}$ be an overall input of the collections $\hat{M}_*$ and $\hat{M}_{\mathsf{spec}}$. Then both collections make the same outputs on all ports to the users and the adversary.*   □

Together, Theorems 2 and 3 prove that the two systems are bisimilar, which finishes our proof of Theorem 1.

5.3 Verification Effort

The manual proof effort in PVS is rather small. The proofs make heavy use of the built-in PVS strategy (grind), which expands definitions and performs automatic case-splitting. The main effort was to figure out the correct parameters for the (grind) command. The proof goals not resolved by (grind) were proved with little manual assistance. However, looking for errors and thinking about the necessary modifications of the machines was a time-consuming task. During our proof attempts, we simultaneously debugged the machines until we finally found the correct specifications of all machines. After that, the proof itself turned out to be quite easy. Altogether, the formalization of the machines in PVS took 2 weeks, and the development of the proofs took another week (given prior familiarity with PVS). A complete checking of the proof takes about one hour on a 600 MHz Athlon processor.

6 Summary and Future Work

We have presented the first abstract specification for secure message transmission preventing message reordering, together with a secure implementation. Its proof of security involved a recently proven composition theorem [16] and a bisimulation which we formally verified using the theorem prover PVS. Our approach furthermore presents a general strategy how to derive real implementations by splitting specifications into smaller systems that can then be refined stepwise using the composition theorem and formal proof systems.

One next step is to verify the claimed integrity property of the systems, i.e., a formula that messages are output in correct order. This requires more theoretical work, e.g., we have to show that integrity properties are in fact preserved under simulatability also in the asynchronous case (this is not trivial even though the synchronous case was already shown in [15]). Also the PVS proof becomes more complicated than the one presented here. A preliminary version of that work can already be seen in [3]. Putting our current paper and those results together, we are confident that our underlying model is well suited for future analysis of larger protocols including real cryptographic primitives, since it supports commonly accepted machine-aided proofs (like the one of [14]) without losing its sound cryptographic semantics.

Concerning further future work, there are innumerous things to do. Obviously, the security of the system presented in this paper is still based on paper-and-pencil proofs such as the composition theorem, the transitivity lemma or the security proof in [16]. Hence, one future step could be the verification of those theorems using formal proof systems. However, we are aware of the difficulty of this task, mostly because of the occurrence of probabilism. In the shorter term, we are turning our attention to a library which should provide sound abstractions of a set of common cryptographic primitives. The library may naturally serve as a construction kit for designing large protocols whose security properties can then easily be validated again by formal proof systems.

References

1. M. Abadi and A. D. Gordon. A calculus for cryptographic protocols: The spi calculus. Information and Computation 148/1 (1999) 1-70.
2. M. Abadi and P. Rogaway. Reconciling two views of cryptography (the computational soundness of formal encryption). IFIP Intern. Conf. on Theoretical Computer Science (TCS 2000), LNCS 1872, Springer-Verlag, 2000, 3–22.
3. M. Backes. Cryptographically sound analysis of security protocols. Ph.D thesis, Computer Science Department, Saarland University, 2002.
4. D. Dolev and A. C. Yao. On the security of public key protocols. IEEE Transactions on Information Theory 29/2 (1983) 198-208.
5. F. J. T. Fabrega, J. C. Herzog, and J. D. Guttman. Strand spaces: Why is a security protocol correct? 1998 IEEE Symposium on Security and Privacy, IEEE Computer Society Press, Los Alamitos 1998, 160-171.
6. C. A. R. Hoare. Communicating sequential processes. International Series in Computer Science, Prentice Hall, Hemel Hempstead 1985.
7. P. Lincoln, J. Mitchell, M. Mitchell, and A. Scedrov. A probabilistic poly-time framework for protocol analysis. 5th ACM Conference on Computer and Communications Security, San Francisco, November 1998, 112–121.
8. P. Lincoln, J. Mitchell, M. Mitchell, and A. Scedrov. Probabilistic polynomial-time equivalence and security analysis. Formal Methods '99, LNCS 1708, Springer-Verlag, 1999, 776–793.
9. G. Lowe. Breaking and fixing the needham-schroeder public-key protocol using FDR. Tools and Algorithms for the Construction and Analysis of Systems (TACAS), LNCS 1055, Springer-Verlag, Berlin 1996, 147-166.
10. N. Lynch. Distributed algorithms. Morgan Kaufmann Publishers, San Francisco 1996.
11. N. Lynch. I/O automaton models and proofs for shared-key communication systems. 12th Computer Security Foundations Workshop (CSFW), IEEE, 1999, 14–29.
12. S. Owre and N. Shankar. Abstract datatypes in PVS. Technical report, Computer Science Laboratory, SRI International, 1993.
13. S. Owre, N. Shankar, and J. M. Rushby. PVS: A prototype verification system. In *CADE 11*, volume 607 of *LNAI*, pages 748–752. Springer, 1992.
14. L. Paulson. The inductive approach to verifying cryptographic protocols. Journal of Computer Security, 6(1):85-128, 1998.
15. B. Pfitzmann and M. Waidner. Composition and integrity preservation of secure reactive systems. 7th ACM Conference on Computer and Communications Security, Athens, November 2000, 245-254.
16. B. Pfitzmann and M. Waidner. A model for asynchronous reactive systems and its application to secure message transmission. IEEE Symposium on Security and Privacy, Oakland, May 2001, 184-202.
17. S. Schneider. Security properties and CSP. 1996 IEEE Symposium on Security and Privacy, IEEE Computer Society Press, Washington 1996, 174-187.
18. A. C. Yao. Protocols for secure computations. 23rd Symposium on Foundations of Computer Science (FOCS) 1982, IEEE Computer Society, 1982, 160-164.

Interference Analysis for Dependable Systems Using Refinement and Abstraction

Claus Pahl

School of Computer Applications, Dublin City University
Dublin 9, Ireland
`cpahl@compapp.dcu.ie`

Abstract. A common requirement for modern distributed and reactive systems is a high dependability guaranteeing reliability and security. The rigorous analysis of dependable systems specifications is of paramount importance for the reliability and security of these systems. A two-layered modal specification notation will allow the specification of services and protocols for distributed dependable systems and their properties. Refinement and its dual – abstraction – will play the key roles in an integrated development and analysis framework. Refinement and abstraction form the basis for an interference analysis method for security properties and for automated test case generation.

1 Motivation

Current software engineering approaches are unlikely to deliver the level of dependability required to construct future distributed, decentralised, and reactive systems such as mobile systems, telecommunications management, communication and process control, or integrated e-business systems. The recent advent of Internet and other intercommunications technologies has made one aspect of properties particularly important: security properties.

We present a notation for the rigorous development and analysis of dependable systems properties. The specification of distributed systems is usually concerned with properties such as reliability or fairness of the communication. In dependable systems with high security requirements other properties are also important. Confidentiality describes that no confidential data is disclosed to unauthorised users. Integrity addresses unauthorised modification. Authentication describes that the identity of participants in a communication can be established. We have dependable systems such as public key infrastructures (PKI) in mind. PKIs are a combination of distributed systems and security technologies, which create an ideal setting to discuss reliability and security issues.

A PKI provides an infrastructure for the management of public keys in cryptographic systems [1]. It deals with entities, protocols and services in those systems. This includes for example services such as the generation, distribution and storage of keys and other secrets. The central concept is that of a certificate. A certificate is a datastructure that associates an identity to a public key by means

L.-H. Eriksson and P. Lindsay (Eds.): FME 2002, LNCS 2391, pp. 330–349, 2002.

of a signature. This concept is used for encryption, signatures and key exchange. The objectives are to guarantee confidentiality, integrity and authentication.

We will analyse some aspects of PKIs, addressing services and protocols based on these services. We will analyse these services and protocols with respect to security issues such as confidentiality, integrity, and authentication. The security analysis is realised as an interference analysis, i.e., it is checked if an intruder can interfere with the system and violate any of the security conditions. The refinement calculus [2,3] forms the framework for the analysis. The analysis is supported by systematic test case generation based on abstraction (abstraction is dual to refinement).

Modal logics, such as temporal or dynamic logics [4,5], have shown their ability to define and reason about important properties of dependable systems, such as safety and liveness, through special modal operators [6,7,8]. Dynamic logic is suitable for the specification of finite aspects, which includes security considerations. Dynamic logic is compositional, i.e., reasoning via structural induction on commands is possible. We will argue that dynamic logic is a suitable tool for security aspects in reactive and distributed systems specification. In combination with a refinement concept it allows the analysis of dependable systems in a novel way. Another advantage of dynamic logic is that it embraces the classical pre/postcondition technique [9], which has become the foundation of various engineering methods and notations such as design-by-contract [10] or the Object Constraint Language OCL [11].

We propose refinement of modal specifications as the central concept for the analysis of dependable systems. The refinement relation can be used to develop systems starting from a simple core, but also to integrate an adversary into the specification in order to detect possible security flaws in a system specification. Refinement essentially guarantees property preservation. Assuming that a property P holds for some specification of a system S, i.e., $P(S)$, we expect a refined specification S' to preserve that property, i.e., $P(S) \Rightarrow P(S')$. Refinement is a classical software engineering technique [2,3] developed to support transformational design and implementation, that has recently been deployed in defining essential concepts for component technology [12,13] and also for interference analysis [14,15]. Here, we will show a novel use of refinement as an analysis tool for detecting undesirable interferences and security violations. The refinement-based approach allows us to combine the traditional transformational development with the unusual applications of interference analyses and test case generation for the context of dependable systems.

We introduce our specification notation in Section 2. In subsections 2.3 and 2.4 we demonstrate the notation by specifying a protocol implementing an authentication service. The principles of refinement and abstraction are introduced in Section 3. An analysis looking at an authentication service is carried out in Section 4 for the protocol described in Section 2.3. Another form of analysis is addressed in Section 5 focussing on confidentiality and integrity in a key establishment and distribution service. We finish with related work and conclusions.

2 The Notation

The actors in communicating distributed systems are agents. Their activities are usually described in terms of the following application-specific basic commands: generate and remember data, establish and close connections, send and receive messages, and guards to protect the execution of operations[1]. In this section, we introduce the notation that we will use to specify and reason about dependability properties. A command language can be based on the constructs listed above. However, we will reduce this language for the sake of simplicity here.

2.1 The Command and Specification Languages

We define the command primitives – *send*, *receive* and a *test*-operator – and the command combinators informally, but we will give axiomatisations later on. This process of configuring the language contributes to a better understanding of the application and its problems. Flexibility in defining basic variations even on this level is important for the analysis of security protocols.

- $snd_{A \to R}(M_1, \ldots, M_n)$: the send operation for agent A. R is the receiver, the M_i denote messages that are sent. The M_i are local variables of the agent. Their value $s(M_i)$ in the current state s is sent to R. The operation fails if there is no variable M_i defined or no communication takes place.
- $rcv_{B \leftarrow S}(M_1, \ldots, M_n)$: the receive operation for agent B. S is sender and the M_i are messages arriving from S. The reception will only be carried out, if data has been sent. The message data is assigned to local variables M_i.
- ϕ?: the test is an operator that involves a quantifier-free formula ϕ. The semantics is to proceed if ϕ is true, and fail otherwise.

We assume that messages are created and assigned to a variable before they are sent. Received messages are assigned to variables, too.

Command combinators are defined inductively. Let c_1, c_2 be command terms:

- $c_1; c_2$ (sequential composition): c_1 is followed by c_2,
- $c_1 + c_2$ (non-deterministic choice): one possibility is chosen and executed,
- c_1^* (iteration): c_1 is iterated a non-deterministically chosen finite number of times,
- $c_1 | c_2$ (parallel composition): c_1 and c_2 are executed concurrently.

The parallel composition differs from the other command combinators in that it is an operator involving two agents composed in parallel, whereas the others can be combinations of commands of one or several agents. A send and a receive operation from two different agents can be synchronised. The two agents communicate by synchronised message passing. On the receiving side, data is assigned to a local name. The following is a parallel composition of two agents:

$$snd_{A \to B}(X); rcv_{A \leftarrow B}(Y) \mid rcv_{B \leftarrow A}(Z); snd_{B \to A}(f(Z))$$

---

[1] Later on, we will also consider cryptographic functionality.

An agent A sends a data item X to B and receives an answer Y from B. The second agent B applies a function f to the received data Z item before sending $f(Z)$ back to A. Agent A receives $f(Z)$ as Y.

The definitions of parallel composition and communication are critical for our analysis. Our semantics allows two agents to communicate, i.e. allows a send and a receive operation to be synchronised, if the types of the in- and out-parameters coincide. Other notations for the specification of communication such as the π-calculus [16] also use dedicated channels between two agents.

Our specification language consists of two sublanguages: a command language to express behaviour and a logical part to specify and reason about properties of command executions. The language is based on dynamic logic [4] – a logic with a notion of state that makes a command language explicit in the notation. Modalities are indexed by programs, which are built from primitive commands such as send and receive. Logical connectors such as conjunction, disjunction or negation are available. There are also mixed operators – the modal operators – combining commands and logical constructs, which make the language different from classical first-order logics. We introduce a box- and a diamond-operator for safety and liveness properties, respectively. Let c be a command.

- $[c]\phi$: whenever c terminates, it must do so in a state satisfying ϕ.
- $\langle c \rangle \phi$: it is possible to execute c and terminate in a state satisfying ϕ.

If c is a simple state transition, e.g. a receive operation, then $\phi \to [c]\ \psi$ and $\phi \to \langle c \rangle\ \psi$ are *contracts* for c with a precondition ϕ and a postcondition ψ^2. If $c \equiv snd_{A \to B}(x)|rcv_{B \leftarrow A}(y)$ is an interaction, then $\phi_x \to [snd_{A \to B}(x)|rcv_{B \leftarrow A}(y)]\ \psi_y$ is a contract for the interaction saying that properties ϕ_x of an output variable x are transferred to ψ_y of an input variable y if the interaction takes place.

We can, for example, specify that an agent B remembers a message X that has been received from A, but an intruder I should not be able to access X,

$$Knows_A(X) \to [snd_{A \to B}(X)\ |\ rcv_{B \leftarrow A}(X)]\ Knows_B(X) \land \neg Knows_I(X)$$

using a predicate $Knows$. We might expect from a key exchange service – the parallel execution of agents A and B – that a shared key is eventually in place. $Knows(key)$ is an invariant for the sender of key.

$$\langle A|B \rangle\ Knows_A(key) \land Knows_B(key)$$

2.2   The Inference Framework

Formulas of our logical language are based on predicates. The equality predicate $t = t'$ is satisfied in a state of a semantic structure if the interpretations of terms t and t' are equal. Let M be a semantic structure and s be a state. A satisfaction $\models$ for the modalities can be defined as follows:

---

[2] The symbol $\to$ stands for implication.

$$M, s \models [p]\phi \quad \text{iff} \quad \text{every terminating computation of } p \text{ starting in } s$$
$$\text{terminates in a state satisfying } \phi \tag{1}$$
$$M, s \models \langle p\rangle\phi \quad \text{iff} \quad \text{exists a computation of } p \text{ starting in state } s$$
$$\text{and terminating in a state that satisfies } \phi$$

We could also define one of the constructors in terms of the other: $\langle p\rangle\phi := \neg[p]\neg\phi$ (or vice versa). With x' we denote the variable x in the previous state of a command execution. This allows us to specify for example increment operations $[incr(x)]\, x = x'+1$. In order to support the formal analysis of specified behaviour, the operations – such as send and receive – shall be axiomatised in terms of the given predicates, e.g., receive $rcv_{A\leftarrow B}$ for a given agent A:

$$[rcv_{A\leftarrow B}(X)]\, Knows_A(X) \tag{2}$$

After receiving the message X from B, the agent A remembers (knows about) X. An axiomatisation can be varied if the given application requires this. These axioms express a developer's assumptions about the environment explicitly.

We can axiomatise the commands combinators:

$$\langle c_1 + c_2\rangle\phi \Leftrightarrow \langle c_1\rangle\phi \vee \langle c_2\rangle\phi \tag{3}$$
$$\langle c_1; c_2\rangle\phi \Leftrightarrow \langle c_1\rangle\langle c_2\rangle\phi \tag{4}$$

There are also dual formulations for the box-operator: $[c_1 + c_2]\phi \Leftrightarrow [c_1]\phi \wedge [c_2]\phi$ and $[c_1; c_2]\phi \Leftrightarrow [c_1][c_2]\phi$. In the literature (e.g. [4]), we typically find axiomatisations of the test-operator such as $\langle\phi?\rangle\psi \Leftrightarrow \phi \wedge \psi$ and $[\phi?]\psi \Leftrightarrow (\phi \rightarrow \psi)$. Due to our non-standard definition of the test-operator, these equivalences do not hold here. There is no simple axiomatisation for the iteration t^*; see [4] for axioms.

The parallel composition $p|q$ of commands p and q of agents A and B, resp., makes our framework different from dynamic logic as presented in [4]. The semantics of $c_1|c_2$ is defined as a pair of component semantics $([\![c_1]\!]_A, [\![c_2]\!]_B)$ if $[\![c_1]\!]_A$ and $[\![c_2]\!]_B$ are the semantics of c_1 and c_2. The following axioms hold:

$$[c_1|c_2]\phi \Leftrightarrow [c_1]\phi \wedge [c_2]\phi \tag{5}$$
$$\langle c_1|c_2\rangle\phi \Leftrightarrow \langle c_1\rangle\phi \vee \langle c_2\rangle\phi \tag{6}$$

This corresponds to the axioms for the non-deterministic choice (3), except that a choice between two commands is interpreted in one structure, whereas the parallel composition is interpreted in two.

2.3   The Needham-Schroeder Protocol Specification

Public key infrastructures provide services such as key generation and distribution, or authentication. A number of these services are implemented by protocols. The Needham-Schroeder protocol is a possible way to implement key exchange and authentication [17]. It allows to bring a shared secret in place, assuming that an encryption mechanism is already in place.

The Needham-Schroeder key exchange protocol is usually introduced using the following informal notation:

$$A \to B : \{A, N_a\}_{K_b}$$
$$B \to A : \{N_a, N_b\}_{K_a}$$
$$A \to B : \{N_b\}_{K_b}$$

Two agents, A and B, attempt to share a secret. A starts by sending its own identity and a randomly chosen number N_a (called a nonce – number used once) to B. A uses B's public encryption key K_b to encrypt the message. B decrypts the message with its own private decryption key and sends the number sent by A, N_a, together with another nonce N_b (created by B itself) back to A – again using encryption, but now A's public key K_a. Since A has used B's public key, only B can decrypt the message. If A receives its nonce N_a, it can be sure that it has communicated with B. In order to allow B to also verify the authenticity of A, A sends the nonce N_b produced by B back to B. Two results should be achieved: authenticity of the participants and confidentiality of the nonces.

We reformulate the informal protocol specification using our command language, before specifying properties. The specification shall be divided into activities of agent A and agent B. Agent A acts as follows:

$$snd_{A \to B}(A, N_a); rcv_{A \leftarrow B}(N_a, N_b); snd_{A \to B}(N_b) \tag{7}$$

A sends a message to B, receives one from B, and sends a second message. The data items received are stored in variables. Here is B's behaviour:

$$rcv_{B \leftarrow A}(A, N_a); snd_{B \to A}(N_a, N_b); rcv_{B \leftarrow A}(N_b) \tag{8}$$

The authenticity of the agents A and B and the confidentiality the nonces is not guaranteed here. Encryption – to be added later – will achieve this.

2.4   Properties of the Needham-Schroeder Protocol

A dynamic logic specification consists of command terms and properties that specify the commands in their behaviour. We can classify security properties into authentication: authenticity of agents is guaranteed, confidentiality: secret data remains secret, and integrity: data remains intact. We use different forms of constraints to address them:

– Firstly, an *access control constraint* describes that a data item is accessible for the receiver, e.g., that data actually arrives if it is sent. This allows us to deal with confidentiality and integrity.
– An *authentication constraint* describes that after a sequence of message exchanges one agent is sure about the identity of another agent. This requires the use of cryptographic methods.
– The *correctness constraint* is a data-specific consistency condition, e.g., that data, which has been sent, satisfies a certain condition.

Later, we add cryptographic constraints. If a message has been encrypted with a public key, then the message can only be decrypted with the corresponding private key. Authentication and confidentiality can be achieved using cryptographic methods, but, still, an intruder attack can violate all these properties.

The receive-operation of agent A in the Needham-Schroeder protocol shall be specified by the following *access control constraint*:

$$[rcv_{A\leftarrow B}(N_a, N_b)] \; Knows_A(N_a, N_b) \tag{9}$$

After receiving data, A remembers the information, i.e., stores it locally in variables N_a and N_b, expressed using the predicate *Knows*. Agent B receives two messages. Each reception is remembered in the corresponding variables:

$$[rcv_{B\leftarrow A}(A, N_a)] \; Knows_B(A, N_a) \tag{10}$$
$$[rcv_{B\leftarrow A}(N_b)] \; Knows_B(N_b) \tag{11}$$

Previous assignments are overwritten, otherwise older assignments are remembered. After discussing single protocol steps, we address the full behaviour of a single agent. After finishing their execution sequences both agents shall share a secret, or at least the same two values[3]. Here are agent A (12) and B (13):

$$[snd_{A\rightarrow B}(A, N_a); rcv_{A\leftarrow B}(N_a, N_b); snd_{A\rightarrow B}(N_b)] \; Knows_A(N_a, N_b) \tag{12}$$
$$[rcv_{B\leftarrow A}(A, N_a); snd_{B\rightarrow A}(N_a, N_b); rcv_{B\leftarrow A}(N_b)] \; Knows_B(N_a, N_b) \tag{13}$$

An agent A *authenticates* another agent B, if A sends a random number N_a to B encrypted with B's public key. If A receives N_a' back from B and $N_a = N_a'$, then A can be sure that only B – the owner of the public key K_B – could have decrypted $K_B(N_a)$ and sent N_a back. We expect

$$[snd_{A\rightarrow B}(K_B(N_A)); rcv_{A\leftarrow B}(K_A(N_A'))] \; N_A = N_A' \tag{14}$$

for the authentication. We define the authentication predicate $Auth_A(B)$ for agent A and a target agent B to become true in that case.

Data sent or received is subjected to constraints in some cases. The first send-operation of agent A is not restricted with respect to a *correctness constraint*,

$$[snd_{A\rightarrow B}(A, N_a)] \; true \tag{15}$$

but A should receive its nonce N_a back from B, i.e., the received value in N_a is the same as the value in the previous state N_a':

$$[rcv_{A\leftarrow B}(N_a, N_b)] \; N_a = N_a' \tag{16}$$

A should only proceed if this is satisfied – expressed using a precondition:

$$N_a = N_a' \rightarrow [snd_{A\rightarrow B}(N_b)] \; true \tag{17}$$

---

[3] The fact that B also remembers the identity of A – see (10) – is not relevant at this stage and therefore neglected.

The first value that A receives must coincide with its own nonce N_a. Similar constraints can be imposed on agent B, e.g., on the second receive operation: $[rcv_{B \leftarrow A}(N_b)] \ N_b = N'_b$.

Access control, authentication, and correctness form different views on the problem – e.g., the accessibility formula $[rcv_{A \leftarrow B}(N_a, N_b)] \ Knows_A(N_a, N_b)$ and the correctness condition $rcv_{A \leftarrow B}(N_a, N_b)] \ N_a = N'_a$ can be combined to the formula $[rcv_{A \leftarrow B}(N_a, N_b)] \ Knows_A(N_a, N_b) \wedge N_a = N'_a$ using inference rules of the logic, see Section 2.2.

3 Refinement and Abstraction

The two main concepts for our interference analysis shall now be introduced. Traditionally, refinement is used to develop a specification step by step. Refinement also serves another purpose in our approach. Security analysis – intruder integration and interference analysis – can also be supported. We use the concept of abstraction – the dual of refinement – to test for interferences. We will briefly show how to add encryption to a simplified protocol specification in order to illustrate the transformational development approach based on refinement. The concepts for interference analysis and testing will be applied in Section 4.

3.1 Refinement

The refinement relation is essentially defined based on implication. A specification is a refinement of another if it implies it, i.e., if the refinement preserves the properties of the original specification. Let ϕ and ψ be formulas: ϕ refines ψ iff $\phi \to \psi$. For commands p and q specified by $\phi \to [c] \ \phi'$ and $\psi \to [c'] \ \psi'$ we define – based on the monotonicity of $[\ . \ ]$, see [4] Th. 4(2) – for the box-operator:

$$c \text{ is refined by } c' \text{, or } c \sqsubseteq c' \text{, iff } \phi \to \psi \wedge \psi' \to \phi' \qquad (18)$$

We have chosen to define a sufficient and necessary condition. An intruder cannot be introduced (using refinement – see Section 4) that violates the refinement, but does not affect the security conditions of the original specification. A violation of a refinement should only occur if security specifications are violated.

We do not constrain the commands c and c' in any way. This allows a single command to be refined by a sequence of commands. We could also insert commands into a sequence of commands without violating the refinement condition. The refinement of commands is here defined on properties of the state that is reached through command execution. More support for a refinement calculus can be based on an inference system for dynamic logic, see [4].

To add encryption to the protocol specification from Section 2.3 using refinement, we define two new functions for encryption and decryption and axiomatise their behaviour. The particular encryption method (RSA, Merkle-Hellman, etc. [18]) shall not matter. We assume that the encryption scheme is secure, i.e., that there are no principal problems such as mathematical flaws. We assume a public key encryption scheme. K_A is A's (public) encryption key and K_A^{-1} is its (private) decryption key (analogously for B). $K_A(X)$ is the encryption operation and $K_A^{-1}(Y)$ the decryption operation[4]. The cryptographic law is:

$$K_A^{-1}(K_A(X)) \; = \; X \qquad (19)$$

In order to fully specify cryptographic basics, we would need to express that not only can the original message be recovered with the corresponding private key, but also that no other key except the corresponding private key can decrypt the message. For the sake of simplicity, we have left out properties like this.

Each agent shall know the public keys of the agents it wants to communicate with securely. In our case, for two agents A and B, the predicates $Knows_A(K_B)$ for A and $Knows_B(K_A)$ for B are true. The specification of agent B, who receives encrypted data from A, now looks as follows:

$$[rcv_{A \leftarrow B}(X, Y)] \; Knows_B(K_B^{-1}(X, Y)) \qquad (20)$$

B tries to decrypt the received pair of two data items X and Y. B should only proceed if the decryption is successful, i.e., results in $K_B^{-1}(X, Y) = (A, N_a)$.

$$[(K_B^{-1}(X, Y) = (A, N_a))?; snd_{B \rightarrow A}(K_A(N_a, N_b))] \; true \qquad (21)$$

Composed in parallel, A and B can communicate – the send and receive operation are synchronised and data is transferred from A to B. After applying the axioms (5) and $true \wedge \phi \Leftrightarrow \phi$ to (15) and (10), the simplified specification

$$[snd_{A \rightarrow B}(A, N_a) \mid rcv_{B \leftarrow A}(A, N_a)] \; Knows_B(A, N_a) \qquad (22)$$

can be refined by

$$[snd_{A \rightarrow B}(K_B(A, N_a)) \mid rcv_{B \leftarrow A}(K_B(A, N_a))] \; Knows_B(K_B^{-1}(K_B(A, N_a))) \qquad (23)$$

With the assumption that a cryptosystem is in place, we get $Knows_B(A, N_a) = Knows_B(K_B^{-1}(K_B(A, N_a)))$ by applying the cryptographic law (19). Thus, the refinement relation is satisfied. We have proved that properties from the original specification (22) are actually preserved by (23).

3.2 Abstraction and Testing

The parallel composition of agents is the essential combinator for our interference analysis. We can automate the analysis by testing the composition of sequential agent behaviours. Each sequential agent behaviour – called a scenario – is a test case for a non-sequential, non-deterministic agent specification. Agents of our ideal protocol have been defined in a sequential deterministic way, but we

---

[4] This notation is not sufficient for cryptographic techniques such as signatures. To keep the notation simple for the given protocol form, we have used this simple form.

assume a non-deterministic behaviour for the intruder. These scenarios shall be
constrained by the abstraction $Spec \sqsupseteq Scen$, i.e., the system specification $Spec$
is abstracted by the scenario $Scen$, or, the specification refines the scenario. We
will systematically try to find intruder scenarios that – in composition with the
protocol agents – violate the refinement relation.

The basic principle of test case generation in the context of the refinement
calculus is that test cases abstract contracts[5]. The *abstraction* is dual to the
refinement relation. c abstracts c' – or c' is abstracted by c – if c' refines c:

$$c' \sqsupseteq c \ := \ c \sqsubseteq c' \wedge c \neq false$$

for any two commands c and c'. $false$ is the trivial abstraction, which should be
excluded. Specifications can involve sequential, iterative and non-deterministic
behaviour. For an intruder, we cannot assume sequential or deterministic behaviour, but we will test the system using various sequential intruder scenarios.

The first step shall be to define a simple input/output test case for a command. A *test case TC_c* for a command c is defined by:

$$TC_c(\alpha, \beta) \ := \ \alpha \to [c] \ \beta$$

α and β are conditions describing input and output values. The following proposition states when a pair of conditions α and β is a suitable test case for a
command, i.e., when it abstracts a command c specified by $\phi \to [c] \ \psi$.

$$c \sqsupseteq TC_c(\alpha, \beta) \ \Leftrightarrow \ (\alpha \to \phi) \wedge (\alpha \wedge \psi) \to \beta \qquad (24)$$

An example shall illustrate this proposition. We assume the following definitions
for the conditions α, β, ϕ and ψ: $\phi \equiv x \geq 0$, $\psi \equiv y = x + 1$, $\alpha \equiv x = 1$, and $\beta \equiv$
$y = 2$. Then, the two constraints formulated in the proposition are satisfied and
we have a proper test case: the condition $\alpha \to \phi$ is satisfied since $x = 1 \to x \geq 0$,
and the condition $(\alpha \wedge \psi) \to \beta$ is satisfied since $(x = 1 \wedge y = x + 1) \to y = 2$.

In order to deal with interaction between agents of a protocol, we expand
our notion of test cases to interactions between two agents.

$$TC_{c_1|c_2}(\alpha_x, \beta_y) := \alpha_x \to [\overline{c_1}\langle x\rangle | c_2(y)] \ \beta_y$$

where α_x and β_y are properties of x and y, respectively. Properties of x are
transferred to y if the interaction takes place. A test case for parallel compositions
requires x and y to have the same type.

$$c_1|c_2 \sqsupseteq TC_{c_1|c_2}(\alpha_x, \beta_y) \ \Leftrightarrow \ \alpha_x \to \beta_y \qquad (25)$$

The key construct to test concurrent non-deterministic agents is a scenario, i.e.,
a sequence of basic commands or interactions of basic commands. We define
a *scenario S* for a specification as a sequence $(c_1; \ldots; c_n)$ of basic commands

---

[5] Most of the concepts here are motivated by [19], but formulated in a different semantical framework and extended to parallel composition.

or interactions of basic commands. We assume an iterative non-deterministic choice to be the basic format of an intruder specification, see also (31). Scenarios abstract iterative choices $(c_1 + \ldots + c_n)^*$ if the scenario itself is executable, i.e., if the last state of the sequence can be reached.

Let c_i be specified by $\phi_i \rightarrow [c_i] \, \psi_i$ and assume $\psi_{i_k} \neq false$ (the last state should be reachable). Then

$$(c_1 + \ldots + c_n)^* \sqsupseteq (c_{i_1}; \ldots; c_{i_k}) \quad \text{if} \quad \psi_{i_j} \rightarrow \phi_{i_{j+1}} \tag{26}$$

with $1 \leq i_j \leq n$ $(j = 1, .., k)$ and $\phi_{i_j} \rightarrow [c_{i_j}] \, \psi_{i_j}$ and $\phi_{i_{j+1}}$ being the precondition of the $(j + 1)$-th element in the scenario sequence.

The next two propositions are corollaries based on the last proposition. They essentially state how to construct scenarios for specifications. The first one shows conditions that makes a basic scenario a test case for an iterative choice. Let $p \wedge \phi_i \rightarrow [c_i] \, \psi_i$ and $\phi_j \rightarrow [c_j] \, \psi_j$. If $p \neq false$ and $\psi_i \rightarrow \phi_j$ then

$$(c_1 + \ldots + c_n)^* \sqsupseteq (c_i; c_j) \tag{27}$$

for $i, j \in 1, .., n$. The next corollary shows how to combine basic scenarios into more complex ones. Let $c_a \wedge \phi_a \rightarrow [c_a] \, \psi_a$, $a \in \{i, j, k\}$. If $(c_1 + \ldots + c_n)^* \sqsupseteq c_i; c_j$ and $(c_1 + \ldots + c_n)^* \sqsupseteq c_j; c_k$ and $c_i \neq false$ and $\psi_i \rightarrow c_i \wedge \phi_j$ and $c_i \neq false$ and $\psi_i \rightarrow c_j \wedge \phi_j$ then

$$(c_1 + \ldots + c_n)^* \sqsupseteq (c_i; c_j; c_k) \tag{28}$$

4 Authentication Analysis

A central PKI service is authentication support through certificates. Therefore, our first analysis addresses a protocol implementing an authentication service.

Security analysis is mostly concerned with safety properties, i.e., something (bad) must never happen (e.g., that the intruder knows a secret – at any time), whereas the development of protocols is more involved with liveness properties, i.e., that something (good) will happen eventually (data arrives, keys are eventually in place). Our dynamic logic provides constructs for both aspects.

We will base our analysis on an accepted and successful methodology – used by most analysis techniques [8,20,21]: formal specification of the ideal behaviour, add the intruder or possible interfering features, state the properties to be guaranteed/analysed, analyse the ideal specification, and vary parameters and analyse again. This justifies to use refinement to add the adversary or new features, but also to vary parameters through repeated use of refinement.

4.1 The Protocol

The full specification of the desired behaviour of the Needham-Schroeder protocol with respect to *authentication* based on the specifications of A and B in isolation, (12) and (13), is:

$$[snd_{A \rightarrow B}(K_B(A, N_a)); rcv_{A \leftarrow B}(K_A(N_a, N_b)); snd_{A \rightarrow B}(K_B(N_b)) \mid$$
$$rcv_{B \leftarrow A}(K_B(A, N_a)); snd_{B \rightarrow A}(K_A(N_a, N_b)); rcv_{B \leftarrow A}(K_B(N_b))]$$
$$Auth_A(B) \wedge Auth_B(A) \tag{29}$$

This is the *ideal* protocol. Any intruder behaviour will be analysed against this specification. The agents themselves behave deterministically, thus we have used the box operator. When the intruder I is integrated, behaviour becomes non-deterministic. The intruder might intercept at any time. Still, we would like to guarantee that A and B eventually authenticate each other, even under interference by an intruder:

$$\langle A|B|I \rangle \; Auth_A(B) \wedge Auth_B(A) \tag{30}$$

We want to prevent that an intruder can interfere with the authentication between A and B. A mutual authentication between A and B shall be achieved. This is an adaptation of Goguen and Meseguer's classical non-interference definition. Here, an intruder does not interfere with another group of agents, if the excution of intruder commands has no effect on the agent's security properties.

4.2 The Adversary

We assume intruders to have capabilities as formulated in the Dolev-Yao model [22]. The Dolev-Yao model is an accepted collection of assumptions about possible intruder behaviour. The intruder can read any message, block further transmission, decompose messages, remember messages, generate fresh data, and compose and send new messages[6]. In principle, the intruder can non-deterministically choose between these operations. The general difficulty with these analyses is to make the right assumptions about the intruder (or about new features in feature interaction analysis) in order to detect possible interferences. This problem can only be solved by the developer or analyser, but the specification and analysis technique should provide the possibility to vary assumptions explicitly.

The mechanism for an intruder to attack a protocol is to intercept the communication between the agents participating in the protocol. This can be modelled by allowing the intruder to be executed in parallel with the agents. Then, the intruder I can communicate with the agents A and B, receiving and sending messages. Let $A := snd_{A \to B}(y)$, $B := rcv_{B \leftarrow A}(y)$ and $I := rcv_{I \leftarrow A}(y); snd_{I \to B}(f(y))$. The parallel composition of A, B and intruder I, $A|B|I$, can result in one of the following executions based on synchronisations of non-deterministically chosen send- and receive-operations. A and B can communicate directly by transferring data from A to B, or A communicates first with I and then I communicates with B sending manipulated data $f(y)$ to B. The first is the desired case, the second is a successful intrusion, or interference, using a man-in-the-middle attack.

Reducing the capabilities of the intruder to two operations here, the general behaviour of an intruder is:

$$(snd_{I \to X}(M_1, \ldots, M_n) + rcv_{I \leftarrow Y}(M_1, \ldots, M_m))^* \tag{31}$$

The intruder chooses repeatedly and non-deterministically between sending and receiving – we cannot make many assumptions about an intruder's behaviour. We assume that the intruder does not block communication between A and B.

---

[6] This does not include the intruder's encryption capabilities.

4.3 The Analysis

In a concrete example, the intruder may execute the following command sequence

$$rcv_{I \leftarrow A}(K_I(A, N_a)); snd_{I \rightarrow B}(K_B(A, N_a));$$
$$rcv_{I \leftarrow B}(K_A(N_a, N_b)); snd_{I \rightarrow A}(K_A(N_a, N_b)) \tag{32}$$

which satisfies (31). The intruder intercepts the communication between A and B. At the beginning, the intruder has to convince A to communicate with him instead of B, i.e., A needs to send data to him and to use his public encryption key. The intruder then forwards this to B imposturing as A, and B's answer to A is again intercepted and forwarded to A. A and B might not suspect an intrusion. In this scenario, A authenticates I, since A uses I's public key and receives N_A back. B authenticates A since N_B encrypted with A's public key is returned. This is where the protocol fails to work securelyfootnoteThis attack has originally been described in [23]..

The intruder can be integrated via refinement. The ideal protocol specification, which specifies the expected secure behaviour, should be preserved. The inclusion of a successful intruder would violate the ideal specification, i.e., would not refine the ideal protocol specification. For instance, the confidentiality constraint could be violated by the intruder behaviour. Refinement is the tool to analyse, i.e., to prove or disprove, the security of a protocol. We would hope to prove that all possible extensions by intruder behaviours are refinements that preserve the properties specified for the protocol. Then, the protocol is secure.

The essential properties have already been discussed. Eventually the agents A and B have authenticated each other: $Auth_A(B) \wedge Auth_B(A)$. Including the intruder I as specified above in formula (32) will satisfy

$$\langle A|B|I \rangle \ Auth_A(I) \wedge Auth_B(A) \tag{33}$$

since the intruder intercepts the communication and is able to imposture as A for B, but this clearly violates the protocol specification (30) – $\langle A|B|I \rangle \ Auth_A(B) \wedge Auth_B(A)$ – which requires that A and B mutually authenticate each other. Seen as a refinement step, we get a violation of the constraint: the predicate $Auth_A(I)$ does obviously not imply $Auth_A(B)$. Besides being used for the stepwise development, refinement is also a tool for analysis – even though our aim now is to violate the refinement constraint in order to detect security flaws.

4.4 Testing

The testing concepts shall now be applied to the authentication analysis of the Needham-Schroeder protocol. Firstly, we would need to summarise the contracts of the basic commands such as $[snd_{A \rightarrow B}(K_B(N_A));$ $rcv_{A \leftarrow B}(K_A(N_A))] \ Auth_A(B)$ or $[snd_{A \rightarrow B}(A, N_a)] \ true$. Then, we list the possible interactions between the two agents of the ideal protocol in (34) and also some of the possible interactions between the two agents and the intruder for the extended protocol in (35).

$$\iota_1 := snd_{A \to B}(A, N_a) \mid rcv_{B \leftarrow A}(A, N_a)$$
$$\iota_2 := rcv_{A \leftarrow B}(N_a, N_b) \mid snd_{B \to A}(N_a, N_b) \qquad (34)$$
$$\iota_3 := \quad snd_{A \to B}(N_b) \mid rcv_{B \leftarrow A}(N_b)$$

A variety of interactions is possible if the non-deterministic intruder is included. A few of them are:

$$\iota_4 := snd_{A \to B}(A, N_a) \mid rcv_{I \leftarrow A}(A, N_a)$$
$$\iota_5 := \quad snd_{I \to B}(I, N_a) \mid rcv_{B \leftarrow I}(I, N_a)$$
$$\iota_6 := rcv_{I \leftarrow B}(N_a, N_b) \mid snd_{B \to I}(N_a, N_b)$$
$$\iota_7 := rcv_{A \leftarrow I}(N_a, N_b) \mid snd_{I \to A}(N_a, N_b) \qquad (35)$$
$$\iota_8 := \quad snd_{A \to B}(N_b) \mid rcv_{I \leftarrow A}(N_b)$$
$$\iota_9 := \quad snd_{I \to B}(N_b) \mid rcv_{B \leftarrow I}(N_b)$$

The interactions $\iota_4, \ldots, \iota_9$ describe a successful intrusion that leads to the described authentication problem – see (32) in Section 4.3. Interactions are the basis of the scenario generation. Interactions are sequentially composed to simple scenarios in the first step. Simple two-element scenarios are $(\iota_4; \iota_5)$, $(\iota_5; \iota_6)$, ..., $(\iota_8; \iota_9)$. These simple scenarios are derived using proposition (27). The simple scenarios are combined to full scenarios based on proposition (28), e.g.,

$$\sigma(\iota_4) := \iota_4$$
$$\sigma(\iota_5) := \iota_4; \iota_5 \qquad (36)$$
$$\sigma(\iota_6) := \iota_4; \iota_5; \iota_6$$

Finally, we can show that the scenario $\sigma(\iota_9) := \iota_4; \ldots; \iota_9$ is an abstraction of the protocol including the intruder.

$$A|B|I \sqsupseteq \iota_4; \ldots; \iota_9 \qquad (37)$$

We can derive the intruder behaviour for this scenario by projecting onto the intruder in the overall sequence of interactions. This sequence is clearly an abstraction of the general intruder behaviour:

$$(snd_{I \to X}(M_1) + rcv_{I \leftarrow Y}(M_2))^* \sqsupseteq$$
$$rcv_{I \leftarrow A}(A, N_a); snd_{I \to B}(I, N_a); rcv_{I \leftarrow B}(N_a, N_b); \qquad (38)$$
$$snd_{I \to A}(N_a, N_b); rcv_{I \leftarrow A}(N_b); snd_{I \to B}(N_b)$$

The inclusion of the intruder does not satisfy the constraint that A and B mutually authenticate each other, see (30). A security flaw is detected.

5   Confidentiality and Integrity Analysis

Besides authentication support, a PKI also provides services concerned with the secure distribution of keys and other secrets. In order to show the versatility of our method, we shall look at confidentiality and integrity issues relating to a key establishment service based on a simplified Diffie-Hellman protocol [18].

5.1   The Protocol

The protocol assumes a common number g. The names a and b denote random values generated by A and B, respectively.

$$snd_{A \to B}(g^a); rcv_{A \leftarrow B}(g^b) \tag{39}$$

A sends g^a to B, and receives g^b from B. Here is B:

$$rcv_{B \leftarrow A}(g^a); snd_{B \to A}(g^b) \tag{40}$$

Here are the access control properties concerning A and B:

$$\begin{array}{l} [snd_{A \to B}(g^a); rcv_{A \leftarrow B}(g^b)] \; Knows_A(a,b) \\ [rcv_{B \leftarrow A}(g^a); snd_{B \to A}(g^b)] \; Knows_B(a,b) \end{array} \tag{41}$$

Thus, we get for the ideal protocol – the parallel composition:

$$\begin{array}{c} [snd_{A \to B}(g^a); rcv_{A \leftarrow B}(g^b) \mid rcv_{B \leftarrow A}(g^a); snd_{B \to A}(g^b)] \\ Knows_A(a,b) \wedge Knows_B(a,b) \end{array} \tag{42}$$

Two values are exchanged. A knows value b of B, and B knows value a of A. This is the full specification of the desired behaviour – the protocol without intruder – based on the specifications of A and B in isolation, (41). Including intruder I

$$[A|B|I] \; \neg Knows_I(a,b) \tag{43}$$

we would not like I to interfere, but would like to achieve

$$\langle A|B|I \rangle \; Knows_A(a,b) \wedge Knows_B(a,b) . \tag{44}$$

We want to prevent that an intruder will ever get hold on the secret (a safety condition) and that A and B will eventually share a secret (a liveness condition).

5.2   The Adversary

We reduce the capabilities of the intruder to the send- and receive-operations: $(snd_{I \to X}(M_1, \ldots, M_n) + rcv_{I \leftarrow Y}(M_1, \ldots, M_m))^*$. The intruder may proceed as specified by the following command sequence:

$$rcv_{I \leftarrow A}(g^a); snd_{I \to B}(g^a); rcv_{I \leftarrow B}(g^b); snd_{I \to A}(g^b) \tag{45}$$

The intruder intercepts the communication between A and B. He will know about the secret shared between A and B – the values g^a and g^b – and he will even about a and b if he knows g or can infer it.

5.3   The Analysis

The intruder is again integrated via refinement. A successful intruder inclusion would violate the security conditions of the ideal specification, i.e., would not refine the ideal protocol specification. We hope that eventually secrets a and b are in place and nobody else knows about them, i.e., $Knows_A(a, b) \wedge Knows_B(a, b)$ and $\neg Knows_I(a, b)$ for any other agent I. Including the intruder I as specified above in formula (45) and assuming that I can infer g will satisfy

$$[A|B|I] \; Knows_I(a, b) \tag{46}$$

since the intruder intercepts the communication and has access to g^a and g^b and can calculate a and b from them, but it also violates the specification $[A|B|I] \; \neg Knows_I(a, b)$, see (43). Assuming that I knows g, we get again a violation of the refinement constraint: $Knows_I(a, b)$ does not imply $\neg Knows_I(a, b)$.

6   Related Work

Most approaches to security systems analysis are essentially adaptations of general frameworks to the security context. Durgin and Mitchell [8] use conventional logics and analysis methods to analyse security protocols. Their specification approach is based on multisets of first-order formulas (called facts). A rewriting technique is used to develop and analyse specifications. State are described by multisets of facts. State transitions are given by rules, essentially relations on multisets of facts. This treatment of states and state transitions is the essential difference between their approach and our framework. We believe that a formal specification framework closer to techniques such as pre/postconditions and refinement is more suitable for a general approach to dependable systems engineering. Common characteristics include the aim to reduce implicit assumptions and to make them explicit, and the use of the explicit intruder method.

The spi-calculus [20] is based on the π-calculus and includes additional cryptographic primitives. Process calculi such as the π-calculus are suitable to model and develop infrastructures for distributed and mobile systems. The key difference to our approach is that the intruder behaviour is not modelled explicitly in the spi-calculus. Security properties of process definitions such as confidentiality (secrecy) and authentication (essentially integrity) are expressed via equivalences to a process specification. Consider the following example. Two processes shall be defined: a process A sending a message M on channel c_{AB} and a process $B := c_{AB}(x).F(x)$ receiving on c_{AB} and then processing the input x. The protocol is the parallel composition of A and B, i.e., $P = \nu c_{AB}.A(M)|B$ with a channel c_{AB} restricted to A and B. We expect B to process M internally, which can be expressed by $B_{spec} := c_{AB}(x).F(M)$. The overall protocol specification is $P_{spec} := \nu c_{AB}.A(M)|B_{spec}$.

- Secrecy: if $F(M) \simeq F(M')$ then $P(M) \simeq P(M')$ for all M, M'. Whatever the message is, an observer cannot distinguish between messages. If B does not leak M within F, then the protocol should not leak M in order to guarantee secrecy.

– Authentication (integrity): $P(M) \simeq P_{spec}(M)$ for all M. The protocol P should behave (under observation) like its specification P_{spec}, i.e., if M is sent, then M arrives unchanged and is processed subsequently.

The equivalence $\simeq$ is testing equivalence. It formalises the idea of observation (by an intruder). Compared to our approach, the spi-calculus is more abstract. It assumes restricted channels to be secure. Our approach does not make this assumption. We offer the possibility of more fine-granular and explicit analyses.

Paulson's Inductive Method [21] uses induction over protocol traces (a trace is a list of events that occur in some run of a protocol). Paulson introduces a specialised notation for security protocols. Standard operators to construct, deconstruct and remember messages are used in the specification of traces. The overall set of traces describing a protocol is defined inductively. Focardi, Ghelli and Gorrieri [24] apply a non-interference approach for the analysis of the Needham-Schroeder protocol. To keep our approach suitable for all forms of dependability aspects and integrated development and analysis, we have included security-specific aspects into a general-purpose framework, providing flexibility and configurability by combining different command features.

Butler [25] describes an approach to security systems analysis similar to ours. Butler bases his framework on a combination of the abstract machine notation AMN (the B method) and CSP. He also uses refinement to introduce the intruder. The correctness of an abstraction invariant AI needs to be checked: $S \sqsubseteq_{AI} T$ if $AI \Rightarrow [T]\langle S \rangle AI$. Butler's approach is based on iterative refinement, i.e., an initial abstraction might need to be strengthened iteratively until suitable. Butler's and our approach are similar in that both use an explicit intruder model and use refinement to introduce encryption and the intruder. Both provide safety and liveness operators and make parallel composition available. The key difference is that Butler's approach is based on data refinement with explicit state, whereas we use an implicit, observation-based notion of state, which creates a more abstract framework. We think that developing our refinements results into refinement laws giving templates for e.g. confidentiality-preserving refinements is a more suitable way. The combination of CSP and FDR, a model checking tool, has been been very fruitful for security analyses, e.g., to detect Lowe's attack [23]. This work has been carried further; [26] is a recent example. However, a proof-theoretic approach can give more insight into why a protocol works or fails than model checking.

We see refinement as an interference analysis tool, not restricted to security analysis, but also suitable for other forms of interference detection. Feature interaction in telephony systems poses a similar problem [14,15]. If a new feature has to be added to an existing system, the main question is whether there are unexpected or undesirable interferences with existing features. Refinement can answer this question. The principle of our analysis method – state the ideal properties, add new behaviour, and analyse possible interferences – is not limited to security analysis. In [15], an investigation into common simple telephone systems and advanced features such as call waiting and call forwarding is carried out. Certain properties (invariants) are proven for the specification of the basic system. A refined specification including advanced features needs to preserve the properties. There is an interference, if this is not possible. Feature interaction is defined as the violation of proof obligations in a refinement.

Our work is based on testing approaches developed in [27,28,29,19]. We have in particular based parts of our test case generation on ideas developed by Aichernig in [19]. He presented his work in a general purpose context, with semantics based on weakest preconditions – essentially based on [3]. We have improved this semantic framework towards a more flexible and expressive modal logic framework. Additionally, we have provided an improved, process-algebra style command language including an explicit parallel composition.

7 Conclusions

Our approach to integrated development and analysis of dependable systems is based on a refinement mechanism for both purposes. Using refinement as an analysis tool is not restricted to security analyses where various intruder behaviours can be analysed. The analysis of any kind of interference such as feature interaction can be carried out. An essential technique for the analysis of interferences is to vary the behaviour. Elements have to be added or removed in a flexible way. We have provided two ways to control this flexibility: firstly, by using refinement to add new elements while preserving properties, and, secondly, by providing a framework where the command language for the communication primitives itself is not fixed, but can be influenced through the introduction and axiomatisation of new commands (or variants of existing ones). This flexibility in reflecting different assumptions about the underlying technology and the intruder is crucial. Another key element is the compositionality of the approach, which supports the required flexibility in modelling and analysing various scenarios through composition and decomposition.

Our main objective has been to illustrate the concepts needed to address reliability and security problems in dependable systems engineering. Two different aspects have been looked at to show the versatility of the approach. Here, we have illustrated concepts using aspects from the well-known security protocols Needham-Schroeder and Diffie-Hellman. In [30], we have investigated a specialised protocol – the Online Certificate Status Protocol OCSP. Due to the compositionality of the dynamic logic framework, the approach is scalable and can be applied to larger systems. We have addressed mechanised analysis support through test case generation, necessary for large systems analysis. An approach to further simplify reasoning, and enable automated or mechanised reasoning in particular, is to reduce the complexity to equational reasoning by defining a refinement between modal formulas where the condition can be reduced to an implication between simple non-modal formulas. Suitable environments for proof support could be tools supporting pre- and postcondition based specification or tools such as tools for the B specification language, which have also been used in [25] and in the feature interaction analysis [15] discussed earlier on.

We have used abstraction-based testing to verify security properties. Since we have used a dynamic logic similar to the modal μ-calculus [31], the question arises whether model checking is another alternative. The modal μ-calculus is a branching time temporal logic that forms the basis of several model checking approaches, see [32]. With a finite state space and finite set of properties, model checking becomes an alternative. If a given model satisfies the ideal protocol specification, then the model also has to satisfy the protocol with intruder. Otherwise, there is a security violation. In [30], we have given semantics to a similar specification notation based on Kripke transition systems and the μ-calculus, enabling model checking as an alternative approach to the automation of the security analysis.

Acknowledgements. The author would like to thank the anonymous reviewers for their valuable comments.

References

[1] IETF PKIX Working Group. Internet X.509 Public Key Infrastructure, 2000. http://www.ietf.org/internet-drafts/draft-ietf-pkix-roadmap-06.txt.

[2] C. Morgan. *Programming from Specifications 2e.* Addison-Wesley, 1994.

[3] R.J.R. Back and J. von Wright. *The Refinement Calculus: A Systematic Introduction.* Springer-Verlag, 1998.

[4] Dexter Kozen and Jerzy Tiuryn. Logics of programs. In J. van Leeuwen, editor, *Handbook of Theoretical Computer Science, Vol. B*, pages 789–840. Elsevier Science Publishers, 1990.

[5] E.A. Emerson. Temporal and Modal Logic. In J. van Leeuwen, editor, *Handbook of Theoretical Computer Science, Vol. B*, pages 995–1072. Elsevier Science Publishers, 1990.

[6] L. Lamport. The Temporal Logic of Actions. *ACM Transactions on Programming Languages and Systems*, 16(3):872–923, May 1994.

[7] K.M. Chandy and J. Misra. *Parallel Program Design.* Addison-Wesley, 1988.

[8] N.A. Durgin and J.C. Mitchell. Analysis of Security Protocols. In M. Broy and R. Steinbruggen, editors, *Calculational System Design*, pages 369–395. IOS Press, 1999.

[9] G.T. Leavens and A.L. Baker. Enhancing the Pre- and Postcondition Technique for More Expressive Specifications. In R. France and B. Rumpe, editors, *Proceedings 2nd Int. Conference UML'99 - The Unified Modeling Language.* Springer Verlag, LNCS 1723, 1999.

[10] Bertrand Meyer. Applying Design by Contract. *Computer*, pages 40–51, October 1992.

[11] J.B. Warmer and A.G. Kleppe. *The Object Constraint Language – Precise Modeling With UML.* Addison-Wesley, 1998.

[12] M. Büchi and E. Sekerinski. Formal Methods for Component Software: The Refinement Calculus Perspective. In *Proceedings 2nd International Workshop on Component-Oriented Programming WCOP '97*. Turku Center for Computer Science, General Publication No.5-97, Turku University, Finland, 1997.

[13] C. Pahl. Components, Contracts and Connectors for the Unified Modelling Language. In *Proc. Symposium Formal Methods Europe 2001, Berlin, Germany.* Springer-Verlag, LNCS-Series, 2001.

[14] B. Mermet and D. Méry. Incremental Specification of Telecommunication Services. In M. Hinchey, editor, *International Conference on Formal Engineering Methods ICFEM*. IEEE Press, 1997.

[15] J.-P. Gibson, G. Hamilton, and D. Méry. Integration Problems in Telephone Feature Requirements. In A. Galloway and K. Taguchi, editors, *Proc. IFM'99 Integrated Formal Methods*. Springer-Verlag, 1999.

[16] R. Milner. *Communicating and Mobile Systems: the π-Calculus*. Cambridge University Press, 1999.

[17] R.M. Needham and M.D. Schroeder. Using Encryption for Authentication in Large Networks of Computers. *Communications of the ACM*, 21(12):993–999, 1978.

[18] W. Stallings. *Cryptography and Network Security*. Prentice Hall, 1999.

[19] B.K. Aichernig. Test-case calculation through abstraction. In J.N. Oliveira and P. Zave, editors, *Proc. FME'2001 Symposium Formal Methods Europe*. Springer-Verlag, LNCS Series No. 2021, 2001.

[20] M. Abadi and A. Gordon. A Calculus for Cryptographic Protocols: the spi Calculus. *Information and Computation*, 148:1–70, 1999.

[21] L.C. Paulson. Proving Properties of Security Protocols by Induction. In *10th IEEE Computer Security Foundations Workshop*, pages 70–83. 1997.

[22] D. Dolev and A. Yao. On the Security of Public-key Protocols. *IEEE Transactions on Information Theory*, 29(2), 1983.

[23] G. Lowe. An attack on the Needham-Schroeder public-key protocol. *Information Processing Letters*, 56:131–133, 1995.

[24] R. Focardi, A. Ghelli, and R. Gorrieri. Using non interference for the analysis of security protocols. In H. Orman and C. Meadows, editors, *DIMACS Workshop on Design and Formal Verification of Security Protocols*. DIMACS, Rutgers University, 1997. http://dimacs.rutgers.edu/Workshops/Security.

[25] M. Butler. On the Use of Data Refinement in the Development of Secure Communications Systems. Technical Report DSSE-TR-2001-1, University of Southampton Declarative Systems and Software Engineering, 2001.

[26] I. Zakiuddin, J. Woodcock, M. Goldsmith, and J. Hulance. Formal Verification for Survivable Key Management Systems. In *Proc. IEEE Information Survivability Workshop*. http://www.cert.org/research/isw/isw2000/, 2000.

[27] J. Peleska. Test automation for safety-critical systems: Industrial applications and future developments. In M.-C. Gaudel and J. Woodcock, editors, *Proc. FME'96 Symposium Formal Methods Europe*. Springer-Verlag, LNCS Series, 1996.

[28] R. Back, A. Mikhajlova, and J. von Wright. Reasoning about interactive systems. In J.M. Wing, J. Woodcock, and J. Davies, editors, *Proc. FME'99 Symposium Formal Methods Europe*. Springer-Verlag, LNCS Series No. 1709, 1999.

[29] J. Derrick and E. Boiten. Testing Refinements of State-based Formal Specifications. *Software Testing, Verification and Reliability*, 9:27–50, 1999.

[30] C. Pahl. Analysing Security Properties using Refinement. In *Proc. International Workshop on Refinement of Critical Systems RCS'02*, 2002. (to appear).

[31] D. Kozen. Results on the propositional mu-calculus. *Theoretical Computer Science*, 27:333–354, 1983.

[32] M. Müller-Olm, D. Schmidt, and B. Steffen. Model Checking – a Tutorial Introduction. In *Proc. 6th Static Analysis Symposium*. Springer-Verlag, LNCS 1694, 1999.

The Formal Classification and Verification of Simpson's 4-Slot Asynchronous Communication Mechanism

N. Henderson[1] and S.E. Paynter[2]

[1] BAE SYSTEMS DCSC, University of Newcastle-Upon-Tyne, UK
neil.henderson@ncl.ac.uk
[2] MBDA UK Ltd, Filton, Bristol, UK
stephen.paynter@mbda.co.uk

Abstract. This paper critiques and extends Lamport's taxonomy of asynchronous registers, [8], [9]. This extended taxonomy is used to characterise Simpson's 4-slot asynchronous communication mechanism (ACM), [15], [16], [17], [18], [19]. A formalisation of the Lamport atomic property and Simpson's original 4-slot implementation is given in the PVS logic [12]. We prove that the 4-slot is atomic using Nipkow's retrieve relation proof rules, [10], [11], [7]. A description is given of the formal proofs, which have been discharged in the PVS theorem prover [13].

Keywords: asynchronous communication, reification, refinement, retrieve relation.

1 Introduction

Asynchronous Communication Mechanisms (ACMs) are inter-process communication devices that support the communication of data between writing and reading processes which are unconstrained in when and at what rate they can access the mechanism. Not only may reads and writes overlap, but multiple consecutive writes may overlap a read and vice versa. ACMs are essentially shared variables or registers, and typically have the properties that: a value written into one may be read many times; and writing a value conceptually destroys (makes unavailable for reading) values previously written.[1]

ACMs are of particular interest for a number of reasons, including:

- They are present whenever systems communicate that do not share a clock. This is even true when there is apparent support for synchronous communication, as such mechanisms need to be built from ACMs, although this may be at the hardware level and hidden from the software.

---

[1] The asynchronous communication that ACMs support is therefore to be distinguished from the model of "asynchronous communication" supported by (infinite) buffers.

L.-H. Eriksson and P. Lindsay (Eds.): FME 2002, LNCS 2391, pp. 350–369, 2002.
© Springer-Verlag Berlin Heidelberg 2002

- They support the integration of sub-systems or processes which run at different frequencies, or which are sporadic.
- They provide a means of decoupling the temporal interactions between systems that communicate. By definition, no process accessing an ACM can hinder another one from also accessing it.
- They provide a means of building systems which are robust against deadlock due the failure of one of the communicating systems.
- They are intellectually fascinating objects, capable of exhibiting both simplicity and beauty, yet even simple ACMs can exhibit surprisingly complex behaviour that is a challenge to characterise and analyse.

This paper introduces a formal taxonomy of ACMs, and uses it to characterise Simpson's 4-slot ACM, a particularly efficient ACM implementation that has been developed and used in the defence sector, [15] and [18]. A formal model of this ACM is given and its correctness is verified against an abstract specification. Previously ACMs, and the 4-slot in particular, have been analysed using complex event based models, for example using CSP, [3], [2], Petri-nets, [21], [22], and Role models, [16]. Here we attempt to produce a more human accessible specification and correctness analysis using pre- and post-conditions and Nipkow's data refinement law [10].

The rest of this paper is organised in the following way. In Section 2 Lamport's hierarchy of asynchronous registers, [8], [9], is introduced and extended to provide a framework in which Simpson's 4-slot ACM can be understood. Section 3 introduces an abstract specification of an "atomic" ACM. Section 4 introduces Simpson's original 4-slot algorithm,[2] Section 5 formalises this ACM and Section 6 defines the retrieve relation between the model and specification and gives the proofs which demonstrate the model reifies the specification. Finally Section 7 draws conclusions and outlines further work.

2   A Critique of Lamport's Hierarchy of Asynchronous Registers

In [9], Lamport defines *safe*, *regular* and *atomic* asynchronous registers, for which he gives the following informal descriptions:

> The weakest possibility is a *safe* register, in which it is assumed only that a read not concurrent with any write obtains the correct value, that is, the most recently written one. No assumption is made about the value obtained by a read that overlaps a write, except that it must obtain one of the possible values of the register. ...
> The next stronger possibility is a *regular* register, which is safe ... and in which a read that overwrites a write obtains either the old or new value. More generally, a read that overlaps any series of writes obtains either

---

[2] Simpson has subsequently introduced a number of variants, for example see [18].

the value in the register before the read starts or a value written by one of the overlapping writes. ...

The final possibility is an *atomic* register, which is safe, and in which reads and writes behave as if they occur in some definite order. In other words, for any execution of the system, there is some way of totally ordering the reads and writes so that the values returned by the reads are the same as if the operations had been performed in that order, with no overlapping.

Safe is a slightly unexpected name for Lamport's first class of register, for which an overlapping read can acquire any valid value (including ones which have never been written!). In our opinion "type safe" or "type compatible" are better terms, and we adopt *type safe* accordingly. *Atomic* is also a slightly unexpected description of any ACM, and is not to be confused with the devices that actually achieve total ordering of reads and writes (not merely the appearance of it) via synchronisation, for example, Hoare's monitors, [5].

It is important to note that these definitions are couched in terms of complete read and write actions. This is in contrast, for example, to Simpson's work on communication protocols, [20], which defines them in terms of critical *release* and *acquire* events within a write and read action, respectively. The acquire event is the abstract point during a read action at which the value that is to be read becomes determined, and the release event is the abstract point during a write action at which the value written is available for reading. Fortunately, this distinction need not concern us, if we limit consideration to those ACMs with well behaved read and write access routines which do not have multiple release or acquire events. When there is only one release and acquire event per read or write, these can be seen as marking the end of read or write (at least, as far as the above definitions of safe, regular, and atomic ACMs are concerned).[3]

Although Lamport claims the weakest (presumably, useful) possibility for an ACM is a type safe one, we consider weaker *persistent* ACMs. A read of a persistent ACM which conflicts with a write cannot even be guaranteed to return a value of the correct type. The intuition here is that the ACM is physically capable of storing more values than there are in the type of the data which is being communicated through it. For example, a two-bit ACM has a base type of four values, but might be used to communicate only a three valued variable. Such an ACM is called "persistent" because, although it is not type safe, it does have the desirable properties of accepting the values written into it by writes, and of keeping the value from the end of one write to the beginning of the next.

An important implementation of a persistent ACM protocol is *dual-port memory*, which is memory which a reader and writer can access independently (effectively it resides on two different processor buses). A read of dual-port memory which clashes with a write may pick-up corrupted values because, for example, it may get part of the old value, and part of the new.

---

[3] Simpson considers this tailoring of Lamport's definitions as critical to the application of Lamport's concepts to his work.

An important implementation of type safe ACM protocols, involves using persistent ACMs with base types the same size as their valid types. Within this class, as Lamport observed, the safe bit variables are notable.

Conceptually, there is an even weaker ACM, which one might call *noisy*. A noisy ACM can autonomously change the value stored in it at any time. No-one would ideally use such an ACM, but there might be occasions when that is the most accurate model of the communication media one has to use, and one wants to reason about the behaviour of a particular protocol which is built on-top of such devices.[4]

One could also imagine ACMs which are only *semi-regular*: they are type safe when reads and writes do not overlap, but when they do, a read might get any value that has previously been written.[5]

These three new classes of ACM, noisy, persistent, and semi-regular, are added to Lamport's, type safe, regular, and atomic to form a hierarchy of ACMs. The following section introduces an abstract specification of atomic ACMs.

3   An Abstract Specification of Atomic ACMs

This section gives a specification, in the PVS logic,[6] [12] of atomic ACMs. In the following it is assumed that the ACM has a single reader and single writer. This means that, although multiple reads and writes can overlap, reads cannot overlap reads and writes cannot overlap writes.

An atomic ACM has the following properties:

1. The reader of the ACM should read items in the order they are written by the writer. This means that once the reader has read a particular item it cannot subsequently read one that was written earlier.
2. The writer can overwrite items. If the writer is faster than the reader, some of the items may be overwritten before they are read.
3. The reader may re-read items if it is faster than the writer.
4. The reader and writer can access the ACM concurrently, and it is possible for a number of writes to overlap with a single read and vice versa.
5. Reads and writes behave as if they occur in some definite order.

Rather than characterising the last property directly, the approach is taken in the following specification, of modelling the data items that have been written

---

[4] Clearly, a usable protocol built on top of such ACMs would need some form of error detection and correction mechanism, such a repetition, confirmation, or checksums. For example the internet protocol (IP) gives no guarantees about the data transmitted, and individual packets may be lost, and it is the TCP package, which is built on the top of IP, that provides the required reliable behaviour of the communications medium.

[5] It is not so much that one would want such a ACM, but that some implementations might exhibit such behaviour.

[6] The PVS logic is used because of the powerful, freely available, PVS theorem prover, [13].

into the ACM as a sequence. The order of the items in the model records the sequence in which they were written. The presence of items in the sequence at any particular moment reflects the possibility of their being read. The specification allows multiple items to be present in situations where it is non-deterministic which item the reader will acquire.

The specification state, which is shown below, also includes two booleans, *writerAccess* and *readerAccess*, to record whether the writer and reader, respectively, are accessing the mechanism at a particular moment.

Val_Sequence: TYPE = [# length: nat1, valseq: sequence[Val] #]

Abs_State: TYPE =
[# vals: Val_Sequence, writerAccess: bool, readerAccess: bool #]

The four operations in our specification, which are described below, are; *start_write, end_write, start_read and end_read*. The following definitions in the PVS logic exploit the encoding of VDM-SL operations developed in [1].

start_write : has a pre-condition that the writer is not already accessing the mechanism. The operation adds the new value that is being written to the head of the sequence, and records that the writer is accessing the ACM.[7]

pre_start_write(prot: Abs_State): bool = prot'writerAccess = FALSE

post_start_write(p: (pre_start_write))(item: Val, prot: Abs_State): bool =
  prot = p WITH [vals := (# length := p'vals'length + 1,
                      valseq := (item^p'vals'valseq) #),
        writerAccess := TRUE]

start_write: [p: (pre_start_write), i: Val → (post_start_write(p))]

It is noted that in concrete ACMs, as described above, subsequent writes destroy items previously written. However this abstract specification exploits the simplification that items are only removed by the *start_read* operation. The collecting together of all of the sequence shortening actions into the *start_read* operation, while impractical in an implementation, simplifies both the operations of the abstract model and the retrieve relation (see Section 6).

end_write : has a pre-condition that the writer is accessing the mechanism. The post-condition establishes that the writer is no longer accessing the ACM.

pre_end_write(prot: Abs_State): bool = prot'writerAccess = TRUE

post_end_write(p: (pre_end_write))(prot: Abs_State): bool =
  prot = p WITH [writerAccess := FALSE]

end_write: [p: (pre_end_write) → (post_end_write(p))]

---

[7] In the PVS logic "p WITH [w := x, y := z]" refers to the composite element that is equal to p, except that the values of its w and y fields are over-ridden with the values x and z. Other fields are unchanged.

start_read : has a pre-condition that the reader is not already accessing the mechanism. This operation removes any items from the sequence that are not available to be read, and records that the reader is accessing the ACM. If the writer is not accessing the ACM when a read starts the only item that is available to the reader is the one written immediately before the read starts: in this case *start_read* removes all of the items from the sequence except for the head item. If the writer is accessing the ACM the reader may also get the item that is being written by the current write, so the first two items are left in the sequence and the rest are removed.

pre_start_read(prot: Abs_State): bool = prot'readerAccess = FALSE

post_start_read(p: (pre_start_read))(prot: Abs_State): bool =
    IF p'writerAccess = FALSE
      THEN prot = p WITH [vals := (# length := 1,
                                  valseq := first(p'vals'valseq) #),
                    readerAccess := TRUE]
      ELSE prot = p WITH [vals := (# length := 2,
                      valseq := (p'vals'valseq(0)^p'vals'valseq(1)) #),
                    readerAccess := TRUE]
    ENDIF

start_read: [p: (pre_start_read) → (post_start_read(p))]

end_read : has a pre-condition that the reader is accessing the mechanism. It returns the item read and records that the reader is no longer accessing the ACM.

pre_end_read(prot: Abs_State): bool = prot'readerAccess = TRUE

post_end_read(p: (pre_end_read))(prot: Abs_State, read_item: Val):
                                                bool =
    ($\exists$ (i: nat1): i < p'vals'length $\land$ read_item = p'vals'valseq(i) $\land$
              prot = p WITH [readerAccess := FALSE])

end_read: [p: (pre_end_read) → (post_end_read(p))]

The ACM is initialised with an initial value, and a sequence length of one, because the first read can occur before the first write and an item must then be available to the reader.

4   Simpson's 4-Slot ACM

In 1990 Simpson published a paper, [15] in which he defined a fully asynchronous communication mechanism that maintained data-coherence and which only used four *slots*: each slot in the mechanism being a persistent ACM in our terminology. The 4-slot can be seen as an implementation of a MASCOT [6], [14] pool, or shared variable. Simpson has given a formal model of the pool in terms of the synchronising behaviour of the reader and writer, [20].

In the 4-slot bit control variables (i.e. binary valued type safe ACMs) are used to ensure that the reader and writer are always directed to different slots, so the reader can never read values composed of partial items from more than one write. The four slot algorithm is deceptively simple, consisting of only five actions in the *write* operation and four actions in the *read* operation, and is shown in Table 1.

Table 1. The 4-slot mechanism

```
mechanism four slot;
    type PairIndex = (p0, p1);
         SlotIndex = (s0, s1);
    var data: array[PairIndex, SlotIndex] of Data;
        slot: array[PairIndex] of SlotIndex;
        latest, reading: PairIndex;
    procedure write (item: data);
    var writepair: PairIndex;
        writeindex: SlotIndex;
    begin
        writepair := not reading;             (writerChoosesPair)
        writeindex := not slot[writepair];    (writerChoosesSlot)
        data[writepair, writeindex] := item;  (write)
        slot[writepair] := writeindex         (writerIndicatesSlot)
        latest := writepair;                  (writerIndicatesPair)
    end;

    function read: Data;
    var readpair: PairIndex;
        readindex: SlotIndex;
    begin
        readpair := latest;                   (readerChoosesPair)
        reading := readpair;                  (readerIndicatesPair)
        readindex := slot[readpair];          (readerChoosesSlot)
        read := data[readpair, readindex];    (read)
    end;
end;
```

The mechanism is described as follows:

1. the slots are organised in two pairs of two slots;
2. an initial value is put into one of the slots in one of the pairs;
3. the mechanism has four single bit control variables:
   reading: which indicates the pair the reader is reading (or last read) from.
   latest: which indicates the pair the writer is writing (or last wrote) to.

slots: a two element array of binary slot indices, which is accessed by the reader to choose the slot to read from in the pair of slots the reader is currently accessing, or by the writer to choose the slot to write to in the current pair of slots the writer is accessing.

4. the writer:
   - chooses the pair and the slot within that pair to which it will write the new value - *writerChoosesPair* and *writerChoosesSlot* in Table 1 (the write pre-sequence). It always chooses to write to the opposite pair to the one the reader last indicated it was reading from;[8]
   - writes the new item to the chosen slot - *write* in Table 1; and
   - indicates the slot and pair it has written the data to - *writerIndicatesSlot* and *writerIndiciatesPair* in Table 1 (the write post-sequence).

5. the reader:
   - chooses to read from the pair of slots last written to (or the pair the initial value was written to), indicates that it is reading from that pair, and then chooses to read from the latest slot in that pair that has had a value written to it - *readerChoosesPair*, *readerIndicatesPair* and *readerChoosesSlot* in Table 1 (the read pre-sequence); and
   - reads the item from the chosen slot - *read* in Table 1.

Simpson, in a later paper, gave a new algorithm for the four slot, which essentially reverses the order in which the reader and writer choose the pair and slot to read from or write to, [18]. That variant, however, is not considered in this paper.

It is the intention of the design of the 4-slot mechanism that the reader and writer cannot access the same slot at the same time, and so in this way the use of persistent ACMs for the slots is adequate to ensure data coherence even when reads and writes to the ACM overlap. It is also intended to support *data freshness* i.e. the reader should read the most recently written item. More precisely the reader will:

- get the last item written prior to the start of the read, when the read does not overlap with a write.[9]
- get the last item written prior to the start of the read or one of the items written by an overlapping write.[10]
- not get staler data than it has previously read.[11]

The requirements for the 4-slot mechanism to maintain data coherence and freshness can be summarised by saying that the 4-slot should be atomic.

Simpson developed a novel analysis method called *role modelling* in [16], [19] to demonstrate that the 4-slot exhibits the data coherence and freshness properties.

---

[8] This will be the pair the initial item was written to until the reader indicates the pair it is reading from for the first time.

[9] This is a property of a persistent ACM.

[10] This is a property of a regular ACM.

[11] This is a property of an atomic ACM.

5   A Formal Model of the 4-Slot ACM

This section describes a formal model, in the PVS logic, of Simpson's 4-slot ACM which was introduced in Section 4.

The state of the model consists of:

1. two binary control variables to indicate the latest pair that has had an item written to it, and the pair of slots that the reader is accessing, called *pairWritten* and *pairReading* respectively;
2. a two element array of binary slot indices, called *slotWritten*, to record the last slot, in each pair of slots, that has had data written to it. This array is accessed by the writer to choose the slot to write to in the pair of slots it is currently accessing, and by the reader to choose the slot to read from in the pair of slots that it is currently accessing;
3. the four slots for communicating the data;
4. variables to record the position the reader and writer have reached in their respective algorithms, *nri* (next read instruction) and *nwi* (next write instruction) respectively; and
5. the reader and writer states that record which of pairs, and slots in those pairs, the reader and writer are accessing when a read or write is taking place.

PairIndex: TYPE = {p_0, p_1}

SlotIndex: TYPE = {s_0, s_1}

NextReadInstruction: TYPE = {rcp, rd}

NextWriteInstruction: TYPE = {wcp, wip}

WriterState: TYPE = [# writerPair: PairIndex, writerSlot: SlotIndex #]

ReaderState: TYPE = [# readerPair: PairIndex, readerSlot: SlotIndex #]

Conc_State: TYPE = [# pairWritten: PairIndex,
                slotWritten: [PairIndex $\rightarrow$ SlotIndex],
                pairReading: PairIndex,
                slots: [PairIndex, SlotIndex $\rightarrow$ Val],
                nri: NextReadInstruction,
                nwi: NextWriteInstruction,
                writer: WriterState,
                reader: ReaderState #]

The 4-slot algorithm in Section 4 consists of five actions by the writer and four reader actions and it is possible for the reader actions to interleave with the writer actions in any way. In this model, we have grouped the actions of the reader into two operations to coincide with the two read operations in the abstract model of atomicness in Section 3. Similarly the actions of the writer have been combined into two operations to coincide with the two write operations in Section 3. The operations in the model are:

startWr : which is equivalent to *start_write*. The pre-condition for this operation is that the writer is not accessing the mechanism (the next write operation is *wcp* - writer chooses pair). The post-condition establishes the particular slot into which the writer will write the new data item (the pair of slots to write to is chosen, and the particular slot in that pair). The new data item is added to the appropriate slot, and the appropriate element of the *slotWritten* array is set to indicate the slot in the current *writer pair* that the writer has accessed. The value of *nwi* (next write instruction) is also changed to *wip* (writer indicates pair) to indicate that the writer is accessing the mechanism. This is the most complex operation, because the writer needs to avoid the reader[12] and then chooses to write to the slot in the pair it is going to access which contains the oldest data item.

pre_startWr(p: Conc_State): bool = p'nwi = wcp

post_startWr(p: (pre_startWr))(val: Val, prot: Conc_State): bool =
IF p'pairReading = p_0
  THEN LET prot1 = p WITH
            [writer := p'writer WITH [writerPair := p_1]] IN
       IF prot1'slotWritten(prot1'writer'writerPair) = s_0
         THEN LET prot2 = prot1
              WITH [writer := prot1'writer WITH [writerSlot := s_1]] IN
              LET prot3 = prot2 WITH [(slots)(prot2'writer'writerPair,
                                        prot2'writer'writerSlot) := val] IN
              prot = prot3 WITH [nwi := wip,
                                    slotWritten(prot3'writer'writerPair) :=
                                        prot3'writer'writerSlot]
         ELSE LET prot2 = prot1 WITH
                  [writer := prot1'writer WITH [writerSlot := s_0]] IN
              LET prot3 = prot2 WITH [(slots)(prot2'writer'writerPair,
                                        prot2'writer'writerSlot) := val] IN
              prot = prot3 WITH [nwi := wip,
                                    slotWritten(prot3'writer'writerPair) :=
                                        prot3'writer'writerSlot]
       ENDIF
  ELSE LET prot1 = p WITH [writer := p'writer WITH
                                    [writerPair := p_0]] IN
       IF prot1'slotWritten(prot1'writer'writerPair) = s_0
         THEN LET prot2 = prot1 WITH [writer := prot1'writer WITH
                                        [writerSlot := s_1]] IN
              LET prot3 = prot2 WITH [(slots)(prot2'writer'writerPair,
                                        prot2'writer'writerSlot) := val]
              IN prot = prot3 WITH [nwi := wip,

---

[12] The writer avoids the reader by choosing to write to the opposite pair to the one the reader last indicated it was reading when the write starts.

$$\text{slotWritten(prot3'writer'writerPair)} :=$$
$$\text{prot3'writer'writerSlot]}$$
$$\text{ELSE LET prot2} = \text{prot1}$$
$$\text{WITH [writer} := \text{prot1'writer WITH [writerSlot} := s_0]] \text{ IN}$$
$$\text{LET prot3} = \text{prot2 WITH [(slots)(prot2'writer'writerPair,}$$
$$\text{prot2'writer'writerSlot)} := \text{val]}$$
$$\text{IN prot} = \text{prot3 WITH [nwi} := \text{wip,}$$
$$\text{slotWritten(prot3'writer'writerPair)} :=$$
$$\text{prot3'writer'writerSlot]}$$
$$\text{ENDIF}$$
$$\text{ENDIF}$$

startWr: [p: (pre_startWr) $\rightarrow$ (post_startWr(p))]

endWr : which is equivalent to *end_write*. The pre-condition for this operation is that the writer is accessing the mechanism (the next write instruction is *wip* - writer indicates pair). The post-condition establishes that the pair the writer has just written to is recorded by *pairWritten*, and that *nwi* has been set to *wcp* (writer chooses pair) to indicate the writer is no longer accessing the mechanism.

pre_endWr(p: Conc_State): bool $= p$'nwi $=$ wip

post_endWr(p: (pre_endWr))(p_1: Conc_State): bool $=$
    LET pair $= p$'writer'writerPair IN
        prot $= p$ WITH [nwi $:=$ wcp, pairWritten $:=$ pair]

endWr: [p: (pre_endWr) $\rightarrow$ (post_endWr(p))]

startRd : which is equivalent to *start_read*. The pre-condition is that the reader is not accessing the mechanism (the next read instruction is *rcp* (reader chooses pair)). The post-condition for the operation is that the reader has chosen the pair of slots it is going to read from, indicated that it is reading from that pair (by writing the name of the pair it is reading to *pairReading*), has chosen the particular slot in the pair that it is going to access and has set *nri* (next read instruction) to *rd* (read) to indicate that it is accessing the mechanism.

pre_startRd(p: Conc_State): bool $= p$'nri $=$ rcp

post_startRd(p: (pre_startRd))(prot: Conc_State): bool $=$
    LET prot1 $= p$ WITH [reader $:= p$'reader WITH
                            [readerPair $:= p$'pairWritten]] IN
        LET prot2 $=$ prot1 WITH [pairReading $:=$ prot1'reader'readerPair] IN
            prot $=$ prot2 WITH [nri $:=$ rd,
                            reader $:=$ prot2'reader WITH [readerSlot $:=$
                            prot2'slotWritten(prot2'reader'readerPair)]]

startRd: [p: (pre_startRd) $\rightarrow$ (post_startRd(p))]

endRd : which is equivalent to *end_read*. This operation has a pre-condition that the reader is accessing the mechanism $(nri = rd)$). It returns the value read and sets nri to rcp to indicate the reader is no longer accessing the mechanism.

pre_endRd(p: Conc_State): bool $= p$'nri $=$ rd

post_endRd(p: (pre_endRd))(p_1: Conc_State, v: Val): bool $=$
    $v = (p$'slots)(p'reader'readerPair)(p'reader'readerSlot) $\wedge$
    prot $= p$ WITH [nri := rcp]

endRd: [p: (pre_endRd) $\rightarrow$ (post_endRd(p))]

6   The Retrieve Relation between the Models

This section gives details of the retrieve relation between the model of the 4-slot in Section 5, which we refer to here as the concrete model, and the abstract specification in Section 3. First we will consider why it is not possible to use a retrieve function in this case.

6.1   A Retrieve Function?

It is usually possible to prove that a more concrete model is a reification of an abstract model by using a retrieve function between the states in the two models. In order to do this there must be a one to one, or many to one, mapping between the concrete and abstract states in both the pre and post states for each operation.

It is not possible to relate the states in our model and specification in this way, however, because there can be a one to many relation between the concrete and abstract states. For instance it is possible for a read to start, and an undetermined number of writes to occur before the read finishes. In the abstract state each of the writes adds a new item to the sequence of items that are available to read, so that each time one of those writes occurs the abstract model moves to a new state. We only know that the *end_read* operation will return one of these items. In the implementation, however, there are only four slots, and some of the values in the sequence in the abstract state may have been overwritten (depending on the number of writes that occur), and the item the reader reads is determined by the manner in which the read and write actions interleave. There is, therefore only a single concrete state that maps to all of these abstract states caused by the writes that occur concurrently with the read.

6.2   The Retrieve Relation

The retrieve relation has been encoded in the PVS logic. The relation is given in full in Appendix A and the means of retrieving the values from the concrete model is shown graphically in Fig. 1.

The relation is explained as follows:

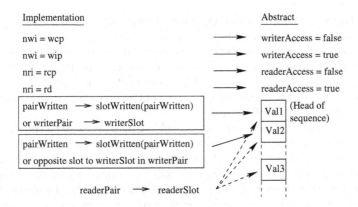

Fig. 1. The retrieve relation between the concrete and abstract models

1. The concrete and abstract models can each be in any one of four states at any time, and the equivalent states can be determined by the values of nwi and nri in the concrete state and $writerAccess$ and $readerAccess$ in the abstract state:
   - in the concrete state nwi and nri are used to record the next write instruction and next read instruction (the position of the writer and reader in their algorithms) respectively;
   - nwi can take the values wcp when the writer is not accessing the mechanism, which is equivalent to $writerAccess = FALSE$ in the abstract state, and wip when the writer is accessing the mechanism, which is equivalent to $writerAccess = TRUE$ in the abstract state; and
   - nri can take the values rcp when the reader is not accessing the mechanism, which is equivalent to $readerAccess = FALSE$ in the abstract state, and rd when the reader is accessing the mechanism, which is equivalent to $readerAccess = TRUE$ in the abstract state.
2. The four equivalent states in the models are:
   - when neither the reader nor writer are accessing the mechanism ($nwi = wcp$ & $nri = rcp \equiv writerAccess = FALSE$ & $readerAccess = FALSE$);
   - when only the writer is accessing the mechanism ($nwi = wip$ & $nri = rcp \equiv writerAccess = TRUE$ & $readerAccess = FALSE$);
   - when only the reader is accessing the mechanism ($nwi = wcp$ & $nri = rd \equiv writerAccess = FALSE$ & $readerAccess = TRUE$); and
   - when both the reader and writer are accessing the mechanism ($nwi = wip$ & $nri = rd \equiv writerAccess = TRUE$ & $readerAccess = TRUE$).
3. The sequence of items in the abstract state can have any number of items in it, depending on how many writes have occurred since the last $start\_read$, and there is always at least one item there.[13] A maximum of two items can

---

[13] The model is initialised with a single value that is immediately available to the reader. The $start\_read$ thereafter shortens the sequence to either a single item if

be retrieved from the concrete state using the writer local state and the mechanism's control variables:

- The head item of the abstract sequence can always be retrieved from the concrete state. If there is a write in progress this item will be pointed to by the writer local variables, *writerPair* and *writerSlot*. Otherwise it will be pointed to by the control variables in the mechanism (*slotWritten(pairWritten)*).
- If the writer is accessing the mechanism when *start_read* occurs the abstract state will be shortened to contain only two items after the operation hes been executed - the item being written and the last item written. The item being written will be pointed to by the writer local variables as described above. The last item will either be in the opposite slot of the pair that the writer is currently accessing, or, if the writer has changed pairs since the last write, it will be in the slot pointed to by *slotWritten(pairWritten)*.[14] If a write is in progress there will always be at least two items in the sequence in the abstract state, and the second item in the sequence can always then be retrieved in this manner until the write finishes. At this stage the previous value is no longer available to the reader in the implementation (it has been overwritten by the writer), and cannot be retrieved from the concrete model.

4. If a read is in progress the reader local variables will be pointing to the value that is going to be read. When a read starts the sequence in the abstract specification is shortened to include at most two items, as described above, so it is only possible for the reader to choose to read one of these items at this stage. Any number of writes can, however, overlap with the read and each write will add a new item to the abstract sequence. It is only possible to know, therefore, that the item the reader will get in the concrete model is in the abstract sequence, but not where it will be in the sequence.[15]

6.3   Correctness Proofs

This section gives details of the correctness proofs that have been discharged in PVS to show that the concrete model in Section 5 is a refinement of the abstract specification in Section 3. We have used Nipkow's retrieve relation proof rules from [10], [11], [7], which are:

$$\forall(as : Abs\_State, cs : Conc\_State) \cdot R(cs, as) \wedge pre\_OPA(as) \Rightarrow pre\_OPC(cs) \tag{1}$$

---

the writer is not accessing the mechanism when the operation is executed, or to two items if the writer is accessing the mechanism when it is executed.

[14] It is possible to check if the writer has swapped pairs for the current write - the values of the control variable *pairWritten* and the writer local variable *writerPair* will be different.

[15] It will be one of the last two items, because all new items are added to the head of the sequence.

$$\forall(\overleftarrow{as}: Abs\_State, \overleftarrow{cs}, cs :Conc\_State) \cdot R(\overleftarrow{cs}, \overleftarrow{as}) \wedge pre\_OPA(\overleftarrow{as}) \wedge post\_OPC(\overleftarrow{cs}, cs) \Rightarrow$$
$$\exists (as : Abs\_State) \cdot post\_OPA(\overleftarrow{as}, as) \wedge R(cs, as)$$
$$(2)$$

where OPA and OPC are the abstract and concrete operations respectively.

These domain and result proof obligations have been discharged in PVS for each the equivalent operations in our specification and model and are described below. The domain proofs are:

$$\forall(as : Abs\_State, cs : Conc\_State) \cdot R(cs, as) \wedge pre\_start\_write(as) \Rightarrow pre\_startWr(cs)$$
$$(3)$$

$$\forall(as : Abs\_State, cs : Conc\_State) \cdot R(cs, as) \wedge pre\_end\_write(as) \Rightarrow pre\_endWr(cs)$$
$$(4)$$

$$\forall(as : Abs\_State, cs : Conc\_State) \cdot R(cs, as) \wedge pre\_start\_read(as) \Rightarrow pre\_startRd(cs)$$
$$(5)$$

$$\forall(as : Abs\_State, cs : Conc\_State) \cdot R(cs, as) \wedge pre\_end\_read(as) \Rightarrow pre\_endRd(cs)$$
$$(6)$$

These proofs are relatively trivial to discharge, because, for example in the case of (3), we are simply showing that $writerAccess = FALSE$ when $nwi = writerChoosesPair$. We know this to be the case, because this means that the writer is not accessing the mechanism in both models. The only complication is that each of the proofs must be discharged by using a *case split*, because the reader may or may not be accessing the mechanism when the writer operations are executed and vice versa.

The result proof obligations are more interesting. They are shown in (7) to (10) and are described below. In each case a case split is required to discharge the proof for the same reason as with the domain proofs above.

$$\forall(\overleftarrow{as}: Abs\_State, \overleftarrow{cs}, cs :Conc\_State) \cdot R(\overleftarrow{cs}, \overleftarrow{as}) \wedge pre\_start\_write(\overleftarrow{as}) \wedge$$
$$post\_startWr(\overleftarrow{cs}, cs) \Rightarrow \exists (as : Abs\_State) \cdot post\_start\_write(\overleftarrow{as}, as) \wedge R(cs, as) \quad (7)$$

$$\forall(\overleftarrow{as}: Abs\_State, \overleftarrow{cs}, cs :Conc\_State) \cdot R(\overleftarrow{cs}, \overleftarrow{as}) \wedge pre\_end\_write(\overleftarrow{as}) \wedge$$
$$post\_endWr(\overleftarrow{cs}, cs) \Rightarrow \exists (as : Abs\_State) \cdot post\_end\_write(\overleftarrow{as}, as) \wedge R(cs, as) \quad (8)$$

$$\forall(\overleftarrow{as}: Abs\_State, \overleftarrow{cs}, cs :Conc\_State) \cdot R(\overleftarrow{cs}, \overleftarrow{as}) \wedge pre\_start\_read(\overleftarrow{as}) \wedge$$
$$post\_startRd(\overleftarrow{cs}, cs) \Rightarrow \exists (as : Abs\_State) \cdot post\_start\_read(\overleftarrow{as}, as) \wedge R(cs, as) \quad (9)$$

$$\forall(\overleftarrow{as}: Abs\_State, \overleftarrow{cs}, cs :Conc\_State) \cdot R(\overleftarrow{cs}, \overleftarrow{as}) \wedge pre\_end\_read(\overleftarrow{as}) \wedge$$
$$post\_endRd(\overleftarrow{cs}, cs) \Rightarrow \exists (as : Abs\_State) \cdot post\_end\_read(\overleftarrow{as}, as) \wedge R(cs, as) \quad (10)$$

The proofs were discharged in each case by *splitting* the consequent to

$$\exists\,(as : Abs\_State) \cdot R(cs, as) \wedge (R(cs, as) \Rightarrow post\_end\_read(\overleftarrow{as}, as)) \qquad (11)$$

Brief details are as follows:[16]

Start Write: This operation adds a new item to the sequence in the abstract state and in the concrete state puts the new item into the slot pointed to by the writer local variables. We assume that the relation holds before the operation and that the post condition for the concrete operation holds. If we therefore amend the concrete state to take into account the changes made by the post condition we can show that, if the retrieve relation holds between the final states, the post condition for the abstract operation must hold (because the new item is added to the head of the sequence). We can then show that the retrieve relation holds between the final states, because the item we have just written will be at the head of the sequence and the last item written will be second in the sequence. These items can be retrieved from the concrete state, as described above. In addition, if the reader is accessing the mechanism we can show that the slot the reader is accessing contains one of the items in the sequence (this part is trivial, because we know it was in the sequence before the operation and all we have done is to add another item to the head of the sequence).

End Write: This operation leaves the sequence unchanged in the abstract state and simply changes the concrete state so that the *pairWritten* control variable changes to point to the pair the writer has just accessed, and to show that the writer is no longer accessing the mechanism. After the operation has been executed we can no longer retrieve the previous item written from the concrete state,[17] otherwise the relationship between the two states is unchanged. It is therefore only necessary to show that the slot that contains the head item of the sequence in the abstract state is pointed to by *slotWritten(pairWritten)*.

Start Read: This operation removes all the unreadable items from the sequence, but the remaining items can be retrieved from the control variables and writer local state as appropriate (and this relationship is unchanged by the operation). It only remains to prove that the item that is going to be read (and is pointed to by the reader local variables) is in fact in the sequence in the abstract state. This is the case, because the reader in the concrete model can only read the item the writer is currently writing, or the item that was written previously. These are the first two items in the abstract sequence.

---

[16] The interested reader can download the PVS theory and proof files from http://www.csr.ncl.ac.uk/fme2002 to see the proofs in full. In addition an extended version of this paper, which includes example proofs, is available as a technical report from http://www.cs.ncl.ac.uk/publications/, [4].

[17] The writer local variables *writerPair* and *writerSlot* will point to the same slot as the control variables in the mechanism. This is the stage at which this previous item has been overwritten in the implementation.

End Read: Here it can be shown that the item returned by the read in the concrete model is in the sequence in the abstract state, because no items are removed from the sequence, and no new items are added, by the operation. The retrieve relation between the states is therefore unchanged, other that the change in the respective variables to show that the reader is no longer accessing the mechanism in the model and specification.

In the work to date we have proved that Simpson's 4-slot ACM is Lamport atomic, subject to the assumption that the reader and writer actions can only interleave in the restricted way as described in Section 5, and further work is planned to extend this proof to cover situations when these restrictions are relaxed.[18]

7   Conclusions

This paper has presented an extension to Lamport's taxonomy of asynchronous registers, which can be used to model the behaviour of an extended range of ACMs. We have given an abstract specification of an atomic ACM, and a model of Simpson's 4-slot ACM (both in PVS) and proved that the 4-slot is atomic subject to certain assumptions about the interleaving of the actions of the reader and writer to the mechanism.[19] Future work is planned to extend our model to relax our assumptions about the possible interleaving of actions of the reader and writer, and to prove that the ACM is truly atomic.

In [16], [19] Simpson introduced a technique, called role model analysis, which he used to prove that the 4-slot preserves coherence of data and that the reader of the mechanism receives the freshest data that was available when the read started. This technique relies on an exhaustive search of the state space (although the state space that it is required to search is restricted in a novel manner), and we aim to prove the same properties using formal models of the ACM. It will be interesting to compare our results with results from Simpson's role model, and also to compare the ease with which the two techniques can be used.

Acknowledgments. MBDA(UK) and the BAE SYSTEMS Dependable Computing Systems Centre funded this research. Our ideas have benefitted from conversations with Profs. C. B. Jones and H.R. Simpson and Drs. J.M. Armstrong and J.S. Fitzgerald. The authors also thank the referees for their helpful comments.

---

[18] So that the reader and writer actions can interleave in any way, as in the implementation.

[19] We have modelled our extended taxonomy in PVS and this model is also available from http://csr.ncl.ac.uk/fme2002.

References

1. S. Angerholm, J. Bicarregui, and S. Maharaj. On the Verification of VDM Specifications and Refinement with PVS. In J.C. Bicarregui, editor, *Proof in VDM: Case Studies*, FACIT. Springer, 1998.
2. P. Brooke, J.L. Jacob, and J.M. Armstrong. Analysis of the Four-Slot Mechanism. In *Proceedings of the BCS-FACS Northern Formal Methods Workshop*, 1996.
3. P.J. Brooke. *A Timed Semantics for a Hierarchical Design Notation*. PhD thesis, Department of Computer Science, University of York, April 1999.
4. Neil Henderson and Stephen Paynter. The formal classification and verification of simpson's 4-slot asynchronous communication mechanism. Technical Report CS-TR-756, University of Newcastle, 2002.
5. C.A.R. Hoare. Monitors: An Operating System Structuring Concept. *Communications of the ACM*, 17(10):549–557, 1974.
6. Joint IECCA and MUF Committee on MASCOT (JIMCOM). *The Official Handbook of MASCOT: Version 3.1 - Issue 1*, June 1987. Crown Copyright.
7. C.B. Jones. *Systematic Software Development Using VDM: Second Edition*. Prentice-Hall International Series in Computer Science, 1990.
8. L. Lamport. On Interprocess Communication - Part 1: Basic Formalism. *Distributed Computing*, 1:77–85, 1986.
9. L. Lamport. On Interprocess Communication - Part 2: Algorithms. *Distributed Computing*, 1:86–101, 1986.
10. T. Nipkow. Non-deterministic data types: Models and implementations. *Acta Informatica*, 22:629–661, 1986.
11. T. Nipkow. *Behavioural Implementation Concepts for Nondeterministic Data Types*. PhD thesis, University of Manchester, May 1987.
12. S. Owre, N. Shanker, J.M. Rushby, and D.W.J. Stringer-Calvert. PVS Language: Version 2.3. Technical report, Computer Science Laboratory - SRI International, September 1999.
13. S. Owre, N. Shanker, J.M. Rushby, and D.W.J. Stringer-Calvert. PVS System Guide: Version 2.3. Technical report, Computer Science Laboratory - SRI International, September 1999.
14. H.R. Simpson. The MASCOT Method. *Software Engineering Journal*, 1(3):103–120, 1986.
15. H.R. Simpson. Four-Slot Fully Asynchronous Communication Mechanism. *IEE Proceedings*, 137 Part E(1):17–30, January 1990.
16. H.R. Simpson. Correctness Analysis for Class of Asynchronous Communication Mechanism. *IEE Proceedings*, 139 Part E(1):35–49, January 1992.
17. H.R. Simpson. Multireader and Multiwriter Asynchronous Communication Mechanisms. *IEE Proceedings of Computer Digital Technology*, 144(4):241–243, July 1997.
18. H.R. Simpson. New Algorithms for Asynchronous Communication. *IEE Proceedings of Computer Digital Technology*, 144(4):227–231, July 1997.
19. H.R. Simpson. Role Model Analysis of an Asynchronous Communication Mechanism. *IEE Proceedings of Computer Digital Technology*, 144(4):232–240, July 1997.
20. H.R. Simpson. Protocols for Process Interaction. Resubmitted to IEE Proceedings on Software, 2001.
21. F Xia. *Supporting the MASCOT method with Petri net techniques for real-time systems development*. PhD thesis, London University, King's College, January 2000.

22. A. Yakovlev, F. Xia, and D. Shang. Synthesis and Implementation of a Signal-Type Asynchronous Data Communication Mechanism. In *Proceedings of the 7th International Symposium on Asynchronous Circuits and Systems (ASYNC 2001) – Salt Lake City*, March 2001.

A   The Retrieve Relation between the Two Models in PVS

Retrieve: THEORY
  BEGIN

  IMPORTING New_Abstract_Protocol, FOUR_SLOT

  R(as: Abs_State, cs: Conc_State): bool =

```
-- The reader and writer are not accessing the ACM. Only the last
-- item written can be retrieved from the model of the
-- implementation and this will be the head of the sequence in the
-- abstract state
```
  (cs'nri = rcp ∧ cs'nwi = wcp ⇒
    ¬ as'readerAccess ∧ ¬ as'writerAccess ∧
    cs'slots(cs'pairWritten, cs'slotWritten(cs'pairWritten)) =
                    first(as'vals'valseq) ∧
      as'vals'length ≥ 1) ∧

```
-- Only the writer is accessing the ACM. Two items can be retrieved
-- from the model of the implementation, the one being written and
-- the previous item written, and these will be the head and second
-- items respectively in the abstract sequence
```
  (cs'nri = rcp ∧ cs'nwi = wip ⇒
    ¬ as'readerAccess ∧ as'writerAccess ∧
    cs'writer'writerSlot = cs'slotWritten(cs'writer'writerPair) ∧
    cs'slots(cs'writer'writerPair, cs'writer'writerSlot) =
                    first(as'vals'valseq) ∧
      IF cs'pairWritten = cs'writer'writerPair
        THEN (cs'writer'writerSlot = s_0 ⇒
              cs'slots(cs'writer'writerPair, s_1) = as'vals'valseq(1)) ∧
              (cs'writer'writerSlot = s_1 ⇒
                  cs'slots(cs'writer'writerPair, s_0) = as'vals'valseq(1))
        ELSE cs'slots(cs'pairWritten, cs'slotWritten(cs'pairWritten)) =
                    as'vals'valseq(1)
      ENDIF
        ∧ as'vals'length ≥ 2) ∧
```
-- Only the reader is accessing the ACM. It may be possible to
-- retrieve two values - the last one written can always be
-- retreived,and we can also retreive the value the reader is
```

```
-- accessing (which may be different from the last one written).
-- It is not possible to know which item in the abstract sequence
-- will be the one that the reader reads, because there can be
-- any number of writes overlapping with the read, each one adding
-- a new item to the sequence
```
$(cs\text{`}nri = rd \land cs\text{`}nwi = wcp \Rightarrow$
$\quad as\text{`}readerAccess \land \neg\ as\text{`}writerAccess \land$
$\quad cs\text{`}reader\text{`}readerPair = cs\text{`}pairReading \land$
$\quad\quad cs\text{`}slots(cs\text{`}pairWritten,\ cs\text{`}slotWritten(cs\text{`}pairWritten)) =$
$\quad\quad\quad\quad first(as\text{`}vals\text{`}valseq) \land$
$\quad\quad\quad (\exists\ (i\colon nat)\colon$
$\quad\quad\quad\quad i < as\text{`}vals\text{`}length \land$
$\quad\quad\quad\quad\quad cs\text{`}slots(cs\text{`}reader\text{`}readerPair,\ cs\text{`}reader\text{`}readerSlot) =$
$\quad\quad\quad\quad\quad\quad as\text{`}vals\text{`}valseq(i))$
$\quad\quad\quad \land\ as\text{`}vals\text{`}length \geq 1 \land$

```
-- Reader and writer both accessing the ACM. Up to three values
-- can be retrieved. The one being written, the last value written
-- and the value the reader is accessing which may be different
-- from these two values.
```
$(cs\text{`}nri = rd \land cs\text{`}nwi = wip \Rightarrow$
$\quad as\text{`}readerAccess \land as\text{`}writerAccess \land$
$\quad\quad cs\text{`}writer\text{`}writerSlot = cs\text{`}slotWritten(cs\text{`}writer\text{`}writerPair) \land$
$\quad\quad cs\text{`}reader\text{`}readerPair = cs\text{`}pairReading \land$
$\quad\quad cs\text{`}slots(cs\text{`}writer\text{`}writerPair,\ cs\text{`}writer\text{`}writerSlot) =$
$\quad\quad\quad\quad first(as\text{`}vals\text{`}valseq) \land$
$\quad\quad$ IF $cs\text{`}pairWritten = cs\text{`}writer\text{`}writerPair$
$\quad\quad\quad$ THEN $(cs\text{`}writer\text{`}writerSlot = s_0 \Rightarrow$
$\quad\quad\quad\quad\quad cs\text{`}slots(cs\text{`}writer\text{`}writerPair,\ s_1) = as\text{`}vals\text{`}valseq(1)) \land$
$\quad\quad\quad\quad (cs\text{`}writer\text{`}writerSlot = s_1 \Rightarrow$
$\quad\quad\quad\quad\quad cs\text{`}slots(cs\text{`}writer\text{`}writerPair,\ s_0) = as\text{`}vals\text{`}valseq(1))$
$\quad\quad\quad$ ELSE $cs\text{`}slots(cs\text{`}pairWritten,\ cs\text{`}slotWritten(cs\text{`}pairWritten)) =$
$\quad\quad\quad\quad\quad\quad as\text{`}vals\text{`}valseq(1)$
$\quad\quad$ ENDIF $\land$
$\quad\quad\quad (\exists\ (i\colon nat)\colon$
$\quad\quad\quad\quad i < as\text{`}vals\text{`}length \land$
$\quad\quad\quad\quad\quad cs\text{`}slots(cs\text{`}reader\text{`}readerPair,\ cs\text{`}reader\text{`}readerSlot) =$
$\quad\quad\quad\quad\quad\quad as\text{`}vals\text{`}valseq(i))$
$\quad\quad\quad \land\ as\text{`}vals\text{`}length \geq 2)$
END Retrieve

Timing Analysis of Assembler Code
Control-Flow Paths

C.J. Fidge

Software Verification Research Centre
The University of Queensland, Australia

Abstract. Timing analysis of assembler code is essential to achieve the
strongest possible guarantee of correctness for safety-critical, real-time
software. Previous work has shown how timing constraints on control-
flow paths through high-level language programs can be formalised using
the semantics of the statements comprising the path. We extend these
results to assembler-level code where it becomes possible to not only determine timing constraints, but also to verify them against the known execution times for each instruction. A minimal formal model is developed
with both a weakest liberal precondition and a strongest postcondition
semantics. However, despite the formalism's simplicity, it is shown that
complex timing behaviour associated with instruction pipelining and iterative code can be modelled accurately.

1 Introduction

The usefulness of formal methods does not end with the construction of a high-
level language program. Here we show how a carefully chosen semantic model
can act as a formal theory for static analysis of the timing characteristics of
assembler-level code. Such a formalism provides the essential theoretical foundation for algorithms and tools [12] aimed at proving timing correctness for
safety-critical, real-time software.

Despite recent advances in real-time programming using high-level languages,
assembler-level programming of real-time systems remains an important concern.
Programmers of safety-critical systems still analyse compiled assembler code to
achieve highly-optimised timing performance and to allay concerns about compiler correctness [1]. Also, much legacy real-time software [5] exists as executable
code only, so the ability to verify code at the assembler level during maintenance
or upgrades is vital. Finally, a significant challenge for *any* attempt to apply
formal methods to real-time programming is that the program's actual timing
performance cannot be known until the final executable code has been produced
and the particular host architecture has been selected. Therefore, it is essential
that formal timing requirements can be carried down to the assembler level,
where they can be fully discharged.

Although formal models of assembler programs have been produced before,
there are still formidable practical challenges. Most notably, RISC architectures
are popular for real-time systems due to their high processing speeds [20], but

L.-H. Eriksson and P. Lindsay (Eds.): FME 2002, LNCS 2391, pp. 370–389, 2002.

the behaviour of such processors is notoriously difficult to formalise due to the presence of complex architectural features such as instruction pipelines [13].

Previously, Hayes *et al.* showed how high-level language programs can be annotated with precise timing requirements [8], how such annotations can be given a weakest-precondition semantics [11], and how particular control-flow paths through a high-level language program can be analysed to extract specific constraints on the compiled code's worst-case execution time [9]. In this paper, we complete this process by showing how such path analyses can also be performed directly on assembler-level code and how the extracted timing constraints can be verified against the specific timing characteristics of each instruction.

In particular, we use a detailed case study to show that a simple semantics is sufficient for timing analysis of control-flow paths through assembler code. Unlike previous assembler instruction formalisms, we do not need to model the behaviour of the instruction pointer because instruction sequencing is predetermined by the path extraction process. Furthermore, it is shown that the influences of instruction pipelining can be incorporated by separately defining the effects of annulled or stalled instructions and ineffective branches. It is then explained how a weakest liberal precondition semantics can be used to extract timing constraints by working backwards through an assembler code path, and how a complementary strongest postcondition semantics can be used to extract the final worst-case execution time by working forwards through the path, thus completing the timing proof.

2   Related Work

Our work builds on research into formal modelling of assembler code, static analysis of program control flow, and timing analysis of real-time software.

Formal models of assembler code have been developed for a number of purposes. Cifuentes *et al.* used Object-Z and the Semantic Specification Language to model instruction semantics as the basis for algorithms that translate legacy code from one instruction set to another [4]. Similarly, Ramsey and Fernández devised the Specification Language for Encoding and Decoding as the formal basis for a toolkit that supports manipulation of RISC instruction set code [17]. Kearney and Utting developed theories for the Ergo theorem prover to characterise pipelined instructions [13] to support their subsequent proof of a simple run-time scheduler's timing behaviour. Assembler code models also feature in formalisations of compiler code generation strategies [18,16].

Control-flow analysis is a fundamential concept in program debugging, static analysis and testing. Techniques for extracting (potential) control-flow paths through high-level language programs are well understood, and tools that subsequently analyse such paths are available [3,10]. Notably, flow analysis is the starting point for algorithms that attempt to predict the worst-case execution time of assembler code fragments [14,7,12].

In particular, Hayes *et al.* devised a formalism for extracting timing constraints from high-level language programs. They defined a predicate-transformer semantics for modelling real-time program statements [11] and used it to give a formal meaning to high-level language program annotations that specify desired timing properties [8]. Control-flow path analysis can then be applied to such annotated programs to extract specific constraints on the worst-case execution time of the final executable code corresponding to each path [9]. Potentially, these timing constraints can be verified against the actual or predicted execution time of the compiled code. However, Hayes *et al.*'s formal model does not go this far, so our goal here is to complete the timing analysis formalism by extending it to the assembler level, and by showing how both timing constraints and worst-case execution times can be derived from the same instruction semantics.

3 High-Level Language Timing Constraint Analysis

To introduce the timing analysis formalism, this section explains how the timing constraint associated with a trivial high-level language program fragment can be determined. The same example is revisited at the assembler level in Section 4.

$$\{\tau \leqslant st\};$$ -- Assumed latest starting time
$$\{4 \leqslant in \leqslant 11\};$$ -- Assumed range of input values
1) $in := in$ **div** 4;   -- Calculate sample size (1 or 2 bytes)
2) $cport := in;$ -- Write to control reg. to start conversion
3) **delay**$(in * 15\mathrm{ms});$ -- Wait until conversion completed
4) $res := dport;$ -- Read result from data register
   deadline$(st + 40\mathrm{ms} + in * 10\mathrm{ms})$ -- Specify latest finishing time

Fig. 1. High-level language program to sample a value from an analogue-to-digital converter. Let absolute time st be a logical constant of type Time; variables in and res be program variables of type Integer; and variables $cport$ and $dport$ be memory-mapped input/output locations

Consider the small program fragment in Fig. 1. It samples data from an analogue-to-digital converter by first writing to a control port to start the conversion, waiting for the conversion to be completed, and then reading the result from a data port. The numbered lines are conventional imperative programming language statements. The **div** operator on line 1 denotes truncating integer division. The **delay** statement on line 3 is a relative delay measured in milliseconds. Thus, the program takes the input value in, divides it to determine how many bytes the sampled value is to occupy, starts the conversion by writing to the control port $cport$, waits an amount of time proportional to the size of the required result, and reads the result from the data port $dport$ into result variable res. Care must be taken with such device-dependent programming to consider the behaviour of the compiled code. We require that variables $cport$, $dport$ and res are declared to be volatile to ensure that their values are always read from and written to memory, rather than held in a data register.

The unnumbered lines in Fig. 1 are non-executable program annotations. The first two are assumptions [15, §8.2] that we expect to be true of the program state when this program fragment begins. The second defines the expected range of the input variable in to be between 4 and 11. Dividing this by 4 (and rounding down) will therefore yield either 1 or 2 as the required number of bytes for the result. The first assumption uses the distinguished 'current time' variable τ to state that the program fragment is expected to start no later than absolute starting time st. Variable τ is part of the real-time semantics and may be used in program annotations to refer to the current time [11]. The last line in Fig. 1 is a **deadline** annotation [8] which expresses the requirement that this point in the program may be reached no later than the stated absolute time. In this case the latest finishing time is expressed in terms of the latest assumed starting time st, and is proportional to the number of bytes required from the conversion, as determined by the value of variable in.

The **deadline** annotation concisely states the programmer's intended timing behaviour for this program fragment but it is not immediately clear how to prove whether this requirement is met or not. Given such a program, 'timing constraint analysis' aims to extract a specific constraint on the worst-case execution time for each control-flow path, in a form that is easily checkable against the measured or predicted worst-case execution time for that path [9]. To formalise this process, however, we need a semantics for the statements in the path and its constructors.

Table 1. Weakest liberal precondition semantics for the basic control-flow path constructors. Let P, Q and R be predicates on the program variables, possibly including time τ. Predicates P and Q may not have free occurrences of primed variables. Also let v be a program variable, or list of variables; I be an indexing set; and S be a statement in our programming language

Construct S	Semantics wlp.$S.R$
$v:[P\,,Q]$	$P \Rightarrow (\forall v', \tau' \bullet (\tau' \geqslant \tau \wedge Q) \Rightarrow R[v', \tau'/v, \tau])$
$S_1 \,;\, S_2$	wlp.S_1.(wlp.S_2.R)
$\sqcap i : I \bullet S^i$	$\bigwedge_{i \in I}$ wlp.S^i.R

Table 1 defines the semantics of the three basic path constructors used herein via their weakest liberal preconditions. Weakest liberal preconditions offer a way of characterising the semantics of a program, provided that the program terminates [6, p. 127]. This is a suitable basis for path analysis since we expect that the extraction process identifies control-flow paths of interest only. Given some statement S and postcondition predicate R, the weakest liberal precondition 'wlp.$S.R$' is a predicate characterising those initial states from which statement S will achieve postcondition R, if S terminates. We construct predicates from the usual propositional operators, with '$\forall v : T \bullet P$' and '$\exists v : T \bullet P$' respectively denoting universal and existential quantification of variable v, of (optional) type T, over predicate P. We also use $P[E/v]$ to denote substitution of expression(s) E for variable(s) v in predicate P [15, §A.2.1].

The first constructor in Table 1 is a 'timed' version of the traditional specification statement [15, §21.3.2]. Specification $v\!:[P\,,Q]$ expresses a requirement to achieve postcondition Q, by modifying variable(s) v, provided that precondition P holds initially. If P is just 'true' it may be omitted. The postcondition predicate Q may contain primed variables 'v'' to denote final values. The timed semantics on the right in Table 1 is the same as the conventional one, except that it allow the implicit current time variable τ to appear in predicates. It also states that the finishing time τ' of the statement can be no earlier than the starting time τ. The semantics of the sequential composition of two statements '$S_1\,;\,S_2$' is standard [15, p. 182]. The final path constructor (used in Section 4) is nondeterministic choice [2]. In particular, path construct '$\sqcap i:I \bullet S^i$' models i repetitions of statement S, where i is chosen nondeterministically from indexing set I, and S^i denotes statement S sequentially-composed with itself i times.

Table 2. Semantics of the high-level language statements used in Fig. 1. Let P and R be predicates on program variables, possibly including time τ, but without free occurrences of primed variables. Also let v be a program variable; E be a high-level language expression which is type-compatible with v; duration D be a non-negative **Time**-valued expression; and absolute time T be an arbitrary **Time**-valued expression

Statement S	Specification	Semantics wlp.$S.R$
$v := E$	$v\!:[v'=E]$	$\forall \tau' \bullet \tau' \geqslant \tau \Rightarrow R[E,\tau'/v,\tau]$
delay(D)	$:[\tau' \geqslant \tau + D]$	$\forall \tau' \bullet \tau' \geqslant \tau + D \Rightarrow R[\tau'/\tau]$
$\{P\}$	$:[P\,,\tau'=\tau]$	$P \Rightarrow R$
deadline(T)	$:[\tau'=\tau \wedge \tau \leqslant T]$	$\tau \leqslant T \Rightarrow R$

Table 2 then defines the meaning of the programming language statements used in our example, as specification statements. (Similar definitions for other programming language statements can be found elsewhere [11].) The most notable feature is the effect each statement has on the time variable τ. An assignment statement not only updates the target variable v, but may also allow time to increase. In a high-level language program, however, we cannot say exactly how long the assignment will take—this depends on the compiled object code and the choice of processor. The **delay** statement is even simpler. It merely ensures that its finishing time τ' is no less than its starting time τ plus the minimum specified delay D. The assumption statement $\{P\}$ expects predicate P to be true, but does not allow time to advance. This is consistent with its role as a non-executable annotation. Similarly, the **deadline** statement cannot change the time τ, but still requires that its finishing time must not exceed the stated deadline T. A **deadline** annotation is thus a formal requirement to prove that the compiled code will indeed satisfy this obligation [8].

The timing analysis then uses this semantics to extract the timing constraint corresponding to each path through the program [9]. Control flow through the program in Fig. 1 is trivial—there is only one possible sequence of statements, so the program *is* a control-flow path. Starting from the **deadline** requirement, the analysis works backwards through the statements in the path and calculates the path's weakest liberal precondition with respect to the **deadline** expression. Given predicates P and Q with free variable(s) v, let $P \Rightarrow Q$ denote predicate implication in all states, i.e., $\forall v \bullet (P \Rightarrow Q)$ [15, p. 23]. Also let $P \equiv Q$ denote predicate equivalence in all states, i.e., $P \Rightarrow Q \wedge Q \Rightarrow P$.

Analysis begins by introducing a time-valued constant ω to denote the finishing time of the path, i.e., the final value of current-time variable τ. The postcondition that must be satisfied to meet the deadline at the end of the path (program) in Fig. 1 is therefore as follows.

$$R_0 \equiv \omega \leqslant st + 40\text{ms} + in * 10\text{ms}$$

Working backwards through the statements on lines 2 to 4 does not change this requirement.

$$
\begin{aligned}
R_1 &\equiv \text{wlp.}(res := dport).R_0 \\
&\equiv \forall \tau' \bullet \tau' \geqslant \tau \Rightarrow R_0[dport, \tau'/res, \tau] \\
&\equiv \omega \leqslant st + 40\text{ms} + in * 10\text{ms} \\
R_2 &\equiv \text{wlp.}(\textbf{delay}(in * 15\text{ms})).R_1 \\
&\equiv \forall \tau' \bullet \tau' \geqslant \tau + 15\text{ms} \Rightarrow R_1[\tau'/\tau] \\
&\equiv \omega \leqslant st + 40\text{ms} + in * 10\text{ms} \\
R_3 &\equiv \text{wlp.}(cport := in).R_2 \\
&\equiv \forall \tau' \bullet \tau' \geqslant \tau \Rightarrow R_2[in, \tau'/cport, \tau] \\
&\equiv \omega \leqslant st + 40\text{ms} + in * 10\text{ms}
\end{aligned}
$$

This is because none of these statements assigns to any of the variables in the **deadline** expression, and none of them tell us anything that helps determine whether the deadline can be met or not. (This might seem strange for the **delay** statement, which clearly specifies its minimum duration, but this information does not help us without knowing when the delay interval started.)

However, traversing the remaining statements does alter the expression. (We handle the two assumptions in one step.) In particular the statement on line 1 assigns to one of the free variables in the postcondition predicate. Let the rounding-down operator $\lfloor n \rfloor$ return the largest integer not exceeding number n.

$$
\begin{aligned}
R_4 &\equiv \text{wlp.}(in := in \ \textbf{div}\ 4).R_3 \\
&\equiv \forall \tau' \bullet \tau' \geqslant \tau \Rightarrow R_3[\lfloor in/4 \rfloor, \tau'/in, \tau] \\
&\equiv \omega \leqslant st + 40\text{ms} + \lfloor in/4 \rfloor * 10\text{ms} \\
R_5 &\equiv \text{wlp.}(\{\tau \leqslant st\} \, ; \, \{4 \leqslant in \leqslant 11\}).R_4 \\
&\equiv (\tau \leqslant st \wedge 4 \leqslant in \leqslant 11) \Rightarrow \omega \leqslant st + 40\text{ms} + \lfloor in/4 \rfloor * 10\text{ms}
\end{aligned}
$$

Thus, provided the two initial assumptions hold, the path in Fig. 1 will meet its deadline if its finishing time ω does not exceed the expression on the right.

The analysis is then completed by identifying a particular execution time for the path, i.e., the difference between finishing time ω and starting time τ, that ensures this predicate will be satisfied [9].

$$\omega - \tau \leqslant 40\text{ms} + \lfloor in/4 \rfloor * 10\text{ms}$$
$$\equiv \omega \leqslant \tau + 40\text{ms} + \lfloor in/4 \rfloor * 10\text{ms}$$
$$\Rightarrow (\tau \leqslant st \wedge 4 \leqslant in \leqslant 11) \Rightarrow \omega \leqslant st + 40\text{ms} + \lfloor in/4 \rfloor * 10\text{ms}$$
$$\equiv R_5$$

The required deadline is therefore guaranteed to be met provided that the worst-case execution time of the program fragment in Fig. 1 does not exceed 40ms + $\lfloor in/4 \rfloor * 10$ms. (Recall that this is a pre-state expression, whereas the original **deadline** annotation was written in terms of the post state.) This outcome is not surprising for this simple program, and could have been determined trivially by inspection. Nevertheless, it confirms the correctness of the formalism. More challenging examples can be found elsewhere [9,11].

Thus, formal path analysis has identified the essential constraint on the compiled code's worst-case execution time. However, this is as far as timing analysis of a high-level language program can go. Without further information, we cannot determine whether the program will meet this constraint at run time or not. Nor can we directly apply the above formalism to assembler code.

4   Assembler Code Analysis

In this section we extend the above analysis technique for high-level language programs into the realm of assembler code. In doing so, we must carefully consider some of the peculiarities of assembler-level programming.

4.1   A Brief Review of Some Pipelining Principles

We assume a pipelined architecture [20], in which consecutive instructions may overlap. This raises the issue of how to measure their execution times.

Consider the two instructions shown in Fig. 2. We assume a simple three-stage pipeline where: the Instruction Fetch stage increments the instruction pointer and decodes the next instruction; the Arithmetic and Logic Unit stage performs instruction-dependent operations on data from registers and memory; and the Write Back stage stores the instruction's results in registers or memory, depending on the instruction type. In the particular case shown in Fig. 2, the 'divide immediate' instruction consumes 4 machine cycles, and the 'indirect store' instruction consumes 5. However, the sequence of a **divi** instruction followed by an **istore** consumes only 7 cycles due to their overlapping execution.

Rather than reasoning about the timing of each stage separately, we adopt the simplifying approach of defining the duration of each instruction with respect to a particular pipeline stage [19], in this case the ALU stage. Thus the **divi** instruction in Fig. 2 is considered to have a duration of 2 cycles and the **istore** instruction takes 3 cycles. In sequence they have a total duration of 5 cycles. The first and last cycles in the right-hand matrix of Fig. 2 will overlap the preceding and succeeding code fragments, respectively. These pipeline *priming* and *flushing* overheads are the same for any instruction sequence and can be overlooked when analysing a code fragment that forms part of some larger program.

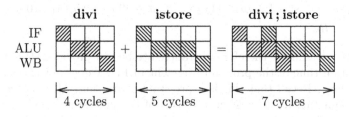

Fig. 2. The influence of instruction pipelining on end-to-end timing

Two consecutive instructions cannot overlap, however, if the results of the first instruction are needed by the second. It is then necessary to *stall* the pipeline so that the WB stage of the first instruction finishes before the ALU stage of the second instruction begins. To avoid frequent stalls due to consecutive instructions that access the same registers, most architectures incorporate a *bypass* path that forwards the results of the first instruction's ALU stage directly to the ALU stage of the second instruction [13]. Nevertheless, instructions that perform complex arithmetic operations or access secondary storage may still stall the pipeline. In particular, we assume below that **load** instructions may cause pipeline stalls.

Another pipelining feature is the need to sometimes *annul* an instruction that has already started executing. This can occur when an instruction occupies a *delay slot*, i.e., it immediately follows a branch instruction. Typically, the architecture is configured so that if the branch is taken, then the following instruction is executed, but if the branch is not taken the following instruction should be ignored. However, since instructions overlap in the pipeline, the following instruction will be partially completed by the time the branching instruction decides which way to go. The solution is to 'annul' the second instruction when it is recognised that the branch will not be followed. This prevents the annulled instruction from performing its WB stage, so the results of its ALU computation are not preserved. We will see how our formalism accommodates this below.

4.2 Timing Constraint Analysis

Here we continue the case study from Section 3 at the assembler level. Fig. 3 shows an assembler program that corresponds to the previous high-level language example. The target register or memory location for each instruction appears last in its operand list.

$$\{\tau \leqslant st\}$$
$$\{4 \leqslant m(`in') \leqslant 11\}$$

a : **load** 'in' A -- Calculate sample size (1 or 2 bytes)
b : **divi** A 4 A
c : **store** A '$cport$'   -- Write to control reg. to start conversion
d : **multi** A 3 B -- Wait until conversion completed
e : **brpos** B e
f : **subi** B 1 B
g : **load** '$dport$' C -- Read result from data register
h : **store** C 'res'
    deadline(st + 20cycles + $A * 5$cycles)

Fig. 3. Assembler code corresponding to the program in Fig. 1. Let data memory m be a total function of type `Identifier` $\to$ `Word`, and registers A, B and C be variables of type `Word`

The timing annotations are modified only slightly. Where high-level language variable in appeared before, it is now replaced by $m(`in')$ which denotes the corresponding machine-level memory location. Data memory is represented by a memory function m which is indexed symbolically by identifiers. We use quotation marks 'v' to denote the memory address associated with high-level language variable v. The **deadline** annotation is unchanged except that we have updated the arithmetic to reflect an assumption that each cycle on the target machine consumes 2 milliseconds, and have replaced the high-level language variable in with the register A which holds its value. (Variable in was not declared as volatile, so its value has not yet been stored in $m(`in')$ at this point.)

The executable instructions correspond closely to the high-level language program. An optimisation was applied to avoid storing and reloading non-volatile variable in after the instruction at location b. However, the most dramatic feature is the iterative sequence of instructions at locations d to f which implement the **delay** statement on line 3 of the high-level language program. The 'multiply immediate' instruction **multi** at location d calculates the number of iterations required to achieve the necessary delay and puts this value into register B— the multiplier 3 is based on knowledge of the actual execution times of the instructions in the loop. The 'branch if positive' instruction **brpos** at location e iterates while the loop counter in register B is greater than zero. The following 'subtract immediate' instruction **subi** occupies the **brpos** instruction's delay slot. Due to the instruction pipeline, it is executed whenever the branch is taken, even though it appears to be 'outside' the loop. The flow graph in Fig. 4 shows the actual control flow through this code.

To accommodate the behaviour of branches not taken, and annulled and stalled instructions, Fig. 4 uses some special case instructions. The 'negated' branch instruction ~~brpos~~ represents the situation where the branch condition fails and the branch is *not* taken. It is helpful to include this in our formalism because knowing that instruction '**brpos** B e' was ineffective tells us something

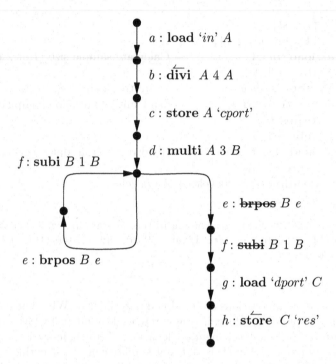

$a : $ **load** $'in'$ A

$b : $ $\overleftarrow{\textbf{divi}}$ A 4 A

$c : $ **store** A $'cport'$

$d : $ **multi** A 3 B

$f: $ **subi** B 1 B

$e : $ ~~**brpos**~~ B e

$f: $ ~~**subi**~~ B 1 B

$g : $ **load** $'dport'$ C

$h : $ $\overleftarrow{\textbf{store}}$ C $'res'$

$e : $ **brpos** B e

Fig. 4. Flow graph for the assembler code in Fig. 3

about the value of register B. Similarly, the 'annulled' subtract instruction ~~**subi**~~ represents the situation where the subtraction in the delay slot is annulled. Even though it does not change the machine state, it is important to include this information in our formalism because the annulled instruction still consumes time. The 'stalled' divide immediate $\overleftarrow{\textbf{divi}}$ and store $\overleftarrow{\textbf{store}}$ instructions are used to model the case where these instructions must wait for the result of a preceding **load** to become available. Again it is important to distinguish such cases to model the delays caused by pipeline stalls. Introducing these special cases as separate instructions in their own right considerably simplifies our formalism.

To duplicate the high-level language timing analysis performed in Section 3, we next need to express the program in Fig. 3 as a control-flow path using the constructors from Table 1. This is done in Fig. 5. The most notable feature of this path is that it contains a loop, expressed using the $\sqcap$ operator. The two instructions that form the loop, '**brpos** B e' and '**subi** B 1 B', are enclosed within a construct that iterates between 0 and B times. This choice of indexing set is informed by our knowledge of this particular loop's structure. The graph in Fig. 4 reminds us that the loop's instructions may not be executed at all, thus providing the lower bound of 0. The fact that the loop is controlled by instruction '**brpos** B e' provides the upper bound of B. (Register B's value is a loop variant.) Similar reasoning can be used to accommodate other common assembler code patterns. Following the iterative construct, the negated branch

$\{\tau \leqslant st\};$
$\{4 \leqslant m(`in') \leqslant 11\};$
(**load** `in` A);
(**$\overleftarrow{\textbf{divi}}$** A 4 A);
(**store** A `cport`);
(**multi** A 3 B);
($\sqcap i : \{n : \mathbb{N} \mid 0 \leqslant n \leqslant B\}$ •
    (**brpos** B e);
    (**subi** B 1 B));
(~~**brpos**~~ B e);
(~~**subi**~~ B 1 B);
(**load** `dport` C);
(**$\overleftarrow{\textbf{store}}$** C `res`);
deadline($st + 20\text{cycles} + A * 5\text{cycles}$)

Fig. 5. The flow graph from Fig. 4 represented as a path

and annulled subtraction appear in the path. The graph in Fig. 4 reminds us that these instructions are always executed, even if the loop is never entered.

Table 3. Semantics of the assembler instructions used in Figs. 3 to 5. Let r be a general-purpose register; m be the data memory array; a be an address in the domain of m; ℓ be an instruction memory address; and i be an integer valued constant

Instruction	Equivalent specification
load a r	$r : [r' = m(a) \wedge \tau' = \tau + 2]$
store r a	$m : [m' = m \oplus (a \mapsto r) \wedge \tau' = \tau + 2]$
multi r_1 i r_2	$r_2 : [r_2' = r_1 * i \wedge \tau + 1 \leqslant \tau' \leqslant \tau + 2]$
divi r_1 i r_2	$r_2 : [r_2' = \lfloor r_1/i \rfloor \wedge \tau + 1 \leqslant \tau' \leqslant \tau + 2]$
subi r_1 i r_2	$r_2 : [r_2' = r_1 - i \wedge \tau' = \tau + 1]$
brpos r ℓ	$: [r > 0 \wedge \tau' = \tau + 1]$
~~**brpos**~~ r ℓ	$: [r \leqslant 0 \wedge \tau' = \tau + 1]$
~~**subi**~~ r_1 i r_2	$: [\tau' = \tau + 1]$
$\overleftarrow{\textbf{divi}}$ r_1 i r_2	$r_2 : [r_2' = \lfloor r_1/i \rfloor \wedge \tau + 2 \leqslant \tau' \leqslant \tau + 3]$
$\overleftarrow{\textbf{store}}$ r a	$m : [m' = m \oplus (a \mapsto r) \wedge \tau' = \tau + 3]$

The assembler-level semantics is completed by providing a meaning for each instruction, as shown in Table 3. The effect of each instruction on the machine's state and the current time τ is expressed as a specification statement. For some function f, let $f \oplus (d \mapsto r)$ denote *overriding* of the function's mapping from domain element d by a mapping with range value r. In general, each instruction definition consists of two conjuncts: the first shows how the instruction updates the machine's state, and the second specifies how many cycles the instruction takes. The execution time of multiplication instructions is assumed to depend on the size of their operands, so a range of values is allowed for their finishing time τ'. Although it does not update the system state, the **brpos** instruction (and its negated form) includes a predicate which tells us the state of the register used to make the decision. The definition of the annulled subtraction instruction ~~subi~~ shows that it consumes one machine cycle, but has no other effect. The execution times of the stalled instructions, $\overset{\smile}{\textbf{divi}}$ and $\overset{\smile}{\textbf{store}}$, are both one cycle longer than their unhindered counterparts. (For brevity, none of the definitions include preconditions. We assume that memory function m is total, so there is no need to check whether an address is in m's domain, and use mathematical, rather than machine-specific, arithmetic so there is no need to check for overflow.)

Notably absent from the definitions in Table 3 is the instruction pointer. In all comparable assembler-level semantic models [18,16,13] the instruction pointer is explicitly modelled so that reasoning can be performed about control flow through the program. Indeed, this has been a major source of difficulty because this is analogous to reasoning about arbitrary **goto** statements. In our application, however, the path through the code is predetermined, so there is no need to incorporate the instruction pointer in the semantics at all.

We can now begin to calculate the weakest liberal precondition of the path in Fig. 5 needed to meet its final deadline. Firstly, we determine the semantics of the embedded loop with respect to an arbitrary postcondition R. The semantics of the two instructions comprising the loop is calculated as follows.

$$
\begin{aligned}
R_0 &\equiv \text{wlp.}(\textbf{subi } B \ 1 \ B).R \\
&\equiv \forall B', \tau' \bullet ((B' = B - 1 \wedge \tau' = \tau + 1) \Rightarrow R[B', \tau'/B, \tau]) \\
&\equiv R[B - 1, \tau + 1/B, \tau] \\
R_1 &\equiv \text{wlp.}(\textbf{brpos } B \ e).R_0 \\
&\equiv \forall \tau' \bullet ((B > 0 \wedge \tau' = \tau + 1) \Rightarrow R_0[\tau'/\tau]) \\
&\equiv B > 0 \Rightarrow (\forall \tau' \bullet (\tau' = \tau + 1 \Rightarrow R[B - 1, \tau' + 1/B, \tau])) \\
&\equiv B > 0 \Rightarrow R[B - 1, \tau + 2/B, \tau]
\end{aligned}
$$

This is exactly the result we would expect. We enter the loop only if register B is positive, and performing the loop once decrements B and consumes 2 cycles.

We now need to calculate the effect of performing these two instructions several times in a row. Let statement X denote '$(\textbf{brpos } B \ e) \,; (\textbf{subi } B \ 1 \ B)$'. In the base case, where the instructions are not performed at all, they have no effect and their semantics is just the identity function.

$$
\text{wlp.}X^0.R \equiv R
$$

The semantics for non-zero cases can be calculated as follows.

$$
\begin{aligned}
\text{wlp.}X^1.R &\equiv B > 0 \Rightarrow R[B - 1, \tau + 2/B, \tau] \\
\text{wlp.}X^2.R &\equiv B > 0 \Rightarrow (B > 0 \Rightarrow R[B - 1, \tau + 2/B, \tau])[B - 1, \tau + 2/B, \tau]
\end{aligned}
$$

$$\equiv B > 0 \Rightarrow R[B - 2, \tau + 4/B, \tau]$$
$$\text{wlp}.X^3.R \equiv B > 0 \Rightarrow R[B - 3, \tau + 6/B, \tau]$$

$$\vdots$$

$$\text{wlp}.X^n.R \equiv B > 0 \Rightarrow R[B - n, \tau + 2 * n/B, \tau]$$

Then we use the semantics of iteration from Table 1 to determine the weakest liberal precondition of the whole loop.

$$\text{wlp}.(\sqcap i : \{n : \mathbb{N} \mid 0 \leqslant n \leqslant B\} \bullet X^i).R$$
$$\equiv R \wedge \bigwedge_{i \in \{n : \mathbb{N} \mid 0 < n \leqslant B\}} (B > 0 \Rightarrow R[B - i, \tau + 2 * i/B, \tau])$$
$$\equiv R \wedge (\forall i \bullet (0 < i \leqslant B \Rightarrow R[B - i, \tau + 2 * i/B, \tau]))$$

We can now use this result when working backwards through the path in Fig. 5, treating the loop as a single statement. As in Section 3 the starting point is the final **deadline** requirement reexpressed in terms of finishing time ω.

$$R_0 \equiv \omega \leqslant st + 20\text{cycles} + A * 5\text{cycles}$$

The final three instructions have no effect on the postcondition because they do not update any of the free variables in the predicate.

$$R_1 \equiv \text{wlp}.(\overleftarrow{\text{store}} \ C \ \text{'res'}).R_0$$
$$\equiv \forall m', \tau' \bullet ((m' = m \oplus (\text{'res'} \mapsto C) \wedge \tau' = \tau + 3) \Rightarrow R_0[m', \tau'/m, \tau])$$
$$\equiv \omega \leqslant st + 20\text{cycles} + A * 5\text{cycles}$$
$$R_2 \equiv \text{wlp}.(\text{load} \ \text{'dport'} \ C).R_1$$
$$\equiv \forall C', \tau' \bullet ((C' = m(\text{'dport'}) \wedge \tau' = \tau + 2) \Rightarrow R_1[C', \tau'/C, \tau])$$
$$\equiv \omega \leqslant st + 20\text{cycles} + A * 5\text{cycles}$$
$$R_3 \equiv \text{wlp}.(\text{subi} \ B \ 1 \ B).R_2$$
$$\equiv \forall \tau' \bullet (\tau' = \tau + 1 \Rightarrow R_2[\tau'/\tau])$$
$$\equiv \omega \leqslant st + 20\text{cycles} + A * 5\text{cycles}$$

Even though the semantics in Table 3 provides exact execution times for each instruction, these do not feature in the calculation of the timing *constraint* on the path. We will see their use in Section 4.3.

Working through the negated branch instruction, however, informs us that the value in register B cannot be positive at this point.

$$R_4 \equiv \text{wlp}.(\text{brpos} \ B \ e).R_3$$
$$\equiv \forall \tau' \bullet ((\tau' = \tau + 1 \wedge B \leqslant 0) \Rightarrow R_3[\tau'/\tau])$$
$$\equiv B \leqslant 0 \Rightarrow \omega \leqslant st + 20\text{cycles} + A * 5\text{cycles}$$

Next we apply the loop semantics calculated above.

$$R_5 \equiv \text{wlp}.(\sqcap i : \{n : \mathbb{N} \mid 0 \leqslant n \leqslant B\} \bullet X^i).R_4$$
$$\equiv R_4 \wedge (\forall i \bullet (0 < i \leqslant B \Rightarrow R_4[B - i, \tau + 2 * i/B, \tau]))$$

$$\equiv (B \leqslant 0 \Rightarrow \omega \leqslant st + 20 + A * 5) \wedge$$
$$(\forall i \bullet (0 < i \leqslant B \Rightarrow (B - i \leqslant 0 \Rightarrow \omega \leqslant st + 20 + A * 5)))$$
$$\equiv (B \leqslant 0 \Rightarrow \omega \leqslant st + 20 + A * 5) \wedge (B > 0 \Rightarrow \omega \leqslant st + 20 + A * 5)$$
$$\equiv \omega \leqslant st + 20\text{cycles} + A * 5\text{cycles}$$

It may seem disappointing after so much effort to return to the predicate we started with. However, this is the result we expect. The assembler loop, like the **delay** statement it implements, merely consumes time, and therefore contributes nothing to the end-to-end timing constraint. (However, the loop's role in Section 4.3 is much more significant.)

The next two instructions similarly have no impact on the constraint.

$$R_6 \equiv \text{wlp.}(\textbf{multi } A\ 3\ B).R_5$$
$$\equiv \forall B', \tau' \bullet ((B' = B * 3 \wedge \tau + 1 \leqslant \tau' \leqslant \tau + 2) \Rightarrow R_5[B', \tau'/B, \tau])$$
$$\equiv \omega \leqslant st + 20\text{cycles} + A * 5\text{cycles}$$
$$R_7 \equiv \text{wlp.}(\textbf{store } A\ \text{`cport'}).R_6$$
$$\equiv \forall m', \tau' \bullet ((m' = m \oplus (\text{`cport'} \mapsto A) \wedge \tau' = \tau + 2) \Rightarrow R_6[m', \tau'/m, \tau])$$
$$\equiv \omega \leqslant st + 20\text{cycles} + A * 5\text{cycles}$$

In the final sequence of instructions, however, register A is updated with memory value $m(\text{`in'})$, thus modifying the postcondition.

$$R_8 \equiv \text{wlp.}(\overleftarrow{\textbf{divi}}\ A\ 4\ A).R_7$$
$$\equiv \forall A', \tau' \bullet ((A' = \lfloor A/4 \rfloor \wedge \tau + 2 \leqslant \tau' \leqslant \tau + 3) \Rightarrow R_7[A', \tau'/A, \tau])$$
$$\equiv \forall A', \tau' \bullet ((A' = \lfloor A/4 \rfloor \wedge \tau + 2 \leqslant \tau' \leqslant \tau + 3) \Rightarrow \omega \leqslant st + 20 + A' * 5)$$
$$\equiv \omega \leqslant st + 20\text{cycles} + \lfloor A/4 \rfloor * 5\text{cycles}$$
$$R_9 \equiv \text{wlp.}(\textbf{load } \text{`in'}\ A).R_8$$
$$\equiv \forall A', \tau' \bullet ((A' = m(\text{`in'}) \wedge \tau' = \tau + 2) \Rightarrow \omega \leqslant st + 20 + \lfloor A'/4 \rfloor * 5)$$
$$\equiv \omega \leqslant st + 20\text{cycles} + \lfloor m(\text{`in'})/4 \rfloor * 5\text{cycles}$$
$$R_{10} \equiv \text{wlp.}(\{\tau \leqslant st\}\ ;\ \{4 \leqslant m(\text{`in'}) \leqslant 11\}).R_9$$
$$\equiv (\tau \leqslant st \wedge 4 \leqslant m(\text{`in'}) \leqslant 11) \Rightarrow$$
$$\omega \leqslant st + 20\text{cycles} + \lfloor m(\text{`in'})/4 \rfloor * 5\text{cycles}$$

This is exactly the same as the weakest liberal precondition calculated in Section 3, given our assumption that each machine cycle consumes 2 milliseconds, thus confirming that we can duplicate high-level language timing constraint analysis at the assembler level, even though the control flow through the assembler code is significantly more complex. Furthermore, as shown in the next section, the additional timing information available in the assembler semantics now allows us to go further and determine whether the assembler code actually satisfies this constraint or not.

4.3   Worst-Case Execution Time Analysis

The constraint calculation above used weakest liberal preconditions to work backwards though the path, making use of the changes to the machine's state in the semantics of each instruction. In this section we follow the complementary approach, working forwards through the path using a strongest postcondition semantics [6], in order to use the timing predicates in each instruction's semantics to calculate the path's worst-case execution time.

Table 4. Strongest postcondition semantics for the basic control-flow path constructors. Operands are the same as in Table 1

Construct S	Semantics sp.S.R
$v: [P, Q]$	$(\exists v, \tau \bullet (P \wedge \tau' \geqslant \tau \wedge Q \wedge R))[v, \tau/v', \tau']$
$S_1 ; S_2$	sp.S_2.(sp.S_1.R)
$\sqcap i : I \bullet S^i$	$\bigvee_{i \in I}$ sp.S^i.R

Table 4 presents the strongest postcondition semantics of each of the basic path constructors. Let sp.S.R be the strongest postcondition derivable from the execution of statement S in a state satisfying precondition predicate R. The definitions complement those in Table 1 in an obvious way. Coupled with the definitions in Table 3, this is sufficient to immediately calculate the strongest postcondition of the path in Fig. 5.

Again we begin by calculating the semantics of the embedded loop. In this case we work forwards through the instruction sequence, for an arbitrary *precondition* R.

$$R_0 \equiv \text{sp.}(\textbf{brpos } B \text{ } e).R$$
$$\equiv (\exists \tau \bullet (B > 0 \wedge \tau' = \tau + 1 \wedge R))[\tau/\tau']$$
$$\equiv (B > 0 \wedge R[\tau' - 1/\tau])[\tau/\tau']$$
$$\equiv B > 0 \wedge R[\tau - 1/\tau]$$
$$R_1 \equiv \text{sp.}(\textbf{subi } B \text{ } 1 \text{ } B).R_0$$
$$\equiv (\exists B, \tau \bullet (B' = B - 1 \wedge \tau' = \tau + 1 \wedge R_0))[B, \tau/B', \tau']$$
$$\equiv (\exists B, \tau \bullet (B = B' + 1 \wedge \tau = \tau' - 1 \wedge$$
$$B > 0 \wedge R[\tau - 1/\tau]))[B, \tau/B', \tau']$$
$$\equiv (B' + 1 > 0 \wedge R[B' + 1, \tau' - 2/B, \tau])[B, \tau/B', \tau']$$
$$\equiv B \geqslant 0 \wedge R[B + 1, \tau - 2/B, \tau]$$

Again, this is the result we anticipate. After these two instructions are executed, register B will be non-negative and the value of B in the precondition will equal its final value plus one. Similarly, the starting time will be 2 cycles less than the finishing time.

Now we calculate the strongest postcondition derivable from performing these instructions zero or more times. Let X denote '$(\textbf{brpos } B \text{ } e)\text{;}(\textbf{subi } B \text{ } 1 \text{ } B)$'. The base case does nothing, and the non-zero cases are straightforward.

$$\mathrm{sp}.X^0.R \equiv R$$
$$\mathrm{sp}.X^1.R \equiv B \geqslant 0 \wedge R[B+1, \tau - 2/B, \tau]$$
$$\mathrm{sp}.X^2.R \equiv B \geqslant 0 \wedge (B \geqslant 0 \wedge R[B+1, \tau - 2/B, \tau])[B+1, \tau - 2/B, \tau]$$
$$\equiv B \geqslant 0 \wedge B + 1 \geqslant 0 \wedge R[B+2, \tau - 4/B, \tau]$$
$$\equiv B \geqslant 0 \wedge R[B+2, \tau - 4/B, \tau]$$
$$\mathrm{sp}.X^3.R \equiv B \geqslant 0 \wedge R[B+3, \tau - 6/B, \tau]$$
$$\vdots$$
$$\mathrm{sp}.X^n.R \equiv B \geqslant 0 \wedge R[B+n, \tau - 2*n/B, \tau]$$

To calculate the semantics of the whole iterative construct, however, we must first resolve a small complication. Set comprehension $\{n : \mathbb{N} \mid 0 \leqslant n \leqslant B\}$ in Fig. 5 is expressed in terms of the *initial* value of register B when the loop is encountered. Now that we are calculating a *postcondition* predicate, references to 'B' will mean its *final* value. Therefore, we temporarily introduce a logical constant N to capture the initial value of B.

$$\mathrm{sp}.(\{N = B\} \,;\, (\sqcap i : \{n : \mathbb{N} \mid 0 \leqslant n \leqslant N\} \bullet X^i)).R$$
$$\equiv R \vee \bigvee_{i \in \{n:\mathbb{N}\mid 0 < n \leqslant N\}} (B \geqslant 0 \wedge R[B+i, \tau - 2*i/B, \tau])$$
$$\equiv R \vee (\exists i \bullet (0 < i \leqslant N \wedge B \geqslant 0 \wedge R[B+i, \tau - 2*i/B, \tau]))$$

We now want to work forwards through the path to calculate its postcondition. As a starting point we introduce an absolute time-valued constant α to capture the starting time of the entire path.

$$R_0 \equiv \tau = \alpha$$

The assumptions tell us something about the input variable and the starting time.

$$R_1 \equiv \mathrm{sp}.(\{\tau \leqslant st\} \,;\, \{4 \leqslant m(`in') \leqslant 11\}).R_0$$
$$\equiv \alpha \leqslant st \wedge 4 \leqslant m(`in') \leqslant 11 \wedge \tau = \alpha$$

The strongest postcondition of the first **load** instruction defines the value of register A and relates the instruction's finishing time τ to the starting time α.

$$R_2 \equiv \mathrm{sp}.(\mathbf{load}\ `in'\ A).R_1$$
$$\equiv (\exists A, \tau \bullet (A' = m(`in') \wedge \tau' = \tau + 2 \wedge$$
$$\tau \leqslant st \wedge 4 \leqslant m(`in') \leqslant 11 \wedge \tau = \alpha))[A, \tau/A', \tau']$$
$$\equiv \alpha \leqslant st \wedge 4 \leqslant m(`in') \leqslant 11 \wedge A = m(`in') \wedge \tau = \alpha + 2$$

The next three instructions further update the processor state and time.

$$R_3 \equiv \mathrm{sp}.(\overleftarrow{\mathbf{divi}}\ A\ 4\ A).R_2$$
$$\equiv (\exists A, \tau \bullet (A = m(`in') \wedge A' = \lfloor A/4 \rfloor \wedge 4 \leqslant m(`in') \leqslant 11 \wedge$$
$$\tau + 2 \leqslant \tau' \leqslant \tau + 3 \wedge \alpha \leqslant st \wedge \tau = \alpha + 2))[A, \tau/A', \tau']$$

$$\equiv \alpha \leqslant st \wedge 4 \leqslant m(`in`) \leqslant 11 \wedge A = \lfloor m(`in`)/4 \rfloor \wedge \alpha + 4 \leqslant \tau \leqslant \alpha + 5$$

$$R_4 \equiv \text{sp.}(\textbf{store } A \ `cport`).R_3$$

$$\equiv (\exists m, \tau \bullet (A = \lfloor m(`in`)/4 \rfloor \wedge m' = m \oplus (`cport` \mapsto A) \wedge$$
$$4 \leqslant m(`in`) \leqslant 11 \wedge \tau' = \tau + 2 \wedge$$
$$\alpha \leqslant st \wedge \alpha + 4 \leqslant \tau \leqslant \alpha + 5))[m, \tau/m', \tau']$$

$$\equiv \text{`provided addresses } `in` \text{ and } `cport` \text{ are distinct'}$$
$$\alpha \leqslant st \wedge 4 \leqslant m(`in`) \leqslant 11 \wedge A = \lfloor m(`in`)/4 \rfloor \wedge$$
$$(\exists m \bullet m' = m \oplus (`cport` \mapsto A))[m/m'] \wedge \alpha + 6 \leqslant \tau \leqslant \alpha + 7$$

$$\equiv \alpha \leqslant st \wedge 4 \leqslant m(`in`) \leqslant 11 \wedge A = \lfloor m(`in`)/4 \rfloor \wedge$$
$$(\exists m'' \bullet m = m'' \oplus (`cport` \mapsto A)) \wedge \alpha + 6 \leqslant \tau \leqslant \alpha + 7$$

$$R_5 \equiv \text{sp.}(\textbf{multi } A \ 3 \ B).R_4$$

$$\equiv (\exists B, \tau \bullet (B' = A * 3 \wedge \tau + 1 \leqslant \tau' \leqslant \tau + 2 \wedge R_4))[B, \tau/B', \tau']$$

$$\equiv \alpha \leqslant st \wedge 4 \leqslant m(`in`) \leqslant 11 \wedge A = \lfloor m(`in`)/4 \rfloor \wedge B = A * 3 \wedge$$
$$(\exists m'' \bullet m = m'' \oplus (`cport` \mapsto A)) \wedge \alpha + 7 \leqslant \tau \leqslant \alpha + 9$$

The existentially quantified predicate defining how memory function m relates to its initial value m'' is awkward, but cannot be simplified due to the lack of an inverse for the '$\oplus$' operator. We cannot 'unoverride' a mapping to recover the original function. At this point the range of execution times is between 7 and 9 cycles, due to the nondeterministic timing of the multiplication instructions.

To apply the loop semantics calculated above, logical constant N is unified with expression $A * 3$ because this is the value of register B in postcondition R_5, i.e., when the loop begins.

$$R_6 \equiv \text{sp.}(\sqcap i : \{n : \mathbb{N} \mid 0 \leqslant n \leqslant N\} \bullet X^i).R_5$$

$$\equiv \text{`substitute } A * 3 \text{ for } N \text{ since } B = A * 3`$$
$$R_5 \vee (\exists i \bullet (0 < i \leqslant A * 3 \wedge B \geqslant 0 \wedge R_5[B + i, \tau - 2 * i/B, \tau]))$$

$$\equiv A = \lfloor m(`in`)/4 \rfloor \wedge 4 \leqslant m(`in`) \leqslant 11 \wedge \alpha \leqslant st \wedge$$
$$(\exists m'' \bullet m = m'' \oplus (`cport` \mapsto A)) \wedge$$
$$((B = A * 3 \wedge \alpha + 7 \leqslant \tau \leqslant \alpha + 9) \vee$$
$$(\exists i \bullet (0 < i \leqslant A * 3 \wedge B \geqslant 0 \wedge \alpha + 7 \leqslant \tau - 2 * i \leqslant \alpha + 9 \wedge$$
$$B + i = A * 3)))$$

$$\equiv \text{`since } A \text{ is non-negative, due to the range of } m(`in`)`$$
$$A = \lfloor m(`in`)/4 \rfloor \wedge 4 \leqslant m(`in`) \leqslant 11 \wedge \alpha \leqslant st \wedge$$
$$(\exists m'' \bullet m = m'' \oplus (`cport` \mapsto A)) \wedge$$
$$((B = A * 3 \wedge \alpha + 7 \leqslant \tau \leqslant \alpha + 9) \vee$$
$$(0 < (A * 3 - B) \leqslant A * 3 \wedge B \geqslant 0 \wedge$$
$$\alpha + 7 + 2 * (A * 3 - B) \leqslant \tau \leqslant \alpha + 9 + 2 * (A * 3 - B)))$$

$$\equiv \alpha \leqslant st \wedge 4 \leqslant m(`in`) \leqslant 11 \wedge A = \lfloor m(`in`)/4 \rfloor \wedge$$
$$(\exists m'' \bullet m = m'' \oplus (`cport` \mapsto A)) \wedge$$
$$((B = A * 3 \wedge \alpha + 7 \leqslant \tau \leqslant \alpha + 9) \vee$$
$$(0 \leqslant B < A * 3 \wedge$$
$$\alpha + 7 + 2 * (A * 3 - B) \leqslant \tau \leqslant \alpha + 9 + 2 * (A * 3 - B)))$$

The part of predicate R_6 which defines the finishing time τ of the loop has been divided into two complex disjuncts at this point. Fortunately, these can be simplified when we work through the negated branch instruction, since it tells us that register B will be zero when the loop terminates (given the initial assumption about $m('in')$).

$R_7 \equiv \text{sp.}(\textbf{brpos } B\ e).R_6$

$\equiv (\exists \tau \bullet (B \leqslant 0 \wedge \tau' = \tau + 1 \wedge R_6))[\tau/\tau']$

$\equiv B \leqslant 0 \wedge R_6[\tau - 1, \tau/\tau, \tau']$

$\equiv A = \lfloor m('in')/4 \rfloor \wedge 4 \leqslant m('in') \leqslant 11 \wedge \alpha \leqslant st \wedge$
$(\exists m'' \bullet m = m'' \oplus ('cport' \mapsto A)) \wedge B \leqslant 0 \wedge$
$((B = A * 3 \wedge \alpha + 8 \leqslant \tau \leqslant \alpha + 10) \vee$
$(0 \leqslant B < A * 3 \wedge$
$\alpha + 8 + 2 * (A * 3 - B) \leqslant \tau \leqslant \alpha + 10 + 2 * (A * 3 - B)))$

$\equiv$ 'since A is positive, due to the range of $m('in')$'
$A = \lfloor m('in')/4 \rfloor \wedge 4 \leqslant m('in') \leqslant 11 \wedge \alpha \leqslant st \wedge$
$(\exists m'' \bullet m = m'' \oplus ('cport' \mapsto A)) \wedge B \leqslant 0 \wedge$
$(0 \leqslant B < A * 3 \wedge$
$\alpha + 8 + 2 * (A * 3 - B) \leqslant \tau \leqslant \alpha + 10 + 2 * (A * 3 - B))$

$\equiv \alpha \leqslant st \wedge 4 \leqslant m('in') \leqslant 11 \wedge A = \lfloor m('in')/4 \rfloor \wedge B = 0 \wedge$
$(\exists m'' \bullet m = m'' \oplus ('cport' \mapsto A)) \wedge \alpha + 8 + A * 6 \leqslant \tau \leqslant \alpha + 10 + A * 6$

The annulled subtraction instruction changes the time only.

$R_8 \equiv \text{sp.}(\textbf{subi } B\ 1\ B).R_7$

$\equiv \alpha \leqslant st \wedge 4 \leqslant m('in') \leqslant 11 \wedge A = \lfloor m('in')/4 \rfloor \wedge B = 0 \wedge$
$(\exists m'' \bullet m = m'' \oplus ('cport' \mapsto A)) \wedge \alpha + 9 + A * 6 \leqslant \tau \leqslant \alpha + 11 + A * 6$

At this point we observe that the instructions that achieve the 'busy wait', from **multi** to **subi** inclusive, consume at least $3 + 1 * 6 = 9$cycles $= 18$ms if register A is 1, and at least $3 + 2 * 6 = 15$cycles $= 30$ms if A is 2, and thus satisfactorily implement the **delay** statement on line 3 of the high-level language program.

The remaining two instructions make obvious updates to register C, the memory array m, and the finishing time τ.

$R_9 \equiv \text{sp.}(\textbf{load } 'dport'\ C).R_8$

$\equiv \alpha \leqslant st \wedge 4 \leqslant m('in') \leqslant 11 \wedge A = \lfloor m('in')/4 \rfloor \wedge B = 0 \wedge$
$C = m('dport') \wedge (\exists m'' \bullet m = m'' \oplus ('cport' \mapsto A)) \wedge$
$\alpha + 11 + A * 6 \leqslant \tau \leqslant \alpha + 13 + A * 6$

$R_{10} \equiv \text{sp.}(\overleftarrow{\textbf{store}}\ C\ 'res').R_9$

$\equiv$ 'provided addresses $'in'$, $'dport'$ and $'res'$ are all distinct'
$\alpha \leqslant st \wedge 4 \leqslant m('in') \leqslant 11 \wedge A = \lfloor m('in')/4 \rfloor \wedge B = 0 \wedge$
$C = m('dport') \wedge (\exists m'' \bullet m = m'' \oplus ('cport' \mapsto A, 'res' \mapsto C)) \wedge$
$\alpha + 14 + A * 6 \leqslant \tau \leqslant \alpha + 16 + A * 6$

$$\equiv \alpha \leqslant st \wedge 4 \leqslant m(\text{`}in\text{'}) \leqslant 11 \wedge A = \lfloor m(\text{`}in\text{'})/4 \rfloor \wedge B = 0 \wedge$$
$$C = m(\text{`}dport\text{'}) \wedge (\exists m'' \bullet m = m'' \oplus (\text{`}cport\text{'} \mapsto A, \text{`}res\text{'} \mapsto C)) \wedge$$
$$\alpha + 14\text{cycles} + \lfloor m(\text{`}in\text{'})/4 \rfloor * 6\text{cycles} \leqslant \tau \wedge$$
$$\tau \leqslant \alpha + 16\text{cycles} + \lfloor m(\text{`}in\text{'})/4 \rfloor * 6\text{cycles}$$

From this result we can see that the largest difference between finishing time τ and starting time α is $16\text{cycles} + \lfloor m(\text{`}in\text{'})/4 \rfloor * 6\text{cycles}$. We can now compare this worst-case execution time with the timing constraint calculated in Section 4.2. Given the initial assumption about the range of values for input $m(\text{`}in\text{'})$, we know that $\lfloor m(\text{`}in\text{'})/4 \rfloor$ is either 1 or 2. If it is 1, then the timing constraint is $20 + 1*5 = 25\text{cycles}$, whereas the worst-case execution time is $16 + 1*6 = 22\text{cycles}$. If it is 2 then the constraint is $20 + 2*5 = 30\text{cycles}$, and the execution time is $16 + 2*6 = 28\text{cycles}$. Therefore, we can finally conclude that the assembler code in Fig. 3 does indeed meet the original timing requirement in Fig. 1.

5   Conclusion

We have seen how a high-level language timing analysis formalism can be adapted to assembler code. It was shown how working backwards along a control-flow path using a weakest liberal precondition semantics yields the path's end-to-end timing constraint, and how working forwards along the path using a strongest postcondition semantics yields the path's worst-case execution time. Comparing the two then tells us whether the assembler code meets the programmer's timing requirement or not. The resulting formalism thus provides a sound basis for justifying algorithms and tools that analyse real-time assembler code.

Acknowledgements. I wish to thank Nam Hien Le for helping identify the problems of assembler code analysis, Geoffrey Watson for correcting errors in this paper, and the FME reviewers. Karl Lermer suggested using the constructors in Tables 1 and 4 for timing analysis. This research was funded by Australian Research Council Large Grant A49937045: *Effective Real-Time Program Analysis*.

References

1. N. C. Audsley, I. J. Bate, and A. Grigg. Portable code for critical systems. In *Proc. 6th International Conference on Real-Time Computing Systems and Applications*, pages 111–118, December 1999.
2. R.-J. R. Back and J. von Wright. Refinement calculus, part I: Sequential nondeterministic programs. In J. W. de Bakker, W.-P. de Roever, and G. Rozenberg, editors, *Stepwise Refinement of Distributed Systems: Models, Formalisms, Correctness (REX Workshop 1989)*, volume 430 of *Lecture Notes in Computer Science*, pages 42–66. Springer-Verlag, 1989.
3. B. Carré. Program analysis and verification. In C. T. Sennett, editor, *High-Integrity Software*, chapter 8, pages 176–197. Plenum Press, 1989.

4. C. Cifuentes, D. Simon, and A. Fraboulet. Assembly to high-level language translation. Technical Report 439, School of Information Technology, The University of Queensland, August 1998.
5. D. Corman, P. Goertzen, J. Luke, and M. Mills. Incremental Upgrade of Legacy Systems (IULS): A fundamental software technology for aging aircraft. In *Fourth Joint DOD/FAA/NASA Conference on Aging Aircraft*, 2000.
6. E. W. Dijkstra and C. S. Scholten. *Predicate Calculus and Program Semantics*. Springer-Verlag, 1990.
7. J. Engblom and A. Ermedahl. Modeling complex flows for worst-case execution time analysis. In *Proceedings of the 21st IEEE Real-Time Systems Symposium*, pages 163–174. IEEE Computer Society, 2000.
8. C. J. Fidge, I. J. Hayes, and G. Watson. The deadline command. *IEE Proceedings—Software*, 146(2):104–111, April 1999.
9. S. Grundon, I. J. Hayes, and C. J. Fidge. Timing constraint analysis. In C. McDonald, editor, *Computer Science '98: Proc. 21st Australasian Computer Science Conference*, pages 575–586. Springer-Verlag, 1998.
10. E. L. Gunter and D. Peled. Path exploration tool. In W. R. Cleaveland, editor, *Tools and Algorithms for the Construction and Analysis of Systems (TACAS/ETAPS'99)*, volume 1579 of *Lecture Notes in Computer Science*, pages 405–419. Springer-Verlag, 1999.
11. I. J. Hayes and M. Utting. A sequential real-time refinement calculus. *Acta Informatica*, 37(6):385–448, 2001.
12. C. A. Healy, D. B. Whalley, and M. G. Harmon. Integrating the timing analysis of pipelining and instruction caching. In *Proc. 16th IEEE Real-Time Systems Symposium*, pages 288–297. IEEE Computer Society Press, December 1995.
13. P. Kearney and M. Utting. A layered real-time specification of a RISC processor. In H. Langmaack, W.-P. de Roever, and J. Vytopil, editors, *Formal Techniques in Real Time and Fault Tolerant Systems*, volume 863 of *Lecture Notes in Computer Science*, pages 455–475. Springer-Verlag, 1994.
14. T. Lundqvist and P. Stenström. An integrated path and timing analysis method based on cycle-level symbolic execution. *Real-Time Systems*, 17(2/3):183–207, November 1999.
15. C. Morgan. *Programming from Specifications*. Prentice-Hall, 1990.
16. M. Müller-Olm. *Modular Compiler Verification: A Refinement-Algebraic Approach Advocating Stepwise Abstraction*, volume 1283 of *Lecture Notes in Computer Science*. Springer-Verlag, 1997.
17. N. Ramsey and M. F. Fernández. Specifying representations of machine instructions. *ACM Transactions on Programming Languages and Systems*, 19(3):492–524, May 1997.
18. A. Sampaio. *An Algebraic Approach to Compiler Design*, volume 4 of *AMAST Series in Computing*. World Scientific, 1997.
19. M. Utting and P. Kearney. Instruction level specification of a MIPS R3000 CPU. Technical Report 93-25, Software Verification Research Centre, The University of Queensland, February 1994.
20. T. Williams. Performance pushes RISC chips into real-time roles. *Computer Design*, pages 79–86, September 1991.

Towards OCL/RT

María Victoria Cengarle[1]* and Alexander Knapp[2]

[1] Technische Universität München
cengarle@in.tum.de
[2] Ludwig–Maximilians–Universität München
knapp@informatik.uni-muenchen.de

Abstract. An extension of the "Object Constraint Language" (OCL) for modeling real-time and reactive systems in the "Unified Modeling Language" (UML) is proposed, called OCL/RT. A general notion of events that may carry time stamps is introduced providing means to describe the detailed dynamic and timing behaviour of UML software models. OCL is enriched by satisfaction operators @η for referring to the value in the history of an expression at the instant when event η occurred, as well as the modalities **always** and **sometime**. The approach is illustrated by several examples. Finally, an operational semantics of OCL/RT is given.

Keywords. Real-time systems, OCL, UML, events

1 Introduction

The "Object Constraint Language" (OCL [25]) provides means to constrain realisations of software models in the "Unified Modeling Language" (UML [3]) by textual specifications in a formal, navigational expression language. OCL specifications complement UML models where constraints for defining meaningful realisations can not or not conveniently be stated diagrammatically. The OCL focusses on the axiomatic specification of consistent system states by invariants and the transformations of system states by means of pre- and post-conditions for operations.

As it stands, OCL thus seems to be well-suited for describing constraints on UML models for conventional business applications [8,2], but shows distinct limitations for specifying reactive, embedded, or real-time systems as the language does not feature time or signal handling constructs, nor is capable of expressing general liveness properties of systems conveniently. Moreover, performance aspects, which play an important role in today's software systems, cannot be easily expressed in the OCL. On the other hand, employment of the UML for describing systems where time, performance, or reactive behaviour is in focus has gained considerable interest [6,7,10] building on the general impact of object-oriented technology in real-time software engineering [21]. In fact, the UML shows some

---

* This research has partially been carried out while at Fraunhofer Institut Experimentelles Software Engineering.

L.-H. Eriksson and P. Lindsay (Eds.): FME 2002, LNCS 2391, pp. 390–409, 2002.
© Springer-Verlag Berlin Heidelberg 2002

support for these kinds of systems by including a signal and an event concept, timed state machines, and collaborations with timing annotations. Moreover, specialised real-time language extensions and profiles have been devised [22,17]. However, most of these UML notions have only been provided with an intuitive semantics and have no formal counterpart. Methodologically, UML reactive and timing specifications, like state machines, tend to be rather concrete; the interspersing of modelling and constraint diagrams may make it hard to grasp the proof obligations.

What therefore may be called for is an enhancement of the OCL by constructs for time and signals in order to also complement UML real-time models by formal and abstract specifications. We propose such an extension to the OCL, called "OCL for real-time" (OCL/RT). In OCL/RT, time evolution as well as signal occurrences are captured by a generalised notion of UML events that carry a time stamp. In accordance with the design principles of the OCL, events are viewed on locally and are associated to instances. Based on this event concept, special satisfaction operators @η enable referring to the system state at the occurrence of an event η and thus provide control over a history of system states. Furthermore, the modalities **always** and **sometime** provide means to specify safety as well as liveness properties. This proposal takes up some of the ideas present in Lano's "Real-time Action Logic" (RAL) for formal object-oriented software development [13] and the work by Trentelman and Huisman on extending the "Java Modeling Language" (JML) by temporal logic [24].

Related work. Several approaches to coping with time and events in OCL and related specification languages for the UML have already been reported in the literature: Conrad and Turowski [5] extend OCL by temporal modalities but do not consider real-time systems proper. Kleppe and Warmer [12], in the same vein as Álvarez et. al. [1] and the "Action Semantics for the UML" integrated with the UML 1.4 specification [19], define a dynamic semantics of UML and its actions using OCL. Though they capture history by local snapshots, they neither provide a notion of time nor a notion of event. These concepts are investigated in detail in the response to the request for proposals "Schedulability, Performance, and Time for the UML" [17], but an extension to the OCL is not discussed. Lavazza, Quaroni, and Venturelli [14] propose the use of "TRIO" real-time specifications to capture the semantics of UML state machines with time annotations; this approach, along the techniques introduced by Lano [13], indeed provides a powerful specification language, but lacks tight integration with conventional notations for UML.

Outline. In Sect. 2 we briefly review the OCL syntax, intended semantics, and expressiveness. The OCL/RT notion of event as well as its relationship to time is motivated in Sect. 3. In Sect. 4 the concepts and syntax of OCL/RT are introduced. We illustrate our proposal in Sect. 5 by means of several typical examples. Sect. 6 defines the formal semantics of OCL/RT. Finally, in Sect. 7, we conclude by drawing advantages and disadvantages of our proposal and hint at possible directions of future work.

2   OCL

We briefly summarise the syntax and semantics of the OCL by means of an example. An introduction to OCL is provided by Warmer and Kleppe [25], the syntax and semantics of OCL 2.0 is discussed in more detail in [16]. The overview of the OCL semantics given here is based on the operational semantics for OCL expressions by the authors [4].

The UML class diagram in Fig. 1 represents the *static structure* of a (over-simplified) model of several automatic teller machines (ATMs) connected to a single bank showing an *association* with according *multiplicities* between the *classes* ATM and Bank. An ATM has a depot *attribute*, holding the current amount of money it can spend; the identification number of the card currently put in, with cardId set to, say, zero if it holds no card; and a state indicating whether an error has occurred during processing. An ATM may spend an amount of money when *operation* spend is called on it. The bank offers two operations: credit withdraws an amount of money from the card holder's account if this amount is covered; requestRefill registers ATMs whose depots are running low.

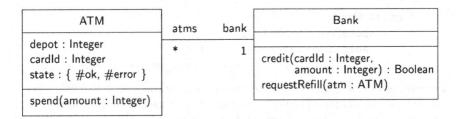

Fig. 1. UML class diagram for ATMs

2.1   Invariants, Pre-/Post-conditions, and Definitions

In OCL, a class *invariant* specifies a condition that has to be satisfied throughout the whole life-time of instances of the class. An OCL invariant for ATMs may require that, whenever the state of an ATM does not indicate an error, there is enough money to spend:

```
context ATM
inv: (self.state = #ok) implies (self.depot >= 100)
```

OCL uses the dot-notation for navigation to attributes and via associations (as well as for operation calls). The OCL expression self denotes the instance the constraint is evaluated on and may be omitted if the navigation reference remains unambiguous. Each OCL type, like Enumeration (for #ok), Integer or the types of the underlying UML static structure, shows a special undefined value **undef**; an expression can be tested whether it results in **undef** using the predefined function **isUndef()**.

An *axiomatic specification* for an operation defines the behaviour of the operation by a pre-/post-condition pair. An OCL axiomatic specification for operation **spend** on an ATM may require that whenever **spend** is called, the ATM must not be in an error state, it must hold some card, the amount of money to be withdrawn is positive, and the depot covers the withdrawal. After **spend** has been executed, the right amount of money must have been spent or some error has occurred:

```
context ATM::spend(amount : Integer)
pre:  (state = #ok) and (cardId <> 0) and
      (amount > 0) and (depot > amount+100)
post: (depot = depot@pre-amount) or (state = #error)
```

The post-condition expression makes use of the OCL operator @pre that yields an expression's value at pre-condition time.

OCL also provides a mechanism to introduce *auxiliary attributes* and (arbitrarily recursive) *operations* not specified in the underlying UML model. A bank may define an operation calculating the sum of the depots in its ATMs:

```
context Bank
def: depotsSum() : Integer =
        self.atms->iterate(i : ATM;
                            sum : Integer = 0 | sum+i.depot)
```

The expression **self.atms** evaluates to a set of instances of class ATM, reflecting the multiplicity of **atms**. The OCL predefined operation **iterate** iterates through a given collection and accumulates the result of evaluating an expression with an iterator variable bound to the current element and an accumulator variable bound to the previous result. Like for all collection operations, e.g., **select**, **reject**, or **collect**, a special arrow notation is used.

2.2 Actions

Kleppe and Warmer [11] have proposed an extension of the original OCL by action clauses for classes and operations; see also [16].

An *action clause for classes* requires that whenever a condition becomes satisfied, an operation has to be called. For example, if an ATM is about to run out of money, it has to request a refill from its bank:

```
context ATM
action: depot < 1000 ==> bank.requestRefill(self)
```

An *action clause for operations* specifies that, when some condition is satisfied at post-condition time, certain other operation calls must have happened while executing the operation. For example, during execution of **spend** operation **credit** must have been called on the bank with the current card identification and the amount of money to be withdrawn:

```
context ATM::spend(amount : Integer)
action: true ==> bank.credit(cardId, amount)
```

An action clause for operations implicitly assumes the pre-condition of the operation.

2.3   Semantics

Formally, the semantics of evaluating an OCL *expression* in a system state may be captured as follows: System states are formalised by *dynamic bases*. A dynamic basis comprises an implementation of the predefined OCL types and their operations as well as the set of current instances of classes together with their attribute valuations, connections to other instances, and implementations of operations. Moreover, a dynamic basis can be extended by implementations of auxiliary, user defined operations. Given an OCL expression e to be evaluated over a dynamic basis ω and a variable environment γ assigning values to variables (including self), we write $\omega; \gamma \vdash e \downarrow v$ for the judgement that e evaluates in this situation to the value v. Structural operational rules [4] define the procedure of evaluating an OCL expression.

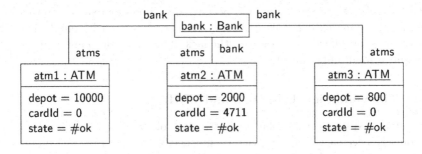

Fig. 2. UML object diagram for a sample ATM configuration

For example, the evaluation of a call to the auxiliary operation depotsSum on the bank bank over a dynamic basis ω corresponding to the system state described by the *object diagram* in Fig. 2 is given by the judgement:

$\omega;$ self $\mapsto$ bank $\vdash$ self.depotsSum() $\downarrow$ 12800

Moreover, the ATM invariant above is satisfied for all instances of ATM, i.e., for $1 \leq i \leq 3$:

$\omega;$ self $\mapsto$ atm$i$ $\vdash$ self.state = #ok implies self.depot >= 100 $\downarrow$ true

OCL *constraints*, i.e., invariants, pre-/post-conditions, and action clauses, restrict the *runs* of systems modelled in UML. These constraints specify safety properties of a system, such that if a constraint is satisfied by a system run, all finite initial segments of the system run satisfy the constraint. Roughly speaking, an OCL constraint has to hold for a (potentially infinite) sequence of dynamic bases $\vec{\omega} = \omega_0, \omega_1, \ldots$ where ω_0 represents the initial system state and ω_n is transformed into ω_{n+1} by a step of the system. However, the OCL semantics does not prescribe at which states of such a run an invariant has to hold indeed — an instance's invariant may be violated if an operation is currently executed on this instance (see, e.g., [15]). Taking some ω_m to be the system state where an operation is called and ω_n with $m \leq n$ the system state where this operation call terminates, a pre-/post-condition pair for this operation holds (cf. [20]) whenever a **true** pre-condition over ω_m implies a **true** post-condition over ω_n with expressions of the form e@pre evaluated over ω_m. But it is unclear how system states are to be identified where an operation is called or where an operation terminates. The interpretation of action clauses shows similar problems.

3   Time and Events

Though the OCL provides sufficient means to describe the functional behaviour of software systems modelled in the UML, its expressiveness is rather limited when it comes to either timing and performance issues or reaction to (external) signals. To some extent, this deficiency can be countered by employing UML diagrams as specifications; however, the lack of formal underpinning of the UML remains a main impediment.

3.1   Time and Signals in OCL and UML

In software systems, time plays a particular role when it is desirable or even absolutely necessary that a service be finished within certain time bounds. For example, the period to be waited for when asking for money at an automatic teller machine, i.e. calling spend on an ATM in the example of the previous section, must not exceed a certain predefined time limit. An OCL solution to such a requirement would be to define an explicit clock attribute requiring the clock to be reset to zero in the pre-condition of spend and putting a constraint on the clock's value in the post-condition:

```
context ATM::spend(amount : Integer)
pre: (clock = 0) and (state = #ok) and ...
post: (clock <= T) and ...
```

Such a solution may become unwieldy when several dependent timing constraints are required. Alternatively, a UML sequence diagram with timing annotations as suggested in the UML specification [18, Sect. 3.64] may be employed, see Fig. 3. The precise meaning, however, is undefined.

Time also plays a role when, the other way round, the occurrence of some (external) signal is waited for during a certain period, and if nothing happens the system has to react in a predefined way. For instance, when inserting the

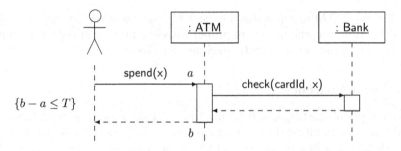

Fig. 3. Sequence diagram with timing constraints for ATM::spend

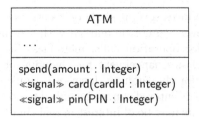

(a) ATM with signals

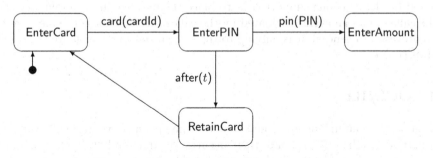

(b) Timed state machine for ATM with signals (fragment)

Fig. 4. UML specifications for ATMs with signals

bank card in an automatic teller machine, if the card holder does not enter the corresponding personal identification number (PIN) within a reasonable time, the card may be retained by the automatic teller machine, which is now ready to accept another card. In order to accommodate for this requirement, in Fig. 4(a) two signals card and pin for class ATM are introduced by defining appropriate UML receptions (which are meant to be asynchronous in contrast to synchronous operations). But OCL does not offer any convenient means to handle the occurrence of signals and thus to specify the intended behaviour. In UML, the deadline for entering the PIN may be expressed by using a state machine with time trig-

gers for class ATM as suggested in the UML specification [18, Sect. 3.74], see
Fig. 4(b). However, the precise meaning is unclear and the specification may be
too concrete in introducing state machines for classes.

3.2 Event Concept

The concepts of starting and finishing time of a service can be used to measure
the duration of fulfilling the service by a system. In the same vein, when waiting
for a signal for a limited amount of time, the occurrence time of a signal can
be used to decide whether the signal arrived in time. It seems natural to reify
these concepts in a system model as *events* that may be accompanied by a *time
stamp*.

In fact, UML introduces several kinds of events as sub-classes of the meta-
class Event that, however, cannot be marked with the time of their occurrence:
meta-class CallEvent for operation calls, meta-class SignalEvent for signal occurrences, and meta-class ChangeEvent for changing of conditions. The UML
meta-class TimeEvent for the running down of a timer that is started when a
state of a state machine is entered cannot be linked to other events. Furthermore,
also other kinds of events may be of interest in real-time or reactive systems: For
example, an assignment to an attribute may be an event. In an object-oriented
environment, an operation invocation may be subdivided into several events,
e.g., an event originated by the caller (i.e., to send a message), an event originated by the run-time support (i.e., to place the message in the input queue of
the callee), and an event originated by the callee (i.e., to choose the message for
its process). In general, it is only up to the system specifier which are the events
of discourse.

4 OCL/RT

In order to open up the event and thus the time perspective for OCL, language
primitives for handling events, their occurrence time, and their sequence have
to be introduced. The detailed structure of the available events may depend on
the system's nature.

4.1 Events

OCL/RT is based on a modification and extension of the original UML abstract
meta-class Event as depicted in Fig. 5. Each event (instance) shows the time
at which it occurred by a link to the new primitive data type Time that represents the global system time. We assume that Time comes with a total ordering
relation $\leq$ for comparing time values, an associative and commutative binary
operation $+$ for adding time values, and a class attribute now that always yields
the current system time. Events are associated to instances (of classifiers), such
that an instance is linked to all its current events. Similar to UML, an event may
carry a list of actual parameters.

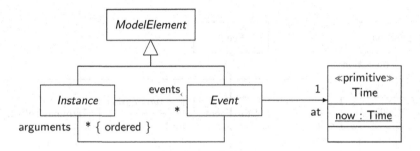

Fig. 5. Event meta-class

We extend OCL by the new types Event and Time that correspond to Event and Time, respectively and that reify their structure in OCL/RT. Each system state complying to an UML model based on the OCL/RT extension thus has to show a current time, which can be accessed by the OCL/RT expression Time.now. For each of the instances in such a system state a set of current events for this instance has to be present, which can be accessed by the OCL/RT expression e.events if e evaluates to an instance. The set of current events is accumulative, i.e., over a system run all events that have been raised for the instance value of e are present in e.events.

4.2   Constraints

For the definition of OCL/RT constraints, which are evaluated over a sequence of systems states, we introduce a new clause

```
context C
constr: c
```

where C is a classifier and c an OCL/RT constraint expression. OCL/RT *constraint expressions* comprise all boolean OCL/RT expressions, but may also show the *modality* always such that always c for a OCL/RT constraint expression is satisfied over a system run when c evaluates to true in all states of the run. As is customary in modal logic, we define a modality sometime by abbreviating not (always (not c)) to sometime c. Finally, OCL/RT expressions may include *satisfaction operators* @η that when applied to an expression correspond to evaluating the expression at the system state where event η occurred.

4.3   Invariants, Pre-/Post-conditions, and Action Clauses

The OCL/RT constraint language is expressive enough to subsume (interpretations of) the original OCL invariant, pre-/post-condition, and action clause constraints. Accepting those interpretations, inv:, pre:, post:, and action: can be used as convenient abbreviations in OCL/RT.

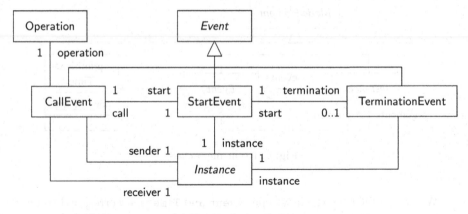

(a) Events for operations

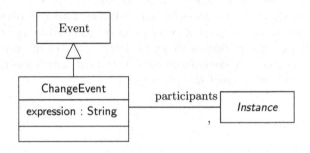

(b) Events for changes

Fig. 6. Event model for OCL

We define a suitably expressive hierarchy of events, i.e. an *event model* for OCL in Fig. 6. For operations, see Fig. 6(a), we assume that a CallEvent (instance) occurs when a sender instance issues a call on operation operation to a receiver instance; it is visible to its sender and receiver. A StartEvent is raised, whenever instance is about to start executing the operation; it is visible to instance. Finally, a TerminationEvent occurs when the execution of an operation is finished; it is again visible to instance. CallEvent and StartEvent show as arguments the actual parameters of the operation call. All three event types are linked: A StartEvent can refer to its causing CallEvent, a TerminationEvent to its causing StartEvent. Moreover, if an operation call terminates, the StartEvent corresponding to starting execution of the operation has to show a link termination to a TerminationEvent. For changes, see Fig. 6(b), we assume that arbitrary expressions can be tested over a system state, and that whenever the expression value changes from `false` to `true`, a ChangeEvent occurs; a ChangeEvent is visible to all the instances of the system state.

Invariants. An OCL specification of an invariant

```
context C
inv: inv
```

may be interpreted as: *inv* must be satisfied for an instance of C, whenever an operation is called on the instance from outside; cf. [15]. In OCL/RT this interpretation, taking calls from the outside to be calls of public operations, reads as follows:

```
context C
def: publicCalls() : Event
        events->select(e |
          e.isTypeOf(StartEvent) and
          e.call.operation.visibility = #public)
constr: always (publicCalls()->forAll(s | inv@s))
```

In particular, an invariant may be violated during execution of an operation.

Pre-/post-conditions. OCL pre-/post-condition specifications

```
context C::o(x₁ : τ₁, ... , xₙ : τₙ)
pre: pre
post: post
```

can be expressed by

```
context C
def: startso() : Event
        events->select(e |
          e.isTypeOf(StartEvent) and
          e.call.operation.name = "o")
constr: always (startso()->forAll(s |
                    (p̃re@s and (not isUndef(s.termination)))
                    implies
                    p̃ost@(s.termination)))
```

The OCL/RT translations $\widetilde{pre}$ and $\widetilde{post}$ of the OCL expressions *pre* and *post* replace each reference to a parameter x_i by `s.arguments->at`(i), i.e. the ith argument of event s representing the start of an operation execution. Moreover, in order to obtain $\widetilde{post}$, each occurrence of @pre is replaced by @s.

Action clauses for classes. An OCL action clause for a class

```
context C
action: cond ==> e.m(e₁, ... , e_k)
```

conveys that whenever condition *cond* becomes satisfied, an operation call on m has to be sent to the instance value of e. In OCL/RT this can be specified as follows, assuming that a short amount of time ε may pass between *cond* becoming satisfied and calling m:

```
context C
def: changes() : Event
        events->select(e | e.isTypeOf(ChangeEvent) and
                           e.expression = "cond")
def: callsm() : Event
        events->select(e |
            e.isTypeOf(CallEvent) and e.operation.name = "m")
constr: always (changes()->forAll(c | sometime
                   (callsm()->exists(m |
                       m.sender = self and m.receiver = e@c and
                       m.arguments->at(1) = e_1@c and ... and
                       m.arguments->at(k) = e_k@c and
                       c.at <= m.at and m.at <= c.at + ε)))))
```

Action clauses for operations. An OCL action clause for an operation

```
context C::o(x_1 : τ_1, ..., x_n : τ_n)
action: cond ==> e.m(e_1, ..., e_k)
```

means that if at termination time of an operation execution for o the condition *cond* holds, then an operation call for operation m on the instance value of e has been raised between the events of starting the operation o and its termination. This can be expressed by the following OCL/RT specification:

```
context C::o(x_1 : τ_1, ..., x_n : τ_n)
def: terminateso() : Event
        events->select(e | e.isTypeOf(TerminationEvent) and
                           e.operation.name = "o")
def: callsm() : Event
        events->select(e |
            e.isTypeOf(CallEvent) and e.operation.name = "m")
constr: always (terminateso()->forAll(t | (cond@t implies
                   callsm()->exists(m | sometime
                       (m.sender = self and m.receiver = ẽ@t and
                       m.arguments->at(1) = ẽ_1@t and ... and
                       m.arguments->at(k) = ẽ_k@t and
                       t.start.at <= m.at and m.at <= t.at)))))
```

where $\tilde{e}, \tilde{e}_1, \ldots, \tilde{e}_k$ are defined as above.

5   Examples

We illustrate the use of OCL/RT by modelling common real-time paradigms, in particular deadlines and timeouts, for UML systems, as discussed in Sect. 3. A *deadline* requires that something must occur before a specified point in time is reached. Similarly, a *timeout* expects that something can occur before a specified point in time is reached and, if this is not the case, then something will occur.

5.1   Deadlines for Operations

We define an OCL/RT constraint for the desired deadline for the operation spend
of class ATM (see Fig. 1) in the ATM example of Sect. 3.1: Executions of the
operation spend have to be finished within a certain time T. The post-condition
of spend (see Sect. 2.1) is rewritten as follows:

```
context ATM::spend(amount:Integer)
pre: ...
post: (depot = depot@pre - amount and
       Time.now <= Time.now@pre+T) or (state = #error)
```

This specification makes use of the abbreviation introduced in Sect. 4.3.

5.2   Deadlines for Reactions to Signals

Deadlines for signals pose a similar problem as the previous example. The essential difference resides in the fact that post-conditions not necessarily are available
for signals. We define an OCL/RT event model for signals in Fig. 7. A SignalEvent
is raised on instance if signal is received by this instance; it is visible to instance.

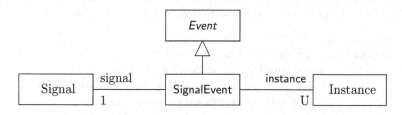

Fig. 7. Event model for signals

Assume a railway level crossing with an automatically controlled gate. Whenever a sensor signals the approach of a train, the gate has to be completely closed
within a certain time limit. After the train has crossed, the gate starts opening.
It may happen that the gate is opening when the next train is detected by the
sensor; in this case, the gate has to stop opening and close again. This example
is taken from [14]. A UML model for gate controllers is given in Fig. 8.

We specify constraints on the reactions to the open and close signals. In
order to enhance readability of these constraints, we introduce several auxiliary
attributes in the context of Gate that collect the signal events for close, the
change events that are raised when angle becomes 0, and the change events that
are raised when angle becomes Real.pi, respectively:

```
context Gate
def: closeSignals : Set(SignalEvent) =
        events->select(e |
          e.isTypeOf(SignalEvent) and e.signal.name = "close")
```

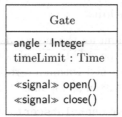

Fig. 8. UML class diagram for gate controllers

```
def: gateDownEvents : Set(ChangeEvent) =
        events->select(e |
            e.isTypeOf(ChangeEvent) and e.expression = "angle=0")
def: gateUpEvents : Set(ChangeEvent) =
        events->select(e | e.isTypeOf(ChangeEvent) and
                            e.expression = "angle=Real.pi")
```

The following constraint checks that, for any close signal, within timeLimit after the signal has arrived the gate is indeed closed. Furthermore, we require that between these two events, namely the arrival of a signal close and the gate reaching a horizontal position, the gate does not become open.

```
context Gate
constr: always (closeSignals->forAll(cs |
            sometime (gateDownEvents->exists(gd |
                cs.at < gd.at and gd.at <= cs.at+timeLimit
                and not gateUpEvents->exists(gu |
                        cs.at < gu.at and gu.at < gd.at)))))
```

For a constraint stating that the gate be opened within timeLimit after a open signal occurred, we could write a dual expression. However, we must ensure that, if the signal close arrives while opening the gate, the gate must start closing immediately. Similarly as for the case of close, we define an abbreviation for the set of open signals.

```
context Gate
def: openSignals : Set(SignalEvent) =
        events->select(e |
            e.isTypeOf(SignalEvent) and e.name = "open")
```

The desired constraint reads as follows:

```
context Gate
constr: always (openSignals->forAll(os |
            sometime (gateUpEvents->exists(gd |
                os.at < gu.at and gu.at <= os.at+timeLimit and
                not gateDownEvents->exists(gd |
                    os.at < gd.at and gd.at < gu.at))))
```

```
xor
sometime (closeSignals->exists(cs |
    cs.at < os.at+timeLimit)))
```

5.3 Timeouts

Timeouts are illustrated using an example consisting of an auctioneer and a set
of bidders, such that goods are offered one after the other for a minimum bid.
Bidders may place a bid greater than the current one for the item now being
offered. Each item is sold to the person who offers the most money for it. The
auction is closed by the auctioneer when no new bid has been placed for certain
period, which represents a timeout. The auctioneer does this by hammering three
times; this closing procedure can be interrupted by a bidder placing a new bid,
and again that certain period where no bid is placed has to elapse in order for
the auctioneer to be able to restart closing the auction. In other words, this
setting presents two nested timeouts. This example is taken from [23]. Let the
UML class Auctioneer be defined as shown in Fig. 9.

Auctioneer
open : Boolean actualBid : Money timeLimit : Time
open(min : Money) acceptBid(m : Money) close()

Fig. 9. UML class diagram for auctioneers

The following OCL/RT invariant constraint requires every auction to remain
open as long as the constant timeLimit has not elapsed with no bid placed.
Moreover, it triggers the operation close if timeLimit elapsed with no valid bid
placed.

```
context Auctioneer
def: lastEvent(se : Set(Event)) : Event =
        se->iterate(e; r = undef |
        if r.isUndef() then e
        else if r.at < e.at then e else r endif endif)
def: openEvents : Set(Event) =
        events->select(e |
            e.isTypeOf(CallEvent) and e.operation.name = "open")
def: validBids : Set(Event) =
```

```
          self.events->select(e |
              e.isTypeOf(CallEvent) and
              e.operation.name = "acceptBid" and
              e.at > lastEvent(openEvents).at and
              e.arguments->at(1) > actualBid@e)
  def: lastBidOrOpen =
          if lastEvent(validBids).isUndef()
          then lastEvent(openEvents)
          else lastEvent(validBids)
          endif
  inv: (not open) iff (lastBidOrOpen.at+timeLimit < Time.now)
  action: lastBidOrOpen.at+timeLimit < Time.now
              ==> self.close()
```

Note that the invariant forbids closing if at regular intervals a joker adds one cent to the last bid.

A further constraint is set on the operation close, which presupposes that the auction is open and that timeLimit has elapsed with no new bid having been placed. The post-condition simply states that the auction is indeed closed.

```
context Auctioneer::close()
pre:   open and lastBidOrOpen.at+timeLimit >= Time.now
post: not open
```

The situation for timeouts on ATMs (see Fig. 4) can be easily specified along the same lines.

6   Semantics

We define an operational semantics for OCL/RT constraints that are evaluated over system runs. This semantics conservatively extends the operational semantics for OCL expressions presented in [4], as sketched in Sect. 2.3.

6.1   Semantic Domains

Given a UML model, we denote by Σ the semantic domain of dynamic bases ω over the UML model. We use a map $\omega(\zeta)$ that for each class type in the UML model yields all instances of ζ that exist in ω.

The semantic domain E reflects a given event model such that, in particular, for each event the occurrence time and its arguments can be retrieved by suitable maps *at* and *arguments*. Moreover, we assume a map *relevant* that, given a set M of events in E and an instance v of a dynamic basis in Σ, yields all those events in M that are relevant or visible for v.

A system run or *trace* ρ is a finite or infinite sequence of pairs of dynamic bases and finite sets of events

$$(\omega_0, H_0), (\omega_1, H_1), (\omega_2, H_2), \ldots \in (\Sigma \times \wp_{\leq \omega} E)^* \cup (\Sigma \times \wp_{\leq \omega} E)^\infty$$

such that $at(\eta) < at(\eta')$ for all $\eta \in H_i$, $\eta' \in H_j$ with $i < j$. The dynamic basis ω_0 defines the initial system state; ω_n is transformed into ω_{n+1} by a single system step where exactly the events in H_n occur. We denote by $\omega(\rho)_n$ the nth dynamic basis in ρ, by $H(\rho)_n$ the nth event set in ρ, that is ω_n and H_n, respectively. Moreover, $\omega(\rho)_\eta$ denotes the dynamic basis where η occurred and $i(\rho)_\eta$ the index of this state, i.e., $\omega(\rho)_\eta$ is ω_k with $\eta \in H_{k-1}$ and $i(\rho)_\eta$ is k. Finally, we write $i(\rho)_v$ for the first state where instance v exists.

Further requirements on traces may be necessary for particular event models. For the OCL event model in Sect. 4.3, call, start, and termination events linked by call and start, respectively, must occur in this order.

6.2   Operational Rules

The operational semantics derives judgements of the form

$$(\rho, i); \gamma \vdash c \downarrow v$$

where ρ is a trace, i is an index in the trace, γ a variable environment, c an OCL/RT constraint, and v a value. Such a judgement conveys the fact that c evaluates to v at the ith system state in the trace ρ using the variable environment γ.

To begin with, the operational rules for deriving OCL/RT judgements comprise all rules of OCL as defined in [4], but generalising these rules to traces. For example, the rules for evaluating self and retrieving an attribute a of an instance originally read:

(Self$^\downarrow$)
$$\omega; \gamma \vdash \text{self} \downarrow \gamma(\text{self})$$

(Feat$^\downarrow$)
$$\frac{\omega; \gamma \vdash e \downarrow v}{\omega; \gamma \vdash e.a \downarrow impl_\omega(a, v)}$$

where $impl_\omega(a, v)$ yields the value of attribute a on instance v in the dynamic basis ω. For OCL/RT, these rules become

(Self$^{\downarrow}$*)
$$(\rho, i); \gamma \vdash \text{self} \downarrow \gamma(\text{self})$$

(Feat$^{\downarrow}$*)
$$\frac{(\rho, i); \gamma \vdash e \downarrow v}{(\rho, i); \gamma \vdash e.a \downarrow impl_{\omega(\rho)_i}(a, v)}$$

In particular, all rules are relativised to the event instance at which an expression currently is to be evaluated.

Furthermore, we define rules for evaluating OCL/RT constraints that contain the special OCL/RT instance attribute `events`, or one of the new operators @η and `always`:

(Evt$^{\downarrow *}$)

$$\frac{(\rho, i); \gamma \vdash e \downarrow v}{(\rho, i); \gamma \vdash e.\texttt{events} \downarrow relevant(\bigcup_{0 \le j \le i} H(\rho)_j, v)}$$

(At$^{\downarrow *}$)

$$\frac{(\rho, i); \gamma \vdash e' \downarrow \eta' \qquad (\rho, i(\rho)_{\eta'}); \gamma \vdash e \downarrow v}{(\rho, i); \gamma \vdash e@e' \downarrow v}$$

(Alw$^{\downarrow *}$)

$$\frac{((\rho, i'); \gamma \vdash c \downarrow v)_{i \le i'}}{(\rho, i); \gamma \vdash \texttt{always } c}$$

Thus `e.events` comprises all events relevant for an instance e that have occurred up to the current state. An expression $e@e'$ evaluates e at the state where event e' occurred. A constraint `always` c must hold at all states after the current state.

Finally, a rule for general OCL/RT constraints is defined as follows:

(Constr$^{\downarrow *}$)

$$\frac{((\rho, i(\rho)_z); \gamma \vdash c \downarrow v_z)_{z \in \bigcup_{0 \le i} \omega(\rho)_i(\zeta)}}{(\rho, i); \gamma \vdash \texttt{context } \zeta \texttt{ constr: } c \downarrow \bigwedge_z v_z}$$

Hence, an OCL/RT constraint has to hold for all instances z of a class ζ at the state where z is created.

7 Conclusions and Outlook

OCL/RT extends OCL by a general notion of events accompanied by time stamps, satisfaction operators on expressions, and modal operators. This extension enables the specification of several common real-time paradigms for UML models. Moreover, OCL/RT provides means to clarify the semantics of OCL invariants, pre-/post-conditions, and action clauses.

Being based on a trace semantics for systems and on a notion of global time, OCL/RT neither takes into account the possibility that events be only partially ordered nor the concept of different observers with local time, as discussed, e.g., in [17]. Partial orderings may turn indispensable for modelling true concurrency, the notion of observer could prove useful for modelling distributed systems. Though, it might be difficult to reconcile these two notions, since different observers may equip event instances with incompatible partial orderings.

The event models presented for OCL and for signals serve as a basis for the development of the chosen examples, but we do not claim them to be complete. Further event notions like assignment events and return events may have to be included. The specification of events could be refined by adding conditions that e.g. ensure that events get meaningful time stamps and are placed in time at the right place. In general, the relation between OCL/RT events and UML actions has to be clarified.

Moreover, OCL/RT does not offer means to specify which events force a state transition in the semantic trace. Right now, a successor state has more events, but apart from the obvious choice of change events that cause a state transition, it might also make sense to choose further events for provoking a state transition as well. For instance, close signals of the Gate example can be such kind of events; in this way, the constraint for the gate closed within a certain time after a close signal has arrived may be written just for the last close signal and not for all of them. Given that such a constraint has to hold always, i.e., in any state of the semantic trace, then this new constraint will be enough as well as more compact. However, for this proposal to make sense, we have to solve the question of two state changing events occurring simultaneously. Independently, OCL/RT may be further improved by including abbreviations that make it easier to write and read constraints. More ambitiously, a modal logic for reasoning on OCL/RT and UML may be devised.

Acknowledgements. We would like to thank the anonymous referees for their insightful comments.

References

1. José M. Álvarez, Tony Clark, Andy Evans, and Paul Sammut. An Action Semantics for MML. In Gogolla and Kobryn [9], pages 2–18.
2. Thomas Baar. Experiences with the UML/OCL-Approach to Precise Software Modeling. In *Proc. Net.ObjectDays*, Erfurt, 2000.
   http://i12www.ira.uka.de/ key/doc/2000/baar00.pdf.gz.
3. Grady Booch, James Rumbaugh, and Ivar Jacobson. *The Unified Modeling Language User Guide*. Addison–Wesley, Reading, Mass., &c., 1998.
4. María Victoria Cengarle and Alexander Knapp. A Formal Semantics for OCL 1.4. In Gogolla and Kobryn [9], pages 118–133.
5. Stefan Conrad and Klaus Turowski. Temporal OCL: Meeting Specification Demands for Business Components. In Keng Siau and Terry Halpin, editors, *Unified Modeling Language: Systems Analysis, Design and Development Issues*, chapter 10, pages 151–166. Idea Publishing Group, 2001.
6. Bruce P. Douglass. *Real-Time UML*. Addison-Wesley, Reading, Mass., &c., 1998.
7. Bruce P. Douglass. *Doing Hard Time*. Addison-Wesley, Reading, Mass., &c., 1999.
8. Desmond F. D'Souza and Alan C. Wills. *Object, Components, Frameworks with UML: The Catalysis Approach*. Addison-Wesley, Reading, Mass., &c., 1998.
9. Martin Gogolla and Cris Kobryn, editors. *Proc. 4th Int. Conf. UML*, volume 2185 of *Lect. Notes Comp. Sci.* Springer, Berlin, 2001.
10. Hassan Gomaa. *Designing Concurrent, Distributed, and Real-Time Systems with UML*. Addison-Wesley, Reading, Mass., &c., 2000.
11. Anneke Kleppe and Jos Warmer. Extending OCL to Include Actions. In Andy Evans, Stuart Kent, and Bran Selic, editors, *Proc. 3rd Int. Conf. UML*, volume 1939 of *Lect. Notes Comp. Sci.*, pages 440–450. Springer, Berlin, 2000.

12. Anneke Kleppe and Jos Warmer. Unification of Static and Dynamic Semantics of UML. Technical report, Klasse Objecten, 2001.
http://www.cs.york.ac.uk/puml/mmf/KleppeWarmer.pdf.

13. Kevin Lano. *Formal Object-Oriented Development*. Formal Approaches to Computing and Information Technology. Springer, London, 1995.

14. Luigi Lavazza, Gabriele Quaroni, and Matteo Venturelli. Combining UML and Formal Notations for Modelling Real-Time Systems. In 8th Europ. Conf. Software Engineering, Wien, 2001.

15. Bertrand Meyer. *Object-Oriented Software Construction*. Prentice Hall, New York, &c., 1988.

16. Response to OMG RfP ad/00-09-03 "UML 2.0 OCL". Submission, OMG, 2001. http://cgi.omg.org/cgi-bin/doc?ad/01-08-01.

17. Response to OMG RfP ad/99-03-13 "Schedulability, Performance, and Time". Revised submission, OMG, 2001. http://cgi.omg.org/cgi-bin/doc?ad/01-06-14.

18. Object Management Group. Unified Modeling Language Specification, Version 1.4. Specification, OMG, 2001. http://cgi.omg.org/cgi-bin/doc?formal/01-09-67.

19. Object Management Group. Unified Modeling Language Specification (Action Semantics), Version 1.4. Specification, OMG, 2002.
http://cgi.omg.org/cgi-bin/doc?ptc/02-01-09.

20. Mark Richters and Martin Gogolla. OCL — Syntax, Semantics and Tools. In Tony Clark and Jos Warmer, editors, *Advances in Object Modelling with the OCL*, volume 2263 of *Lect. Notes Comp. Sci.*, pages 38–63. Springer, Berlin, 2002.

21. Bran Selic, Garth Gullekson, and Paul T. Ward. *Real-Time Object-Oriented Modeling*. John Wiley & Sons, New York, 1994.

22. Bran Selic and James Rumbaugh. Using UML for Modeling Complex Real-Time Systems. White paper, Rational Software Corp., 1998.
http://www.rational.com/media/whitepapers/umlrt.pdf.

23. Shane Sendall and Alfred Strohmeier. Specifying Concurrent System Behavior and Timing Constraints Using OCL and UML. In Martin Gogolla and Cris Kobryn, editors, *Proc. 4th Int. Conf. UML*, volume 2185 of *Lect. Notes Comp. Sci.*, pages 391–405. Springer, Berlin, 2001.

24. Kerry Trentelman and Marieke Huisman. Extending JML Specifications with Temporal Logic. In *Proc. 9th Int. Conf. Algebraic Methodology And Software Technology*, 2002. To appear.

25. Jos Warmer and Anneke Kleppe. *The Object Constraint Language*. Addison–Wesley, Reading, Mass., &c., 1999.

On Combining Functional Verification and Performance Evaluation Using CADP

Hubert Garavel[1] and Holger Hermanns[2]

[1] INRIA Rhône-Alpes / VASY, 655, avenue de l'Europe
F-38330 Montbonnot Saint-Martin, France
[2] Formal Methods and Tools Group, University of Twente,
P.O. Box 217, NL-7500 AE Enschede, The Netherlands

Abstract. Considering functional correctness and performance evaluation in a common framework is desirable, both for scientific and economic reasons. In this paper, we describe how the CADP toolbox, originally designed for verifying the functional correctness of LOTOS specifications, can also be used for performance evaluation. We illustrate the proposed approach by the performance study of the SCSI-2 bus arbitration protocol.

1 Introduction

The design of models suited for performance and reliability analysis of systems is difficult because of their increase in size and complexity, in particular for systems with a high degree of irregularity. Traditional performance models like Markov chains and queueing networks are not easy to apply in these areas, mainly because they lack hierarchical composition and abstraction means. Therefore, if attempts are nowadays made to assess performance of complex designs, they are most often isolated from the system design cycle. This *insularity problem* of performance evaluation [10] is undesirable.

On the other hand, to describe and analyse the functional properties of designs, various specification formalisms exist, which enable systems to be modelled in a compositional, hierarchical manner. A prominent example of such specification formalisms is the class of *process algebras*, which provide abstraction mechanisms to treat system components as black boxes, making their internal implementation details invisible.

Among the many process algebras proposed in the literature, LOTOS [27,7,35] has received much attention, due to its technical merits and its status of ISO/IEC International Standard. CADP (*Caesar/Aldebaran Development Package*) [17] is a widespread tool set for the design and verification of complex systems. CADP supports the process algebra LOTOS for specification, and offers various tools for simulation and formal verification, including equivalence checkers (bisimulations) and model checkers (temporal logics and modal μ-calculus).

Facing these advanced means to construct correct models of complex systems, it appears most interesting to investigate how performance evaluation can be carried out on the basis of such models, and this is what the present paper is

L.-H. Eriksson and P. Lindsay (Eds.): FME 2002, LNCS 2391, pp. 410–429, 2002.
© Springer-Verlag Berlin Heidelberg 2002

about. Functional correctness and performance evaluation being two facets of the same problem, which is the proper functioning of a system, it is desirable to address them together, both for scientific and economic reasons. This requires *(i)* a common theoretical framework, *(ii)* a common language for modelling both functional and performance aspects, *(iii)* a common methodology for combining both aspects, and *(iv)* software tools implementing the appropriate algorithms.

To arrive at this joint consideration of functionality and performance, we follow the approach advocated in [23]. We start from a functionally verified LOTOS specification, in which we introduce timing related information, which expresses that certain events are delayed by a random time (governed by an exponential distribution or, more generally, a phase-type distribution).

To support this methodology, we use the existing software components of CADP, as well as a novel tool named BCG_MIN, which we developed for minimising stochastic models. We illustrate the approach with an industrial case study: the bus arbitration protocol used in the SCSI-2 [2] standard.

We are not the first to advocate a joint consideration of functional verification and performance evaluation. This idea has driven the development of stochastic Petri nets [1], stochastic process algebras [24,29,26,4,20], as well as other approaches, e.g., [6]. Our proposal can be considered as a pragmatic outcome of research on stochastic algebras, other tools in this context being the PEPA-workbench [14], TWOTOWERS [3], and the TIPPTOOL [21]. Although on a superficial level all these tools implement an approach similar to ours, only TWOTOWERS provides support for both functional verification as well as performance evaluation. Moreover, we are not aware of any publication considering both functional correctness and performance properties for industrial scale applications, with the exception of [23], where a verified LOTOS specification of a telephone system is studied with respect to performance properties. One conclusion of [23] was a lack of tool support for doing industrial strength case studies, a problem that we address here explicitly.

This paper is organised as follows. Section 2 explains how the process algebra LOTOS can be used for modelling Markovian aspects, and describes extensions of CADP to support performance evaluation. The functional part of the SCSI-2 case study is introduced in Section 3, while Section 4 covers the performance-related modelling and analysis aspects for the SCSI protocol. Finally, Section 5 concludes the paper.

2   The Proposed Approach

Our approach to combining functional verification and performance evaluation is pragmatic in the sense that, instead of developing new models, new languages and new tools, it is, to a large extent, based on prior work for 'classical' (i.e., non-stochastic) process algebras, and especially the CADP tools. However, to address performance aspects, the CADP tools (originally designed for functional verification only) must be extended and combined with performance tools. To do so, several challenging issues must be addressed. In this section, we present the principles of our approach and their practical implementation.

2.1   Interactive Markov Chains

To define the operational semantics of process algebras, the usual model is that of *labelled transition systems* (LTS for short). An LTS is a directed graph whose vertices denote the global *states* of the system and whose edges correspond to the *transitions* permitted by the system. Each transition is labelled by an *action*, and there is one distinguished state considered as the *initial state*.

As regards functional verification, many verification techniques (such as those implemented in CADP) are based on the LTS model.

As regards performance evaluation, many stochastic models derived from state-transition diagrams have been proposed. Our approach is based on the *Interactive Markov Chains* model [19] (IMC for short), which is well-adapted to process algebras. An IMC is simply an LTS whose transitions can be either labelled with an action (as in an 'ordinary' LTS) or with special labels of the form "rate λ", where λ belongs to the set of positive reals. A transition "rate λ" going out of some state S is called a *delay transition* and expresses an internal delay in state S. More precisely, it indicates that the time t spent in S follows a so-called *negative exponential distribution function* $Prob\{t \leq x\} = 1 - e^{-\lambda x}$, to be read as: the probability that state S is exited at time x the latest equals $1 - e^{-\lambda x}$. The parameter λ of the distribution is called a *Markov delay*; it is also referred to as the *rate* of the distribution (the rate being the reciprocal value of the mean duration of an exponentially distributed delay). The IMC model is very general in several respects:

- It contains, as two particular cases, the LTS model (which is obtained when there is no delay transition) and the well-known *Continuous Time Markov Chain* model (which is obtained when there are only delay transitions). The latter model (CTMC for short) has been extensively studied in the literature and is equipped with various efficient evaluation strategies (see, e.g. [34]).
- The IMC model allows nondeterminism in states, i.e., two identical action transitions leaving the same state. Nondeterminism is an important feature if the IMC model is to be generated automatically from higher-level languages such as process algebra.
- Unlike some stochastic models (e.g. [26,4]), the IMC model does not require a strict alternation between actions and delays. It is therefore permitted to have several successive actions not separated by a delay in between. It is also permitted to have several delays interspersed between actions. This is practically useful: by combining several exponential distributions one can define a more general class of distributions, so-called *phase-type distributions*. Concretely, each CTMC fragment with an *absorbing* state (i.e., a state without rate-successors) can be used to represent a phase-type distribution, which describes the time needed to reach the absorbing state from the initial state. For instance, the following example:

$$\dots \circ \xrightarrow{A} \circ \xrightarrow{\text{rate } 10} \circ \xrightarrow{\text{rate } 10} \circ \xrightarrow{\text{rate } 10} \circ \xrightarrow{B} \circ \dots$$

expresses that the occurrence of action B after witnessing action A is delayed by an Erlang-3 distribution. This is an important feature, as phase-type distributions can approximate arbitrary distributions arbitrarily close [32].

There is a subtle, but important difference between the LTS and IMC models. In the LTS model, given an action A and two states S_1 and S_2, there is *at most one* transition labelled by A going from S_1 to S_2. It is not possible to have several identical transitions between the same states, because transitions are usually defined by a relation over *States × Actions × States*. Technically, it would be easy to allow identical transitions by using a *multirelation* over *States × Actions × States* instead. But this is not the standard approach, as the usual means of observing LTSs (bisimulations, μ-calculus, SOS rules that define the semantics of process algebraic operators used to compose LTSs) only check for the existence of transitions and, thus, would not make any difference between one and several identical transitions.

The situation is different in the stochastic setting. Multiplicity of identical transitions is making a difference in the case of delay transitions. Given a rate λ and two states S_1 and S_2, the co-existence of two transitions labelled "rate λ" expresses that there are two competing ways to reach S_2. According to this so-called *race interpretation*, which is widely used to explain the behaviour of Markov chains over time, these two delay transitions could be merged into a unique transition "rate 2λ" that cumulates their rates.

Concretely, in our approach, LTSs and IMCs are encoded in the BCG (*Binary Coded Graphs*) file format. BCG is a compact format for storing very large LTSs. It plays a pivotal role in the CADP tool set, which provides programming interfaces and a comprehensive collection of software tools to handle BCG files. The BCG format can handle identical transitions according to the multirelation semantics because, for time efficiency reasons, transitions are stored inside the BCG format as a list-like data structure, without checking for duplicates.

2.2   Using LOTOS to Express Interactive Markov Chains

Although it is possible to specify performance aspects directly at the IMC level, this is not always suitable for complex systems, which are more easily described using higher level languages. Our approach is based on the LOTOS process algebra, which we briefly present hereafter.

LOTOS is a formal description technique for specifying communication protocols and distributed systems at a high abstraction level and with a strong mathematical basis. Its definition [27] features two parts.

The *data part* is based on the theory of algebraic data types. It allows the definition of data structures described by *sorts*, which represent value domains, and *operations*, which are mathematical functions defined on these domains using algebraic *equations*. Sorts, operations, and equations are grouped in modules called *types*, which can be combined together using importation, renaming, parameterisation, and actualisation. The underlying semantics is that of initial algebras.

The *behaviour part* combines the best features of the pioneering process algebras, notably Milner's CCS and Hoare's CSP. It is used to describe concurrent processes that synchronise and communicate by rendezvous message-passing. LOTOS has a small set of basic operators (sequential composition, non-deterministic choice, guard, parallel composition, etc.), which can be combined together to express complex behaviours. The semantics of LOTOS is defined operationally in terms of (finite or infinite) LTSs. We refer to [7,35] for further reading.

As LOTOS is mainly intended for functional aspects (data and behaviours), it provides no built-in support for quantitative time nor performance modelling. It is worth noticing that the recent E-LOTOS standard [28], which introduces quantitative time, still lacks support for performance aspects. In particular, a concept like *randomness* or *probability* has not been included.

At this point, we are confronted to a crucial choice: either designing a new process algebra containing stochastic extensions (as done with TIPP [15], PEPA [26], or EMPA [4]), or taking LOTOS as is and extend it orthogonally with stochastic features. The former approach requires to develop a whole set of new tools, which we want to avoid for time/cost reasons. We therefore chose the latter approach, so as to reuse existing tools already available for LOTOS, in particular the CÆSAR.ADT [11] and CÆSAR [13] tools of CADP.

CÆSAR.ADT and CÆSAR are two complementary LOTOS to C compilers, the former for the data part, the latter for the behaviour part of LOTOS. The C code generated by these compilers is then used by other CADP tools for various purposes: simulation, random execution, on the fly verification, test generation, etc. Additionally, CÆSAR can generate the LTS corresponding to a LOTOS specification, if of finite size. This LTS is encoded in the BCG format and can be verified using bisimulations and/or model-checking of μ-calculus or temporal logic formulas.

Extending LOTOS with stochastic constructs would imply deep changes in the existing compilers in order to cope with delay transitions. Still guided by pragmatism, we found a lighter approach, which does not modify the syntax of LOTOS and requires no change in the CÆSAR.ADT and CÆSAR compilers. The principle is the following. Starting from a LOTOS specification whose functional correctness has been already verified, the user should, at every place in the LOTOS specification where a Markov delay λ_i should occur, insert an action Λ_i, where Λ_i is a new LOTOS *gate* (i.e., action name) expressing a communication with the external environment. The user should declare as many new gates Λ_i as there exists different rates λ_i. It is also possible to declare a single new gate Λ to which different parameter values will be associated (e.g., "Λ !i").

To ensure that introducing Markov delays does not corrupt the functional behaviour of the original specification, one can check that the LOTOS specification obtained after hiding the Λ_i gates (i.e., renaming these gates to τ) is equivalent to the original LOTOS specification modulo a weak equivalence (e.g., branching equivalence), or that both satisfy the same set of properties expressed in temporal logic or μ-calculus.

After the special gates Λ_i have been inserted in the LOTOS specification, CÆSAR and CÆSAR.ADT are invoked as usual to generate the corresponding LTS. This LTS is then turned into an IMC (still encoded in the BCG format) by replacing all its action transitions Λ_i with delay transitions "rate λ_i". This is done using the BCG_LABELS tool of CADP, which performs hiding and/or renaming on the labels attached to the transitions of a BCG file, according to a set of regular expression and substitution patterns specified by the user.

Our approach operates in two successive steps, first generating an LTS parameterised with action names Λ_i, then instantiating the Λ_i parameter with actual Markov delays. This is practically useful, as one often needs to try several values for each rate parameters when evaluating the performance of a system. With our approach, the highest cost (generating the parameterised LTS) occurs only once, while the instantiation costs are negligible in comparison.

One might wonder whether this two step approach is theoretically sound. For most LOTOS operators (sequential composition, non-deterministic choice, process instantiation, etc.), there is no problem because the IMC model has been designed as an orthogonal extension of standard process algebra [19,23,20]. Yet, two points must be clarified:

- As regards parallel composition, there are various possible semantics for the synchronisation on a common action [25,20]. To avoid any ambiguity, we do not allow synchronisation on the special gates Λ_i. It is the user's responsibility not to synchronise these gates. For the same reason, the LOTOS parallel operator "| |", which forces synchronisation for all visible gates, should be avoided as well.
- With respect to the above discussion on multirelation semantics for transitions, it is true that the standard semantics of LOTOS [27] is defined in terms of LTSs, contrary to stochastic process algebras, which rely (explicitly or implicitly) on multirelation semantics. However, LOTOS could equally well be equipped with a multirelation semantics without disturbing its sound algebraic theory, given that both standard and multirelation semantics cannot be distinguished by strong bisimulation.

  Concretely, if a LOTOS specification contains identical transitions (e.g., "Λ; stop [] Λ; stop"), a LOTOS compiler such as CÆSAR can generate an LTS with one or two Λ-transitions, both solutions being equivalent modulo strong bisimulation; the number of Λ-transitions will mainly depend on the degree of optimisations done by the compiler internally. The user can safely avoid this issue by using, instead of Λ, two different gate names Λ_1 and Λ_2, which will be later instantiated with the same Markov delay.

There is another approach to extend a LOTOS specification with stochastic timing information, besides the direct insertion of Markov delays in the specification text. This alternative approach is based on the use of *specification styles* [36] for LOTOS, and especially the *constraint-oriented* style, which allows to refine the behaviour of an existing LOTOS process by synchronising it with one (or several) concurrent process(es) expressing a set of temporal constraints on the ordering of actions. It has been suggested in [23] that the constraint-oriented style can be used to incorporate Markov delays (or even more complex phase-type distributions) between the actions of a LOTOS specification, without modifying the specification text itself; see also [6] for a similar suggestion. Following this idea, a general operator for expressing time constraints compositionally has been proposed in [19, Section 5.5]. In this paper, we will illustrate both approaches, i.e., both the direct insertion of Markov delays in the LOTOS text (see Section 3) and the superposition of time constraints specified externally (see Section 4).

2.3   Minimisation of Interactive Markov Chains

After generating an LTS from a LOTOS specification and converting this LTS to an IMC by instantiating Markov delays with their actual values, the next step of our methodology consists in *minimising* this IMC, i.e., aggregating its state space. This minimisation is based on the (closely related) notions of bisimulation (on LTS) and *lumpability* (on CTMCs), and is of interest for at least three reasons:

- It brings the IMC to a minimal number of states, still retaining its essential properties; this improves the efficiency of performance evaluation tools applied later to the minimised IMC;
- It replaces all delay transitions between a given pair of states by a single transition that cumulates the rates of these transitions; in particular, it removes identical transitions, so that multirelation semantics is no longer needed after minimisation.
- It may reduce (or even eliminate) nondeterminism, a concept not supported by performance evaluation algorithms; however, nondeterminism is not guaranteed to vanish after minimisation.

Although minimisation is practically useful, a lack of tool support to minimise large IMCs or CTMCs has been identified (e.g., in [23] where the minimisation tool used could not handle more than 4,000 states). To account for this, we developed a software tool called BCG_MIN (3,000 lines of C code) for minimising LTSs and IMCs encoded in the BCG format:

- As regards LTSs, BCG_MIN performs efficient minimisation with respect to either strong or branching bisimulation. According to independent experts, BCG_MIN is *"the best implementation of the standard [i.e., Groote & Vaandrager] algorithm for branching bisimulation"* [18]. Using BCG_MIN we have been able to minimise an LTS with 8 million states and 43 million transitions on a standard PC.
- As regards IMCs, BCG_MIN implements both *stochastic strong bisimulation* and *stochastic branching bisimulation*. In a nutshell, stochastic strong (resp. branching) bisimulation combines lumpability on the delay transitions with strong (resp. branching) bisimulation on the action transitions. Consequently, BCG_MIN can be used to minimise CTMCs modulo lumpability. A formal definition of stochastic strong bisimulation and stochastic weak bisimulation (a variant of stochastic branching bisimulation) can be found in [19].

Apart from LTSs, CTMCs, and IMCs, BCG_MIN can handle a wide range of other models, including *(i)* stochastic models containing transitions labelled by (action, rate) pairs, which allows to minimise TIPP [15], PEPA [26], and EMPA [4] models modulo strong equivalence and Markovian bisimulation, *(ii)* probabilistic systems containing transitions labelled by action, probabilities, and/or (action, probability) pairs, which allows to minimise discrete time Markov chains (and various probabilistic transition systems) modulo lumpability (respectively probabilistic bisimulation), and *(iii)* Markov decision processes [33], which can be minimised modulo lumpability. We refer to the BCG_MIN manual page[1] for a detailed description of the features of BCG_MIN.

2.4 Compositional Generation of Interactive Markov Chains

Both functional verification and performance evaluation are confronted to the well-known *state explosion* problem, which occurs when state spaces or Markov chains become too large for being generated exhaustively. As regards functional verification, the CADP tool set provides various strategies to address the state explosion problem, one of these being *compositional generation* (also known as *compositional minimisation*), see e.g. [16]. This approach consists in dividing the system into a set of concurrent processes, then generating the LTSs corresponding to these processes, minimising these LTSs using an equivalence relation (such as strong or branching bisimulation), and finally combining the minimised LTSs in parallel so as to generate the LTS of the whole system.

Compositional generation has been adapted to performance evaluation, both in the context of CTMCs, where bisimulation is known to agree with the notion of lumpability [26], and in the context of LOTOS and IMCs [23]. Compared to [23], our approach is novel in several respects:

- Using the BCG_MIN tool, which did not exist at the time of [23], we are now able to minimise IMCs effectively.
- To compute the IMC corresponding to a set of IMCs combined together using LOTOS parallel composition operators (without synchronisation on delay transitions as mentioned above), we resort to the EXP.OPEN tool[2] developed by Laurent Mounier. The EXP.OPEN tool is also used to combine a LOTOS specification with a set of IMCs expressing delays to be incorporated in a constraint-oriented style.
- Finally, we take advantage of SVL [12,31], a new scripting language for compositional and on-the-fly verification. SVL provides a high-level interface to all CADP tools (including CÆSAR, CÆSAR.ADT, BCG_LABELS, BCG_MIN, EXP.OPEN, etc.), thus enabling an easy description and execution of complex performance studies.

2.5 Numerical Analysis of Interactive Markov Chains

After constructing a minimised IMC, the last step of our methodology consists in applying performance evaluation analysis algorithms, so as to compute interesting performance metrics out of the model. To analyse the IMC models, one can use either model checking algorithms, such as those implemented in ETMCC [22] or PRISM [30][3], or more standard analysis algorithms for CTMCs, such as

---

[1] http://www.inrialpes.fr/vasy/cadp/man/bcg_min.html

[2] http://www.inrialpes.fr/vasy/cadp/man/exp.open.html

[3] IMC models containing nondeterminism require rather involved algorithms as described in [33,9]

those available in the TIPPTOOL [21] developed at the University of Erlangen-Nuremberg. Note however that in general the IMC models contain nondeterminism, and thus one needs rather involved algorithms as described in [33,9].

We decided to stick to standard CTMC analysis algorithms. A connection of the TIPPTOOL analysis engine to the BCG format was developed, which enables the use of the TIPPTOOL to carry out analysis of (moderate size) IMCs generated using CADP. This connection allows to study the time dependent (*transient*) behaviour, as well as the long run average (*steady-state*) behaviour of a model. Transient analysis uses a numerical algorithm known as *uniformisation*, while steady-state analysis is carried out using either the *power*, *Gauss-Seidel* or *SOR* method; see [34] for a thorough introduction to these algorithms.

3   The SCSI-2 Bus Arbitration Protocol

To illustrate our approach, we consider an industrial case-study brought to our attention by Massimo Zendri while he was working in the VASY team. This case-study is about a storage system developed by Bull in the early 90's. This system consists of at most 8 *devices* (7 hard disks and one disk controller) connected by a bus implementing the SCSI-2 (*Small Computer System Interface*) standard [2]. Each device is assigned a unique SCSI number between 0 and 7.

During the testing phase, Bull engineers discovered potential starvation problems for disks having SCSI numbers smaller than the SCSI number of the disk controller. Practically, this problem was solved by instructing system manufacturers to install the controller with the SCSI number 0 systematically. In parallel, research was initiated to understand the issue. This problem was first modelled by Massimo Zendri, who developed a Markovian queueing model to study performance issues [37]. Later, the functional aspects of the SCSI-2 bus arbitration protocol were formalised in LOTOS by Hubert Garavel, with an emphasis on modelling arbitration concisely using LOTOS multiway rendezvous. This LOTOS specification[4] served as a basis for model-checking verification by Radu Mateescu (thus, enabling to discover the starvation problem mechanically) and automated test generation by Solofo Ramangalahy. See also [5] for a discussion of fairness issues in the SCSI-3 bus arbitration protocol. In the present paper, we complement these functional verification efforts by enhancing the LOTOS model so as to study performance issues.

In the SCSI-2 system, the controller can send randomly to the disk n a message "CMD !n" (*command*) indicating a transfer request (read/write a block of data from/to the disk). After processing this command, the disk sends back to the controller a message "REC !n" (*reconnect*). We do not model the detailed contents (e.g., type or data) of these messages. The CMD and REC messages are stored in eight-place FIFO queues (see Figure 1). Since we abstract from the message contents, it is sufficient to model these queues as simple counters.

Arbitration mechanism. The CMD and REC messages circulate on the SCSI bus, which is shared by all devices. To avoid access conflicts, the SCSI-2 standard

---

[4] See http://www.inrialpes.fr/vasy/verdon for details

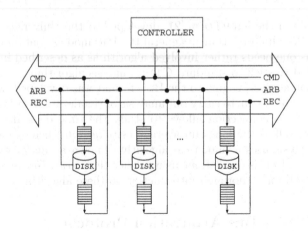

Fig. 1. Architecture of the SCSI-2 system.

defines a bus arbitration policy ensuring that at any time at most one device is allowed to access the bus. Before sending a message over the bus, each device must first request and obtain exclusive bus access. Arbitration is based on fixed priorities: if several devices want to access the bus simultaneously, the device with the highest SCSI number is granted access. Arbitration is also decentralised: contrary to other bus protocols (e.g., PCI) there is no centralised arbiter responsible for granting bus access. To ensure exclusive access in a distributed way, the arbitration mechanism is physically implemented by eight electrical wires, the voltage level of which (high or low) can be consulted by all devices. Each wire is owned by a particular device, and is set to high voltage when this device requests bus access. Before using the bus, each device examines the eight wires' voltage level during a certain amount of time (the *arbitration period*) to ensure that no other device with a higher SCSI number has its wire set to high voltage.

Modelling the SCSI-2 arbitration policy in a precise, concise, yet understandable way is a challenge, especially for languages providing binary communication paradigms only (such as FIFO queues, remote procedure calls, or binary synchronisations).

Yet, this problem can be solved elegantly using the advanced features of LOTOS (namely, multiway rendezvous with value negotiation based on pattern-matching). Assuming that the arbitration period is short enough, arbitration can be modelled by a single, eight-party rendezvous between all devices on a gate named ARB. During every arbitration period, all devices must synchronise to indicate whether they request bus access or not. Syntactically, each device must propose an action of the form "ARB ?W:WIRE [C_n(W, n)]", where n is the SCSI number of the device, where variable W of type WIRE is an eight-tuple ($w_0, w_1, \ldots, w_7$) of booleans corresponding to the voltage levels on the wires[5], and where predi-

---

[5] The boolean values *false* and *true* correspond to low and high voltage, respectively.

cate $C_n(W, n)$ belongs to a set of three possible constraints relating W and n. These three constraints are: *(i)* the constraint $C\_PASS(W, n) := \neg w_n$ is true iff device n does not request the bus; *(ii)* the constraint $C\_WIN(W, n) := w_n \wedge \neg \bigvee_{i=n+1}^{i=7} w_i$ is true iff device n requests the bus and succeeds to be the highest priority competitor; *(iii)* the constraint $C\_LOSS(W, n) := w_n \wedge \bigvee_{i=n+1}^{i=7} w_i$ is true iff device n requests the bus but fails to gain access. When the eight devices synchronise together on gate ARB, their individual, distributed constraints are combined into a logical conjunction $\bigwedge_{i=0}^{i=7} C_i(W, i)$, which determines a unique solution W agreed by all the devices unanimously.

Disk devices. Each disk is described as an instance of a generic LOTOS process (noted DISK) parameterised by the SCSI number N, the number L of CMD messages waiting to be processed in the disk's input FIFO queue (initially, L = 0), and by a boolean variable READY which is true iff the device has processed a CMD message and is ready to send the result back to the controller (initially, READY = *false*). The behaviour of the DISK process is a nondeterministic selection between five branches: *(i)* the disk may receive a CMD message and increment L (a flow control mechanism implemented in the controller avoids overflows in the disks' input queues); *(ii)* if the disk is not ready, it may take part in the arbitration mechanism without requesting the bus, which enables lower priority devices to access the bus; *(iii)* if the disk is not ready and if its input queue is not empty, it may process a command stored in the queue (which takes a Markov delay noted "MU !N"), then decrement L and become ready; *(iv)* and *(v)* if the disk is ready, it requests the bus repeatedly until it is granted; once successful, it sends a corresponding REC message and returns to its non-ready state.

```
process DISK [ARB, CMD, REC, MU] (N:NUM, L:NAT, READY:BOOL):noexit :=
    CMD !N;
        DISK [ARB, CMD, REC, MU] (N, L+1, READY)
    []
    ARB ?W:WIRE [not (READY) and C_PASS (W, N)];
        DISK [ARB, CMD, REC, MU] (N, L, READY)
    []
    [not (READY) and (L > 0)] ->
        MU !N; (* Markov delay inserted here *)
            DISK [ARB, CMD, REC, MU] (N, L-1, true)
    []
    ARB ?W:WIRE [READY and C_LOSS (W, N)];
        DISK [ARB, CMD, REC, MU] (N, L, READY)
    []
    ARB ?W:WIRE [READY and C_WIN (W, N)];
        REC !N;
            DISK [ARB, CMD, REC, MU] (N, L, false)
endproc
```

Controller device. The controller is described by a LOTOS process (noted CONTROLLER) parameterised by the SCSI number NC of the controller and by two variables PENDING and T. PENDING contains the SCSI number of the disk to which the controller has to send a CMD message (initially, PENDING = NC, which means that the controller is idle). T is a table (i.e., an array) used for flow control, so as to avoid overflow of the disks' input queues. The n-th element of T (noted "VAL (T, n)''", where n is a SCSI number different from NC) stores the number of commands waiting to be processed by disk n, i.e., the difference between the number of "CMD !n" messages sent and the number of "REC !n" messages received by the controller. ZERO denotes the initial value of the table, with all elements equal to 0. INCR (T, n) and DECR (T, n) denote the table T in which the n-th element is incremented or decremented, respectively.

As with the disk, the behaviour of the CONTROLLER process is a selection between five branches: *(i)* if the controller is idle, it may take part in the arbitration mechanism without requesting the bus; *(ii)* if the controller is idle, it may also select (nondeterministically) some disk N with less than eight unprocessed commands and assign N to PENDING; in practice, this selection is triggered by a transfer request sent to the controller by its external environment; we introduce a Markov delay noted "LAMBDA !N" in order to model the load stress imposed on the controller; *(iii)* and *(iv)* if the controller is not idle, it requests the bus repeatedly until it is granted; once successful, it sends a CMD message to the disk indicated by PENDING, then increments T accordingly and returns to its idle state; *(v)* the controller may receive REC messages and decrement T accordingly.

```
process CONTROLLER [ARB, CMD, REC, LAMBDA] (NC:NUM, PENDING:NUM,
                                            T:TABLE) : noexit :=
    ARB ?W:WIRE [(PENDING == NC) and C_PASS (W, NC)];
        CONTROLLER [ARB, CMD, REC, LAMBDA] (NC, PENDING, T)
    []
    (
    choice N:NUM []
        [(PENDING == NC) and (N <> NC)] ->
            [VAL (T, N) < 8] ->
                LAMBDA !N; (* Markov delay inserted here *)
                    CONTROLLER [ARB, CMD, REC, LAMBDA] (NC, N, T)
    )
    []
    ARB ?W:WIRE [(PENDING <> NC) and C_LOSS (W, NC)];
        CONTROLLER [ARB, CMD, REC, LAMBDA] (NC, PENDING, T)
    []
    ARB ?W:WIRE [(PENDING <> NC) and C_WIN (W, NC)];
        CMD !PENDING;
            CONTROLLER [ARB, CMD, REC, LAMBDA] (NC, NC, INCR (T, PENDING))
    []
    REC ?N:NUM [N <> NC];
        CONTROLLER [ARB, CMD, REC, LAMBDA] (NC, PENDING, DECR (T, N))
endproc
```

System architecture. The architecture of the SCSI-2 system is described by composing in parallel the seven disk processes and the controller process. All these processes synchronise together using an eight-way rendezvous on the ARB gate. The disks communicate with the controller using binary rendezvous on gates CMD and REC. Although the seven disks are competing with each other for achieving a rendezvous on gates CMD and REC with the controller, the "!n" parameters associated to these gates allow to identify the corresponding disk. Finally, as explained in Section 2.2, the MU and LAMBDA gates must not be synchronised.

```
(
DISK [ARB, CMD, REC, MU] (0, 0, false)
| [ARB] |
DISK [ARB, CMD, REC, MU] (1, 0, false)
| [ARB] |
  ...
| [ARB] |
DISK [ARB, CMD, REC, MU] (6, 0, false)
)
| [ARB, CMD, REC] |
CONTROLLER [ARB, CMD, REC, LAMBDA] (7, 7, ZERO)
```

4 Performance Model Aspects

The SCSI-2 specification as introduced above incorporates already some timing parameters, namely the Markov delays LAMBDA and MU. This section motivates the timing characteristics of the model. It further discusses the approach followed to generate and analyse the model numerically, together with some interesting performance figures we obtained.

4.1 SCSI-2 Timing Parameters

Based on the timing parameters given in definition of the SCSI-2 architecture, we identified three parameters as most relevant for a performance study.

- The Markov delay LAMBDA put in the controller models the load (transfer requests issued by the controller) that stimulates the whole SCSI-2 system. It is the main parameter we vary in our experiments.
- The Markov delay MU put in the disk corresponds to the *disk servicing time*, i.e., the time needed by an individual disk to fetch or store the requested data. The mean servicing time depends on the size of the data blocks to be transferred, and also varies from one disk manufacturer to another. Its value ranges from 1500 μs to about 4500 μs [37].
- Finally, the *bus inter-arbitration time* (or *bus delay*, for short) determines the delay between two consecutive bus arbitration periods. This delay is minimally 2.5 μs and depends on the amount of data transmitted on the bus after an arbitration.

To incorporate the bus delay into the SCSI specification, we use the constraint-oriented style mentioned earlier. As the bus delay elapses between any two consecutive ARB actions, it will be incorporated by running the SCSI system in parallel with an additional, very simple process BUS, which forces any two consecutive ARB actions to be separated by a Markov delay NU:

```
process BUS [ARB, NU]:noexit :=
  ARB; NU; BUS [ARB, NU]
endproc
```

Both the SCSI system and the BUS process are synchronised on gate ARB. Note that this approach allows one to experiment with different, phase-type distributed delays in a flexible way, such as with an Erlang-5 distributed delay:

```
process BUS_5 [ARB, NU]:noexit :=
  ARB; NU; NU; NU; NU; NU; BUS_5 [ARB, NU]
endproc
```

We carried out several experiments with such delays, and found that as long as the mean value of the distributions used stays unchanged, the influence of the distributions on the numerical results is marginal. As regards the LAMBDA and MU delays, experimenting with other distributions is not so straightforward, because any change in the distribution implies a change in the LOTOS specification, and hence a proof obligation that the functional behaviour is still as intended. The constraint-oriented style reliefs this burden, since it preserves the functional behaviour: the resulting LTS obtained after parallel composition is branching bisimilar to the original one provided that the Markov delays are hidden (i.e., renamed to τ) [19].

4.2 Performance Results

Among the studies we performed, we here focus on the behaviour of a SCSI-2 system under heavy load, since the system exhibits some interesting aspects of unfairness in extreme situations. Note that due to the distributed priority mechanism governing the bus arbitration protocol, the system can not be expected to behave perfectly fair under all circumstances.

We study a system with 3 disks. The load imposed on the system varies between 10 and 800 requests per seconds and per disk. Unless otherwise stated, we assume the average servicing time of the disks to be 2,500 μs, and the bus delay to range between 2.5 μs and 2,500 μs.

First, we study a system in which the controller is assigned the SCSI number 7, and observe the throughput of each disk under increasing load. The resulting throughputs are plotted in Figure 2, for four different bus delay parameters. The left plot shows the high priority disk 2, and the right one shows the low priority disk 0. We observe that the bus bandwidth is shared in a load dependent way, and we further observe that the higher the bus delay, the lower the throughputs of the disks. Interestingly, the lower disks' throughputs may collapse if the bus delay is very long and load is heavy. The high priority disk does not exhibit such a phenomenon. This reveals the unfairness of the arbitration mechanism.

To study this phenomenon further, we analyse the effect of the controller SCSI number on the throughputs of the high and low priority disk. Figure 3 plots the throughputs of the low and high priority disks under extreme bus delays. If the controller is in the highest position (SCSI number 7), we find back one of the scenarios studied in Figure 2: the high priority disk dominates the low priority disk, and makes the throughput of the latter collapse. If on the other hand, the

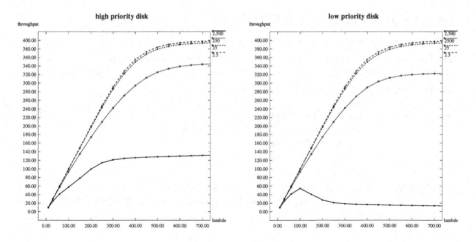

Fig. 2. Throughput of disk 2 (left) and disk 0 (right) under increasing load with bus delay ranging from 2.5 μs (dashed) to 2.5 ms (solid), and controller having number 7.

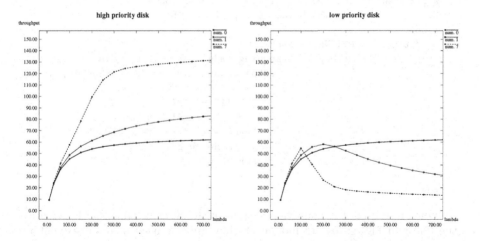

Fig. 3. Throughput of high priority disk (left) and low priority disk (right) under increasing load with bus delay 2.5 ms, and controller having lowest (solid), middle, and highest (dashed) number.

controller is in the lowest position (SCSI number 0), the achieved throughputs of high and low priority disk are rather balanced, and in particular the low priority throughput does not degrade nor collapse.

This study allows us to draw the conclusion that assigning SCSI number 0 to the controller makes the system balanced. Otherwise, disks in a position lower than the controller are disfavoured. This conclusion is in line with the experimental observations made by the Bull engineers; our studies allow a quantification of the influence of the disk position on the throughput.

4.3   An SVL Session with CADP

This section discusses how the Markov chains under study are generated from the LOTOS specification using the CADP toolbox. To explain how we proceed, we list below the main fragment of the SVL-script used to distill the lumped Markov chain used for the plots in Figure 2.

```
"scsi.bcg" = branching reduction of                          (1)
                total rename "ARB !.*" -> ARB   in
                    hide CMD, REC in
                        "scsi.lotos";

"model.bcg" = hide all but LAMBDA, MU, NU in                 (2)
                ("scsi.bcg" |[ARB]| "erlang.lotos":BUS [ARB, NU]);



% for SPEED in .4 2 4 40 400                                 (3)
% do
    % for LOAD in .01 .03 .06 .1 .15 .2 .25 .3 .35 \
    %             .4 .45 .5 .55 .6 .65 .7 .75 .8
    % do
        % BCG_MIN_OPTIONS="-rate"
        "res-$SPEED.bcg" = branching reduction with bcg_min of   (4)
                            total rename "NU" -> "rate $SPEED",
                                "MU !0" -> "DISK_L; rate .4",
                                "MU !1" -> "DISK_M; rate .4",
                                "MU !2" -> "DISK_H; rate .4",
                                "LAMBDA !.*" -> "rate $LOAD" in
                                    "model.bcg";
        % seidel -v $LOAD "res-$SPEED.bcg"                   (5)
    % done
% done
```

During step (1) the transition system of the SCSI specification is generated, the CMD and REC gates are hidden as they are not needed in subsequent processing, and the arbitration events are uniformly renamed into a new action named ARB. Then, the resulting state space is minimised according to branching bisimulation, and stored in a file named "scsi.bcg".

Step (2) incorporates the bus delay via the process BUS [ARB, NU] taken from file "erlang.lotos". Afterwards, all gates are hidden, except those corresponding to Markov delays (i.e., LAMBDA, MU, and NU). The result is stored in file "model.bcg".

Step (3) initiates two nested loops that compute a two-dimensional matrix of performance results. The outer loop varies the SPEED parameter, which is the inverse of the bus delay expressed in milliseconds, ranging from $1/2.5$ μs to $1/2.5$ ms. The inner loop varies the LOAD parameter, imposing between 0.01 and 0.8 requests per millisecond on each disk.

Step (4) instantiates, for each pair (SPEED, LOAD), the Markov delays LAMBDA, MU, and NU present in file "model.bcg" with concrete values. The resulting IMC is then minimised using BCG_MIN according to stochastic branching bisimulation, which eliminates nondeterminism. This results in a Markov chain stored in file "res-$SPEED.bcg".

Step (5) calls the TIPPTOOL solver seidel, a numerical solution engine implementing the Gauss-Seidel linear equation solver for Markov chains. It computes the equilibrium (steady-state) probabilities for the states of the Markov chain. From these probabilities, seidel calculates the transition throughputs for each Markov delay marked with a distinguished label. These labels have been incorporated into the transition system in step (4); they indicate a high (DISK_H), medium (DISK_M), or low (DISK_L) priority disk being active.

The largest state space produced during the execution of the SVL script is the LTS generated from "scsi.lotos", which has 56,169 states and 154,752 transitions. The size of the Markov chains solved (i.e., files "res-*.bcg") ranges from 10,666 to 17,852 states.

5 Concluding Remarks

This paper has presented a practical methodology for studying the performance of a concurrent system, starting from an already verified functional specification of this system. Compared to prior works on stochastic Petri nets and stochastic process algebras, our approach is original in several respects:

- We have chosen not to design a new formalism to model stochastic systems, because the effort required to develop appropriate software tools would have been very high. Instead, we reuse a non-stochastic process algebra (LOTOS), which we adapt to the stochastic framework by introducing a few additional operators (such as relabelling, restriction, time constraints, and minimisation). This approach provides the user with a high-level language (LOTOS) to describe both control and data aspects (contrary to, e.g., the TIPPTOOL, which only supports a subset of LOTOS without data structures). Furthermore, existing LOTOS tools can be used to perform functional verification before undertaking performance analysis.
- To translate LOTOS specifications into labelled transition systems, we use the CÆSAR.ADT and CÆSAR compilers of the CADP tool set. To perform relabelling, we also reuse an existing CADP tool, BCG_LABELS. Our major development effort is BCG_MIN, an efficient tool implementing several minimisation algorithms for ordinary, stochastic, and probabilistic transition systems. BCG_MIN plays a central role in connecting the CADP tools to the stochastic setting, and supports the compositional approach proposed in [23], in which concurrent processes are generated, then minimised separately so as to handle large state spaces.
- In order to automate the performance studies, in which stochastic parameters are varied in multiple dimensions, we take advantage of the scripting language SVL. Originally developed for compositional verification of non-stochastic systems, SVL is also useful in the stochastic settings, and provides convenient means to integrate the various tools transparently.

We have presented an application of these principles to an industrial problem: the SCSI-2 bus arbitration protocol, which we managed to model elegantly using the expressiveness of LOTOS multiway negotiated rendezvous. After verifying the functional correctness of the LOTOS specification using the CADP tools, we turned this specification into a performance model, which we analysed automatically by combining the CADP tools and the solution engine of the TIPPTOOL. This performance study allowed us to quantify the unfairness of the SCSI-2 bus arbitration protocol, and to show how the respective disk thoughputs depend on the SCSI number assigned to the controller. These results are in line with the experimental observations on the real SCSI-2 disk system.

As regards future work, more efforts are foreseen on the model solution side. So far, we are resorting to the TIPPTOOL, but in a near future we shall investigate model checking approaches to Markov models, notably by linking the ETMCC Markov chain model checker [22] to CADP. Also, MTBDD- or Kronecker-based Markov chain representations [30,8] are promising directions to enable the analysis of even larger models, in combination with our compositional approach.

Acknowledgements. We are grateful to Massimo Zendri for bringing the SCSI-2 example to our attention, and to Moëz Cherif (formerly at INRIA/VASY) for helping us to develop the BCG_MIN tool. We are also grateful to Frédéric Lang (INRIA/VASY) and the anonymous referees for their remarks about this paper.

References

1. A. Marsan, G. Balbo, and G. Conte. A Class of Generalized Stochastic Petri Nets for the Performance Evaluation of Multiprocessor Systems. *ACM Trans. on Comp. Sys.*, 2(2), 1984.
2. ANSI. Small Computer System Interface-2. Standard X3.131-1994, American National Standards Institute, 1994.
3. M. Bernardo, W.R. Cleaveland, S.T. Sims, and W.J. Stewart. TwoTowers: A Tool Integrating Functional and Performance Analysis of Concurrent Systems. In *Proc. FORTE'98*, IFIP, North-Holland, 1998.
4. M. Bernardo and R. Gorrieri. A Tutorial on EMPA: A Theory of Concurrent Processes with Nondeterminism, Priorities, Probabilities and Time. *Th. Comp. Sci.*, 202:1–54, 1998.
5. D. Bert. *Preuve de propriétés d'équité en B : Preuve de l'algorithme d'arbitrage du bus SCSI-3*. In *Proc. AFADL'2001* (Nancy, France), pages 221–241, June 2001.
6. L. Blair, G. Blair, and A. Andersen. Separating Functional Behaviour and Performance Constraints: Aspect-Oriented Specification. Technical Report MPG-98-07, Computing Department, Lancaster University, 1998.
7. T. Bolognesi and E. Brinksma. Introduction to the ISO Specification Language LOTOS. *Comp. Netw. and ISDN Sys.*, 14(1):25–59, 1988.
8. P. Buchholz, G. Ciardo, S. Donatelli, and P. Kemper. Complexity of memory-efficient Kronecker operations with applications to the solution of Markov models. *INFORMS J. on Comp.*, 13(3):203–222, 2000.
9. L. de Alfaro. How to specify and verify the long-run average behavior of probabilistic systems. In *Proc. Symp. on Logic in Computer Science*, 1998.

10. D. Ferrari. Considerations on the Insularity of Performance Evaluation. *IEEE Trans. on Softw. Eng.*, SE–12(6):678–683, June 1986.
11. H. Garavel. Compilation of LOTOS abstract data types. In *Proc. FORTE'89*, pages 147–162. IFIP, North-Holland, 1989.
12. H. Garavel and F. Lang. SVL: A Scripting Language for Compositional Verification. In *Proc. FORTE'2001*, pages 377–392. IFIP, Kluwer Academic, 2001. Full version available as INRIA Research Report RR-4223.
13. H. Garavel and J. Sifakis. Compilation and verification of LOTOS specifications. In *Proc. PSTV'90*, pages 379–394. IFIP, North-Holland, 1990.
14. S. Gilmore and J. Hillston. The PEPA Workbench: A Tool to Support a Process Algebra-Based Approach to Performance Modelling. In *Proc. TOOLS'94*, 1994.
15. N. Götz, U. Herzog, and M. Rettelbach. Multiprocessor and distributed system design: The integration of functional specification and performance analysis using stochastic process algebras. In *Tutorial Proc. PERFORMANCE '93*. Springer, LNCS 729, 1993.
16. S. Graf, B. Steffen, and G. Luettgen. Compositional Minimization of Finite State Systems. *Formal Asp. of Comp.*, 8(5):607–616, 1996.
17. H. Garavel, F. Lang, and R. Mateescu. An Overview of CADP 2001. INRIA Technical Report RT-254, December 2001.
18. J.F. Groote and J. van de Pol. State space reduction using partial τ-confluence. In *Proc. MFCS'2000*, pages 383–393. Springer, LNCS 1893, 2000.
19. H. Hermanns. *Interactive Markov Chains*. PhD thesis, Universität Erlangen-Nürnberg, 1998. revised version to appear as Springer LNCS monograph.
20. H. Hermanns, U. Herzog, and J.-P. Katoen. Process algebra for performance evaluation. *Th. Comp. Sci.*, 274(1-2):43–87, 2002.
21. H. Hermanns, U. Herzog, U. Klehmet, V. Mertsiotakis, and M. Siegle. Compositional performance modelling with the TIPPtool. *Perf. Eval.*, 39(1-4):5–35, January 2000.
22. H. Hermanns, J.-P. Katoen, J. Meyer-Kayser, and M. Siegle. A Markov Chain Model Checker. In *Proc. TACAS'2000*, pages 347–362, Springer, LNCS 1785, 2000.
23. H. Hermanns and J.P. Katoen. Automated compositional Markov chain generation for a plain-old telephony system. *Sci. of Comp. Prog.*, 36(1):97–127, 2000.
24. O. Hjiej, A. Benzekri, and A. Valderruten. From Annotated LOTOS specifications to Queueing Networks: Automating Performance Models Derivation. Decentralized and Distributed Systems (North Holland), 1993.
25. J. Hillston. The Nature of Synchronisation. In *Proc. PAPM'94*, Arbeitsberichte des IMMD, Universität Erlangen-Nürnberg. pages 51–70, 1994.
26. J. Hillston. *A Compositional Approach to Performance Modelling*. Cambridge University Press, 1996.
27. ISO/IEC. LOTOS — A Formal Description Technique based on the Temporal Ordering of Observational Behaviour. International Standard 8807, ISO - Information Processing Systems - Open Systems Interconnection, 1988.
28. ISO/IEC. Enhancements to LOTOS (E-LOTOS). International Standard 15437:2001, ISO - Information Technology, 2001.
29. A. Marsan, A. Bianco, L. Ciminiera, R. Sisto, and A. Valenzano. A LOTOS Extension for the Performance Analysis of Distributed Systems. IEEE/ACM Trans. on Networking, 2(2), 151–164, 1994.
30. M. Kwiatkowska, G. Norman, and D. Parker. Probabilistic Symbolic Model Checking with PRISM: A Hybrid Approach. In *Proc. TACAS'2002*, pages 52–66, 2002, Springer LNCS 2280.

31. F. Lang. Compositional Verification using SVL Scripts. In *Proc. TACAS'2002*, pages 465–469, 2002, Springer LNCS 2280.
32. M.F. Neuts. *Matrix-geometric Solutions in Stochastic Models–An Algorithmic Approach*. The Johns Hopkins University Press, 1981.
33. M.L. Puterman. *Markov Decision Processes*. John Wiley, 1994.
34. W.J. Stewart. *Introduction to the numerical solution of Markov chains*. Princeton University Press, 1994.
35. K. J. Turner, editor. *Using Formal Description Techniques – An Introduction to ESTELLE, LOTOS, and SDL*. John Wiley, 1993.
36. C. Vissers, G. Scollo, M. van Sinderen, and E. Brinksma. Specification styles in distributed systems design and verification. *Th. Comp. Sci.*, 89(1):179–206, 1991.
37. M. Zendri. *Studio ed implementazione di un modello del bus SCSI*. Laurea thesis, Politecnico di Milano, Facoltà di Ingegneria, Dip. di Elettronica, 1992.

Synthesizing Certified Code

Michael Whalen[1], Johann Schumann[2], and Bernd Fischer[2]

[1] Department of Computer Science and Engineering
Univ. of Minnesota, Minneapolis, MN 55455
whalen@cs.umn.edu
[2] RIACS / NASA Ames, Moffett Field, CA 94035
{schumann|fisch}@email.arc.nasa.gov

Abstract. Code certification is a lightweight approach for formally demonstrating software quality. Its basic idea is to require code producers to provide formal *proofs* that their code satisfies certain quality properties. These proofs serve as *certificates* that can be checked independently. Since code certification uses the same underlying technology as program verification, it requires detailed annotations (e.g., loop invariants) to make the proofs possible. However, manually adding annotations to the code is time-consuming and error-prone.
We address this problem by combining code certification with automatic program synthesis. Given a high-level specification, our approach simultaneously generates code and *all* annotations required to certify the generated code. We describe a certification extension of AUTOBAYES, a synthesis tool for automatically generating data analysis programs. Based on built-in domain knowledge, proof annotations are added and used to generate proof obligations that are discharged by the automated theorem prover E-SETHEO. We demonstrate our approach by certifying operator- and memory-safety on a data-classification program. For this program, our approach was faster and more precise than PolySpace, a commercial static analysis tool.

Keyword: automatic program synthesis, program verification, code certification, proof-carrying code, automated theorem proving.

1 Introduction

Code certification is a lightweight approach to formally demonstrate software quality. It concentrates on aspects of software quality that can be defined and formalized via properties, e.g., operator safety or memory safety. Its basic idea is to require code producers to provide formal *proofs* that their code satisfies these quality properties. The proofs serve as *certificates* which can be checked independently, either by the code consumer or by certification authorities.

Code certification is an alternative to other, more established validation and verification techniques. It is more formal than code inspection and can show stronger properties than static analysis. In contrast to testing, code certification demonstrates that the properties of interest hold for all possible execution paths

L.-H. Eriksson and P. Lindsay (Eds.): FME 2002, LNCS 2391, pp. 431–450, 2002.

of the program. It also complements software model checking, which works on a different set of properties (typically liveness properties such as absence of dead-locks). Moreover, model checking does not produce explicit certificates: while it can produce counter-examples if a property is violated, validity follows only indirectly from the claim of an exhaustive search through the state space that cannot be checked independently.

In essence, code certification is a more tractable version of traditional ax-iomatic or Hoare-style program verification. It uses the same basic technology: the program is annotated with an axiomatic specification, the annotated pro-gram is fed into a verification condition generator (VCG) which produces a series of proof obligations, the proof obligations are proven or *discharged* by an automated theorem prover (ATP). The difference, however, is in the details: the certified properties are much simpler and much more regular than full be-havioral specifications. Both aspects are crucial: Since the properties are much simpler, the resulting proof obligations are much simpler as well. Consequently, discharging them is also much easier; in many cases, all proof obligations can be shown fully automatically. Since the properties are much more regular, the annotations can be derived schematically from an explicitly formulated *safety policy*. Consequently, the specification effort—which can become overwhelming in traditional verification—is also much smaller.

However, code certification shares not only the underlying technology with Hoare-style program verification but also a fundamental limitation: in order to certify non-trivial programs or non-trivial properties, auxiliary annotations (e.g., loop invariants) are required. Since these annotations describe program-specific properties, the VCG cannot derive them automatically from the safety policy; instead, they must be provided manually by the software designer. This severe-ly limits the practical usability of current certification approaches like proof-carrying code (PCC) [26].

In this paper we address this problem by combining code certification with automatic code generation from high-level specifications. Our idea is to use the high-level domain information "known" to the code generator to generate not only code but also *all* annotations required to certify that code. We believe that this idea is generally applicable to template-based code-generation systems through embedding additional properties into code templates. We demonstrate this embedding process for a particular program synthesis system, showing that the system formalizes enough high-level domain knowledge to generate all nec-essary annotations required to satisfy safety policies for complex programs. This domain knowledge cannot be recovered from the program by a certifying compil-er as used in PCC. We further illustrate that state-of-the-art automated theorem provers can solve the verification conditions arising from the certification of such automatically synthesized annotated code. Moreover, we demonstrate that our approach can improve on conventional certification technology based on static program analysis.

This work represents an important step towards our long-term goal of ex-tending a program synthesis system such that all generated programs can be certified completely automatically, thus relieving the users from having to annotate their code. This combination of program synthesis and program verification offers some unique benefits:

- It provides *independent verification* that automatically generated programs are safe.
- It can certify properties that are too "low-level" to be practically verified by the usual correct-by-construction arguments of the synthesis approaches.
- It can certify more complex properties and larger programs than certifying compilers.
- It can be tailored to provide proofs that function as audit trails for specific properties that are required for safety-critical software by regulatory agencies.

The remainder of the paper is organized as follows. In Section 2, we briefly describe methods and techniques underlying our approach: property verification, proof carrying code, and program synthesis. Section 3 contains a detailed architectural description of the certifying synthesizer. We specifically focus on how the safety-policy is reflected in extended Hoare-rules and how the annotations are produced and propagated during the synthesis process. We furthermore give a short description of the automated prover E-SETHEO and discuss results from processing the generated verification conditions. Section 4 covers related work and compares our approach to a conventional certification approach based on static analysis techniques. In Section 5 we conclude and sketch out future work.

2 Background

2.1 Property Verification

Traditionally, program verification has focused on showing the functional equivalence of (full) specification and implementation. However, this verification style is very demanding, because of the involved specification and proof efforts, respectively. Therefore, more recent approaches concentrate on showing specific *properties* that are nevertheless important for software safety. For example, model checking has been used successfully to verify liveness and safety aspects of distributed software systems [36]. We extend this property-oriented verification style in two key aspects. First, we use automated theorem provers for full first-order logic that do not require abstractions and that produce the necessary "real" proofs that can be checked independently. Second, we investigate how this approach can be extended towards a broader set of properties.

While many mechanisms and tools for verifying program properties have been published, especially for distributed systems, relatively little attention has been paid to the properties themselves. The related work in this area is usually concerned with computer security [32]; we are interested in all "useful" properties. To help guide our research, we have created an initial taxonomy of verifiable aspects of programs.

We first distinguish between *functional* and *property-based* verification. Functional verification is necessary to show that a program correctly implements a high-level specification. Typically, these proofs are performed by showing that a program is equivalent to, or a refinement of, some higher-level specification. Property-based verification, on the other hand, ensures that the programs have desirable features (e.g., absence of certain runtime errors), but does not show program correctness in the traditional sense. These properties are often much simpler to verify than full functional correctness; however, functional verification and property-based verification are not *fundamentally* different—in fact, many of the properties are necessary to show functional correctness.

These properties can be grouped into four categories: safety, resource-limit, liveness, and security properties. *Safety properties* prevent the program from performing illegal or nonsensical operations. Within this category, we further subdivide into five different aspects of safety:

Memory safety properties assert that all memory accesses involving arrays and pointers are within their assigned bounds.

Type safety properties assert that a program is "well typed" according to a type system defined for the language. This type system may correspond to the standard type system for the language, or may enforce additional obligations, such as ensuring that all variables representing physical quantities have correct and compatible units and dimensions [21].

Numeric safety properties assert that programs will perform arithmetic correctly. Potential errors include: (1) using partial operators with arguments outside their defined domain (e.g., division by zero), (2) performing computations that yield results larger or smaller than are representable on the computer (overflow/underflow), and (3) performing floating point operations which cause an unacceptable loss of precision.

Exception handling properties ensure that all exceptions that can be thrown within a program are handled within the program.

Environment compatibility properties ensure that a program is compatible with its target environment. Compatibility constraints specify hardware, operating systems, and libraries necessary for safe execution. Parameter conventions define constraints on program communication and invocation.

Resource limit properties check that the required resources (e.g., stack size) for a computation are within some bound. *Liveness/progress properties* are used to show that the program will eventually perform some required activity, or will not be permanently blocked waiting for resources. *Security properties* prevent a program from accidental or malicious tampering with the environment. Security policies regulate access to system resources, and are often enforced by authentication procedures, which determine the identity of the program or user involved.

Clearly, there is overlap between these categories; for example, many security flaws are due to safety violations. Our list also includes many properties that are difficult or impossible to automatically verify in the general case; we plan to extend and clarify this taxonomy in future work. For this paper, we have chosen to investigate two safety properties: array bounds checks and numeric partial operator/function domain errors.

2.2 Proof-Carrying Code

Proof-carrying code [26,1] is a certification approach especially suited for mobile code. Many distributed systems (e.g., browsers, cellular phones) allow the user to download executable code and run it on the local machine. If, however, the origin of this code is unknown, or the source is not trustworthy, this poses a considerable risk: the dynamically loaded code may not be compatible with the current system status (e.g., operating system version, available resources), or the code can destroy (on purpose or not) critical data.

The concept of proof-carrying code has been developed to address the problem of showing certain properties (i.e., a safety policy) efficiently at the time when the software is downloaded. The developer of the software annotates the program which is subsequently compiled into object-code using a certifying compiler. Such a compiler (e.g., Touchstone [6]) carries over the source code annotations to the object-code level. A verification condition generator processes the annotated object code together with the public safety policy and produces a large number of proof obligations. If all of them are proven (by a theorem prover), the safety policy holds for this program. However, since these activities are performed by the producer, the provided proofs are not necessarily trustworthy. Therefore, the annotated code and a compressed copy of the proofs are packaged together and sent to the user. The user reconstructs the proof obligations and uses a proof checker to ensure that the conditions match up with the proofs as delivered with the software. Both the local VCG and the proof checker need to be trusted in this approach. However, since a proof checker is much simpler in its internal structure than a prover, it is simpler to design and implement it in a correct and trustworthy manner. Furthermore, checking a proof is very efficient, in stark contrast to finding the proof in the first place—which is usually a very complex and time-consuming process.

A number of PCC-approaches have been developed, particularly focusing on the compact and efficient representation of proofs (e.g., using LCF [26] or HOL [1]). However, as mentioned earlier, all of these approaches are in practice restricted to very simple properties. More intricate properties require the producer of the program to provide elaborate annotations and to carry out complicated formal proofs manually.

2.3 Program Synthesis

Automated program synthesis aims at automatically constructing executable programs from high-level specifications. Although a variety of approaches exist [19], we will focus in this paper on a specific system, AUTOBAYES [11]. AUTOBAYES generates complex data analysis programs (currently up to 1200 lines of C++ code) from compact specifications. Throughout this paper, we will use a simple but realistic classification example to introduce the application domain and to describe the main features of the underlying synthesis process.

Assume our task is to analyze spectral data measurements, e.g., from a star. Our instrument registers photons and their energy. All we know is that a photon originates from one of M different sources which emit photons at different energy levels. The energy of each photon is not defined sharply but described by a normal distribution with a certain mean value and standard deviation. However, we do not know the mean and standard deviation for each source, nor do we know their relative strength (i.e., the percentage of photons coming from each individual source). Figure 1 shows an example data set for $M = 3$ (see [4] for the physical background).

A statistical model can be written down easily and in a compact way. For the measurements $x_0, ..., x_{N-1}$ we know that each point is normal (Gaussian) distributed around the mean value μ with a standard deviation σ for the class (individual source) c_i to which the photon belongs, i.e., $x_i \sim N(\mu_{c_i}, \sigma_{c_i}^2)$ These class assignments c_i and the relative class percentages ϕ are not known. All we know is that all photons belong to one of the classes, i.e., $\sum_{i=1}^{M} \phi_i = 1$, and that summing up the class assignments results in the desired percentages. These four formulas comprise the core of the problem specification.

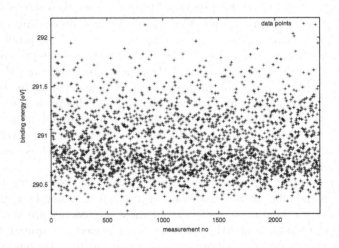

Fig. 1. Example spectral data for three sources ($M = 3$). The parameters are $\mu_1 = 290.7, \sigma_1 = 0.15, \phi_1 = 0.61$, $\mu_2 = 291.13, \sigma_2 = 0.18, \phi_2 = 0.33$, and $\mu_3 = 291.55, \sigma_3 = 0.21, \phi_3 = 0.06$ (modeled after the spectrum of NH_3 molecules; cf. [4])

AUTOBAYES takes a specification similar to the formulas above (a total of 19 lines including all declarations, see [11] for details) and generates executable C++ code of roughly 380 lines (including comments but not annotations) in less than a second on a 1000 MHz. SunBlade workstation. The implementation requires an iterative numerical algorithm[1] which approximates the values of the desired variables μ, σ, and ϕ.

AUTOBAYES synthesizes code by exhaustive, layered application of *schemas*. A schema consists of a program fragment with open slots and a set of applicability conditions. The slots are filled in with code pieces by the synthesis system calling schemas in a recursive way. The conditions constrain how the slots can be filled; they must be proven to hold in the given specification before the schema can be applied. Some of the schemas contain calls to symbolic equation solvers, others contain entire skeletons of statistical or numerical algorithms. By recursively invoking schemas and composing the resulting code fragments, AUTOBAYES is able to automatically synthesize programs of considerable size and internal complexity.

```
schema( max P(U|V) wrt V, Code_fragment↑ ) :-
    ...                                          (* applicability constraints *)
    → Code_fragment =
      begin
        ⟨guess values for c[i]⟩                  (* Initialize *)
        for i:=1 to N do for j:=1 to M do q[i,j] := 0;
        for k:=1 to M do q[k,c[k]] := 1;
        while-converging(V) do
            ⟨ max P({q,U}|V) wrt V⟩              (* M-step *)
            q[i,j] := ⟨...⟩                       (* E-step: calculate P(q|{U,V}) *)
        end                                       (* end while-converging *)
      end
```

Fig. 2. EM-Schema (Fragment)

Let us consider the schema which is automatically selected as the core to solve our example. This schema, presented in a Prolog notation in Figure 2 above, solves the task to estimate the desired parameters (ϕ, μ, σ in our example) by maximizing their probability with respect to certain random variables (for a detailed description of the statistical background see [12]).

This task description is provided as a formal input parameter to the schema in Figure 2. The output parameter *Code_fragment*↑ returns the synthesized code. After checking that the schema can be applied, the parts of the EM-algorithm are assembled. First, we generate a randomized initialization for the array q, then the iteration code starts. As in most numerical optimization algorithms (cf. [15,29]), we update the local array q until we have reached our desired accuracy (abbreviated as while-converging). The code fragments for the initialization of q and to calculate the updates (M-Step and E-Step) are constructed by recursively calling schemas on the respective subproblems. In Figure 2, these parts are included in ⟨...⟩. Text set in typewriter font denotes code fragments in the target language; underlined words (like max) are keywords from AUTOBAYES's specification language.

---

[1] Currently, an EM (expectation maximization) algorithm is generated.

While we cannot present details of the synthesis process here, we want to emphasize that the code is assembled from building blocks which are obtained by symbolic computation or schema instantiation. The schemas clearly lay out the domain knowledge and important design decisions. As we will see later on, they can be extended in such a way that the annotations required for the certification are also generated automatically.

2.4   Why Certify Synthesized Code?

Program synthesis systems are usually built on the notion of "correctness-by-construction." This means that the systems always produce code which correctly implement the user's specifications. Hence, the idea of explicitly certifying the synthesized code appears to be redundant. However, in practice, the notion of correctness-by-construction has two major problems which are mitigated by our approach.

First, the correctness-by-construction argument relies on only a single certificate—the synthesis proof. This proof is often extremely large and filled with artifacts from the domain theory. However, regulatory agencies overseeing the development of critical software systems describe very specific safety properties which need to be verified or tested [31]. Trying to extract the specific (sub-) proofs of these properties is difficult, if they are at all captured by the synthesis proof. Our approach allows a separation of proof concerns: any number of explicit and much smaller proofs can be generated, tailored towards the required safety properties.

Second, the validity of correctness-by-construction hinges on the correctness and consistency of the underlying synthesis engine and the domain theory. The synthesis engine is concerned with assembling schemas in a way that satisfies the constraints of the domain theory; thus, it ensures that the fragments of the program are correctly *assembled*. However, the code included in or constructed by the schemas for each fragment is not directly verified by the synthesis proof, so coding errors that are contained in the domain theory may be propagated through the synthesis process. Thus, users must in practice "trust" schemas to produce correct code, without independent verification of correctness. For safety/security sensitive code, e.g., for navigation/state estimation [39], this level of trust is not acceptable. Our approach provides an automatic and independent verification path for important properties of the generated code.

3   System Architecture

The architecture of our certifying synthesis system is somewhat similar to a typical proof-carrying code architecture. However, since we are currently not dealing with proof validation aspects, we only have three major building blocks (see Figure 3): the synthesis system AUTOBAYES (which replaces the certifying compiler), the verification condition generator MOPS, and the automated theorem prover E-SETHEO. All system components used in certification will be described in more detail below.

The system's input is a statistical model which defines the data analysis task as shown above. This specification need not be modified for certification—the process is thus completely transparent to the user. AUTOBAYES then attempts to synthesize code using the schemas described above. These schemas are extended appropriately (cf. Section 3.3) to support the automatic generation of code annotations. AUTOBAYES produces Modula-2 code[2] which carries the annotations as formal comments. Annotations and code are then processed by the verification condition generator MOPS. Its output is a set of proof obligations in first order predicate logic which must be proven to show the desired properties. In order to do so, a domain theory in form of an axiom set defining all operations and functions in the proof tasks must be added to the formulas. Finally, these extended proof obligations are fed into the automated theorem prover E-SETHEO.

For our prototype implementation, we added several small "glue" modules which convert the syntactical representation between all components. These are implemented in lex/yacc, awk, and Unix shell sh.

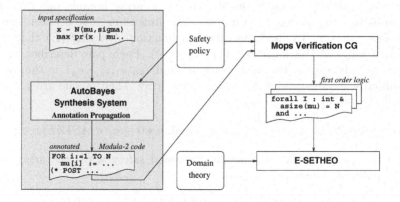

Fig. 3. AutoBayes system architecture, extended for code certification

3.1 Safety Policy

The first step in certification is to define precisely what constitutes safe behavior for the programs. In our case, we must define notions of memory and operator safety as predicates within a logic. Then a mechanism must be defined to transform a program into a series of verification conditions that are valid if and only if the safety properties are satisfied. In the sections below, we formulate the safety properties and describe the mechanism for creating the verification conditions.

---

[2] We extended AUTOBAYES to generate the Modula-2 code used by MOPS. Usually, AUTOBAYES synthesizes C++/C programs for Octave [25] and Matlab [23].

Hoare rules [40] form the foundation of our approach. Hoare rules are triples of the form $\{P\}\ C\ \{Q\}$ where C is a statement in an imperative programming language, and P and Q are predicates. The statement acts as a *predicate transformer*, that is, it describes how predicate P is transformed into predicate Q by the execution of C. Our idea, following Dijkstra's well-defined expression predicate *Def* [8], is to strengthen the preconditions of the Hoare rules by adding explicit memory- and operator-safety constraints. The rules for our policy are shown in Figure 4.

Array Bounds Safety Policy. To show array bounds safety, we need to define variables within the assertion language that represent the notion of array bounds. Given these variables, we can test that each subscript expression within a statement is within the appropriate dimension for the array. More concretely, we assume that given an array x of dimension $n+1$, all array dimensions $0 \leq k \leq n$ have the lower bound zero, and a size that is represented by $ASIZE(x, k)$. The $ASIZE(x, k)$ notation is used to denote the unique variable representing that array size.

We can then determine what it means for an expression to be array-bounds safe. Given an expression E, we say that it is array bounds safe if every array subscript expression for variable x in dimension k is between zero and $ASIZE(x, k) - 1$. To check, we define a function $ArrayRefs(E)$ that returns a set of pairs of the form $(x, \langle e_0, e_1, \ldots, e_n \rangle)$. Each pair describes an array reference, where x is the array variable and $\langle e_0, e_1, \ldots, e_n \rangle$ is the sequence of subscript expressions used to access the array. Then, a safe array reference $SafeRef(x, \langle e_0, e_1, \ldots, e_n \rangle)$ is:

$$SafeRef(x, \langle e_0, e_1, \ldots, e_n \rangle) \equiv \forall a : 0..n \bullet 0 \leq e_a < ASIZE(x, a)$$

From this predicate, we can define expression safety w.r.t. the array bounds safety policy as follows:

$$SafeExpr_A(E) \equiv \forall (x, seq) \in ArrayRefs(E) \bullet SafeRef(x, seq)$$

These two predicates state that, for each array reference, every subscript expression is within bounds.

Unfortunately, the $SafeRef$ and $SafeExpr_A$ predicates are higher-order, as they quantify over expressions in the program syntax. Since $ArrayRefs(E)$ yields a finite set, we can expand these quantified predicates over variables and expressions into a sequence of first-order predicates. For example, given the statement:

$$q[k, c[k]] := 1/v; \tag{1}$$

$SafeExpr_A(E)$ yields the following safety predicate, once expanded:

$$0 \leq k \wedge k < ASIZE(q, 0) \wedge 0 \leq c[k] \wedge c[k] < ASIZE(q, 1) \wedge$$
$$0 \leq k \wedge k < ASIZE(c, 0)$$

By checking that all array subscripts are within bounds for each array reference for each expression, we can determine array bounds safety for the entire program.

Operator Safety Policy. To show operator safety, we only need to show that all divisors are different from zero. All other partial operators, such as square root, are implemented as standard library functions, and not as programming language language constructs. The domain constraints on these functions are enforced by the respective procedure pre- and post-conditions.

To check for zero divisors, a function $divisors(E)$ is defined. This function returns the set of subexpressions of an expression E that are used as divisors. From this function, we can define expression safety with respect to the operator safety policy as follows:

$$SafeExpr_O(E) \equiv \forall e \in divisors(E) \bullet e \neq 0$$

So, given the statement (1), $SafeExpr_O(E)$ yields the safety predicate $v \neq 0$, once expanded.

Extended Hoare rules. Given definitions for operator and array bounds safety for expressions, we can extend the Hoare rules with respect to these policies. First, we define $SafeExpr(E)$ as:

$$SafeExpr(E) \equiv SafeExpr_A(E) \wedge SafeExpr_O(E)$$

Then the Hoare rules can be formulated as shown in Figure 4.

The first rule applies to array declarations. As described earlier, we create a variable $ASIZE(x, k)$ to refer to the size of array x at dimension k. The declaration of an array is an assignment of values to these variables. The rule works by replacing instances of $ASIZE(x, k)$ in the postcondition of a statement with the variable declaration expression. For example, given an array declaration

$$\textbf{var } c: \textbf{ array}[nclasses] \textbf{ of REAL}$$

and a postcondition $ASIZE(x, 0) = nclasses$, this rule generates the precondition $nclasses = nclasses$ which is obviously true.

The second rule, assignment of scalars, is the same as the standard Hoare assignment rule, except that it has a strengthened precondition that checks that the assignment expression is safe w.r.t. our safety policies.

The third rule describes assignment of array cells. Unlike scalar assignment, array cell assignment cannot be handled by simple substitution, because of the possibility of aliasing of array cells. Instead, we think of the array as describing a mapping function from cells to values. An assignment to a cell is an update of the mapping function, written as $x\{(e_0, e_1, \ldots, e_n) \to e\}$. This approach is the standard extension of the Hoare calculus to handle arrays and is described fully in [22]. We strengthen the precondition of this rule to ensure that both the

Array Declaration:

$$\left\{ \begin{array}{l} P[e_0/ASIZE(x,0),\ldots,e_n/ASIZE(x,n)] \wedge \\ SafeExpr(e_0) \wedge SafeExpr(e_1) \wedge \\ \vdots \\ SafeExpr(e_n) \end{array} \right\} \text{var } x: \text{ array}[e_0,\ldots,e_n] \text{ of } Y \ \{P\}$$

Scalar Assignment: $\{P[e/x] \wedge SafeExpr(e)\}\ x := e\ \{P\}$

Array Assignment: $\left\{ \begin{array}{l} P[x\{(e_0,\ldots,e_n) \to e\}] \wedge \\ SafeExpr(e) \wedge \\ SafeExpr(x[e_0,\ldots,e_n]) \end{array} \right\} x[e_0,\ldots,e_n] := e\ \{P\}$

Conditional Stmt:
$$\frac{\{P \wedge b \wedge SafeExpr(b)\}\ c\ \{Q\} \qquad (P \wedge \neg b \wedge SafeExpr(b) \implies Q)}{\{P \wedge SafeExpr(b)\} \text{ if } b \text{ then } c\ \{Q\}}$$

While Loop:
$$\frac{\{P \wedge b \wedge SafeExpr(b)\}\ c\ \{P \wedge SafeExpr(b)\}}{\{P \wedge SafeExpr(b)\} \text{ while } b \text{ do } c\ \{P \wedge \neg b \wedge SafeExpr(b)\}}$$

For Loop:
$$\frac{\left\{ \begin{array}{l} P \wedge e_0 \leq x \leq e_1 \\ \wedge SafeExpr(e_0) \\ \wedge SafeExpr(e_1) \end{array} \right\} C \left\{ \begin{array}{l} P[(x+1)/x] \wedge SafeExpr(e_0) \\ \wedge SafeExpr(e_1) \end{array} \right\}}{\left\{ \begin{array}{l} P[e_0/x] \wedge SafeExpr(e_0) \\ e_0 \leq e_1 \wedge SafeExpr(e_1) \end{array} \right\} \text{ for } x := e_0 \text{ to } e_1 \text{ do } C \left\{ \begin{array}{l} P[(e_1+1)/x] \wedge SafeExpr(e_0) \\ \wedge SafeExpr(e_1) \end{array} \right\}}$$

Sequence:
$$\frac{\{P\}\ s_0\ \{R\} \quad \{R\}\ s_1\ \{Q\}}{\{P\}\ s_0; s_1\ \{Q\}}$$

Rule of Conseq:
$$\frac{P' \implies P \quad \{P\}\ C\ \{Q\} \quad Q \implies Q'}{\{P'\}\ C\ \{Q'\}}$$

Fig. 4. Hoare rules with safety policy extensions

subscript expressions in the left-hand side and the assignment expression are safe.

The next three rules describe conditional and loop statements. They are the same as the standard Hoare rules, with strengthened preconditions to show that their expressions are safe. Finally, we define the standard Hoare rule of consequence, which states that we can always legally strengthen the precondition or weaken the postcondition of a statement. Soundness of all rules is obvious.

3.2   The Verification Condition Generator

In practical proof-carrying code approaches, the safety policy is hardcoded into the VCG component of the certifying compiler. In our approach all required annotations are generated so that *any* VCG can be used. For our experiments, we used the VCG of the *Modula Proving System* MOPS [17]. MOPS is a Hoare-calculus based verification system for a large subset of the programming language Modula-2 [41], including pointers, arrays, and other data structures. The verification of REAL-arithmetics is idealized and ignores possible round-off errors. MOPS supports the verification of arbitrary program segments and not only procedures or modules. The verification segments can be nested to break large proofs into manageable pieces.

MOPS uses a subset of VDM-SL [7] as its specification language; this is interpreted here only as syntactic sugar for classical first-order logic. All annotations are written as Modula-2 comments enclosed in (*{ ... }*). Pre- and post-conditions start with the keywords `pre` and `post`, respectively, loop invariants with a `loopinv`, and additional assertions with an `assert` (cf. Figure 5.)

3.3   Annotations and Their Propagation

Annotating the large programs created by AUTOBAYES requires careful attention to detail and many annotations. There are potentially dozens of loops requiring an invariant, and nesting of loops and if-statements can make it difficult to determine what is necessary to completely annotate a statement. The schema-guided synthesis mechanism of AUTOBAYES makes it easy to produce annotations *local* to the current statement, as the generation of annotations is tightly coupled to the individual schema. For this reason, we split the task of creating the statement annotations into two parts: creating local annotations during the run of AUTOBAYES, and propagating the annotations through the code.

Local Annotations. The local annotations for a schema describe the changes in variables made by the schema, without needing to describe all of the global information that may later be necessary for proofs.

During synthesis (i.e., at the time when the schemas are instantiated), the annotations are produced locally for each statement. Each loop is annotated with a schematic invariant and schematic pre- and postconditions describing how it changes variables within the program. The specific form of the invariants and assertions depends on the safety policy supported by the synthesis system. For example, the precondition in lines 1–3 in Figure 5 is required to show memory safety, more specifically, the safety of the nested array access in line 26. The fact that this precondition is actually required is part of our domain knowledge and thus encoded within the schema. Obviously, a modification or extension of the supported safety policy requires corresponding modifications or extensions of the schemas.

```
01  (*{ pre
02       (forall a: int &
03          (0 <= a and a < N) => 0 <= c[a] <= M) }*)
04  (*{ loopinv
05       0 <= i and i <= N - 1 and
06       0 <= j and j <= M - 1 and
07       (forall a,b : int &
08          ((0 <= a and a < i) and (0 <= b and b < j))
09             => q[a,b] = 0.0) }*)
10  FOR i := 0 TO N - 1 DO
11    FOR j := 0 TO M - 1 DO
12        q[i,j] := 0.0;
13      END;
14  END;
15  (*{ assert
16        i = N and j = M and
17        (forall a,b : int &
18          ((0 <= a and a < N) and (0 <= b and b < M))
19             => q[a,b] = 0.0) }*)
20  (*{ loopinv
21        0 <= k and k <= N - 1 and
22        (forall a, b: int &
23          ((0 <= a and a < N) and (0 <= b and b < M))
24             => 0 <= q[a,b] and q[a,b] <= 1.0) }*)
25  FOR k := 0 to N - 1 DO
26      q[k,c[k]] := 1.0;
27  END
28  (*{ post
29        (forall a,b : int &
30          ((0 <= a and a < N) and (0 <= b and b < M))
31             => 0 <= q[a,b] and q[a,b] <= 1.0) }*)
```

Fig. 5. Code fragment with annotations for the initialization of the intermediate arrays (q and c) as defined in the schema in Figure 2.

Propagation of Annotations. Unfortunately, these local annotations are in general insufficient to prove the postcondition at the end of a larger code fragment. For example, at line 26 in the code (cf. Figure 5), we do not necessarily know what invariants hold prior to the loop. To overcome this problem, we *propagate* any unchanged information through the annotations. Because program synthesis restricts aliasing to few, known places, the test for which statements influence which annotations can be accomplished easily without full static analysis of the synthesized program.

In our example, we propagate the initial condition about the vector c (lines 1–3) and add it to the loop invariant and post-assertion for the first loop (lines 15–19). Since the second loop does not change variable c, this condition is propagated forward into invariant and post-condition of the second loop.

The propagation algorithm (shown in Figure 6) works on a tree. The tree nodes are initially labeled with the AUTOBAYES-generated local annotations. The tree edges describe the locations of the annotations relative to one another in the code according to a lexicographic ordering which obeys the nesting of the language constructs. Each node may have many children in two categories: one *sibling* node and zero or more *child* nodes, corresponding to the lexical placement of the annotations in the code. The edges are labeled by the set of variables that have been assigned between the annotations.

```
procedure propagate(root: Vertex, inherited: predicate set)
   annotation(root) := annotation(root) ∪ inherited;
   forall c in children(root)
      c_inherits := {};
      vars := vars_assigned(edge(root,c));
      forall a in annotations(root)
         if variables(a) ∩ vars = {}
            c_inherits := c_inherits ∪ a;
      propagate(c,c_inherits);
```

Fig. 6. The annotation propagation algorithm

The algorithm starts from the top of the tree and performs a recursive depth-first traversal. The parameters to the algorithm are the current root node of the tree ($root$) and the set of inherited formulas ($inherited$). The algorithm first updates the annotations associated with the root node, $annotation(root)$, to include the parent-node formulas. Then, for each child, it creates a set of inherited predicates ($c\_inherits$) and calls itself recursively. The set $c\_inherits$ is a set of all predicates from $annotation(root)$ that do not contain variables modified by the intervening code. This information is extracted from the labeling of the edge between the root node and node c.

3.4   The Automated Prover

For our experiments we used the automated theorem prover E-SETHEO, version csp01 [5]. E-SETHEO is a compositional theorem prover for formulas in first order logic, combining the systems E [33] and SETHEO [20,24]. The subsystems are based on the superposition, model elimination, and semantic tree calculi. Depending on syntactic characteristics of the input formula, an optimal schedule for each of the different strategies is selected. These different schedules have been computed from experimental data using machine learning techniques [35]. Because all of the subsystems work on formulas in clausal normal form (CNF), the first order formula is first converted into CNF using the module Flotter [38]. E-SETHEO is one of the most powerful ATP systems available as has been shown in recent international theorem proving competitions [5].

Out of the 69 proof tasks of our example, E-SETHEO initially could solve 65 automatically with a run-time limit of 120 seconds on a 1000 Mhz. SunBlade workstation. The remaining four proof tasks required some relatively simple preprocessing (splitting up the formula into two separate proof tasks) before they could be proven automatically. Most of the tasks could be solved in about one second, but several tasks took up to 20 seconds. The overall proof time of 323 seconds indicates that our approach is feasible.

4 Related Work

We are not aware of any other work to automatically extract knowledge about the program under construction from the synthesis process, whether for certification or for other purposes. However, there is a large number of different approaches which share either techniques or goals with our work.

The approach most closely related to ours is proof-carrying code which has already been discussed in Section 2.2. However, due to its focus on mobile code, PCC covers many aspects we are (currently) not interested in, e.g., efficient proof representation and proof checking. It also works on the level of object code or typed intermediate languages (e.g., Flint [34]) and is thus complementary to our approach. Certifying compilers as Touchstone [6] or Cyclone [16] could consequently be used to show that the safety policy established on the source code level is not compromised by the compilation step.

Lowry et al. [21] present an approach for certifying domain-specific properties which is based on abstract interpretation. They check programs for *frame safety*, an extended type safety property. Other safety properties can also be encoded in extended type systems and then checked via (extended) type inference algorithms. Such approaches have been used to show, for example, unit and dimensional safety [30,18] and memory safety [42]. However, these approaches usually also require additional annotations, e.g., type declarations. Moreover, most of them are restricted to a specific safety policy and thus less general than proof-based certification approaches.

Many reverse engineering approaches try to recover formal specifications from code. Gannod and Cheng [14] use a strongest postcondition predicate transformer to support different reverse engineering tasks but their approach still requires additional manual annotations (e.g., loop invariants). Ernst et al. [9] try to infer such invariants dynamically, using a generate-and-test approach: potential invariants are generated from a set of patterns and checked against previously collected run-time trace information. However, the inferred predicates are not proven to be actually invariant so that the approach is not suitable for certification purposes. Flanagan and Leino [13] describe a similar system, Houdini, to support their ESC/Java verification system. Houdini also uses a generate-and-test approach but the test phase relies on ESC/Java to prove the invariants. However, Houdini does not use domain knowledge in the generate phase and is thus restricted in the kind of invariants it can recover.

Obviously, our research is also related to standard program verification. However, program verification concentrates on showing full functional equivalence or refinement between specifications and programs. This is true especially for integrated development/proof environments as for example the KIV system [37], and SPARK Ada [2]. Unlike our approach, program verification systems usually offer no support to find and formalize the functional specifications and auxiliary annotations. Our work could be used as a front-end, providing the necessary annotations for safety properties to these kinds of systems.

It is sometimes possible to encode aspects of the safety policy into the logic used in a program verification system. For example, if VDM is not interpreted as mere syntactic sugar for classical logic but as notation for the three-valued logic of partial functions (LPF) [3], a partial correctness proof in MOPS already gives operator safety. Partial operators provide a uniform notion applicable for several safety properties, but they also preclude our ability to create small, separate proofs for different partial operator properties and require additional tool support.

Certification tools based on static analysis techniques try to show which parts of the code are safe with respect to a (usually hard-wired) safety policy. All necessary information is extracted from the code; hence, no annotations or domain knowledge are required. In order to compare our approach to static analysis, we analyzed the equivalent C-version of our example program with the tool PolySpace [28]. PolySpace was capable of declaring most of the code safe with respect to memory/operator safety. However, it could not clear several important parts of the code, most notably the nested indexing (q[k,c[k]], see line 26 in Figure 5) and the initialization of some variables in the main loop. In these cases, certification requires annotation propagation as it is done in our work; PolySpace does not require or support annotations. On the other hand, PolySpace detected a possible integer overflow error of a loop counter in the synthesized code, something that our safety policy does not (yet) check. The runtime of PolySpace for this example (about one hour of wall-clock time on the same machine as used for our experiments) demonstrates that our approach can be competitive to commercial tools.

5   Conclusions

In this paper, we have described a novel combination of automated program synthesis and automated program verification. Our basic idea is to generate the program together with detailed formal annotations which are required for a fully automatic correctness proof. This approach is facilitated by the knowledge of the domain and the program under construction which are formalized in the program synthesis system. Since it is virtually impossible to re-generate this information from the synthesized program only, our approach is much more powerful and "smarter" than a certifying compiler and allows us to certify complex properties for mid-sized programs fully automatically.

We have demonstrated the feasibility of our approach by certifying operator safety and memory safety for an automatically generated iterative data classification program. The synthesized program consists of roughly 380 lines of code, 90 of which are auto-generated comments to explain the code. With all annotations (including propagated annotations), it grows to 2,116 lines of code—a clear indication than manual annotation is out of question. The annotated program induces 69 proof tasks in first-order logic. After some minor preprocessing steps, all these tasks can be solved automatically in relatively short time, using the theorem prover E-SETHEO. In contrast, certification of this program using the commercial tool PolySpace took approximately one hour and was incomplete with respect to our chosen safety policy.

Our long-term goal is to extend AUTOBAYES such that all generated programs can be certified completely automatically. We are confident that our approach can also be extended to other program synthesis systems, because they generally encode enough abstract knowledge about the domain and the program under construction. We see a number of benefits from this combination of program synthesis and program verification. For the user of such a certifying synthesis system, the major benefit is obviously the additional verification of (important aspects of) the synthesized code; moreover, it comes at no cost for the user, and it can be double-checked independently.

This independent verification complements the notion of "correctness-by-construction" generally built into program synthesis systems. This notion means that the system always produces code which correctly implements the user's specification. However, its validity depends on the correctness and consistency of the underlying synthesis engine and the domain theory. Because these are large and complex artifacts—comparable to a compiler—current technology cannot *guarantee* their correctness. Thus, a user must in reality "trust" that the synthesis system produces correct code. Our approach provides a tool and methodology to demonstrate important properties of the code in an automatic and independently re-checkable way.

Our system is still a prototype; the certification extension covers only those parts of the domain theory required to generate EM-variants. However, we see no fundamental obstacles in extending the approach to the entire (still growing) domain theory. Also, the safety-policy is hard-coded in the way the annotations are generated within the synthesis schemas. We will work on ways to explicitly represent safety policies (e.g., using higher-order formulations) and use this to tailor the annotation generation in AUTOBAYES. Our propagation algorithm can be viewed as a mechanism for managing proof context information. We are investigating more complex proof frameworks, such as program window inference [27] that provide rules for managing this information, making the propagation step of our approach unnecessary. Our architecture also relies on the correctness of E-SETHEO. We are planning to extend our system to incorporate a small and verified proof checker which is able to give us the certainty that the proofs produced by E-SETHEO are indeed correct. Furthermore, we plan to implement a small and trustworthy verification condition generator.

Acknowledgements. We would like to thank the reviewers for their detailed and helpful comments. This work is supported by the NASA, grant 749–10–11 (Thinking Systems / Program Synthesis); M. Whalen was supported by the RIACS SSRP program.

References

1. A. W. Appel and A. P. Felty. A semantic model of types and machine instructions for proof-carrying code. In *Proc. 27th ACM Symp. Principles of Programming Languages*, pp. 243–253. ACM Press, 2001.
2. J. Barnes. *High Integrity Ada: The SPARK Approach.* Addison-Wesley, 1997.

3. H. Barringer, J. H. Cheng, and C. B. Jones. A logic covering undefinedness in program proofs. *Acta Informatica*, 21(3):251–269, Oct. 1984.
4. J. Berkowitz. *Photoabsorption, Photoionization, and Photoelectron Spectroscopy.* Academic Press, 1979.
5. CASC-JC theorem proving competition. http://www.cs.miams.edu/~tptp/CASC/JC.
6. C. Colby, P. Lee, G. C. Necula, F. Blau, M. Plesko, and K. Cline. A certifying compiler for Java. *ACM SIGPLAN Notices*, 35(5):95–107, 2000.
7. J. Dawes. *The VDM-SL Reference Guide.* Pitman, London, 1991.
8. E. W. Dijkstra. *A Discipline of Programming.* Prentice-Hall, 1976.
9. M. D. Ernst, J. Cockrell, W. G. Griswold, and D. Notkin. Dynamically discovering likely program invariants to support program evolution. *IEEE Trans. Software Engineering*, 27(2):1–25, Feb. 2001.
10. M. S. Feather and M. Goedicke (eds.) *Proc. 16th Intl. Conf. Automated Software Engineering*, IEEE Comp. Soc. Press, 2001.
11. B. Fischer and J. Schumann. AutoBayes: A system for generating data analysis programs from statistical models. *J. Functional Programming*, 2002. To appear. Preprint available at http://ase.arc.nasa.gov/people/fischer/.
12. B. Fischer, J. Schumann, and T. Pressburger. Generating data analysis programs from statistical models (Position Paper). In W. Taha (ed.), *Proc. Intl. Workshop Semantics, Applications, and Implementation of Program Generation*, Lect. Notes Comp. Sci. 1924, pp. 212–229. Springer, 2000.
13. C. Flanagan and K. R. M. Leino. Houdini, an annotation assistant for ESC/Java. In J. Oliveira and P. Zave (eds.), *Proc. Intl. Symp. Formal Methods Europe 2001: Formal Methods for Increasing Software Productivity*, Lect. Notes Comp. Sci. 2021, pp. 500–517. Springer, 1997.
14. G. C. Gannod, Y. Chen, and B. H. C. Cheng. An automated approach for supporting software reuse via reverse engineering. In D. F. Redmiles and B. Nuseibeh (eds.), *Proc. 13th Intl. Conf. Automated Software Engineering*, pp. 79–86. IEEE Comp. Soc. Press, 1998.
15. P. Gill, W. Murray, and M. Wright. *Practical Optimization.* Academic Press, 1981.
16. L. Hornof and T. Jim. Certifying compilation and run-time code generation. *Higher-Order and Symbolic Computation*, 12(4):337–375, 1999.
17. T. Kaiser, B. Fischer, and W. Struckmann. Mops: Verifying Modula-2 programs specified in VDM-SL. In *Proc. 4th Workshop Tools for System Design and Verification*, pp. 163–167. 2000.
18. A. Kennedy. *Programming Languages and Dimensions.* PhD thesis, University of Cambridge, Apr. 1996. Published as UCCL TR391.
19. C. Kreitz. Program synthesis. In W. Bibel and P. H. Schmitt (eds.), *Automated Deduction - A Basis for Applications*, Vol III, pp. 105–134. Kluwer, 1998.
20. R. Letz, J. Schumann, S. Bayerl, and W. Bibel. SETHEO: A high-performance theorem prover. *J. Automated Reasoning*, 8(2):183–212, 1992.
21. M. Lowry, T. Pressburger, and G. Rosu. Certifying domain-specific policies. In Feather and Goedicke [10], pp. 118–125.
22. D. C. Luckham and N. Suzuki. Verification of array, record, and pointer operations in Pascal. *ACM Trans. Programming Languages and Systems*, 1(2):226–244, 1979.
23. C. B. Moler, J. N. Little, and S. Bangert. *PC-Matlab Users Guide.* Cochituate Place, 24 Prime Park Way, Natick, MA, USA, 1987.
24. M. Moser, O. Ibens, R. Letz, J. Steinbach, C. Goller, J. Schumann, and K. Mayr. The model elimination provers SETHEO and E-SETHEO. *J. Automated Reasoning*, 18:237–246, 1997.

25. M. Murphy. Octave: A free, high-level language for mathematics. *Linux Journal*, 39, July 1997.
26. G. C. Necula and P. Lee. Efficient representation and validation of logical proofs. In *Proc. 13th Annual IEEE Symp. Logic in Computer Science*, pp. 93–104. IEEE Comp. Soc. Press, 1998.
27. R. Nickson and I. J. Hayes. Supporting contexts in program refinement. *Science of Computer Programming*, 29(3):279–302, 1997.
28. PolySpace technologies. http://www.polyspace.com, 2002.
29. W. H. Press, B. P. Flannery, S. A. Teukolsky, and W. T. Vetterling. *Numerical Recipes in C*. Cambridge Univ. Press, Cambridge, UK, 2nd. edition, 1992.
30. M. Rittri. Dimension inference under polymorphic recursion. In *Proc. 7th Conf. Functional Programming Languages and Computer Architecture*, pp. 147–159, ACM Press, 1995.
31. *Software Considerations in Airborne Systems and Equipment Certification*. Radio Technical Commission for Aeronautics, 1992.
32. F. B. Schneider. Enforceable security policies. Computer Science Technical Report TR98-1644, Cornell University, Computer Science Department, September 1998.
33. S. Schulz. System abstract: E 0.3. In H. Ganzinger (ed.), *Proc. 16th Intl. Conf. Automated Deduction*, Lect. Notes Artificial Intelligence 1421, pp. 297–301. Springer, 1999.
34. Z. Shao, C. League, and S. Monnier. Implementing typed intermediate language. In *Proc. 1998 ACM SIGPLAN Intl. Conf. Functional Programming*, pp. 313–323. 1998.
35. G. Stenz and A. Wolf. E-SETHEO: Design configuration and use of a parallel theorem prover. In N. Foo (ed.), *Proc. of the 12th Australian Joint Conf. on Artificial Intelligence*, Lect. Notes Artificial Intelligence 1747, pp. 231–243. Springer, 1999.
36. W. Visser, K. Havelund, G. Brat, and S. Park. Model checking programs. In P. Alexander and P. Flener (eds.), *Proc. 15th Intl. Conf. Automated Software Engineering*, pp. 3–12. IEEE Comp. Soc. Press, 2000.
37. W. Reif. The KIV Approach to Software Verification. In M. Broy and S. Jähnichen (eds.), *KORSO: Methods, Languages and Tools for the Construction of Correct Software*, Lect. Notes Comp. Sci. 1009, pp. 339–370. Springer, 1995.
38. C. Weidenbach, B. Gaede, and G. Rock. Spass and Flotter version 0.42. In M. A. McRobbie and J. K. Slaney (eds.), *Proc. 13th Intl. Conf. Automated Deduction*, Lect. Notes Artificial Intelligence 1104, pp. 141–145. Springer, 1996.
39. J. Whittle, J. Van Baalen, J. Schumann, P. Robinson, T. Pressburger, J. Penix, P. Oh, M. Lowry, and G. Brat. Amphion/NAV: Deductive synthesis of state estimation software. In Feather and Goedicke [10], pp. 395–399.
40. G. Winskel. *The Formal Semantics of Programming Languages: An Introduction*. The MIT Press, 1993.
41. N. Wirth. *Programming in Modula-2*. Springer, 4th edition, 1988.
42. H. Xi and F. Pfenning. Eliminating array bound checking through dependent types. In *Proc. ACM Conf. on Programming Language Design and Implementation 1998*, pp. 249–257. ACM Press, 1998. Published as SIGPLAN Notices 33(5).

Refinement in *Circus*

Augusto Sampaio[1], Jim Woodcock[2], and Ana Cavalcanti[1]

[1] Centro de Informática/UFPE
Recife PE Brazil
[2] University of Kent
Canterbury England - UK

Abstract. We describe refinement in *Circus*, a concurrent specification language that integrates imperative CSP, Z, and the refinement calculus. Each *Circus* process has a state and accompanying actions that define both the internal state transitions and the changes in control flow that occur during execution. We define the meaning of refinement of processes and their actions, and propose a sound data refinement technique for process refinement. Refinement laws for CSP and Z are directly relevant and applicable to *Circus*, but our focus here is on new laws for processes that integrate state and control. We give some new results about the distribution of data refinement through the combinators of CSP. We illustrate our ideas with the development of a distributed system of co-operating processes from a centralised specification.

Keywords: Z, CSP, distribution, unifying theories of programming.

1 Introduction

A recent, interesting, and challenging trend in computing is the combination of theories and tools. One important topic in this research context is language integration, with the major objective of addressing the several facets (data, control, time) of realistic software engineering problems.

In particular, much work has been done in combining Z [21] and process algebras, including CSP [8]; Fischer gives a survey of some of this research [4]. Such a combination has obvious advantages: Z is useful for describing rich information structures in a state, and process algebra is useful for describing the behavioural patterns of communication and synchronisation. Some interesting work has been undertaken, but very little has been accomplished in terms of understanding the formal development of programs starting from such mixed specifications.

Circus [18] combines Z and CSP, and includes specification constructs usually found in refinement calculi (as, for instance, in [10]) and Dijkstra's language of guarded commands [3]. As a result, *Circus* is a unified programming language for presenting specifications, designs, and programs. Specifications are based on the use of Z constructs and specification statements. These constructs can be combined with executable commands, like assignments, conditionals, and loops; reactive behaviour, including communication, parallelism, and choice, is defined with the use of CSP constructs. All existing combinations of Z with a process

L.-H. Eriksson and P. Lindsay (Eds.): FME 2002, LNCS 2391, pp. 451–470, 2002.

algebra model concurrent programs as communicating abstract data types, but we do not insist on identifying events with operations on the state. The result is a general programming language adequate for developing concurrent programs.

There are several complex issues to be considered in the integration of languages: syntax, semantics, proof theory, development methods, structuring techniques, and reuse, among others. *Circus* already has a well-defined syntax and a formal semantics [18,20] based on unifying theories of programming [9], together with case studies that illustrate its expressive power [19].

The central aim of this paper is to describe a development method for *Circus*, based on refinement. A refinement calculus for *Circus* should clearly extend similar work for CSP [15] and Z [2], since *Circus* integrates these two languages. In addition, however, new laws are necessary to deal directly with *Circus* processes, which combine state and control behaviour. The focus of this paper is on describing some of these new laws for processes.

We propose a refinement strategy whose typical starting point is a centralised specification of an application. In the development process, we move towards a distributed solution. The strategy is supported by two families of laws that allow the incremental splitting of *Circus* processes using parallelism. The overall approach is illustrated by a case study that, although simple, is interesting enough to demonstrate the proposed strategy in all its relevant details.

In the next section, we present *Circus*: its syntax and semantics. Our main results are in sections 3 and 4, where we present the notions of refinement appropriate for *Circus* and refinement laws. In Section 5, we present a case study, and conclude in Section 6 with a discussion of related and future work.

2   *Circus*

A *Circus* program is a sequence of paragraphs: a Z paragraph, a channel definition, a channel set definition, or a process definition. In Figure 1 we present the BNF description of the syntax of *Circus*. CircusPar* is a possibly empty list of elements of the syntactic category CircusPar of *Circus* paragraphs; similarly for PPar*. We use N^+ for a comma-separated list of Z identifiers (elements of N), and similarly for Exp^+. The syntactic categories Par, Schema-Exp, Exp, Pred, and Decl include the Z paragraphs, schema expressions, expressions, predicates, and declarations defined in [16]. The syntactic category CSExp of channel set expressions contains the empty set of channels {| |}, channel enumerations enclosed in {| and |}, and expressions involving the usual set operators.

To illustrate the use of *Circus*, we give a specification of a simple bounded reactive buffer that is used to store natural numbers. The maximum size of the buffer is a positive constant.

$$|\quad maxbuff : \mathbb{N}_1$$

Inputs and outputs are taken from two different channels.

channel $input, output : \mathbb{N}$

Program	::=	CircusPar*
CircusPar	::=	Par | **channel** CDecl | **chanset** N == CSExp |
	|	**process** N $\widehat{=}$ Proc
CDecl	::=	SimpleCDecl | SimpleCDecl; CDecl
SimpleCDecl	::=	N^+ | N^+ : Exp | Schema-Exp
Proc	::=	**begin** PPar* • Action **end** | N | Proc; Proc | Proc $\square$ Proc
	|	Proc $\sqcap$ Proc | Proc $[\![$ CSExp $]\!]$ Proc | Proc $\|\|\|$ Proc | Proc \ CSExp
	|	Decl $\odot$ Proc | Proc$\lfloor$Exp$^+\rfloor$ | Process$[N^+ := N^+]$
	|	Decl • Proc | Proc(Exp$^+$) | $[N^+]$Proc | Proc[Exp$^+$]
PPar	::=	Par | N $\widehat{=}$ Action
Action	::=	Schema-Exp | CSPAction | Command
CSPAction	::=	*Skip* | *Stop* | *Chaos* | Comm → Action | Pred & Action
	|	Action; Action | Action $\square$ Action | Action $\sqcap$ Action
	|	Action $[\![$ CSExp $]\!]$ Action | Action $\|\|\|$ Action
	|	Action \ CSExp | μ N • Action | Decl • Action | Action(Exp$^+$)
Comm	::=	N CParameter*
CParameter	::=	? N | ? N : Predicate | ! Expression | . Expression
Command	::=	N^+ : [Pred, Pred] | N^+ := Exp$^+$
	|	**if** GActions **fi** | **var** Decl • Action | **con** Decl • Action
GActions	::=	Pred → Action | Pred → Action $\square$ GActions

Fig. 1. *Circus* syntax

The basic form of process definition describes the process's state and operations, as in a Z specification. In *Circus*, we use process paragraphs; the operations are called "actions" and can be specified using schemas, CSP operators, and guarded commands. The nameless action at the end of a process description defines its behaviour; we refer to this action as the "main action" of the process.

In our example, we have a process *Buffer*, whose state components are the contents of the buffer and its size.

process *Buffer* $\widehat{=}$ **begin**

$BufferState \widehat{=} [\, buff : \text{seq}\,\mathbb{N};\ size : 1 \mathinner{\ldotp\ldotp} maxbuff \mid size = \#buff \leq maxbuff \,]$

Initially, the buffer is empty.

$BufferInit \widehat{=} [\, BufferState' \mid buff' = \langle\rangle \land size' = 0 \,]$

Input is possible if there is space in the buffer; the input element is appended to the bounded sequence and the size incremented.

```
┌─ InputCmd ─────────────────────────────────────────────────────────
│ ΔBufferState
│ x? : ℕ
├────────────────────────────────────────────────────────────────────
│ size < maxbuff ∧ buff' = buff ⌢ ⟨x?⟩ ∧ size' = size + 1
└────────────────────────────────────────────────────────────────────
```

$Input \,\widehat{=}\, size < maxbuff \;\&\; input?x \rightarrow InputCmd$

The *Output* action is enabled providing the buffer is not empty. It outputs the head of the buffer, giving the FIFO discipline, and updates the size accordingly.

```
┌─ OutputCmd ────────────────────────────────────────────────────────
│ ΔBufferState
├────────────────────────────────────────────────────────────────────
│ size > 0
│ buff' = tail buff ∧ size' = size − 1
└────────────────────────────────────────────────────────────────────
```

$Output \,\widehat{=}\, size > 0 \;\&\; output!(head\;buff) \rightarrow OutputCmd$

Finally, the main action initialises the *Buffer* and repeatedly offers the choice of input and output.

- $BufferInit;\; \mu X \bullet (Input \,\square\, Output);\; X$

end

The guards guarantee that *Input* is available only if the buffer is not full, and *Output*, only if the buffer is not empty.

CSP operators can also be applied to processes: their states are conjoined and their main actions are combined using the operator applied. An unusual operator available in *Circus* is indexing: a process as $i : T \odot P$ behaves like P, but uses different channels. For each channel c of P, we have a fresh channel c_i that communicates pairs of values: the first element is the index, a value of type T, and the second element is the value originally communicated through c. The instantiation $(i : T \odot P)\lfloor e \rfloor$ behaves like P, but the first element of the pairs communicated is the value of the index expression e.

We also have a renaming operator in *Circus*. For example, in $P[oldc := newc]$, the communications of P through channel $oldc$ are done through the channel $newc$ instead. An example of the use of the indexing and renaming operators is found in our case study (Section 5).

The semantics of *Circus* [20,17] is based on unifying theories of programming [9]: an alphabetised relational model for imperative programming, concurrency, and communication. In our work, Z is the concrete syntax for the relational model, so that a *Circus* program denotes a Z specification. Each process corresponds to a part of that specification characterised by a state definition. Actions are modelled as operations over this state.

In the unifying theory, distinguished variables are used to describe relevant observations. In the semantics of *Circus*, these variables comprise the state components of a process denotation. In addition to the state components in the process specification, there are components to model behaviour: stability from divergence (*okay*), termination (*wait*), a history of interaction with the environment (*tr*), and a set of events that can be refused (*ref*). This is a state-based, failures-divergences model, with embedded imperative features.

To illustrate the unifying theory, we give a description of the semantics of the simple prefixing operator. Consider the process $P = a \rightarrow Skip$; we explain P's behaviour by case analysis on the observational variables *okay* and *wait*.

Suppose that *okay* is false; in this case, P has been activated in the final state of a process that is diverging. Divergence is a left-zero for sequential composition, so the only thing that P can guarantee is that it leaves the final value of tr as an extension of its initial value: tr prefix tr'.

Suppose instead that *okay* is true and so P's predecessor is not diverging. There are two cases to consider: the predecessor may or may not have terminated; this is described by the observation *wait*. Suppose that *wait* is true and so the predecessor has not terminated, then P has no effect on the observations.

Suppose instead that *wait* is false and so the predecessor has terminated. There are two possible states: P itself may or may not have terminated. Suppose that *wait'* is true and so P has not terminated. P must leave the trace tr unchanged, but it must not be refusing the event a: $tr' = tr \wedge a \notin ref'$.

Finally, suppose that *wait'* is false and so P has terminated. P must have added the event a to the trace: $tr' = tr \frown \langle a \rangle$. The final value of the refusal set is irrelevant, since P has now terminated and can do nothing further. In all these *okay* cases, the state variables are left unchanged and P doesn't diverge.

3   Refinement Notions

In the unifying theory, refinement is expressed as implication; that is, an implementation P satisfies a specification S, providing that $[P \Rightarrow S]$, where the square brackets denote universal quantification over the alphabet, which must be the same for both implementation and specification. In *Circus*, this notion is used to formalise the situation when one action B refines another A ($\sqsubseteq_A$).

Definition 1 (Action refinement). *Suppose that A and B are actions on the same state space. Action A is refined by action B if, and only if, every observation of B is permitted by A as well: $A \sqsubseteq_A B$ iff $[B \Rightarrow A]$.*   □

The state of a process is encapsulated; therefore, when refining a process we may change the local state if we wish. In the standard theory of data refinement [11], this possibility is handled by regarding the states as existing in local blocks. In *Circus*, as a result of hiding the details of the states of two processes P and Q, we are left with two main actions with a common alphabet; this allows us to define process refinement in terms of action refinement of local blocks ($\sqsubseteq_P$).

Let $P.st$, $P.init$, and $P.act$ denote the local state, initialisation, and main action of a process P, respectively.

Definition 2 (Process refinement). *We define* $P \sqsubseteq_{\mathcal{P}} Q$ *to mean that process* P *is refined by process* Q *if, and only if,*

$$(\exists P.st;\ P.st' \bullet P.init \wedge P.act) \sqsubseteq_{\mathcal{A}} (\exists Q.st;\ Q.st' \bullet Q.init \wedge Q.act) \qquad \square$$

The techniques of data refinement are well-known for proving the correctness of a development step involving local blocks. They require the formalisation of a link between abstract and concrete states, usually referred to as as *forwards* and *backwards simulations* [7,5,21]. A well-established result is that the completeness of data refinement requires both techniques; however, in this paper, we restrict ourselves to the most widely-used technique of forwards simulation, and leave backwards simulation as a topic for further work.

Definition 3 (Forwards simulation). *A forwards simulation between actions* A *and* B *of processes* P *and* Q *is a relation* R *satisfying*

1. (initialisation) $[\forall Q.st \bullet Q.init \Rightarrow (\exists P.st \bullet P.init \wedge R)]$
2. (correctness) $[\forall P.st;\ Q.st;\ Q.st' \bullet R \wedge B \Rightarrow (\exists P.st' \bullet R' \wedge A)]$

A forwards simulation between P *and* Q *is a forwards simulation between their main actions.* $\qquad \square$

In this definition, there is no applicability requirement concerning preconditions, as would usually be found in the definition of forwards simulation. This is because the semantics of actions are total.

The next theorem ensures that, if we provide a forwards simulation between processes P and Q, then we can substitute Q for occurrences of P in a program.

Theorem 1 (Forwards simulation is sound). *Whenever a forwards simulation exists between two processes* P *and* Q, *we also have that* $P \sqsubseteq_{\mathcal{P}} Q$.

Proof

$$\exists Q.st;\ Q.st' \bullet Q.init \wedge Q.act$$
$$\Rightarrow \exists P.st;\ Q.st;\ Q.st' \bullet P.init \wedge R \wedge Q.act \qquad \text{[initialisation]}$$
$$\Rightarrow \exists P.st;\ P.st';\ Q.st;\ Q.st' \bullet P.init \wedge R \wedge R' \wedge P.act \qquad \text{[correctness]}$$
$$\Rightarrow \exists P.st;\ P.st' \bullet P.init \wedge P.act \qquad \text{[schema calculus]}$$

$\square$

We still need, however, support for the proof that a particular relation R is a forwards simulation.

Definition 3 imposes proof obligations related to the main actions of the processes. To support a calculational approach and the reuse of well-established techniques, it is useful to be able to prove simulation for primitive actions and rely on distribution properties through the action combinators. More specifically, we want to be able to be assured of the existence of a simulation by discharging proof obligations for schema expressions, as in Z, but keeping the structure of the main action. This is the approach supported by the following theorems.

First of all, data refinement leaves *Skip*, *Stop*, and *Chaos* unchanged. If an action is described by a schema, then the familiar proof obligations of Z apply.

Theorem 2 (Forwards simulation of schema expressions). *The following are sufficient conditions for the forwards simulation of schema expressions.*

1. (applicability) $[\forall P.st;\ Q.st \bullet R \wedge \text{pre } PSExp \Rightarrow \text{pre } QSExp]$

2. (correctness) $\left[\begin{array}{l} \forall P.st;\ Q.st;\ Q.st' \bullet \\ R \wedge \text{pre } PSExp \wedge QSExp \Rightarrow (\exists P.st' \bullet R' \wedge PSExp) \end{array} \right]$

Proof *From the semantics of schema expressions.*   □

Results exist about the distribution of data refinement through the combinators of sequential programming languages [11,12], and some of these have been re-expressed in the unifying theory [9]. More interesting is the distribution through the combinators of CSP; in this paper, we have space for demonstrating a few cases: sequential composition, prefixing, and concurrency.

Theorem 3 (Data refinement distributes through sequential composition). *Suppose that R is a forwards simulation between A_1 and B_1 and between A_2 and B_2, then R is also a forwards simulation between $A_1;\ A_2$ and $B_1;\ B_2$.*

Proof

$R(P.st, Q.st) \wedge (B_1(Q.st, Q.st');\ B_2(Q.st, Q.st'))$

$\Leftrightarrow \exists\, Q.st_0 \bullet R(P.st, Q.st) \wedge B_1(Q.st, Q.st_0) \wedge B_2(Q.st_0, Q.st')$

$\hspace{6cm}$ *[sequential composition]*

$\Rightarrow \exists\, P.st_0, Q.st_0 \bullet R(P.st_0, Q.st_0) \wedge A_1(P.st, P.st_0) \wedge B_2(Q.st_0, Q.st')$

$\hspace{9cm}$ *[assumption]*

$\Rightarrow \exists\, P.st_0, P.st' \bullet R(P.st', Q.st') \wedge A_1(P.st, P.st_0) \wedge A_2(P.st_0, P.st')$

$\hspace{9cm}$ *[assumption]*

$\Leftrightarrow \exists\, P.st' \bullet R(P.st', Q.st') \wedge (A_1(P.st, P.st');\ A_2(P.st, P.st'))$

$\hspace{7cm}$ *[sequential composition]*

□

The proof of the last theorem is given in the relational calculus; the proof in the schema calculus is rather longer.

We consider the simple prefixing action $c.pxp \rightarrow Skip$, where c is a channel name and pxp is an expression in terms of the abstract state denoting a communicable value on that channel. The abstract description of the event $c.pxp$ must be transformed into a concrete description $c.qxp$ of the same event. Externally, the same value is communicated; it is the description in terms of the internal state that has to change in a data refinement.

The correctness of replacing pxp by qxp may be explained by considering an expression as an interrogation of the state; that is, $[\Xi P.st;\ o! : V \mid o! = pxp]$. The assumption in the following theorem is then a consequence of the simulation of these interrogations: pxp and qxp are equal, modulo R.

Theorem 4 (Data refinement distributes through simple prefixing). *Suppose that pxp and qxp are expressions in terms of the states $P.st$ and $Q.st$ of processes P and Q, respectively, and that R is a forwards simulation between these processes. If the expressions are equal, modulo R,*

$$\forall P.st;\ Q.st \bullet R \Rightarrow pxp = qxp$$

then we have that the relation R is also a forwards simulation between the simple prefixed actions $c.pxp \rightarrow Skip$ and $c.qxp \rightarrow Skip$.

Proof

$$R \wedge (c.qxp \rightarrow Skip)$$
$$\Leftrightarrow R \wedge (\,(x' = x \wedge okay' \wedge$$
$$\qquad (Id \lhd wait \rhd (tr' = tr \wedge c.qxp \notin ref' \lhd wait' \rhd tr' = tr \,^\frown \langle c.qxp \rangle)))$$
$$\qquad\quad \lhd okay \rhd tr \text{ prefix } tr'\,) \qquad\qquad\qquad\qquad\qquad\qquad [\textit{definition}]$$
$$\Leftrightarrow R \wedge (\,(x' = x \wedge okay' \wedge$$
$$\qquad (Id \lhd wait \rhd (tr' = tr \wedge c.pxp \notin ref' \lhd wait' \rhd tr' = tr \,^\frown \langle c.pxp \rangle)))$$
$$\qquad\quad \lhd okay \rhd tr \text{ prefix } tr'\,) \qquad\qquad\qquad\qquad\qquad\qquad [\textit{assumption}]$$
$$\Leftrightarrow \exists P.st' \bullet$$
$$\qquad R' \wedge (\,(nx' = x \wedge okay' \wedge$$
$$\qquad (Id \lhd wait \rhd (tr' = tr \wedge c.pxp \notin ref' \lhd wait' \rhd tr' = tr \,^\frown \langle c.pxp \rangle)))$$
$$\qquad\quad \lhd okay \rhd tr \text{ prefix } tr'\,) \qquad\qquad\qquad\quad [\textit{existential introduction}]$$
$$\Leftrightarrow \exists P.st' \bullet R' \wedge (c.pxp \rightarrow Skip) \qquad\qquad\qquad\qquad\qquad [\textit{definition}]$$

□

Prefixing is defined in terms of sequential composition and simple prefixing.

Corollary 1 (Data Refinement distributes through prefixing). *Suppose that pxp and qxp are expressions in terms of the states $P.st$ and $Q.st$ of processes P and Q, and that R is a forwards simulation between these processes and their actions A and B. If the expressions are equal, modulo R, then R is a forwards simulation between the actions $c!pxp \rightarrow A$ and $c!qxp \rightarrow B$.*

Proof *Directly from Theorems 3 and 4.*   □

The parallel composition $A_1 \parallel C \parallel A_2$ describes two actions synchronising on events in the set C. The resulting action is formed by merging the observations and conjoining the state changes. The traces are merged to produce a trace where the events in C occur synchronously. An event is refused if either component refuses it, divergence arises if either component diverges, and termination occurs when both components terminate. To achieve distribution of data refinement through parallelism, we must show its effect on the conjunction of state changes.

The assumptions for distributing data refinement through concurrency require that we can partition the state space in a particular way to avoid interference, so that A_1 has precedence in one partition, and A_2 has precedence in the other. More formally, there is a sub-space S of the abstract state such that $A_1 \upharpoonright S' \Rightarrow A_2 \upharpoonright S'$. (Here, $A_1 \upharpoonright S'$ is the *projection* of A_1 onto the variables of S'; the complementary operation is $A_1 \setminus S'$, which is A_1 with the variables of S' *hidden*.) In other words, every result that A_1 can produce in S' is acceptable to A_2. Furthermore, every result that A_2 can produce in the complement of S' is acceptable to A_1; that is, $A_2 \setminus S' \Rightarrow A_1 \setminus S'$. In general, this allows each action to make compatible changes in the other's partition. Furthermore, the simulation R must respect the same noninterference properties between A_1 and A_2, so that, for example, $(A_1 \upharpoonright S') \mathbin{\fatsemi} R \Rightarrow (A_2 \upharpoonright S') \mathbin{\fatsemi} R$. Moreover, R must respect the partition by identifying a corresponding region T in the concrete state space.

Theorem 5 (Data Refinement distributes through concurrency). *Suppose that R is a forwards simulation between A_1 and B_1 and between A_2 and B_2. Furthermore, suppose that the after-variables can be partitioned as follows:*

$$A_1 \upharpoonright S' \Rightarrow A_2 \upharpoonright S' \qquad\qquad (A_1 \upharpoonright S') \mathbin{\fatsemi} R = (A_1 \mathbin{\fatsemi} R) \upharpoonright T'$$
$$A_2 \setminus S' \Rightarrow A_1 \setminus S' \qquad\qquad (A_1 \setminus S') \mathbin{\fatsemi} R = (A_1 \mathbin{\fatsemi} R) \setminus T'$$
$$(A_1 \upharpoonright S') \mathbin{\fatsemi} R \Rightarrow (A_2 \upharpoonright S') \mathbin{\fatsemi} R \qquad\qquad (A_2 \upharpoonright S') \mathbin{\fatsemi} R = (A_2 \mathbin{\fatsemi} R) \upharpoonright T'$$
$$(A_2 \setminus S') \mathbin{\fatsemi} R \Rightarrow (A_1 \setminus S') \mathbin{\fatsemi} R \qquad\qquad (A_2 \setminus S') \mathbin{\fatsemi} R = (A_2 \mathbin{\fatsemi} R) \setminus T'$$

Then R is also a forwards simulation between $A_1 \llbracket\, C \,\rrbracket A_2$ and $B_1 \llbracket\, C \,\rrbracket B_2$.

Proof *Our result follows directly from the schema calculus and our assumptions.*

$$R \mathbin{\fatsemi} (B_1 \wedge B_2)$$
$$\Rightarrow (R \mathbin{\fatsemi} B_1) \wedge (R \mathbin{\fatsemi} B_2) \qquad\qquad [schema\ calculus]$$
$$\Rightarrow (A_1 \mathbin{\fatsemi} R) \wedge (A_2 \mathbin{\fatsemi} R) \qquad\qquad [hypothesis]$$
$$\Leftrightarrow (((A_1 \mathbin{\fatsemi} R) \upharpoonright T') \vee ((A_1 \mathbin{\fatsemi} R) \setminus T')) \wedge (((A_2 \mathbin{\fatsemi} R) \upharpoonright T') \vee ((A_2 \mathbin{\fatsemi} R) \setminus T'))$$
$$[T'\ and\ its\ complement\ partition\ the\ state\ space]$$
$$\Leftrightarrow (((A_1 \mathbin{\fatsemi} R) \upharpoonright T') \wedge ((A_2 \mathbin{\fatsemi} R) \upharpoonright T')) \vee (((A_1 \mathbin{\fatsemi} R) \setminus T') \wedge ((A_2 \mathbin{\fatsemi} R) \setminus T'))$$
$$[schema\ calculus]$$
$$\Leftrightarrow ((A_1 \upharpoonright S') \mathbin{\fatsemi} R) \vee ((A_2 \setminus S') \mathbin{\fatsemi} R) \qquad\qquad [assumption]$$
$$\Leftrightarrow ((A_1 \upharpoonright S') \vee (A_2 \setminus S')) \mathbin{\fatsemi} R \qquad\qquad [schema\ calculus]$$
$$\Leftrightarrow (((A_1 \upharpoonright S') \wedge (A_2 \upharpoonright S')) \vee ((A_1 \setminus S') \wedge (A_2 \setminus S'))) \mathbin{\fatsemi} R \qquad [assumption]$$
$$\Leftrightarrow (((A_1 \upharpoonright S') \vee (A_1 \setminus S')) \wedge ((A_2 \upharpoonright S') \vee (A_2 \setminus S'))) \mathbin{\fatsemi} R \quad [schema\ calculus]$$
$$\Leftrightarrow (A_1 \wedge A_2) \mathbin{\fatsemi} R \qquad\qquad [S'\ and\ its\ complement\ partition\ the\ state\ space]$$

□

The next result ensures that algorithmically refining an action (Definition 1) is a proper way of refining the process as a whole, justifying the use of action refinements in developments. As usual, we must prove the initialisation and applicability theorems.

Theorem 6 (Feasible refinement). *Suppose we have have a process P with actions A and B. If $A \sqsubseteq_A B$, then the identity is a forwards simulation between A and B, provided P satisfies the Z initialisation theorem and its schema actions are feasible.*

Proof *Direct from definitions.* □

The results just presented are applied in the case study in Section 5.

4   Refinement Laws

Both laws of CSP and laws of Z, for which we have a refinement calculus [2], are relevant to our work; nevertheless, our focus here are on the laws of processes. Our approach to the refinement of *Circus* specifications is guided by the progressive and incremental distribution of a specification originally centralised. Surprisingly, perhaps, such a strategy can be supported by simple laws that allow the splitting of processes. Here we present two families of refinement laws.

4.1   Process Splitting

The first family of laws, called *process splitting*, applies to processes whose state components can be partitioned in such a way that each partition has its own set of process paragraphs. The result is three processes: each of the first two include a partition of the state and the corresponding paragraphs, and the third process has the same behaviour as the original one.

Let *pd* stand for the process declaration below, where we use $Q.pps$ and $R.pps$ to stand for the process paragraphs of the processes Q and R; and F for an arbitrary context (function on processes). This is the general form of processes to which the process split laws apply.

> **process** $P \cong$ **begin**
> $\quad State \cong Q.st \wedge R.st$
> $\quad Q.pps \uparrow R.st$
> $\quad R.pps \uparrow Q.st$
> $\quad \bullet F(Q.act, R.act)$
> **end**

The state of P is defined as the conjunction of two other state schemas: $Q.st$ and $R.st$. The actions of P are $Q.pps \uparrow R.st$ and $R.pps \uparrow Q.st$, which handle the partitions of the state separately. In $Q.pps \uparrow R.st$, each schema expression in $Q.pps$ is conjoined with $\Xi R.st$. This means that these process paragraphs do not change the state components of $R.st$; similarly for $R.pps \uparrow Q.st$.

Let *qd* and *rd* stand for the declarations of the processes Q and R, determined by $Q.st$, $Q.ppS$, and $Q.act$, and $R.st$, $R.pps$, and $R.act$, respectively. We can formulate our family of laws as follows.

Law 1 (Process splitting)

$$pd = (\textbf{ process } P \mathrel{\widehat{=}} F(Q.act, R.act))$$

provided Q.pps and R.pps are disjoint with respect to R.st and Q.st.   □

We say that two sets of process paragraphs *pps* and *pps'* are disjoint with respect to states s and s' if, and only if, $pps = pps \uparrow s'$ and $pps' = pps' \uparrow s$, and no command nor CSP action expression in *pps* refers to components of s' or to paragraph names in *pps'*; further, no command nor CSP action expression in *pps'* refers to components of s or to paragraph names in *pps*.

4.2 Process Indexing

The second family of laws applies to processes defined using the promotion technique of Z. Broadly, the technique is based on defining the specification of an abstract data type (with its operations) and then using this as the type of the elements of a more elaborate data structure (like sets, sequences, maps, etc.).

By convention, the basic (element) type is referred to as *local*, whereas the collection is called *global*. When the local type is completely encapsulated (as an abstract data type) in the global type, we say that the promotion is *free*; otherwise it is called *constrained* [21]. Here we are concerned solely with free promotions.

The proposed family of laws refines a specification structured using a free promotion to an indexed family of processes, each one representing an element of the local type.

One of the contributions of this work is to extend the Z technique of promotion to *Circus* actions. Below we give an inductive definition of the relevant promotion patterns; where L stands for the local process, G for the global process, and *Promotion* for the promotion schema.

For simplicity, we assume that the global state is a function f from elements of an arbitrary type *Range* to elements of the local state; so, a local element is identified in the global state as $f(i)$. Promotion of schema expressions is as in Z.

$$\textbf{promote}(SExp) \mathrel{\widehat{=}} \exists\, \Delta L.st \bullet SExp \wedge Promotion$$

The promotion of *Skip*, *Stop*, and *Chaos* leaves them unchanged.

$$\textbf{promote}(A) \mathrel{\widehat{=}} A, \qquad \text{for } A \in \{\, Skip, Stop, Chaos \,\}$$

To promote a communication $c.e$, we need to communicate an extra value: the identifier of the value e in the collection. Therefore, for each channel c, there is a corresponding promoted channel pc that communicates a pair formed by the identifier and the value. The latter may also need to be promoted, as it may include references to elements of the local state.

$$\textbf{promote}(c.e \rightarrow A) \mathrel{\widehat{=}} pc.\textbf{promote}(e) \rightarrow \textbf{promote}(A)$$

Promotion for expressions is defined below; for the other forms of prefixing, the definition is similar. Promotion distributes through the other action operators. For a guarded action, we need to promote the guard. Promotion of predicates has an inductive definition based on promotion of expressions. For parallelism and hiding, the channels are replaced with corresponding promoted channels.

If a variable x is not local state component, it does not need to be changed.

$$\mathbf{promote}(x) \mathrel{\widehat{=}} x, \qquad \text{provided } x \text{ is not a component of } L.st$$

If it is, then we need to access it through the global state.

$$\mathbf{promote}(x) \mathrel{\widehat{=}} f(i).x, \qquad \text{if } x \text{ is a component of } L.st$$

Finally, promotion distributes through the expression operators; the simple but lengthy definition is omitted. If the local state includes components x, y, and z, for instance, a promoted assignment like $f(i).x := e$ is an abbreviation for

$$f := f \oplus \{i : Range;\ l : L.st \mid l.x = e \wedge l.y = f(i).y \wedge l.z = f(i).z\}$$

Promotion of multiple assignments may lead to aliasing if more than one component of the local state is being updated. For example, promotion of $x, y := 2, 3$ leads to $f(i).x, f(i).y := 2, 3$. A specification statement with a frame containing x and y is also problematic. We assume that actions like these are not used.

Let pd stand for the following process declaration. The family of process indexing laws applies to processes of this form.

> **process** $P \mathrel{\widehat{=}}$ **begin**
> $State \mathrel{\widehat{=}} [\, f : Range \nrightarrow L.st \mid pred \,]$
> $L.action_k \uparrow State$
> $L.act \mathrel{\widehat{=}} \mu X \bullet F(L.action_k); X$
> $Promotion \mathrel{\widehat{=}}$
> $[\, \Delta L.st;\ \Delta State;\ i? : Range \mid$
> $i? \in \mathrm{dom}\, f \wedge \theta L.st = f(i?) \wedge f' = f \oplus \{i? \mapsto \theta L.st'\}\,]$
> $action_k \mathrel{\widehat{=}} \mathbf{promote}(L.action_k)$
> $\bullet\ (\, \mu X \bullet F(action_k); X \,)$
> **end**

As discussed before, the global state component is a function from $Range$ to a local state $L.st$. Actions $L.action_k$ over the local state do not affect the global state. The main local action $L.act$ is defined recursively, as is the main global action. Both have the same structure, but the former uses the actions $L.action_k$ on the local states, and the latter, the corresponding promoted actions $action_k$. There is a promoted action $action_k$ for every local action $L.action_k$. We note that for each channel c used by the $action_k$, the corresponding promoted action uses a corresponding promoted channel pc. A topic for further work is the generalisation of the process indexing family of laws in terms of the data structure used in the global state and the main action of both the local and the global states.

Consider also the indexed process *IL* below.

process $IL \mathrel{\widehat{=}} i : Range \odot L[c\_i := pc]$

The process $i : Range \odot L$ acts on indexed channels c_i, where L acts on a channel c. Like the promoted channels pc used in P, they communicate pairs of values: the index and the original value. Above, we rename each channel c_i to pc. In this way, we can use *IL* in the refinement of P.

The family of laws for process indexing is as follows.

Law 2 (Process indexing)

$pd = $ **process** $P \mathrel{\widehat{=}} \ ||| \ i : Range \odot IL\lfloor i \rfloor$

provided L.pps and pps are disjoint with respect to L.st and State.   □

Here, the local state is available through the indexed processes *IL*. Due to interleaving, there is no interference among the individual elements of the collection.

5   Refining the Reactive Buffer

In this section, we develop an implementation for the bounded reactive buffer abstract specification presented in Section 2. The structure of the final implementation is a ring of cells with a central controller and a cached head. Broadly, the refinement progresses as follows: after a standard data refinement, we decompose the original process into a controller and a centralised ring (Law 1); through a second data refinement step, the centralised ring is redesigned as a *promotion* of individual ring cells. Finally, we apply Law 2 to decompose the ring process into the interleaving of ring cell, each one storing a single value.

5.1   A Centralised Ring Buffer

Our first development step is a data refinement, in which we introduce a *cache* and a *ring* to represent the internal state of the process *Buffer*. When the buffer is non-empty, the cache stores the head of the buffer. In a circular array, the two ends are considered to be joined. We maintain two indexes into this array: a *bottom* and a *top*, to delimit the relevant values. This part of the array is a concrete representation of the tail of the original bounded buffer.

This step can be justified applying Theorems 2 and 3, Corollary 1, and other similar theorems. For conciseness we omit the details of this data refinement which is very much like a standard Z data refinement. The resulting state is as follows. Its definition is partitioned because we aim at applying Law 1.

process *CBuffer* $\mathrel{\widehat{=}}$ **begin**

```
┌─ ControllerState ─────────────────────────────────
│ size : 0 .. maxbuff
│ cache : ℕ
│ ringsize : 0 .. maxring;  top, bot : 1 .. maxring
├───────────────────────────────────────────────────
│ ringsize = max{0, size − 1}
│ ringsize mod maxring = (top − bot) mod maxring
└───────────────────────────────────────────────────
```

$RingState \mathrel{\widehat{=}} [\, ring : \operatorname{seq} \mathbb{N} \mid \#ring = maxring \,]$

$BufferState \mathrel{\widehat{=}} ControllerState \land RingState$

The constant $maxring$, defined as $maxbuff - 1$, gives the bound for the ring. There is a subtle situation when the bottom and the top indexes coincide; in this case it is not possible to distinguish whether the ring has reached its maximum storage capacity or whether it is empty. As a consequence, we need to keep a separate record of the number of values stored in the ring.

The structure of the main action is exactly that used in the abstract specification in Section 2. The primitive actions, however, are changed to act on the concrete state.

5.2   Isolate Access to the Ring Component

According to Theorem 6, we can also refine the individual actions of the *Buffer*. Indeed, in our second and third development steps we refine these actions with the aim of obtaining two independent sets of paragraphs. One set of paragraphs accesses exclusively the *ring* and is, in the next step, promoted into an independent process. The other set of paragraphs accesses the remaining components, and is, also in the next step, turned into a controller process which remains unchanged up to the end of the development.

In some circumstances, this partitioning of the state space is not direct. For example, the *StoreInput* operation updates both *top* and *ring*. Splitting it into two operations is not immediate, because the operation that is concerned with updating the *ring* needs the input value ($x?$) and the current value of *top*. The main design tool to solve such data dependencies is introduction of communication. We need two new channels, as follows.

channel $write, read : (1 .. maxring) \times \mathbb{N}$

These channels are hidden in the *Buffer* design and implementation.

The first set of paragraphs has *ControllerState* as its state space, whilst preserving *RingState*. The initialisation is for an empty buffer.

$ControllerInit \mathrel{\widehat{=}} [\, ControllerState' \mid size' = 0 \land bot' = 1 \land top' = 1 \,]$

In the case the buffer is empty, an input is cached. The ring indexes do not change and the buffer now contains a single item.

```
┌─ CacheInput ─────────────────────────────────
│ ΔControllerState
│ ΞRingState
│ x? : ℕ
├──────────────────────────────────────────────
│ size = 0
│ size' = 1 ∧ cache' = x?
│ bot' = bot ∧ top' = top
└──────────────────────────────────────────────
```

If the buffer is not empty, the *cache* is not changed; the indexes and the size of the ring are updated, but the ring itself is not changed.

```
┌─ StoreInputController ───────────────────────
│ ΔControllerState
│ ΞRingState
│ x? : ℕ
├──────────────────────────────────────────────
│ 0 < size < maxbuff
│ size' = size + 1 ∧ cache' = cache
│ bot' = bot ∧ top' = (top mod maxring) + 1
└──────────────────────────────────────────────
```

The action below gets the new input and, if necessary, sends it to the ring using channel *write*.

$$InputController \ \widehat{=}$$
$$\quad size < maxbuff \ \& \ input?x \rightarrow$$
$$\qquad size = 0 \ \& \ CacheInput$$
$$\qquad \square$$
$$\qquad size > 0 \ \& \ write.top!x \rightarrow StoreInputController$$

The extra value communicated through *write* identifies the position in which the input is to be stored in the *ring*.

The handling of outputs by the controller can be specified in a similar way. For conciseness, we omit the definition of the action *OutputController*. The behaviour of the controller is as follows.

$$ControllerAction \ \widehat{=} \ ControllerInit;$$
$$\qquad\qquad \mu X \bullet (InputController \ \square \ OutputController); \ X$$

After initialisation, inputs and outputs are offered repeatedly, whenever possible.

The second set of paragraphs has as its state space *RingState*, whilst preserving *ControllerState*. The next action stores a value in the *ring*.

```
┌─ StoreRingCmd ───────────────────────────────
│ ΔRingState
│ ΞControllerState
│ i? : 1 .. maxring
│ x? : ℕ
├──────────────────────────────────────────────
│ ring' = ring ⊕ {i? ↦ x?}
└──────────────────────────────────────────────
```

Although all state components are in scope, we confine the direct access to *RingSate* and receive the current value of *top* through the *write* internal channel.

$$StoreRing \mathrel{\widehat{=}} write?i?x \rightarrow StoreRingCmd$$

To send the value stored at a given position of the *ring* requires no state change.

$$NewCacheRing \mathrel{\widehat{=}} read?i!ring[i] \rightarrow Skip$$

In its main action, the ring repeatedly offers the external choice between *StoreRing* and *NewCacheRing* actions.

$$RingAction \mathrel{\widehat{=}} \mu X \bullet (StoreRing \,\square\, NewCacheRing);\ X$$

The control behaviour of the process *Buffer* is given by the parallel execution of the controller and the ring, hiding the internal channels.

• (*ControllerAction* $[\![\,\{\!|\ write, read, |\!\}\,]\!]$ *RingAction*) \ $\{\!|\ write, read\ |\!\}$

end

This is actually a significant refinement step, but it involves no change of data representation. To prove that it is valid, we need to compare the above main action to that of the data refined buffer, which was obtained by data refining the actions *BufferInit*, *Input*, and *Output* presented in the previous section. We could appeal to Definition 1, but the purpose is not to prove such obligations directly from the semantics of actions. Rather, the relevant tools are the algebraic laws of CSP (adapted for actions); however, they are not our concern here, as we concentrate on laws which relate processes.

5.3   Split Centralised Buffer into a Controller and a Ring

As a result of the previous development step, the process *Buffer* has two disjoint sets of paragraphs with respect to *ControllerState* and *RingState*. Therefore, with an application of Law 1, *Buffer* can be split into two independent processes: a controller and a ring process .

We call the first process *Controller*; its paragraphs include *ControllerState*, *ControllerInit*, *CacheInput*, *StoreInputController*, *InputController*, those that define *OutputController*, and *ControllerAction*. The latter is the main action. The second process, *Ring*, includes *RingState*, *StoreRingCmd*, *StoreRing*, *New-CacheRing*, and *RingAction*, which is the main action. The main action of *Buffer* is the basis for its new definition.

process *Buffer* $\mathrel{\widehat{=}}$ (*Controller* $[\![\,\{\!|\ write, read\ |\!\}\,]\!]$ *Ring*) \ $\{\!|\ write, read\ |\!\}$

This step is a direct application of Law 1.

5.4   The Ring Process as a Promotion of Ring Cells

In this step, we introduce the concept of a ring cell as an abstract data type and restructure the process *Ring* as a promotion of ring cells. The ring cells communicate over channels *rd* and *wrt*.

channel *rd*, *wrt* : $\mathbb{N}$

process *Ring* $\widehat{=}$ **begin**

A ring cell is required to store only a natural number; the *ring* is simply a sequence of cells.

$CellState \widehat{=} [\, val : \mathbb{N} \,]$

$RingState \widehat{=} [\, ring : \text{seq } CellState \mid \#ring = maxring \,]$

There are two actions on the ring cell state. *Read* merely outputs *val*.

$Read \widehat{=} rd!val \rightarrow Skip$

The *Write* action updates *val*.

$CellWrite \widehat{=} [\, \Delta CellState;\; x? : \mathbb{N} \mid val' = x? \,]$

$Write \widehat{=} wrt?x \rightarrow CellWrite$

The ring cell allows either *Read* or *Write* actions.

$RingCellController \widehat{=} \mu X \bullet (Read \; \Box \; Write);\; X$

The promotion schema relates the local state of ring cells with the sequence of cells. The relevant ring cell in the collection is that indexed by *i?*.

$$\begin{array}{|l}
\_\,Promotion\,\rule[-0.2em]{0pt}{0pt}\_\! \\
\Delta CellState \\
\Delta RingState \\
i? : 1 \,..\, maxring \\
\hline
\theta CellState = ring[i?] \\
ring' = ring \oplus \{i? \mapsto \theta CellState'\} \\
\end{array}$$

StoreRingCmd is defined as a promotion of *CellWrite*, in a standard way.

$StoreRingCmd \widehat{=} \exists\, CellState \bullet CellWrite \land Promotion$

The *StoreRing* action is not touched. It is a prefixing involving the action *StoreRingCmd*, which has already been promoted. The values it communicates are not in the local state, and so are not affect by promotion.

$StoreRing \widehat{=} write?i?x \rightarrow StoreRingCmd$

If we consider that the promotion of the channel *wrt* is the channel *write*, then *StoreRing* is the result of promoting *Write*.

The *NewCacheRing* action is defined by promoting *Read* in a similar way.

$$NewCacheRing \mathrel{\widehat{=}} read?i!ring[i] \to Skip$$

The promotion of *rd* is *read*. Promoting *val* we get $ring[i]$.

The main action of the promoted ring is defined by the same CSP expression as the original process.

$$RingAction \mathrel{\widehat{=}} \mu X \bullet (StoreRing \;\square\; NewCacheRing); \; X$$

$\bullet$ *RingAction*

end

The actions involved, however, have been promoted. This step can be justified by a simulation relating the sequence of cells to the sequence of natural numbers.

5.5 A Distributed Cached-Head Ring Buffer

This is the final step of the development process, where each ring cell is implemented as an independent *Circus* process as the result of an application of Law 2 to *Ring*. We observe that a sequence is a special case of a partial function, which is the kind of global component actually considered in the presentation of Law 2.

A process *RingCell* is defined to include the paragraphs *CellState*, *Read*, *CellWrite*, *Write*, and *RingCellController* as the main action. An indexed ring cell is defined as follows.

process $IRCell \mathrel{\widehat{=}} (i : 1 .. maxring \odot RingCell)[rd\_i, wrt\_i := read, write]$

The indexed process operates on the channels rd_i and wrt_i, which have type $(1 .. maxring) \times \mathbb{N}$. We rename them to *read* and *write*, respectively. The indexed ring cell behaves like a ring cell, except that the communications $rd!val$ and $wrt?x$ are replaced by $read.i!val$ and $write.i?x$.

The ring is constructed by interleaving the indexed ring cells.

process $Ring \mathrel{\widehat{=}} \mathbin{\vert\vert\vert} i : 1 .. maxring \odot IRCell\lfloor i \rfloor$

There is no interaction between the ring's cells, so the definition is appropriate as a refinement of a sequence. This results from a direct application of Law 2.

6 Related and Future Work

In this paper, we outlined a process for developing distributed implementations from centralised *Circus* specifications. Although the application domain is concurrent programming, the process is similar in spirit to the development techniques used for sequential programming.

We gave a semantic definition of refinement and a forwards simulation rule for proving refinements correct. We presented laws for distributing data refinement through some of the combinators of CSP and laws for splitting processes. These laws are new contributions. In particular, we single out Law 2, which establishes a connection (original to our knowledge) between the Z promotion technique (for sequential programming) and the indexed interleaving of the promoted elements, which are processes in *Circus*. Expressing this law has required a generalisation of promotion of schemas to promotion of actions.

Previous work in this area includes that of Back [1], who has applied the refinement calculus to the stepwise development of parallel and reactive programs. In his work, action systems are used as the basic program model: they may be regarded as sequential programs, but they can be implemented as parallel programs. Back's parallel refinement uses techniques originally developed for the sequential refinement calculus. Our work differs in that it is based on concepts taken from CSP, rather than action systems.

The assumptions in Theorem 5 require freedom from interference between two parallel actions in a manner that is essentially the same as a free promotion in Z [21]. In the work of Owicki and Gries [13,14], noninterference also plays an important rôle. Their theory extends Hoare's deductive system for partial correctness of sequential programs [6] by adding parallelism in the form of co-blocks, synchronisation, mutual exclusion, and wait statements. In their method, processes are considered in isolation and a proof of sequential correctness is obtained. These proofs must then be shown to be free from interference: no wait statement or assignment outside a wait statement in one process interferes with the proof of any other. The specification of the parallel program is then the conjunction of the preconditions and the postconditions of the components.

In their later work, the use of critical regions reduces much of the burden of the proofs of interference freedom. An invariant is required for each shared variable, and proofs of invariance replace proofs of noninterference. The difference between our notion of interference and that in the Owicki-Gries work is that we are interested in a design pattern that guarantees noninterference; the design pattern (promotion) is introduced by data refinement.

Our current work includes a weakest precondition semantics for *Circus*, and the indications are that this leads to simpler proofs for the soundness of the laws of refinement. We have already shown that the notion of refinement in this predicate transformer model is equivalent to that in the unifying theory. We shall continue to explore this matter. We also intend to address the completeness of data refinement by considering backwards simulation. Finally, adaptation of algebraic laws of CSP for actions is required to allow us to justify the refinement steps in detail, leading to a refinement calculus for *Circus*.

Acknowledgements. This work is partially supported by the EPSRC grant GR/R43211/01 on "Refinement calculi for sequential and concurrent programs". The work of Ana Cavalcanti and Augusto Sampaio is partially supported by CNPq: grants 520763/98-0 and 521039/95-9. We are grateful to Arthur Hughes for his suggestions.

References

1. R. J. R. Back. Refinement of parallel and reactive programs. In *Proceedings of the Summer School on Program Design Calculi*, Lecture Notes in Computer Science. Springer-Verlag, 1992.
2. A. L. C. Cavalcanti and J. C. P. Woodcock. ZRC - A Refinement Calculus for Z. *Formal Aspects of Computing*, 10(3):267 – 289, 1999.
3. E. W. Dijkstra. Guarded commands, nondeterminacy and the formal derivation of programs. *Communication of the ACM*, 18:453 – 457, 1975.
4. C. Fischer. How to Combine Z with a Process Algebra. In J. Bowen, A. Fett, and M. Hinchey, editors, *ZUM'98: The Z Formal Specification Notation*. Springer-Verlag, 1998.
5. J. He, C. A. R. Hoare, and J. W. Sanders. Data Refinement Refined. In G. Goos and H. Hartmants, editors, *ESOP'86 European Symposium on Programming*, volume 213 of *Lecture Notes in Computer Science*, pages 187 – 196, March 1986.
6. C. A. R. Hoare. An Axiomatic Basis for Computer Programming. *Communications of the ACM*, 12:576 – 580, 1969.
7. C. A. R. Hoare. Proof of Correctness of Data Representations. *Acta Informatica*, 1:271 – 281, 1972.
8. C. A. R. Hoare. *Communicating Sequential Processes*. Prentice-Hall International, 1985.
9. C. A. R. Hoare and He Jifeng. *Unifying Theories of Programming*. Prentice-Hall, 1998.
10. C. C. Morgan. *Programming from Specifications*. Prentice-Hall, 2nd edition, 1994.
11. C. C. Morgan and P. H. B. Gardiner. Data Refinement by Calculation. *Acta Informatica*, 27(6):481 – 503, 1990.
12. J. M. Morris. A Theoretical Basis for Stepwise Refinement and the Programming Calculus. *Science of Computer Programming*, 9(3):287 – 306, 1987.
13. S. Owicki and D. Gries. An axiomatic proof technique for parallel programs I. *Acta Informatica*, 6:319 – 340, 1976.
14. S. Owicki and D. Gries. Verifying properties of parallel programs: an axiomatic approach . *Communications of the ACM*, 19(5):279 – 285, 1976.
15. A. W. Roscoe. *The Theory and Practice of Concurrency*. Prentice-Hall Series in Computer Science. Prentice-Hall, 1998.
16. J. M. Spivey. *The Z Notation: A Reference Manual*. Prentice-Hall, 2nd edition, 1992.
17. J. C. P. Woodcock and A. L. C. Cavalcanti. *Circus*: a concurrent refinement language. Technical report, Oxford University Computing Laboratory, Wolfson Building, Parks Road, Oxford OX1 3QD UK, July 2001.
18. J. C. P. Woodcock and A. L. C. Cavalcanti. A concurrent language for refinement. In Andrew Butterfield and Claus Pahl, editors, *IWFM'01: 5th Irish Workshop in Formal Methods*. Computer Science Department, Trinity College Dublin, July 2001.
19. J. C. P. Woodcock and A. L. C. Cavalcanti. The steam boiler in a unified theory of Z and CSP. In *8th Asia-Pacific Software Engineering Conference (APSEC 2001)*, 2001.
20. J. C. P. Woodcock and A. L. C. Cavalcanti. The Semantics of Circus. In *ZB 2002 International Conference*, 2002. To appear.
21. J. C. P. Woodcock and J. Davies. *Using Z – Specification, Refinement, and Proof*. Prentice-Hall, 1996.

Forward Simulation for Data Refinement of Classes

Ana Cavalcanti[1] and David A. Naumann[2]

[1] Centro de Informática
Universidade Federal de Pernambuco, P.O. Box 7851 50740-540 Recife PE Brazil
alcc@cin.ufpe.br   www.cin.ufpe.br/~alcc
[2] Department of Computer Science
Stevens Institute of Technology, Hoboken NJ 07030 USA
naumann@cs.stevens-tech.edu   www.cs.stevens-tech.edu/~naumann

Abstract. Simulation is the most widely used technique to prove data refinement. We define forward simulation for a language with recursive classes, inheritance, type casts and tests, dynamic binding, class based visibility, mutable state (without aliasing), and specification constructs from refinement calculi. It is a language based on sequential Java, but it also includes specification and deseign mechanisms appropriate for the construction of programs based on refinement. We show simulation to be sound for data refinement of classes in this language.

Keywords: object-orientation, data refinement, soundness of simulation, program analysis and verification.

1 Introduction

Simulation is a well-established technique for showing data refinement (or equivalence) between systems. Its use is ubiquitous in program analysis, verification of hardware and software systems, and theoretical studies. It is also the basis for standard definitions of behavioral subclassing [24,20].

Our contribution is to define and prove sound a notion of simulation for proving refinement of class implementations in a sequential object-oriented language. We extend simulation to a considerably richer language than has been treated hitherto, including several core features refinement calculi [26] and Java-like languages: class-oriented visibility, inheritance, dynamic binding, mutable state, type casts and tests (`instanceof`), and specification statements. Our language has recursive methods and mutually recursive class declarations.

Our work is part of a project addressing program development, transformation, and compilation. We are concerned with refinement laws that capture stepwise development and refactoring [13] of class hierarchies. In this context, the ability to treat specifications as program fragments is important; it is useful in modular program analysis [12], compilation by transformation [17], stepwise development [26], and specification of callback patterns [5,35,21]. However, our result does not depend on the presence of specifications.

L.-H. Eriksson and P. Lindsay (Eds.): FME 2002, LNCS 2391, pp. 471–490, 2002.

For expressiveness, specification statements are usually combined with angelic variables (logical constants). Because these specification constructs prescribe observable behavior without implementation, they cannot be directly interpreted in standard operational or denotational models, e.g., specification statements need not be continuous. We give a predicate transformer semantics, extending the standard model of imperative refinement calculi [3,26]. In previous work [6,7] we showed that the semantics can be defined using transformers that act on predicate formulas, which is convenient for direct application in program development [26]. To prove soundness of simulation, however, we need to construct induced simulation relations that are difficult to express and manipulate as formulas. For the present work, we adapted the semantics to one using sets of states as in, e.g., [3]; this is discussed in depth in [9].

Class refinement is a form of data abstraction. Our notion is based on the traditional notion of data refinement for imperative programs [15,11]. For a class declaration *cdc* to be a refinement of an alternative declaration *cda* for the same class means that replacing *cda* by *cdc* in the context of any complete program yields a refinement of that program. Refinement of programs is algorithmic refinement with respect to pre-post specifications. Simulation provides a means of proving class refinement without having to consider all contexts.

Our main result is a soundness theorem, which says that class refinement follows from simulation, or more precisely, from the existence of a coupling invariant that is a simulation for the methods of the classes. Thus, to prove that *cdc* improves *cda* in all contexts, it suffices to prove simulation for the methods of *cda* and *cdc*. The coupling invariant is a predicate on a *cdc* object and a *cda* object, and simulation for commands has the usual definition [15,11].

Unlike recent work on verification of Java programs, our result does not depend on behavioral subclassing. By contrast with class refinement, behavioral subclassing is concerned with two coexisting classes, one declared to be a subclass of the other. As we discuss in [7], the formulation of behavioral subclassing in terms of contexts is not obvious in the presence of type casts and tests. Several authors sidestep such complications by taking simulation, which we view as a proof technique, to be the definition of behavioral subclassing [24]. Moreover, formal treatments in the literature typically ignore type casts and tests.

To see the difficulty, suppose *CPt* is a declared subclass of *Pt* and expression *e* has static type *Pt*. A context including the command

if *e* **is** *CPt* → **abort** [] ¬(*e* **is** *CPt*) → **skip** **fi**

precludes us from using objects of *CPt* as if they were of class *Pt*, regardless of how the methods of *CPt* are defined. There has been extensive work on typing systems that avoid the need for type tests (and casts, which pose similar problems); but we are interested in correctness of programs in Java-like languages. Our result shows that casts and test do not pose a problem for simulation.

The precise definition of simulation is asymmetric; it caters for refinement by reducing nondeterminacy and failure. In the presence of nondeterminacy, this notion of simulation is incomplete: there are refinements for which no simulation exists. The term forward is used to distinguish this notion from the backward simulations that are needed for completeness [25,11]. We consider only forward simulation, although our language includes nondeterministic guarded commands and specification statements. Forward simulations exist for most practical examples. Many works restrict attention to forward simulation (or even the special case of functional relations [28,21]), even taking it to be the definition of data refinement [3] or behavioral subclassing [24].

Soundness and completeness results are known for many languages, including general transition systems [25], first order imperative languages [11], higher order functional [32] and imperative languages [36,29], and applicative object-oriented languages [22]. For concurrent (first order) programs, nondeterminacy poses interesting challenges for completeness, but formalizing the notion of simulation is straightforward: each of the two programs is in a fixed state space, for which the coupling invariant is given. The same is true of standard treatments of first order imperative programs [15,11]. By contrast, the type constructors of functional languages require coupling invariants to be type-indexed families of relations, usually induced from given relations on the base types [30]. The inductive construction is more complicated for recursively defined data types, and thus, for the recursively defined classes addressed here.

In early work, coupling invariants are restricted to functions, and functional simulations are still widely used (e.g., [12]) due to their ease of manipulation. Later work allowed relations, subject to conditions such as totality and surjectivity that were later found unnecessary in some settings [15]. Our work has brought to light new healthiness conditions related to the inductive construction of relations as well as the need for totality and surjectivity to treat specification constructs. Surjectivity is also used in our treatment of local variables, but it is avoidable as discussed in Section 5.

As in previous work on data refinement, our language does not include pointers. We treat object values as nested tuples (trees); assignment and parameter passing have copy rather than reference semantics. In verification-oriented work, an explicit model of the heap is typically used, and this works as well for object-oriented languages [1,12,31]. Aliasing, in general, violates encapsulation and invalidates simulation; only recently practical restrictions have been found to constrain aliasing sufficiently to achieve encapsulation [4,23]. Here we choose copy semantics to focus on the nontrivial challenges posed by other features. Section 5 discusses promising prospects for adding pointers.

Section 2 describes the syntax and semantics of the language, called ROOL; it also includes the definition of class refinement. Section 3 defines simulation and Section 4 proves the main results. Section 5 gives our conclusions. Complete definitions and proofs of all results can be found in [8]. A detailed presentation of the semantics appears in [9].

class *Stack*
  prot *elt* : **int**; *empty* : **bool**
  pri *rest* : *Stack*
  meth *push* $\widehat{=}$ (**val** *e* : **int** •
      var *t* : *Stack* •
          t := **new** *Stack*;
          t.rest := *rest*; *t.elt* := *elt*; *t.empty* := *empty*;
          rest := *t*; *elt* := *e*; *empty* := false
      end)
  meth *top* $\widehat{=}$ (**res** *e* : **int** • *e* : [¬ *empty*, *e* = *elt*])
  meth *sum* $\widehat{=}$ (**res** *s* : **int** •
      if *empty* → *s* := 0
      [] ¬ *empty* → *rest.sum*(*s*); **var** *x* : **int** • **self**.*top*(*x*); *s* := *s* + *x* **end**
      fi)
end
class *IncStack* **extends** *Stack*
  meth *top* $\widehat{=}$ (**res** *e* : **int** • **if** ¬ *empty* → *e* := *elt* + 1 **fi**)
end
• **var** *s* : *Stack* • *s* := **new** *IncStack*; *s.push*(*x*); *s.push*(*y*); *s.sum*(*z*) **end**

Fig. 1. ROOL program example, with global variables x, y, z : **int**.

2   Syntax, Semantics, and Refinement

This section describes the syntax of our language, including the typing judgements on which the semantics is defined. Afterwards, we define class refinement and conclude with a sketch of the semantics.

2.1   Language and Typing

A program in ROOL takes the form *cds* • *c* where *cds* is a sequence of class declarations and *c* is the main command, whose free variables represent the inputs and outputs. In the example in Figure 1, the main command has free variables x, y, z. The class *Stack* in Figure 1 contains three attributes: *elt*, recording the element at the top, *empty*, a boolean that records whether the stack is empty or not, and *rest*, recording the other elements. The first two attributes are protected: visible in *Stack* and in its subclasses; the last attribute is private to *Stack*. Classes can also have public attributes. The type of *rest* is *Stack*, so this is a recursive class. Attributes are implicitly initialized to 0, false, or **null** as in Java.

The method *push* in *Stack* has an integer value parameter *e*. ROOL also has result parameters, to model return values, and value-result parameters which are needed for expressiveness, as assignment has copy semantics. Method bodies are parameterized commands in the style of [2,10]. In *push*, a local variable *t* of type *Stack* is initialized to hold a new *Stack* and its attributes are initialized to those of the current (*Stack*) object. Because of the copy semantics, this is equivalent to the assignment $t :=$ **self**, where t is initialized with a copy of the current object **self**. Nevertheless, we are primarily interested in reasoning about programs as they are written in a language with reference semantics.

In the body of the method *top* we have a specification statement. The result parameter e is specified to take the value of the element at the top of the stack, if it is not empty. If it is, the behavior of *top* is unpredictable.

The method *sum* calculates the sum of the elements of the stack. It is recursive, as it calls itself on the object *rest*. Also, it calls the method *top* of *Stack* on the current object. We refer to these calls as **self** method calls.

Class *IncStack* is a subclass of *Stack*, redefining method *top* so that, if the stack is not empty, it returns through e the value at the top plus 1. This illustrates that our results do not require behavioral subclassing The method *top* of *IncStack* does not refine that of *Stack*, so *IncStack* does not refine *Stack*.

The main command constructs an *IncStack* and assigns it to a local variable s. The first two method calls push the values x and y. The inherited method *push* constructs *Stack* objects, so s has type *IncStack*, but $s.rest$ has type *Stack*. The call $s.sum$ assigns to z the value $x + (y + 1)$, due to dynamic binding for **self**.*top*.

The example is designed to illustrate ROOL, not class refinement. In the next section we present another definition for *Stack* that refines that in Figure 1.

We formalize the syntax using a relation $\Gamma, \Sigma, N \rhd c : \mathbf{com}$, which characterizes the commands c that are well-typed in the context defined by type environment Γ, local signature Σ, and class N. To characterize typing for the main commands, we use a class name **main**, distinct from all declared classes. We refrain from giving the detailed definition for type environments Γ; they are symbol tables that record the declared classes, their attributes and methods, the typing and visibility declarations, and the class hierarchy. A local signature records method parameters and local variables in scope, as well as the visible attributes of the current class N. The typing judgement $\Gamma, \Sigma, N \rhd c : \mathbf{com}$ means that c can occur in the body of a method of N, whose parameters are recorded in Σ, if the local variables in Σ are in scope. As an example, the local signature for the inner scope of method *push* is *elt* : **int**; *empty* : **bool**; *rest* : *Stack*; e : **int**; t : *Stack*.

We also have a relation $\Gamma, \Sigma, N \rhd pc : \mathbf{pcom}(pds)$ for well-typed parameterized commands pc with parameters pds. There are relations for expressions and predicates as well. Typing rules and definitions for auxiliary functions can be found in [7,8]. As an example, we give the typing rule for **self** method calls.

$$\frac{\Gamma, \Sigma, N \rhd \mathbf{self}.m : \mathbf{pcom}(pds) \qquad \Gamma, \Sigma, N \rhd e : T}{\Gamma, \Sigma, N \rhd \mathbf{self}.m(e) : \mathbf{com}}$$
$$norep(rvrargs\ pds\ e) \qquad aptype\ \Gamma\ pds\ e\ T$$

The call **self**.$m(e)$ is well-typed if e is a well-typed (list of) expressions and **self**.m is well-typed: m is declared or inherited in N with parameter declarations pds. Result and value-result arguments cannot be repeated; this is enforced by the condition $norep(rvrargs\ pds\ e)$, using auxiliary functions $norep$ and $rvrargs$.

The types of the arguments have to be compatible with those of the parameters. This is enforced by the condition *aptype Γ pds e T*.

Finally, a program *cds $\bullet$ c* is well-typed in the context of a signature Σ, written $\Sigma \triangleright cds \bullet c : \textbf{program}$, provided that c is typable as $\Gamma, \Sigma, \textbf{main} \triangleright c : \textbf{com}$ for the fictitious class **main**. The local signature records the global variables of c. The typing environment Γ records the information in *cds*.

Besides characterizing well-typed programs, the typing judgements record context information that is used in the semantic definitions. The semantics is discussed in Section 2.3.

2.2   Refinement

The semantics $[\![\Sigma \triangleright cds \bullet c : \textbf{program}]\!]$ of a complete program in the context of a signature Σ is the semantics $[\![\Gamma, \Sigma, \textbf{main} \triangleright c : \textbf{com}]\!]$ of its main command c, where Γ is the typing environment determined by the class declarations in *cds*. The command denotes a predicate transformer. We write $\sqsubseteq$ for the pointwise order on predicate transformers; this models algorithmic refinement.

We also write $\sqsubseteq$ for program refinement, a relation we define below. It is the basic notion of refinement on which we base our study of class refinement.

Definition 1 (Program Refinement). *For sequences of class declarations cds and cds', and commands c and c' with global variables Σ, we define*

$$(cds \bullet c) \sqsubseteq (cds' \bullet c')$$

if and only if

$$[\![\varnothing, \Sigma \triangleright (cds \bullet c) : \textbf{program}]\!] \sqsubseteq [\![\varnothing, \Sigma \triangleright (cds' \bullet c') : \textbf{program}]\!]$$

One way to refine a program is to refine its command part. In this paper, we are concerned with the other way: refining classes in *cds*.

Class refinement requires that any complete program that uses the original abstract class declaration is refined when it is replaced with the alternative concrete declaration. Program refinement, however, compares programs that act on the same state space: the same global variables. For this reason, this state space cannot contain values of the refined class.

To formalize this restriction we define *N-free types*. A variable of such a type cannot have as value or as component an object of N or of its subclasses. For a value, attribute, parameter, or local variable of a class type, we use the term *component* for its attributes, the attributes of its object-valued attributes, and so on. The components of a class are its attributes and their components.

Definition 2 (Class Refinement). *For a sequence of class declarations cds, and class declarations cda and cdc, that introduce a class called N, for instance, we define cds $\triangleright$ cda $\preccurlyeq$ cdc if and only if (a) cds cda and cds cdc are both well-formed; (b) for all commands c that use only methods in cds and cda and whose global variables have types that are N-free, if c is well-typed for cds cda, **main**, then c is well-typed for cds cdc, **main**; and (cds cda $\bullet$ c) $\sqsubseteq$ (cds cdc $\bullet$ c).*

```
class Stack
    prot elt : int; empty : bool
    pri others : seq int
    meth push ≙ (val e : int • others := ⟨elt⟩ ⌢ others; elt := e; empty := false)
    meth top ≙ (res e : int • e : [¬ empty, e = elt])
    meth sum ≙ (res s : int •
        if empty → s := 0
        [] ¬ empty → var x : int • self.top(x); s := x + (sums others) end
        fi)
end
```

Fig. 2. New definition for class *Stack*

The typing requirement ensures that the methods provided by *cdc* include those provided by *cda*, with the same signatures.

To see why the restriction to global variables that are *N*-free is necessary, consider *c* with a global variable of some class with an attribute of type *Stack*. The semantics of *c* in the context *cds cdc* is different from its semantics in context *cds cda*, so it does not make sense to compare them by algorithmic refinement ⊑. The restriction allows, however, that stacks appear in (components of) local variables of *c*, and also in parameters and local variables of methods called (directly or indirectly) by *c*. In Section 5 we discuss a less restrictive treatment.

For simple functional languages, it is easy to express that values of the refined class are used only internally: the class type does not appear in the program's type. For simple imperative languages, many sources consider a local variable [26] or a model thereof [15,11] for internalization. In practice, modules are used to encapsulate data structures and definitions of abstract data types that can be multiply instantiated. Our class construct is of this kind.

As an example, we present in Figure 2 a new definition for the class *Stack* presented in the previous section. It has the same protected attributes as before. Its private attribute *rest*, however, is replaced with a sequence of integers *others*. The methods *push* and *sum* are changed accordingly; we use a built-in function *sums* that calculates the sum of a sequence of integers. This new definition of *Stack* refines the previous one: a fact we can prove using our main results.

In this example, the declarations are equivalent: each refines the other. If, however, we change the definition of the method *top* in Figure 2 so that it does not abort when the stack is empty, then we have a proper refinement. In another example, we can have a bounded array implementation, whose *push* operation aborts if the array size is exceeded. It is properly refined by the implementations in both Figure 1 and 2, since their *push* methods do not abort.

2.3 Semantics

The semantics is based on states of methods. A state is a partial function that gives values to attributes of the current object, and to parameters and local variables; it also records the class of the current object in an extra attribute *myclass*. For example, a state of method *push* acting on an object of class *Stack* in Figure 1 has $\sigma\,myclass = Stack$, and also maps *elt*, *empty*, *rest*, *e*, and *t* to their values.

For each type T, we define the set $\mathcal{V}[\![\Gamma, T]\!]$ of values of type T. Like the semantic domains defined in the sequel, this one depends on an environment Γ which is needed in the case that T is a class name. For a class type N, the values $\mathcal{V}[\![\Gamma, N]\!]$ include the object values of that class: **null** and partial functions like states that, however, give only values to attributes of N or one of its subclasses. The values of the attributes are given in accordance with their types in Γ.

The set $\mathcal{S}[\![\Gamma, \Sigma, N]\!]$ contains all states for N and its subclasses, and for the signature Σ. For an empty signature we have $\mathcal{S}[\![\Gamma, \varnothing, N]\!] = \mathcal{V}[\![\Gamma, N]\!]\backslash\{\textbf{null}\}$. Similarly, if the signature contains only the visible attributes (*vattr Γ N*) of N, but no parameters or local variables, then $\mathcal{S}[\![\Gamma, (vattr\ \Gamma\ N), N]\!] = \mathcal{V}[\![\Gamma, N]\!] \backslash \{\textbf{null}\}$. The role of these attributes in the signatures is just to simplify typing rules.

A predicate on Γ, Σ, N is an element of $\mathbb{P}\,\mathcal{S}[\![\Gamma, \Sigma, N]\!]$. The set $\mathcal{T}[\![\Gamma, \Sigma, N]\!]$ of predicate transformers for Γ, Σ, N contains the total monotonic functions on such predicates.

For a parameter declaration *pds*, we define the set $\mathcal{PC}[\![\Gamma, \Sigma, N, pds]\!]$ of parameterized command meanings by induction on *pds*, following the approach of [2]. If *pds* is empty, this is $\mathcal{T}[\![\Gamma, \Sigma, N]\!]$. If *pds* has the form **val** $x\,:\,T$; *pds'*, then $\mathcal{PC}[\![\Gamma, \Sigma, N, pds]\!]$ is the set of functions from $\mathcal{V}[\![\Gamma, T]\!]$ to $\mathcal{PC}[\![\Gamma, \Sigma, N, pds']\!]$. Finally, if *pds* has the form **res** $x\,:\,T$; *pds'* or **vres** $x\,:\,T$; *pds'*, the meaning is the set of functions from names (result and value-result arguments) y to $\mathcal{PC}[\![\Gamma, (\Sigma \cup (y{:}T)), N, pds']\!]$. This is a dependent function space: applying a parameterized command to a result or value-result argument y yields a parameterized command meaning in a state space $\Sigma\cup(y{:}T)$ that includes y. We impose technical restrictions to ensure that, if y already occurs in Σ, then it has type T there, so the union yields a well-formed local context. In [8] we show that the semantics using this dependent function space is an accurate model for parameter passing, given mild restrictions on the use of names.

The function spaces above model a multi-parameter command as a curried function. Nonetheless, parameterized commands are always applied to all of their arguments, in the form of a list. As shown below, this mismatch is reconciled in the semantics of method calls using an auxiliary function *uncurry*.

Due to the presence of method calls, the semantics of commands depends on that of the methods in each class. The set $\mathcal{E}[\![\Gamma]\!]$ contains all the environments η that record, for each class N in Γ, meanings for all methods m inherited or declared by N. Thus $\eta\ N\ m$ is a parameterized command meaning in $\mathcal{PC}[\![\Gamma, \varnothing, N, pds]\!]$, where *pds* is the parameter declaration of m.

The semantics is defined by induction on typing rules; there is one rule for each syntactic construct. For η in $\mathcal{E}[\![\Gamma]\!]$, we define $[\![\Gamma, \Sigma, N \rhd c\,:\,\textbf{com}]\!]\eta$ to be an element of $\mathcal{T}[\![\Gamma, \Sigma, N]\!]$. Most definitions are adaptations of the standard ones for simple imperative programs [26]. The semantics of method calls is more interesting; we give that of **self**.$m(e)$.

Without loss of generality, we consider the signature $(vattr\ \Gamma\ N)$; Σ to distinguish the visible attributes $(vattr\ \Gamma\ N)$ of N from the local variables and parameters Σ. For any state σ in $\mathcal{S}[\![\Gamma, ((vattr\ \Gamma\ N); \Sigma), N]\!]$ and subset ψ of the same state space, we define

$$\sigma \in [\![\Gamma, ((vattr\ \Gamma\ N); \Sigma), N \triangleright \mathbf{self}.m(e) : \mathbf{com}]\!]\eta\ \psi \Leftrightarrow$$
$$\sigma \in lift\ vs\ pt\ (\psi \cap \mathcal{S}[\![\Gamma, \Sigma, N']\!])$$

where

$$N' = \sigma\ myclass, \quad pds = \Gamma.meth\ N'\ m$$
$$arglist = args\ \Gamma\ ((vattr\ \Gamma\ N); \Sigma)\ N\ pds\ e\ \sigma$$
$$pt = uncurry\ (\eta\ N'\ m)\ arglist, \quad rs = rvrargs\ pds\ e, \quad vs = rs \triangleleft \Sigma$$

The class N' is the dynamic class of **self**. The parameterized command meaning $(\eta\ N'\ m)$ is applied to the list of arguments $arglist$ to get an appropriate predicate transformer pt; $arglist$ is determined from e by the function $args$, that evaluates the arguments passed by value and keeps the variables passed by result or value-result. Application requires an iterated form of uncurrying, as explained above.

The predicate transformer pt is for a signature that contains the visible attributes of N' and the parameters. The function $lift$ extends it to the signature at the point of the call. Result and value-result arguments rs do not need to be considered because the application of the parameterized command meaning produces a predicate transformer for these variables. Therefore, we lift pt to vs, the signature obtained by removing rs from Σ. The symbol $\triangleleft$ denotes the domain subtraction operator. Finally, the intersection of ψ with $\mathcal{S}[\![\Gamma, \Sigma, N']\!]$ ensures that the lifted pt is applied in its domain: sets of states of the subclass N' of N.

The semantics thus defined is, of course, the basis for our main soundness result presented later on.

3   Forward Simulation

We formulate forward simulation for class declarations of the form defined below. Two class declarations, cda and cdc, which we call the abstract and concrete declarations, respectively, are involved. Both declare the same class Ns. The private attributes of cda include avs, and those of cdc include cvs. For any declaration vs, we write $\alpha(vs)$ for the set of variables declared.

Definition 3 (Compatible). *A sequence of class declarations cds, class declarations cda and cdc, a class name Ns, and variable declarations avs and cvs are compatible if: (1)cds cda and cds cdc are well-formed; (2) cda and cdc declare class Ns, with the same superclass; (3) $\alpha(avs) \cap \alpha(cvs) = \varnothing$; (4) the private attributes of cda include avs, and those of cdc include cvs; (5)cdc includes at least the same methods as cda, with the same parameters.*

In this section we consider compatible *cds*, *cda*, *cdc*, *Ns*, *avs*, and *cvs*. We also assume that Γ (resp. Γ') records the class declarations in *cds cda* (resp. *cds cdc*), and η (resp. η') the meanings of the methods in these classes. We denote by va_N and va'_N the signatures (*vattr Γ N*) and (*vattr Γ' N*), respectively, for any N. They contain the visible attributes of N according to Γ and Γ'.

A coupling invariant relates states of a pair of class declarations. As an example, let *cda* be the linked list implementation of stacks in Figure 1 and *cdc* the declaration that uses an array in Figure 2. For an object o in $[\![\Gamma, Stack]\!]$ and o' in $[\![\Gamma', Stack]\!]$, a suitable coupling is the following.

$$o.elt = o'.elt \wedge o.empty = o'.empty \wedge elems(o.rest) = o'.others$$

The function *elems* gives the sequence of elements in a stack. We define it as $elems(o) = (\textbf{if } o.empty \textbf{ then } \langle\rangle \textbf{ else } o.elt \frown elems(o.rest))$. In practice the coupling invariant is given by the programmer as a formula as above. For our purposes, we consider it as a mathematical relation on values.

The soundness theorem guarantees that class refinement follows from the fact that the simulation property, which we formalize later on, holds for the corresponding implementations of the methods of *Stack*. Informally, this means that, for each of these methods, related initial states lead to related final states. Refinement ensures that a client using only the methods of *Stack* can only be improved if we replace the first declaration of this class by the second.

In the proof of soundness, we need to compare the state spaces of the clients in the presence of *cda* and *cdc*. They are different for a client that has a component that is not *Ns*-free. To compare them, we need relations induced from the coupling invariant at all types. For a coupling invariant *ci*, the value coupling *vci T* is defined as follows. We write $N_1 \leq_\Gamma N_2$ when N_1 is a subclass of N_2 according to the typing environment Γ.

Definition 4 (Coupling of Values). *For a type T and a relation ci that is a subset of $\mathcal{S}[\![\Gamma, va_{Ns}, Ns]\!] \times \mathcal{S}[\![\Gamma', va'_{Ns}, Ns]\!]$, we define vci T as a subset of the cartesian product $(\mathcal{V}[\![\Gamma, T]\!] \cup \{\textbf{error}\}) \times (\mathcal{V}[\![\Gamma', T]\!] \cup \{\textbf{error}\})$, as follows.*

$vci\ T = \{(v,v) \mid v \in (\mathcal{V}[\![\Gamma, T]\!]\ \cup \{\textbf{error}\})\}$, *if T is primitive*

$vci\ N = \{(\textbf{error},\textbf{error}),(\textbf{null},\textbf{null})\} \cup (ci \cap \mathcal{S}[\![\Gamma, va_N, N]\!] \times \mathcal{S}[\![\Gamma', va'_N, N]\!])$, *if $N \leq_\Gamma Ns$*

$vci\ N = \{(\textbf{error},\textbf{error}),(\textbf{null},\textbf{null})\}\ \cup$
  $\{(\sigma,\sigma') \mid \sigma \in \mathcal{V}[\![\Gamma, N]\!] \setminus \{\textbf{null}\} \wedge \sigma' \in \mathcal{V}[\![\Gamma', N]\!] \setminus \{\textbf{null}\} \wedge$
    $\text{dom}\,\sigma = \text{dom}\,\sigma' \wedge \sigma\ myclass = \sigma'\,myclass \wedge$
      $\forall x : \text{dom}\,\sigma \setminus \{myclass\} \bullet (\sigma\ x, \sigma'\ x) \in vci\ T \text{ where } \Gamma.attr\ N\ x = T$
  $\}$, *if $\neg (N \leq_\Gamma Ns)$*

If T is primitive, *vci T* is the identity relation; if T is a subclass of *Ns*, then *vci T* is *ci* itself restricted to the appropriate state space, but also relates **error** and **null** to themselves; finally, if T is not a subclass of *Ns*, then *vci T* relates objects of the same class whose attributes are related, and **error** and **null** to themselves. In summary, related values are equal if they have a primitive type or do not have components of type *Ns*; these have to be related by *ci*.

Below, we formalize the notion of coupling invariant as a relation that satisfies a few healthiness conditions.

Definition 5 (Coupling Invariant). *A coupling invariant ci is a subset of $S[\![\Gamma, va_{Ns}, Ns]\!] \times S[\![\Gamma', va'_{Ns}, Ns]\!]$ for which the following healthiness conditions are satisfied: (H1) only states for the same class are related; (H2) the initial states of all classes are related; (H3) in related states, attributes other than avs and cvs are related by vci; (H4) if the coupling invariant relates two states, it relates all others that give the same value to the simulated attributes and give related values to the other ones; (H5) surjective; (H6) total.*

The formalization of the healthiness conditions is simple and can be found in [8]. Most of them are intuitive: H1 expresses that we are comparing different representations for the same class. The condition H2 is standard for simulations in any context. The conditions H3 and H4 are concerned with the attributes other than those being refined, and are needed for inductive arguments about recursive classes and subclasses. Firstly, H3 expresses that these attributes are related inductively. Secondly, H4 is a convexity condition expressing the sense in which the relation is independent from them.

The need for surjectivity and totality came as a surprise. Initial works on simulation imposed this sort of restriction on couplings invariants [16,19], but later developments have lifted them [15]. However, works on imperative programming do not include structured data like objects, and works on functional programming languages do not include specification constructs.

In practice, as illustrated in our example above, we expect the coupling invariant to be given as a relation just on states for Ns, not including states for its proper subclasses. For such a relation, an inductive definition similar to that for vci gives a coupling invariant that satisfies H1 to H6. We refrain from phrasing things that way because it is more complicated and we are focusing on foundations, not on development methods.

We are now in a position to define the relation induced for all state spaces from a coupling invariant. The relation $vci\ T$ associates values and ci associates states of the simulated class Ns and its subclasses. The relation $gci\ N\ vs$ defined below relates states for an arbitrary class N (and its subclasses) and the signature determined by the declaration vs of parameters and local variables. It is this relation that is used to compare states of the client classes.

Definition 6 (Generalized Coupling Invariant). *For a class N and parameters and local variables in scope vs, we define $gci\ N\ vs$ as a subset of $S[\![\Gamma, (va_N;\ vs), N]\!] \times S[\![\Gamma', (va'_N;\ vs), N]\!]$ as follows.*

$$(\sigma, \sigma') \in gci\ N\ vs \Leftrightarrow (\alpha(vs) \lhd \sigma, \alpha(vs) \lhd \sigma') \in ci \land$$
$$\forall x : \alpha(vs) \bullet (\sigma\ x, \sigma'\ x) \in vci\ T, \text{ with } \Gamma, (va_N;\ vs), N \rhd x : T$$
$$\text{if } N \leq_\Gamma Ns$$
$$(\sigma, \sigma') \in gci\ N\ vs \Leftrightarrow \text{dom}\,\sigma = \text{dom}\,\sigma' \land \sigma\ myclass = \sigma'\ myclass \land$$
$$\forall x : \text{dom}\,\sigma \setminus \{myclass\} \bullet (\sigma\ x, \sigma'\ x) \in vci\ T, \text{ with } \Gamma, (va_N;\ vs), N \rhd x : T$$
$$\text{if } \neg\,(N \leq_\Gamma Ns)$$

If N is a subclass of Ns, we cannot define $gci\ N\ vs$ to be ci because of the extra parameters and local variables vs. If we remove them, then we can require the resulting states to be related by ci. The values assigned to the variables of vs have to be related. Recall that $\lhd$ denotes domain subtraction. If N is not a subclass of Ns, the states have to be for the same class, and the values they assign to attributes, parameters, and local variables have to be related.

Simulation $ci, N, vs \rhd pt \preccurlyeq pt'$ of transformers pt and pt' holds, if and only if, for all ψ we have $gci\ N\ vs\ (\!|\ pt\ \psi\ |\!) \subseteq pt'(gci\ N\ vs\ (\!|\ \psi\ |\!))$. This is the usual definition [14] of simulation for predicate transformers, but uses $gci\ N\ vs$. Here $(\!|\ -\ |\!)$ denotes the direct image of a relation on a set.

Simulation $ci, N, vs \rhd f \preccurlyeq f'$ of parameterized command meanings f and f' uses a coupling for arguments: it relates value arguments when vci does, and relates result and value-result arguments to themselves. Simulation holds if, when applied to related arguments, f and f' yield related parameterized command meanings or transformers.

To structure the soundness proof of class simulation, we introduce the notion of environment simulation.

Definition 7 (Environment Simulation). *For environments $\eta \in \mathcal{E}[\![\Gamma]\!]$ and $\eta' \in \mathcal{E}[\![\Gamma']\!]$, we define $ci \rhd \eta \preccurlyeq \eta'$, if and only if, for all N and m we have $ci, N, \varnothing \rhd (\eta\ N\ m) \preccurlyeq (\eta'\ N\ m)$.*

In the definition of class simulation, we require that the meaning recorded in η for each method of cda and cdc is simulated by the meaning recorded in η'.

Definition 8 (Class Simulation). *We define $ci \rhd cda \preccurlyeq cdc$ if and only if for each method m of cda and cdc, we have that $ci, Ns, \varnothing \rhd (\eta\ Ns\ m) \preccurlyeq (\eta'\ Ns\ m)$.*

For each method, there are no parameters or local variables in scope.

Soundness establishes that if two class declarations are related by simulation as defined above, then they are also related by refinement (Definition 2).

4   Soundness

The proof of soundness relies on preservation and identity extension. We explain these in terms of the stack example. The coupling invariant presented previously is a simulation for the corresponding bodies of *push*, *top*, and *sum*. Preservation implies that it is also a simulation for calls to these methods, and for any command or parameterized command that acts on the stack using only these method calls: control constructs and parameterization preserve simulation. More specifically, the client programs preserve the induced coupling invariants.

The identity extension lemma says that the induced coupling invariants are the identity on state spaces that do not contain values of the simulated type. For identity coupling invariants, the simulation property reduces to algorithmic refinement.

To prove class refinement, we need to compare only programs that use the refined class internally. Their main command is a client whose state space does include objects of the refined class, and so algorithmic refinement follows. The details of this proof are presented in this section.

Preservation of simulations by parameterized commands depends on preservation by expressions, predicates, and commands. We give each result separately.

Expressions. The semantics of expressions is a function from states to values. For $\sigma \in S[\![\Gamma, \Sigma, N]\!]$, and derivable $\Gamma, \Sigma, N \rhd e : T$, we define $[\![\Gamma, \Sigma, N \rhd e : T]\!]\sigma$, the value of e in state σ. It is an element of $V[\![\Gamma, T]\!] \cup \{\mathbf{error}\}$. We assume that for every built-in function $f : T \to U$, a semantics is given. It should be a total function $V[\![\Gamma, T]\!] \to (V[\![\Gamma, U]\!] \cup \{\mathbf{error}\})$. The definition of $[\![\Gamma, \Sigma, N \rhd e : T]\!]\sigma$ is simple and can be found in [7,8].

Lemma 1 (Preservation by expressions). *For a class N different from Ns, parameters and local variables vs, an expression e of type T, and states σ and σ',*

$$(\sigma, \sigma') \in gci\ N\ vs \Rightarrow$$
$$([\![\Gamma, (va_N;\ vs), N \rhd e : T]\!]\sigma, [\![\Gamma', (va'_N;\ vs), N \rhd e : T]\!]\sigma') \in vci\ T$$

Proof By induction on the structure of e. We present a few cases; the others can be found in [8].

Case **new** N'. We have that $[\![\Gamma, (va_N;\ vs), N \rhd \mathbf{new}\ N' : N']\!]\sigma = init\ \Gamma\ N'$, the initial state of N'. If N' is a subclass of Ns, by the healthiness condition H2, $(init\ \Gamma\ N', init\ \Gamma'\ N') \in ci$. If N' is not a subclass of Ns, we observe that $init\ \Gamma\ N' = init\ \Gamma'\ N'$ because the atributes of N' are the same in Γ and Γ'. We have that $init\ \Gamma\ N'$ and $init\ \Gamma\ N'$ are elements of $V[\![\Gamma, N']\!]$ and $V[\![\Gamma', N']\!]$, respectively, have the same domain, and associate *myclass* to N'. Moreover, for each attribute x of N', if its type is primitive, then $init\ \Gamma\ N'\ x = init\ \Gamma'\ N'\ x$. If the type of x is a class N'', then $init\ \Gamma\ N'\ x = init\ \Gamma'\ N'\ x = \mathbf{null}$.

Case $f(e)$. By the induction hypothesis, we have that $[\![\Gamma, (va_N;\ vs), N \rhd e : T]\!]\sigma$ and $[\![\Gamma', (va'_N;\ vs), N \rhd e : T]\!]\sigma'$ are related by $vci\ T$. Since, by assumption, T is a primitive type, these values are actually equal. Therefore, the result of the application of the semantics of f to them is the same. Since we also assume that the type of this result is primitive, they are also related.

Case e **is** N''. By the induction hypothesis, $[\![\Gamma, (va_N;\ vs), N \rhd e : N']\!]\sigma$ and $[\![\Gamma', (va'_N;\ vs), N \rhd e : N']\!]\sigma'$ are related by $vci\ N'$. So these values may be both **error**, both **null**, or both different from **error** and **null**. In the first two cases, the values are equal and related because they are primitive (booleans). In the third case, we have to consider whether the type N' of e is a subclass of Ns or not. If it is, then $[\![\Gamma, (va_N;\ vs), N \rhd e : N']\!]\sigma$ and $[\![\Gamma', (va'_N;\ vs), N \rhd e : N']\!]\sigma'$ are related by ci and the healthiness condition H1 guarantees that they have the same value at *myclass*. If it is not, then the definition of $vci\ N'$ guarantees the same property. As a consequence, $[\![\Gamma, (va_N;\ vs), N \rhd e\ \mathbf{is}\ N' : \mathbf{bool}]\!]\sigma$ and $[\![\Gamma', (va'_N;\ vs), N \rhd e\ \mathbf{is}\ N' : \mathbf{bool}]\!]\sigma'$ are equal and so related by $vci\ \mathbf{bool}$.

Similar reasoning applies to the cases $(N'')e$, $e.x$, and $(e;\ x:e')$. For $e.x$ we rely on H3, and for $(e;\ x:e')$, on H4. $\square$

To extend the language to include built-in functions on class types, we have to impose a parametricity condition on their semantics for the above lemma to hold. For example, the lemma would not hold for a built-in exact equality test of object values. An object might be simulated by two different objects; in this case, equality holds for two copies of the object, but not for the related objects.

Predicate. The semantics $[\![\Gamma,\Sigma,N \triangleright \psi : \mathbf{pred}]\!]$ of a formula is a subset of the state space $\mathcal{S}[\![\Gamma,\Sigma,N]\!]$. Its definition is standard and can be found in [7,8].

Lemma 2 (Preservation by predicates). *For a class N different from Ns, parameters and local variables vs, a predicate formula φ, and states σ and σ',*

$$(\sigma,\sigma') \in gci\ N\ vs \Rightarrow$$
$$\sigma \in [\![\Gamma,(va_N;\ vs),N \triangleright \varphi : \mathbf{pred}]\!] \Leftrightarrow \sigma' \in [\![\Gamma',(va'_N;\ vs),N \triangleright \varphi : \mathbf{pred}]\!]$$

Proof By induction on φ. Most cases are a simple consequence of the definitions and the induction hypothesis. For boolean expressions we rely on the previous lemma. For universal quantification, we need surjectivity and totality of ci, from which we have surjectivity and totality for vci. The details are in [8]. $\square$

Commands. The semantics of commands depends on the environment. Preservation of simulation for commands, therefore, depends on the corresponding environments being related by simulation as well. This is a hypothesis for the following lemma. In the proof of soundness, we use the fact that class simulation implies environment simulation.

Lemma 3 (Preservation by commands). *If $ci \triangleright \eta \preccurlyeq \eta'$, then for a class N different from Ns, parameters and local variables vs, and a command c,*

$$ci,N,vs \triangleright [\![\Gamma,(va_N;\ vs),N \triangleright c : \mathbf{com}]\!]\eta \preccurlyeq [\![\Gamma',(va'_N;\ vs),N \triangleright c : \mathbf{com}]\!]\eta'$$

Proof By induction on the structure of c. In most cases we use the definition of simulation at the level of states and predicates, giving the argument for an arbitrary $\sigma' \in \mathcal{S}[\![\Gamma',(va'_N;\ vs),N]\!]$ and predicate $\psi \in \mathbb{P}\mathcal{S}[\![\Gamma,(va_N;\ vs),N]\!]$. We present below just a few interesting cases. In this proof and in others that follow, we omit the typing of commands and parameterized commands, and the environment η for the sake of conciseness.

Case $x:[\varphi_1,\varphi_2]$. For this we need surjectivity of ci, and due to the use of Lemma 2, totality as well. The operator $\oplus$ is function overriding.

$$\sigma' \in gci\ N\ vs\ (\!|\ [\![\Gamma,(va_N;\ vs),N \triangleright x:[\varphi_1,\varphi_2]]\!]\psi\ |\!)$$
$$\Leftrightarrow \exists \sigma \bullet (\sigma,\sigma') \in gci\ N\ vs \wedge \quad \text{[property of relational image and semantics]}$$
$$\sigma \in [\![\Gamma,(va_N;\ vs),N \triangleright \varphi_1]\!] \wedge \forall v:\mathcal{V}[\![\Gamma,T]\!] \bullet$$
$$\sigma \oplus \{x \mapsto v\} \in [\![\Gamma,(va_N;\ vs),N \triangleright \varphi_2]\!] \Rightarrow \sigma \oplus \{x \mapsto v\} \in \psi$$

$$\Leftrightarrow \sigma' \in [\![\Gamma', (va'_N;\ vs), N \triangleright \varphi_1]\!] \wedge \qquad \text{[Lemma 2 and predicate calculus]}$$
$$\exists \sigma \bullet (\sigma, \sigma') \in gci\ N\ vs \wedge \forall v : \mathcal{V}[\![\Gamma, T]\!] \bullet$$
$$\sigma \oplus \{x \mapsto v\} \in [\![\Gamma, (va_N;\ vs), N \triangleright \varphi_2]\!] \Rightarrow \sigma \oplus \{x \mapsto v\} \in \psi$$

$$\Rightarrow \sigma' \in [\![\Gamma', (va'_N;\ vs), N \triangleright \varphi_1]\!] \wedge \qquad \text{[property of } gci \text{ and predicate calculus]}$$
$$\forall v : \mathcal{V}[\![\Gamma, T]\!];\ v' : \mathcal{V}[\![\Gamma', T]\!] \bullet \exists \sigma \bullet (v, v') \in vci\ T \Rightarrow$$
$$(\sigma \oplus \{x \mapsto v\}, \sigma' \oplus \{x \mapsto v'\}) \in gci\ N\ vs \wedge$$
$$(\sigma \oplus \{x \mapsto v\} \in [\![\Gamma, (va_N;\ vs), N \triangleright \varphi_2]\!] \Rightarrow \sigma \oplus \{x \mapsto v\} \in \psi)$$

$$\Leftrightarrow \sigma' \in [\![\Gamma', (va'_N;\ vs), N \triangleright \varphi_1]\!] \wedge \qquad \text{[Lemma 2 and predicate calculus]}$$
$$\forall v : \mathcal{V}[\![\Gamma, T]\!];\ v' : \mathcal{V}[\![\Gamma', T]\!] \bullet \exists \sigma \bullet (v, v') \in vci\ T \Rightarrow$$
$$(\sigma \oplus \{x \mapsto v\}, \sigma' \oplus \{x \mapsto v'\}) \in gci\ N\ vs \wedge$$
$$(\sigma' \oplus \{x \mapsto v'\} \in [\![\Gamma', (va'_N;\ vs), N \triangleright \varphi_2]\!] \Rightarrow \sigma \oplus \{x \mapsto v\} \in \psi)$$

$$\Rightarrow \sigma' \in [\![\Gamma', (va'_N;\ vs), N \triangleright \varphi_1]\!] \wedge$$
$$\forall v' : \mathcal{V}[\![\Gamma', T]\!] \bullet \exists v : \mathcal{V}[\![\Gamma, T]\!] \bullet (v, v') \in vci\ T \wedge$$
$$((v, v') \in vci\ T \Rightarrow \exists \sigma \bullet$$
$$(\sigma, \sigma' \oplus \{x \mapsto v'\}) \in gci\ N\ vs \wedge$$
$$(\sigma' \oplus \{x \mapsto v'\} \in [\![\Gamma', (va'_N;\ vs), N \triangleright \varphi_2]\!] \Rightarrow \sigma \in \psi)$$
$$\text{[surjectivity of } vci \text{ and predicate calculus]}$$

$$\Rightarrow \sigma' \in [\![\Gamma', (va'_N;\ vs), N \triangleright \varphi_1]\!] \wedge \qquad \text{[predicate calculus]}$$
$$\forall v' : \mathcal{V}[\![\Gamma', T]\!] \bullet \sigma' \oplus \{x \mapsto v'\} \in [\![\Gamma', (va'_N;\ vs), N \triangleright \varphi_2]\!] \Rightarrow$$
$$\exists \sigma \bullet \sigma \in \psi \wedge (\sigma, \sigma' \oplus \{x \mapsto v'\}) \in gci\ N\ vs$$

$$\Rightarrow \sigma' \in [\![\Gamma', (va'_N;\ vs), N \triangleright x : [\varphi_1, \varphi_2]]\!]\ (gci\ N\ vs\ (\!|\ \psi\ |\!))$$
$$\text{[property of relational image and semantics]}$$

Case **self**.$m(e)$.

$$\sigma' \in gci\ N\ vs\ (\!|\ [\![\Gamma, (va_N;\ vs), N \triangleright \textbf{self}.m(e)]\!]\psi\ |\!)$$
$$\Leftrightarrow \exists \sigma \bullet (\sigma, \sigma') \in gci\ N\ vs \wedge \sigma \in lift\ vs_1\ pt\ (\psi \cap [\![\Gamma, vs, N_1]\!])$$
$$\text{[property of relational image and semantics]}$$

In this step we are using the following definitions inside the scope of σ, and also their dashed counterparts for semantics for Γ', η', and σ'.

$$N_1 = \sigma\ myclass, \quad pds = \Gamma.meth\ N_1\ m,$$
$$pt = uncurry(\eta\ N_1\ m)\ arglist, \quad arglist = args\ \Gamma\ (va_N;\ vs)\ N\ pds\ e\ \sigma,$$
$$rs = rvrargs\ pds\ e, \quad vs_1 = rs \triangleleft vs$$

Below, we list a number of facts about these definitions.

1. $N_1 = \sigma'\ myclass = N'_1$, by $(\sigma, \sigma') \in gci\ N\ vs$, the definition of gci, and H1.

2. Since the methods in cda and cdc have the same parameters, $pds = pds'$.
3. $arglist$ is pointwise related to $arglist'$, by induction on lists, Lemma 1, and the definition of coupling for arguments.
4. By Fact 2, above, $rs = rs'$ and $vs_1 = vs_1'$.
5. By hypothesis, $ci \vartriangleright \eta \preccurlyeq \eta'$, so by definition of environment simulation, $ci, N_1, \varnothing \vartriangleright (\eta\ N_1\ m) \preccurlyeq (\eta'\ N_1\ m)$. Therefore, by Facts 1, 3 and the definition of simulation of parameterized command meanings, $ci, N_1, \varnothing \vartriangleright pt \preccurlyeq pt'$.

We proceed as follows. The operator $\lfloor$ restricts the state space of a predicate. For a predicate ψ on $\Gamma, (\Sigma;\ x\ :\ T), N$, the predicate $\psi \lfloor x$ on Γ, Σ, N is defined as $\sigma \in \psi \lfloor x \Leftrightarrow \exists v : [\![T]\!]_\Gamma \bullet \sigma \oplus \{x \mapsto v\} \in \psi$. The substitution in $\psi[\sigma\ (\mathrm{dom}\ vs_1) /\!\!/ \mathrm{dom}\ vs_1]$ is a multiple substitution on ψ in which the value of each variable x in $\mathrm{dom}\ vs_1$ is replaced with the value $\sigma\ x$.

$$\exists \sigma \bullet (\sigma, \sigma') \in gci\ N\ vs \wedge \sigma \in lift\ vs_1\ pt\ (\psi \cap [\![\Gamma, vs, N_1]\!])$$

$\Leftrightarrow \exists \sigma \bullet (\sigma, \sigma') \in gci\ N\ vs \wedge$ \hfill [definition of $lift$]
$$(\mathrm{dom}\ vs_1) \vartriangleleft \sigma \in pt((\psi \cap [\![\Gamma, vs, N_1]\!])[\sigma\ (\mathrm{dom}\ vs_1) /\!\!/ \mathrm{dom}\ vs_1] \lfloor (\mathrm{dom}\ vs_1))$$

$\Rightarrow \exists \sigma \bullet (\sigma, \sigma') \in gci\ N\ vs \wedge (\mathrm{dom}\ vs_1) \vartriangleleft \sigma' \in pt'(gci\ N\ ((\mathrm{dom}\ vs_1) \vartriangleleft vs)$
$$(\!(\psi \cap [\![\Gamma, vs, N_1]\!])[\sigma\ (\mathrm{dom}\ vs_1) /\!\!/ \mathrm{dom}\ vs_1] \lfloor (\mathrm{dom}\ vs_1)\ )\!)) \hfill \text{[Fact 5]}$$

$\Rightarrow (\mathrm{dom}\ vs_1) \vartriangleleft \sigma' \in$ \hfill [properties of gci and Fact 1]
$$pt'(((gci\ N\ vs\ (\!(\psi)\!)) \cap [\![\Gamma', vs, N_1']\!])[\sigma\ (\mathrm{dom}\ vs_1) /\!\!/ \mathrm{dom}\ vs_1]) \lfloor \mathrm{dom}\ vs_1)$$

$\Leftrightarrow (\mathrm{dom}\ vs_1') \vartriangleleft \sigma' \in$ \hfill [Fact 4]
$$pt'(((gci\ N\ vs\ (\!(\psi)\!)) \cap [\![\Gamma', vs, N_1]\!])[\sigma\ (\mathrm{dom}\ vs_1') /\!\!/ \mathrm{dom}\ vs_1']) \lfloor \mathrm{dom}\ vs_1')$$

$\Leftrightarrow \sigma' \in [\![\Gamma', (va_N';\ vs), N \vartriangleright \mathbf{self}.m(e)]\!]\ (gci\ N\ vs\ (\!(\psi)\!))$
\hfill [definition of $lift$ and semantics]

$\square$

As pointed out before, preservation of simulation by environments is necessary for the application of the lemma above. This is the result stated below.

Lemma 4 (Preservation by environments). *If $ci \vartriangleright cda \preccurlyeq cdc$ then*

$$ci \vartriangleright \eta \preccurlyeq \eta'$$

This is based on Lemma 3, and also the facts that fixpoints and parameterization preserve simulation. We refrain from formally stating those results. They are standard and can be found in [8].

The second main result we need in the proof of our main theorem is the identity extension lemma below.

Lemma 5 (Identity extension). *For a class N that is not a subclass of Ns, parameters and local variables vs, if all attributes of N and all variables declared in vs are Ns-free, then $gci\ N\ vs$ is the identity relation.*

Proof By definition, if σ and σ' are related by $gci\ N\ vs$, then they have the same domain and value at *myclass*. Moreover, the values v and v' associated to a variable x in σ and σ' are related by *vci* T, where T is the type of x in $\Gamma, (va_N; vs), N$.

By induction on the structure of T, we prove that *vci* T is the identity. If T is a primitive type, this is direct from the definition. The type T of x cannot possibly be *Ns* or any of its subclasses as the hypothesis guarantees that there are no local variables of such a type. Finally, if T is a class N', it is not a subclass of *Ns*, then by definition of *vci* T we have three possibilities: v and v' are both **error**, both **null**, or they are object values with the same domain and value at *myclass*. Also, the values associated to an attribute y in the domain of v (and v') are related by *vci* T', where T' is the type of y in $\Gamma, (va_N; vs), N$. By the induction hypothesis, *vci* T' is the identity. $\square$

This is a relatively simple consequence of the definitions.

Finally, we can present our soundness theorem.

Theorem 1 (Soundness). *If $ci \triangleright cda \preccurlyeq cdc$, then $cds \triangleright cda \preccurlyeq cdc$.*

Proof Well-formedness of $cds\ cda$ and $cds\ cdc$ follows from compatibility. We prove that, for all commands c that use only methods of cds and cda, with no global variables whose type is not *Ns*-free, and well-typed for $cds\ cda$, **main**, (1) c is well-typed for $cds\ cdc$, **main**; and (2) $(cds\ cda \bullet c) \sqsubseteq (cds\ cdc \bullet c)$.

We have (1) because cdc has at least the methods of cda. For (2), from $ci \triangleright cda \preccurlyeq cdc$, we have $ci \triangleright \eta \preccurlyeq \eta'$, by Lemma 4. Therefore, by Lemma 3, we have

$$ci, \textbf{main}, vs \triangleright [\![\Gamma, vs, \textbf{main} \triangleright c : \textbf{com}]\!]\eta \preccurlyeq [\![\Gamma', vs, \textbf{main} \triangleright c : \textbf{com}]\!]\eta'$$

where vs records the global variables of c. This means, by definition,

$$gci\ \textbf{main}\ vs\ (\!|\ [\![\Gamma, vs, \textbf{main} \triangleright c]\!]\eta\ \psi\ |\!) \subseteq [\![\Gamma', vs, \textbf{main} \triangleright c]\!]\eta'\ (gci\ \textbf{main}\ vs\ (\!|\ \psi\ |\!))$$

Since vs does not include variables whose type is not *Ns*-free, by Lemma 5, we have that $gci\ \textbf{main}\ vs$ is the identity, and hence

$$[\![\Gamma, vs, \textbf{main} \triangleright c]\!]\eta\ \psi \subseteq [\![\Gamma', \textbf{main}, vs \triangleright c]\!]\eta'\ \psi.$$

Therefore, by the semantics of programs, we have that

$$[\![\varnothing, vs \triangleright (cds\ cda \bullet c) : \textbf{program}]\!]\ \psi \subseteq [\![\varnothing, vs \triangleright (cds\ cdc \bullet c) : \textbf{program}]\!]\ \psi$$

as required for (2). $\square$

The argument for this proof is relatively simple. The main difficulty is in the proof of Lemma 3, in the presence of method calls and dynamic binding.

The need for the generalized coupling invariant also posed a few difficulties. We could not find a straightforward way of expressing this invariant as a formula. From a practical point of view, however, this is not a problem. Using our technique, the programmer needs to define only the coupling invariant and prove that the alternative class declarations are related by simulation. The generalized coupling invariant is used in our proof of soundness, but it is not used in the application of the simulation technique.

5 Conclusion

Our main results are preservation, identity extension, and soundness of forward simulation for a Java-like language including recursive classes, type casts and tests, mutable state, class-oriented visibility control, and specification constructs. Previous work on simulation for object-oriented languages has treated simpler languages; e.g., one of the most advanced works [33] has instance-oriented visibility and has no type casts or specification constructs. As for major features of Java that we do not treat, we know of no work dealing with concurrency together with features like classes and dynamic dispatch, nor any on reflection.

Our result can potentially be extended for behavioral subclassing. Such results are known only for more restricted languages than that considered here. This is a topic for future work. For now, we remark only that our result is an implication: class refinement follows from simulation of methods of the refined class. To prove simulation for those methods, preservation rules need to be used together with ordinary verification rules (see, e.g., [26,27]) and some form of behavioral subclassing is probably needed for the latter rules to be tractable [1, 12,31].

Our notion of class refinement does not allow the refined type to occur in global variables; it is based on the standard notion of algorithmic refinement. We believe it is possible to adapt our proofs to a definition that uses a notion of refinement that builds in the hiding of private attributes, in which case no restriction to N-free types is needed for them. We have found this adaptation to be advantageous in our ongoing work on behavioral subclassing.

Our most questionable omission is pointers. Building on the insights gained in the present work, and on recent progress in reasoning about pointers [34,18], Banerjee and Naumann recently obtained results similar to ours for a Java-like language with pointers [4]. That work uses a state-transformer model and does not treat specification constructs. It uses simulation for program equivalence rather than refinement. We believe the present semantics can be extended to encompass pointers, but that is left as future work.

It was surprisingly difficult to find workable formalizations for typing, semantics, and simulation, and the result exhibits ideas drawn from a number of independent lines of research on simulation. Two surprising healthiness conditions, totality and surjectivity, came to light. They seem to be a consequence of the fact that, even though private attributes of an object are not directly accessible from the clients, semantically they are available for manipulation by the methods. It may be possible to drop these restrictions if we restrict our attention only to the values that can be obtained by initializing an object and calling its methods.

Surjectivity and totality are needed only for specification constructs. In particular, our proof of Lemma 3 uses surjectivity for the case of local variables, but that is because we treat the block construct from refinement calculi [26] that makes an unboundedly nondeterministic choice of initial values. Surjectivity is not needed for initialized local variables, which are the norm in Java-like languages (and are also used in [29]).

With the aim of providing a foundation for specification disciplines intended to ensure behavioral subclassing, we avoided the requirement that classes have specifications or that they exhibit behavioral subclassing. If such requirements are imposed, alternative healthiness conditions are possible; this is the subject of future work as well.

References

1. Martín Abadi and K. Rustan M. Leino. A logic of object-oriented programs. In *Proceedings, TAPSOFT 1997.* Springer-Verlag, 1997. Expanded in DEC SRC report 161.
2. R. J. R. Back. Procedural Abstraction in the Refinement Calculus. Technical report, Department of Computer Science, Åbo - Finland, 1987. Ser. A No. 55.
3. R. J. R. Back and J. Wright. *Refinement Calculus: A Systematic Introduction.* Graduate Texts in Computer Science. Springer-Verlag, 1998.
4. Anindya Banerjee and David Naumann. Representation independence, confinement and access control. In *POPL2002*, pages 166 – 177, 2001.
5. Martin Büchi and Wolfgang Weck. The greybox approach: When blackbox specifications hide too much. Technical Report 297, Turku Center for Computer Science, August 1999. http://www.abo.fi/~mbuechi/publications/TR297.html.
6. A. L. C. Cavalcanti and D. Naumann. A Weakest Precondition Semantics for an Object-oriented Language of Refinement. In J. M. Wing, J. C. P. Woodcock, and J. Davies, editors, *FM'99: World Congress on Formal Methods*, volume 1709 of *Lecture Notes in Computer Science*, pages 1439 – 1459. Springer-Verlag, September 1999.
7. A. L. C. Cavalcanti and D. A. Naumann. A Weakest Precondition Semantics for Refinement of Object-oriented Programs. *IEEE Transactions on Software Engineering*, 26(8):713 – 728, August 2000.
8. A. L. C. Cavalcanti and D. A. Naumann. Forward Simulation for Data Refinement of Classes - Extended Version. Technical Report 2001-4, Computer Science, Stevens Institute of Technology, 2001.
   http://www.cs.stevens-tech.edu/~naumann/tr2001-4.ps.
9. A. L. C. Cavalcanti and David A. Naumann. On a specification-oriented model for object-orientation. In *Proceedings of the VI Brazilian Symposium on Programming Languares*, 2002. To appear.
10. A. L. C. Cavalcanti, A. C. A. Sampaio, and J. C. P. Woodcock. Procedures and Recursion in the Refinement Calculus. *Journal of the Brazilian Computer Society*, 5(1):1 – 15, 1998.
11. Willem-Paul de Roever and Kai Engelhardt. *Data Refinement: Model-Oriented Proof Methods and their Comparison.* Cambridge University Press, 1998.
12. David L. Detlefs, K. Rustan M. Leino, Greg Nelson, and James B. Saxe. Extended static checking. Technical Report Report 159, Compaq Systems Research Center, December 1998.
13. Martin Fowler. *Refactoring: Improving the Design of Existing Code.* Addison-Wesley, 1999.
14. P. H. B. Gardiner and C. C. Morgan. Data Refinement of Predicate Transformers. *Theoretical Computer Science*, 87:143 – 162, 1991.
15. J. He, C. A. R. Hoare, and J. W. Sanders. Prespecification in Data Refinement. *Information Processing Letters*, 25(1), 1987.

16. C. A. R. Hoare. Proof of Correctness of Data Representations. *Acta Informatica*, 1:271 – 281, 1972.
17. C. A. R. Hoare, J. He, and A. Sampaio. Normal form approach to compiler design. *Acta Informatica*, 30:701–739, 1993.
18. Samin Ishtiaq and Peter W. O'Hearn. BI as an assertion language for mutable data structures. In *POPL*. ACM Press, 2001.
19. C. B. Jones. *Software Development: A Rigorous Approach*. Prentice-Hall, 1980.
20. G. T. Leavens and W. E. Weihl. Specification and verification of object-oriented programas using supertype abstraction. *Acta Informatica*, 32, 1995.
21. Gary T. Leavens, K. Rustan M. Leino, Erik Poll, Clyde Ruby, and Bart Jacobs. JML: notations and tools supporting detailed design in Java. In *OOPSLA 2000 Companion, Minneapolis, Minnesota*, pages 105–106. ACM, October 2000.
22. Gary T. Leavens and Don Pigozzi. A complete algebraic characterization of behavioral subtyping. *Acta Informatica*, 36:617–663, 2000.
23. K.R.M Leino, A. Poetzsch-Heffter, and Y. Zhou. Using data groups to specify and check side effects. In *Programming Language Design and Implementation 2002*, 2002. To appear.
24. B. H. Liskov and J. M. Wing. A Behavioural Notion of Subtyping. *ACM Transactions on Programming Languages and Systems*, 16(6), 1994.
25. Nancy Lynch and Frits Vaandrager. Forward and backward simulations part I: Untimed systems. *Information and Computation*, 121(2), 1995.
26. C. C. Morgan. *Programming from Specifications*. Prentice-Hall, 2nd edition, 1994.
27. C. C. Morgan and P. H. B. Gardiner. Data Refinement by Calculation. *Acta Informatica*, 27(6):481 – 503, 1990.
28. P. Müller. *Modular Specification and Verification of Object-Oriented Programs*. PhD thesis, FernUniversität Hagen, 2001. Available from www.informatik.fernuni-hagen.de/pi5/publications.html.
29. David A. Naumann. Soundness of data refinement for a higher order imperative language. *Theoretical Computer Science*, 278(1–2):271–301, 2002.
30. Gordon Plotkin. Lambda definability and logical relations. Technical Report SAI-RM-4, University of Edinburgh, School of Artificial Intelligence, 1973.
31. A. Poetzsch-Heffter and P. Müller. A programming logic for sequential Java. In S. D. Swierstra, editor, *Programming Languages and Systems (ESOP '99)*, volume 1576 of *Lecture Notes in Computer Science*, pages 162–176. Springer-Verlag, 1999.
32. John Power and Edmund Robinson. Logical relations and data abstraction. In *Computer Science Logic*, 2000.
33. U. S. Reddy. Objects and classes in Algol-like languages. In *Fifth Intern. Workshop on Foundations of Object-oriented Languages*, Jan 1998. Full version to appear in Information and Computation.
34. John C. Reynolds. Intuitionistic reasoning about shared mutable data structure. In *Millenial Perspectives in Computer Science*. Palgrave, 2001.
35. Clemens Szyperski. *Component Software: Beyond Object-Oriented Programming*. ACM Press Books. Addison-Wesley, 1999.
36. R. D. Tennent. Correctness of data representations in Algol-like languages. In A. W. Roscoe, editor, *A Classical Mind: Essays Dedicated to C. A. R. Hoare*. Prentice-Hall, 1994.

A Formal Basis for a Program Compilation Proof Tool

Luke Wildman

Software Verification Research Centre,
The University of Queensland, Australia

Abstract. This paper presents a case study in verified program compilation from high-level language programs to assembler code using the Cogito formal development system. A form of window-inference based on the Z schema is used to perform the compilation. Data-refinement is used to change the representation of integer variables to assembler word locations.

1 Introduction

As a solution to the problem of verified compilation, several [1,2,3] propose that rather than attempt to verify the correctness of a compiler directly, a verified compilation strategy be produced for deriving object code from a high-level program. In this paper, a compilation strategy is described in the Cogito formal development method [4]. The high-level language program is described in the broad spectrum modelling language Sum [5] which includes a Z like high-level requirements specification language and an intermediate programming language (IL) [6]. The object code is a form of assembler (interpreted by some abstract machine and with symbolic addressing) and is described as an extension of the Sum IL. A stack-machine model similar to that adopted by Microsoft's .NET CIL [7] language is assumed.

A compilation strategy is presented as a 'data refinement' [8,9] from the high-level programming language to the assembler code and its associated environment of instruction pointer, evaluation stack, local store, etc. Data refinement of Sum modules has been presented previously [6]. However that work focused on the data refinement of abstract specifications to concrete specifications rather than from programs to assembler as developed here.

Previously [1,3] a compilation strategy has been presented as an algorithm refinement in a predicate-transformer model [10]. This previous work is extended in this paper by situating it in a Z-like predicative programming model [9,11] and by adding the transformation from high-level to low level data representations. A form of window-inference based on the Z schema is introduced here. This will form the theoretical basis of an automatic tool for producing verified assembler code using the Ergo theorem prover[12].

L.-H. Eriksson and P. Lindsay (Eds.): FME 2002, LNCS 2391, pp. 491–510, 2002.

The following section introduces the case study and explains the Sum specification notation and IL semantics. The target assembler code is then presented before proceeding with the data refinement from IL program to assembler code. This is followed by further discussion and comparison to related work.

2   Program to Be Compiled

As a motivational example we consider a simple program to calculate the remainder of integer division by repeated subtraction [1]. The programmer's task is to implement the following Sum specification.

$$
\begin{array}{|l}
\hline \text{\_\_} remainder\_spec \text{_____} \\
\quad\begin{array}{|l} \hline \text{\_\_} state \text{_____} \\ \quad p, q, r : int \\ \hline \end{array} \\[4pt]
\quad init == [true] \\[4pt]
\quad\begin{array}{|l} \hline \text{\_\_} op\ rem \text{_____} \\ \quad \mathrm{pre}(p \geq_c 0_c \wedge q >_c 0_c) \wedge \\ \quad p =_c \lfloor p/_c q \rfloor_c *_c q +_c r' \wedge \\ \quad changes\_only\{r\} \\ \hline \end{array} \\
\hline
\end{array}
$$

The Sum module *remainder_spec* is comprised of a state, an initialisation *init*, and a single operation *rem*. The state, initialisation, and operation are described by schemas (like Z). The initialisation operation *init* is trivial and will be elided in the sequel. The state machine interpretation of Z schemas is codified in Sum by making the state global to all operations without the explicit $\Delta State$ notation.

The state is comprised of p the dividend, q the divisor, and r the remainder, and the operation *rem* calculates r. The subscripts ($\_c$) denote computational versions of the given theoretical operators/constants and are explained further in Section 2.1. The *changes_only* predicate states that the operation only changes the value of state variable r. In the context of the module *remainder_spec* it may be expanded to $p' = p \wedge q' = q$. As usual, primed variables denote final values and unprimed variables denote initial values.

To achieve the task, the programmer develops a high-level language program implementing the specification - this is the starting point for our verified compilation. It is expressed in the Sum intermediate language (IL).

$$
\begin{array}{|l}
\hline \text{\_\_} remainder \text{_____} \\
\quad\begin{array}{|l} \hline \text{\_\_} state \text{_____} \\ \quad p, q, r : int \\ \hline \end{array} \\[4pt]
\quad\begin{array}{|l} \hline \text{\_\_} op\ rem \text{_____} \\ \quad \mathrm{pre}(p \geq_c 0_c \wedge q >_c 0_c) \wedge \\ \quad (r := p \ ;; \ \mathbf{while}\ r \geq_c q\ \mathbf{do}\ r := r -_c q\ \mathbf{od}) \\ \hline \end{array} \\
\hline
\end{array}
$$

2.1   Computational Types

The type of the variables used above is the computational (finite) type *int* representable by a machine. Computational integers are used in order to justify the change of representation to assembler words later on. Computational integers are defined as the subset of the integers between two machine dependent constants *minint* and *maxint*.

$$int == \{z : \mathbb{Z} \mid minint \leq z \leq maxint\}$$

All operators op_c used in the *rem* operation are computational operators rather than Sum's general operators for $\mathbb{Z}$ and $\mathbb{N}$ types. Computational operators are defined so that results are guaranteed to be defined only when the results are in range. For example, $-_c$ is a computational subtraction operator specified in terms of mathematical subtraction as follows.

$$-_c : int \times int \nrightarrow int$$

$$\forall x, y : int \bullet (minint \leq x - y \wedge x - y \leq maxint) \Rightarrow x -_c y = x - y$$

Note that the result of the computational subtraction is defined when the theoretical difference is within bounds. Other computational arithmetic (and boolean) operators may be characterised similarly. Note that the constant 0_c is the *int* representation of zero.

2.2   Intermediate Language

A notable feature of the *rem* operation is that the IL program is embedded into the schema "below the line", i.e., in the predicate part. This key syntactic feature of the Sum broad spectrum language distinguishes it from other approaches for refinement in Z [9,13,14].

The IL constructs include an explicit precondition (pre(_)), (multiple) assignment (_ := _), sequential composition (_ ;; _), iteration (**while** _ **do** _ **od**), and conditional (**ifc** _ **then** _ **else** _ **fi**).

An operation is *feasible* if the explicit precondition $pre(P)$ implies the calculated precondition (*cpre*) of the Body. The calculated precondition is defined in Sum using existential schema quantification.

$$cpre(Body) == \exists State' \bullet Body \setminus outputs$$

This expression characterises the collection of *before* states and inputs for which some *after* state can be shown to exist. The explicit precondition is intended to be used as a simplified version of the calculated precondition. The notation pre(P) simply reminds us that P only constrains the initial state.

The expansion of the initial assignment $r := p$ is $r' = p \wedge changes\_only\{r\}$. Sequential composition is defined as a demonic relational composition [11].

$$A \;;; B == (A \, {}^\circ_\circ B) \wedge_z (A \rhd cpre(B))$$

Here $(A \, ; B)$ is ordinary relational composition for Z:

$$A \, ; B == \exists \, State'' \bullet A[State''/State'] \wedge B[State''/State]$$

and $(A \, \triangleright \, cpre(B))$ means that every final state of A satisfies the calculated precondition of B given that:

$$A \triangleright B == \forall \, State' \bullet A \Rightarrow B'$$

Demonic composition eliminates magical behaviour. That is, the undefined behaviour of the program A applied outside its precondition can not be corrected by the subsequent program B.

The while loop in our example is expanded as a fixed point as follows.

$$\mu X \bullet \textbf{ifc } r \geq_c q \textbf{ then } (r := r -_c q) \,;; \, X \textbf{ else } skip \textbf{ fi}$$

Sum's conditional operator **ifc** is strict.

$$\textbf{ifc } G \textbf{ then } S \textbf{ else } T \textbf{ fi} == (G \wedge S) \vee (notc(G) \wedge T)$$

If the test G is undefined $notc(G)$ will be undefined and the overall effect undefined. This is reflected in the definition of $notc$.

$$notc(x) = if(x =?, ?, not(x))$$

The value '?' is the undefined value which is used in a similar way to Functional Logic [15]. The undefined value provides a means for reasoning about partial functions however it does not extend the logic; the logic is two-valued.

3   Target Assembler Code

The compilation involves a data refinement to an assembler program running on an abstract stack machine similar to that used by the .NET assembler language CIL [7]. The data in the abstract stack machine is described by the Sum module *assembler* with a state containing an instruction pointer ip, next instruction address $next$, local variables $local$, an evaluation stack $stack$, and stack pointer sp. The positions of instructions are represented by symbolic addresses ($Addr$). $Block$ represents the addresses allocated to the program. Several constant addresses $a \ldots f$ are declared for use as labels for instructions. The types of the compiled data are words ($Word$). The type ($\text{seq}_0 \, Word$) denotes finite sequences of words numbered $0..n$. It is assumed that the stack pointer sp is representable by a single word. All operations on the stack pointer are word-ops.

The assembler module also contains the compiled operation rem and several other schemas giving the definitions of the several .NET assembler instructions used in rem. The precondition of rem asserts that $p \geq 0$ and $q > 0$ and that the location of the first instruction executed is labelled a. This final conjunct captures the notion that the assembler is only a refinement of the abstract rem program if it is entered at the first instruction.

The unoptimised assembler code works as follows. In the initialisation at addresses $a \ldots b$, the dividend p at local storage location 2 is loaded onto the stack and then stored into local storage location 0 representing the remainder r. Control then branches to the loop test at locations $e \ldots e + 2$. In the test, q and r are loaded from local storage locations 1 and 0 and placed on the stack. If r is greater than q then control branches to the body of the loop at addresses $c \ldots d$, otherwise it exits and the result is r at local storage location 0. In the loop body q and r are loaded from local storage locations 1 and 0 and placed on the stack. The subtraction operation replaces the operands with the result $r - q$ which is then stored into local storage location 0 representing the remainder r.

__ $assembler[Block : \mathbb{P}\ Addr]$ _____

$a \ldots f : Block$

> __ $state$ _____
>
> $ip, next : Addr;$
> $sp : Word;$
> $local, stack : \text{seq}_0\ Word$
>
> ---
> $sp \geq_w 0_w \land ip \in Block$

> __ $op\ rem$ _____
>
> $\text{pre}(local(2) \geq_w 0_w \land local(1) >_w 0_w \land ip =_a a) \land$
> $a \qquad : \textbf{ldloc.2}\ \downarrow_{a+1}$
> $a + 1 : \textbf{stloc.0}\ \downarrow_b$
> $b \qquad : (\textbf{br.s}\ [e/l?])\ \downarrow_e$
> $c \qquad : \textbf{ldloc.1}\ \downarrow_{c+1}$
> $c + 1 : \textbf{ldloc.0}\ \downarrow_{c+2}$
> $c + 2 : \textbf{sub}\ \downarrow_d$
> $d \qquad : \textbf{stloc.0}\ \downarrow_e$
> $e \qquad : \textbf{ldloc.1}\ \downarrow_{e+1}$
> $e + 1 : \textbf{ldloc.0}\ \downarrow_{e+2}$
> $e + 2 : (\textbf{bge.s}\ [c/l?])\ \downarrow_f$

> __ $\textbf{ldloc.n}$ _____
>
> $sp, stack(sp +_w 1), ip := sp +_w 1, local(n), next$

> __ $\textbf{stloc.n}$ _____
>
> $\text{pre}(sp >_w 0_w) \land$
> $sp, local(n), ip := sp -_w 1, stack(sp), next$

> __ $\textbf{sub}$ _____
>
> $\text{pre}(sp >_w 1_w) \land$
> $sp, stack(sp -_w 1_w), ip :=$
> $\qquad sp -_w 1, stack(sp) -_w stack(sp -_w 1_w), next$

---

br.s _____

$l? : Addr$

$\text{pre}(l? \in Block) \wedge ip := l?$

---

bge.s _____

$l? : Addr$

$\text{pre}(l? \in Block \wedge sp >_w 2) \wedge$
ifc $(stack(sp) \geq_w stack(sp -_w 1_w))$ **then** $sp, ip := sp -_w 2, l?$
else $sp, ip := sp -_w 2, next$ **fi**

The body of the compiled *rem* operation consists of a sequence of assembler instructions. The assembler notation used is explained below. The .NET assembler instructions are defined using Sum IL schemas operating on the assembler-level data variables. The schema **ldloc.n** describes the four .NET "load local" instructions operating on the local stack at positions **n** = 1 through 4. Each **ldloc.n** instruction pushes a value $local(n)$ onto the stack. Similarly for **stloc.n** except that it pops the value off the stack. The **sub** operation replaces the two topmost stack values by their difference.

The two branch instruction **br.s** and **bge.s** take a parameter $l?$ for the target of the jump. The target must be a valid address (within the allocated block). Note that the expansion for (concrete) array assignment $stack(sp) := local(n)$ is defined using function overriding as follows.

$$stack' = stack \oplus \{sp \mapsto local(n)\} \wedge changes\_only\{stack\}$$

In multiple assignments any expression evaluations on the left and right side of the assignment are performed in the unprimed state.

3.1   Assembler Model

To model assembler code sequences, statements can be prefixed by a label consisting of the set of instruction addresses at which the compiled code will reside, and suffixed by a single label denoting the address of the following instruction. A vertically displayed list of labelled statements is then interpreted as a virtual machine that selects statements under the control of the instruction pointer [1, 3].

$$
\begin{aligned}
a \ldots b : S_1 \downarrow_c \;&== \; \textbf{do} \; ip \in a \ldots b \rightarrow next := c \;;; \; S_1 \\
c \ldots d : S_2 \downarrow_e \;&\quad\;\; \square \; ip \in c \ldots d \rightarrow next := e \;;; \; S_2 \\
&\quad\;\; \textbf{od}
\end{aligned}
$$

This differs from Lermer and Fidge's approach [16] in that an initial assignment to the variable *next* is used to control the exit of the statement, rather than a coercion as used in their description based on predicate transformers. This modification is needed due to the limited expressiveness of the relational model for programs. Note that if the statement S is a jump or branch instruction, it is free to assign a different next address to ip.

The semantics of the do-loop is defined using recursion as follows.

do $G_1 \rightarrow S_1 \square \ldots G_i \rightarrow S_i$ **od**

$==$

$\mu X \bullet (\text{pre}(G1) \wedge S_1 ;; X) \vee \ldots \vee (\text{pre}(G_i) \wedge S_i ;; X) \vee$
$(\text{pre}(notc(G1) \vee \ldots \vee notc(G_i)) \wedge skip)$

Several laws are given for introducing, merging, and collapsing nested loops by Lermer and Fidge [17]. Similar laws will be introduced as necessary in the following compilation.

To satisfy the strategy of program compilation adopted here, the statement labels must satisfy two important properties: they must be ordered and there must be a way to insert new labelled instructions between existing labelled instructions as statements are decomposed into their equivalent assembler. Several approaches to this problem exist, including hierarchical numbering systems [17] and initial use of unknown constants followed by a second pass [18]. We intend to use the latter in our implementation.

4   Data Refinement in Cogito

Data refinement in Cogito occurs via a data refinement module which maps the abstract module to the concrete module. For our example, the mapping is as follows.

```
┌─ remainderAC[Block : ℙ Addr] ──────────────────────────
│  import remainder as A;
│  import assembler[Block] as C;
│  visible A, C;
│  ┌──────────────────────────────
│  │ wc : word ⤚→ int
│  ├──────────────────────────────
│  │ ∀ w1, w2 : Word •
│  │     wc(w1) −c wc(w2) = w1 −w w2 ∧
│  │     wc(w1) ≥c wc(w2) ⟺ w1 ≥w w2
│  └──────────────────────────────
│  remₐ == ∃ C.state • A.rem
│
│  rem_C == ∃ A.state • C.rem
│
│  remₐ_ipa == [C.state; remₐ | pre(C.ip = C.a)]
│  ┌─ ACreln ──────────────────
│  │ A.state; C.state
│  ├──────────────────────────────
│  │ p = wc(local(2)) ∧ q = wc(local(1)) ∧ r = wc(local(0))
│  └──────────────────────────────
└──────────────────────────────────────────────────────
```

Both the abstract and concrete modules are imported and made visible, effectively including the contents of both modules. The bijection wc maps word representations to integers. It must deal with both simulation over a variety of arithmetic operators, and conversion between words and integers. Large integers may require multi-word representations. We have assumed a uniform word-size for integers to simplify the discussion. This puts a bound on the computational integers $maxint$ and $minint$.

The schema $ACreln$ defines the relationship between concrete and abstract states. It is equivalent to the information contained in a compiler's symbol table.

4.1   Generalisation

The operations rem_A and rem_C are the *generalisations* [19] of the corresponding operations from the abstract and concrete modules respectively. Generalisation raises the operations to the combined state $A.state \wedge C.state$. Generalisation is required because the operations are defined with a *closed-world* view of variables other than those explicitly changed. That is, use of $changes\_only\{r\}$ insists that all other variables in scope are unchanged by the operation. When the operation is imported into the expanded context, the scope expands also. Generalisation allows a closed-world view to be changed to an *open-world* view, that is, nothing is said about the new variables in the context extension. The effect of the generalisation of $A.rem$ is to convert all occurrences of $changes\_only\{r\}$ to open-world version $changes\_only(\{r\}, A.state)$ which limits the view to variables occurring in the original context.

4.2   Extended Abstract Context

The operation rem_{A_ipa} extends rem_A with the precondition that the instruction pointer is at location a. This context extension captures the idea that we only refine the abstract program when it is invoked with $ip = a$, this being the label of the address of the first assembler instruction. However, this context extension is not a refinement. It is actually a *realisation* step [20].

Alternatively, others [16] assign $ip := a$ as the first step of the assembled procedure. However, this does not accurately reflect the idea that a procedure call is implemented as a jump to the starting address of the procedure.

4.3   Data Refinement Laws

In Sum (and Z), the data refinement above requires the proof of the following three postulates: Applicability, Correctness, and Initialisation [6].

A: $cpre(rem_{A\_ipa}) \wedge ACreln \Rightarrow cpre(rem_C)$
C: $cpre(rem_{A\_ipa}) \wedge ACreln \wedge rem_C \Rightarrow (\exists\, A.state' \bullet rem_{A\_ipa} \wedge ACreln')$
I: $C.init \Rightarrow (\exists\, A.state' \bullet init_A \wedge ACreln')$

In the case that the retrieve relation *ACReln* is *Functional* (which it is), the proof obligations may be simplified to:

F: $\exists! A.state \bullet ACReln$
A: $cpre(rem_A\_ipa) \wedge ACReln \Rightarrow cpre(rem_C)$
C: $cpre(rem_A\_ipa) \wedge ACReln \wedge rem_C \wedge ACReln' \Rightarrow rem_A\_ipa$
I: $init_C \wedge ACReln' \Rightarrow init_A$

In our situation of refining programs to assembler, the proof obligations for applicability *App* and initialisation *Init* are easily discharged, but the correctness *Cor* obligation is prohibitively difficult because it involves an unfolding of the meaning of the high-level language program and the compiled assembler.

For this reason, we do not attempt to perform the data refinement in this way. Instead, we proceed by calculating the assembler program by applying refinement rules and delaying the data refinement step until it can be applied to simple statements. This can be achieved because the least refined specification [8] of the compiled assembler can be defined as follows.

$$rem_C\_sp == \exists A.state; \; A.state' \bullet ACReln \wedge rem_A\_ipa \wedge ACReln'$$

The definition of rem_C_sp may be verified by substituting it for rem_C in the above proof obligations. The compilation proceeds by showing that $rem_C\_sp \sqsubseteq rem_C$. It is possible at this stage to perform a substitution of abstracted concrete variables for abstract variables thereby removing *ACReln* and *ACReln'*. However, this approach requires the use of the concrete variables throughout the compilation where we prefer to use the abstract variables where possible.

The refinement and inference step are presented in a window inference [21] style. However, before proceeding with the compilation, we introduce a form of window inference based on schemas.

5   Sum Window Inference

Window inference [22] is a form of hierarchical reasoning supporting transformations. Program window inference [21] extends window inference with support for the sort of declarations found in programs and calculates preconditions at each point of the program, thus allowing transformation of sub-programs based on local information. It provides a formal basis for tool support for refinement and allows program refinement and proof to be carried out in the same framework.

In general, a focus V may be transformed to U, preserving relation e, if a transformation rule $P \Rightarrow V \; e \; U$ can be found where premise P may be discharged in the current context. In Sum window inference the schema signature and explicit precondition record the available contextual information about variable declarations and preconditions. That is, in Sum window inference, the window is the schema.

Refinement of predicate P to predicate Q with respect to a specific signature *Sig* is defined by the following inference rule.

$$\frac{[Sig \mid (cpre(P) \Rightarrow_z (cpre(Q) \wedge (Q \Rightarrow_z P)))]}{[Sig \mid P \sqsubseteq Q]} \quad [\, defref \,]$$

That is, refinement on schemas having the same signature is defined by refinement on the predicates. Here, we use the schema $[Sig \mid P]$ as a *window* on the state of the proof of $[Sig \mid P \sqsubseteq Q]$ were Q is the as yet unknown goal of the refinement, predicate P is the focus, and '$\sqsubseteq$' is the window relation.

The definition of rem_C_sp above must be restated as a schema in order to get it into a form suitable for Sum window inference.

$$W1 = [sig(\Delta C) \mid \exists[\Delta A \mid ACreln \wedge rem_A\_ipa \wedge ACreln']]$$

The following abbreviations are used for the combined pre and post states for the remainder of this paper.

$\Delta A == A.state; \ A.state'$
$\Delta C == C.state; \ C.state'$
$\Delta AC == C.state; \ C.state'; \ A.state; \ A.state'$

The schema numbered $W1$ represents our starting window. Numbered schemas will be used for subsequent windows (proof states) as the compilation develops. Sum window inference is based on two types of rules. *Opening rules* describe how to change the contexts Sig' and C' (signature and precondition for IL programs) and relation e' of the sub-schema (window) in order to preserve the correctness of the relation e of the parent schema.

$$\frac{[Sig' \mid C' \wedge V \ e' \ U]}{[Sig \mid C[V] \ e \ C[U]]} \quad [\, open\_X\_N \,]$$

Following a transformation $V \ e' U$ in the sub-schema, the sub-schema is *closed* and the result of the transformation U replaces the *focus* V, in the parent schema. Opening rules are systematically named with X referring to the structure of C and N referring to the place of V within C.

For example, the opening rule for focusing on the body P of an existential quantifier $\exists[x : T \mid P]$ and transforming P to Q via relation '$\Leftrightarrow$' is as follows.

$$\frac{[Sig; \ x : T \mid P \Leftrightarrow Q]}{[Sig \mid \exists[x : T \mid P] \Leftrightarrow \exists[x : T \mid Q]]} \quad [\, open\_exi\_2 \,]$$

where x is not free in Sig. Applying this rule to schema $W1$ and simplifying gives the new schema $W2$ representing the new goal P to be refined to Q in the extended context.

$$W2 = [sig(\Delta AC) \mid ACreln \wedge rem_A\_ipa \wedge ACreln']$$

Note that the relation ($\Leftrightarrow$) does not match the window relation ($\sqsubseteq$), however, because it is stronger, it may be used as a replacement.

Transformation rules transform a focus directly. Transformation rules have the form

$$\frac{[Sig \mid P]}{[Sig \mid V \ e \ U]} \quad [\, X \,]$$

where V must match the current focus and e matches the window relation. For instance the combined rule for associativity of pre-conditions and post-conditions follows.

$$\frac{}{[Sig \mid (\text{pre}(A) \wedge (S \,;; \ T) \wedge A') = (\text{pre}(A) \wedge S \,;; \ T \wedge A')]} \quad [\, asprepos \,]$$

After expanding the body of rem_A_ipa, this rule can be applied to get the following schema.

W3
$sig(\Delta AC)$

$(pre(ACreln \wedge p \geq_c 0 \wedge q >_c 0 \wedge ip =_a a) \wedge r := p) \,;;$
$(\textbf{while } r \geq_c q \ \textbf{do } r \ := \ r -_c q \ \textbf{od} \wedge ACreln')$

Note that as $ACreln$ only involves unprimed variables it is included in the precondition.

5.1   Programs

Several opening rules and refinement rules (transformation rules preserving the refinement relation) are defined here for hierarchical refinement of programs. The opening rule for the first component of a sequential composition is

$$\frac{[Sig \mid \text{pre}(P) \wedge S \sqsubseteq U]}{[Sig \mid (\text{pre}(P) \wedge S \,;; \ T) \sqsubseteq (\text{pre}(P) \wedge U \,;; \ T)]} \quad [\, open\_sem\_1 \,]$$

This rule relies on the monotonicity of $(\_ \,;; \ \_)$ with respect to refinement in the first parameter. Note that the precondition information of the entire composition may be used to transform the first part of the composition. A refinement rule for maintaining an invariant follows.

$$\frac{[Sig \mid (\text{pre}(A) \wedge cpre(S)) \Rightarrow cpre(S \wedge A')]}{[Sig \mid (\text{pre}(A) \wedge S) \sqsubseteq (\text{pre}(A) \wedge S \wedge A')]} \quad [\, maintinv \,]$$

Opening on the first component of the composition in schema W3 above and applying the refinement rule gives the following schema.

W4
$sig(\Delta AC)$

$\text{pre}(ACreln \wedge p \geq_c 0 \wedge q >_c 0 \wedge ip =_a a) \wedge r := p \wedge ACreln'$

However the proof obligation must be discharged.

Proof. The proof-obligation states a requirement to show the following.

$$\forall\, Sig \bullet ACreln \wedge cpre(r := p) \Rightarrow cpre(r := p \wedge ACreln')$$

The calculated precondition for an assignment is *true*. As $ACreln'$ is independent of $r := p$, the proof follows from the following simplification.

$$cpre(r := p \wedge ACreln') = cpre(r := p) \wedge cpre(ACreln')$$

♡

Closing the schema replaces the original component with the transformed component. The distribution of $ACreln$ is completed by the application of the following rule for inserting a precondition into a sequential composition.

$$\frac{[Sig \mid (S \rhd pre(P))]}{[Sig \mid S\,;;\ T = S\,;;\ (pre(P) \wedge T)]} \quad [\,inspre\,]$$

Proof. The proof-obligation follows immediately from its expansion in terms of the focus.

$$\forall[A.State';\ C.state' \mid pre(ACreln) \wedge r := p \wedge ACreln'] \bullet ACreln'$$

♡

Alternatively, the related opening rule for opening the second component of a sequential composition could have been used and the second component transformed directly. The opening rule for the second component of a sequential composition follows.

$$\frac{[Sig \mid (pre(sp(S, P)) \wedge T) \sqsubseteq U]}{[Sig \mid (pre(P) \wedge S\,;;\ T) \sqsubseteq (pre(P) \wedge S\,;;\ U)]} \quad [\,open\_sem\_2\,]$$

Predicate $sp(S, P)$ is the strongest post-condition [23] of statement S from precondition P. Let $initial(State)$ be the signature made up from the unprimed variables in Sig. Substituting the strongest-postcondition for $pre(P)$ satisfies the proof-obligation of the rule $[inspre]$.

$$sp(S, P) == pre(undash(\exists[initial(State) \mid pre(P) \wedge S]))$$

6   Verified Compilation

The compilation of the remainder program begins with the steps already described above which result in the following.

```
┌─ W5 ─────────────────────────────────────────────────
│  sig(ΔAC)
│  ─────────────────────────────────────────────────────
│  pre(ACreln ∧ p ≥_c 0 ∧ q >_c 0 ∧ ip =_a a) ∧
│  (ACreln ∧ r := p ∧ ACreln') ;;
│  (ACreln ∧ while r ≥ q do r := r − q od ∧ ACreln')
└───────────────────────────────────────────────────────
```

The next step is to introduce statement labelling. The refinement rule to introduce labels has one antecedent that establishes the entry and termination of the labelled statement. Variable names i, j, and k are reserved for use as meta-variables in rule definitions in the sequel.

$$\frac{[Sig \mid \text{pre}(P \Rightarrow ip \in i \ldots j - 1 \wedge i < j - 1 < j)]}{[Sig \mid \text{pre}(P) \wedge S \sqsubseteq_{Sig} \text{pre}(P) \wedge i \ldots j - 1 : S \downarrow_j]} \quad [\; labintro \;]$$

Proof obligation $\text{pre}(ip \in i \ldots j - 1)$ justifies the use of labels $i \ldots j - 1$ for the assembled instructions of S. Label i is intended for use as the entry point of S.

Termination of the labelled statement $i \ldots j - 1 : S \downarrow_j$ relies on the termination of S and the assignment to ip of address j outside of $i \ldots j - 1$, that is, $j > i \wedge j - 1 < j$. Constraints such as this are accumulated throughout the compilation and are used at its completion to determine a valid set of addresses to use for the symbolic labels. When applying [labintro] the proof obligation is satisfied by $ip = a$. Addresses a to $f - 1$ are set aside for compilation of the procedure. The "magically" well-ordered choice of names for the symbolic addresses in the following compilation reflects the expectation of a subsequent parse to instantiate symbolic addresses according to the introduced constraints and thus discharging the proof obligation.

W6

$sig(\Delta AC)$

$\text{pre}(ACreln \wedge p \geq_c 0 \wedge q >_c 0 \wedge ip =_a a) \wedge$
$a \ldots f - 1 : ((ACreln \wedge r := p \wedge ACreln') \;;;$
$\qquad\qquad (ACreln \wedge \textbf{while } r \geq q \textbf{ do } r := r - q \textbf{ od} \wedge ACreln')) \downarrow_f$

The next step is to split the labelled statement into two sections. The law *Compile Sequence* [1] for splitting the labels follows.

$$\frac{[sig \mid \text{pre}(P \Rightarrow ip \in i \ldots j - 1 \wedge i < j - 1 < j < k - 1 < k)]}{\begin{array}{l}[Sig \mid \text{pre}(P) \wedge i \ldots k - 1 : (S \;;; \; T) \downarrow_k \\ \quad \sqsubseteq_{Sig} \\ \quad \text{pre}(P) \wedge i \ldots j - 1 : S \downarrow_j \\ \qquad\quad j \ldots k - 1 : T \downarrow_k]\end{array}} \quad [\; cseq \;]$$

The obligation $ip \in i \ldots j - 1$ ensures that the statement S is executed before T, thus preserving the semantics of $S \;;; \; T$. Applying the splitting rule to the focus results in the following schema. The new labels are comprised of $a \ldots b - 1$ for the initial assignment to r, and $b \ldots f - 1$ for the while loop.

W7

$sig(\Delta AC)$

$\text{pre}(ACreln \wedge p \geq_c 0 \wedge q >_c 0 \wedge ip =_a a) \wedge$
$a \ldots b - 1 : (ACreln \wedge r := p \wedge ACreln') \downarrow_b$
$b \ldots f - 1 : (ACreln \wedge \textbf{while } r \geq_c q \textbf{ do } r := r -_c q \textbf{ od} \wedge ACreln') \downarrow_f$

6.1   Compiling the Loop

First of all we focus on the loop. The following rule for opening a window on a labelled statement does not assume anything about any other surrounding statements as it assumes that a labelled statement may be the target of a jump from anywhere.

$$\frac{[Sig \mid (\mathrm{pre}(ip = j) \wedge T) \sqsubseteq U]}{[Sig \mid i \ldots j-1 : S \downarrow_j \;\; \sqsubseteq \;\; i \ldots j-1 : S \downarrow_j}{j \ldots k-1 : T \downarrow_k \quad\quad j \ldots k-1 : U \downarrow_k]} \quad [\; open\_lab\_2 \;]$$

The new precondition context $\mathrm{pre}(ip = j)$ allows us to assume that execution starts at the beginning of T when refining it to U.

Applying this opening rule gives the following schema.

__ W8 _____

$sig(\Delta AC)$

$\mathrm{pre}(ip = b) \wedge$
$ACreln \wedge \textbf{while } r \geq_c q \textbf{ do } r := r -_c q \textbf{ od} \wedge ACreln'$

Here we assume that a label allows the possibility of jumping directly to a statement without executing the previous statement. However, the compilation of goto-less programs does not allow arbitrary jumps. Therefore we may as well have used a stronger rule which required that S was executed before T. This would be useful if the post-condition of the previous statement was required (as would be the case if code optimisation were being performed). However, we do not require this contextual information as we are doing a simple compilation.

Before the body of the loop can be compiled, $ACreln$ must be distributed into the body of the loop. Unfolding the fix-point definition of the loop produces

$$[sig(\Delta AC) \mid \mathrm{pre}(ACreln) \wedge$$
$$\mu X \bullet \textbf{if } r \geq_c q \textbf{ then } (r := r -_c q \;;; \; X) \textbf{ fi} \wedge ACreln']$$

and the following rule allows us to transform the expanded loop.

$$\frac{}{[Sig \mid (\mathrm{pre}(A) \wedge \textbf{ifc } C \textbf{ then } P \textbf{ fi}) =}{(\textbf{ifc } \mathrm{pre}(A) \wedge C \textbf{ then } \mathrm{pre}(A) \wedge P \textbf{ fi})]} \quad [\; preif \;]$$

Rules [$maintinv$] and [$inspre$] allow us to complete the distribution of $ACreln$ via the following transformation.

$$(\mathrm{pre}(ACreln) \wedge r := r -_c q) \;;; \; X$$
$$\sqsubseteq$$
$$(\mathrm{pre}(ACreln) \wedge r := r -_c q \wedge ACreln') \;;;$$
$$\mathrm{pre}(ACreln) \wedge X$$

Reintroducing a labelling with rule [$labintro$] produces the following schema.

```
┌─ W9 ──────────────────────────────────────────
│ sig(ΔAC)
├───────────────────────────────────────────────
│ pre(ip = b) ∧
│ b...f − 1 : (while ACreln ∧ (r ≥_c q) do
│                  ACreln ∧ r := r −_c q ∧ ACreln'od) ↓_f
└───────────────────────────────────────────────
```

The data refinement is completed on the guard to produce the new guard $local(0) \geq_w local(1)$. The following law *Compile iteration* [1] is then applied.

$$\frac{[Sig \mid \mathrm{pre}(P \Rightarrow ip = i \wedge i < i + 1 < j - 1 < j < k - 1 < k)]}{\begin{array}{l}[Sig \mid \\ \mathrm{pre}(P) \wedge i \ldots k - 1 : \textbf{while } B \textbf{ do } S \textbf{ od } \downarrow_k \\ \sqsubseteq \\ \mathrm{pre}(P) \wedge i : \textbf{br.s}[j/l?] \downarrow_j \\ \qquad i + 1 \ldots j - 1 : S \downarrow_j \\ \qquad j \ldots k - 1 : \textbf{evalbr}[i +_w 1, B/l?, b?]) \downarrow_k] \end{array}} \quad [\, citer \,]$$

The pseudo-assembler instruction $\textbf{evalbr}[i +_w 1, B/l?, b?]$ evaluates the expression B and if the result is $true_w$ jumps to address $i +_w 1$. It place the result of evaluating the high-level language expression B on the top of the evaluation stack. (However, it allows the stack to be used for evaluation of B). Domain restriction $(\_ \lhd \_)$ is used to extract the prefix the stack.

```
┌─ evalbr ───────────────────────────────────────
│ l? : Addr
│ b? : Word
├───────────────────────────────────────────────
│ pre(l? ∈ Block) ∧
│ sp' = sp ∧
│ (1 .. sp) ◁ stack' = (1 .. sp) ◁ stack ∧
│ ifc b? =_w true_w then ip' = l? else ip' = next fi ∧
│ changes_only{sp, stack, ip}
└───────────────────────────────────────────────
```

Applying rule [citer] to schema $W12$ results in the following schema.

```
┌─ W10 ──────────────────────────────────────────
│ sig(ΔAC)
├───────────────────────────────────────────────
│ pre(ip = b) ∧
│ b : br.s[e/l?] ↓_e
│ c...d : (ACreln ∧ r := r −_c q ∧ ACreln') ↓_e
│ e...f − 1 : (evalbr[c, local(0) ≥_w local(1)/l?, b?]) ↓_f
└───────────────────────────────────────────────
```

Label b is set aside for initial jump to the loop test and labels $e .. f − 1$ are set aside for the loop test itself. This leaves $c .. d$ for the loop body.

6.2   Compiling the Loop Body

We compile the body of the loop after using an opening rule similar to $[open\_lab\_2]$.

$$\begin{array}{|l} \hline \_W11_____ \\ sig(\Delta AC) \\ \hline \mathrm{pre}(ip =_a c) \wedge \\ c \ldots d : (ACreln \wedge r := r -_c q \wedge ACreln') \downarrow_e \\ \hline \end{array}$$

Focusing on the body of this labelled statement, the data refinement can now be completed. We assume that the integers r and q are representable by single words, that is, the size of a local register, in order to complete this data refinement. The following schema DR shows the transformation we wish to perform.

$$\begin{array}{|l} \hline \_DR_____ \\ sig(\Delta AC) \\ \hline \mathrm{pre}(ip = c) \\ (ACreln \wedge r := r -_c q \wedge ACreln') \sqsubseteq \\ \quad local(0) := local(0) -_w local(1) \\ \hline \end{array}$$

The refinement holds by virtue of the refinement definition $[defref]$.

Proof. Unfolding $ACreln$ and the assignment and further simplification via substitution and the definition of wc gives the following simplified predicate for the specification (left side of the refinement).

$$local'(0) = local(0) -_w local(1) \wedge local'(2) = local(2) \wedge local'(1) = local(1)$$

The desired implementation is an array assignment with semantics as follows.

$$local' = local \oplus \{0 \mapsto (local(0) -_w local(1))\}$$

The desired array assignment is stronger than the specification (left side). Because the calculated preconditions of both assignments is the predicate $true$, the implementation satisfies the definition of refinement rule $[defref]$.$\heartsuit$

The assignment to $local$ will now be compiled into assembler. Law *Compile Assignment* [1] is applied for the special case of $local(0)$.

$$\frac{[Sig \mid \mathrm{pre}(P \Rightarrow ip = i \wedge i < j - 1 < j < k)]}{\begin{array}{l} [Sig \mid \mathrm{pre}(P) \wedge i \ldots j : (local(0) := E) \downarrow_k \\ \quad \sqsubseteq \\ \quad\quad \mathrm{pre}(P) \wedge i \ldots j - 1 : (\mathbf{eval}\ [E/e?]) \downarrow_j \\ \quad\quad\quad j : \mathbf{stloc.0}\ \downarrow_k] \end{array}} \ [\,cass\,]$$

That is, an expression evaluation followed by a store to $local(0)$. The effect of the pseudo-assembler instruction **eval**$[E/e?]$ is modelled by the following schema.

```
  eval
 e? : Word

 sp' = sp +_w 1 ∧
 (1 .. (sp +_w 1)) ◁ stack' = ((1 .. sp) ◁ stack) ⌢ ⟨e?⟩ ∧
 ip' = next ∧
 changes_only{sp, stack, ip}
```

After closing the result of the data refinement of the assignment, application of rule [*cass*] to the transformed schema $W11$ results in the following schema.

```
  W12
 sig(ΔAC)

 pre(ACreln ∧ r ≥_c q ∧ ip =_a c) ∧
 c ... d − 1 : (eval [(local(0) −_w local(1))/e?]) ↓_d
 d : stloc.0 ↓_e
```

The **eval** pseudo instruction is compiled into a stack based operation using law *compile subtraction*. The assumption about the size of local registers justifies the use of the single word subtraction.

$$\frac{[Sig \mid \mathrm{pre}(P \Rightarrow ip = i \wedge i < j − 1 \wedge i < i + 1 < i + 2 < j)]}{\begin{array}{l} [Sig \mid \\ \mathrm{pre}(P) \wedge i \ldots j − 1 : (\textbf{eval}\ [(local(0) −_w local(1))/e?]) \downarrow_j \\ \sqsubseteq \\ \mathrm{pre}(P) \wedge\ i : (\textbf{ldloc.1})\ \downarrow_{i+1} \\ \qquad\qquad i + 1 : (\textbf{ldloc.0})\ \downarrow_{i+2} \\ \qquad\qquad i + 2 : \textbf{sub}\ \ \downarrow_j] \end{array}} \quad [\ csubs\ ]$$

Now we close the window completing the transformation to schema $W10$. We then focus on the end of the loop and open a window on the **evalbr**.

Law *Compile branch ge* is applied to complete the compilation of the loop.

$$\frac{[Sig \mid \mathrm{pre}(P \Rightarrow ip = i \wedge i < j − 1 \wedge i < i + 1 < i + 2 < j)]}{\begin{array}{l} [Sig \mid \\ \mathrm{pre}(P) \wedge i \ldots j − 1 : (\textbf{evalbr}[k, local(0) ≥_w local(1)/l?, b?]) \downarrow_j \\ \sqsubseteq \\ \mathrm{pre}(P) \wedge\ i : (\textbf{ldloc.1})\ \downarrow_{i+1} \\ \qquad\qquad i + 1 : (\textbf{ldloc.0})\ \downarrow_{i+2} \\ \qquad\qquad i + 2 : \textbf{bge.s}\ k\ \downarrow_j] \end{array}} \quad [\ cbge\ ]$$

Closing the window and completing the compilation of the initial assignment completes the compilation of the high-level language program from Section 2, to the assembler code in Section 3.

7   Conclusion

This paper describes the theoretical basis for the implementation of verified compilation using the Cogito theories of the Ergo theorem prover[12]. We have extended the syntax of the Sum Intermediate Language (IL) with a small stack-based assembly language similar to .NET CIL [7]. The assembly operations have been defined in the existing Sum IL. We have restated laws developed elsewhere [1] into the predicative programming language used by Cogito [6], and introduced a new form of window inference based on schemas to capture the transformation of Sum IL code to assembler.

The compiled code is data refined by calculation in a style mixing data refinement and algorithmic refinement as do others [10]. As the retrieve relation is functional, the distribution of the retrieve relation throughout the abstract program can be simplified to the equivalent substitution. Since this is generally the case for compilation, this approach may be used in the automatic tool. Others [24] have explored extensions to window inference that support mixing data refinement with algorithmic refinement.

Window inference rules for Sum have been presented. These rules are fashioned after the tactics provided by the Cogito refinement theories [5]. As with Program Window Inference [21], contextual information, such as predicates holding in the pre-state of a program specification, are used to discharge the proof obligations of specification/program transformations. Opening rules describe how such contextual information may be inferred from the surrounding program.

We have presented rules that assume a single point of entry and another that does not. The former are useful when considering compilation of structured programs whereas the latter would also be useful for optimising assembler where arbitrary jumps are assumed. The window inference style allows both sorts of rules to be presented.

Transformations depending on preconditions concerning variables other than the instruction pointer are rarely used in compilation steps because they are often very simple. However, preconditions are useful if code transforming optimisations are attempted. For instance they allow $x := y \;;;\; x := y$ to be optimised to $x := y \;;;\; skip$. Future development incorporating equivalence preserving optimisations of the assembler code will make more use of the contextual information concerning the precondition.

The current set of rules require labels to be introduced on every statement. Reasoning about labelled statements is awkward because of the possibility that they may be target of any jump. In the implementation we will provide rules that do not require the introduction of so many labels simplifying the compilation. In addition, the production of a consistent set of labels, currently informal, needs further work.

Acknowledgements. This research was funded by Australian Research Council Large Grant A00104650, Verified Compilation Strategies for Critical Computer Programs. Thanks are due to Colin Fidge, Geoff Watson and Karl Lermer whose comments on drafts of this paper have led to several improvements.

References

1. C. J. Fidge. Modelling program compilation in the refinement calculus. In D. J. Duke and A. S. Evans, editors, *2nd BCS-FACS Northern Formal Methods Workshop*, Electronic Workshops in Computing. Springer-Verlag, 1997.

2. Markus Müller-Olm. *Modular Compiler Verification*, volume 1283 of *LNCS*. Springer, 1997.

3. A. Sampaio. *An Algebraic Approach to Compiler Design*, volume 4 of *AMAST Series in Computing*. World Scientific, 1997.

4. O. Traynor, D. Hazel, P. Kearney, A. Martin, R. Nickson, and L. Wildman. The Cogito development system. In M. Johnson, editor, *Algebraic Methodology and Software Technology (AMAST'97)*, volume 1349 of *LNCS*. Springer-Verlag, December 1997.

5. A. Bloesch, E. Kazmierczak, P. Kearney, J. Staples, O. Traynor, and M. Utting. A formal reasoning environment for Sum – a Z based specification language. In Kotagiri Ramamohanarao, editor, *Proceedings of the Nineteenth Australasian Computer Science Conference (ACSC'96)*. Australian Computer Science Communications, 1996.

6. P. Kearney and L. Wildman. From formal specifications to Ada programs. In J. Edwards, editor, *Computer Science: Proc. of the 22nd Australasian Computer Science Conference (ACSC'99)*, pages 193–204. Springer, 1999.

7. ECMA TC39/TG3. ECMA standardisation. http://msdn.microsoft.com/net/ecma.

8. Mark B. Josephs. The data refinement calculator for Z specifications. *Information Processing Letters*, 27, February 1988.

9. Jim Woodcock and Jim Davies. *Using Z, Specification, Refinement, and Proof.* International Series in Computer Science. Prentice Hall, 1996.

10. C. Morgan. *Programming from Specifications*. International Series in Computer Science. Prentice Hall, 2nd edition, 1995.

11. Emil Sekerinski. A calculus for predicative programming. In R.S. Bird, C.C. Morgan, and J.C.P. Woodcock, editors, *Mathematics of Program Construction, Second International Conference, Oxford, U.K.*, volume 669 of *LNCS*. Springer-Verlag, New York, N.Y., June/July 1993.

12. A. Martin, R. Nickson, and M. Utting. A tactic language for Ergo. In *Proceedings Formal Methods Pacific (FMP'97)*. Springer-Verlag.

13. D.T. Jordan, C.J. Locke, J.A. McDermid, C.E. Parker, B.A. Sharp, and I. Toyn. Literate Formal Development of Ada from Z for Safety Critical Applications. In *SAFECOMP*, 1994.

14. S. King. Z and the refinement calculus. In *VDM and Z – Formal Methods in Software Development, LNCS 428*, pages 164–188. Springer-Verlag, 1990.

15. John Staples, Peter J. Robinson, and Daniel Hazel. A functional logic for higher level reasoning about computation. *Formal Aspects of Computing, BCS*, 6, 1996.

16. K. Lermer and C. J. Fidge. A formal model of real-time program compilation. *Theoretical Computer Science*, 2001. In press.

17. K. Lermer and C. J. Fidge. Compilation as refinement. In L. Groves and S.Reeves, editors, *In Proceedings Formal Methods Pacific (FMP'97)*. Springer-Verlag, 1997.

18. T.S. Norvell. Machine code programs are predicates too. In D.Till, editor, *sixth refinement workshop*. Springer-Verlag, 1994.

19. Nigel Ward. Adding specification constructors to the refinement calculus. In J. P. Woodcock and P. G. Larsen, editors, *First International Symposium of Formal Methods Europe FME'93*, volume 670 of *LNCS*, Odense, Denmark, April 1993. Springer-Verlag.

20. G. Smith. Stepwise development from ideal specifications. In J. Edwards, editor, *Australasian Computer Science Conference*, Los Alamitos, California, January 2000. IEEE Computer Society.

21. R. Nickson and I. Hayes. Supporting contexts in program refinement. *Science of Computer Programming 29*, 1997.

22. P.J. Robinson and J. Staples. Formalising the hierachical structure of practical mathematical reasoning. *Journal of Logic and Computation*, 3(1), 1993.

23. E.W. Dijkstra and C.S. Scholten. *Predicate Calculus and Program Semantics*. Springer-Verlag, 1990.

24. Ray Nickson. Window inference for data refinement. In *Fifth Australasian Refinement Workshop*, University of Queensland, April 1996.

Property Dependent Abstraction of Control Structure for Software Verification

Thomas Firley and Ursula Goltz*

Technical University of Braunschweig, Germany
{firley,goltz}@ips.cs.tu-bs.de

Abstract. In this paper we present a technique to compute abstract models for formal system verification. The method reduces the state space by eliminating those parts of a system model which are not required to check a property. The abstract model depends on the property, which is a formula of the next-less fragment of CTL^*. The algorithm reads a system description, annotates it with abstract sub-models for the statements, which are finally composed as abstract model for the system. In the paper we introduce the core algorithm and illustrate it by an example.

Keywords: software verification, property oriented abstraction, algorithmic construction of abstract semantics.

1   Introduction

In the field of software development, formal methods for the verification of system properties become more and more essential. Software systems get complexer and harder to develop or to maintain. Especially automated techniques, such as model checking, gain importance, since they allow programmers without much theoretical background to use these techniques.

Due to the so called state explosion problem, the state space is often much too large, so that the core model checking cannot be used. Different techniques have been invented to overcome this problem. One group of these techniques can be gathered under the term *abstraction*. These techniques have in common, that they reduce the state space by hiding some of the behavioural information [CGL92,LGS+95,DGG97,CGP99].

In this paper a technique is introduced which mainly reduces the state space introduced by control structure of parts of the system, which are not relevant for a property. Unlike many other techniques, we do not construct a general model suitable for a class of properties, as for instance in [CGL92,ABA01]. Rather we will construct models, which are suited for one property at a time. In contrast to works like [JQKP97,JG00,PVE+00,SS00], where the abstract model has been

---

* This work is connected to our research for SFB 562 (Robotersysteme für Handhabung und Montage)

constructed manually, it should be stressed that our technique can be used fully automatically without intermediate user interactions.

Basically we annotate the parse tree of the system description with abstract models for each statement. Depending on the property of interest, we adapt these abstract models, which are finally composed as abstract model for the system.

Closely related to our idea are those of Balarin, Sangiovanni-Vincentelli [BSV93] and Kurshan [Kur94, p.170]. They also try to find an abstract model by refining a general abstraction. They do the abstraction process-wise, where each abstract model of a process has as many states as its concrete counterpart (but possibly more transitions, however yielding a smaller BDD representation). They find the necessary refinements by analysing the failure reports of intermediate verification attempts.

In [CGP99] this kind of technique is called *cone of influence reduction*. There it is described for electronic circuits (resp. a set of Boolean equations). A set of variables is calculated on which the property depends. As in the works of the previous paragraph, the circuits (equations) are considered as concurrent processes and either a process is included into the abstract model or not. The proof of correctness is done via a bisimulation relation between the abstract and the concrete model.

[ABA01] uses a similar technique to verify *ACTL* properties. The verification process requires intermediate model checking runs, whose results are analysed. Instead of an exact abstract model, an under-approximation and an over-approximation are used as abstract representation of the system.

In [YG00], two abstraction techniques are introduced, which construct an abstract model for an imperative system description. The *path reduction* identifies computation steps which have only one successor and which do not influence the property. Those steps are merged into one abstract step. The *dead variable reduction* ignores variables, whose value will change anyway until the next use of the variable.

Another technique whose idea is very close to ours is called *splicing* and was originally intended for software engineering and debugging. In [HCD+99] the technique, which is incorporated into the Bandera tool-set, is applied to a simple programming language for concurrent, imperative programs. The program code is reduced considering statements, which are relevant for the property according to different dependence relations. Then, the residual program code is simplified and afterwards used for verification purpose.

In this paper we concentrate on presenting the core of our abstraction idea and its illustration. Some points should be stressed here, since we think, they are the main contribution of this paper. Our algorithm can be implemented in such a way, that it works fully automatic. It is intended for reactive systems, which may read external variables, changing their values at any time without notice. The resulting model is guaranteed to be finite, leaving only the termination of loops to be verified separately. The construction itself is rather efficient, since no intermediate model checking runs are necessary. It is also guaranteed to terminate. Furthermore the construction is rather simple and easy to implement.

The paper is structured as follows. In the next section, we will introduce the language, which we will use throughout the paper to specify the system behaviour. In Section 3 we will introduce the abstraction idea and the realisation by means of an algorithmic description. In Section 4 we will illustrate the use and the benefit of the algorithm by an example. Section 5 finally will conclude the paper with some remarks on how this algorithm can be optimised, which are the advantages compared to other abstraction techniques, and what will be done in the future.

2 Language

In this section, we will introduce the language, that we will use for our investigations. This is a simplified version of the language presented by Manna and Pnueli in [MP92].

2.1 Syntax

The syntax is defined by a number of BNF grammar rules. A program starts with a declaration section and continues with a behavioural section. In the behavioural section, there is a parallel composition of a number of statements, which are also called processes.

$$\langle \text{program} \rangle ::= \langle \text{declaration} \rangle^* \langle \text{statement} \rangle_1 \,||\, \ldots \,||\, \langle \text{statement} \rangle_n$$

All variables, which are used in the program body, have to be declared in the declaration part with declaration statements of the form:

$$\langle \text{declaration} \rangle ::= \langle \text{mode} \rangle \; [\langle \text{variable list} \rangle \colon \langle \text{type} \rangle \; [\textbf{where} \; \langle \text{constraint} \rangle]]^+$$

The two valid modes for variables are **in** and **out**. Variables marked as **in** are external read-only variables, which may be changed by the environment, those marked as **out** can be used for internal calculations and are observable from the outside. Constraints for internal variables determine the initial value of this variable, constraints for external variables restrict the domain of that variable.

The basic data types are *integer* and *boolean*. For this paper we assume, that external variables range over a finite domain, such as the type *boolean* or a finite subset of the type *integer* (declared with a constraint such as $n_1 \leq v \leq n_2$).

The constraints in the declaration are Boolean expressions, which hold in the initial state of the system. They can be formed using the variable to be defined, integer constants (positive or negative), Boolean constants (*false* or *true*) and the Boolean operations $\wedge$, $\vee$, $\neg$, the integer operations $+$, $-$, $*$, **div**, **mod**, and comparison operations $=$, $\neq$, $<$, $\leq$, $>$, $\geq$. An empty constraint corresponds to the constraint *true*. In the declarations part, a comma ',' may be used instead of the $\wedge$ symbol as and-operator.

Each process is represented by a statement. A statement can either be an atomic statement or a compound one. Statements are defined as follows:

⟨statement⟩ ::= **skip**
  | ⟨variable⟩ := ⟨expression⟩
  | **await** ⟨condition⟩
  | ⟨statement⟩₁; ⟨statement⟩₂
  | **if** ⟨condition⟩ **then** ⟨statement⟩₁ **else** ⟨statement⟩₂ **fi**
  | **while** ⟨condition⟩ **do** ⟨statement⟩ **od**

Several side constraints have to hold, to make a statement valid. Expressions are built using the standard infix notation. All variables used in expressions have to be defined in the declarations part. The type of the expression in an assignment has to fit to the type of the assigned variable. The variables on the left side of an assignment have to be declared as **out**. A condition is a Boolean expression.

2.2 Semantics

Each statement S is associated with two labels denoted by $pre(S)$ and $post(S)$. Each of these labels represent a control location. $pre(S)$ represents the control location before the statement S and $post(S)$ represents the control location after the statement S.

Since some of the labels for control locations are redundant, we introduce equivalence classes of such labels. For instance in the sequential composition S_1; S_2, the two labels $post(S_1)$ and $pre(S_2)$ should represent the same control location. We define a label equivalence relation $\sim_L$ by the smallest relation, which satisfies the following conditions:

– For a concatenation $S \equiv S_1$; S_2, we have:
  $post(S_1) \sim_L pre(S_2)$, $pre(S) \sim_L pre(S_1)$, and $post(S) \sim_L post(S_2)$.
– For a conditional $S \equiv$ **if** c **then** S_1 **else** S_2 **fi**, we have:
  $post(S) \sim_L post(S_1) \sim_L post(S_2)$.
– For a while loop $S \equiv$ **while** c **do** S_1 **od**, we have:
  $post(S_1) \sim_L pre(S)$.

An equivalence class of of such labels is a control location. For a control location label ℓ, we denote its control location by $[\ell]$. We denote the set of all control locations by $\mathcal{L}$.

Example. The statement $S \equiv S_1$; S_2 has got three control locations. The first one is before S, represented by the two labels $pre(S)$ and $pre(S_1)$. The second one is between S_1 and S_2, represented by $post(S_1)$ and $pre(S_2)$. The third one is after the statement S and is represented by the two labels $post(S_2)$ and $post(S)$.

Program Counter. Besides explicitly declared internal and external data variables, there is one implicit control variable $pc \subseteq \mathcal{L}$. The variable pc contains all locations at which the control of the system is. Since all control locations in a program are distinct, we use a set to represent the current locations for different processes. The number of elements in pc is determined by the number of concurrent processes.

States. A state s of the program is defined as mapping from variables to values. We denote the set of all states by Σ^c. We only consider internal variables to be part of a state. External variables may be read, but since they may change their value without notice, they are considered to determine the state of the environment, not the state of the system. We define the concrete interpretation function with $I_s^c(v) := s(v)$.

Transitions. We will now define the transition relation $T^c \subseteq \Sigma^c \times \Sigma^c$ of the system. For each statement in the system, we will define a subset of the transition relation. The union of all these subsets is T^c. We will give the subsets in terms of equations. The unprimed identifiers refer to variables in the source state. The primed identifiers refer to those in the target state. Implicitly, we assume that variables whose values are not explicitly specified are identical in both states.

Furthermore, we introduce labels for each transition. The function L^c maps every transition to its label. Later, we will need the label, to identify a relation between the semantic model and the abstract model. We will have two kinds of labels. The first one is of the form $x := e$, indicating, that the value of variable x has changed to e, the other one is of the form $[c]$, indicating, that the transition is only enabled, if c will be evaluated to *true*. Both, c and e are expressions without external variables.

- For $S \equiv$ **skip**, transitions are defined by
  $[pre(S)] \in pc \wedge pc' = pc \cup \{[post(S)]\} \setminus \{[pre(S)]\}$ with label $[true]$.
- For $S \equiv v := e$, transitions are defined by
  $[pre(S)] \in pc \wedge pc' = pc \cup \{[post(S)]\} \setminus \{[pre(S)]\} \wedge v' = e$ with label $v := e$.
  Note, that for every possible value of external variables, that occur in the expression e, a different transition will be introduced, since we do not know their values in advance.
- For $S \equiv$ **await** c, transitions are defined by
  $[pre(S)] \in pc \wedge c \wedge pc' = pc \cup \{[post(S)]\} \setminus \{[pre(S)]\}$ with label $[c]$.
- For $S \equiv$ **if** c **then** S_1 **else** S_2 **fi**, transitions are defined by
  $[pre(S)] \in pc \wedge c \wedge pc' = pc \cup \{[pre(S_1)]\} \setminus \{[pre(S)]\}$ with label $[c]$
  or by $[pre(S)] \in pc \wedge \neg c \wedge pc' = pc \cup \{[pre(S_2)]\} \setminus \{[pre(S)]\}$ with label $[\neg c]$.
- For $S \equiv$ **while** c **do** S_1 **od**, transitions are defined by
  $[pre(S)] \in pc \wedge c \wedge pc' = pc \cup \{[pre(S_1)]\} \setminus \{[pre(S)]\}$ with label $[c]$
  or by $[pre(S)] \in pc \wedge \neg c \wedge pc' = pc \cup \{[post(S)]\} \setminus \{[pre(S)]\}$ with label $[\neg c]$.

For concatenation, we do not need to introduce new transitions.

Initial states. The initial states can be calculated by the conjunction of all where-clauses in the declaration part. The pc variable is the union of $[pre(P_i)]$ for all processes P_i. If the where-clause of some variables is omitted, it is equivalent to *true*. Note, that in general there is more than one initial state, since often not all variables are initialised. The set of all initial states is denoted by S_0^c.

2.3   Concrete Model

After having defined the set of states, the transition relation and the set of initial states, we are able to give the notation for the concrete model of a system. The concrete model is denoted by $M^c = (\Sigma^c, T^c, S_0^c, L^c)$, where Σ^c is the set of states, T^c is the transition relation, S_0^c is the set of initial states, and L^c is the mapping from transitions to transition labels.

Of course the number of reachable states may be infinite. On the one hand, loops may not terminate and thus produce infinitely many states, which leads to an infinite depth of the transition system. On the other hand, if we do not restrict the possible values of external variables, the branching structure may be infinite.

3   Abstraction

To be able to use automatic verification methods such as model checking, we need a finite model. In this section, we will introduce an algorithm, which constructs a finite model for a system description and a property. If the property holds in the abstract model, it will also hold in the concrete model.

The main idea of this method is to take an abstract model of the system, to look at the properties of interest, and to adapt the abstract model in such a way, that it preserves these properties. The adaptation steps will be applied iteratively, so that different properties can be investigated in one abstract model. This is necessary, if properties depend on other properties. The resulting abstract model preserves all the properties, that it preserved before and additionally the new properties. During the process of refining the abstract model, it will get larger in the number of states and its behaviour will get closer to that of the concrete model.

We will associate an abstract model to each statement (to be precise: to each node in the parse tree) of the system description. We start with a generic abstraction. Then we will identify important atomic statements, for which we will exchange the generic abstract model by a more concrete abstract model. The abstract models for the composed statements, which depend on the changed atomic statements, have to be re-calculated. At the end an abstract model is constructed, which preserves exactly the interesting properties.

We will introduce this abstraction technique in several steps. First we will explain the abstract model. We introduce the automata-based representation and an alternative representation, which is better suited to perform certain operations on the model. In the next step, we will introduce how to calculate and compose abstract models depending on the system description. Then we will introduce rules when to extend the abstract model by giving an algorithm, which iterates over the properties. Each iteration adapts the model for one property.

3.1   Abstract Model

The abstract model is a simplified representation of the system behaviour. We will use superscript a to indicate that we refer to the abstract model $M^a =$

$(\Sigma^a, T^a, s_0^a, L^a)$, where Σ^a is the set of abstract states, $T^a \subseteq \Sigma^a \times \Sigma^a$ is the transition relation, s_0^a is a single initial state, and L^a is the mapping from abstract transitions to transition labels.

Abstract States. The set of states Σ^a is a subset of $P(\mathcal{L}) \times N^*$. The first component of the tuple is the power-set of control locations in the system description. This component is an abstract representation for the program counter variable. It reduces the amount of information about where the control of the system actually is.

The second component of the tuple is a word over the alphabet N, where N is an arbitrary, countable set of adequate size including one special symbol $|$. We will call words over N *data words*, since they represent abstract information about the values of data variables. States which differ only in a data variable can be distinguished by different data words. The application of $P(\mathcal{L})$ and N^* will become clear in the examples below.

Furthermore, in the abstract model, there is only one initial state $s_0^a \in \Sigma^a$.

Basic Model. Instead of doing our calculations directly on the automata-based abstract model, we will use a different representation, which will simplify certain operations. The *basic model* is a tuple $BM = (\Sigma^a, G, s_0^a, F, L^b)$, where Σ^a is the set of abstract states, G is a set of transition generators, s_0^a is the initial state, F is the set of final states, and L^b is the abstract labelling function for transition generators. This representation induces an automata-based abstract model as introduced above, and it simplifies compositionality.

- *Transition generators* are tuples of $(\mathcal{L} \times N^*) \times (\mathcal{L} \times N^*)$. As introduced before, $\mathcal{L}$ is a set of locations in the system description. N^* is the set of words over the alphabet N. Each element of the set of transition generators will induce possibly many transitions of the abstract model.
- We have introduced a set of *final states* $F \subseteq \Sigma^a$, which simplifies compositionality. This set has to be non-empty, which can always be achieved by adding a non-reachable state.
- Furthermore, we will use a *labelling function*, that tells us, what effect a transition has. The function L^b will map transition generators to labels. We consider three kind of labels. The first one is of the form $x := v$, which indicates that variable x is changed to value v. The second kind is of the form $[c]$, where c is a Boolean condition. This transition is only enabled if c will be evaluated to true. The third kind is τ for transitions, which do not exist in the concrete model.

Induction Rule. The induction rule defines, which abstract model is induced by a basic model. If $BM = (\Sigma^a, G, s_0^a, F, L^b)$ is a basic model of a system description, then $M^a = (\Sigma^a, T^a, s_0^a, L^a)$ is an abstract model of the same system description, where the transitions T^a and their labels L^a are induced by the following rule.

For every generator $g = ((l, \nu), (l', \nu')) \in G$ and for every two states $(L, \mu_0 \nu \mu_1), (L', \mu_0 \nu' \mu_1) \in \Sigma^a$ with $l \in L$, $l' \in L'$, and $\mu_0, \mu_1 \in N^*$, the transition

$t = ((L, \mu_0 \nu \mu_1), (L', \mu_0 \nu' \mu_1)) \in T^a$ is induced. If μ_1 is a non-empty word, it starts with the special symbol |.

For every transition generator g and every transition t, which is induced by g, the labels are the same $L^a(t) = L^b(g)$.

The induction rule shows the main advantage of the transition generators. Even if the set of locations may be extended in an abstract state and even if a common prefix or suffix is added to the words of some states, the transition generators need not to be changed. We will illustrate this advantage by two examples.

Example 1. We concentrate on the set of locations and omit the data words in the first example. The line numbers serve as labels for locations. Consider the following program:

```
1  x := 4;
2  y := 5;
3  z := 6
```

We assume, that previous calculations have given three abstract models for the assignments. In the graphical representation, we have annotated the abstract transition graphs with their respective statements.

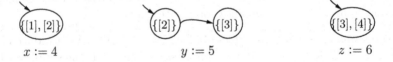

$x := 4$ $y := 5$ $z := 6$

Note, that there is only one transition for these assignments. In the case of the basic model, the transition generator is $(([2], \varepsilon), ([3], a))$, which induces the abstract transition $((\{[2]\}, \varepsilon), (\{[3]\}, a))$.

Now, we want to consider how the sequential composition for the ;-operator can be achieved. Obviously, we have to join the set of locations of the final state of the first operand with those of the initial state of the second operand respectively. As a result, we get the state $(\{[1], [2]\}, \varepsilon)$. Analogously, we merge the final state of the second assignment with the initial state of the third assignment. This gives the new state $(\{[3], [4]\}, a)$.

The sets of transition generators have to be joined as well. Since the set of states has changed, a different abstract transition is induced by the generator. In this case there is only one abstract transition, namely $((\{[1], [2]\}, \varepsilon), (\{[3], [4]\}, a))$. The composed abstract model thus is:

$x := 4; \ y := 5; \ z := 6$

Example 2. Whereas in the first example we omitted the data words, we will now investigate how these words will help composing the abstract model. Suppose, we want to compose the abstract model for the following system:

1 **if** B **then**
2 $x := 1$
3 **else**
4 $x := 2$
5 **fi**;
6 $y := x$

We assume, that the abstract models for the conditional statement with its substatements and the final assignment have been calculated beforehand.

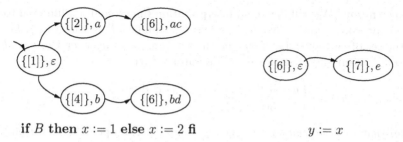

if B then $x := 1$ else $x := 2$ fi $y := x$

As one can see, the states of the then-branch are prefixed with a, the states of the else-branch are prefixed with b. We will use fresh prefixes for every branching structure. (Fresh prefixes means elements of N, which have not been used before.) Note that the two branches remain split after the if-statement, giving two final states. The conditional has got four transition generators:

$$(([1], \varepsilon), ([2], a)), \quad (([1], \varepsilon), ([4], b)), \quad (([2], \varepsilon), ([6], c)), \quad (([4], \varepsilon), ([6], d))$$

and the final assignment has got one transition generator:

$$(([6], \varepsilon), ([7], e))$$

Note, that all these generators have empty data words in their first component.

In this example, it is not sufficient, to join the locations of the states. We have to deal with two final states of the conditional. Although both final states involve the location [6], we have to distinguish them, since the data of both are different. Hence the states of each branch of the conditional get a different prefix. If we want to compose the two abstract models, we have to duplicate the second model for each final state of the first one, to keep track of the different data. On the one hand, we have to join the locations of each final state with those of the second initial state. On the other hand, we duplicate the second abstract model by prefixing each state in the second model with the respective data word. The composed abstract model now is:

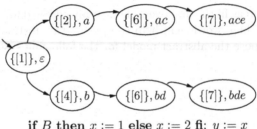

if B then $x := 1$ else $x := 2$ fi; $y := x$

Again the sets of generators simply have to be joined. The generator of the final assignment $((([6], \varepsilon), ([7], e))$ now induces two abstract transitions, namely:

$$((\{[6]\}, ac), (\{[7]\}, ace)) \quad \text{and} \quad ((\{[6]\}, bd), (\{[7]\}, bde))$$

Interpretation. We will define an interpretation function and a function to evaluate expressions. Let $Val = boolean \cup integer$ and $Val' = Val \cup \{\bot\}$. Let Var be the set of variables. Let $Expr$ be the set of expressions over $Var \cup Val'$. We extend domain and range for every operator $\circ$ with

$$\circ(x_1, \dots, x_n) = \begin{cases} y & \text{if } y = \circ(x_1, \dots, x_n) \text{ is defined,} \\ \bot & \text{otherwise.} \end{cases}$$

Note, that in case that any of the x_i equals $\bot$, the operator $\circ$ is usually not defined and $\circ(x_1, \dots, x_n) = \bot$.

For every function $f \subseteq Var \times \Sigma^a \to Val'$ mapping variables to values, we define a function $f' \subseteq Expr \times \Sigma^a \to Val'$ mapping expressions to values with

$$f'(e, s) := \begin{cases} f(e, s) & \text{if } e \in Var, \\ e & \text{if } e \in Val', \\ \circ(f'(x_1, s), \dots, f'(x_n, s)) & \text{if } e = \circ(x_1, \dots, x_n) \in Expr. \end{cases}$$

The function f is an *interpretation function* for an abstract model $M^a = (\Sigma^a, T^a, s_0^a, L^a)$ with initial constraints ξ if and only if $f \subseteq Var \times \Sigma^a \times Val'$, and for all variables v the following holds. For every non-reachable state s the function evaluates to $f(v, s) = \bot$. For every reachable state s:

$$f(v, s) = w \neq \bot \quad \text{implies}$$
$$(\forall (s', s) \in T^a : ((L^a(s', s) \equiv v := e \Rightarrow f'(e, s') = w)$$
$$\wedge (L^a(s', s) \not\equiv v := e \Rightarrow f(v, s') = w)))$$
$$\wedge (s = s_0^a \Rightarrow (\xi \Rightarrow v = w)).$$

That means, the value of a variable in each state is consistent for every incoming transition and initial constraint. There are possibly many interpretation functions satisfying these conditions. We define a partial order $\preceq$ on the set of all interpretation functions. Let

$$f \preceq g :\Leftrightarrow (\forall v, s : f(v, s) \neq \bot \Rightarrow f(v, s) = g(v, s)),$$

where f and g are interpretation functions.

Lemma 1. *For an abstract model, the greatest interpretation function exists and is unique.*

Let f be the greatest interpretation function for the model M^a. Then we define $I_s^a(v) := f(v, s)$.

Proof: (1) Existence of an interpretation function: The trivial interpretation function maps every variable in every state to $\perp$.

(2) Greatest interpretation function is unique: We assume, that there are two interpretation functions $f \neq g$ and there is no h with $f \preceq h$ or $g \preceq h$. Then there is at least one state s_n and one variable v with $\perp \neq f(v, s_n) \neq g(v, s_n) \neq \perp$. Let $s_0 s_1 \ldots s_n$ be the finite path from the initial state s_0 to s_n. Suppose $s_n \neq s_0$, then

- If $L^a(s_{n-1}, s_n) \equiv v := e$, then there is at least one variable v' in expression e with $\perp \neq f(v', s_{n-1}) \neq g(v', s_{n-1}) \neq \perp$. Investigate state s_{n-1} and v' in this case.
- If $L^a(s_{n-1}, s_n) \not\equiv v := e$, then $\perp \neq f(v, s_{n-1}) \neq g(v, s_{n-1}) \neq \perp$. Investigate state s_{n-1} and variable v in this case.

Suppose $s_n = s_0$. Either the initial constraint ξ implies $v = w \neq \perp$. Than either f or g is not an interpretation function. Or ξ does not imply any value for v, then both f and g are not interpretation functions.

Since the path $s_0 \ldots s_n$ is finite, eventually the case $s_n = s_0$ will occur.   ∎

3.2   Composition

In the two examples above, we have composed systems which are connected by sequential composition. In this section we will introduce the generic abstract model as well as the composed abstract model for each statement formally.

Generic Abstract Model. There is one abstract model which can be considered to represent the behaviour of every possible process. This abstract model has one state, which is also the initial state, and no transition. In our notation we denote it by $M^a = (\{s_0\}, \emptyset, s_0, \emptyset)$. Of course the locations in s_0 vary for every system, but the data word is always ε. This model is not suited to show any behavioural properties, but since it is so universal, we will use it as starting point for the refinement of our abstraction technique. The basic representation of this model is $BM = (\{s_0\}, \emptyset, s_0, \{s_0\}, \emptyset)$.

Expanded Abstract Model. To define the expanded abstract models for each statement, we will start by introducing three auxiliary functions. Two functions are called *addprefix*. One is operating on states, the other one is operating on sets of states. Both modify states, by adding a prefix to the data word of each state.

$$addprefix(s, \nu_0) = (L, \hat{\nu}) \quad \text{where } \hat{\nu} = \nu_0 \nu \text{ and } (L, \nu) = s$$
$$addprefix(\Sigma, \nu_0) = \{(L, \hat{\nu}) | \hat{\nu} = \nu_0 \nu \text{ and } (L, \nu) \in \Sigma\}$$

The third function merges two states into one target state. The set of locations of both states are joined, the data words are concatenated.

$$merge((L_1, \nu_1), (L_2, \nu_2)) = (L, \nu) \quad \text{with } \nu = \nu_1 \nu_2 \text{ and } L = L_1 \cup L_2$$

With the help of these functions, we can define the composition of sub-systems. For each statement we will give the respective composition rule.

To capture expressions which refer to external variables, we introduce two notations. If e is an expression, we will write $\bar{e}$ to denote the set of expressions, where in each element $e' \in \bar{e}$, the occurrences of external variables have been replaced by actual values. The union of all these values is equal to the domain of that variable. We will write $\bigvee \bar{e}$ to denote the disjunction of all expressions in $\bar{e}$ under the condition, that all these expressions are Boolean expressions.

We write $S.BM$ to express that the basic model $S.BM$ is an attribute of the statement S.

– $S \equiv \mathbf{skip}$.

$$s_0 = (\{[pre(S)]\}, \varepsilon)$$
$$s_1 = (\{[post(S)]\}, \nu) \quad \nu \text{ is fresh}$$
$$g = (([pre(S)], \varepsilon), ([post(S)], \nu))$$
$$S.BM = (\{s_0, s_1\}, \{g\}, s_0, \{s_1\}, \{g \mapsto [true]\})$$

– $S \equiv x := e$.

$$s_0 = (\{[pre(S)]\}, \varepsilon)$$
$$F = \{(\{[post(S)]\}, \nu) | \nu \text{ is fresh for each element of } \bar{e}\}$$
$$\Sigma = \{s_0\} \cup F$$
$$G = \{(([pre(S)], \varepsilon), (l, w)) \mid (\{l\}, w) \in F\}$$

For each generator g in G we define a label $L^b(g) = (x := e')$, where $e' \in \bar{e}$.

$$S.BM = (\Sigma, G, s_0, F, L^b)$$

– $S \equiv \mathbf{await} \; b$.

$$s_0 = (\{[pre(S)]\}, \varepsilon)$$
$$s_1 = (\{[post(S)]\}, \nu) \quad \nu \text{ is fresh}$$
$$g = (([pre(S)], \varepsilon), ([post(S)], \nu))$$
$$S.BM = (\{s_0, s_1\}, \{g\}, s_0, \{s_1\}, \{g \mapsto [\bigvee \bar{b}]\})$$

– $S \equiv S_0; \; S_1$. Let $S_0.BM = (\Sigma_0, G_0, s_0, F_0, L_0^b)$ be the basic model for S_0 and $S_1.BM = (\Sigma_1, G_1, s_1, F_1, L_1^b)$ for S_1. For each final state $s_f \in F_0$ we define the sets Σ_{s_f} and F_{s_f}, where ν_0 is the data word of s_f.

$$\Sigma_{s_f} = addprefix(\Sigma_1 \setminus \{s_1\}, \nu_0) \cup \{merge(s_f, s_1)\}$$
$$F_{s_f} = addprefix(F_1, \nu_0)$$

The expanded model for this statement is then

$$S.BM = ((\Sigma_0 \setminus F_0) \cup \bigcup_{s_f \in F_0} \Sigma_{s_f}, G_0 \cup G_1, s_0, \bigcup_{s_f \in F_0} F_{s_f}, L_0^b \cup L_1^b)$$

- $S \equiv \textbf{if } b \textbf{ then } S_0 \ S_1 \textbf{ fi}$. Let $S_0.BM = (\Sigma_0, G_0, s_0, F_0, L_0^b)$ be the basic model of sub-term S_0 and $S_1.BM = (\Sigma_1, G_1, s_1, F_1, L_1^b)$ be the basic model of sub-term S_1. Let ν and μ be fresh data words. Let s be $(\{[pre(S)]\}, \varepsilon)$. Let l_0 be $pre(S_0)$ and l_1 be $pre(S_1)$.

$$\Sigma = addprefix(\Sigma_0, \nu) \cup addprefix(\Sigma_1, \mu) \cup \{s\}$$
$$G = G_0 \cup G_1 \cup \{(([pre(S)], \varepsilon), (l_0, \nu)), (([pre(S)], \varepsilon), (l_1, \mu))\}$$
$$F = addprefix(F_0, \nu) \cup addprefix(F_1, \mu)$$

Let L^b be the union of L_0^b and L_1^b and mappings for the new transitions. The transition for the then-branch is labelled with $[\bigvee \bar{b}]$. The transition for the else-branch is labelled with $[\bigvee \neg \bar{b}]$.

$$S.BM = (\Sigma, G, s, F, L^b)$$

- $S \equiv \textbf{while } b \textbf{ do } S_0 \textbf{ od}$. Let $S_0.BM = (\Sigma_0, G_0, s_0, F_0, L_0^b)$ be the basic model of sub-term S_0. Let s_b be $(\{[pre(S)]\}, \varepsilon)$ and s_f be $(\{[post(S)]\}, \mu)$, where μ is fresh.

$$\Sigma = addprefix(\Sigma_0, \nu) \cup \{s_b, s_f\}, \text{ where } \nu \text{ is a fresh prefix}$$
$$G = G_0 \cup \{(([pre(S)], \varepsilon), ([post(S)], \mu)), (([pre(S)], \varepsilon), ([pre(S_0)], \nu))\}$$
$$\cup \{((post(S_0), w), ([pre(S)], \varepsilon)) \mid (L, w) \in F_0\}$$
$$F = \{s_f\}$$

The transition to enter the loop is labelled with $[\bigvee \bar{b}]$. The transition to skip the loop is labelled with $[\bigvee \neg \bar{b}]$. The transitions from final states of the loop-body back to the loop-condition are labelled with τ.

$$S.BM = (\Sigma, G, s_b, \{s_f\}, L^b)$$

- $S \equiv S_0 \parallel S_1$. Let $S_0.BM = (\Sigma_0, G_0, s_0, F_0, L_0^b)$ be the basic model of sub-term S_0 and $S_1.BM = (\Sigma_1, G_1, s_1, F_1, L_1^b)$ be the basic model of sub-term S_1. Let s be $(L_0 \cup L_1, \nu_0 | \nu_1)$. L_i is the set of locations of s_i and ν_i is its data word $(i \in \{0, 1\})$.

$$\Sigma = \{(L_0 \cup L_1, \nu_0 | \nu_1) \mid (L_0, \nu_0) \in \Sigma_0, (L_1, \nu_1) \in \Sigma_1\}$$
$$G = G_0 \cup G_1$$
$$F = \{(L_0 \cup L_1, \nu_0 | \nu_1) \mid (L_0, \nu_0) \in F_0, (L_1, \nu_1) \in F_1\}$$
$$L^b = L_0^b \cup L_1^b$$
$$S.BM = (\Sigma, G, s, F, L^b)$$

The composition rules allow to compose the abstract model from the respective sub-models. They also allow to compose sub-models, where some of them are still generic abstract models.

3.3   Algorithm

After having defined the composition rule for every statement, we are ready to define the algorithm, which expands the model for each property. The result of the algorithm is the basic model, which induces the desired abstract model. Each iteration of the algorithm operates on the system description. We will use the parse tree of the system description, which we have attributed with the basic model for each node.

Every node in the parse tree has got a basic model representation, either the representation for the generic abstract model, or that defined by the composition rule given in the previous section.

Initial Basic Models. Initially all nodes in the parse tree are attributed with the generic basic abstraction. This includes the top node which is the basic model of the whole system. Thus initially the basic model of the system is the generic one.

Note however, that we can use any basic model as starting point for our investigations. If we have several similar properties to check, we can recycle the resulting abstract model for consecutive abstraction runs. Except for the size of the resulting model, it does not matter if parts of the initial model are already expanded.

Expansion Algorithm. The expansion algorithm identifies those statements in the program code, which are relevant for the property and replaces their generic abstract models by the newly constructed ones.

The algorithm uses the set C of relevant requirements, which have to be checked in the abstract model. Thus the algorithm will expand the abstract model so that all properties in C are preserved by the abstraction. Since the algorithm also adds new relevant properties to C, we introduce the set D of properties which already have been analysed. The algorithm will terminate, when $C \setminus D$ becomes empty. In our setting, C and D contain variables, on which the requirement depends.

The functions *change* and *query* map each node S to a set of variables, which are changed by the statement S or which are queried in S. The function *change* is used to determine, if the basic model for node S has to be expanded. Note, that this function identifies only those variables, which are changed directly. Variables which are changed in a sub-statement are not in the set. The function *query* is used, to determine which other properties might be important for the property under consideration.

Furthermore the attribute *expanded* is introduced, to indicate if a basic model of a statement has been changed. The parent statement will look at this attribute, to decide whether it has to be expanded itself.

```
1  while C \ D ≠ ∅ do
2      v := one element of C \ D
3      reset all S.expanded to false
4      for each node S in the parse tree (post order) do
```

```
5            if v ∈ change(S) or S.expanded then
6                expand basic model of node S
7                C := C ∪ query(S)
8                set S.expanded to true
9            fi
10       od
11       D := D ∪ {v}
12 od
```

The algorithm will terminate, since the size of set C is limited by the number of variables in the system.

4 Example

We will illustrate the abstraction techniques and its benefits by an example. The subject of this example is an *'intelligent house'*, which controls certain devices by measuring certain values of the environment. The state of the light and the heating will depend on the presence of a human being in the room.

In our simple example, we will have three measuring devices (the light switch, the temperature, and the presence detector), two controlled devices (the light and the heating), and a controlling unit.

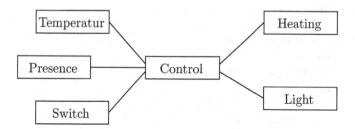

Fig. 1. Structure of the devices

The light will be illuminated, if the switch is in position 'on' and someone is present in the room, otherwise the light will be off. The heating is working, if someone is present and the current temperature is below 20°C, or in any case, if the temperature is below 18°C.

As the devices are physically distributed, we have modelled them as different components of a system. The components will communicate over well defined interfaces. In our example we will use shared variables for that purpose.

In the following the implementation of the system will be given. The sensors will look like:

```
1 while true do
2         skip;
3             value_dev := measured_value
4 od
```

Where $dev \in \{temperature, presence, switch\}$.

The controlled devices will look like:

```
1 while true do
2         if command_dev = on
3         then
4                 device_dev := on
5         else
6                 device_dev := off
7         fi
8 od
```

Where $dev \in \{light, heating\}$.

The controller is a loop, in which all measured values are checked and if necessary a command is sent to one of the controlled devices.

```
1  local_light := off;
2  local_heating := off;
3  while true do
5          if value_switch = on ∧ value_presence = yes ∧ local_light = off
6          then
7                  command_light := on;
8                  local_light := on
9          else skip fi;
11         if (value_switch = off ∨ value_presence = no) ∧ local_light = on
12         then
13                 command_light := off;
14                 local_light := off
15         else skip fi;
17         if (value_temperature < 18°C ∨ (value_temperature < 20°C
18             ∧value_presence = yes)) ∧ local_heating = off
19         then
20                 command_heating := on;
21                 local_heating := on
22         else skip fi;
24         if ((value_temperature > 18°C ∧ value_presence = no)
25             ∨value_temperature > 20°C) ∧ local_heating = on
26         then
27                 command_heating := off;
28                 local_heating := off
29         else skip fi;
31 od
```

In the main loop, there are four cases. Two cases will control the light, the other two will control the heating. Note, that there are local variables, which remember the state of the light or heating. Thus it is neither necessary to query the status of the light, nor will there be unnecessary communication actions.

We will now perform the operations, that the abstraction algorithm would take. We start with the initial abstract model, which has got one state. We will perform the abstraction steps for each component separately.

Suppose we want to check the property 'if nobody is present, the lights will go out'. More formally, with the temporal logic CTL^* this property can be written as '$AG(value_{presence} = no \rightarrow AF(device_{light} = off \lor value_{presence} = yes)$.

As we can see, two variables occur in the formula. Thus the set C should contain these variables.

Execution of the Algorithm. In the beginning, model M^a is the generic abstract model, D is empty and $C = \{value_{presence}, device_{light}\}$. We start to explain, what will happen during the execution of the algorithm. We only will investigate those processes, whose models are changed within an iteration.

Iteration 1. Let $v = value_{presence}$. The presence detector process is the only process, which changes this value. The assignment, which changes this variable, refers to an external variable. Since the domain of this variable contains two elements, two transitions are inserted for the assignment. Afterwards, the loop has to be expanded.

Iteration 2. Let $v = device_{light}$. We perceive, that this variable is only changed in the light device process. There, it has got two occurrences, both are assignments of constants. The super statement of these two assignments is an if-statement. When this if-statement is expanded, the variable $command_{light}$ will be added to the set C.

Iteration 3. Let $v = command_{light}$. The value of $command_{light}$ is changed in two places. The two super statements are expanded as well and the variables $value_{presence}$, $value_{switch}$ and $local_{light}$ are added to C. The first of these variables already has been investigated. The other two still have to be done in the next two iterations.

Iteration 4. Let $v = value_{switch}$. This iteration expands the light switch process as it has happened to the presence detector process in iteration 1. This expansion is in fact not necessary. A more sophisticated evaluation in iteration 3 would have recognised, that this variable does not have influence on the interesting variables.

Iteration 5. Let $v = local_{light}$. This variable expands two assignments in the control process.

After these iterations, the set $C \setminus D$ is empty. The algorithms stops and we can look at the abstract model. We will not give the whole abstract model. Instead we indicate in Figure 2 which of the components have been refined and which have been left to the generic abstract model. As we can see, only those components of

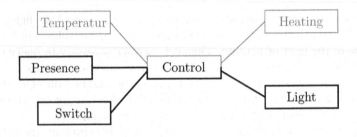

Fig. 2. Important parts for the verification

the system, which influence the state of the light have been refined. As already said, a more sophisticated selection of interesting variables could even improve this choice.

It is clear, that the abstraction for this example can easily be done manually by splitting the control unit into two independent parts. However, we demonstrated how this can be done automatically. Depending on how sophisticated the calculation of the set C is done, a similar abstract model constructed manually would require thorough efforts of a specialist.

5   Conclusion

In the paper we introduced an abstraction algorithm and illustrated its use by an example. The algorithm reduces the state space of the semantic model of a system to a finite size. It works for systems, whose behaviour is given by means of a simple imperative programming language and is intended for properties of the next-less fragment of CTL^*. This implies, that the algorithm also can handle CTL and LTL without next operator. In a forthcoming paper, we prove formally that these properties are preserved by the abstraction technique.

We did not yet consider synchronous communication, procedures with recursion, object orientation. However, we think, that most of these issues can easily be embedded in our framework. On the property side, we can not handle the next operator, which is caused by the nature of abstracting calculation steps. For the same reason, we cannot handle bounded liveness properties.

The works of Balarin, Sangiovanni-Vincentelli [BSV93] and Kurshan [Kur94, p. 170] also provide iterative algorithms to refine an abstract model to be able to verify a particular property. In contrast to their works, we do not have a problem in finding the processes influencing the required property. Since our generic abstraction has got only one state and no transitions, additional processes do not contribute to the state explosion. Hence we do not need heuristics to exclude some of the processes from the abstract model and thus to find the appropriate refinements. Secondly we do not use intermediate verification attempts to analyse the resulting failure reports, instead we calculate the dependencies directly. However, the calculation steps within one process may be much complexer than in the hardware oriented setting of for instance in [CGP99].

The technique, which seems to be closest to our idea is the *splicing* technique [HCD$^+$99]. In that paper, the program description is reduced according to a property of interest and statements, on which it depends. In contrast to our approach, the splicing technique is much more complicated since six dependence relations have to be evaluated and statements have to be deleted or replaced according to them. Afterwards the program code has to be analysed and trivial jumps and unreachable code has to be removed. The abstract model can then be constructed according to the regular semantics of the residual program code. It is hence not guaranteed to be finite.

One thing that we consider to be an important value of this work is the possibility to combine our result with other abstraction techniques and to use it as a basic framework and starting point for further investigations.

Besides the formal investigation of the property preservation, which is analysed in a forthcoming paper, there are two main directions which we will tackle in the future. On the one hand, we will extend the algorithm mainly with techniques for data abstraction. Not only will the state space profit from both abstractions as they are, but hopefully the combination of these techniques will yield an even larger state space reduction. On the other hand, we will investigate the usability of our algorithms by case studies. This will primarily be done in consideration of the extensions mentioned above. The results will be compared to the original algorithms and will give a quantitive measurement of usability. Currently we are implementing the algorithm which will give its output to the SMV model checker.

References

[ABA01]   Alexander Asteroth, Christel Baier, and Ulrich Aßmann. Model checking with formula-dependent abstract models. In *Computer Aided Verification (CAV '01)*, 2001.

[BSV93]   Felice Balarin and Alberto L. Sangiovanni-Vincentelli. An iterative approach to language containment. In Courcoubetis, editor, *Proceedings of Computer Aided Verification (CAV '93)*, volume 697 of *Lecture Notes in Computer Science*, pages 29–40. Springer, 1993.

[CGL92]   Edmund M. Clarke, Orna Grumberg, and David E. Long. Model checking and abstraction. In *Conference record of the Nineteenth Annual ACM SIGPLAN-SIGACT Symposium on Principles of Programming Languages*, pages 343–354. ACM Press, 1992.

[CGP99]   Edmund M. Clarke, Orna Grumberg, and Doron Peled. *Model Checking*. MIT Press, 1999.

[DGG97]   Dennis Dams, Orna Grumberg, and Rob Gerth. Abstract interpretation of reactive systems. *ACM Transactions on Programming Languages and Systems*, 19(2):253–291, 1997.

[HCD$^+$99]   John Hatcliff, James C. Corbett, Matthew B. Dwyer, Stefan Sokolowski, and Hongjun Zheng. A formal study of slicing for multi-threaded programs with JVM concurrency primitives. In *Proceedings of the International Symposium on Static Analysis (SAS '99)*, 1999.

[JG00]   Michael Jones and Ganesh Gopalakrishnan. Verifying transaction or-
            dering properties in unbounded bus networks through combined deduc-
            tive/algorithmic methods. In *Formal Methods in Computer-Aided Design*,
            pages 505–519, 2000.

[JQKP97]   Jae-Young Jang, Shaz Qadeer, Matt Kaufmann, and Carl Pixley. Formal
            verification of FIRE: A case study. In *Design Automation Conference*,
            pages 173–177, 1997.

[Kur94]   Robert P. Kurshan. *Computer-Aided Verification of Coordinating Pro-
            cesses*. Princeton University Press, 1994.

[LGS+95]   Claire Loiseaux, Susanne Graf, Joseph Sifakis, Ahmed Bouajjani, and Sad-
            dek Bensalem. Property preserving abstractions for the verification of
            concurrent systems. *Formal Methods in System Design*, 6:1–35, 1995.

[MP92]   Zohar Manna and Amir Pnueli. *The Temporal Logic of Reactive and Con-
            current Systems, Specification*. Springer, 1992.

[PVE+00]   John Penix, Willem Visser, Eric Engstrom, Aaron Larson, and Nicholas
            Weininger. Verification of time partitioning in the DEOS scheduler kernel.
            In *International Conference on Software Engineering*, pages 488–497, 2000.

[SS00]   Natalia Sidorova and Martin Steffen. Verification of a wireless atm medium
            access protocol. Technical Report TR ST 00 3, University of Kiel, Ger-
            many, May 2000.

[YG00]   Karen Yorav and Orna Grumberg. Static analysis for state-space reduc-
            tions preserving temporal logics. Technical Report CS-2000-03, Technion,
            Israel, 2000.

Closing Open SDL-Systems for Model Checking with DTSpin

Natalia Ioustinova[1]*, Natalia Sidorova[2], and Martin Steffen[3]

[1] Department of Software Engineering, CWI
P.O. Box 94079, 1090 GB Amsterdam, The Netherlands
Natalia.Ioustinova@cwi.nl
[2] Department of Mathematics and Computer Science
Eindhoven University of Technology
Den Dolech 2, P.O. Box 513,
5612 MB Eindhoven, The Netherlands
n.sidorova@tue.nl
[3] Institute of Computer Science and Applied Mathematics
Christian-Albrechts-Universität
Preußerstraße 1–9,
24105 Kiel, Germany
ms@informatik.uni-kiel.de

Abstract. Model checkers like Spin can handle closed reactive systems, only. Thus to handle open systems, in particular when using assume-guarantee reasoning, we need to be able to close (sub-)systems, which is commonly done by adding an environment process. For models with asynchronous message-passing communication, however, modelling the environment as separate process will lead to a combinatorial explosion caused by all combinations of messages in the input queues.

In this paper we describe the implementation of a tool which automatically closes DTPromela translations of SDL-specifications by embedding the timed chaotic environment into the system. To corroborate the usefulness of our approach, we compare the state space of models closed by embedding chaos with the state space of the same models closed with chaos as external environment process on some simple models and on a case study from a wireless ATM medium-access protocol.

Keywords: model checking, SDL, DTSpin, open communication systems, abstractions.

1 Introduction

Model checking is becoming an increasingly important part of the software design process [10]. Modern commercial SDL design tools like OBJECTGEODE [30] and the TAU SDL suite [1] allow validation of SDL specifications through simulation and testing. Since errors in telecommunication systems are expensive, there is a need for additional ways of verification and debugging, and model checking of SDL specifications is an area of active research, cf. e.g. [19,6,4,21,22,18,35].

---

* Supported by the CWI-project "Systems Validation Centre (SVC)".

L.-H. Eriksson and P. Lindsay (Eds.): FME 2002, LNCS 2391, pp. 531–548, 2002.
© Springer-Verlag Berlin Heidelberg 2002

Despite all algorithmic advances in model checking techniques and progress in raw computing power, however, the state explosion problem limits the applicability of model-checking [8,31,9] and thus *decomposition* and *abstraction* are indispensable when confronted with checking large designs. Following a decompositional approach and after singling out a subcomponent to check in isolation, the next step often is to *close* the subcomponent with an environment, since most model checkers cannot handle open systems.

Closing is generally done by adding an overapproximation of the real environment in the form of an external process. To allow the transfer of positive verification results from the constructed closed model to the real system, the environment process must be a safe abstraction [12,13] of the real environment, i.e., it must exhibit at least all the behaviour of the real environment. In the simplest case this means the closing environment behaves *chaotically.*

In an asynchronous communication model, just adding an external chaos process will not work, since injecting arbitrary message streams to the unbounded input queues will immediately lead to an infinite state space, unless some restrictions on the environment behaviour or on the maximal queue length are imposed in the closing process. Even so, external chaos results in a combinatorial explosion caused by all combinations of messages in the input queues.

In [32], we describe a simple approach which avoids the state-space penalty in the queues by "embedding" the external chaos into the component under consideration. We use *data abstraction,* condensing data from outside into a single abstract value to deal with the infinity of environmental data. By removing reception of chaotic data, we nevertheless must take into account the cone of influence of the removed statements, lest we get less behaviour than before. Therefore, we use *data-flow analysis* to detect instances of chaotically influenced variables and timers. Furthermore, since we are dealing with the discrete-time semantics [22,4] of SDL, special care must be taken to ensure that the chaos also shows more behaviour wrt. *timing* issues such as timeouts and time progress. Using the result of the analysis, the transformation yields a *closed* system which is a safe abstraction of the original one in terms of traces.

Based on these earlier theoretical results, the main contribution of this paper is the description of a tool implementing the embedded closing ideas and the presentation of experimental results that corroborate the usefulness of the approach. The implementation is targeted towards the verification with DTSpin, a discrete time extension of the well-known Spin model checker, therefore we chose to close DTPromela translations of SDL specifications. The experiments performed with DTSpin confirmed that the proposed method leads to a significant reduction of the state space and the verification time.

The rest of the paper is organized as follows. In the following Section 2, we sketch the formal background of the method. Afterwards, in Sections 3 and 4, we present the toolset we use, its extension, and the experimental results of a few smaller examples as well as the results on a larger case study. We conclude in Section 5 with discussing related work.

2   Embedding Chaos

In this section, we recapitulate the ideas underlying the program transformation to yield a closed system. A more detailed account of the underlying theory can be found in [32]. We start with fixing syntax and semantics and proceed with program transformation and data-flow analysis required for the transformation.

2.1   Semantics

Our operational model is based on asynchronously communicating state machines (processes) with top-level concurrency. Since we take SDL as a source and DTPromela as target language, the operational model gives the semantics of a subset of SDL that does not allow procedure calls and dynamic process creation, and also suits as semantics for a subset of DTPromela that is a target of translation from IF to DTPromela.

A program *Prog* is given as the parallel composition $\Pi_{i=1}^{n} P_i$ of a finite number of processes. A process P is described by a four-tuple ($Var, Loc, \sigma_{init}, Edg$), where *Var* denotes a finite set of variables, and *Loc* denotes a finite set of *locations* or control states. We assume the sets of variables Var_i of processes P_i in a program $Prog = \Pi_{i=1}^{n} P_i$ to be disjoint. A mapping of variables to values is called a valuation; we denote the set of valuations by $Val : Var \to D$. We assume standard data domains such as $\mathbb{N}$, *Bool*, etc., and write D when leaving the data-domain unspecified, and silently assume all expressions to be well-typed. $\Sigma = Loc \times Val$ is the set of states, where a process has one designated initial state $\sigma_{init} = (l_{init}, Val_{init}) \in \Sigma$. An *edge* of the state machine describes a change of configuration resulting from performing an *action* from a set *Act*; the set $Edg \subseteq Loc \times Act \times Loc$ denotes the set of edges.

As actions, we distinguish (1) *input* of a signal s containing a value to be assigned to a local variable, (2) *sending* a signal s together with a value described by an expression to a process P', and (3) *assignments*. In SDL, each transition starts with an input action, hence we assume the inputs to be unguarded, while output and assignment can be *guarded* by a boolean expression g, its guard. The three classes of actions are written as $?s(x)$, $g \rhd P!s(e)$, and $g \rhd x := e$, respectively, and we use $\alpha, \alpha' \ldots$ when leaving the class of actions unspecified. For an edge $(l, \alpha, \hat{l}) \in Edg$, we write more suggestively $l \longrightarrow_\alpha \hat{l}$.

Time aspects of a system behaviour are specified by actions dealing with *timers*. In SDL, timeouts are often considered as specific timeout *messages* kept in the input queue like any other message, and timer-expiration consequently is seen as adding a timeout-message to the queue. We use an equivalent presentation of this semantics, where timeouts are not put into the input queue, but are modelled more directly by guards. The equivalence of timeouts-by-guards and timeouts-as-messages in the presence of SDL's asynchronous communication model is argued for in [4]. The time semantics chosen here is not the only one conceivable (see e.g. [7] for a broader discussion of the use of timers in SDL). The semantics we use is the one described in [22,4], and is also implemented in DTSpin [3,14].

Each process has a finite set of timer variables (with typical elements $t, t_1', \dots$) which consist of a boolean flag indicating whether the timer is active or not, and a natural number value. A timer can be either *set* to a value $on(v)$ (rule SET), i.e., it is activated to run for the designated period, or deactivated (rule RESET)), i.e., it has a value *off*. Setting and resetting are expressed by guarded actions of the form $g \triangleright set\ t := e$ and $g \triangleright reset\ t$. If a timer expires, i.e., the value of a timer becomes zero, it can cause a *timeout*, upon which the timer is reset. The timeout action is denoted by $g_t \triangleright reset\ t$, where the timer guard g_t expresses the fact that the action can only be taken upon expiration (rule TIMEOUT). A possible discard of a timeout signal is imitated by analogous action (rule TDISCARD).

In SDL's asynchronous communication model, a process receives messages via a single associated input queue. We call a state of a process together with its input queue a *configuration* (σ, q). We write ϵ for the empty queue; $(s, v) :: q$ denotes a queue with message (s, v) (consisting of a signal s and a value v) at the head of the queue, i.e., (s, v) is the message to be input next; likewise the queue $q :: (s, v)$ contains (s, v) most recently entered. The behaviour of a single process is then given by sequences of configurations $(\sigma_{init}, \epsilon) = (\sigma_0, q_0) \to_\lambda (\sigma_1, q_1) \to_\lambda \cdots$ starting from the initial one, i.e., the initial state and the empty queue. The step semantics $\to_\lambda \subseteq \Gamma \times Lab \times \Gamma$ is given as a labelled transition relation between configurations. The labels differentiate between internal τ-steps, "*tick*"-steps, which globally decrease all active timers, and communication steps, either input or output, which are labelled by a triple of process (of destination/origin resp.), signal, and value being transmitted. Depending on location, valuation, the possible next actions, and the content of the input queue, the possible successor configurations are given by the rules of Table 1.

An input of a signal is enabled if the signal at the head of the queue matches signal expected by the process. Inputting results in removing the signal from the head of the queue and updating the local valuation according to parameters of the signal. In rule INPUT $\eta \in Val$, and $\eta[x \mapsto v]$ stands for the valuation equalling η for all $y \in Var$ except for $x \in Var$, where $\eta[x \mapsto v](x) = v$ holds instead. The rule DISCARD captures a specific feature of SDL92: if the signal from the head of the queue does not match any input defined as possible for the current (input) location, the signal is removed from the queue without changing the location and the valuation. Unlike input, output is guarded, so sending a message involves evaluating the guard and the expression according to the current valuation (rule OUTPUT). In OUTPUT, P' stands for the process identity of the destination and P is the identity of the sender. Assignment in ASSIGN works analogously, except that the step is internal. Receiving a message by asynchronous communication simply means putting it into the input queue where in the RECEIVE-rule, P is the identity of the process and P' is the identity of a sender. We assume for the non-timer guards, that at least one of them evaluates to true for each configuration.

The *global* transition semantics for a program $Prog = \Pi_{i=1}^n P_i$ is given by a standard product construction: configurations and initial states are paired, and

Table 1. Step semantics for process P

$$\frac{l \longrightarrow_{?s(x)} \hat{l} \in Edg}{(l, \eta, (s, v) :: q) \to_\tau (\hat{l}, \eta_{[x \mapsto v]}, q)} \text{ INPUT} \qquad \frac{l \longrightarrow_{?s'(x)} \hat{l} \in Edg \Rightarrow s' \neq s}{(l, \eta, (s, \_) :: q) \to_\tau (l, \eta, q)} \text{ DISCARD}$$

$$\frac{l \longrightarrow_{g \,\triangleright\, P'!(s,e)} \hat{l} \in Edg \qquad [\![g]\!]_\eta = true \qquad [\![e]\!]_\eta = v}{(l, \eta, q) \to_{P'!P(s,v)} (\hat{l}, \eta, q)} \text{ OUTPUT}$$

$$\frac{v \in D}{(l, \eta, q) \to_{P?P'(s,v)} (l, \eta, q :: (s, v))} \text{ RECEIVE}$$

$$\frac{l \longrightarrow_{g \,\triangleright\, x:=e} \hat{l} \in Edg \qquad [\![g]\!]_\eta = true \qquad [\![e]\!]_\eta = v}{(l, \eta, q) \to_\tau (\hat{l}, \eta_{[x \mapsto v]}, q)} \text{ ASSIGN}$$

$$\frac{l \longrightarrow_{g \,\triangleright\, set\, t:=e} \hat{l} \in Edg \qquad [\![g]\!]_\eta = true \qquad [\![e]\!]_\eta = v}{(l, \eta, q) \to_\tau (\hat{l}, \eta_{[t \mapsto on(v)]}, q)} \text{ SET}$$

$$\frac{l \longrightarrow_{g \,\triangleright\, reset\, t} \hat{l} \in Edg \qquad [\![g]\!]_\eta = true}{(l, \eta, q) \to_\tau (\hat{l}, \eta_{[t \mapsto off]}, q)} \text{ RESET}$$

$$\frac{l \longrightarrow_{g_t \,\triangleright\, reset\, t} \hat{l} \in Edg \qquad [\![t]\!]_\eta = on(0)}{(l, \eta, q) \to_\tau (\hat{l}, \eta_{[t \mapsto off]}, q)} \text{ TIMEOUT}$$

$$\frac{(l \longrightarrow_\alpha \hat{l} \in Edg \Rightarrow \alpha \neq g_t \triangleright reset\, t) \qquad [\![t]\!]_\eta = on(0)}{(l, \eta, q) \to_\tau (l, \eta_{[t \mapsto off]}, q)} \text{ TDISCARD}$$

Table 2. Parallel composition of P_1 and P_2

$$\frac{(\sigma_1, q_1) \to_{P_2!P_1(s,v)} (\hat{\sigma}_1, \hat{q}_1) \qquad (\sigma_2, q_2) \to_{P_2?P_1(s,v)} (\hat{\sigma}_2, \hat{q}_2)}{(\sigma_1, q_1) \times (\sigma_2, q_2) \to_\tau (\hat{\sigma}_1, \hat{q}_1) \times (\hat{\sigma}_2, \hat{q}_2)} \text{ COMM}$$

$$\frac{(\sigma_1, q_1) \to_{P_1?P_2'(s,v)} (\hat{\sigma}_1, \hat{q}_1) \qquad P_2' \neq P_2}{(\sigma_1, q_1) \times (\sigma_2, q_2) \to_{P_1?P_2'(s,v)} (\hat{\sigma}_1, \hat{q}_1) \times (\sigma_2, q_2)} \text{ INTERLEAVE}_1$$

$$\frac{(\sigma_1, q_1) \to_{P_2'!P_1(s,v)} (\hat{\sigma}_1, \hat{q}_1) \qquad P_2' \neq P_2}{(\sigma_1, q_1) \times (\sigma_2, q_2) \to_{P_2'!P_1(s,v)} (\hat{\sigma}_1, \hat{q}_1) \times (\sigma_2, q_2)} \text{ INTERLEAVE}_2$$

$$\frac{(\sigma_1, q_1) \to_\tau (\hat{\sigma}_1, \hat{q}_1)}{(\sigma_1, q_1) \times (\sigma_2, q_2) \to_\tau (\hat{\sigma}_1, \hat{q}_1) \times (\sigma_2, q_2)} \text{ INTERLEAVE}_\tau$$

$$\frac{blocked(\sigma)}{\sigma \to_{tick} \sigma_{[t \mapsto (t-1)]}} \text{ TICK}_P$$

---

global transitions synchronize via their common labels. The global step relation $\to_\lambda \subseteq \Gamma \times Lab \times \Gamma$ is given by the rules of Table 2.

Asynchronous communication between the two processes uses signal s to exchange a common value v, as given by rule COMM. As far as τ-steps and non-matching communication steps are concerned, each process can proceed on its own by the interleaving rules; each of these rules has a symmetric counterpart, which we elide.

Time elapses by counting down active timers till zero, which happens in case no untimed actions are possible. In rule TICK$_P$, this is expressed by the predicate *blocked* on configurations: *blocked*(σ) holds if no move is possible by the system except either a clock-tick or a reception of a message from the outside. Note in passing that due to the discarding feature, *blocked*(σ, q) implies $q = \epsilon$. The counting down of the timers is written $\eta[t \mapsto (t-1)]$, by which we mean, all currently active timers are decreased by one, i.e., $on(n + 1) - 1 = on(n)$, non-active timers are not affected. Note that the operation is undefined for $on(0)$, since a configuration can perform a tick only if not timer equals $on(0)$.

2.2   Abstracting Data

Next we present a straightforward dataflow analysis marking variable and timer instances that may be influenced by the environment.

The analysis uses a simple *flow graph* representation of the system, where each process is represented by a single flow graph whose nodes n are associated with the process' actions and the flow relation captures the intra-process data dependencies. Since the structure of the language we consider is rather simple, the flow-graph can be easily obtained by standard techniques.

The analysis works on an abstract representation of the data values, where $\top$ is interpreted as value chaotically influenced by the environment and $\bot$ stands for a non-chaotic value. We write $\eta^\alpha, \eta_1^\alpha, \ldots$ for abstract valuations, i.e., for typical elements from $Val^\alpha = Var \to \{\top, \bot\}$. The abstract values are ordered $\bot \leq \top$, and the order is lifted pointwise to valuations. With this ordering, the set of valuations forms a finite complete lattice, where we write $\eta_\bot$ for the least element, given as $\eta_\bot(x) = \bot$ for all $x \in Var$, and we denote the least upper bound of $\eta_1^\alpha, \ldots, \eta_n^\alpha$ by $\bigvee_{i=1}^n \eta_i^\alpha$.

Each node n of the flow graph has associated an abstract transfer function $f_n : Val^\alpha \to Val^\alpha$. The functions are given in Table 3, where α_n denotes the action associated with the node n. The equations describe the change of the abstract valuations depending on the sort of the action at the node. The only case deserving mention is the one for $?s(x)$, whose equation captures the inter-process data-flow from a sending to a receiving actions and where Sig_{ext} are the signals potentially sent by the environment. It is easy to see that the functions f_n are monotone.

Upon start of the analysis, at each node the variables' values are assumed to be defined, i.e., the initial valuation is the least one: $\eta_{init}^\alpha(n) = \eta_\bot$. We are interested in the least solution to the data-flow problem given by the following constraint set:

Table 3. Transfer functions/abstract effect for process P

$$f(?s(x))\eta^\alpha = \begin{cases} \eta^\alpha[x \mapsto \top] & s \in Sig_{ext} \\ \eta^\alpha[x \mapsto \bigvee\{[\![e]\!]_{\eta^\alpha} \mid \alpha_{n'} = g \triangleright P!s(e) \text{ for some node } n'] & \text{else} \end{cases}$$

$$f(g \triangleright P!s(e))\eta^\alpha = \eta^\alpha$$
$$f(g \triangleright x := e)\eta^\alpha = \eta^\alpha[x \mapsto [\![e]\!]_{\eta^\alpha}]$$
$$f(g \triangleright set\ t := e)\eta^\alpha = \eta^\alpha[t \mapsto on([\![e]\!]_{\eta^\alpha})]$$
$$f(g \triangleright reset\ t)\eta^\alpha = \eta^\alpha[t \mapsto off]$$
$$f(g_t \triangleright reset\ t)\eta^\alpha = \eta^\alpha[t \mapsto off]$$

$$\eta^\alpha_{post}(n) \geq f_n(\eta^\alpha_{pre}(n))$$
$$\eta^\alpha_{pre}(n) \geq \bigvee\{\eta^\alpha_{post}(n') \mid (n', n) \text{ in flow relation}\} \tag{1}$$

For each node n of the flow graph, the data-flow problem is specified by two inequations or constraints. The first one relates the abstract valuation η^α_{pre} before entering the node with the valuation η^α_{post} afterwards via the abstract effects of Table 3. The least fixpoint of the constraint set can be solved iteratively in a fairly standard way by a *worklist algorithm* (see e.g., [24,20,29]), where the worklist steers the iterative loop until the least fixpoint is reached (cf. Fig. 1).

```
input : the flow-graph of the program
output : η^α_pre, η^α_post ;

η^α(n) = η^α_init(n) ;
WL = {n | α_n =?s(x), s ∈ Sig_ext} ;

repeat
    pick n ∈ WL;
    let  S = {n' ∈ succ(n) | f_n(η^α(n)) ⊄ η^α(n')}
    in
        for all  n' ∈ S:  η^α(n') := f(η^α(n));
        WL := WL\n ∪ S;
until  WL = ∅;

η^α_pre(n) = η^α(n) ;
η^α_post(n) = f_n(η^α(n))
```

Fig. 1. Worklist algorithm

The algorithm starts with the least valuation on all nodes and an initial worklist containing nodes with input from the environment. It enlarges the valuation within the given lattice step by step until it stabilizes, i.e., until the worklist is empty. If adding the abstract effect of one node to the current state enlarges the valuation, i.e., the set S is non-empty, those successor nodes from S are (re-)entered into the list of the unfinished one. After termination the algorithm yields two mappings $\eta^\alpha_{pre}, \eta^\alpha_{post} : Node \to Val^\alpha$. On a location l, the result of the analysis is given by $\eta^\alpha(l) = \bigvee\{\eta^\alpha_{post}(\tilde{n}) \mid \tilde{n} = \tilde{l} \longrightarrow_\alpha l\}$, also written as η^α_l.

2.3   Program Transformation

Based on the result of the analysis, we transform the given system S into an optimized one, denoted by $S^\sharp$, which is closed, which does not use the value $\top$, and which is in a simulation relation with the original system.

The transformation is given as a set of transformation rules (see Table 4) for each process P. The transformation is straightforward: guards potentially influenced by the environment are taken non-deterministically, i.e., a guard g at a location l replaced by $true$, if $[\![g]\!]_{\eta^\alpha_l} = \top$. Assignments of expressions are either left untouched or replaced by $skip$, depending on the result of the analysis concerning the left-hand value of the assignment (rules T-ASSIGN$_1$ and T-ASSIGN$_2$). For timer guards whose value is indeterminate because of outside influence, we work with a 3-valued abstraction: off, when the timer is deactivated, a value $on(\top)$ when the timer is active with arbitrary expiration time, and a value $on(\top^+)$ for active timers whose expiration time is arbitrary except immediate timeout: the latter two abstract values are represented by $on(0)$ and $on(1)$, respectively, and the non-deterministic behaviour of the timer expiration is captured by arbitrary postponing a timeout by setting back the value of the timer to $on(1)$ according to T-NOTIMEOUT.

We embed the chaotic nature of the environment by adding to each process P a new timer variable t_P, used to guard the input from outside.[1] These timers behave in the same manner as the "chaotic" timers above, except that we do not allow the new t_P timers to become deactivated (cf. rules T-INPUT$_2$ and T-NOINPUT). Since for both input and output, the communication statement using an external signal is replaced by a $skip$, the transformation yields a *closed* system. Outputs to the environment are just removed (rule T-OUTPUT$_2$).

3   Extending the Vires Toolset

The Vires toolset was introduced for verification of industrial-size communication protocols. Its architecture is targeted towards the verification of SDL specifications and it provides an automatic translation of SDL-code into the input language of a discrete-time extension of the well-known Spin model-checker. Design, analysis, verification, and validation of SDL specifications is supported by OBJECTGEODE, one of the most advanced integrated SDL-environments.

---

[1] Note that the action $g_{t_P} \triangleright reset\ t_P;\ set\ t_P := 0$ in rule T-INPUT$_2$ corresponds to the do-nothing step $g_{t_P} \triangleright skip$.

Table 4. Transformation rules

$$\frac{l \xrightarrow{\ }_{g \,\triangleright\, x:=e} \hat{l} \in Edg^{\top} \qquad [\![e]\!]_{\eta_l^{\alpha}} \neq \top \qquad g^{\sharp} = [\![g]\!]_{\eta_l^{\alpha}}}{l \xrightarrow{\ }_{g^{\sharp} \,\triangleright\, x:=e} \hat{l} \in Edg^{\sharp}} \; \text{T-ASSIGN}_1$$

$$\frac{l \xrightarrow{\ }_{g \,\triangleright\, x:=e} \hat{l} \in Edg^{\top} \qquad [\![e]\!]_{\eta_l^{\alpha}} = \top \qquad g^{\sharp} = [\![g]\!]_{\eta_l^{\alpha}}}{l \xrightarrow{\ }_{g^{\sharp} \,\triangleright\, skip} \hat{l} \in Edg^{\sharp}} \; \text{T-ASSIGN}_2$$

$$\frac{l \xrightarrow{\ }_{?s(x)} \hat{l} \in Edg^{\top} \qquad s \notin Sig_{ext}}{l \xrightarrow{\ }_{?s(x)} \hat{l} \in Edg^{\sharp}} \; \text{T-INPUT}_1$$

$$\frac{l \xrightarrow{\ }_{?s(x)} \hat{l} \in Edg^{\top} \qquad s \in Sig_{ext}}{l \xrightarrow{\ }_{g_{t_P} \,\triangleright\, reset\, t_P} \xrightarrow{\ }_{set\, t_P:=0} \hat{l} \in Edg^{\sharp}} \; \text{T-INPUT}_2$$

$$\frac{}{l \xrightarrow{\ }_{g_{t_P} \,\triangleright\, reset\, t_P} \xrightarrow{\ }_{set\, t_P:=1} l \in Edg^{\sharp}} \; \text{T-NOINPUT}$$

$$\frac{l \xrightarrow{\ }_{g \,\triangleright\, P'!(s,e)} \hat{l} \in Edg^{\top} \qquad s \notin Sig_{ext} \qquad g^{\sharp} = [\![g]\!]_{\eta_l^{\alpha}}}{l \xrightarrow{\ }_{g^{\sharp} \,\triangleright\, P'!(s,e)} \hat{l} \in Edg^{\sharp}} \; \text{T-OUTPUT}_1$$

$$\frac{l \xrightarrow{\ }_{g \,\triangleright\, P'!(s,e)} \hat{l} \in Edg^{\top} \qquad s \in Sig_{ext} \qquad g^{\sharp} = [\![g]\!]_{\eta_l^{\alpha}}}{l \xrightarrow{\ }_{g^{\sharp} \,\triangleright\, skip} \hat{l} \in Edg^{\sharp}} \; \text{T-OUTPUT}_2$$

$$\frac{l \xrightarrow{\ }_{g \,\triangleright\, set\, t:=e} \hat{l} \in Edg^{\top} \qquad g^{\sharp} = [\![g]\!]_{\eta_l^{\alpha}} \qquad [\![e]\!]_{\eta_l^{\alpha}} \neq \top}{l \xrightarrow{\ }_{g^{\sharp} \,\triangleright\, set\, t:=e} \hat{l} \in Edg^{\sharp}} \; \text{T-SET}_1$$

$$\frac{l \xrightarrow{\ }_{g \,\triangleright\, set\, t:=e} \hat{l} \in Edg^{\top} \qquad g^{\sharp} = [\![g]\!]_{\eta_l^{\alpha}} \qquad [\![e]\!]_{\eta_l^{\alpha}} = \top}{l \xrightarrow{\ }_{g^{\sharp} \,\triangleright\, set\, t:=0} \hat{l} \in Edg^{\sharp}} \; \text{T-SET}_2$$

$$\frac{l \xrightarrow{\ }_{g \,\triangleright\, reset\, t} \hat{l} \in Edg^{\top} \qquad g^{\sharp} = [\![g]\!]_{\eta_l^{\alpha}}}{l \xrightarrow{\ }_{g^{\sharp} \,\triangleright\, reset\, t} \hat{l} \in Edg^{\sharp}} \; \text{T-RESET}$$

$$\frac{l \xrightarrow{\ }_{g_t \,\triangleright\, reset\, t} \hat{l} \in Edg^{\top} \qquad g_t^{\sharp} = [\![g_t]\!]_{\eta_l^{\alpha}}}{l \xrightarrow{\ }_{g_t^{\sharp} \,\triangleright\, reset\, t} \hat{l} \in Edg^{\sharp}} \; \text{T-TIMEOUT}$$

$$\frac{[\![t]\!]_{\eta_l^{\alpha}} = \top}{l \xrightarrow{\ }_{g_t \,\triangleright\, reset\, t} \xrightarrow{\ }_{set\, t:=1} l \in Edg^{\sharp}} \; \text{T-NOTIMEOUT}$$

OBJECTGEODE also provides code generation and testing of real-time and distributed applications.

Spin [23] is a state-of-the-art, enumerative model-checker with an expressive input-language Promela. In an extensive list of industrial applications, Spin and Promela have proven to be useful for the verification of industrial systems. Spin can be used not only as a simulator for rapid prototyping that supports random, guided and interactive simulation, but also as a powerful state space analyzer for proving user-specified correctness properties of the system. As standard Spin

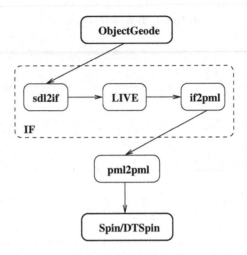

Fig. 2. Toolset components

does not deal with timing aspects of protocols, DTSpin, a discrete time extension of Spin has been developed [3,14], that can be used for verification of properties depending on timing parameters. The extension is compatible with the standard untimed version of the Spin validator, except for the timeout statement, which has different semantics and its usage is no longer allowed (nor necessary) in discrete-time models.

IF [5] bridges the gap between OBJECTGEODE and Spin/DTSpin. It contains a translator, SDL2IF of SDL specifications into the intermediate representation IF. A static analyzer Live [27] performs optimization of IF-representation to reduce the state space of the model. IF-specifications can be translated to DTPromela models with the help of IF2PML-translator [4] and verified by DTSpin.

The PML2PML-translator takes care of the automatic closing of a subcomponent and implements the theory presented before. The tool post-processes the output from the translation from the SDL-specification to Promela, where the implementation covers the subset of SDL described abstractly in Section 2. The translator works fully automatic and does not require any user interaction, except that the user is required to indicate the list of external signals. The extension is implemented in Java and requires JDK-1.2 or later. The package can be downloaded from http://www.cwi.nl/~ustin/EH.html.

4   Experimental Results

Before we present the results on a larger example — the control-part of a medium-access protocol — we show the effect of the transformation on the state space using a few artificial, small examples.

4.1 Simple Motivating Examples

In this subsection we take some simple open systems modelled in DTPromela, close them with chaos as separate process and illustrate how the state space grows with the buffer length and with the number of signals involved into the communication with the environment.

First, we construct a DTPromela model of a process that receives signals a, b, and c from the outside, and reacts by sending back d, e, and f, respectively.

```
proctype proc(){
    start: goto q;
    q: atomic{ if
               :: envch?a ->  proch!d; goto q;
               :: envch?b ->  proch!e; goto q;
               :: envch?c ->  proch!f; goto q; fi;
               }
}
```

A closing environment will send the messages a, b, and c to the process, and conversely receive d, e, and f in an arbitrary manner. As explained in Section 2, the environment must behave chaotically also wrt. the timing behaviour. Therefore, in order to avoid zero-time cycles, the sending actions are guarded by a timeout and an extra clause is added when no more signals are to be sent in the current time slice. A specification of such an environment process is given below:

```
s: atomic{ if
   :: expire(t) -> set(t, 1); goto s; /* stop sending
                           signals until the next time slice */
   :: expire(t) -> envch!a; set(t, 0); goto s;
   . . . . . . . . . . .
   :: proch?f -> goto s;
   fi }
}
```

The queues in the verification model, however, have to be bounded. There are two options in Spin for handling queues. The first one is to block a process attempting to send a message to a full queue until there is a free cell in the queue. With this option, our "naive" closing leads to a deadlock caused by an attempt of a process to send a message to the full queue of the environment while the environment is trying to send a message to the full process queue. Another option is to lose new messages in case the queue is full. In this case large number of messages gets lost (see Table 5). Many properties cannot be verified using this option. Moreover, there is a large class of systems where messages should not get lost, for this would lead to non-realistic behaviour of the system. Still, even when this option is applicable, time and memory consumption grow tremendously fast with the buffer size, as shown in Table 5.

Table 5. Different buffer sizes, unlimited number of signals per time slice

option	buffer	states	transitions	lost messages	memory (MB)	time
block	3	deadlock				
loose	3	3783	13201	5086	2.644	00.24 s
loose	4	37956	128079	47173	3.976	01.97 s
loose	5	357015	1.18841e+06	428165	18.936	20.49 s
loose	6	3.27769e+06	1.08437e+07	3.86926e+06	170.487	4 min 04.74 s

We can avoid the deadlock in the system above if we limit a number of messages sent by the environment per a time slice. For this purpose we introduce an integer variable n set to the queue size and modify the options of the *if* statement in such a way that sendings are enabled only if n is positive; n is counted down with every message sent and n is revived every time before a new time slice starts.

```
:: (n>0 && expire(t)) -> envch!a; n = n-1; set(t, 0); goto ea;
......................
:: expire(t) -> set(t, 1); n= BUFFSIZE; goto ea;
```

Verification results for the system closed in such a way are shown in Table 6. And again, though more slowly than in the previous example, the number of states, transitions, memory usage, and time required for the verification grow with the queue length very fast.

Table 6. Different buffer sizes (4 signals per time slice)

option	buffer	states	transitions	nemory (MB)	time
block	3	328	770	2.542	00.06 s
block	4	1280	3243	2.542	00.10 s
block	5	4743	12601	2.747	00.24 s
block	6	16954	46502	3.259	00.78 s

Next we fix the length of the queue at 4 and vary the number of different messages sent from the process to the environment and from the environment to the process. Table 7 shows the experimental results. Note that the growth of the state space of the system is now caused by the combinatorial explosion in the queues. (The maximal number of messages that can be sent per a time slice is still equal to the length of the queue.)

In the experiments for the same process with the environment embedded and not external, the number of states is constant for all the cases considered and equal to 4. As one might have expected, closing system by a separate environment process behaving chaotically, leads to a state space explosion even

Table 7. Different numbers of message types

n-messages	states	transitions	memory (MB)	time
4	3568	9041	2.644	00.22 s
5	8108	20519	2.849	00.42 s
6	16052	40569	3.156	00.75 s
7	28792	72683	3.771	01.36 s
8	47960	120953	4.590	02.45 s
9	75428	190071	5.819	03.86 s

for very simple small systems. Tailoring the environment process such that only "relevant" messages can be sent makes the environment process large and complicated, which can also cause the growth of the state space or lead to errors caused by mistakes in the environment design.

4.2   Case Study: A Wireless ATM Medium-Access Protocol

To validate our approach, we applied the PML2PML-translator in a series of experiments to the industrial protocol Mascara [36].

Located between the ATM-layer and the physical medium, Mascara is a medium-access layer or, in the context of the ISDN reference model, a transmission convergence sub-layer for wireless ATM communication in local area networks. A crucial feature of Mascara is the support of *mobility*. A mobile terminal (MT) located inside the area cell of an access point (AP) is capable of communicating with it. When a mobile terminal moves outside the current cell, it has to perform a so-called *handover* to another access point covering the cell the terminal has move into. The handover must be managed transparently with respect to the ATM layer, maintaining the agreed quality of service for the current connections. So the protocol has to detect the need for a handover, select a candidate AP to switch to, and redirect the traffic with minimal interruption.

Composed of various protocol layers and sub-entities, Mascara is a large protocol. With the current state-of-the-art in automatic verification it is not possible to model check it as a whole — the compositional approach and abstractions are necessary. Since the model of Mascara is not trivial, already the state space of the obtained submodels with only several processes is large.

This protocol was the main case study in the Vires project; the results of its verification can be found e.g. in [4,19,33]. Here, we are not interested in the verification of Mascara's properties but in the comparison of the state space of a model of the *Mascara control* entity (MCL) at the mobile terminal side when closed with the environment as a separate chaotic process and the state space of the same entity closed with embedded chaos.

The *Mascara control* entity is responsible for the protocol's control and signaling tasks. It offers its services to the ATM-layer above while using the services of the underlying segmentation and reassembly entity, the sliding-window entities, and in general the low-layer data-pump. It carries out the periodical monitoring of the current radio link quality, gathering the information about radio link qualities of its neighbouring access points to be able to handover to one of them quickly in the case of deterioration of the current association link quality, and switching from one access point to another in the handover procedure.

In [33] we were closing MCL by embedding the chaotic environment *manually*. Not surprisingly, verifying properties of MCL closed with chaos yielded false negatives first in many cases — the completely chaotic environment was too abstract. Therefore, the traces leading to these false negatives were analyzed, which resulted in a refined environment. The refinement was done by identifying signals that could not be exchanged chaotically lest the verification property was violated, then constructing a specific environment process handling only these signals, and finally closing the obtained still open system by embedding the residual chaos. The conditions imposed on sending the detached signals are in fact the conditions imposed on the behaviour of the rest of the protocol, which formed later the verification properties for the other protocol entities. Thus, by constructing the environment process we only produce an abstraction of the real environment, keeping it as abstract as possible and leaving the whole model still open, which means that the environment prescribes the order of sendings and receivings for a part of signals, only. In this way, we could still benefit from embedding the chaos into the process.

Of course, closing the system manually is time-consuming and error-prone. With the implemented translator, it became possible to reproduce the same series of experiments quickly, without looking for typos and omissions introduced during the manual closing. Moreover, we performed the same experiments for MCL closed with the chaotic environment modelled as a process. In our experiments we used DTSpin version 0.1.1, an extension of Spin 3.3.10, using the partial-order reduction and compression options. All the experiments were run on a Silicon Graphics Origin 2000 server on a single R10000/250MHz CPU with 8GB of main memory. Our aim was to compare the state space and resource consumption for the two closing approaches. Therefore, we did not verify any LTL properties.

Table 8. Model checking MCL with chaos as a process and embedded chaos

bs	states	transitions	mem.	time	states	transitions	mem.	time
2	9.73e+05	3.64e+06	40.842	15:57	300062	1.06e+06	9.071	1:13
3	5.24e+06	2.02e+07	398.933	22:28	396333	1.85e+06	11.939	1:37
4	2.69e+07	1.05e+08	944.440	1:59:40	467555	2.30e+06	14.499	2:13

Table 8 gives the results for the model checking of MCL with chaos as external process on the left and embedded on the right. The first column gives the buffer size for process queues. The other columns give the number of states, transitions, memory and time consumption, respectively. As one can see, the state space as well as the time and the memory consumption are significantly larger for the model with the environment as a process, and they grow with the buffer size much faster than for the model with embedded chaos. The model with embedded environment has a relatively stable state-space size and other verification characteristics.

5   Conclusion

In this paper we described the implementation of a tool which allows to automatically close DTPromela translations of SDL-specifications by embedding the timed chaotic environment into the system. Our experiments performed on the Mascara case study show the efficiency of the chaos closing method.

Closing open (sub-)systems is common for software *testing*. In this field, a work close to ours in spirit and techniques is the one of [11]. It describes a dataflow algorithm for closing program fragments given in the C-language with the most general environment, eliminating the external interface at the same time. The algorithm is incorporated into the *VeriSoft* tool. Similar to the work presented here, they assume an asynchronous communicating model, but do not consider *timed* systems and their abstraction. Similarly, [17] consider partial (i.e., open) systems which are transformed into closed ones. To enhance the precision of the abstraction, their approach allows to close the system by an external environment more specific than the most general, chaotic one, where the closing environment can be built to conform to given assumptions, which they call filtering [15]. A more fundamental approach to model checking open systems is known as *module* checking [26,25]. Instead of transforming the system into a closed one, the underlying computational model is generalized to distinguish between transitions under control of the module and those driven by the environment. MOCHA [2] is a model checker for reactive modules, which uses alternating-time temporal logic as specification language.

In the context of the IF-toolset [5], live variable analysis has been proven useful [27] to counter the state explosion. Slicing, a well-known program analysis technique, which resembles the analysis described in this paper, is explored in [28] to speed up model checking and simulation in Spin. Likewise in the context of LTL model checking, [16] use slicing to cut away irrelevant program fragments but the transformation yields a safe, property-preserving abstraction and potentially a smaller state space.

For the future, we will extend the subset of SDL our translator can handle, including complex data types, procedures and process creation. Based on the results from [34], another direction for future work is to the extend the PML2PML implementation to handle environments more refined than just chaos with building an environment process communicating to the system synchronously.

References

1. Telelogic TAU SDL Suite. http://www.telelogic.com/products/sdl/, 2002.
2. R. Alur, T. A. Henzinger, F. Mang, S. Qadeer, S. K. Rajamani, and S. Tasiran. Mocha: Modularity in model checking. In A. J. Hu and M. Y. Vardi, editors, *Proceedings of CAV '98*, volume 1427 of *Lecture Notes in Computer Science*, pages 521–525. Springer-Verlag, 1998.
3. D. Bošnački and D. Dams. Integrating real time into Spin: A prototype implementation. In S. Budkowski, A. Cavalli, and E. Najm, editors, *Proceedings of Formal Description Techniques and Protocol Specification, Testing, and Verification (FORTE/PSTV'98)*. Kluwer Academic Publishers, 1998.
4. D. Bošnački, D. Dams, L. Holenderski, and N. Sidorova. Verifying SDL in Spin. In S. Graf and M. Schwartzbach, editors, *TACAS 2000*, volume 1785 of *Lecture Notes in Computer Science*. Springer-Verlag, 2000.
5. M. Bozga, J.-C. Fernandez, L. Ghirvu, S. Graf, J.-P. Krimm, and L. Mounier. IF: An intermediate representation and validation environment for timed asynchronous systems. In J. Wing, J. Woodcock, and J. Davies, editors, *Proceedings of Symposium on Formal Methods (FM 99)*, volume 1708 of *Lecture Notes in Computer Science*. Springer-Verlag, Sept. 1999.
6. M. Bozga, J.-C. Fernandez, L. Ghirvu, S. Graf, J.-P. Krimm, and L. Mounier. IF: A validation environment for timed asynchronous systems. In E. A. Emerson and A. P. Sistla, editors, *Proceedings of CAV '00*, volume 1855 of *Lecture Notes in Computer Science*. Springer-Verlag, 2000.
7. M. Bozga, S. Graf, A. Kerbrat, L. Mounier, I. Ober, and D. Vincent. SDL for real-time: What is missing? In Y. Lahav, S. Graf, and C. Jard, editors, *Electronic Proceedings of SAM'00*, 2000.
8. E. Clarke, O. Grumberg, and D. Long. Model checking and abstraction. *ACM Transactions on Programming Languages and Systems*, 16(5):1512–1542, 1994. A preliminary version appeared in the Proceedings of POPL 92.
9. E. M. Clarke and E. A. Emerson. Design and synthesis of synchronisation skeletons using branching time temporal logic specifications. In D. Kozen, editor, *Proceedings of the Workshop on Logic of Programs 1981*, volume 131 of *Lecture Notes in Computer Science*, pages 244–263. Springer-Verlag, 1982.
10. E. M. Clarke and J. M. Wing. Formal methods: State of the art and future directions. *ACM Computing Surveys*, Dec. 1996. Available also as Carnegie Mellon University technical report CMU-CS-96-178.
11. C. Colby, P. Godefroid, and L. J. Jagadeesan. Automatically closing of open reactive systems. In *Proceedings of 1998 ACM SIGPLAN Conference on Programming Language Design and Implementation*. ACM Press, 1998.
12. P. Cousot and R. Cousot. Abstract interpretation: A unified lattice model for static analysis of programs by construction or approximaton of fixpoints. In *Fourth Annual Symposium on Principles of Programming Languages (POPL) (Los Angeles, Ca)*, pages 238–252. ACM, January 1977.
13. D. Dams, R. Gerth, and O. Grumberg. Abstract interpretation of reactive systems: Abstraction preserving ∀CTL*,∃CTL*, and CTL*. In E.-R. Olderog, editor, *Proceedings of PROCOMET '94*. IFIP, North-Holland, June 1994.
14. Discrete-time Spin. http://win.tue.nl/~dragan/DTSpin.html, 2000.
15. M. Dwyer and D. Schmidt. Limiting state explosion with filter-based refinement. In *Proceedings of the 1st International Workshop in Verification, Abstract Interpretation, and Model Checking*, Oct. 1997.

16. M. B. Dwyer and J. Hatcliff. Slicing software for model construction. In *Proceedings of the ACM SIGPLAN Workshop on Partial Evaluation and Semantics-Based Program Manipulation (PEPM'99)*, Jan. 1999.

17. M. B. Dwyer and C. S. Pasareanu. Filter-based model checking of partial systems. In *Proceedings of the 6th ACM SIGSOFT Symposium on the Foundations of Software Engineering (SIGSOFT '98)*, pages 189–202, 1998.

18. A. B. F. Regensburger. Formal verification of SDL systems at the Siemens mobile phone department. In B. Steffen, editor, *Proceedings of TACAS '98*, number 1384 in Lecture Notes in Computer Science, pages 439–455. Springer-Verlag, 1998.

19. J. Guoping and S. Graf. Verification experiments on the Mascara protocol. In M. B. Dwyer, editor, *Model Checking Software, Proceedings of the 8th International SPIN Workshop (SPIN 2001), Toronto, Canada*, Lecture Notes in Computer Science, pages 123–142. Springer-Verlag, 2001.

20. M. S. Hecht. *Flow Analysis of Programs*. North-Holland, 1977.

21. U. Hinkel. Verification of SDL specifications on the basis of stream semantics. In Y. Lahav, A. Wolisz, J. Fischer, and E. Holz, editors, *Proceedings of the 1st Workshop of the SDL Forum Society on SDL and MSC (SAM'98)*, pages 241–250, 1998.

22. G. Holzmann and J. Patti. Validating SDL specifications: an experiment. In E. Brinksma, editor, *International Workshop on Protocol Specification, Testing and Verification IX (Twente, The Netherlands)*, pages 317–326. North-Holland, 1989. IFIP TC-6 International Workshop.

23. G. J. Holzmann. *Design and Validation of Computer Protocols*. Prentice Hall, 1991.

24. G. Kildall. A unified approach to global program optimization. In *Proceedings of POPL '73*, pages 194–206. ACM, January 1973.

25. O. Kupferman and M. Y. Vardi. Module checking revisited. In O. Grumberg, editor, *CAV '97, Proceedings of the 9th International Conference on Computer-Aided Verification, Haifa. Israel*, volume 1254 of *Lecture Notes in Computer Science*. Springer, June 1997.

26. O. Kupferman, M. Y. Vardi, and P. Wolper. Module checking. In R. Alur, editor, *Proceedings of CAV '96*, volume 1102 of *Lecture Notes in Computer Science*, pages 75–86, 1996.

27. L. G. M. Bozga, J. Cl. Fernandez. State space reduction based on Live. In A. Cortesi and G. Filé, editors, *Proceedings of SAS '99*, volume 1694 of *Lecture Notes in Computer Science*. Springer-Verlag, 1999.

28. L. I. Millet and T. Teitelbaum. Slicing promela and its application to model checking, simulation, and protocol understanding. In E. Najm, A. Serhrouchni, and G. Holzmann, editors, *Electronic Proceedings of the Fourth International SPIN Workshop, Paris, France*, Nov. 1998.

29. F. Nielson, H.-R. Nielson, and C. Hankin. *Principles of Program Analysis*. Springer-Verlag, 1999.

30. ObjectGeode 4. http://www.csverilog.com/products/geode.htm, 2000.

31. J. P. Queille and J. Sifakis. Specification and verification of concurrent systems in CESAR. In M. Dezani-Ciancaglini and U. Montanari, editors, *Proceedings of the 5th International Symposium on Programming 1981*, volume 137 of *Lecture Notes in Computer Science*, pages 337–351. Springer-Verlag, 1982.

32. N. Sidorova and M. Steffen. Embedding chaos. In P. Cousot, editor, *Proceedings of the 8th Static Analysis Symposium (SAS'01)*, volume 2126 of *Lecture Notes in Computer Science*, pages 319–334. Springer-Verlag, 2001.

33. N. Sidorova and M. Steffen. Verifying large SDL-specifications using model checking. In R. Reed and J. Reed, editors, *Proceedings of the 10th International SDL Forum SDL 2001: Meeting UML*, volume 2078 of *Lecture Notes in Computer Science*, pages 403–416. Springer-Verlag, Feb. 2001.
34. N. Sidorova and M. Steffen. Synchronous closing of timed SDL systems for model checking. In A. Cortesi, editor, *Proceedings of the hird International Workshop on Verification, Model Checking, and Abstract Interpretation (VMCAI) 2002*, volume 2294 of *Lecture Notes in Computer Science*, pages 79–93. Springer-Verlag, 2002.
35. H. Tuominen. Embedding a dialect of SDL in Promela. In D. Dams, R. Gerth, S. Leue, and M. Massink, editors, *Theoretical and Practical Aspects of SPIN Model Checking, Proceedings of 5th and 6th International SPIN Workshops, Trento/Toulouse*, volume 1680 of *Lecture Notes in Computer Science*, pages 245–260. Springer-Verlag, 1999.
36. A wireless ATM network demonstrator (WAND), ACTS project AC085. http://www.tik.ee.ethz.ch/~wand/, 1998.

A Generalised Sweep-Line Method for Safety Properties

Lars Michael Kristensen[1]* and Thomas Mailund[2]

[1] School of Electrical and Information Engineering, University of South Australia
Mawson Lakes Campus, SA 5095, AUSTRALIA
lars.kristensen@unisa.edu.au
[2] Department of Computer Science, University of Aarhus
IT-parken, Aabogade 34, DK-8200 Aarhus N, DENMARK
mailund@daimi.au.dk

Abstract. The recently developed sweep-line method exploits progress present in many concurrent systems to explore the full state space of the system while storing only small fragments of the state space in memory at a time. A disadvantage of the sweep-line method is that it relies on a monotone and global notion of progress. This prevents the method from being used for many reactive systems. In this paper we generalise the sweep-line method such that it can be used for verifying safety properties of reactive systems exhibiting local progress. The basic idea is to relax the monotone notion of progress and to recognise the situations where this could cause the state space exploration not to terminate. The generalised sweep-line method explores all reachable states of the system, but may explore a state several times. We demonstrate the practical application of the generalised sweep-line method on two case studies demonstrating a reduction in peak memory usage to typically 10 % compared to the use of ordinary full state spaces.

Keywords: explicit state space exploration methods, reachability analysis, state space reduction methods, theoretical foundations, practical use and tool support.

1 Introduction

Computer memory is in many cases the limiting factor in verification based on state spaces. This has motivated the development of several *state space reduction methods* to alleviate the *state explosion problem* (see e.g., [25] for a survey). An important class of state space reduction methods is based on the paradigm of deleting and/or throwing away information about the states encountered during the state space exploration. The recently developed sweep-line method [5] belongs to this class of methods. Other examples of state space reduction methods belonging to this class are the *bit-state hashing method* [10, 11] and the *state space caching method* [12]. Deletion of visited states has also been investigated

---

* Supported by the Danish Natural Science Research Council.

L.-H. Eriksson and P. Lindsay (Eds.): FME 2002, LNCS 2391, pp. 549–567, 2002.
© Springer-Verlag Berlin Heidelberg 2002

in [21] based on the identification of *pseudo-root* states. A heuristic for deletion of states based on revisiting degree has been investigated in [17]. Recently [2], heuristics for deleting states based on structural techniques of Petri Nets have been developed for *partial state space exploration*. Other examples of state space reduction methods are partial order reduction methods [22,24,27] and the symmetry method [6,7,15].

The novelty of the sweep-line method is the intriguingly simple idea of exploiting a certain kind of *progress* exhibited by many concurrent systems. Exploiting progress makes it possible to investigate the full state space of the system, while only storing small fragments of the state space in memory at a time. The idea is to guide the state space exploration by a *progress measure*, which maps states into *progress values* and which is compatible with the reachability relation. This makes it possible to *garbage collect* states that are not reachable from the current unexplored states. Intuitively, a *sweep-line* is dragged through the full state space, reachable states is calculated in front of the sweep-line, and states are deleted behind the sweep-line. This is in contrast to conventional state space methods which store the entire state space (or a large subset of it) in memory. The verification of properties is then done on-the-fly during the sweep through the state space. Some first case studies [5] indicate reduction in the memory requirement by factors of 10 to 100 and the time spent on the verification by a factor of 10, compared with conventional state space methods.

The main limitation of the basic sweep-line method [5] is that fully reactive systems cannot be handled due to the monotone notion of progress exploited. Usually fully reactive systems react to some event by performing a number of actions, after which they return to their initial state. While the series of actions performed can be considered a kind of progress, the edges back to the initial state prevents the sweep-line method from being applied to these systems. The contribution of this paper is to present a generalised sweep-line method that reconciles fully reactive systems and the sweep-line method. This significantly broadens the class of the systems that can be handled with the sweep-line method. In fact, the method can now be applied to any system, and the progress exploited determines the reduction in peak memory usage. The idea is to detect *regress-edges* that violate the progress condition of the original sweep-line method, on-the-fly during the sweep through the state space. The state space exploration along regress-edges is postponed, and destination states of regress-edges are used as roots in a subsequent sweep. This results in an algorithm consisting of multiple sweeps that still ensures that each reachable state is visited at least once making it suitable for reasoning about safety properties, e.g., determining whether the system can enter a state satisfying a given predicate on states. Safety properties constitute an important class of properties of concurrent systems and can for instance be used to check mutual exclusion properties.

The paper is organised as follows. Section 2 recalls the basic sweep-line method from [5]. Section 3 introduces the generalised sweep-line method and the concept of regress-edges. Section 4 presents the algorithm for state exploration with the generalised sweep-line method. Section 5 introduces a variant of the method exploiting *persistence predicates*. Section 6 presents experimental results on some example systems. Finally, Sect. 7 contains the conclusions and a further discussion of related and future work. The reader is assumed to be familiar with the basic ideas of state space methods.

2   Background

The sweep-line method has been developed in the context of Coloured Petri Nets (CP-nets or CPNs) [13, 19]. The method is, however, not specific to CP-nets, but applicable to a wide range of modelling languages and formalisms. To make the presentation of the generalised sweep-line method independent of any concrete modelling language, we assume that the systems we are considering can be characterised as a tuple $\mathcal{S} = (S, T, \Delta, s_I)$, where S is a finite set of *states*, T is a finite set of *transitions*, $\Delta \subseteq S \times T \times S$ is the *transition relation*, and $s_I \in S$ is the *initial state*. Most models of concurrent systems including CPN models, fall into this category of systems.

Let $s, s' \in S$ be two states and $t \in T$ a transition. If $(s, t, s') \in \Delta$ we say that t is *enabled* in s, and that the *occurrence* of t in the state s leads to the state s'. This is also written $s \xrightarrow{t} s'$. A state s_n is *reachable* from a state s_1 iff there exists states $s_2, s_3, \ldots, s_{n-1}$ and transitions $t_1, t_2, \ldots t_{n-1}$ such that $(s_i, t_i, s_{i+1}) \in \Delta$ for $1 \leq i \leq n - 1$. If state s' is reachable from state s we write $s \rightarrow^* s'$. In particular: $s \rightarrow^* s$. For a state s, $\mathsf{reach}(s) = \{\, s' \in S \mid s \rightarrow^* s' \,\}$ denotes the set of states reachable from s. The set of *reachable states* of $\mathcal{S}$ is then $\mathsf{reach}(s_I)$. The *state space* of a system is the directed graph (V, E) where $V = \mathsf{reach}(s_I)$ is the set of nodes and $E = \{(s, t, s') \in \Delta \mid s, s' \in V\}$ is the set of edges. In the rest of this paper we will assume that we are given a system $\mathcal{S} = (S, T, \Delta, s_I)$.

The sweep-line method is based on the concept of *progress measure*. A progress measure specifies a *total order* $(O, \sqsubseteq)$ on the states of the system, and a *progress mapping* ψ assigning a *progress value* $\psi(s) \in O$ to each state s. Moreover, the ordering is required to preserve the reachability relation $\rightarrow^*$ of the system.

Definition 1. *(Def. 1 in [5]) A **progress measure** is a tuple $\mathcal{P} = (O, \sqsubseteq, \psi)$ such that $(O, \sqsubseteq)$ is a total order and $\psi : S \rightarrow O$ is a progress mapping from states into O satisfying: $\forall s, s' \in \mathsf{reach}(s_I) : s \rightarrow^* s' \Rightarrow \psi(s) \sqsubseteq \psi(s')$.* □

In the original definition [5], $(O, \sqsubseteq)$ was a *partial order*. To simplify the presentation we consider a total order in this paper. Furthermore, all concrete examples that we have experimented with have been based on a total order. The important property of progress measures is that for all reachable states $s, s' \in \mathsf{reach}(s_I)$, if $\psi(s) \sqsubset \psi(s')$ then $s \notin \mathsf{reach}(s')$. This means that the progress measure $\mathcal{P}$ provides a conservative estimate of the reachability relation. In conventional state space exploration, the states are kept in memory to recognise already visited states. However, states with a progress value strictly less than the progress values of states yet to be processed can never be reached again. It is therefore safe to delete such states. Saving memory by deleting these states is the basic idea underlying the sweep-line method.

The state space exploration algorithm for the basic sweep-line method is listed in Fig. 1. The algorithm is derived from the standard algorithm for state space exploration by including deletion of states that can no longer be reached from the states that are still to be processed, and by exploring the states according to their progress values. The structure UNPROCESSED keeps track of the states for which successors are still to be calculated. In each iteration (lines 3-15) a new unprocessed state is selected (line 4), such that this state has a minimal progress value among the states in UNPROCESSED. The states explored so far are stored in NODES, and states are only added to UNPROCESSED (lines 9-12) if they are not already in NODES. After a state has been processed, states with a progress value strictly less that the minimal progress value among the states in UNPROCESSED can be deleted (line 14). The function GARBAGECOL-LECT removes the nodes (in NODES) with progress value strictly less than the argument. The argument is the smallest progress value among the unprocessed nodes. The condition that the progress measure preserves the reachability relation is checked on-the-fly when the successors of a state are being calculated (line 6-8). If the condition is violated, the generation is stopped giving a triple (s, t, s') demonstrating why the progress measure was not valid.

```
1: UNPROCESSED ← {s_I}
2: NODES.ADD(s_I)
3: while ¬ UNPROCESSED.EMPTY() do
4:    s ← UNPROCESSED.GETMINELEMENT()
5:    for all (t, s') such that s →ᵗ s' do
6:       if ψ(s) ⋢ ψ(s') then
7:          STOP("Progress measure rejected:",(s, t, s'))
8:       end if
9:       if ¬(NODES.CONTAINS(s')) then
10:         NODES.ADD(s')
11:         UNPROCESSED.ADD(s')
12:      end if
13:   end for
14:   NODES.GARBAGECOLLECT(min{ψ(s) | s ∈ UNPROCESSED})
15: end while
```

Fig. 1. The basic sweep-line algorithm.

Figure 2 illustrates the sweep-line method. The states are ordered left to right according to their progress value. Initially (a), only the initial state s_I is stored and the sweep-line (the dashed vertical line), is to the left of the state space. Successors of s_I are then calculated and marked as unprocessed. After s_I has been processed, s_1 is selected for processing since s_1 has a minimal progress value among the unprocessed states (s_1, s_2, and s_3). After s_1 has been processed, all states with the initial progress value (s_I and s_1) have been processed (b), and the sweep-line can move to the right. As it does this, the states with progress value strictly less than the minimal progress value (s_I and s_1) among the unprocessed

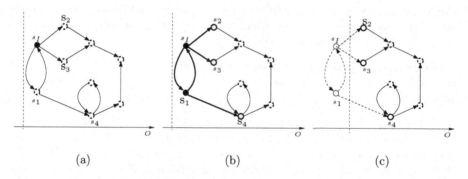

Fig. 2. Snapshots of the sweep-line method.

states (s_2, s_3, and s_4) are deleted (c). After this either s_2 or s_3 can be selected for processing and the exploration continues. Intuitively, a sweep-line is dragged through the state space, while new states are generated in front of the line and old states are deleted behind the line.

3 Regress-Edges and Generalised Progress Measures

For systems with progress, the sweep-line method offers significant savings in memory usage during state space explorations as demonstrated by case studies in [5]. However, for systems with, e.g., a state space with a single strongly connected component (which constitutes a large class of important systems) there is no progress in the formal sense of Def. 1. The problem is that if the state space has one strongly connected component, all states are required to have the same progress value as a consequence of Def. 1. Hence, it is not possible to delete states.

The problem with *monotone progress measures* as required by Def. 1 is that they disallow occurrences of transitions leading from a state s to a state s' with a strictly lower progress value than s. If the state space contains an edge from a state with a high progress value to a state with a low progress value, deleting states with lower progress values than the current minimal progress value among the unprocessed states will no longer be safe. The reason is that such states are potentially needed for comparison with newly generated states, and deleting them could cause the state space exploration algorithm in Fig. 1 not to terminate. Such *regress-edges* leading from a state with high progress value to a state with a lower progress value play a key role in the generalised sweep-line method.

Definition 2. *Let $\mathcal{S} = (S, T, \Delta, s_I)$ be a system. The triple $(s, t, s') \in \Delta$ is a **regress-edge** for a progress mapping $\psi : S \to O$ if and only if $\psi(s) \sqsupset \psi(s')$.* □

The first step towards handling regress-edges and exploiting local progress is to relax the definition of progress measures by removing the requirement that the progress measure preserves the transition relation, and simply require that it orders the states. The next step (which we will return to in Sect. 4) is to modify the sweep-line exploration algorithm.

Definition 3. *A **generalised progress measure** is a tuple* $\mathcal{P} = (O, \sqsubseteq, \psi)$ *such that* $(O, \sqsubseteq)$ *is a total order and* $\psi : S \rightarrow O$ *is a progress mapping from states into* O. $\quad\square$

With this relaxed definition even reactive systems with a fully connected state space can have a non-trivial progress measure. This allows us to exploit progress even when the progress is not global for the entire state space. However, there is no longer any guarantee that the algorithm in Fig. 1 terminates. The problem is that regress-edges can lead to previously visited, but now deleted states. If we do not recognise this situation, we risk exploring the same parts of the state space over and over, never completing the state space exploration. The next section shows how such situations can be recognised and presents an algorithm for state space exploration based on generalised progress measures.

4   State Space Exploration

The key to ensuring that state space exploration with generalised progress measures terminates is to detect the regress-edges on-the-fly during the state space exploration. The idea is to temporarily truncate the state space exploration along a regress-edge and then use the destination states of the regress-edges identified during the sweep as starting points (roots) for the next sweep. Moreover, whenever a regress-edge is identified, its destination state is marked as *persistent* to prevent it from being garbage collected again. In this way, we will explore (i.e., calculate successors of) a destination state of a regress-edge for the last time once we explore the regress-edge. The algorithm works as illustrated in Fig. 3. The state space considered is the same as the one considered in Fig. 2 except that two additional states (s_9 and s_{10}) with associated arcs have been added, and a regress-edge has been added from state s_8 to state s_6. While examining the last nodes s_7 and s_8 in the state space (a), a regress-edge from s_8 to the deleted state s_6, and a regress-edge from s_8 to the unexplored state s_9 are discovered. The states s_6 and s_9 are marked as *persistent*, which ensures that they will not be garbage collected in subsequent sweeps. States s_6 and s_9 are also set aside as *roots* for the next sweep. When the current sweep terminates (b), the algorithm initiates a new sweep using s_6 and s_9 as starting points (c). When the regress-edge from s_8 to s_6 is rediscovered in this sweep, s_6 will not have been garbage collected since it was marked as persistent in the previous sweep. Similarly for the regress-edge from s_8 to s_9. Multiple sweeps are needed, since we cannot distinguish a regress-edge leading to a previously explored state (s_6) from a regress-edge leading to a state (s_9) not explored in a previous sweep.

Figure 4 lists the generalised sweep-line algorithm. The sweep-line is dragged through the state space as in the basic algorithm, except that regress-edges are identified during the sweep. The destination nodes of the regress-edges that are

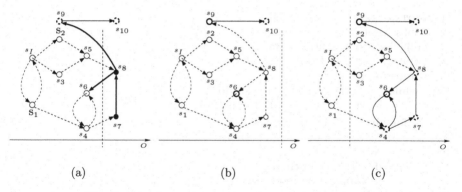

(a)   (b)   (c)

Fig. 3. Snapshots of the generalised sweep-line method.

not identified as previously explored in one sweep are added to a set of nodes
that will constitute the roots for the next sweep. When a node is identified as a
root it is marked as persistent to prevent it from being used as a root again in
a later sweep. The algorithm performs a number of sweeps (lines 3-21) similar
to the basic method, but in each sweep regress-edges are identified (line 11),
and the destination states of regress-edges are marked as persistent and used
as root states for the next sweep (lines 12-13). Once a node has been marked
as persistent, it cannot be deleted by the garbage collection in line 19. Since
all destinations of regress-edges are automatically marked as persistent, a state
that has been used as a root in one sweep will never be used as such again in
any subsequent sweep.

As Fig. 3 shows, a state may be explored (i.e., added to UNPROCESSED and
successor states calculated) several times during the state space exploration.
The following theorem gives an upper bound on the number of times a state
may be explored, and states that all reachable states will indeed be visited by
the generalised sweep-line algorithm.

Theorem 1. *The generalised sweep-line algorithm in Fig. 4 terminates after
having explored at most* $(|B|+1) \cdot |V|$ *states, where B denotes the destinations of
regress-edges:* $B = \{\, s' \mid s \to s' \wedge \psi(s') \sqsubset \psi(s) \,\}$ *and V denotes the nodes in the
state space:* $V = \mathsf{reach}(s_I)$. *Upon termination all states reachable from* s_I *have
been explored at least once.*

Proof. The inner loop (lines 6-20) is a conventional graph traversal, exploiting
progress as in the basic sweep-line algorithm. This graph traversal will explore
the subgraph reachable from the nodes in ROOTS, exploring each node once
giving an upper bound of $|V|$ on the number of states explored. The outer loop
(lines 3-21) is executed initially and repeated whenever the inner loop recognises
at least one regress-edge leading to a state not previously marked as persistent.
Since each node added to ROOTS is marked as persistent, and therefore will
never be added to ROOTS again, $|B|$ is an upper bound on the number of nodes

```
1:  ROOTS ← {s_I}
2:  NODES.ADD(s_I)
3:  while ¬ (ROOTS.EMPTY()) do
4:      UNPROCESSED ← ROOTS
5:      ROOTS ← ∅
6:      while ¬ (UNPROCESSED.EMPTY()) do
7:          s ← UNPROCESSED.GETMINELEMENT()
8:          for all (t, s') such that s →ᵗ s' do
9:              if ¬(NODES.CONTAINS(s')) then
10:                 NODES.ADD(s')
11:                 if ψ(s) ⊐ ψ(s') then
12:                     NODES.MARKPERSISTENT(s')
13:                     ROOTS.ADD(s')
14:                 else
15:                     UNPROCESSED.ADD(s')
16:                 end if
17:             end if
18:         end for
19:         NODES.GARBAGECOLLECT(min{ψ(s) | s ∈ UNPROCESSED}))
20:     end while
21: end while
```

Fig. 4. The generalised sweep-line algorithm.

that will be added to ROOTS after the initial state. $|B| + 1$ is therefore an upper bound on the number of times the outer loop is repeated.

Now assume that there exists reachable states that are not explored, and choose among these a state s such that the length of a shortest path from s_I to s is minimal among the unexplored states. This implies that there exists a sequence $s_0 \xrightarrow{t_1} s_1 \xrightarrow{t_2} \cdots \xrightarrow{t_n} s_n$ where $s_0 = s_I$ and $s_n = s$, such that for all $i < n$, s_i is visited. Since s_I is trivially explored $s \neq s_I$ so $n > 0$ and we can consider the last edge in this sequence, $s_{n-1} \xrightarrow{t_n} s$. If $\psi(s_{n-1}) \sqsubseteq \psi(s)$ the processing of s_{n-1} would discover s, store it in UNPROCESSED, and later visit it during the inner loop. Hence, if $\psi(s_{n-1}) \sqsubseteq \psi(s)$ then s_{n-1} cannot have been explored, which contradicts our choice of s, and we must conclude $\psi(s_{n-1}) \sqsupset \psi(s)$. But if this is the case, then the processing of s_{n-1} would identify $s_{n-1} \xrightarrow{t_n} s$ as a regress-edge and add s to the set of roots, and s would be visited in the next sweep. Again, this implies that s_{n-1} cannot have been explored which contradicts the choice of s. Hence, no such s exists and all states are explored. □

At first sight the complexity of the algorithm looks high, considering that $|B|$ could be of the order of the number of vertices $|V|$ of the state space. In practice, however, each sweep seems to discover more than a single regress-edge, and the number of regress-edges is not high for a "good" progress measure. To examine this further we consider *regress-edge connectedness*:

Definition 4. *Let* $\mathcal{P} = (O, \sqsubseteq, \psi)$ *be a generalised progress measure and* $\mathcal{S} = (S, T, \Delta, s_I)$ *a system.* $\mathcal{S}$ *is* n-**regress-edge connected** *iff it is possible to reach all the reachable states by following at most* n *regress-edges, i.e., for all states* $s \in \mathsf{reach}(s_I)$ *there exists a sequence* $s_I = s_0 \overset{t_1}{\to} s_1 \overset{t_2}{\to} \cdots \overset{t_m}{\to} s_m = s$ *such that* $\big|\{\, i \mid \psi(s_{i-1}) \sqsupset \psi(s_i) \,\}\big| \leq n$, *where* $i \in \{1, 2, \ldots m\}$ □

A 0-regress-edge connected state space is said to be *monotonically connected*, since all states are reachable through occurrence sequences with monotonically increasing progress values.

As a refinement of the proof of Thm. 1 it can be observed that after m iterations of the outer loop (i.e m sweeps), we have explored all states reachable through at most $m - 1$ regress-edges. Hence, for an n-regress-edge connected state space, all states have been visited after $n + 1$ sweeps. Unfortunately, since the last persistent states are not recognised as such until the last sweep, they can still be added as roots for an additional sweep despite the fact that they have already been explored once, so the number of sweeps for an n-regress-edge connected state space is $n + 2$, the $n + 1$ to explore all states, and the last sweep to recognise this.

Corollary 1. *For an* n-*regress-edge connected state space, the generalised sweep-line algorithm terminates after having explored at most* $((n + 2) \cdot |V|)$ *states.*   □

Both Thm. 1 and Corollary 1 above are concerned with the number of states explored which determines the time it takes to complete the state space exploration. The peak memory usage, i.e., maximum number of states stored simultaneously in memory during the sweep, depends on how the progress measure partitions the set of reachable states, and on the graph structure of the state space. If no regress-edges exists, a trivial lower bound for states simultaneously stored in memory is the maximum number of reachable states mapped to the same progress value. This situation can be compared to the use of Binary Decision Diagrams (BDDs) [1,20] in state space exploration, where the peak number of BDD nodes is also unpredictable in the general case. However, unlike BDDs, the peak memory usage with the sweep-line method cannot exceed the memory usage of storing the full state space.

5   Persistence Predicates

Ignoring the states s_9 and s_{10} in the state space in Fig. 3 can be used to illustrate the problem of the last redundant sweep. If s_9 and s_{10} and their associated arcs are removed, then the state space becomes monotonically connected and contains a single regress-edge. At the time this regress-edge is recognised, the destination node s_6 has been deleted, so the algorithm assumes that the state is a new, unexplored state, and adds it to the set of roots for the next sweep. The next sweep, however, only visits previously explored states. The problem is that in general we cannot recognise destinations of regress-edges before we see the regress-edge itself, at which time the destination node is potentially garbage collected. To improve on this we can extend the method with a state predicate π. The purpose of the state predicate is to discover states that are believed to be destinations of regress-edges and mark these as persistent before the corresponding regress-edge is explored. We define a *generalised progress measure with persistence predicate* as follows.

Definition 5. *A **generalised progress measure with persistence predicate** is a tuple $\mathcal{P} = (O, \sqsubseteq, \psi, \pi)$ such that $(O, \sqsubseteq, \psi)$ is a* generalised progress measure *and π is a* persistence predicate *on states given by $\pi : S \to \{\mathsf{tt}, \mathsf{ff}\}$.* □

The two pieces of code that need to be added to the generalised sweepline algorithm from Fig. 4 in order to exploit persistence predicates are listed in Fig. 5. The persistence predicate is used to mark potential destinations of regress-edges as persistent and thereby prevent these from being deleted during garbage collection. Lines 1-3 should be added between line 2 and 3 in Fig. 4 to ensure that the initial state is marked as persistent if it satisfies the predicate. Lines 5-7 should be added between line 10 and 11 in Fig. 4 to ensure that newly generated states are marked as persistent if they satisfy the predicate.

```
1: if π(s_I) then
2:     NODES.MARKPERSISTENT(s_I)
3: end if
4:
5: if π(s') then
6:     NODES.MARKPERSISTENT(s')
7: end if
```

Fig. 5. Extending the generalised sweep-line method with a persistence predicate.

If the persistence predicate is selected wisely, a number of sweeps and thereby re-exploration of states is avoided. If the predicate is chosen poorly, however, not only will the runtime performance not improve significantly, a number of states that are not destinations of regress-edges could also be selected and stored permanently, with no benefit to the state space generation. We use the following terminology:

Definition 6. *Let $\mathcal{P} = (O, \sqsubseteq, \psi, \pi)$ be a generalised progress measure with persistence predicate and $S = (S, T, \Delta, s_I)$ a system. Let $\overline{S} = \{ s' \in \mathsf{reach}(s_I) \mid \exists s \in \mathsf{reach}(s_I) \land \exists t \in T : s \xrightarrow{t} s' \land \psi(s) \sqsupseteq \psi(s') \}$ and $\pi(S) = \{ s \in \mathsf{reach}(s_I) \mid \pi(s) \}$. The predicate π is **exact** if $\pi(S) = \overline{S}$, π is an **over-approximation** of the persistent states if $\pi(S) \supseteq \overline{S}$, and π is an **under-approximation** of the persistent states if $\pi(S) \subseteq \overline{S}$.* □

Since an over-approximative persistence predicate ensures that no destination of a regress-edge is ever garbage collected, the redundant sweep at the end of the generalised sweep-line method, which will only re-explore previously visited states, is avoided. For a state space which is not monotonically connected, a regress-edge may however still lead to a state which have not yet been explored (e.g. s_9 in Fig. 3 (a)), and we get the following result:

Corollary 2. *For an n-regress-edge connected state space, the generalised sweep-line algorithm extended with an over-approximative or exact persistence predicate terminates after having explored at most $(n+1) \cdot |V|$ states. For a monotonically connected state space the states explored with an over-approximative or exact persistence predicate is $|V|$, which equals the states explored with the basic sweep-line method.*   □

Choosing an over-approximative persistence predicate favours runtime over memory usage. All persistent states will be recognised at first sight and will therefore never be deleted and subsequently re-explored. Choosing an under-approximative predicate, on the other hand, favours memory usage over runtime, since no superfluous states are marked as persistent, but a state might not be recognised as persistent until a corresponding regress-edge is explored. An exact predicate recognises exactly the states that will need to be saved as persistent.

6   Experimental Results

This section presents experimental results for two example systems using a prototype implementation of the generalised sweep-line method. The two example systems were modelled using Coloured Petri Nets (CP-nets or CPNs) [13, 19]. The prototype has been implemented on top of the Design/CPN state space tool [4], and is a further development of the prototype for the basic sweep-line method reported on in [5]. In the prototype implementation, the STANDARD ML (SML) [23] programming language is available to the user for specifying progress measures. The user provides a progress mapping to the tool by writing an SML function mapping a state into an integer. SML support for unbounded integers is exploited as the co-domain for progress mappings. The ordering on progress values is the usual total ordering on integers. The user can provide a persistence predicate by writing an SML function mapping a state into a boolean. All results presented in this section were obtained on a Pentium II 166 Mhz with (only) 160 Mb of RAM.

The prototype implementation uses a simple algorithm for garbage collection during the sweep: Whenever n new states have been added to the state space, a garbage collection is initiated. The garbage collection is implemented as a copying collector: When collecting, the states that should not be deleted are copied (including the persistent states) into a new state space. This new state space then becomes the current state space, and the old state space is deleted. This scheme was chosen since it is simple to implement on top of the data structures for state storage in the current version of Design/CPN. It has the drawback that it requires space for two copies of the states that are not deleted, and it does an unnecessary visit and copy of states which cannot yet be garbage collected. The figures for state space exploration time reported on in this section could

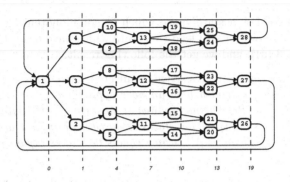

Fig. 6. State space for database transaction protocol ($|D| = 3$).

therefore be improved significantly with a different garbage collection scheme
that avoids visiting and copying states that are not to be deleted.

Database Transaction Protocol. The first example considered is a CPN model
of a database transaction protocol taken from [13]. The CPN model describes
the communication between a set of database managers $D = \{d_1, d_2, \ldots, d_n\}$
for maintaining consistent copies of a database in a distributed system. The
idea of the protocol is that when a database manager updates its local copy
of the database, requests are sent to the other database managers for updating
their copy of the database. Upon each having updated their copy, the database
managers send an acknowledgement back to the initiating database manager to
confirm that the update has now been performed. A database manager in the
protocol can either be in a state Waiting (for acknowledgement), Performing (an
update requested by another database manager) or Inactive after having sent the
acknowledgement back. All database managers are initially Inactive.

The progress measure for this protocol is based on the internal state and
control flow of the database managers. A database manager either goes from an
Inactive to a Waiting state (by initiating an update) and then back to Inactive, or,
from an Inactive to a Performing (a requested update) state and then back to an
Inactive state when sending the acknowledgment for the update. This progress is
also reflected in the state space which is shown for 3 database managers in Fig. 6.
Node 1 corresponds to the initial state. In this state any of the database managers
may initiate an update by going from an Inactive state to a Waiting state (leading
to nodes 2, 3, and 4). The two remaining managers may now (in any interleaved
order) perform their update, and send back the acknowledgement. When all
managers have sent their acknowledgement (nodes 26, 27, 28), the initiating
manager changes its state from Waiting to Inactive. The dashed vertical lines in
Fig. 6 will be explained shortly.

Intuitively, the system progresses from the update being initiated towards
more and more of the database managers having performed an update and sent
their acknowledgement. This intuition can be formalised into a progress measure

for the protocol by counting the number of managers which are in state Waiting, Performing, and Acknowledged and using n-ary arithmetic. A manager is considered to be in state Acknowledged when having sent the acknowledgement back to the initiating manager. Let $s(\mathsf{Waiting}, d)$ denote that database manager d is Waiting in the state s (and similarly for the states Performing and Acknowledged). A progress mapping ψ_D on the protocol can be defined as:

$$\psi_D(s) = |\{d \in D \mid s(\mathsf{Waiting}, d)\}| * |D|^0 +$$
$$|\{d \in D \mid s(\mathsf{Performing}, d)\}| * |D|^1 +$$
$$|\{d \in D \mid s(\mathsf{Acknowledged}, d)\}| * |D|^2$$

The progress measure for each state of the database example is illustrated with the dashed vertical lines. For example, the states corresponding to nodes 2, 3, and 4 all have the progress value 1. We observe that the system returns to the initial state when the initiating manager has received all acknowledgements. Hence, a persistence predicate which is satisfied only in the initial state can be used. This persistence predicate is exact since it captures all states at the end of a regress-edge.

The experimental results obtained with the above progress measure are listed in Table 1 for different numbers of managers. The table consists of five main columns and compares the full state space with the use of the sweep-line method with and without the use of a persistence predicate. The |D| column gives the configuration under consideration, i.e., the number of managers. The Full State Spaces part lists the size of the full state space and the CPU time it took to generate it. The generation time is written on the form $mm{:}ss$ where mm is minutes and ss is seconds. The Persistence Pred. part specifies the peak number of states stored using the persistence predicate and the CPU time it took to conduct the sweep. The number in parentheses after the peak number of states shows (in percentage) the peak number of states divided by the total number of states in the state space. Similarly, the number in parentheses after the exploration time shows the state space exploration time with the sweep-line method divided by the generation time for the full state space. The number of states explored using the persistence predicate is the same as the number of states in the full state space since the persistence predicate is exact. The No Persistence Pred. part gives the total number of states explored, peak number of states stored, and the time it took to conduct the exploration without a persistence predicate. The GC column gives the garbage collection threshold.

Table 1 shows that using a persistence predicate decreases peak states stored ranging from 37.5 % to 57.2 % at the expense of a 66.7 % to 100 % increase in time. For a fixed problem size, it can be seen that it is possible to trade memory usage for run-time by increasing the garbage collection threshold. Not using the persistence predicate is twice as expensive in time compared to using the persistence predicate. The reason is that the state space of the protocol is explored twice (node 1 becomes persistent after the full state space has been explored once). The peak number of states stored is however the same with and

Table 1. Database transaction protocol.

|D|	Full State Spaces		No Persistence Pred.			Persistence Pred.		GC
	States	Time	States	Peak	Time	Peak	Time	
3	28	00:01	56	16	00:02	16 (57.2 %)	00:01 (100.0 %)	1
4	109	00:01	218	53	00:02	53 (48.6 %)	00:01 (100.0 %)	1
5	407	00:01	812	174	00:02	174 (42.8 %)	00:01 (100.0 %)	5
6	1,459	00:03	2,918	583	00:11	583 (40.0 %)	00:06 (200.0 %)	10
6	1,459	00:03	2,918	669	00:10	669 (45.9 %)	00:05 (166.7 %)	100
7	5,104	00:17	10,208	1,913	01:11	1,913 (37.5 %)	00:35 (205.9 %)	100
7	5,104	00:17	10,208	2,189	01:01	2,189 (42.9 %)	00:31 (182.4 %)	500

without the persistence predicate. For $|D| = 3$ the peak number of states stored is 16 which comes from the point during state space exploration where nodes 11 to 25 (see Fig. 6) and the persistent state node 1 is stored in memory.

The results obtained with the above progress measure can be improved by taking into account the identity of the managers. As an example, we can consider a state in which d_1 is in a Waiting state to be higher than any state where d_2 (or d_3) is waiting. This can be formalised in the same way as above using a n-ary arithmetic and assigning weights to the managers. In terms of Fig. 6 this has the effect of exploring the states reachable via node 2 before the states reachable via node 3 which in turn is explored before the states reachable via node 4.

Table 2 shows the experimental results obtained with this progress measure. The table compares full state spaces with the sweep-line method using a progress measure that takes the identity of managers into account and uses the persistence predicate which makes the initial state persistent. A dash in an row indicates that the corresponding full state space was not generated. The size of the full state space was obtained from [14]. The case where the persistence predicate is not used has been omitted from this table since it gives no new insight compared to the results in Table 1. Without the persistence predicate the state space is explored twice leading to a doubling in exploration time compared to using the persistence predicate. The Time column specifies the total time used for the exploration, and the GC-T column shows the amount of the total time that was used for the stop-and-copy garbage collection. The figure is a lower bound on the time spent on deleting states since it may not include the time used by the SML system's garbage collector. It can be seen that taking the identity of the database managers into account significantly reduces peak states stored which is now in the range from 6.8 % to 16.4 %. For larger state spaces the penalty in exploration time is also less significant. The reason for this is that since there are significantly fewer states stored at any time, there are also fewer states to compare with when determining whether a "new" state is already stored compared to the use of full state space.

BANG & OLUFSEN *BeoLink System.* The second example is taken from an industrial case-study [3] in which state spaces of timed CP-nets and Design/CPN were used to validate vital parts of the BANG & OLUFSEN BeoLink system. The

Table 2. Progress measure exploiting identities of database managers.

|D|	Full State Spaces		Persistence Predicate				GC
	States	Time	Peak States	Time		GC-T	
6	1,459	00:03	100 (6.8 %)	00:08	(212.5 %)	00:05	10
6	1,459	00:03	140 (9.6 %)	00:04	(133.3 %)	00:01	50
7	5,104	00:17	350 (6.8 %)	00:22	(129.4 %)	00:06	100
7	5,104	00:17	750 (14.6 %)	00:18	(105.9 %)	00:02	500
8	17,497	01:21	1,737 (9.9 %)	01:32	(113.6 %)	00:10	1000
8	17,497	01:21	2,737 (15.6 %)	01:29	(109.8 %)	00:06	2000
9	59,050	09:49	5,196 (8.8 %)	07:50	(79.8 %)	00:42	3000
9	59,050	09:49	9,694 (16.4 %)	07:37	(77.6 %)	00:20	7500
10	196,832	-	16,570 (8.4 %)	42:45	-	02:30	10000

BeoLink system makes it possible to distribute audio and video throughout a home via a network. A central component of the BeoLink system is the *lock management protocol* used to grant devices exclusive access to various services in the system. The exclusive access is implemented based on the notion of a *key*. A device is required to possess the key in order to access services, and it is the obligation of *video* and *audio master* devices to manage the keys.

The progress measure for this system is based on the control flow of the devices in the lock management protocol which start out being idle, then request the key, obtain the key, and use it for a while after which they release the key and go back to idle. This can be formalised into a progress measure in the same way as for the database protocol taking the identity of the devices into account. Table 3 lists the experimental results obtained for different configurations of the BeoLink system. Configurations with one video master are written as V:n, where n is the total number of devices in the system. Configurations with one audio master are written as A:n. The behaviour of this system was too complex to come up with a useful persistence predicate, so the results in Table 3 are all for the sweep-line method without persistence predicate.

The results show that the peak states stored are reduced to between 9.7 % and 18.8 % at the expense of a penalty in exploration time in the range from 38.7 % to 227.8 %. It can be seen that for the configuration with a high overhead in runtime, the overhead was primarily due to the expensive stop-and-copy garbage collection. Although not shown in the table, the number of persistent states was 995 for a V:3 configuration which required 77 sweeps. This clearly indicates that more than one regress-edge is captured in each sweep. The number of persistent states for an A:3 configuration was 2,634 and the exploration required 58 sweeps. The results also show that the number of states explored is increased less than 6.3 % despite a persistence predicate not being used.

7   Conclusion and Future Work

We have presented a generalised sweep-line method by relaxing the monotone notion of progress required by the original sweep-line method. This significantly

Table 3. BANG & OLUFSEN BeoLink system.

Con	Full SS		Sweep-Line Method				
	States	Time	States Explored	Peak States	GC-T	Time	GC
V:2	274	00:02	283 (103.3 %)	41 (15.0 %)	00:02	00:04 (200.0 %)	1
A:2	346	00:02	355 (102.6 %)	65 (18.8 %)	00:01	00:04 (200.0 %)	1
V:3	10,713	02:19	11,385 (106.3 %)	1,057 (9.7 %)	02:48	04:48 (207.2 %)	50
V:3	10,713	02:19	11,385 (106.3 %)	1,089 (10.2 %)	01:43	03:44 (161.2 %)	100
V:3	10,713	02:19	11,385 (106.3 %)	1,137 (10.6 %)	00:46	02:48 (120.9 %)	500
A:3	27,246	06:54	28,356 (104.1 %)	2,687 (9.7 %)	17:28	22:37 (327.8 %)	50
A:3	27,246	06:54	28,356 (104.1 %)	2,724 (10.0 %)	11:26	16:47 (243.2 %)	100
A:3	27,246	06:54	28,385 (104.1 %)	2,840 (10.4 %)	04:13	09:34 (138.7 %)	500

broadens the class of systems where the sweep-line method is applicable. The relaxation was achieved at the expense of possibly exploring some states several times. The generalised sweep-line method has been implemented in Design/CPN, and experiments have been conducted with promising results.

That a state may be explored several times makes the generalised sweep-line method closely related to the state space caching method [12]. The experimental results in [8] showed that to be feasible for large systems, state space caching needs to be combined with partial-order methods [27] to reduce the number of re-explorations. The problem is that the re-exploration of states caused by the limited size of the state cache induces an explosion in runtime. Judging from our practical experiments, the sweep-line method seems effective in keeping the number of re-explorations low even without the use of partial-order methods. As demonstrated in this paper, re-exploration of states can sometimes be totally avoided with the sweep-line method using persistence predicates, and for 0-regress-edge connected state spaces the re-exploration of states is avoided altogether. This means that the sweep-line method can be considered an alternative to state space caching for modelling languages where partial-order methods are not available. This is for instance the case for Coloured Petri Nets [13] where partial-order methods have been shown to be expensive [18], and for Timed Coloured Petri Nets [16] where there is currently no known partial-order method. As part of future work it would be interesting to make a more direct comparison between the sweep-line method and state space caching, to study how they perform in the trade-off between memory and runtime, and to investigate whether partial-order methods can also be used to improve the performance of the sweep-line method.

Our experiments have established the stop-and-copy garbage collection implemented in the prototype as the primary source of runtime overhead. Datastructures to support efficient deletion of states is a topic of future work. By exploiting the progress mapping as part of the hash function used in the datastructure for state storage, it should be possible to ensure that deletion of states is linear in the number of states to be deleted.

The sweep-line algorithm as presented is aimed at checking safety properties as it explores all states in the state space at least once. It can however be observed that for monotone progress measures, all states of a cycle will have the same progress value, and hence all states in a cycle will reside in memory simultaneously. This suggests that the results can be extended to conduct LTL model checking which can be seen as searching for cycles in the composition of Büchi automata [26]. It is currently an open problem whether LTL model checking is possible with generalised progress measures.

A main topic of future work is also the generation of error-traces. With the sweep-line method, part of the path leading from the initial state to a state satisfying a given state predicate might have been deleted, and needs to be reconstructed to obtain an error-trace. Combining the sweep-line method with disk-based storage seems a promising approach to obtain error-traces with the sweep-line method. With the sweep-line method, states can be written to disk as they are garbage collected from memory, and there is no need to search for states on disk. In this way, the usual runtime penalty encountered in disk-based searches is avoided altogether. To obtain the error-trace one can work backwards (on disk) from the state satisfying the state predicate to the initial state. If states are stored on disk such that each state has a pointer to one of its predecessor states which is closer to the initial state, this backwards search will be inexpensive. This approach may not give the shortest error-trace in terms of occurrences of transitions, but it can be used to obtain a shortest error-trace in terms of how far the system has progressed according to the progress measure.

It should be noted that disk-based storage as outlined above will store a state as many times on disk as the sweep-line method visits the state. Another interesting combination of conventional disk-based storage and the sweep-line method is therefore to reduce the expensive searching for states on disk by observing that it is only necessary to search for states on disk which are destination states of regress-edges; other states are guaranteed by the progress measure to be in memory. These searches for destination states of regress-edges could even be done in parallel with the current sweep since the destination states of regress-edges will not be needed before the subsequent sweep. If the destination state of a regress-edge is stored on disk, there is no need to use it as root in the subsequent sweep.

The approach taken in this paper relies on the user specifying the progress measure and possibly the persistence predicate. It is therefore relevant to ask how difficult it is to come up with a progress measure for a given system. In our experience, if there is progress present in the system, then the modeller has in most cases an intuition about this which can be formalised into a progress measure and provided to the tool. As part of the work presented in this paper, we have identified the control flow of the processes as an origin of progress. Other sources of progress are sequence numbers in data packets and time in certain modelling languages with time. A recent study on the use of the basic sweep-line method on the Wireless Application Protocol (WAP) [9] has identified re-transmission counters as another source of progress. Judging from examples considered in this paper, it was straightforward to specify the progress measure because the control flow of the processes was explicitly modelled. In fact, writing a progress measure can be considered less complicated than writing for instance a formula in temporal logic expressing some property of the system to be investigated.

The automatic derivation of progress measures and persistence predicate is a topic of a forthcoming paper. The approach we have taken to automatic generation of progress measure (and persistence predicates) is to consider a compositional setting where systems are composed of one or more parallel processes. Each process in the parallel composition is assumed to be such that either its state space can be computed in isolation (and a progress measure can then be computed from it) or the process is specified in some process description language in which case the line numbers in the process code can be used as a control flow-based progress measure. The automatically computed progress measure for each process is then composed to obtain a progress measure for the full system. This makes the sweep-line method fully automatic, and also applicable to action-based modelling languages such as process algebras.

Acknowledgements. The authors would like to thank Dr. Laure Petrucci, Dr. Charles Lakos, Prof. Jonathan Billington, and the anonymous referees for valuable comments on earlier versions of this paper.

References

1. R.E. Bryant. Graph Based Algorithms for Boolean Function Manipulation. *IEEE Transactions on Computers*, C-35(8):677–691, 1986.
2. R. Carvajal-Schiaffino, G. Delzanno, and G. Chiola. Combining Structural and Enumerative Techniques for the Validation of Bounded Petri Nets. In *Proceedings of TACAS 2001*, volume 2031 of *LNCS*, pages 435–449. Springer-Verlag, 2001.
3. S. Christensen and J.B. Jørgensen. Analysis of Bang and Olufsen's BeoLink Audio/Video System Using Coloured Petri Nets. In *Proceedings of ICATPN'97*, volume 1248 of *LNCS*, pages 387–406. Springer-Verlag, 1997.
4. S. Christensen, J.B. Jørgensen, and L.M. Kristensen. Design/CPN - A Computer Tool for Coloured Petri Nets. In *Proceedings of TACAS'97*, volume 1217 of *LNCS*, pages 209–223. Springer-Verlag, 1997.
5. S. Christensen, L.M. Kristensen, and T. Mailund. A Sweep-Line Method for State Space Exploration. In *Proceedings of TACAS 2001*, volume 2031 of *LNCS*, pages 450–464. Springer-Verlag, 2001.
6. E.M. Clarke, R. Enders, T. Filkorn, and S. Jha. Exploiting Symmetries in Temporal Logic Model Checking. *Formal Methods in System Design*, 9(1/2):77–104, 1996.
7. E.A. Emerson and A.P. Sistla. Symmetry and Model Checking. *Formal Methods in System Design*, 9(1/2):105–131, 1996.
8. P. Godefroid. *Partial-Order Methods for the Verification of Concurrent Systems, An Approach to the State-Explosion Problem*, volume 1032 of *LNCS*. Springer-Verlag, 1996.
9. S. Gordon, L.M. Kristensen, and J. Billington. Verification of a Revised WAP Wireless Transaction Protocol. In *Proceedings of ICATPN 2002*, LNCS. Springer-Verlag, 2002. To appear.

10. G.J. Holzmann. *Design and Validation of Computer Protocols.* Prentice-Hall International Editions, 1991.
11. G.J. Holzmann. An Analysis of Bitstate Hashing. *Formal Methods in System Design,* 13(3):287–305, 1998.
12. C. Jard and T. Jeron. Bounded-memory Algorithms for Verification On-the-fly. In *Proceedings of CAV'91,* volume 575 of *LNCS,* pages 192–202. Springer-Verlag, 1991.
13. K. Jensen. *Coloured Petri Nets. Basic Concepts, Analysis Methods and Practical Use. Volume 1: Basic Concepts.* Monographs in Theoretical Computer Science. Springer-Verlag, 1992.
14. K. Jensen. *Coloured Petri Nets. Basic Concepts, Analysis Methods and Practical Use. Volume 2: Analysis Methods.* Monographs in Theoretical Computer Science. Springer-Verlag, 1994.
15. K. Jensen. Condensed State Spaces for Symmetrical Coloured Petri Nets. *Formal Methods in System Design,* 9(1/2):7–40, 1996.
16. K. Jensen. *Coloured Petri Nets. Basic Concepts, Analysis Methods and Practical Use. Volume 3: Practical Use.* Monographs in Theoretical Computer Science. Springer-Verlag, 1997.
17. S. Katz and H. Miller. Saving Space by Fully Exploiting Invisible Transitions. *Formal Methods in System Design,* 14(3):311–332, 1999.
18. L. M. Kristensen and A. Valmari. Finding Stubborn Sets of Coloured Petri Nets Without Unfolding. In *Proceedings of ICATPN'98,* volume 1420 of *LNCS,* pages 104–123. Springer-Verlag, 1998.
19. L.M. Kristensen, S. Christensen, and K. Jensen. The Practitioner's Guide to Coloured Petri Nets. *International Journal on Software Tools for Technology Transfer,* 2(2):98–132, 1998.
20. K. L. McMillan. *Symbolic Model Checking.* Kluwer Academic Publishers, 1993.
21. A.N. Parashkevov and J. Yantchev. Space Efficient Reachability Analysis Through Use of Pseudo-Root States. In *Proceedings of TACAS'97,* volume 1217 of *LNCS,* pages 50–64. Springer-Verlag, 1997.
22. D. Peled. All from One, One for All: On Model Checking Using Representatives. In *Proceedings of CAV'93,* volume 697 of *LNCS,* pages 409–423. Springer-Verlag, 1993.
23. J.D. Ullman. *Elements of ML Programming.* Prentice-Hall, 1998.
24. A. Valmari. A Stubborn Attack on State Explosion. In *Proceedings of CAV'90,* volume 531 of *LNCS,* pages 156–165. Springer-Verlag, 1990.
25. A. Valmari. The State Explosion Problem. In *Lectures on Petri Nets I: Basic Models,* volume 1491 of *LNCS,* pages 429–528. Springer-Verlag, 1998.
26. M. Vardi and P. Wolper. An Automata-Theoretic Approach to Automatic Program Verification. In *In Proc. of IEEE Symposium on Logic in Computer Science,* pages 322–331, 1986.
27. P. Wolper and P. Godefroid. Partial Order Methods for Temporal Verification. In *Proceedings of CONCUR'93,* volume 715 of *LNCS.* Springer-Verlag, 1993.

Supplementing a UML Development Process with B

Helen Treharne

Department of Computer Science, Royal Holloway,
University of London, Egham, Surrey, TW20 0EX, UK.

helen@cs.rhul.ac.uk

Abstract. This paper discusses our experiences of using UML and B together through an illustrative case study. Our approach to using UML and B centers around stereotyping UML classes in order to identify which classes should be modelled in B. We discuss the tensions between the notations, and the compromises that need to be reached in order for B to supplement a UML development. The case study begins from the initial conception of a library system and its use case view in order to demonstrate how the classes were identified.

Keywords: B-Method, UML Class Diagrams, Stereotyping.

1 Introduction

This paper discusses our experiences of using the existing notations of the Unified Modeling Language (UML) [13] and the B-Method [2] in software development. Our experiences result from developing a course on object-oriented modelling [17] at Royal Holloway, University of London. Our aim was to develop an object-oriented modelling approach which increases the applicability of formal methods in object-oriented development and thus their potential use. Our aim was not to provide a formal semantics for UML using B but rather to use the notations together in a development process. The main contribution of the approach is the mapping of stereotyped UML classes into B. The benefit of the resulting B model is that it supplements the UML class model by making explicit any assumptions which may be implicit in the UML model. Furthermore, we can use the animation facilities of a supporting B toolkit [11] to examine parts of a UML model interactively. However, since B is not really an object-oriented language this mapping is not going to be straightforward in practice.

Through a case study described in the paper we aim to promote discussion, highlight similarities and areas of difficulties when attempting to map from a stereotyped UML class model to a B model. The case study follows the stages of identifying which parts of a UML model are appropriate for modelling in B and then systematically derives an appropriate B model. We draw on the work of [5,7,20] in order to achieve this supplementary state-model.

L.-H. Eriksson and P. Lindsay (Eds.): FME 2002, LNCS 2391, pp. 568–586, 2002.
© Springer-Verlag Berlin Heidelberg 2002

This paper is organised as follows: Section 2 introduces the B-Method; Section 3 introduces the UML notation that we used in the case study; Section 4 outlines the case study, the initial UML development and how to systematically map an appropriate part of the system from UML to B; Section 5 provides summarising comments on the case study and guiding principles, and Section 6 ends with a discussion of related work.

2   Overview of the B-Method

The B-Method is a collection of mathematically based techniques for the specification of software modules. Systems are modelled as a collection of interdependent abstract machines. An abstract machine is described using the Abstract Machine Notation (AMN). A *machine* encapsulates some local state and a collection of modules called *operations* which define the machine's interface. The operations of a machine can be preconditioned recording the assumptions about when it is safe to call an operation. They have the form *pre P then T end*, where P is a precondition and T describes the effect of invoking the *operation*.

Large machines can be constructed from other machines (lower level machines) using *includes, sees* and other structuring constructs in order to provide a hierarchical structure to a specification. The *promotes* construct allows operations from lower level machines to become part of the interface of a larger machine. Operations which are not promoted from lower level machines can be called within newly defined operations and are akin to method calls in programming languages.

The B-Method also supports the design and implementation of software modules. This refinement transforms an abstract description of the software into a more concrete description. Hence, it can add more detail to the original specification, or it can be closer to an implementation. Further details of the B-Method can be found in [2,7,16].

3   Overview of UML

UML is accepted as the most commonly used modelling language for software development and thus it needs little introduction. Nonetheless we need to make clear which parts of the notation we need in our proposed approach for supplementing UML with B. Our approach extends beyond the scope of focusing on UML class diagrams where much of the relationship between UML and B is currently concentrated [6,20,21]. The reason being is that we need to categorise classes in order to aid our mapping into B. Therefore, not only do we need to consider the design view of UML where class diagrams are described we also need to consider the use case view of the 4+1 view model of a system's architecture.

A use case view is defined as being *the view of the system's architecture that encompasses use cases that describe the behaviour of the system* [14]. The sequence of actions described by a use case results in the system being updated and/or important information being retrieved. The initiator of these sequence of actions or recipient of the results is referred to as an actor. Typically an actor is seen as a user of the system but can be another system with which the system under development communicates. One of the most important aspects of this view is the identification of the system boundary. This means that a resulting UML class model is more likely to include a definition of information that is required from and/or passed to another system. Hence, requirements on the interfaces of other components can be explicitly captured. The process of deriving an initial class model of a system from a use case view is known as *Use Case Analysis* (also known as Robustness Analysis [12]).

3.1 UML Classes

In UML, classes are used to describe appropriate encapsulations of state and operations which update and query that state. In a UML development process a class is seen as the most basic building block of the system. It is used throughout the design process from the initial conception of an object model through to providing a straightforward mapping to code.

The goal of an initial design is to make an attempt at an initial set of classes which interact with each other in order to form the basis of an object model (achieved via a Use Case Analysis). Of course, in practice, the state and operations which form a class are not completely identified immediately. Nonetheless, we can at least group the classes into three types

- Boundary Classes
- Entity Classes
- Control Classes

Boundary classes capture the functionality of the system required to deal with user interfaces. Commonly there will be at least one boundary class for each use case/actor pair. Entity classes store and manage information in the system. They represent the key concepts being developed and capture the logical structure of the system. They are not specific to one use case. Control classes facilitate co-ordinating behaviour in a system. They provide an effective mechanism for protecting the system from changes in its interface. As with entity classes a control class is not specific to one use case. However, collectively the control classes must provide enough operations to realise the functionality required by the use cases of a system.

The above stereotyping of classes will allow us to gain an insight as to what part of the model we need to build a complementary B model.

3.2 Associations

We have already mentioned above that classes interact. Two classes are associated if object instances of those classes have an association relation. These associations are as a result of one object needing the interaction of another in order to carry out its operations. For example, one object may want to access

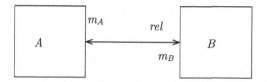

Fig. 1. Associations

another object's information and achieves this by sending it a message for a particular action to occur. If there is an association between A and B, as shown in Figure 1, then the relation is declared by $rel : A \leftrightarrow B$. m_B is the multiplicity associated with B, i.e. the number of B's associated with each A. It can be understood as a set of numbers. For example,

- 0..1 is $\{0, 1\}$,
- 1 is $\{1\}$
- $*$ is $\mathbb{N}$
- 1..$*$ is $\mathbb{N}_1$
- $i..j$ is $i..j$

Then the constraint is translated to:

$$\forall a.(a \in A \Rightarrow card(rel[\{a\}]) \in m_B)$$

Similarly, the other multiplicity is captured on the inverse relation by:

$$\forall b.(b \in B \Rightarrow card(rel^{-1}[\{b\}]) \in m_A)$$

The above is a general scheme which can be applied to all binary associations. Some of the binary associations can be described succinctly as particular kinds of functions. Patterns for representing UML multiplicities and associations have been documented elsewhere in the literature, for example [5,8].

4   Example

This section presents a case study as a running example throughout the rest of the paper. We begin by describing the informal requirements of a simple library logging system. We acknowledge that it is not a large system but it is simple enough to be self contained and serves as a concise way of illustrating the main points when providing an underlying B model for part of a UML development.

All books have a name and an unique identifier. There is a central catalogue which keeps information about such books. There can be several copies of the same book in the library up to a maximum of ten. Copies of books can either be out on loan or on the shelf. Copies of books can be added or removed from the library whereas adding new books to the catalogue is outside the scope of the

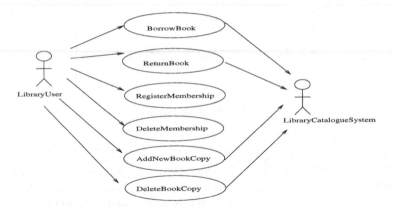

Fig. 2. Example Use Case Diagram

logging system. Members of the library have a name associated with them and are recorded as either being students or staff. Only library members can take books out of the library. Student members can have up to five books on loan whereas staff members can have up to eight books on loan at any one time.

The first step in the development process is to develop a use case diagram for the system. An appropriate diagram for the above system is shown in Figure 2. It illustrates the fact that user is an initiating actor and that the other actor is another system which will need to be queried. We have deliberately limited the users of the system to one kind of user.

Use cases are often documented using only brief descriptions comprising of sentences. A more structured way of documenting them is by recording the flow of events. They should include pre and post conditions on the state of the system to indicate when and how the use case begins and ends. Normally, a detailed description of a use case evolves as more detail is added to the UML model and the overall requirements become clearer. For example, we would expect there to be a precondition for de-registering a membership in order to ensure that the member is present in the system and similarly in the case of a library user wanting to borrow a book. An appropriate postcondition for the *returnBook* use case is that after a successful return of a book it is released for further loans. If the above preconditions are added during an iteration step in the UML development process then the B model would also have to be revisited. In particular, we would expect an impact on the robustness of the underlying B operations and the strengthening of some associated AMN preconditions. Furthermore, use case postconditions can be checked in a B animation scenario. Typically the consistency of post conditions would not be checked in the UML model of a system explicitly.

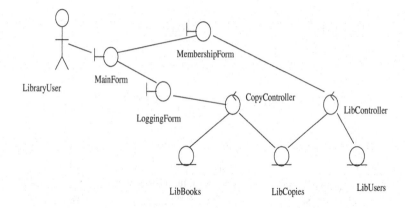

Fig. 3. Example Analysis Classes

4.1   Identifying Analysis Classes

Now that we have the use case diagram we need to identify the major classes of the library logging system. Firstly, let us consider any appropriate interfaces. They will typically be web interfaces or menu driven systems with various options and sub-menus. For example, we would expect there to be a separate sub-menu for taking out books and the house keeping of membership details. Therefore, we identify three boundary classes - the main form, the membership form and the logging form as shown in Figure 3. The different types of classes are represented using different graphical icons as used within Rational Rose [1]. The lines between the stereotyped classes in Figure 3 identify logical flow. The boundary classes provide a way of separating information capture from the user and the updating of the internal state of a system. Notice that we permit hierarchical decomposition of boundary classes as supported by Rose but such interaction between boundary objects is not strictly permitted in Robustness Analysis [12].

In the use case diagram, in Figure 2, there is another actor. This is an abstraction of the interface to another system and therefore no boundary class is linked to it. Instead, this abstraction is represented as an entity class (*LibBooks*) and as we have already said it allows us to clearly identify the dependency on the interfaces of an external system. The other two logical structures are those capturing details of the individual copies of the books (*LibCopies*) and the membership details of the student and staff library members (*LibUsers*).

The final set of classes to be identified are those which effectively de-couple the interface from the entity classes. We have identified two possible controllers. The *LibController* and the *CopyContoller* update the *LibUsers* and *LibCopies* entities respectively.

---

[1] http://www.rational.org

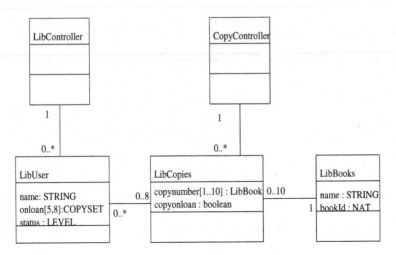

Fig. 4. Example Class Diagram

4.2   Building a Class Diagram

From our initial object model in the previous section we can now focus on developing a class diagram for the main functionality. We need not consider the boundary classes in our diagram because these are not going to be modelled in B. Methods/operations to capture data input from an interface, e.g. a GUI, are not central to a formal specification of the core functionality of a system. B's strength is to focus on predicates on the state of the model so that safety properties can be expressed. Therefore, having constrained the scope of our class diagram one such possible diagram for our system is given in Figure 4.

The main feature of the diagram is that each controller is closely coupled with an underlying entity. We could make it even more explicit by adding a strict aggregation (black diamond) at the base of the *LibController* class. This would constrain all *LibUsers* entity objects to be under *LibController*'s control and thus unable to exist on their own. Similarly, we could make *LibCopies* an integral part of *CopyController*. In this example there will always be only one object instance of a controller class but this cannot be made explicit in the class diagram.

The other associations in the diagram capture the constraints outlined in the informal requirements. Notice, however, that it is difficult on the diagram to express the exact association between members and the copies of the books they have on loan. Clearly, this association is dependent on the value of the *status* attribute of each object. We can resolve some of the ambiguity by including a multiplicity on the *onloan* attribute. It will be of the type of a copy object, *COPYSET*, and in programming terms will either represent a pointer to an array of size five or eight elements of such objects. However, the exact link between the attributes remains informal as an annotation in the class specification. In

MACHINE *LibBooks*
SEES *String_TYPE* , *Bool_TYPE*
SETS *BOOKSET*
VARIABLES *booksobj* , *name* , *bookId*
INVARIANT *booksobj* $\subseteq$ *BOOKSET* $\wedge$
name $\in$ *booksobj* $\rightarrow$ *STRING* $\wedge$
bookId $\in$ *booksobj* $\rightarrowtail$ $\mathbb{N}$
INITIALISATION
   BEGIN *booksobj* := $\varnothing$ $\|$ *name* := $\varnothing$ $\|$ *bookId* := $\varnothing$ **END**

OPERATIONS
   createLibBook (*bobj*) $\widehat{=}$
    PRE *bobj* $\notin$ *booksobj* $\wedge$ *bobj* $\in$ *BOOKSET*
    THEN
       ANY *nn* , *ii* **WHERE** *nn* $\in$ *STRING* $\wedge$ *ii* $\in$ $\mathbb{N}$ **THEN**
         booksobj := *booksobj* $\cup$ { *bobj* } $\|$
         name := *name* $\cup$ { *bobj* $\mapsto$ *nn* } $\|$
         bookId := *bookId* $\cup$ { *bobj* $\mapsto$ *ii* }
       END
     END ;
   setName (*bobj* , *nn*) $\widehat{=}$
    PRE *bobj* $\in$ *booksobj* $\wedge$ *nn* $\in$ *STRING* **THEN**
       name (*bobj*) := *nn*
     END ;
   nn $\longleftarrow$ **getName** (*bobj*) $\widehat{=}$
    PRE *bobj* $\in$ *booksobj* **THEN**
       nn := *name* (*bobj*)
     END ;
   bb $\longleftarrow$ **isName** (*bname*) $\widehat{=}$
    PRE *bname* $\in$ *STRING* **THEN**
       bb := bool (*bname* $\in$ ran (*name*))
     END
END

Fig. 5. *LibBooks* Machine

B we will be able to use our general scheme for associations to represent this constraint between attributes formally.

4.3   Mapping UML to B

Now that we have the static structure of the design view in place we can systematically translate the UML class diagram into a B model. We begin by representing the entity classes. The classes *LibUsers* and *LibCopies* form the core data of the system and *LibBooks* is an abstraction of the external system with which the logging system will communicate. Information about books is captured in the *LibBooks* machine, which is defined in Figure 5. Book objects are tracked in the variable *booksobj* and the set of possible book objects is the set *BOOKSET*. Initially no such objects exist. The attributes of an object are represented as mappings from some source object to its target value. They will commonly be relations but sometimes particular kinds of functions. This style of specification, i.e. using functions to represent attributes of objects, is commonly used [7,6,19, 20]. In our example a book which has an unique identifier can be captured as an injective function. We have not made this explicit in the UML because it would simply be an annotation on the attribute diagram. Laleau and Polack [5] have used a key annotation $\{k\}$ to make such constraints explicit on a UML diagram. However, to the best of our knowledge this kind of annotation is not widely used and is more commonly captured in the informal text.

Four operations are offered by the *LibBooks* machine; *createLibBook* mimics the dynamic creation of a new object with a random initialisation of its attributes; *setName* is a primitive setting operation and two query operations *getName* and *isName*. We have omitted the ones querying *bookId* for reasons of space. The operations provided reflect primitive query and modify operations which are standard in object-oriented design and the operations that are typically generated by the Base Generators of the B-Toolkit [11] for a particular data structure. In the development of our logging system the *LibBooks* machine should only be used to query its state, i.e. all messages to the machine should be read access only. Furthermore, the developer should define only the operations needed so that it is clear what information needs to be retrieved from the external system.

The dynamic information about particular copies of books is introduced in the *LibCopies* machine defined in Figure 6. Objects and their associated attributes are defined as variables as before. We also document the association using our general scheme introduced in Section 3.2. We have simplified the fact that all copy objects are associated with only one book from the following predicate

$$\forall\, a.(a \in \text{copiesobj} \Rightarrow \text{card}(\text{copynumber}[\{a\}]) \in \{1\})$$

to simply be a total function between *copiesobj* and *booksobj*.

Two kinds of operations are typically offered by an entity machine. Firstly, we have object creation and deletion operations - *createCopy* and *deleteCopy* are such examples in *LibCopies*. The delete operation mimics a destructor. Often destructors will not be needed but the *DeleteBookCopy* use case removes a particular copy of a book and thus the system will need to remove any unnecessary book copy objects. Secondly, primitive operations which set and query the attributes of a particular object - examples of which are *setOnLoan* and *setNotOnLoan*. These operations pass the object as a parameter mirroring the notion of scoping a method call with an object prefix (a typical pro forma would be *objectname.methodname*). These primitive modify/access operations are straightforward to extract automatically given the data structure.

The last entity which needs to be mapped to a machine is the *LibUsers* entity as shown in Figures 7 and 8. It follows the same pattern as the *LibCopies*

MACHINE *LibCopies*
SEES *String_TYPE* , *Bool_TYPE*
USES *LibBooks*
SETS *COPYSET*
VARIABLES *copiesobj* , *copynumber* , *copyonloan*
INVARIANT
  copiesobj $\subseteq$ *COPYSET* $\land$ *copyonloan* $\in$ *copiesobj* $\rightarrow$ *BOOL* $\land$
  copynumber $\in$ *copiesobj* $\rightarrow$ *booksobj* $\land$
  $\forall$ *bb* . (*bb* $\in$ ran (*copynumber*) $\Rightarrow$ card (ran (*copynumber* $\triangleright$ { *bb* })) $\leq$ *10*)
INITIALISATION
  BEGIN *copiesobj* := $\varnothing$ $\|$ *copyonloan* := $\varnothing$ $\|$ *copynumber* := $\varnothing$ **END**

OPERATIONS
  createCopy (*cobj* , *bobj*) $\hat{=}$
    PRE *cobj* $\notin$ *copiesobj* $\land$ *cobj* $\in$ *COPYSET* $\land$ *bobj* $\in$ *booksobj* $\land$
      card (*copynumber* $^{-1}$ [{ *bobj* }]) < *10*
    THEN
      copiesobj := *copiesobj* $\cup$ { *cobj* } $\|$
      copyonloan := *copyonloan* $\cup$ { *cobj* $\mapsto$ *FALSE* } $\|$
      copynumber := *copynumber* $\cup$ { *cobj* $\mapsto$ *bobj* }
    END ;
  deleteCopy (*cobj*) $\hat{=}$
    PRE *cobj* $\in$ *copiesobj* $\land$ *cobj* $\in$ *COPYSET* $\land$ *copyonloan* (*cobj*) = *FALSE*
    THEN
      copiesobj := *copiesobj* $-$ { *cobj* } $\|$
      copyonloan := { *cobj* } $\lhd$ *copyonloan* $\|$
      copynumber := { *cobj* } $\lhd$ *copynumber*
    END ;
  setOnLoan (*cobj*) $\hat{=}$
    PRE *cobj* $\in$ *copiesobj* $\land$ *copyonloan* (*cobj*) = *FALSE* **THEN**
      copyonloan (*cobj*) := *TRUE*
    END ;
  setNotOnLoan (*cobj*) $\hat{=}$
    PRE *cobj* $\in$ *copiesobj* $\land$ *copyonloan* (*cobj*) = *TRUE* **THEN**
      copyonloan (*cobj*) := *FALSE*
    END
END

Fig. 6. *LibCopies* Machine

entity. There are two creation operations and four primitive operations. The two creation operations demonstrate that B can reflect the notion of a default constructor and parameterised constructors. Unfortunately, some concessions have to be made in the naming convention of these constructors because B does not allow the reuse of operation names. A delete operation is not needed in this machine.

MACHINE *LibUsers*
SEES *String_TYPE* , *Bool_TYPE*
USES *LibCopies*
SETS *MEMBERSET* ; *LEVEL* = { *staff* , *student* }
CONSTANTS *default_name*
PROPERTIES *default_name* ∈ *STRING*
VARIABLES *membersobj* , *memberName* , *onloan* , *status*
INVARIANT *onloan* ∈ *membersobj* ↔ *COPYSET* ∧
ran (*onloan*) = dom (*copyonloan* ▷ { *TRUE* })
∧ *membersobj* ⊆ *MEMBERSET* ∧
memberName ∈ *membersobj* → *STRING* ∧
status ∈ *membersobj* → *LEVEL* ∧
∀ *mm* . (*mm* ∈ *membersobj* ∧ *status* (*mm*) = *student* ⇒
            card (*onloan* [{ *mm* }]) ≤ 5) ∧
∀ *mm* . (*mm* ∈ *membersobj* ∧ *status* (*mm*) = *staff* ⇒
            card (*onloan* [{ *mm* }]) ≤ 8)
INITIALISATION
BEGIN
    onloan := ∅ ∥ *membersobj* := ∅ ∥ *memberName* := ∅ ∥ *status* := ∅
END

Fig. 7. *LibUsers* Machine

Notice that the invariant of the machine in Figure 7 contains two universally quantified predicates. These predicates provide a more accurate representation of the relationship between the number of books a staff and student member has out on loan.

Now we can focus on mapping the control classes. We present only the *LibController* but the *CopyController* is very similar in style. The *LibController* machine associated with the control class (of the same name) is presented in Figure 9.

Notice that we do not need to refer to object instances this time because there will only be one instance of this machine and hence the machine itself can be considered as the instance. Notice also that the *LibUsers* machine loses its identify and becomes under the direct control of the controller whereas *Lib-Copies* and *LibBooks* are only queried. The *includes* mechanism means that the controller can determine which operations from *LibUsers* will form part of the overall interface. A style we have adopted in this example is that the operational interface of a controller (not including constructors and destructors) should be robust whenever possible. Therefore, only typing predicates and predicates which state that objects are dynamically recognized are allowed within preconditions. Concessions on this robustnesss are made as a result of assumptions in the flow of events of a use case description. For example, in Section 4, we stated that a de-registration of a member only happens provided that member is already in

OPERATIONS
  create (*mobj*) $\hat{=}$
    PRE *mobj* $\notin$ *membersobj* $\wedge$ *mobj* $\in$ *MEMBERSET* **THEN**
      membersobj := *membersobj* $\cup$ { *mobj* } ‖
      memberName := *memberName* $\cup$ { *mobj* $\mapsto$ *default_name* } ‖
      status := *status* $\cup$ { *mobj* $\mapsto$ *staff* } ‖
      onloan := $\varnothing$
    END ;
  createAndRegister (*mobj* , *mm* , *st*) $\hat{=}$
    PRE *mobj* $\notin$ *membersobj* $\wedge$ *mobj* $\in$ *MEMBERSET* $\wedge$
    mm $\in$ *STRING* $\wedge$ *mm* $\neq$ *default_name* $\wedge$ *st* $\in$ *LEVEL* **THEN**
      membersobj := *membersobj* $\cup$ { *mobj* } ‖
      memberName := *memberName* $\cup$ { *mobj* $\mapsto$ *mm* } ‖
      status := *status* $\cup$ { *mobj* $\mapsto$ *st* }
    END ;
  registerMember (*mobj* , *mm* , *st*) $\hat{=}$
    PRE *mobj* $\in$ *membersobj* $\wedge$ *mm* $\in$ *STRING* $\wedge$
    mm $\neq$ *default_name* $\wedge$ *st* $\in$ *LEVEL* **THEN**
      memberName (*mobj*) := *mm* ‖
      status (*mobj*) := *st*
    END ;
  deRegisterMember (*mobj* , *mm*) $\hat{=}$
    PRE *mobj* $\in$ *membersobj* $\wedge$ *mm* $\in$ *STRING* $\wedge$ *mm* $\neq$ *default_name*
    THEN
      memberName := *memberName* $-$ { *mobj* $\mapsto$ *mm* } ‖
      status := { *mobj* } $\lhd$ *status* ‖
      membersobj := *membersobj* $-$ { *mobj* } ‖
      onloan := { *mobj* } $\lhd$ *onloan*
    END ;
  takeOutCopy (*mobj* , *cc*) $\hat{=}$
    PRE *mobj* $\in$ *membersobj* $\wedge$ *cc* $\in$ *copiesobj* $\wedge$
    (*status* (*mobj*) = *student* $\Rightarrow$ card (*onloan* [{ *mobj* }]) < 5) $\wedge$
    (*status* (*mobj*) = *staff* $\Rightarrow$ card (*onloan* [{ *mobj* }]) < 8)
    THEN
      onloan := *onloan* $\cup$ { *mobj* $\mapsto$ *cc* }
    END ;
  returnACopy (*mobj* , *cc*) $\hat{=}$
    PRE *mobj* $\in$ *membersobj* $\wedge$ *cc* $\in$ ran (*onloan*) **THEN**
      onloan := *onloan* $-$ { *mobj* $\mapsto$ *cc* }
    END
END

Fig. 8. *LibUsers* Machine (continued)

the system. This is already an assumption of the *deRegisterMember* operation and because of this we can simply promote the operation.

MACHINE *LibController*
SEES *String_TYPE* , *Bool_TYPE*
USES *LibCopies* , *LibBooks*
INCLUDES *LibUsers*
PROMOTES *create* , *createAndRegister* , *registerMember* , *deRegisterMember*
SETS *REPORT* = { *OK* , *FAILED* }

OPERATIONS
   rep ⟵ **takeOutBook** (*mobj* , *bname*) ≙
    PRE *mobj* ∈ *membersobj* ∧ *bname* ∈ *STRING* **THEN**

       IF *FALSE* ∈ *copyonloan* [*copynumber* $^{-1}$ [*name* $^{-1}$ [{ *bname* }]]] ∧
       (*status* (*mobj*) = *student* ⇒ card (*onloan* [{ *mobj* }]) < 5) ∧
       (*status* (*mobj*) = *staff* ⇒ card (*onloan* [{ *mobj* }]) < 8) **THEN**
       ANY *cc* **WHERE** *cc* ∈ *copynumber* $^{-1}$ [*name* $^{-1}$ [{ *bname* }]]
       THEN
        takeOutCopy (*mobj* , *cc*)
       END ‖
       rep := *OK*
      ELSE
       rep := *FAILED*
      END
     END ;
   rep ⟵ **returnBook** (*mobj* , *bid*) ≙
    PRE *mobj* ∈ *membersobj* ∧ *bid* ∈ ℕ **THEN**
    IF *copynumber* $^{-1}$ (*bookId* $^{-1}$ (*bid*)) ∈ ran (*onloan*) **THEN**
    returnACopy (*mobj* , *copynumber* $^{-1}$ (*bookId* $^{-1}$ (*bid*))) ‖
    rep := *OK*
    ELSE
     rep := *FAILED*
    END
   END
END

Fig. 9. *LibController* Machine

In our example *takeOutCopy* and *returnACopy* are not robust and these lower level operations need to be protected from unsafe invocation (assuming that no further assumptions are included in any use case documentation). They need the protection of *if* statement wrappers around their invocations. The boolean conditions within the *if* statements make use of B's ability to allow direct read access to the other objects. This is one place where the relationships between object-oriented methods and B conflicts. In an O-O language we would expect to invoke query operations in order to retrieve the relevant information. Due to B's semi-hiding principle at the abstract specification level we do not need to make use of such query operations because state can be accessed directly.

Nonetheless, during refinement the scope of visibility is reduced and we do need such operations. For example, a simple query operation *howManyOnLoan* would need be included to inspect the appropriate attribute of a member object in order to find out how many books a particular member had out on loan. The direct read access in *takeOutCopy* also refers explicitly to the book copy objects. The predicate

$$FALSE \in copyonloan\ [\ copynumber\ ^{-1}\ [\ name\ ^{-1}\ [\ \{\ bname\ \}\ ]\ ]\ ]$$

iterates over all copy objects. This means that an implementation of a controller would have to provide an iterator query method, say *isAvailable*, to extract the information captured in the above predicate and return a boolean result. To make this dependency explicit at the abstract level we would have to identify an appropriate class in which to define the iterator query operation. The most natural place for it would be in a control class definition and in turn the corresponding controller machine. For example, the *CopyController* machine is an appropriate place for *isAvailable*. The disadvantage of this is that the coupling between objects is now lifted to inter-dependency between controller objects. However, this is permitted in the Robustness Analysis approach to class design.

5   General Principles and Open Issues

In this section we identify principles from the example in the previous section which can be applied when mapping from a UML stereotyped class diagram to a B model. Then we shall elaborate on compromises and open issues resulting from identifying these principles.

1. Boundary classes can be left out from a B model,
2. An entity class is represented using a single entity machine. Attributes of a class are captured using relations. An entity class should mainly contain creation/deletion operations and simple get/set operations.
3. Abstractions of system boundaries are captured using entity machines. Their interaction with other machines should be restricted via the *sees* and *uses* mechanisms.
4. A control class is represented using a single control machine with only one instance. It can update only one entity machine (using *includes*) but have read access to many other entity machines and control machines.
5. Control classes should only include control logic and associations (see 9 below). They should not introduce any important state information which could be represented as an entity.
6. Control classes should incorporate the preconditions of a use case description within the preconditions of their own operation definitions. If there are no such preconditions to consider then the operations should aim to be robust.
7. Control classes should not promote operations liberally when taking ownership of an entity class. Since entity classes provide a rich set of access and query operation it is likely that not all of them need to become part of the

global interface of the system. Only operations which contribute to the flow of events of a use case need to be included.

8. Iterator methods should be identified early and explicitly captured.
9. Associations between objects are captured using a relation scheme and quantified predicates capture cardinality information. If there are no multiplicities on attributes associations should be placed in controller machines. This enables individual entities to exist independently and their co-ordinating behaviour to be naturally captured in the appropriate control class.

   Multiplicities on attributes give rise to cardinality constraints which should be captured in the relevant entity machine. In the cases when multiplicities are attached to attributes duplicating (or elaborating upon) the binary associations between objects may not always be necessary in the related controller machine. For example, the fact that a library user could be associated with up to eight books was captured with finer granularity within the *LibUsers* entity machine and thus we did not need to duplicate the association in the *LibController* machine.

The second and eighth principles allude to a possible compromise when identifying an appropriate place for iterator definitions within the B model. This compromise arises when a controller needs to update more than one object from the same entity machine. For example, we may want to recall all copies of a book and set the status of those copies to *FALSE*, i.e. not on loan. This means that in the *CopyController* machine we would want to call the operation *setNotOnLoan* of the *LibCopies* machine repeatedly but the B structuring mechanisms do not allow this at the abstract level. This means that we have to compromise and define a new operation, e.g. *setAllNotOnLoan* below, to mimic the idea of an iterator within the *LibCopies* machine.

$$\textbf{setAllNotOnLoan} \mathrel{\widehat{=}} copyonloan := \mathsf{dom} \ (\ copyonloan\ ) \times \{\ FALSE\ \}$$

Therefore, we can expand on the eighth principle in the above list by saying that, control classes should contain the query iterator methods and entity classes must contain any update iterator methods. As a complete alternative to using B to capture the control class, our current research is the application of our work on combining CSP and B [22,18] to support descriptions of more complex UML controller classes and their underlying entity classes. This would eliminate the need to write awkward B because we could capture the sequencing of methods naturally. Even so, there would still be the unresolved issues of describing associations between classes within CSP controllers.

The fourth principle is needed because the limited structuring mechanisms in B force some restrictions upon the possible UML class diagrams we can develop and hence limits object interaction. We cannot allow more than one controller to update the same entity object. In general, this could be dangerous because we may cause the same state to be updated in different ways which would violate the invariants. Therefore, a compromise must be made in the B model when two controllers wish to update the same object in the UML model, i.e. the B model must merge the controller machines into one large controller machine. However, there may be situations where the individual invariants are preserved because each controller is updating different state within an object (see Lano [9]). In such situations we could allow multiple inclusion of machines in B so that we could retain the separation of concerns and hence reflect the UML structure in the B model. Unfortunately, this is currently not possible within the B-Method. There is no reason in principle why this could not be allowed, it is more a pragmatic issue to keep the proof obligations manageable.

The library logging system presented in Section 4 includes a great deal of inter-relationship. Such tight coupling of objects is generally not recommended as good style in an object-oriented development. Therefore, we should generalise the particular dependency between member objects and the fact that they take out books. It would be more appropriate to capture a relationship between member objects and another (generic) object. Initial investigations indicate that a UML model could be designed using an interface pattern [3] so that the relationship between a member and a general object can be expressed. The particular kind of object would then become a derived class at a later stage in the development - this would involve inheritance. The key point is that a *LibUsers* object need not know the particular kinds of objects it is tracking in the *onloan* attribute but simply that it does need to keep track of it. In B we could reflect this by capturing the target type of the *onloan* relation as a parameter of *LibUsers* machine as has been suggested by Lano in [9]. The resultant effect is a decoupling between *LibUsers* and *LibCopies* objects. However, the issue of relating this with an inheritance structure remains open.

The library logging system is also restricted to one kind of user. If we were to generalise the use case diagram in Figure 2 in order to explicitly state that only specialised users are allowed to manage memberships and books we would have to introduce another actor as shown in Figure 10. This clearly indicates that the class model should have a general notion of a user forming a base class from which a normal user could be instantiated and from which an administrator class could be derived. Developing an entity/control structure for a group of different objects wanting to perform similar tasks is ongoing work.

6   Related Work

In this paper the technique of stereotyping classes proved invaluable in order to derive a structured B model comprising of only the relevant functionality. Therefore, this paper supports the view of Ambler [1] that UML stereotypes *increases the communication value* of the model. Many other researchers have been looking at linking UML with formal techniques but few use the notion of stereotyping. To the best of our knowledge Liu *et al.* [10] only use the classification of boundary and control classes. Our use of entity classes to provide an abstraction of the system boundary (e.g. the use of *LibBooks* to represent the library catalogue system) is akin to their use of boundary classes to capture the physical objects of the external environment. Snook and Butler [20] have produced a prototype tool, U2B, which supports the translation of state diagrams and class diagrams

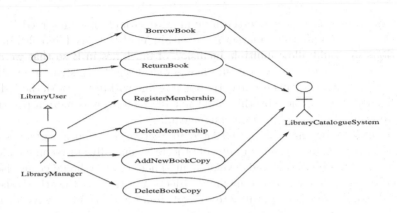

Fig. 10. Specialised Use Case Diagram

into B machines. The latest version of U2B supports the work of this paper by including stereotyping and the translation of control and entity classes. Other work which is looking at UML/B is [21] and is proposing to provide tool support to extract a UML class diagram from a B abstract machine (its development is in the initial stages). No results are known to us to indicate that stereotyping of classes is currently proposed to assist in the generation of the underlying B machines within this tool support.

Satpathy et al. [15] conclude that UML is not sufficient to specify complex and rigorous requirements. We agree that the UML notation may not be sufficient but the informality of a UML development process allows the opportunity for adding textual annotations to any part of a UML description. This enables requirements capture even when the notation itself is not strong enough to support such information. We saw one such example in Section 4.2 when attempting to clarify how many books a particular type of library member could borrow. In Section 4.3 we showed that by supplementing the class diagram with an underlying B model the ambiguity is eliminated and the rigour of an invariant predicate supplements the UML model. To achieve this in the UML model alone we would have had to generalise the model to include an inheritance structure so that each type of member is a different class. This would then allow further associations to be added to breakdown the relationships appropriately. The drawback with this generalisation is that the design may then become over-engineered.

In this paper we have shown that it is possible to extract a B model given a rigid structure, i.e. one without inheritance and with aggregation but with varied associations. We have demonstrated the concept of using the division of classes to guide a B specification structure and that a formal specification forces us to think very carefully about the relationships between the classes. We have also noted the fact that a B model should not ignore assumptions regarding the behaviour of the system recorded in different UML views (in particular the use case view) since the overall style of the B specification is likely to be influenced by this extra information.

Acknowledgements. Thanks to the referees for valuable comments and suggestions, and also to Damien Karkinsky and Steve Schneider for much discussion and comments on earlier drafts.

References

1. Ambler S. *The Object Primer* 2nd Edition, New York CUP 2001.
2. Abrial J. R.: *The B Book: Assigning Programs to Meaning*, CUP, 1996.
3. Cooper J. W.: *Java Design Patterns: A tutorial*, Addison-Wesley, 2000.
4. Facon P., Laleau R. and Nguyen H. P.: *Derivation de specification formelles B partir de specification semi-formelles de systems d'information*. In Habrias H. (ed), Proceedings of the 1st Conference on the B Method, France, 1996.
5. Laleau R., Polack F.: *Specification of Integrity-Preserving Operations in Information Systems by Using a Formal UML-based Language*. Information and Software Technology, 43(12), pp 693-704,November 2001.
6. Laleau R., Polack F.: *Coming and Going from UML to B: A Proposal to Support Traceability in Rigorous IS Development*, In Bert D., Bowen J. P., Henson M. C. and Robinson K. (eds.) ZB2002, LNCS 2272, pp 517-534, Springer-Verlag, 2002.
7. Lano K. C.: *Specification in B: An Introduction Using the B Toolkit*, IC Press, 1996.
8. Lano K., Bicarregui J. and Evans A.: *Structured Axiomatic Semantics for UML Models*, ROOM 2000 Workshop, Springer-Verlag, EWICS, 2000.
9. Lano K.: *Limitations of B Structuring*, unpublished, November, 2001.
10. Liu J., Dong J. S, Mahony B. and Shi. K: *Linking UML with Integrated Formal Techniques*, chapter in book: Unified Modeling Language: Systems Analysis, Design, and Development Issues (Editors: K. Siau and T. Halpin), 2001.
11. Neilson D., Sorensen I. H.: *The B-Technologies: a system for computer aided programming*, B-Core (UK) Limited, Kings Piece, Harwell, Oxon, OX11 0PA, 1999, `http://www.b-core.com`
12. Rosenburg D., Scott K.: *Use Case Driven Object Modelling with UML: A Practical Approach*, Addison-Wesley, 1999.
13. Rumbaugh J., Jacobson I. and Booch G.: *The Unified Modeling Language Reference Manual*, Addison-Wesley, 1999.
14. Rumbaugh J., Jacobson I. and Booch G.: *The Unified Modeling Language User Guide*, Addison-Wesley, 1999.
15. Satpathy M., Snook C., Harrison R., Butler M., Krause P.: *A Comparative Study of Formal and Informal Specification through an Industrial Case Study*. In Dumke, Abran (eds.) Proc IEEE/IFIP Workshop on Formal Specification of Computer Based Systems (FSCBS'01), 2001.
16. Schneider S.: *The B-Method: An Introduction*, Palgrave, 2001.
17. Schneider S., Treharne H.: *Object-Oriented Modelling Lecture Notes*, Computer Science Department, Royal Holloway, University of London, 2001, `http://www.cs.rhul.ac.uk/ug/second_year/CS225/info.html`.
18. Schneider S., Treharne H.: *Combining B Machines*, In Bert D., Bowen J. P., Henson M. C. and Robinson K. (eds.) ZB2002, LNCS 2272, pp 416-435, Springer-Verlag, 2002.

19. Shore R.: *An object-oriented approach to B*. In Habrias H. (ed), Proceedings of the 1st Conference on the B Method, France, 1996.
20. Snook C., Butler M. J.: *Tool-Supported Use of UML for Constructing B Specifications*, http://www.ecs.soton.ac.uk/~mjb/.
21. Tatibouet B., Voisinet J. C.: *jbTools and B2UML: a platform and a tool to provide a UML Class Diagram since a B specification*, http://lifc.univ-fcomte.fr/~tatibouet/JBTOOLS/index.html.
22. Treharne H., Schneider S.: *Using a Process Algebra to control B OPERATIONS*. In K. Araki, A. Galloway and K. Taguchi (eds.), IFM'99, York, Springer, 1999.

Semantic Web for Extending and Linking Formalisms

Jin Song Dong, Jing Sun, and Hai Wang

School of Computing,
National University of Singapore,
dongjs,sunjing,wangh@comp.nus.edu.sg

Abstract. The diversity of various formal specification techniques and the need for their effective combinations requires an extensible and integrated supporting environment. The Web provides infrastructure for such an environment for formal specification and design because it allows sharing of various design models and provides hyper textual links among the models. Recently the Semantic Web Activity proposed the idea of having data on the web defined and linked in a way that it can be used for automation, extension and integration. The success of the Semantic Web may have profound impact on the web environment for formal specifications, especially for extending and integrating different formalisms. This paper demonstrates how RDF and DAML can be used to build a Semantic Web environment for supporting, extending and integrating various formal specification languages. Furthermore, the paper illustrates how RDF query techniques can facilitate specification comprehension.

Keywords: specification environment, Semantic Web

1 Introduction

Many formal specification techniques exist for modeling different aspects of software systems and it's difficult to find a single notation that can model all functionalities of a complex system [21,34]. For instance, B/VDM/Z are designed for modeling system data and states, while CSP/CCS/π-calculus are designed for modeling system behaviour and interactions. Various formal notations are often extended and combined for modeling large and complex systems. In recent years, *formal methods integration* has been a popular research topic [1,13]. In the context of combining state-based and event-based formalisms, a number of proposals have been presented [8,11,12,19,26,28,29,32]. Our general observations on these works are that

> Various formal notations can be used in an effective combination if the semantic links between those notations can be clearly established. The semantic/syntax integration of those languages would be a consequence when the semantic links are precisely defined. Due to different motivations, there are possible different semantic links between two formalisms, which lead to different integrations between the two.

L.-H. Eriksson and P. Lindsay (Eds.): FME 2002, LNCS 2391, pp. 587–606, 2002.

Unlike UML,an industrial effort for standardising diagrammatic notations, a single dominating integrated formal method may not exist in the near future. The reason may be partially due to the fact that there are many different well established individual schools, e.g., VDM forum, Z/B users, CSP group, CCS/π-calculus family and etc. Another reason may be due to the open nature of the research community, i.e. FME (www.fmeurope.org), which is different from the industrial 'globalisation' community, i.e. OMG (www.omg.org).

Regardless of whether there will be or there should be an ultimate integrated formal method (like UML), *diversity* seems to be the current reality for formal methods and their integrations. Such a diversity may have an advantage, that is, different formal methods and their combinations may be effective for developing various kinds of complex systems[1]. The best way to support and popularise formal methods and their effective combinations is to build a widely accessible, extensible and integrated environment.

The World Wide Web provides an important infrastructure for a promising environment for various formal specification and design activities because it allows sharing of various design models and provides hyper textual links among the models. Recently the Semantic Web Activity [2] proposed the idea of having data on the web defined and linked in a way that it can be used for automation and integration. The success of the Semantic Web may have profound impact on the web environment for formal specifications, especially for extending and integrating different formal notations. This paper demonstrates an approach on how RDF [18] and DAML [30] can be used to build a Semantic Web environment for supporting, checking, extending and integrating various formal specification languages. Furthermore, based on this Semantic Web environment, specification comprehension (queries for review/understanding purpose) can be supported.

The reminder of the paper is organised as follows. Section 2 firstly introduces RDF/DAML and demonstrates how DAML environment can be built for formal specification languages such as Z and CSP[2]. Then it illustrates how the DAML environments for Z and CSP can be extended for Object-Z and TCSP. Section 3 demonstrates how various integration approaches for combining Object-Z and (T)CSP can be supported by the Semantic Web environment. Section 4 illustrates how specification comprehension can be supported by RDF queries. Section 5 discusses related work and concludes the paper.

2   Semantic Web for Formal Specifications

Following the success of XML [31], W3C's primary focus is on Semantic Web. Currently, one of the major Semantic Web activities at W3C is the work on

---

[1] In fact, one of the difficult tasks of OMG is to resist many good new proposals for extending UML — a clear consequence and drawback of pushing a single language for modeling all software systems.

[2] Specific formal notations used in this paper are mainly for demonstrating the ideas, other formalisms can also be supported.

Resource Description Framework (RDF) [18] and the DARPA Agent Markup Language (DAML) [30].

RDF is a foundation for processing metadata; it provides interoperability between applications that exchange machine-understandable information on the Web. RDF uses XML to exchange descriptions of Web resources and emphasises facilities to enable automated processing. In fact, the RDF descriptions provide a simple ontology system to support the exchange of knowledge and semantic information on the Web. RDF Schema [7] provide the basic vocabulary to describe RDF vocabularies. RDF Schema can be used to define properties and types of the web resources. Similar to XML Schema which give specific constraints on the structure of an XML document, RDF Schema provide information about the interpretation of the RDF statements. DAML is a semantic markup language based on RDF and XML for Web resources. DAML currently combines Ontology Interchange Language (OIL) and features from other ontology systems.

In this section we use Z [33] and CSP [15] as examples to demonstrate how a Semantic Web environment for formal specification languages can be developed. These environments can be further extended and integrated.

2.1 Semantic Web Environment — RDFS/DAML for Z

Firstly, a customised RDFS/DAML definition for Z language is developed according to its syntax and static semantics. This definition (a DAML ontology itself) provides information about the interpretation of the statements given in a Z-RDF instant data model. Part of the RDFS definitions (for constructing a Z schema) is as follows:

```
<rdf:RDF
  xmlns:rdf = "http://www.w3.org/1999/02/22-rdf-syntax-ns#"
  xmlns:rdfs = "http://www.w3.org/2000/01/rdf-schema#"
  xmlns:xsd = "http://www.w3.org/2000/10/XMLSchema#"
  xmlns:daml = "http://www.daml.org/2001/03/daml+oil#"
  xmlns:z = "http://nt-appn.comp.nus.edu.sg/fm/zdaml/Z#">

<!-- some definition omitted -->

  <rdfs:Class rdf:ID="Schemadef">
    <rdfs:label>Schemadef</rdfs:label>
  </rdfs:Class>
  <rdfs:Class rdf:ID="Schemabox">
    <rdfs:label>Schemabox</rdfs:label>
      <rdfs:subClassOf rdf:resource="#Schemadef"/>
      <rdfs:subClassOf>
        <daml:Restriction daml:cardinalityQ="1">
          <daml:onProperty rdf:resource="#name"/>
        </daml:Restriction> </rdfs:subClassOf>
      <rdfs:subClassOf>
```

```
    <daml:Restriction daml:minCardinality="0">
      <daml:onProperty rdf:resource="#del"/>
      <daml:toClass rdf:resource="#Schemadef"/>
    </daml:Restriction> </rdfs:subClassOf>

  <!-- some definition omitted -->
  <rdfs:subClassOf>
    <daml:Restriction daml:minCardinality="0">
      <daml:onProperty rdf:resource="#decl"/>
    </daml:Restriction> </rdfs:subClassOf>
  <rdfs:subClassOf>
    <daml:Restriction daml:minCardinality="0">
      <daml:onProperty rdf:resource="#predicate"/>
    </daml:Restriction>
  </rdfs:subClassOf>
</rdfs:Class>
```

(note that xmlns stands for XML name space)

The DAML class Schemadef represents the Z schemas. The class Schemabox, a subclasses of Schemadef, represents the Z schemas defined in schema box form. The class Schemabox models a type whose instance may consist of a name, a number of declarations decl and some predicate definitions. In addition, a Schemabox instance may also have zero or more properties del whose value must be another Schemadef instance (for capturing the Z Δ-convention). As the paper focuses on demonstrating the approach, other Semantic Web environments for Z constructs are left out but can be found at:

http://nt-appn.comp.nus.edu.sg/fm/zdaml/Z.daml

Under the Semantic Web environment for the Z language, Z specifications as RDF instant files can be edited (by any XML editing tool).

The Z notation contains a rich set of mathematical symbols. Those symbols can be presented directly in Unicode which is supported by RDF (XML). A set of entity declarations is defined to map those Z symbols to their Unicode correspondents (with a Z LATEX compatible name) as follows.

```
<!ENTITY cat "&#x2040;">
<!ENTITY mem "&#x2208;">
<!ENTITY uni "&#x222a;">
```

One benefit of using Unicode is for visualisation purposes, for example, we have developed an XSLT program (http://nt-appn.comp.nus.edu.sg/fm/zdaml/rdf2zml.xsl) to transform the RDF environment into ZML [27][3], an XML environment for display/browsing Z on the web directly (using the IE web browser).

---

[3] Our previous work, ZML, was developed mainly for visualising Z on the web and tranforming Object-Z to UML(XMI) [27].

The following is a simple *Buffer* schema and a *Join* operation.

[*MSG*]

```
┌─ Buffer ──────────────────         ┌─ Join ──────────────────
│ max : ℤ                            │ ΔBuffer
│ items : seq MSG                    │ i? : MSG
├──────────────────                  ├──────────────────
│ #items ≤ max                       │ #items < max ∧
│                                    │ items' = ⟨i?⟩ ⌢ items ∧
│                                    │ max' = max
└──────────────────                  └──────────────────
```

The corresponding RDF definition is as following.

```
<z:Type rdf:ID="msg">
  <z:type>MSG</z:type>
</z:Type>
<z:Schemabox rdf:ID="buffer">
  <z:name>Buffer</z:name>
    <z:decl> <z:Decl z:name="max" z:dtype="&integer;"/> </z:decl>
    <z:decl> <z:Decl z:name="items" z:dtype="&seq; MSG"/> </z:decl>
    <z:predicate> #items &leq; max </z:predicate>
</z:Schemabox>
<z:Schemabox rdf:ID="join">
  <z:name>Join</z:name>
  <z:del rdf:resource="#buffer"/>
  <z:decl> <z:Decl z:name="i?" z:dtype="MSG"/> </z:decl>
  <z:predicate>#items &lt; max  &land;
    items'=  {i?} &cat; items &land; max' = max </z:predicate>
</z:Schemabox>
```

Note that the RDF file is in XML format which can be edited by XML editing tools, i.e. XMLSpy. Alternatively, this RDF specification can be treated as an interchange format which can be generated from ZML via our XSL tool or from Latex (a tool is in the development stage).

2.2 Semantic Web Environment — RDFS/DAML for CSP

Similarly a Semantic Web environment for CSP can be constructed based on its definition. Part of the RDFS/DAML definitions (for constructing a CSP process) is as follows:

```
<!-- some definition omitted -->
    <rdfs:Class rdf:ID="Event">
        <rdfs:label>Event</rdfs:label> </rdfs:Class>
    <rdfs:Class rdf:ID="Process">
        <rdfs:label>Process</rdfs:label> </rdfs:Class>
```

```
<rdfs:Class rdf:ID="Simevent">
    <rdfs:label>SimpleEvent</rdfs:label>
    <!-- some definition omitted -->
</rdfs:Class>

<rdfs:Class rdf:ID="Communication">
    <rdfs:label>Communication</rdfs:label>
    <rdfs:subClassOf rdf:resource="#Event"/>
    <!-- some definition omitted -->
</rdfs:Class>

<!--STOP process-->
<rdfs:Class rdf:ID="Stop">
    <rdfs:label>STOP</rdfs:label>
    <rdfs:subClassOf rdf:resource="#Process"/>
</rdfs:Class>
<!--prefix process-->
<rdfs:Class rdf:ID="PrefixPro">
    <rdfs:label>prefixPro</rdfs:label>
    <rdfs:subClassOf rdf:resource="#Process"/>
    <rdfs:subClassOf>
        <daml:Restriction>
            <daml:onProperty rdf:resource="#prefix"/>
            <daml:toClass rdf:resource="#Event"/>
        </daml:Restriction> </rdfs:subClassOf>
    <rdfs:subClassOf>
        <daml:Restriction>
            <daml:onProperty rdf:resource="#toProc"/>
            <daml:toClass rdf:resource="#Process"/>
        </daml:Restriction> </rdfs:subClassOf>
</rdfs:Class>
```

It states that there are two major kinds of constructs in CSP, events and processes. Events can be classified into simple ones and communications containing channels and messages. Processes can be classified into various forms including a special event STOP, prefix, sequential etc.

The main contribution of these Semantic Web environments is that they provide formal specifications on the web together with additional semantic information. Furthermore, they facilitate web browsing, collaborative formal design and some static semantics checking. For instance, given two CSP processes P_1 and P_2, the following incorrect CSP expression

$$P_1 \to P_2$$

will be detected by the CSP Semantic Web environment via RDF validator. In this paper we will focus on how these environments can be easily extended and integrated to form new environments for the extension and combination of formalisms.

2.3   Extending Z to Object-Z

Object-Z [10,25] is an object-oriented extension to Z. A Z specification defines a number of state and operation schemas. In contrast, Object-Z associates individual operations with one state schema. The collective definition of a state schema with its associated operations constitutes the definition of a class. Each class has one state schema, at most one initial schema and number of operation schema. The state schema can be viewed as a nameless Z schema. The initial schema can be viewed as a Z schema which only contains some predicate properties. The following demonstrates parts of the Semantic Web environment for Object-Z. It extends the Z's environment.

```
<?xml version="1.0" encoding="UTF-8"?>
<rdf:RDF
xmlns:rdf="http://www.w3.org/1999/02/22-rdf-syntax-ns#"
xmlns:rdfs="http://www.w3.org/2000/01/rdf-schema#"
xmlns:xsd="http://www.w3.org/2000/10/XMLSchema#"
xmlns:daml="http://www.daml.org/2001/03/daml+oil#"
xmlns:oz="http://nt-appn.comp.nus.edu.sg/fm/zdaml/OZ#"
xmlns:z="http://nt-appn.comp.nus.edu.sg/fm/zdaml/Z#"
xmlns="http://nt-appn.comp.nus.edu.sg/fm/zdaml/OZ#">
    <daml:Ontology rdf:about="">
        <daml:imports rdf:resource=
            "http://nt-appn.comp.nus.edu.sg/fm/zdaml/Z"/>
    </daml:Ontology>
    <rdfs:Class rdf:ID="State">
        <rdfs:label>State</rdfs:label>
        <rdfs:subClassOf rdf:resource="z:Schemabox"/>
        <rdfs:subClassOf>
            <daml:Restriction>
                <daml:onProperty rdf:resource="z:name"/>
                <daml:hasValue>
                    <xsd:string rdf:value=""/> </daml:hasValue>
            </daml:Restriction> </rdfs:subClassOf>
    </rdfs:Class>
    <rdfs:Class rdf:ID="Init">
        <rdfs:label>INIT</rdfs:label>
        <!-- some definition omitted -->
    </rdfs:Class>
    <rdfs:Class rdf:ID="OP">
        <rdfs:label>OP</rdfs:label>
        <!-- some definition omitted -->
    </rdfs:Class>

    <rdfs:Class rdf:ID="Message">
        <rdfs:label>Message</rdfs:label>
```

```
            <rdfs:subClassOf rdf:resource="#OP"/>
            <rdfs:subClassOf>
                <daml:Restriction daml:cardinality="1">
                    <daml:onProperty rdf:resource="oz:receiver"/>
                </daml:Restriction> </rdfs:subClassOf>
            <rdfs:subClassOf>
                <daml:Restriction daml:cardinality="1">
                    <daml:onProperty rdf:resource="#method"/>
                    <daml:toClass rdf:resource="#OP"/>
                </daml:Restriction> </rdfs:subClassOf>
    </rdfs:Class>

    <!-- some definition omitted -->
    <rdfs:Class rdf:ID="Classdef"/>

    <rdfs:Class rdf:ID="Classdef1">
        <rdfs:label>Classdef1</rdfs:label>
        <rdfs:subClassOf rdf:resource="#Classdef"/>
        <rdfs:subClassOf>
            <daml:Restriction daml:cardinality="1">
                <daml:onProperty rdf:resource="z:name"/>
            </daml:Restriction> </rdfs:subClassOf>
    <!-- some definition omitted -->
        <rdfs:subClassOf>
            <daml:Restriction>
                <daml:maxCardinality>1</daml:maxCardinality>
                <daml:onProperty rdf:resource="#state"/>
                <daml:toClass rdf:resource="#State"/>
            </daml:Restriction> </rdfs:subClassOf>
        <rdfs:subClassOf>
            <daml:Restriction>
                <daml:onProperty rdf:resource="#op"/>
                <daml:toClass rdf:resource="#OP"/>
            </daml:Restriction> </rdfs:subClassOf>
    </rdfs:Class>
    <daml:DatatypeProperty rdf:ID="delObj">
        <rdfs:range rdf:resource=
        "http://www.w3.org/2000/10/XMLSchema#string"/>
    </daml:DatatypeProperty>
</rdf:RDF>
```

This Object-Z Semantic Web environment imports the definition of Z. Note that Message class is used to define message passing. It consists of a receiver property (object reference) and a method property (the operation of the declared class of the receiver).

A `Classdef1` class (an Object-Z class defined by a class box) was defined to have the following properties.

- a `name` property,
- a `state` property whose value must be a `State` class object,
- some `op` properties which value must be `OP` class object etc.

The `State` class is a subclass of `Schemabox` (class for a Z schema defined in schema box form). That is a `State` object is a special `Schemadef` object satisfying the restriction that the `name` property has no value. The `OP` class is the same as class `Schemadef` (for Z schema) except a new property `delObj` was added to it. This is due to the difference between the semantic requirements of Δ list in Z and Object-Z. In Z the entity following Δ is the name of state schema name, and in Object-Z the entity following the Δ are variables defined in the class state schema.

Consider the buffer example in Object-Z:

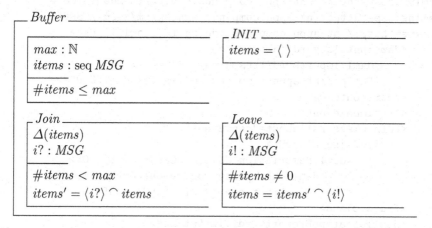

under the Semantic Web environment this Buffer class can be edited as the following RDF file.

```
<oz:Classdef1 rdf:ID="buffer">
  <z:name>Buffer</z:name>
    <oz:state>
      <oz:State>
        <z:decl> <z:Decl z:name="max" z:dtype="&integer;"/> </z:decl>
        <z:decl> <z:Decl z:name="items" z:dtype="&seq; MSG"/> </z:decl>
        <z:predicate>#items &leq; max</z:predicate>
      </oz:State>
    </oz:state>
    <!-- some definition omitted -->
    <oz:op><oz:OP rdf:ID="join">
      <z:name>Join</z:name>
      <oz:delObj> items</oz:delObj>
      <z:decl> <z:Decl z:name="i?" z:dtype="MSG"/> </z:decl>
```

```
    <z:predicate>#items &lt; max  &land;
                items'= {i?} &cat; items </z:predicate>
  </oz:OP></oz:op>
</oz:Classdef1>
```

2.4 Extending CSP to TCSP

The extension from CSP to TCSP can be achieved in a similar way. The following
is part of the Semantic Web environment for TCSP.

```
<?xml version="1.0" encoding="UTF-8"?> <rdf:RDF
xmlns:rdf="http://www.w3.org/1999/02/22-rdf-syntax-ns#"
xmlns:rdfs="http://www.w3.org/2000/01/rdf-schema#"
xmlns:xsd="http://www.w3.org/2000/10/XMLSchema#"
xmlns:daml="http://www.daml.org/2001/03/daml+oil#"
xmlns:tcsp="http://nt-appn.comp.nus.edu.sg/fm/zdaml/TCSP#"
xmlns:csp="http://nt-appn.comp.nus.edu.sg/fm/zdaml/CSP#"
xmlns="http://nt-appn.comp.nus.edu.sg/fm/zdaml/TCSP#">
    <daml:Ontology rdf:about="">
        <daml:imports rdf:resource=
        "http://nt-appn.comp.nus.edu.sg/fm/zdaml/CSP"/>
    </daml:Ontology>
    <!--timed event-->
    <rdfs:Class rdf:about="csp:Event">
        <rdfs:subClassOf>
            <daml:Restriction daml:minCardinality="0">
                <daml:onProperty rdf:resource="#etime"/>
            </daml:Restriction> </rdfs:subClassOf>
    </rdfs:Class>
    <daml:DatatypeProperty rdf:ID="etime">
        <rdfs:range rdf:resource=
        "http://www.w3.org/2000/10/XMLSchema#string"/>
    </daml:DatatypeProperty>
    <!--Wait process-->
    <rdfs:Class rdf:ID="Wait">
        <rdfs:label>WAIT</rdfs:label>
        <rdfs:subClassOf rdf:resource="#process"/>
        <daml:Restriction daml:minCardinality="0">
            <daml:onProperty rdf:resource="#etime"/>
        </daml:Restriction> </rdfs:Class>
    <!-- some definition omitted -->
```

This TCSP environment is derived by first importing the definition of CSP, and
then defining a new property etime for the events in CSP. The property etime
shows the time of occurrence of events. Several new types of process are also
defined. For example, the WAIT process is just a subclass of a general process.

One interesting point is that the physical size or number of 'subclass' clauses in the DAML file (above) may provide an indication of the degree of extension (how much modification and extension has been developed in the new language). Such a concrete number or ratio may give us some quantitive comparison, perhaps indicating how new (or faithful) is Object-Z relative to Z, TCSP to CSP or VDM++ to VDM.

In the next section, we will focus on the essential part of this paper – the use of the Semantic Web for linking formalisms.

3   Semantic Web for Linking Formalisms

Various modeling methods can be used in an effective combination for designing complex systems if the semantic links between those methods can be clearly established and defined. Given two sets of formalisms, say state-based ones and event-based ones, it's not too surprising to see that different possible integrations are more than the cross-product of the two sets. This is simply because the different semantic links between the two formalisms lead to different integrations. Furthermore, the semantic links can be directional and bi-directional.

Let's consider the case of linking Object-Z and CSP. Smith and Derrick's approach [26] is to identify Object-Z operations with CSP channel/events and Object-Z classes with CSP processes. The CSP-OZ approach taken by Fischer and Wehrheim [11] is similar to Smith and Derrick's approach except that it divides each Object-Z operation into two separate operations (enable and effect events). The TCOZ approach [19] identifies Object-Z operations with CSP processes[4].

Despite the differences, all those integrations are useful for modeling different kinds of complex systems. For example, Smith and Derrick's approach is good at modeling a system with a group of simple passive components and complex concurrent interactions (at a system level) between those components. On the other hand, TCOZ is good at modeling system with complex components which may have their own thread of control and support multi-layer compositions and concurrency.

In this paper, we will demonstrate how the Object-Z and (T)CSP Semantic Web environments can be linked to support Smith/Derrick and TCOZ approaches.

3.1   *Class* $\Longrightarrow$ *Process*

In Smith/Derrick's approach [26], Object-Z classes are modeled as CSP processes and the Object-Z operations are modeled as CSP events. The event corresponding to an operation is a communication event with the operation name as the channel and the mapping from its parameters to their values as the value passed on that channel. In this approach any two operations with the same name and

---

[4] TCOZ is an integration of Object-Z and TCSP[24].

parameters will be modelled by identical events when their parameters have same values and hence will be able to synchronize. There are two main phases in specifying a concurrent system.

- The first phase is to decompose the complex system into components and specify each of these components using Object-Z.
- The second phase involves the specification of the system using CSP operators.

Consider the specification of two communicating buffers, the following model demonstrates this approach:

$$Buffer_1 \cong Buffer[Transfer/Leave]$$
$$Buffer_2 \cong Buffer[Transfer/Join]$$
$$System \cong Buffer_1 \parallel [Transfer]Buffer_2$$

where the two buffers ($Buffer_1$ and $Buffer_2$) communicate through channel $Transfer$.

The semantic environment for this approach can be achieved in the following way:

```
<?xml version="1.0" encoding="UTF-8"?>
<rdf:RDF xmlns:rdf="http://www.w3.org/1999/02/22-rdf-syntax-ns#"
xmlns:rdfs="http://www.w3.org/2000/01/rdf-schema#"
xmlns:xsd="http://www.w3.org/2000/10/XMLSchema#"
xmlns:daml="http://www.daml.org/2001/03/daml+oil#"
xmlns:oz="http://nt-appn.comp.nus.edu.sg/fm/zdaml/OZ#"
xmlns:csp="http://nt-appn.comp.nus.edu.sg/fm/zdaml/CSP#"
xmlns:app1="http://nt-appn.comp.nus.edu.sg/fm/zdaml/APP1#">
    <daml:Ontology rdf:about="">
        <daml:imports rdf:resource=
         "http://nt-appn.comp.nus.edu.sg/fm/zdaml/OZ"/>
        <daml:imports rdf:resource=
         "http://nt-appn.comp.nus.edu.sg/fm/zdaml/CSP"/>
    </daml:Ontology>
    <rdfs:Class rdf:about="oz:Classdef">
        <rdfs:subClassOf rdf:resource="csp:Pro"/> </rdfs:Class>
    <rdfs:Class rdf:about="oz:OP">
        <rdfs:subClassOf rdf:resource="csp:Event"/> </rdfs:Class>
    <!--operation is one kind of process-->
</rdf:RDF>
```

It firstly imports the definition of CSP and Object-Z. The Object-Z class is declared as a subclass of the CSP process and the Object-Z operation (extended from Z operation schema) is declared as a subclass of the CSP event. The above two buffers example can be encoded in the Semantic Web environment as following.

```
<oz:Classdef2 rdf:ID="buffer1">
  <z:name>Buffer1</z:name>
  <oz:rename> Transfer/Leave</oz:rename>
  <oz:eqclass rdf:resource="#buffer"/> </oz:Classdef2>
<oz:Classdef2 rdf:ID="buffer2">
  <z:name>Buffer2</z:name>
  <oz:rename> Transfer/Join</oz:rename>
  <oz:eqclass rdf:resource="#buffer"/> </oz:Classdef2>
<oz:Classdef2 rdf:ID="system">
  <z:name>System</z:name>
  <oz:eqclass>
      <csp:ParallelPro>
          <csp:subprocess rdf:resource="buffer1"/>
          <csp:subprocess rdf:resource="buffer2"/>
          <csp:ParaSync>Transfer</csp:ParaSync>
      </csp:ParallelPro> </oz:eqclass> </oz:Classdef2>
```

3.2   *Operation* $\Longleftrightarrow$ *Process*

TCOZ approach is to identify Object-Z operations as CSP processes and all the communication must go through the explicitly declared channels. The behaviour of an active object is explicitly captured by a CSP process. To achieve this approach several new elements are introduced. They are:

Chan. A channel is declared in an object's state.
Main. This process defines the dynamic control behaviour of an active object.

The environment for this approach can be achieved in the following way:

```
<?xml version="1.0" encoding="UTF-8"?> <rdf:RDF
xmlns:rdf="http://www.w3.org/1999/02/22-rdf-syntax-ns#"
xmlns:rdfs="http://www.w3.org/2000/01/rdf-schema#"
xmlns:xsd="http://www.w3.org/2000/10/XMLSchema#"
xmlns:daml="http://www.daml.org/2001/03/daml+oil#"
xmlns:tcoz="http://nt-appn.comp.nus.edu.sg/fm/zdaml/TCOZ#"
xmlns:oz="http://nt-appn.comp.nus.edu.sg/fm/zdaml/OZ#"
xmlns:csp="http://nt-appn.comp.nus.edu.sg/fm/zdaml/CSP#"
xmlns="http://nt-appn.comp.nus.edu.sg/fm/zdaml/TCOZ#">
    <daml:Ontology rdf:about="">
        <daml:imports rdf:resource=
          "http://nt-appn.comp.nus.edu.sg/fm/zdaml/OZ"/>
        <daml:imports rdf:resource=
          "http://nt-appn.comp.nus.edu.sg/fm/zdaml/CSP"/>
    </daml:Ontology>
    <rdfs:Class rdf:about="oz:State">
        <rdfs:subClassOf>
            <daml:Restriction daml:minCardinality="0">
```

```
          <daml:onProperty rdf:resource="csp:chan"/>
        </daml:Restriction> </rdfs:subClassOf>
      <!-- the channel can be declared in sate schema-->
   </rdfs:Class>
   <daml:ObjectProperty rdf:ID="MAIN">
       <rdfs:range rdf:resource="csp:Process"/>
       <rdfs:domain rdf:resource="#Classdef"/>
   </daml:ObjectProperty>
   <rdfs:Class rdf:about="oz:OP">
       <rdfs:subClassOf rdf:resource="csp:Process"/>
   </rdfs:Class>
   <rdfs:Class rdf:about="csp:Process">
       <rdfs:subClassOf rdf:resource="oz:OP"/>
   </rdfs:Class>
   <!--operation is one kind of process-->
</rdf:RDF>
```

Note that the DAML allows the subclass-relation between classes to be cyclic, since a cycle of subclass relationships provides a useful way to assert equality between classes. In TCOZ, the two communicating buffer system (with timing constraints on input and output operations) can be modelled as:

$$
\begin{array}{|l}
\hline
\textit{TBuffer} \\\\
\textit{Buffer} \\\\
\begin{array}{|ll}
\hline
\textit{left, right} : \textbf{chan} & \text{[input and output channels]} \\\\
t_j, t_l : \mathbb{T} & \text{[time durations for Join and Leave operations]} \\\\
\hline
\end{array} \\\\
\textsc{Main} \;\widehat{=}\; \mu\, Q \bullet ([i : MSG] \bullet \textit{left}?i \rightarrow \textit{Join} \bullet \textsc{Deadline}\, t_j \;\square \\\\
\qquad\qquad [\textit{size} \neq 0] \bullet \textit{right}!\textit{last}(\textit{items}) \rightarrow \textit{Leave} \bullet \textsc{Deadline}\, t_l);\; Q \\\\
\hline
\end{array}
$$

$$
\begin{array}{|l}
\hline
\textit{TSystem} \\\\
\begin{array}{|l}
\hline
l : \textit{TBuffer}[\textit{middle}/\textit{right}] \\\\
r : \textit{TBuffer}[\textit{middle}/\textit{left}] \\\\
\hline
\end{array} \\\\
\textsc{Main} \;\widehat{=}\; l \,\|[\, \textit{middle}\,]\|\, r \\\\
\hline
\end{array}
$$

In the Semantic Web environment, the class *TSystem* can be encoded as follows.

```
<oz:Classdef1 rdf:ID="tsystem">
  <z:name>TSystem</z:name>
  <oz:state> <oz:State>
    <z:decl>
      <z:Decl z:name="l" z:dtype="TBuffer[middle/right]"/></z:decl>
    <z:decl>
```

```
      <z:Decl z:name="r" z:dtype="TBuffer[middle/left]"/></z:decl>
  </oz:State> </oz:state>
  <oz:MAIN>
    <csp:parallelPro>
      <csp:subprocess> <oz:Message oz:receiver="l"
        oz:method="#TBMAIN"></oz:Message> </csp:subprocess>
      <csp:subprocess> <oz:Message oz:receiver="r"
        oz:method="#TBMAIN"></oz:Message> </csp:subprocess>
      <csp:ParaSync>middle</csp:ParaSync>
    </csp:parallelPro> </oz:MAIN>
  </oz:Classdef1>
```

Clearly, unlike Smith and Derrick's approach, TCOZ is not a simple integra-tion of Object-Z and TCSP, like CSP-OZ, TCOZ extends the two base notations with some new language constructs. Another distinct difference is that the se-mantic link between operation vs process in TCOZ is bi-directional ($\Longleftrightarrow$), while in Smith and Derrick's approach, the semantic link between class and process has a single direction ($\Longrightarrow$). By building the Semantic Web environments for the two approaches, one can improve the understanding of the difference. Such a Semantic Web environment is applicable for many other integrated formalisms.

4   Specifiation Comprehension

One of the major contributions of the RDF model introduced by the Semantic Web community, is that it allows us to do more accurate and more meaningful searching. This strength of RDF can be applied in the specification context leading to the notion of *specification comprehension*. Useful RDF queries can be formulated for comprehending specification models particularly when models are large and complex.

There are many RDF query systems available or under development. In this paper the RDFQL [16], a RDF query language developed by Intellidimension, is used to demonstrate some queries which can be achieved in the environment.

Based on our simple *Buffer* and *TBuffer* examples, the following demon-strates various queries expressed in RDFQL.

4.1   Inter-class Queries

Two typical queries can be formulated for search/understanding class relation-ships, such as inheritance hierarchy and composition structure.

(Inheritance) Find all the sub-classes derived from the class *Buffer* (Figure 1)

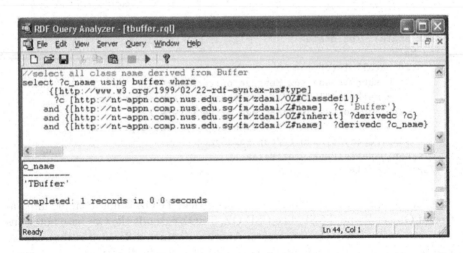

Fig. 1. Find all the sub-classes

Query:
```
select ?c_name using buffer where
    {[http://www.w3.org/1999/02/22-rdf-syntax-ns#type]
       ?c [http://nt-appn.comp.nus.edu.sg/fm/zdaml/OZ#Classdef1]}
and {[http://nt-appn.comp.nus.edu.sg/fm/zdaml/Z#name]  ?c 'Buffer'}
and {[http://nt-appn.comp.nus.edu.sg/fm/zdaml/OZ#inherit] ?derivedc ?c}
and {[http://nt-appn.comp.nus.edu.sg/fm/zdaml/Z#name]  ?derivedc ?c_name}
```
Result: TBuffer

(Composition:) Find all classes containing *Buffer* instances (as attributes)

Query:
```
select ?c_name using buffer where
    {[http://www.w3.org/1999/02/22-rdf-syntax-ns#type]
       ?c [http://nt-appn.comp.nus.edu.sg/fm/zdaml/OZ#Classdef1]}
and {[http://nt-appn.comp.nus.edu.sg/fm/zdaml/Z#name]  ?c ?c_name}
and {[http://nt-appn.comp.nus.edu.sg/fm/zdaml/OZ#state] ?c ?s}
and {[http://nt-appn.comp.nus.edu.sg/fm/zdaml/Z#decl] ?s ?d}
and {[http://nt-appn.comp.nus.edu.sg/fm/zdaml/Z#dtype] ?d ?dt}
and (INSTR(?dt, 'Buffer') = 1)
```
Result: TSystem

4.2   Intro-class Queries

A number of queries can be built for search/understanding class content (this is useful particularly when a class is large and has many operations).

Find all the operations which may change the attribute *items*:

```
Query:
 select ?op_name using buffer where
     {[http://www.w3.org/1999/02/22-rdf-syntax-ns#type]
         ?c [http://nt-appn.comp.nus.edu.sg/fm/zdaml/OZ#Classdef1]}
 and {[http://nt-appn.comp.nus.edu.sg/fm/zdaml/Z#name] ?c 'Buffer'}
 and {[http://nt-appn.comp.nus.edu.sg/fm/zdaml/OZ#op]   ?c ?op}
 and {[http://nt-appn.comp.nus.edu.sg/fm/zdaml/OZ#delObj]  ?op 'items'}
 and {[http://nt-appn.comp.nus.edu.sg/fm/zdaml/Z#name]  ?op ?op_name}
Result: Join, Leave
```

Find all the constant attributes in a class:

```
Query:
 select ?att using buffer where
     {[http://nt-appn.comp.nus.edu.sg/fm/zdaml/OZ#state] ?c ?sta}
 and {[http://nt-appn.comp.nus.edu.sg/fm/zdaml/Z#decl] ?sta ?decl}
 and {[http://nt-appn.comp.nus.edu.sg/fm/zdaml/Z#name]  ?decl ?att}
 and {[http://nt-appn.comp.nus.edu.sg/fm/zdaml/OZ#delObj]  ?op ?att1}
 and (?att <> ?att1)
Result: max
```

Find all the operations which have the same interface (with common base names for output and input):

```
Query:
 select ?op_name1 ?op_name2 using buffer where
     {[http://nt-appn.comp.nus.edu.sg/fm/zdaml/OZ#op]  ?c1 ?op1}
 and {[http://nt-appn.comp.nus.edu.sg/fm/zdaml/OZ#op]  ?c2 ?op2}
 and {[http://nt-appn.comp.nus.edu.sg/fm/zdaml/Z#name]  ?op1 ?op_name1}
 and {[http://nt-appn.comp.nus.edu.sg/fm/zdaml/Z#name]  ?op2 ?op_name2}
 and {[http://nt-appn.comp.nus.edu.sg/fm/zdaml/Z#decl]  ?op1 ?d1}
 and {[http://nt-appn.comp.nus.edu.sg/fm/zdaml/Z#name]   ?d1 ?n1}
 and {[http://nt-appn.comp.nus.edu.sg/fm/zdaml/Z#decl]  ?op2 ?d2}
 and {[http://nt-appn.comp.nus.edu.sg/fm/zdaml/Z#name]   ?d2 ?n2}
 and (?op1 <> ?op2) and (STRCMP(regexp(?n1,'*!'), regexp(?n2,'*?'))= 0)
Result: 'Join'    'Leave'
```

5 Related Work, Conclusion, and Further Work

One of the early work by Bicarregui and Matthews [4] has proposed ideas to integrate SGML (earlier version of XML) and EXPRESS for documenting control systems design. Z notation on the web based on HTML and Java applets has been investigated by Bowen and Chippington [5] and Cinancarini, Mascolo and Vitali [9]. HTML has been successful in presenting information on the Internet, however the lack of content information has made the retrieval and exchange of resource more difficult to perform. Our previous work was to improve on those issues by taking an XML approach [27]. Recently, the Community Z Tools Initiative [20] has stated to consider to build a XML interchange format for Z according to Z standards. However, the focus of all those approaches (based on HTML and XML) was mainly for displaying and browsing Z/Object-Z specifications on the web without concern for semantic issues and integration with other formalisms. The aim of this paper is different, it focuses on building a Semantic Web (RDF/DAML) environment for supporting, extending and integrating many different formalisms. Such a *meta integrator* may bring together the strengths of various formal methods communities in a flexible and widely accessible fashion. The Semantic Web environment for formal specifications may lead to many benefits. One novel application which has been demonstrated in this paper is the notion of specification comprehension based RDF query techniques. The review process of a large specification can be facilitated by various RDF queries.

Using the terminology from Jackson and Wing [17], this paper has demonstrated the potential for constructing a lightweight supporting environment and tools for all formal specification languages and their various (existing or even possible future) integrations. Recent efforts and success in formal methods have been focused on building 'heavy' tools for formal specifications, such as proof tools (e.g. Mural[3] for VDM, EVE[23] for Z etc) and model checkers (e.g. FDR [22] for CSP). Although those tools are essential and important for applications of formal methods, in order to achieve wider acceptance, the development of light weight tools such as the Semantic Web environment for formal specifications is also important. Interfacing such a web environment with proof tools and model checkers would be an interesting future work. Another interesting different research direction will be to investigate how formal specification techniques can facilitate web-based ontology design such that formal methods not only can benefit from web technologies but also can contribute to the web applications.

Acknowledgements. We would like to thank Hugh Anderson, DSTA staffs and anonymous referees for many helpful comments. This work is supported by the Academic Research grant *Integrated Formal Methods* from National University of Singapore and Defence Innovative Research grant *Formal Design Methods and DAML* from Defence Science & Technology Agency (DSTA) Singapore.

References

1. K. Araki, A. Galloway, and K. Taguchi, editors. *IFM'99: Integrated Formal Methods, York, UK.* Springer-Verlag, June 1999.
2. T. Berners-Lee, J. Hendler, and O. Lassila. The semantic web. Scientific American, May 2001.
3. J.C. Bicarregui, J.S. FitzGerald, P.A. Lindsay, R. Moore, and B. Ritchie. *Proof in VDM: A practioners Guide.* Springer Verlag, 1994.
4. J.C. Bicarregui and B. M. Matthews. Integrating EXPRESS and SGML for Document Modelling in Control Systems Design. In *EUG'95, 5th Annual EXPRESS User Group International Conference*, 1995.

5. J. P. Bowen and D. Chippington. Z on the Web using Java. In Bowen et al. [6], pages 66–80.

6. J. P. Bowen, A. Fett, and M. G. Hinchey, editors. *ZUM'98: The Z Formal Specification Notation, 11th International Conference of Z Users, Berlin, Germany, 24–26 September 1998*, volume 1493 of *Lect. Notes in Comput. Sci.* Springer-Verlag, 1998.

7. D. Brickley and R.V. Guha (editors). Resource description framework (rdf) schema specification 1.0.
http://www.w3.org/TR/2000/CR-rdf-schema-20000327/, March, 2000.

8. M. Butler. csp2B: A Practical Approach To Combining CSP and B. In J. Wing, J. Woodcock, and J. Davies, editors, *FM'99: World Congress on Formal Methods*, Lect. Notes in Comput. Sci., Toulouse, France, September 1999. Springer-Verlag.

9. P. Ciancarini, C. Mascolo, and F. Vitali. Visualizing Z notation in HTML documents. In Bowen et al. [6], pages 81–95.

10. R. Duke and G. Rose. *Formal Object Oriented Specification Using Object-Z.* Cornerstones of Computing. Macmillan, March 2000.

11. C. Fischer and H. Wehrheim. Model-Checking CSP-OZ Specifications with FDR. In Araki et al. [1].

12. A. J. Galloway and W. J. Stoddart. An operational semantics for ZCCS. In Hinchey and Liu [14], pages 272–282.

13. W. Grieskamp, T. Santen, and B. Stoddart, editors. *IFM'00: Integrated Formal Methods,*, Lect. Notes in Comput. Sci. Springer-Verlag, October 2000.

14. M. Hinchey and S. Liu, editors. *the IEEE International Conference on Formal Engineering Methods (ICFEM'97)*, Hiroshima, Japan, November 1997. IEEE Computer Society Press.

15. C.A.R. Hoare. *Communicating Sequential Processes.* International Series in Computer Science. Prentice-Hall, 1985.

16. Intellidimension Inc. Rdfql reference manual.
http://www.intellidimension.com/RDFGateway/Docs/rdfqlmanual.asp, 2001.

17. D. Jackson and J. Wing. Lightweight formal methods. *IEEE Computer*, April 1996.

18. O. Lassila and R. R. Swick (editors). Resource description framework (rdf) model and syntax specification. http://www.w3.org/TR/1999/REC-rdf-syntax-19990222/, Feb, 1999.

19. B. Mahony and J. S. Dong. Timed Communicating Object Z. *IEEE Transactions on Software Engineering*, 26(2):150–177, February 2000.

20. Andrew P. Martin. Community z tools initiative.
http://web.comlab.ox.ac.uk/oucl/work/andrew.martin/CZT/, 2001.

21. R. Paige. Formal method integration via heterogeneous notations. PhD Dissertation, University of Toronto, 1997.

22. A.W. Roscoe. *The Theory and Practice of Concurrency.* Prentice-Hall, 1997.

23. M. Saaltink. Z and EVES. In *Proceedings of Sixth Annual Z-User Meeting*, University of York, Dec 1991.

24. S. Schneider, J. Davies, D. M. Jackson, G. M. Reed, J. N. Reed, and A. W. Roscoe. Timed CSP: Theory and practice. In J. W. de Bakker, C. Huizing, W. P. de Roever, and G. Rozenberg, editors, *Real-Time: Theory in Practice*, volume 600 of *Lect. Notes in Comput. Sci.*, pages 640–675. Springer-Verlag, 1992.

25. G. Smith. *The Object-Z Specification Language.* Advances in Formal Methods. Kluwer Academic Publishers, 2000.

26. G. Smith and J. Derrick. Specification, refinement and verification of concurrent systems - an integration of Object-Z and CSP. *Formal Methods in System Design*, 18:249–284, 2001.

606   J.S. Dong, J. Sun, and H. Wang

27. J. Sun, J. S. Dong, J. Liu, and H. Wang. Object-Z Web Environment and Projections to UML. In *WWW-10: 10th International World Wide Web Conference*, pages 725–734. ACM Press, May 2001.
28. K. Taguchi and K. Araki. The State-Based CCS Semantics for Concurrent Z Specification. In Hinchey and Liu [14], pages 283–292.
29. H. Treharne and S. Schneider. Using a Process Algebra to control B OPERATIONS. In Araki et al. [1].
30. F. van Harmelen, P. F. Patel-Schneider, and I. Horrocks (editors). Reference description of the daml+oil ontology markup language. Contributors: T. Berners-Lee, D. Brickley, D. Connolly, M. Dean, S. Decker, P. Hayes, J. Heflin, J. Hendler, O. Lassila, D. McGuinness, L. A. Stein, ..., March, 2001.
31. World Wide Web Consortium (W3C). Extensible markup language (xml). http://www.w3.org/XML.
32. J. Woodcock and A. Cavalcanti. The steam boiler in a unified theory of Z and CSP. In *The 8th Asia-Pacific Software Engineering Conference (APSEC'01)*, pages 291–298. IEEE Press, 2001.
33. J. Woodcock and J. Davies. *Using Z: Specification, Refinement, and Proof.* Prentice-Hall International, 1996.
34. P. Zave and M. Jackson. Where do operations come from?: A multiparadigm specification technique. *IEEE Transactions on Software Engineering*, 22(7):508–528, July 1996.

A Language for Describing Wireless Mobile Applications with Dynamic Establishment of Multi-way Synchronization Channels

Takaaki Umedu[1], Yoshiki Terashima[1], Keiichi Yasumoto[2],
Akio Nakata[1], Teruo Higashino[1], and Kenichi Taniguchi[1]

[1] Graduate School of Info. Sci. & Tech., Osaka Univ., Osaka 560-8531, Japan
`(umedu,nakata,higashino,taniguchi)@ist.osaka-u.ac.jp`
[2] Graduate School of Info. Sci., Nara Inst. of Sci. & Tech., Nara 630-0101, Japan
`yasumoto@is.aist-nara.ac.jp`

Abstract. In this paper, we define a new language called LOTOS/M which enables dynamic establishment of multi-way synchronization channels among multiple agents (processes running on mobile hosts) on ad hoc networks, and show how it can be applied to designing wireless mobile applications. In LOTOS/M, a system specification is given by a set of independent agents. When a pair of agents is in a state capable of communicating with each other, a synchronization relation on a given gate (channel) list can dynamically be assigned to them by a new facility of LOTOS/M: (i) advertisement for a synchronization peer on a gate list and (ii) participation in the advertised synchronization. The synchronization relation on the same gate list can also be assigned to multiple agents to establish a multi-way synchronization channel incrementally so that the agents can exchange data through the channel. When an agent goes in a state incapable of communication, a synchronization relation assigned to the agent is canceled and it can run independently of the others. By describing some examples, we have confirmed that typical wireless mobile systems can easily be specified in LOTOS/M, and that they can be implemented efficiently with our LOTOS/M to Java compiler.

1 Introduction

Owing to recent maturity of wireless transmission technologies and popularity of personal mobile devices (e.g., cellular phones, PDA, etc), wireless mobile applications are becoming more and more important. Various applications have been proposed, for example, location aware systems [5] in ubiquitous networks, virtual meeting on ad hoc networks [7], and so on.

Such wireless mobile applications need dynamic communication facilities with which channels are dynamically allocated between mobile hosts and they can communicate via the channels when they happen to meet in a common radio range (communication area). Therefore, languages and tools for design and implementation of mobile applications which have dynamic communication facilities are desired.

L.-H. Eriksson and P. Lindsay (Eds.): FME 2002, LNCS 2391, pp. 607–624, 2002.

LOTOS [6] is one of the formal specification languages for communication protocols, which has the powerful operators such as choice, parallel and interruption among multiple processes. With the parallel operators, we can specify *multi-way synchronization* which enables several parallel processes to execute the specified events synchronously to exchange data. With multi-way synchronization, we can easily handle complicated mechanisms such as broadcast/multi-cast communication and mutual exclusion for accessing resources in distributed systems. It also allows us to describe systems incrementally as a main behavior and a set of behavioral constraints (called the *constraint oriented style* [2,12]). So, multi-way synchronization seems useful to design and develop wireless mobile systems.

However, standard LOTOS does not have the facility for dynamic channel establishment among processes when those processes are in a state capable of communicating with each other (e.g., by approaching in a common radio range). Since mobile systems require such dynamic communication, it is difficult to apply LOTOS to design and implement such systems.

On the other hand, in π calculus [8] which is a process algebra including a dynamic channel allocation mechanism between processes, and in M-LOTOS [4, 9] which is an extension of LOTOS introducing the above mechanism of π calculus, dynamic channel establishment among processes can be specified. However, multi-way synchronization cannot be specified among processes.

In this paper, we propose a new language called LOTOS/M which enables dynamic establishment of channels for multi-way synchronization among multiple mobile processes. In LOTOS/M, a system specification is given by a set of independent multiple agents (processes running on mobile hosts).

When a pair of agents is in a state capable of communicating with each other, a synchronization relation on a given gate (channel) list can dynamically be assigned to them by a new facility of LOTOS/M: (i) advertisement for a synchronization peer with a gate list and (ii) participation in the advertised synchronization. The pair of combined agents (agents with synchronization relation) is regarded as a single agent, and thus can combine with another agent on a gate list. The synchronization relation on the same gate list can also be assigned to multiple agents to enable multi-way synchronization. The group of combined agents is called the *agent group*, and its member agents can communicate with each other by multi-way synchronization until the synchronization relation is canceled. When an agent (or a sub agent group) goes in a state incapable of communication, the synchronization relation assigned to the agent is canceled and it can run independently of the others.

In LOTOS/M, the agents in an agent group form a binary tree (called the *synchronization tree*) where each node corresponds to the synchronization operator of LOTOS or an agent itself. This property makes it easy to implement specifications based on the existing techniques of our standard LOTOS compiler [14]. The current version of our LOTOS/M compiler generates from a given LOTOS/M specification, multiple Java programs which run on corresponding mobile hosts. We assume that data types and functions specified in LOTOS/M specifications are available as the corresponding Java methods. So, our compiler provides only a mechanism to invoke those methods. Thus, our compiler can be used as a tool for developing concurrent Java programs with a multi-way synchronization mechanism.

In the following Sect. 2, we outline the LOTOS language and problems to describe mobile systems in it. In Sect. 3, we define LOTOS/M language and give its formal semantics. In Sect. 4, we describe typical mobile applications in the proposed language to show applicability of LOTOS/M. Sect. 5 outlines our implementation technique. Finally, Sect. 6 concludes the paper.

2   LOTOS and Its Applicability to Mobile Systems

2.1   Outline of LOTOS

LOTOS [6] is a formal description language for communication protocols and distributed systems, which has been standardized by ISO. In LOTOS, a system specification can be described by a parallel composition of several (sequential) processes. The behavior of each process is described by a *behavior expression*, which specifies execution sequences of *events* (actions observable to the external environment), *internal events* (unobservable actions), and process invocations. Here, an event is an interaction (input/output of data) between a process and an external environment, which occurs at an interaction point called a *gate*.

To specify the ordering of execution, the operators such as action prefix $(a; B)$, choice $(B1[]B2)$, parallel $(B1|[G]|B2)$[1], interleaving $(B1|||B2)$, disabling $(B1[> B2)$ ($B2$ can interrupt $B1$) and sequential composition $(B1 >> B2)$ ($B2$ starts when $B1$ successfully terminates) are specified at each pair of sub-expressions. Especially, using the parallel operator, we can specify *multi-way synchronization*, that is, multiple (possibly more than two) processes executing events on the same gate simultaneously and exchanging data at the gates. In addition, we can restrict the execution of B by a boolean expression *guard* by denoting "$[guard] - > B$". Also, we can create new gates gl used only in B by denoting "**hide** gl **in** B".

By specifying multi-way synchronization among multiple nodes of a distributed system, we can easily describe systems with complicated mechanism such as broadcasting/multicasting and/or mutual exclusion[2] for accessing resources [14]. Moreover, it is known that using multi-way synchronization, some facilities such as step-by-step addition of behavioral constraints among nodes by the constraint-oriented specification style [2,12] are available. Therefore, it is also desirable to use multi-way synchronization among agents of mobile systems.

---

[1] Hereafter, we say that in $B1|[G]|B2$, a *synchronization relation* on gate list G is assigned between $B1$ and $B2$.

[2] Sometimes two-way synchronization may be enough, e.g., $R|[G]|(C1|||C2|||...|||Cn)$

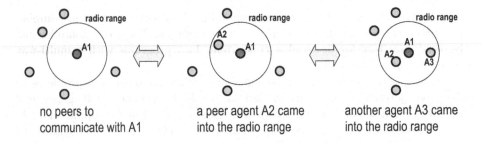

no peers to
communicate with A1

a peer agent A2 came
into the radio range

another agent A3 came
into the radio range

Fig. 1. Dynamic change of agent combinations capable of communication

2.2   Problems for Describing Mobile Systems in LOTOS

In a wireless mobile system, as shown in Fig.1, combinations of agents capable of communicating with each other dynamically change since they move around. Thus, to describe such a system in LOTOS, the following problems arise.

(1) There is no facility to allocate channels to a combination of agents only when they are in a state capable of direct communication (e.g., when they are in a common radio range).
(2) There exist a lot of possible combinations of agents, depending on their locations, on the number of agents participating in the same multi-way synchronization, or so on. In LOTOS, basically we must describe all of such combinations of agents statically in a behavior expression.

In [11], a mobile telephony system including roaming services is described in LOTOS. However, the system is restricted to use only one-to-one communications between mobile hosts and base stations, and solve the above problem partly by dynamically exchanging IDs of each mobile host and each base station.

To solve the problem essentially, we think that we need a language support to dynamically assign among any combination of agents a synchronization relation for multi-way synchronization though which the agents can communicate by executing events synchronously.

3   Proposal of LOTOS/M

In order to solve the problems in the previous section, we propose a new language called *LOTOS/M* suitable to describe wireless mobile applications.

3.1   Definition of LOTOS/M

We show new constructs and their informal semantics of LOTOS/M in Table 1. In LOTOS/M, the entire mobile system is given as a set of independent agents $A := A_1 \mid A_2 \mid ... \mid A_n$ where each A_i does not know how to communicate

Table 1. Extended syntax and informal semantics

Syntax	Semantics
$A1 \mid A2 \mid ... \mid An$	Parallel execution of n agents $A1, ..., An$ independently of each other.
agent $A[G](E) := B$ **endagent**	Definition of the behavior expression of agent A.
sync $!G : sid\ IO\ Guard$ **in** B **endsync**	Advertisement for a synchronization peer with gatelist G and definition of behavior expression B to be executed after the peer agent has been found.
sync $?H : sid\ IO\ Guard$ **in** B **endsync**	Acceptance for an advertisement and definition of behavior expression B to be executed after the acceptance has been approved.
$disc!sid;\ B$	Disconnection of a channel (cancellation of a synchronization relation) established with $ID = sid$ and definition of behavior expression B to be executed after the disconnection.
$g!P; ...\ \|[g]\|_{sid}\ g?Q : process; ...$	Exchange of a process name among agents.

with other agents. We define the operational semantics of $A_1 \mid A_2 \mid ... \mid A_n$ (also denoted by $\|\{A_1, ..., A_n\}$) as follows (Act is the set of all events used in $A_1, ..., A_n$).

$$\frac{A_i \xrightarrow{a} A'_i, \quad a \in Act \cup \{sync, disc\}}{\|\{A_1, ..., A_n\} \xrightarrow{a} \|\{A_1, ..., A'_i, ..., A_n\}}$$

The behavior expression of each agent A_i is specified with a new construct "**agent ... endagent**" where the expression includes only operators of standard LOTOS and "**sync ... endsync**" (i.e., "$\mid$" cannot be used).
Channel establishment. In order to allocate channels (assign a synchronization relation) between a pair of agents only when they can physically communicate with each other, LOTOS/M provides the following special actions: (i) an advertisement for a synchronization peer (**sync** $!G : sid\ IO\ Guard$ **in** $B1$ **endsync**) and (ii) participation in a synchronization advertisement (**sync** $?H : sid\ IO\ Guard$ **in** $B2$ **endsync**).

Here, G and H denote gate lists, "$: sid$" represents a variable for keeping the ID for the synchronization relation between agents and is used for active cancellation of the synchronization relation with $disc!sid$ action. "IO" represents a list of input and output parameters (e.g., $!E1?x1?x2$), and "$Guard$" is the boolean expression denoted by $[f(c1, c2, ...x1, x2, ...)]$ where constants $c1, c2, ...$ and parameters $x1, x2, ...$ in IO may be used. IO and $Guard$ are used to restrict only specific agents to be combined. "IO" and "$Guard$" may be omitted.

If the following conditions hold for a pair of agents, then a synchronization relation on a given gate list G is assigned between the agents (we also say that the two agents are *combined* (or *joined*) on gate list G).

- one agent $\mathcal{A}_1$ is ready to execute the *sync* action "B1:=**sync** !G : $IO1$ $Guard1$ **in** $B1'$ **endsync**" (called *host agent*) and the other agent $\mathcal{A}_2$ can execute "B2:=**sync** ?H : sid $IO2$ $Guard2$ **in** $B2'$ **endsync**" (called *participant agent*).
- the numbers of gates in G and H are the same.
- the numbers of parameters in $IO1$ and $IO2$ are the same, and each pair of the corresponding parameters consist of an input (?x) and an output (!E) where their types must match.
- both of $Guard1$ and $Guard2$ hold after assigning the value of each output parameter to the corresponding variable of the input parameter (e.g., when the parameters are $?x$ and $!E$, the value of expression E is assigned to variable x).
- the two agents are in a state capable of communicating with each other physically[3].

The succeeding behavior is equivalent to $\mathcal{A}_1[B1'/B1] \ ||[G]||_{sid} \ \mathcal{A}_2[B2'[G/H]/B2]$. Here, $||[G]||_{sid}$ is the new operator called *ad hoc parallel* operator which is equivalent to $||[G]||$ except that its operands can be separated by *disc*!*sid* action. $\mathcal{A}[B'/B]$ is the entire behavior expression of agent $\mathcal{A}$ obtained by replacing subbehavior expression B with B', and $B2[G/H]$ is a behavior expression obtained by replacing every gate in H appearing in $B2$ with the corresponding gate in G.

Also, note that G must be created with *hide* operator of LOTOS (or G may be the gate list received from another agent by *sync*?G) before used in *sync*!G. Also, in *sync*?H, H must not be included in environment gates of the agent (e.g., interaction points to the user).

The combined agents are treated as one agent and called the *agent group*. Each agent group can be combined incrementally with another agent by executing *sync* !G (or *sync* ?H) action. As an example, Fig. 2 illustrates that the following three agents are combined in a step-by-step manner.

```
A1 | A2 | A3
where
  A1:= sync !{g} in g; stop endsync
  A2:= sync ?{h} in
          sync !{h} in h; stop endsync
        endsync
  A3:= sync ?{f} in f; stop endsync
```

(Here, *disc* action is omitted).

---

[3] In LOTOS/M, whether each agent is currently able to communicate with another agent is treated as an implementation matter. As a process algebra treating location information to check capability of direct communication, for example, [1] is proposed.

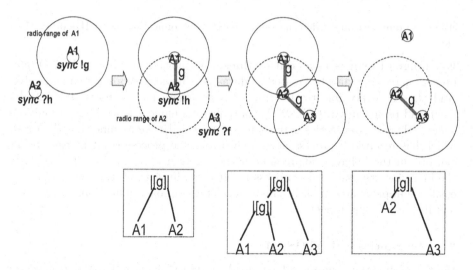

Fig. 2. Assignment/cancellation of the synchronization relation among agents

Channel disconnection. Each agent group can be separated into several agents/agent groups by executing active/passive disconnection. We define the effect of disconnection to internal behavior of each agent as follows.

(1) Active disconnection. By executing *disc!sid* action, each agent can disconnect the specified channel (synchronization relation) spontaneously. This is called *active disconnection*. When an agent goes into a state incapable of communication, e.g., by moving out of a common radio range, we think that active disconnection is executed by the agent.

(2) Passive disconnection. When an agent executes *disc!sid*, *pdisc!sid* is executed at each member agent in its agent group to inform about the channel disconnection. This is called *passive disconnection*.

(3) Synchronization of channel disconnection. *disc!sid* and *pdisc!sid* must be executed synchronously among agents.

In each agent's behavior expression B, we can describe an appropriate processing after each channel disconnection, as an exception handling process when the corresponding *disc!sid* or *pdisc!sid* is executed. Below, we show an example where the behavior stops by *disc!sid* but continues by *pdisc!sid*.

```
sync ?G:sid in
(   B'
||| pdisc!sid; exit
)
[>
   disc!sid; exit
endsync
```

(Here, we omit exception description by passive disconnections with IDs other than *sid*).

Exchange of processes as data values.   As shown in Table 1, in LOTOS/M, process names can also be treated as data-type like higher-order π calculus [10]. And thus it is possible to describe systems where mobile hosts dynamically download programs. In LOTOS/M, only process names are exchanged between agents (therefore semantics extension is not needed). We assume that the agent which has received a process name can invoke the process (that is, each agent can obtain the behavior expression of the received process). How to exchange the behavior expression of a process is left as an implementation matter (it can easily be implemented in Java language). The example applications using these features are shown in Sect. 4.

3.2   Semantics of LOTOS/M

Here, we define the semantics of extended constructs, *sync* action and *disc(pdisc)* action as follows. We also define a structured operational semantics in Table 2 to provide a precise formal definition of the semantics.

- Identifier *sid* is issued for each execution of a *sync* action so that *disc* action with the issued *sid* can cancel the assigned synchronization relation.
- When an agent A executes *disc!sid* action, the operand of the ad hoc parallel operator with $ID = sid$ (the sub-agent group including A) leaves from the entire agent group and the separated two agents run independently. At the time, the corresponding synchronization relation is canceled and the cancellation is informed to all the agents in the agent group.

Combining. When there exist a host agent executing *sync !G* and a participant agent executing *sync ?X*, these two agents are combined and a synchronization relation on G is assigned by the inference rule **Agent-Join** in Table 2. X is a list of formal gate parameters, which are replaced with the actual gate list G when combined. *id* is issued for this synchronization relation, which can be disconnected by the *disc* action with the same *id*. Table 3 shows how inference rules are applied when three agents A_1, A_2 and A_3 are combined into one agent group.

Isolation. When an agent executes *disc!id*, it must be separated from its agent group (this is called *isolation*).

Inference rules for agent isolation in Table 2 have the following meaning.

- **Agent-Leave-1** is the rule for the case when *sid* matches the ID of the current ad hoc parallel operator. This rule removes the ad hoc parallel operator with $ID = sid$ after registering it as an auxiliary term, and makes the peer agent execute *pdisc!sid*.
- **Agent-Leave-2** is the rule for the case when *sid* does not match the ID of the current ad hoc parallel operator. This rule makes the disconnection request work outside of agent group $A_1|[G]|_{sid'} A_2$. This also makes the peer agent execute *pdisc!sid*.

Table 2. Structured operational semantics for LOTOS/M

Agent-Join

$$\frac{A_i \stackrel{sync!G}{\longrightarrow} A_i', \quad A_j \stackrel{sync?X}{\longrightarrow} A_j', \quad G = \{g_1, ..., g_k\}, \quad X = \{x_1, ..., x_k\}}{|\{A_1, ..., A_k\} \stackrel{sync!G}{\longrightarrow} (A_i' \,|[G]|_{sid}\, A_j'[G/X] \quad | \quad |\{A_1, ..., A_k\} - \{A_i, A_j\})}$$

Here, A_i (also, A_j) is the behavior expression of each agent/agent group. $sync!G$ and $sync?H$ can be replaced each other in A_i and A_j. $B[G/X]$ is obtained from B by replacing each free occurrence of formal gate parameters in $X = \{x_1, ..., x_k\}$ used in the B with the corresponding actual gate parameters in $G = \{g_1, ..., g_k\}$. Since the semantics of the guard expressions specified in $sync$ action is the same as LOTOS, it is omitted here.

Agent-Leave-1

$$\frac{A_1 \stackrel{disc!sid}{\longrightarrow} A_1', \quad A_2 \stackrel{pdisc!sid}{\longrightarrow} A_2'}{[A_1|[G]|_{sid}A_2 \stackrel{disc!sid}{\longrightarrow} A_2', A_1']}$$

Agent-Leave-2

$$\frac{A_1 \stackrel{disc!sid}{\longrightarrow} A_1', \quad A_2 \stackrel{pdisc!sid}{\longrightarrow} A_2', \quad sid <> sid'}{A_1|[G]|_{sid'}A_2 \stackrel{disc!sid}{\longrightarrow} A_1'|[G]|_{sid'}A_2'}$$

Agent-Leave-3

$$\frac{[A_1 \stackrel{disc!sid}{\longrightarrow} A_1', A_3], \quad A_2 \stackrel{pdisc!sid}{\longrightarrow} A_2', \quad sid <> sid'}{[A_1|[G]|_{sid'}A_2 \stackrel{disc!sid}{\longrightarrow} A_1'|[G]|_{sid'}A_2', A_3]}$$

Agent-Leave-4

$$\frac{[A \stackrel{disc!sid}{\longrightarrow} A', A'']}{A \stackrel{disc!sid}{\longrightarrow} A'|A''}$$

Agent-Leave-5

$$\frac{A_1 \stackrel{pdisc!sid}{\longrightarrow} A_1', \quad A_2 \stackrel{pdisc!sid}{\longrightarrow} A_2', \quad sid <> sid'}{A_1|[G]|_{sid'}A2 \stackrel{pdisc!sid}{\longrightarrow} A_1'|[G]|_{sid'}A_2'}$$

Here, $A, A', A_1, A_2, ...$ represent the behavior expressions of agents/agent groups. The auxiliary term $[A \stackrel{disc!sid}{\longrightarrow} A', A'']$ is the same as the transition relation $A \stackrel{disc!sid}{\longrightarrow} A'$ except that the extra information A'' (agent to be isolated) are attached. In **Agent-Leave-1–5**, $disc$ and $pdisc$ can be replaced each other in A_1 and A_2.

- **Agent-Leave-3** is the rule which brings the disconnected agent in the auxiliary term to the upper node in the syntax tree and makes the peer agent execute $pdisc!sid$.
- **Agent-Leave-4** is the rule which makes the disconnected agent in an auxiliary term work as an independent agent.
- **Agent-Leave-5** is the rule which represents that $A_1|[G]|_{sid'}A_2$ can execute $pdisc!sid$ only if A_1 and A_2 can execute $pdisc!sid$.

Table 3. Applying inference rules when agents combine

When $A_1 \xrightarrow{sync!G} A_1'$, $A_2 \xrightarrow{sync?F} A_2'$, $A_3 \xrightarrow{sync!F} A_3' \xrightarrow{sync?G} A_3''$,

$A_1 \mid A_2 \mid A_3$

$\xrightarrow{sync!F:1} A_1 \mid (A_2' \; \|[F]\|_1 \; A_3')$

$\xrightarrow{sync!G:2} A_1' \; \|[G]\|_2 \; (A_2' \; \|[F]\|_1 \; A_3'')$

Suppose that an agent group $(A_1\|[g]\|_1 A_2)\|[h]\|_2 A_3$ is the result after A_1 and A_2 have combined on $g(sid = 1)$ and then A_1 and A_3 have combined on $h(sid = 2)$. In Table 4, we show how inference rules are applied when each agent leaves from the above agent group with different sid.

(1) When A_2 is isolated with $sid = 1$, that is, $A_2 \xrightarrow{disc!1} A_2'$:
Inference rules are applied as shown in Example1 of Table 4. As a result, A_2 leaves from the agent group, and $pdisc!1$ is executed in A_1 and A_3 so that they know the active disconnection from A_2 with $sid = 1$.

(2) When A_2 is isolated with $sid = 2$, that is, $A_2 \xrightarrow{disc!2} A_2'$:
Inference rules are applied as shown in Example2 of Table 4. As a result, A_2 is separated as a sub-agent group $(A_1\|[g]\|_1 A_2)$ from A_3, and A_1 and A_3 know the fact by execution of $pdisc!2$.

(3) When A_3 is isolated with $sid = 2$, that is, $A_3 \xrightarrow{disc!2} A_3'$:
Inference rules are applied as shown in Example3 of Table 4. As a result, A_3 is separated from $(A_1\|[g]\|_1 A_2)$, and A_1 and A_2 know the fact by execution of $pdisc!2$.

Note that the semantics in Table 2 enables us to construct an LTS from a given LOTOS/M specification where each node of the LTS corresponds to a tuple of the current agent behaviors (e.g., $A1 \mid (A2' \; \|[F]\|_1 \; A3')$) and each label corresponds to an event, $sync$ or $disc(pdisc)$ action.

Reason why the above semantics were chosen

In [3] Groote proved that if the inference rules of a given operational semantics satisfy one of the following conditions, the semantics preserves the congruence relation.

$$\frac{t_1 \xrightarrow{a_1} y_1, t_2 \xrightarrow{a_2} y_2, \dots}{f(t_1, t_2, \dots) \xrightarrow{a} t'} \qquad \frac{t_1 \xrightarrow{a_1} y_1, t_2 \xrightarrow{a_2} y_2, \dots}{x \xrightarrow{a} t'}$$

Although rule **Agent-Join** satisfies the above sufficient condition, rule **Agent-Leave** does not. This is because we think that any agent should be able to leave from its agent group to whatever ad hoc parallel operator $(\|[G]\|_{id})$ it connects. If we modify rule **Agent-Leave** so that it can be applied only to the root operator of the syntax tree of the agent group (i.e., the agents can be separated only in reverse order when they combined), we can construct the semantics which preserves the congruence relation. However, in actual mobile

Table 4. Applying inference rules when agents are isolated

Example1

$$\frac{\dfrac{A_2 \xrightarrow{disc!1} A_2' \quad A_1 \xrightarrow{pdisc!1} A_1'}{[A_1|[g]|_1 A_2 \xrightarrow{disc!1} A_1', A_2']} \left(\begin{array}{c}\textbf{Agent-}\\\textbf{Leave-1}\end{array}\right) \quad A_3 \xrightarrow{pdisc!1} A_3' \quad 1 <> 2}{\dfrac{[(A_1|[g]|_1 A_2)|[h]|_2 A_3 \xrightarrow{disc!1} (A_1'|[h]|_2 A_3'), A_2']}{(A_1|[g]|_1 A_2)|[h]|_2 A_3 \xrightarrow{disc!1} (A_1'|[h]|_2 A_3')|A_2'}}\left(\begin{array}{c}\textbf{Agent-}\\\textbf{Leave-3}\end{array}\right)}$$

$$(\textbf{Agent-Leave-4})$$

Example2

$$\frac{\dfrac{A_2 \xrightarrow{disc!2} A_2' \quad A_1 \xrightarrow{pdisc!2} A_1' \quad 2 <> 1}{A_1|[g]|_1 A_2 \xrightarrow{disc!2} A_1'|[g]|_1 A_2'}\left(\begin{array}{c}\textbf{Agent-}\\\textbf{Leave-2}\end{array}\right) \quad A_3 \xrightarrow{pdisc!2} A_3'}{\dfrac{[(A_1|[g]|_1 A_2)|[h]|_2 A_3 \xrightarrow{disc!2} A_3', A_1'|[g]|_1 A_2']}{(A_1|[g]|_1 A_2)|[h]|_2 A_3 \xrightarrow{disc!2} A_3'|(A_1'|[g]|_1 A_2')}}\left(\begin{array}{c}\textbf{Agent-}\\\textbf{Leave-1}\end{array}\right)}$$

$$(\textbf{Agent-Leave-4})$$

Example3

$$\frac{A_3 \xrightarrow{disc!2} A_3' \quad \dfrac{\dfrac{A_1 \xrightarrow{pdisc!2} A_1' \quad A_2 \xrightarrow{pdisc!2} A_2' \quad 2 <> 1}{A_1|[g]|_1 A_2 \xrightarrow{pdisc!2} A_1'|[g]|_1 A_2'}(\textbf{Agent-Leave-5})}{}(\textbf{Agent-Leave-1})}{\dfrac{[(A_1|[g]|_1 A_2)|[h]|_2 A_3 \xrightarrow{disc!2} A_1'|[g]|_1 A_2', A_3']}{(A_1|[g]|_1 A_2)|[h]|_2 A_3 \xrightarrow{disc!2} (A_1'|[g]|_1 A_2')|A_3'}}(\textbf{Agent-Leave-4})}$$

applications, we cannot expect in what order agents are leaving from the agent group, we think that such modification makes no sense. That's a reason why the semantics in Table 2 were chosen.

4 Describing Wireless Mobile Systems in LOTOS/M

Location Aware System. In order to develop a location aware system [5], mechanisms (i) for detecting each agent's location and (ii) for providing a different service depending on each location are required. In LOTOS/M, (i) is realized by the dynamic channel establishment mechanism that a base station (host agent) advertises for a synchronization peer in its radio range and a mobile host responds it. Similarly, (ii) is easily realized by the process name exchange mechanism so that a mobile host can download a specific behavior expression from a base station.

An example of a location aware system is depicted in Fig. 3. We also show an example specification in LOTOS/M in Table 5.

In the example, there are three base stations $S1, S2$ and $S3$ and multiple mobile hosts $A1, A2, ..., An$. Gates f and g are used as interaction points between each base station and each agent. In the system, $S1$ advertises for syn-

618   T. Umedu et al.

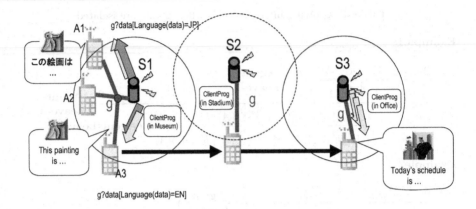

Fig. 3. Example of a location aware system

chronization peers in its radio range for a while (it is described in sub-process *Service* by iterative execution of *sync* !{f, g} action). After some time elapses ($[StartTime()]->...$), $S1$ sends through gate f a program (f!ClientProg) to the agents which participated in the advertised synchronization (*sync* ?{h, g} action in agent $A1$). Then $S1$ starts transmitting through gate g information in several languages in parallel ($Transmit[g](JapaneseInfo)$ ||| ...). Data is transmitted to all participated agents at the same time with the property of multi-way synchronization. Since each user selects his/her mother language ($u?lang$), only information in the specified language are displayed ($[Language(data) = lang]->...$). When some of the participated agents move out of the radio range or execute *disc*, only the agents are isolated (the behavior of agents are initialized by ...[> ($disc!sid; A1[u][]pdisc!sid; A1[u]$)), and the other agents can keep receiving service.

Like this example, by sending/receiving process names, programs can be down-loaded on demand to each mobile host. It contributes efficient use of memory in mobile hosts with poor resources. Also, using properties of multi-way synchronization, we can develop an application where the multiple users interact with a base station at the same time cooperating with each other (e.g., interactive games, quiz competition, and so on).

4.1 Routing in Wireless Ad Hoc Networks

In wireless ad hoc networks, each mobile agent can communicate with another distant agent via some intermediate agents by repeating broadcasting to their radio ranges. Here, based on Dynamic Source Routing [7], we describe a routing protocol to find a path from a source agent to a destination agent in wireless ad hoc networks.

In this protocol, as shown in Fig. 4, when an agent (source agent) wants to obtain a path to a particular agent, it broadcasts a request message to its radio

Table 5. Example specification of a location aware system

```
specification LocationAware: noexit
behavior
A1 | A2 | ... | S1 | S2 | S3
where
  agent A1[u] : exit:= (* A2, A3 are similar *)
   sync ?{h,j}:sid in
     (h?ClientProg:process; u?lang; ClientProg[j](lang))
     [> (disc!sid; A1[u] [] pdisc!sid; A1[u])
   endsync
  endagent
  agent S1 :exit:=
   hide f,g in
     Service[f,g]
  where
   process Service[f,g] : exit:=
    sync !{f,g}:sid in
      [not(StartTime())]- >
        (Service[f,g] ||| (disc!sid; exit [] pdisc!sid; exit))
      [] [StartTime()] - > f!ClientProg; ProvideInfo[g])
    endsync
   endproc
   process ProvideInfo[g] :noexit:=
     Transmit[g](JapaneseInfo)
   ||| Transmit[g](EnglishInfo)
   ||| ...
   endproc
   process ClientProg[g](lang) :noexit:=
    g?data;
      ([Language(data) = lang]; ... (* display information *)
      [] [Language(data) <> lang]; exit (* skip information *)
      ) >> ClientProg[g](lang)
   endproc
   ...
  endagent
  agent S2 :noexit:=
   ...
  agent S3 :noexit:=
   ...
endspec
```

(Here, behavior expressions of processes $S2, S3$ and *Transmit* are omitted. *StartTime*() is an ADT function which becomes true when the service starting time has come)

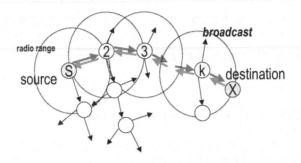

Fig. 4. Routing in wireless ad hoc networks

range. Each agent which has received the request message re-broadcasts it. In such a way, message flooding is carried out until reaching the destination agent. The request message includes the path from the source to the current node (each intermediate agent adds its ID as the last entry of list variable *route_record*). Since the message includes the complete path from the source to the destination when it has reached to the destination agent, then it returns the path information to the source along the reverse direction of the path.

At each stage, each agent executes one of the following action sequences.

(1) at a source node, it inputs the destination agent's ID (*u?dest_id*) and broadcasts a request message asking for a path to the destination.
(2) at an intermediate node, it receives the request message and forwards it by re-broadcasting.
(3) at a destination node, it receives the request message and returns the complete path information to the source node.
(4) at an intermediate node, it receives the return message and forwards it towards the source node according to the return path.
(5) at a source node, it receives the return message and provides the obtained path to its user (*u!route*).

A message broadcast by an agent (sender) can be described by a multiway synchronization between the sender and other agents in its radio range. So, here, we describe the sender agent to advertise for other agents by executing *sync !{b}* repeatedly during a time interval, and to broadcast a message by multiway synchronization among agents which has participated in the advertisement. The above broadcast mechanism can be described as the following LOTOS/M process.

```
process Broadcast[b](msgtype, dest_id, data): exit:=
  sync !{b}:sid!msgtype in
    [not(TimerExpired())]− >
      Broadcast(dest_id, msgtype, data) >> disc!sid; exit
    [] [TimerExpired()]− > b!msgtype!dest_id!data; disc!sid; exit
  endsync
endproc
```

(here, *TimerExpired*() is an ADT function which becomes true when the preset timer has expired)

Among the above behavior, in (2), to avoid the message replication, each agent must forward the message only when the current path attached to the message does not include itself (*not(included(route_record, my_id))*).

In (3), (4) and (5), each intermediate agent must send the path information only to the next agent in the return path towards the source agent. So, the ID of the next agent is used as the I/O parameter in *sync* action so that only the intended pair of agents can be combined (*sync* !{*b*}!*Return*!*last(route_record)* and *sync* ?{*a*}?*msg*?*id*[*msg* = *Return and id* = *my_id*]).

The whole description of the agent behavior in LOTOS/M is shown in Table 6.

5   Implementation of LOTOS/M Specifications and Experimental Results

5.1   LOTOS/M Compiler

We have developed a LOTOS/M compiler where a given LOTOS/M specification is implemented as a set of Java programs executed at the corresponding nodes, respectively. Since we aim at modeling behavior of wireless mobile systems, only the control part of a given specification is automatically implemented. We assume that functions used in the specification (which are supposed to be described in abstract data types in LOTOS [6]) are available as the corresponding "methods" in the given Java class libraries and Java programs generated by our compiler just invoke the methods appropriately. Since the details of the compiler can be found in [13], here we outline the basic ideas on how to establish multi-way synchronization channels and execute events synchronously among mobile agents.

(1) Dynamic establishment of channels. As explained in Sect. 3, a multi-way synchronization channel among multiple agents is established incrementally. So, we adopt the following procedure: (i) the host agent broadcasts a message to advertise for a synchronization peer in its radio range periodically until receiving a participation message from at least one agent; and (ii) if it has received the participation messages from multiple agents, it selects one agent among them and sends the acceptance message only to the selected agent.

(2) Execution of events by multi-way synchronization. In order to calculate what event tuples can be executed synchronously among agents when those agents request execution of events, we construct the *synchronization tree* for each agent group. Here the synchronization tree corresponds to the syntax tree where each intermediate node corresponds to an ad hoc parallel operator and each leaf node does an agent. To enable communication along the syntax tree, we let the host agent to be the *responsible node* where it receives request messages from the participant agent and evaluates the synchronization condition for each pair of events requested from the host agent and the participant agent on given gate list *G*. Since a responsible node is assigned to each operator node

Table 6. Example specification of a path finding protocol based on Dynamic Source
Routing

```
agent DSR[u](my_id): noexit:=
hide b in
(
  (* (1) sending route request with destination node ID *)
  u?dest_id:int;
  Broadcast(Search,dest_id,{my_id})
[] (* (2) forwarding route request *)
sync?{a}:sid?msg[msg=Search] in
  a!Search?dest_id?route_record
  [(dest_id<>my_id) and not(included(route_record,my_id))]);
  disc!sid;
  Broadcast(Search, dest_id, route_record+{my_id})
[] (* (3) when route request reaches the destination node *)
  a!Search?dest_id?route_record[dest_id = my_id];
  disc!sid;
  (sync !{b}:sid2!Return!last(route_record) in
    b!Return!route_record+{my_id}!route_record; disc!sid2; exit
  endsync
)
endsync
[] (* (4) forwarding of route information *)
sync?{a}:sid?msg?id[msg=Return and id=my_id] in
  a!Return?route?return_path
  [included(return_path,my_id) and return_path <> my_id];
  disc!sid;
  (sync !b:sid2!Return!last(return_path-{my_id}) in
    b!Return!route!return_path-{my_id}; disc!sid2; exit
  endsync
  )
  [] (* (5) when the source node receives route info. *)
  a!Return?route?return_path[return_path={my_id}];
  u!route;
endsync
) >> DSR[u](my_id)
endagent
```

(*included*(*list, item*) and *last*(*list*) are ADT functions calculating whether *item* is included in *list* or not and returning the last item of *list*, respectively. Exception behavior
by executing *pdisc* is omitted.

in the tree, according to standard LOTOS semantics, the executable events can
be calculated by examining conditions at each intermediate node along the path
from the leaves to the root. In [14], we have proposed an implementation method
of standard LOTOS and a compiler where a similar algorithm is used to check

executability of multi-way synchronization. So, the above algorithm could easily be implemented by extending the algorithm used in our existing compiler.

(3) Isolation of agents. To handle this issue, the mechanisms (1) for detecting an agent (or a sub-agent group) isolated from the agent group and for (2) reconstructing the synchronization tree are required. For (1), we have implemented a mechanism to periodically send a polling signal to members of the agent group. In (2), there are some complicated cases for reconstructing the tree: e.g., when an intermediate responsible node has been isolated. For this case, we have implemented a detection mechanism to save some of children agents which are still alive (capable of communicating with at least one member of the agent group). [13] describes the details.

5.2 Experimental Results

With the Java programs generated by our compiler, we have measured (1) time for a channel establishment, (2) time for executing each event on the established channel, and (3) data transmission rate on the channel (we used four note PCs with MMX Pentium 233MHz to Celeron 333MHz on IEEE 802.11b wireless LAN, 11Mbps).

For (1), it took about 2.6ms for a channel establishment between a pair of agents. For (2), when the numbers of combined agents is 2 to 4, 60 to 140 events were executed among agents per second. For (3), the achieved rate was 0.9 to 2.3Mbps when the number of agents is two to four. Since data transmission rates between two agents when using http and ftp protocols on the same environment were 692.9 Kbps and 3471.9 Kbps, respectively, we think our compiler generate efficient code enough for practical use. The details of our compiler are reported in [13].

6   Conclusion

In this paper, we have proposed a new language called LOTOS/M suitable for description and implementation of wireless mobile applications.

In LOTOS/M, we can describe dynamic establishment of multi-way synchronization channels among agents so that the agents which happen to meet in a common radio range can dynamically communicate by multi-way synchronization. Also, LOTOS/M can naturally handle the case that some of the combined agents are dynamically isolated (e.g., by leaving from a radio range).

Through some experiments, we have confirmed that our proposed technique is enough applicable to describe and implement wireless mobile applications.

Since our LOTOS/M compiler generates Java programs, it will be easy to implement LOTOS/M specifications on cellular phones and PDAs which can execute Java programs with IEEE802.11 or Bluetooth interfaces (such devices are already available). As part of future work, we would like to develop more practical applications such as video conferences on ad hoc networks consisting of those devices.

References

1. Ando, T., Takahashi, K., Kato, Y. and Shiratori, N.: A Concurrent Calculus with Geographical Constraints, *IEICE Trans. on Fundamentals*, Vol. E81-A, No. 4, pp. 547–555 (1998).
2. Bolognesi, T.: Toward Constraint-Object-Oriented Development, *IEEE Trans. on Soft. Eng.*, Vol. 26, No. 7, pp. 594 – 616 (2000).
3. Groote, J. F.: Transition System Specification with Negative Premises, *Theoretical Computer Science*, Vol.118, No.2, pp.263-299 (1993).
4. Fevrier, A., Najm, E., Leduc, G. and Leonard, L.: Compositional Specification of ODP Binding Objects, *Proc. of 6th IFIP/ ICCC Conf.* (1996).
5. Hodes, T.D., Katz, R.H., Schreiber, E.S. and Rowe, L.: Composable Ad-hoc Mobile Services for Universal Interaction, *Proc. of Mobile Computing and Networking(MOBICOM'97)* (1997).
6. ISO : Information Processing System, Open Systems Interconnection, LOTOS - A Formal Description Technique Based on the Temporal Ordering of Observational Behaviour, *ISO 8807* (1989).
7. Johnson, D. B., Maltz, D. A., Hu., Y. C. and Jetcheva, J. G. : The Dynamic Source Routing Protocol for Mobile Ad Hoc Networks, *IETF Internet Draft, http://www.ietf.org/internet-drafts/draft-ietf-manet-dsr04.txt* (2000).
8. Milner, R., Parrow, J., Walker, D.: A Calculus of Mobile Processes: Parts I & II, *Information and Computation 100*, pp. 1– 77 (1992).
9. Najm, E., Stefani, J.B. and Fevrier, A.: Towards a Mobile LOTOS, *Proc. of 8th IFIP Intl. Conf. on Formal Description Techniques (FORTE'95)* (1995).
10. Sangiorgi, D.: From π-calculus to Higher-Order π-calculus — and back, *Proc. of Theory and Practice of Software Development (TAPSOFT'93)*, Lecture Notes in Computer Science Vol. 668, pp. 151 – 166 (1993).
11. Tuok, R., Logrippo, L.: Formal Specification and Use Case Generation for a Mobile Telephony System, *Computer Networks*, Vol. 30, No. 11, pp. 1045-1063 (1998).
12. Vissers, C. A., Scollo, G. and Sinderen, M. v.: Architecture and Specification Style in Formal Descriptions of Distributed Systems, *Proc. 8th Int. Conf. on Protocol Specification, Testing, and Verification (PSTV'88)*, pp. 189 – 204 (1988).
13. Umedu, T., Yasumoto, K., Nakata, A., Yamaguchi, H., Higashino, T. and Taniguchi, K.: Middleware for Supporting Multi-way Synchronization in Wireless Ad Hoc Networks, submitted for publication. (the technical report version can be found in *http://www-higashi.ist.osaka-u.ac.jp/~umedu/papers/middleware.pdf*).
14. Yasumoto, K., Higashino, T. and Taniguchi, K.: A compiler to implement LOTOS specifications in distributed environments, *Computer Networks*, Vol. 36, No.2-3, pp. 291-310 (2001).

Author Index

Lecture Notes in Computer Science

For information about Vols. 1–2302
please contact your bookseller or Springer-Verlag